Human Development Report 2013

The Rise of the South:
Human Progress in a Diverse World

UN
DP

Empowered lives.
Resilient nations.

Published for the
United Nations
Development
Programme
(UNDP)

Human Development Reports 1990–2013

Regional Human Development Reports: Over the past two decades, regionally focused HDRs have also been produced in all major areas of the developing world, with support from UNDP's regional bureaus. With provocative analyses and clear policy recommendations, regional HDRs have examined such critical issues as political empowerment in the Arab states, food security in Africa, climate change in Asia, treatment of ethnic minorities in Central Europe and challenges of inequality and citizens' security in Latin America and the Caribbean.

National Human Development Reports: Since the release of the first national HDR in 1992, national HDRs have been produced in 140 countries by local editorial teams with UNDP support. These reports—some 700 to date—bring a human development perspective to national policy concerns through local consultations and research. National HDRs have covered many key development issues, from climate change to youth employment to inequalities driven by gender or ethnicity.

ISBN 978-92-1-126340-4

A catalogue record for this book is available from the British Library and the Library of Congress.

Printed in Canada by Gilmore Printing Services Inc. on Forest Stewardship Council certified and elemental chlorine-free papers. Printed using vegetable-based inks and produced by means of environmentally compatible technology.

MIX
Paper from
responsible sources
FSC® C100205

Editing and production: Communications Development Incorporated, Washington DC
Design: Melanie Doherty Design, San Francisco, CA

For a list of any errors or omissions found subsequent to printing, please visit our website at http://hdr.undp.org

Human Development Report 2013 Team

Director and lead author
Khalid Malik

Research and statistics
Maurice Kugler (Head of Research), Milorad Kovacevic (Chief Statistician), Subhra Bhattacharjee, Astra Bonini, Cecilia Calderón, Alan Fuchs, Amie Gaye, Iana Konova, Arthur Minsat, Shivani Nayyar, José Pineda and Swarnim Waglé

Communications and publishing
William Orme (Chief of Communications), Botagoz Abdreyeva, Carlotta Aiello, Eleonore Fournier-Tombs, Jean-Yves Hamel, Scott Lewis and Samantha Wauchope

National Human Development Reports
Eva Jespersen (Deputy Director), Christina Hackmann, Jonathan Hall, Mary Ann Mwangi and Paola Pagliani

Operations and administration
Sarantuya Mend (Operations Manager), Ekaterina Berman, Diane Bouopda, Mamaye Gebretsadik and Fe Juarez-Shanahan

Foreword

The 2013 Human Development Report, *The Rise of the South: Human Progress in a Diverse World* looks at the evolving geopolitics of our times, examining emerging issues and trends and also the new actors which are shaping the development landscape.

The Report argues that the striking transformation of a large number of developing countries into dynamic major economies with growing political influence is having a significant impact on human development progress.

The Report notes that, over the last decade, all countries accelerated their achievements in the education, health, and income dimensions as measured in the Human Development Index (HDI)—to the extent that no country for which data was available had a lower HDI value in 2012 than in 2000. As faster progress was recorded in lower HDI countries during this period, there was notable convergence in HDI values globally, although progress was uneven within and between regions.

Looking specifically at countries which lifted their HDI value substantially between 1990 and 2012 on both the income and non-income dimensions of human development, the Report examines the strategies which enabled them to perform well. In this respect, the 2013 Report makes a significant contribution to development thinking by describing specific drivers of development transformation and by suggesting future policy priorities that could help sustain such momentum.

By 2020, according to projections developed for this Report, the combined economic output of three leading developing countries alone—Brazil, China and India—will surpass the aggregate production of Canada, France, Germany, Italy, the United Kingdom and the United States. Much of this expansion is being driven by new trade and technology partnerships within the South itself, as this Report also shows.

A key message contained in this and previous Human Development Reports, however, is that economic growth alone does not automatically translate into human development progress. Pro-poor policies and significant investments in people's capabilities—through a focus on education, nutrition and health, and employment skills—can expand access to decent work and provide for sustained progress.

The 2013 Report identifies four specific areas of focus for sustaining development momentum: enhancing equity, including on the gender dimension; enabling greater voice and participation of citizens, including youth; confronting environmental pressures; and managing demographic change.

The Report also suggests that as global development challenges become more complex and transboundary in nature, coordinated action on the most pressing challenges of our era, whether they be poverty eradication, climate change, or peace and security, is essential. As countries are increasingly interconnected through trade, migration, and information and communications technologies, it is no surprise that policy decisions in one place have substantial impacts elsewhere. The crises of recent years—food, financial, climate—which have blighted the lives of so many point to this, and to the importance of working to reduce people's vulnerability to shocks and disasters.

To harness the wealth of knowledge, expertise, and development thinking in the South, the Report calls for new institutions which can facilitate regional integration and South–South cooperation. Emerging powers in the developing world are already sources of innovative social and economic policies and are major trade, investment, and increasingly development cooperation partners for other developing countries.

Many other countries across the South have seen rapid development, and their experiences and South–South cooperation are equally an inspiration to development policy. UNDP is able to play a useful role as a knowledge broker, and as a convener of partners—governments, civil society and multinational companies—to share experiences. We have a key role too in facilitating learning and capacity building. This Report offers very useful insights for our future engagement in South–South cooperation.

Finally, the Report also calls for a critical look at global governance institutions to promote a fairer, more equal world. It points to outdated structures, which do not reflect the new economic and geopolitical reality described, and considers options for a new era of partnership. It also calls for greater transparency and accountability, and highlights the role of global civil society in advocating for this and for greater decision-making power for those most directly affected by global challenges, who are often the poorest and most vulnerable people in our world.

As discussion continues on the global development agenda beyond 2015, I hope many will take the time to read this Report and reflect on its lessons for our fast-changing world. The Report refreshes our understanding of the current state of global development, and demonstrates how much can be learned from the experiences of fast development progress in so many countries in the South.

Helen Clark
Administrator
United Nations Development Programme

Acknowledgements

The Human Development Report is the product of a collective effort by the United Nations Development Programme (UNDP) Human Development Report Office (HDRO) and many valued external advisors and contributors. However, the findings, analysis and policy recommendations of this Report, as with previous Reports, are those of the authors alone.

The publication of this Report in March 2013 represents a return to the original schedule of the Human Development Reports, with its global launch and distribution in the first part of the year. This timing allows the Report's composite indices to incorporate the most current statistical indicators and provides greater opportunity for discussions of the Report's key findings and messages during the year.

Preparation of this Report was guided by a careful re-reading of the first Human Development Reports by Mahbub ul Haq. In that spirit, the Report opens with a review of the current "state of human development", looking at key human development trends and issues in the world today. It also benefited greatly from the wise counsel of Amartya Sen and Frances Stewart, Mahbub's close collaborators, who generously provided both critical advice and written contributions.

We are pleased that this Report features signed contributions from New York City Mayor Michael Bloomberg, Japan International Cooperation Agency President Akihiko Tanaka and Turkey's Minister of Development Cevdet Yılmaz, among others. We would like to express special gratitude to the authors of research papers commissioned by HDRO, who greatly enriched our understanding of the issues we set out to address: Fred Block, Nader Fergany, Ilene Grabel, Khalil Hamdani, Patrick Heller, Barry Hughes, Inge Kaul, Peter Kragelund, Shiva Kumar, Wolfgang Lutz, Deepak Nayyar, Leonce Ndikumana and Ngaire Woods.

Throughout the preparation of the Report, we received invaluable insights and guidance from our distinguished HDRO Advisory Panel, especially Edward S. Ayensu, Cristovam Buarque, Michael Elliott, Jayati Ghosh, Patrick Guillaumont, Nanna Hvidt, Rima Khalaf, Nora Lustig, Sir James Alexander Mirrlees, Rajendra K. Pachauri, Samir Radwan, Rizal Ramli, Gustav Ranis, Frances Stewart, Miguel Székely and Kandeh K. Yumkella.

We would also like to thank HDRO's statistical panel, which provided expert advice on methodologies and data choices related to the calculation of the Report's human development indices: Anthony Atkinson, Rachid Benmokhtar Benabdellah, Enrico Giovannini, Peter Harper, Anthony K.M. Kilele, Ben Paul Mungyereza, Hendrik Van der Pol, Marcia Quintsler and Eduardo Sojo Garza-Aldape.

The Report's composite indices and other statistical resources rely on the expertise of the leading international data providers in their specialized fields, and we express our gratitude for their continued collegial collaboration with the Human Development Report. To ensure accuracy and clarity, the Report's statistical analysis also benefited from an external review of statistical findings by Akmal Abdurazakov, Sabina Alkire, Virginija Cruijsen, Kenneth Harttgen and Claudio Montenegro.

The consultations held around the world during preparation of the Report relied on the generous support of many institutions and individuals who are too numerous to mention here. Consultations were held between September 2011 and June 2012 in Addis Ababa, Bonn, Brasilia, Colombo, Geneva, New York, Rabat, Santiago and Tokyo. Support from partnering institutions, including UNDP country and regional offices, listed at http://hdr.undp.org/en/reports/hdr2013/consultations, is acknowledged with much gratitude.

Many of our UNDP colleagues around the world—as members of the HDRO Readers Group and the Executive Group—provided invaluable insights into the preparation and final drafting of the Report. We would especially like to thank Adel Abdellatif, Ajay Chhibber, Pedro Conceição, George Gray Molina, Rebeca Grynspan, Selim Jehan, Olav Kjørven, Natalia Linou, Kamal Malhotra, Abdoulaye Mar Dieye, Charles McNeill, Shantanu Mukherjee, Heraldo Muñoz, Madi Musa, Thangaval Palanivel, Anuradha Rajivan, Turhan Saleh,

Heather Simpson, Ben Slay, Mounir Tabet, Antonio Vigilante and Kanni Wignaraja.

Several hard working, talented young colleagues made important contributions to the thorough fact checking of the Report. These include Philip Bastian, Joshua Greenstein, Ni Gu, Diana Jimenez, Wanshan Li, Veronica Postal and Alyssa Vladimir.

The Report has been blessed with many "friends of HDRO" who have gone out of their way to help strengthen it. Apart from a critical read of the draft Report by Frances Stewart and Jomo Kwame Sundaram and extensive review by Khalil Hamdani, Shiva Kumar, Terry McKinley, Pedro Conceição and Peter Stalker, we are grateful for the painstaking work of our editors at Communications Development Incorporated, led by Bruce Ross-Larson, with Meta de Coquereaumont, Christopher Trott and Elaine Wilson, and of designer Melanie Doherty.

Most of all, I am profoundly grateful to the HDRO team for their dedication and commitment in producing a report that meets the highest standards of scholarship.

Khalid Malik
Director
Human Development Report Office

Contents

FIGURES

MAPS

TABLES

"It is when we all play safe
that we create a world
of utmost insecurity."

Dag Hammarskjold

Overview

One of the most heartening developments in recent years has been the broad progress in human development of many developing countries and their emergence onto the global stage: the "rise of the South". This growing diversity in voice and power is challenging the principles that have guided policymakers and driven the major post–Second World War institutions. Stronger voices from the South are demanding more-representative frameworks of international governance that embody the principles of democracy and equity.

Just as important, many developing countries are reshaping ideas about how to attain human development. The rise of the South has resulted not from adhering to a fixed set of policy prescriptions, but from applying pragmatic policies that respond to local circumstances and opportunities—including a deepening of the developmental role of states, a dedication to improving human development (including by supporting education and social welfare) and an openness to trade and innovation. Even so, future progress will require policymakers to play close attention to such issues as equity, voice and accountability, environmental risks and changing demography.

Over the past decades, countries across the world have been converging towards higher levels of human development, as shown by the Human Development Index (HDI), a composite measure of indicators along three dimensions: life expectancy, educational attainment and command over the resources needed for a decent living. All groups and regions have seen notable improvement in all HDI components, with faster progress in low and medium HDI countries. On this basis, the world is becoming less unequal. Nevertheless, national averages hide large variations in human experience. Wide disparities remain within countries of both the North and the South, and income inequality within and between many countries has been rising.

Although most developing countries have done well, a large number of countries have done particularly well—in what can be called the "rise of the South". Some of the largest countries have made rapid advances, notably Brazil, China, India, Indonesia, South Africa and Turkey. But there has also been substantial progress in smaller economies, such as Bangladesh, Chile, Ghana, Mauritius, Rwanda and Tunisia.

The South has risen at an unprecedented speed and scale. For example, the current economic takeoffs in China and India began with about 1 billion people in each country and doubled output per capita in less than 20 years—an economic force affecting a much larger population than the Industrial Revolution did.[1] By 2050, Brazil, China and India combined are projected to account for 40% of world output in purchasing power parity terms.

During these uncertain times, countries of the South are collectively bolstering world economic growth, lifting other developing economies, reducing poverty and increasing wealth on a grand scale. They still face formidable challenges and are home to many of the world's poor. But they have demonstrated how pragmatic policies and a strong focus on human development can release the opportunities latent in their economies, facilitated by globalization.

A changing world, a more global South

To the casual observer, the state of affairs in 2013 may appear as a tale of two worlds: a resurgent South—most visibly countries such as China and India, where there is much human development progress, growth appears to remain robust and the prospects for poverty reduction are encouraging—and a North in crisis—where austerity policies and the absence of economic growth are imposing hardship on millions of unemployed people and people deprived of benefits as social compacts come under intense pressure. There are also deeper problems, shared by North and South: growing inequality in many countries, both developed and developing, which threatens global recovery and the sustainability of future progress and limits poverty reduction, as well as serious concerns about the environment.

While focusing on the rise of the South and its implications for human development, this Report is also about this changing world, driven in large measure by the rise of the South. It examines the progress being made, the challenges arising (some as a result of that very success) and the opportunities emerging for representative global and regional governance.

The headline story of a resurgent South is both uplifting and in some ways misleading. The South needs the North, and increasingly the North needs the South. The world is getting more connected, not less. Recent years have seen a remarkable reorientation of global production, with much more destined for international trade, which, by 2011, accounted for nearly 60% of global output. Developing countries have played a big part: between 1980 and 2010, they increased their share of world merchandise trade from 25% to 47% and their share of world output from 33% to 45%. Developing regions have also been strengthening links with each other: between 1980 and 2011, South–South trade increased from less than 8% of world merchandise trade to more than 26%.

Yet the United States remains the largest economy in the world in monetary terms and will remain so for the foreseeable future. If the US recovery hesitates and Europe is unable to pull itself out of its current economic and social doldrums, there will be a large knock-on effect on the developing world. Global challenges such as climate change and stressed ecosystems require countries to cooperate even more than before. While the rise of the South is reshaping power relations in many important respects, hard-won gains in human development will be more difficult to protect if cooperation fails and difficult decisions are postponed.

Indeed, one can go further and state that there is a "south" in the North and a "north" in the South. Elites, whether from the North or the South, are increasingly global and connected, and they benefit the most from the enormous wealth generation over the past decade, in part due to accelerating globalization. They are educated at the same universities and share similar lifestyles and perhaps values.

The changing global economy is creating unprecedented challenges and opportunities for continued progress in human development. Global economic and political structures are in flux at a time when the world faces recurrent financial crises, worsening climate change and growing social unrest. Global institutions appear unable to accommodate changing power relations, ensure adequate provision of global public goods to meet global and regional challenges and respond to the growing need for greater equity and sustainability.

This phenomenon, coupled with the diverse development paths followed by these countries from the South, presents an opportunity: the principles that have driven post–Second World War institutions and guided policymakers need recalibration, if not a reset, to accommodate the growing diversity in voice and power and to sustain development progress over the long term. These principles require reconsideration, and global institutions need greater flexibility to reinforce directions that put people first and nudge institutions to aim forcefully at a fairer, more just world. Potentially, the growing diversity in development patterns is creating space, even demands, for such a global dialogue and restructuring. There is scope then for innovation, and the emergence of global, regional and national governance frameworks that embody principles of democracy, equity and sustainability.

The developmental paths of Brazil, China and India, as well as less well recognized success stories such as Bangladesh, Mauritius and Turkey, are reshaping ideas about how to attain human development. The success of these countries calls into question the notion of "right" policies, but that does not mean that valuable lessons cannot be drawn from the experiences of these successful countries. On the contrary, key drivers and principles of development begin to emerge from the diversity of development paths that include deepening the developmental role of states, dedication to human development and social welfare, and openness to trade and innovation. And while this Report acknowledges the positive aspects of the rise of the South, it also underlines the imperatives of ensuring that concerns of equity and sustainability are fully incorporated into future policies and strategies. As the 2011

The South needs the North, and increasingly the North needs the South

Human Development Report also stressed, continued human development progress is unlikely if inequality and environmental destruction are not moved to the forefront of policy discussions. Under worst case scenarios, a business as usual approach to development combined with environmental crises could reverse human development gains in the South or make this progress unsustainable.

Concerns for the future apply in the North as well, where low economic growth, high unemployment rates and austerity measures threaten the high levels of human development. In both the North and the South, ruling elites cannot afford to ignore these threats to social inclusion and social welfare, given the rising call for fairness and accountability—from citizens, communities and civil organizations at home and abroad, facilitated by the explosion of social media.

To support policymaking and research that adequately address these contemporary and emerging global realities, measures and analytics are needed that broaden the human development concept. The Human Development Report and the family of human development indices must meet this challenge by moving beyond a focus on measuring individual capabilities to incorporate society-level capacities, concerns and perceptions. Individual achievements in health, education and income, while essential, do not guarantee progress in human development if social conditions constrain individual achievements and if perceptions about progress differ. The turmoil in several countries in the Arab States is a reminder that people, especially the young, who are better educated and healthier than previous generations put a high premium on meaningful employment, on exercising a voice in affairs that influence their lives and on being treated with respect.

Furthermore, the promotion of social cohesion and social integration, a stated objective of development strategies of countries such as Brazil, is based on evidence of the positive development impact of a unified society. More-equal societies tend to do better in most measures of human development—from teenage pregnancies to suicide rates—than do unequal societies. This finding is borne out by studies in both developed and developing countries. These society-level aspects of development have been underappreciated in past conceptualizations of development but are proving to be essential elements of any viable and desirable long-term development path.

Helping other countries catch up

All developing countries are not yet participating fully in the rise of the South. The pace of change is slower, for instance, in the majority of the 49 least developed countries, especially those that are landlocked or distant from world markets. Nevertheless, many of these countries have also begun to benefit from South–South trade, investment, finance and technology transfer. For example, there have been positive growth spillovers from China to other countries, particularly close trading partners. To some extent, this has offset slackening demand from developed countries. Growth in low-income countries would have been an estimated 0.3–1.1 percentage points lower in 2007–2010 had growth fallen at the same rate in China and India as in developed economies.[2]

Many countries have also benefited from spillovers into important human development sectors, especially health. Indian firms, for example, are supplying affordable medicines, medical equipment, and information and communications technology products and services to countries in Africa. Brazilian and South African companies are having a similar impact.

Rising competitive pressures

Nevertheless, the arrival of exports from larger countries can also have disadvantages. Large countries generate competitive pressures that might stifle economic diversification and industrialization in smaller countries. Yet there are examples of industrial revival following such competitive jolts. A competitive role today may easily turn into a complementary role in the future. Moving from competition to cooperation seems to depend on policies that enable local agents to make the most of the new situation.

Increasingly, the most important engine of growth for countries of the South is their domestic market. The middle class is growing in size and median income. By 2025, annual consumption in emerging markets is estimated

Individual achievements in health, education and income, while essential, do not guarantee progress in human development if social conditions constrain individual achievements and if perceptions about progress differ to rise to $30 trillion. By then, the South will account for three-fifths of the 1 billion households earning more than $20,000 a year. Nevertheless, such expansion will be hampered as well as marred by significant pockets of deprivation. These disparities in the South's expansion are not only undesirable in themselves; they also undermine the sustainability of progress, not least by creating social and political tensions.

These trends are leading to a more balanced world. Instead of having a centre of industrialized countries and a periphery of less developed countries, there is now a more complex and dynamic environment.

While there is much awareness at the global and regional levels that the world is in transition, leaders, institutions and academics seemingly find it difficult to put forward principles, institutions and policy recommendations that can secure the next steps in creating a more just and sustainable world. This may be in part because the world is changing so rapidly and on so many fronts, making shared assessments difficult and collective action elusive. This Report contributes to this conversation by critically assessing the contemporary global context and by promoting principles and concepts that can help a diverse world move towards human development strategies that meet the new challenges of the 21st century, reduce or even eliminate poverty and advance progress for all.

Policies, partnerships, principles

How have so many countries in the South been able to transform their human development prospects? Across most of these countries, there have been three notable drivers of development: a proactive developmental state, tapping of global markets, and determined social policy innovation. These drivers do not spring from abstract conceptions of how development should work; rather, they are demonstrated by the transformational development experiences of many countries in the South. Indeed, they challenge preconceived and prescriptive approaches: on the one hand, they set aside a number of collectivist, centrally managed precepts; on the other hand, they diverge from the unfettered liberalization espoused by the Washington Consensus.

Success is likely to be the result of gradual integration with the world economy and accompanied by investment in people, institutions and infrastructure

Driver 1: a proactive developmental state

A strong, proactive and responsible state develops policies for both public and private sectors—based on a long-term vision and leadership, shared norms and values, and rules and institutions that build trust and cohesion. Achieving enduring transformation requires countries to chart a consistent and balanced approach to development. However, countries that have succeeded in igniting and sustaining growth in incomes and human development have not followed one simple recipe. Faced with different challenges, they have adopted varying policies dealing with market regulation, export promotion, industrial development and technological progress. Priorities need to be people-centred and to promote opportunities while protecting people against downside risks. Governments can nurture industries that would not otherwise emerge because of incomplete markets. Despite posing some risks of rent seeking and cronyism, this has enabled several countries of the South to turn inefficient industries into early drivers of export success as their economies became more open.

In large and complex societies, the outcome of any particular policy is inevitably uncertain. Developmental states therefore need to be pragmatic and test a range of different approaches. Some features stand out: for instance, people-friendly developmental states have expanded basic social services. Investing in people's capabilities—through health, education and other public services—is not an appendage of the growth process but an integral part of it. Rapid expansion of quality jobs is a critical feature of growth that promotes human development.

Driver 2: tapping of global markets

Global markets have played an important role in advancing progress. All newly industrializing countries have pursued a strategy of "importing what the rest of the world knows and exporting what it wants". But even more important are the terms of engagement with these markets. Without investment in people, returns from global markets tend to be limited. Success is more likely to be the result not of a sudden opening but of gradual and sequenced integration with the world economy, according to national circumstances, and accompanied by investment in people, institutions and infrastructure. Smaller economies have successfully focused on niche products, whose success is often the fruit of years of state support built on existing competencies or the creation of new ones.

Driver 3: determined social policy innovation

Few countries have sustained rapid growth without impressive levels of public investment —not just in infrastructure, but also in health and education. The aim should be to create virtuous circles where growth and social policies reinforce each other. Growth is generally much more effective in reducing poverty in countries where income inequality is low than in countries with high inequality. Promoting equality, particularly among different religious, ethnic or racial groups, also helps minimize social conflict.

Education, health care, social protection, legal empowerment and social organization all enable poor people to participate in growth. Sectoral balance—especially paying attention to the rural sector—and the nature and pace of employment expansion are critical in determining how far growth spreads incomes. But even these basic policy instruments may not empower disenfranchised groups. The poor fringes of society struggle to voice their concerns, and governments do not always ensure that services actually reach everyone. Social policy has to promote inclusion—ensuring nondiscrimination and equal treatment is critical for political and social stability—and provide basic social services that can underpin long-term economic growth by supporting the emergence of a healthy, educated labour force. Not all such services need to be provided publicly. But the state should ensure that all citizens have secure access to the basic requirements of human development.

An agenda for development transformation is thus multifaceted. It expands poor people's assets by increasing public expenditures on basic services. It improves the functioning of state and social institutions to promote both growth and equity. It reduces bureaucratic and social constraints on economic action and social mobility. It involves communities in setting budget priorities and holding leadership accountable.

Sustaining the momentum

Many countries of the South have demonstrated much success. But even in the higher achieving countries, future success is not guaranteed. How can countries in the South continue their progress in human development, and how can the progress be extended to other countries? This Report suggests four important areas to facilitate this: enhancing equity, enabling voice and participation, confronting environmental challenges and managing demographic change. This Report points to the high cost of policy inaction and argues for greater policy ambition.

Enhancing equity

Greater equity, including between men and women and among other groups, is not only essential in itself, but also important for promoting human development. One of the most powerful instruments for this purpose is education, which boosts people's self-confidence and enables them to find better jobs, engage in public debate and make demands on government for health care, social security and other entitlements.

Education also has striking impacts on health and mortality. Research for this Report shows that a mother's education level is more important to child survival than is household income. Projections also show that policy interventions have a greater impact in countries and regions where education outcomes are initially weaker. This has profound policy implications, potentially shifting the emphasis from efforts to boost household income to measures to improve girls' education.

This Report makes a strong case for policy ambition. An accelerated progress scenario suggests that low HDI countries can converge towards the levels of human development achieved by high and very high HDI countries. By 2050, aggregate HDI could rise 52% in Sub-Saharan Africa (from 0.402 to 0.612) and 36% in South Asia (from 0.527 to 0.714). Such

Few countries have sustained rapid growth without impressive levels of public investment—not just in infrastructure, but also in health and education policy interventions will also have a positive impact on the fight against poverty. By contrast, the costs of inaction will rise, especially in low HDI countries, which are more vulnerable. For instance, failing to implement ambitious universal education policies will adversely affect many essential pillars of human development for future generations.

Enabling voice and participation

Unless people can participate meaningfully in the events and processes that shape their lives, national human development paths will be neither desirable nor sustainable. People should be able to influence policymaking and results—and young people in particular should be able to look forward to greater economic opportunities and political participation and accountability.

Dissatisfaction is increasingly high in both the North and the South as people call for more opportunities to voice their concerns and influence policy in order to ensure basic social protection and social progress. Among the most active protesters are young people. In part this is a response to limited employment opportunities for educated young people. History is replete with popular rebellions against unresponsive governments. Such upheaval can derail human development—as unrest impedes investment and growth and autocratic governments divert resources to maintaining law and order.

It is hard to predict when societies will reach a tipping point. Mass protests, especially by educated people, tend to erupt when people feel excluded from political influence and when bleak economic prospects lower the opportunity cost of engaging in such protests. These effort-intensive forms of political participation are then easily coordinated by new forms of mass communication.

Confronting environmental challenges

Environmental threats such as climate change, deforestation, air and water pollution, and natural disasters affect everyone. But they hurt poor countries and poor communities most. Climate change is already exacerbating chronic environmental threats, and ecosystem losses are constraining livelihood opportunities, especially for poor people.

Although low HDI countries contribute the least to global climate change, they are likely to endure the greatest loss in annual rainfall and the sharpest increase in its variability, with dire implications for agricultural production and livelihoods. The magnitude of such losses highlights the urgency of adaptation measures.

The cost of inaction will likely be high. The longer the inaction, the higher the cost. To ensure sustainable economies and societies, new policies and structural changes are needed that align human development and climate change goals in low-emission, climate-resilient strategies and innovative public-private financing mechanisms.

Managing demographic change

Between 1970 and 2011, world population increased from 3.6 billion to 7 billion. As that population becomes more educated, its growth rate will slow. Moreover, development prospects are influenced not just by the total number of people, but also by the population's age structure. An increasingly critical concern is a country's dependency ratio—that is, the number of younger and older people divided by the working-age population ages 15–64.

Some poorer regions could benefit from a "demographic dividend" as the share of the working-age population rises, but only if there is strong policy action.[3] Girls' education is a critical vehicle of a possible demographic dividend. Educated women tend to have fewer, healthier and better educated children; in many countries educated women also enjoy higher salaries than do uneducated workers.

By contrast, the richer regions of the South confront a very different problem: as their population ages, the share of the working-age population falls. The rate of population ageing matters because developing countries will struggle to meet the needs of an older population if they are still poor. Many developing countries now have only a short window of opportunity to reap the full benefits of the demographic dividend.

Demographic trends are not destiny, however. They can be altered through education policies in particular. This Report presents two scenarios for 2010–2050: a base case scenario, in which current education trends continue, and a fast track scenario, in which the countries with the lowest initial levels embrace ambitious education targets. For low HDI countries, the decline in the dependency ratio under the fast track scenario is more than twice that under the base case scenario. Ambitious education policies can enable medium and high HDI countries to curb projected increases in their dependency ratio, thus easing the demographic transition towards an ageing population.

Addressing these demographic challenges will require raising educational attainment levels while expanding productive employment opportunities—by reducing unemployment, promoting labour productivity and increasing labour force participation, particularly among women and older workers.

Governance and partnerships for a new era

The rise of the South is providing both opportunities and challenges for the formidable problems of an increasingly interconnected world. Challenges such as management of climate change; use of global commons; and regulation of trade, finance and migration have cross-border consequences. Some elements of global public goods can be provided at the regional level, but effective provision usually requires considerable multilateral coordination and cooperation. Neither the North nor the newly influential South can sit out the regional or global dialogues needed to forge agreement on these issues. Countries of the South are in a position not just to contribute financial resources towards strengthening regional and multilateral processes, but also to bring the substantial experience gained through their human development achievements and pragmatic policies in many of these areas.

The South has promoted new arrangements and institutions such as bilateral and regional trade agreements and financial mechanisms. Consequently, today's systems of international governance are a mosaic of old structures and new arrangements. And they may become even more diverse: international cooperation is likely to involve an ever more complex web of bilateral, regional and global processes.

Many of the current institutions and principles for international governance were designed for a world very different from today's. One consequence is that they underrepresent the South. To survive, international institutions need to be more representative, transparent and accountable. Indeed, all intergovernmental processes would be invigorated by greater participation from the South, which can bring substantial financial, technological and human resources as well as valuable solutions to critical world problems.

In all of this, governments are understandably concerned with preserving national sovereignty. While appropriate in some cases, this focus can encourage zero-sum thinking. A better strategy would be "responsible sovereignty", whereby countries engage in fair, rule-based and accountable international cooperation, joining in collective endeavours that enhance global welfare. Responsible sovereignty also requires that states ensure the human rights security and safety of their citizenry. According to this view, sovereignty is not just a right, but also a responsibility.

The current context has profound implications for the provision of public goods. Among the areas meriting urgent attention are those related to trade, migration and climate change. In some cases, public goods can be delivered by regional institutions, which can avoid the polarization that sometimes slows progress in larger, multilateral forums. But increasing regional cooperation may have disadvantages—adding to a complex, multilevel and fragmented tapestry of institutions. The challenge therefore is to ensure "coherent pluralism"—so that institutions at all levels work in a broadly coordinated fashion.

International governance institutions can be held to account not just by member states, but also by global civil society. Civil society organizations have already influenced global transparency and rule setting on such issues as aid, debt, human rights, health and climate change. Networks of civil society now take advantage of new media and new communications technologies. Yet civil society organizations also face questions about their legitimacy and accountability and may take undesirable forms.

All intergovernmental processes would be invigorated by greater participation from the South, which can bring substantial financial, technological and human resources as well as valuable solutions to critical world problems

Nevertheless, the future legitimacy of international governance will depend on institutions' capabilities to engage with citizen networks and communities.

Priorities for a new era

Through all this, the fundamental principles of human development remain critical. As ever, the aim is to expand choices and capabilities for all people, wherever they live. Many countries of the South have already demonstrated what can be done. But they have gone only part of the way. For the years ahead, this Report suggests five broad conclusions.

Rising economic strength in the South must be matched by a full commitment to human development

Investments in human development are justified not only on moral grounds, but also because improved health, education and social welfare are key to success in a more competitive and dynamic world economy. In particular, these investments should target the poor—connecting them to markets and increasing their livelihood opportunities. Poverty is an injustice that can and should be remedied by determined action.

Good policymaking also requires a focus on enhancing social capacities, not just individual capabilities. Individuals function within social institutions that can limit or enhance their development potential. Policies to change social norms that limit human potential, such as gender discrimination, early marriages and dowry requirements, open up opportunities for individuals to reach their full potential.

Less developed countries can learn and benefit from the success of emerging economies of the South

The unprecedented accumulation of financial reserves and sovereign wealth funds in both the North and South provides an opportunity to accelerate broad-based progress. A small portion of these funds should be dedicated to human development and poverty eradication. At the same time, South–South trade and investment flows can leverage foreign markets in new ways that enhance development opportunities, such as by participating in regional and global value chains.

Burgeoning South–South trade and investment in particular can lay the basis for shifting manufacturing capacity to other less developed regions and countries. Recent Chinese and Indian joint ventures and startup manufacturing investments in Africa could be a prelude to a much expanded force. International production networks provide opportunities to speed development by allowing countries to leap-frog to more sophisticated production modes.

New institutions can facilitate regional integration and South–South relationships

New institutions and partnerships can help countries share knowledge, experiences and technology. This can be accompanied by new and stronger institutions to promote trade and investment and accelerate experience sharing across the South. One step would be to establish a new South Commission to bring a fresh vision of how the South's diversity can be a force for solidarity.

Greater representation for the South and civil society can accelerate progress on major global challenges

The rise of the South is leading to a greater diversity of voice on the world stage. This presents an opportunity to build governance institutions that fully represent all constituencies and that would make productive use of this diversity in finding solutions to world problems.

New guiding principles for international organizations are needed that incorporate the experience of the South. The emergence of the Group of 20 is an important step in this direction, but the countries of the South also need more equitable representation in the Bretton Woods institutions, the United Nations and other international bodies.

Active civil society and social movements, both national and transnational, are using the media to amplify their calls for just and fair governance. The spread of movements and the increase in platforms for vocalizing key

The unprecedented accumulation of financial reserves provides an opportunity to accelerate broad-based progress messages and demands challenge governance institutions to adopt more-democratic and more-inclusive principles. More generally, a fair and less unequal world requires space for a multiplicity of voices and a system of public discourse.

The rise of the South presents new opportunities for generating a greater supply of public goods

A sustainable world requires a greater supply of global public goods. Global issues today are increasing in number and urgency, from mitigation of climate change and international economic and financial instability to the fight against terrorism and nuclear proliferation. They require a global response. Yet in many areas, international cooperation remains slow and at times dangerously hesitant. The rise of the South presents new opportunities for more effectively providing global public goods and for unlocking today's many stalemated global issues.

Publicness and privateness are in most cases not innate properties of a public good but social constructs and as such represent a policy choice. National governments can step in when there is underprovision at the national level. But when global challenges arise, international cooperation is necessary—and can happen only through the voluntary actions of many governments. Given the many pressing challenges, progress in determining what is public and what is private will require strong, committed personal and institutional leadership.

*   *   *

This Report presents the contemporary global context and charts a path for policymakers and citizens to navigate the increasing interconnectedness of the world and to face the growing global challenges. It describes how the dynamics of power, voice and wealth in the world are changing—and identifies the new policies and institutions necessary to address these 21st century realities and promote human development with greater equity, sustainability and social integration. Progress in human development requires action and institutions at both the global and national levels. At the global level, institutional reforms and innovation are required to protect and provide global public goods. At the national level, state commitment to social justice is important, as is the understanding that one-size-fits-all technocratic policies are neither realistic nor effective given the diversity of national contexts, cultures and institutional conditions. Nevertheless, overarching principles such as social cohesion, state commitment to education, health and social protection, and openness to trade integration emerge as means of navigating towards sustainable and equitable human development.

The rise of the South presents new opportunities for more effectively providing global public goods and for unlocking today's many stalemated global issues

"Across the globe, people are uniting in a common struggle: to participate freely in the events and processes that shape their lives."

Mahbub ul Haq

Introduction

When developed economies stopped growing in the 2008–2009 financial crisis but developing economies kept on growing, the world took notice.[1] The rise of the South, seen within the developing world as an overdue global rebalancing, has been much commented on since. This discussion has typically focused narrowly on gross domestic product (GDP) and trade growth in a few large countries. Yet there are broader dynamics at play, involving many more countries and deeper trends, with potentially far-reaching implications for people's lives, for social equity and for democratic governance at the local and global levels. As this Report shows, the rise of the South is both the result of continual human development investments and achievements and an opportunity for still greater human progress for the world as a whole. Making that progress a reality will require informed and enlightened global and national policymaking, drawing on the policy lessons analysed in this Report.

The rise of the South is unprecedented in its speed and scale. Never in history have the living conditions and prospects of so many people changed so dramatically and so fast. Great Britain, where the Industrial Revolution originated, took 150 years to double output per capita; the United States, which industrialized later, took 50 years.[2] Both countries had a population below 10 million when they began to industrialize. In contrast, the current economic takeoffs in China and India began with about 1 billion people in each country and doubled output per capita in less than 20 years—an economic force affecting a hundred times as many people as the Industrial Revolution did.[3]

The rise of the South must be understood as the story of a dramatic expansion of individual capabilities and sustained human development progress in the countries that are home to the vast majority of the world's people. When dozens of countries and billions of people move up the development ladder, as they are doing today, it has a direct impact on wealth creation and broader human progress in all countries and regions of the world. There are new opportunities for catch-up for less developed countries and for creative policy initiatives that could benefit the most advanced economies as well.

A close look at the diverse pathways that successful developing countries have pursued enriches the menu of policy options for all countries and regions while providing insights into values and world views that can inform future development cooperation and constructive responses to the most severe global challenges. The goal, as always, is to accelerate, wherever possible, broad-based progress that raises standards and expands people's choices in all countries and communities in all key dimensions of human development, from health and education and livelihoods to the personal freedom to control and improve one's own life.

Transforming the South requires changing the rules that underpin global relationships. Most multilateral organizations were designed to reflect an international order newly emerging from the Second World War. That world view no longer resonates with the 21st century rebalancing of global demographics, wealth and geopolitical influence. The growing policy-shaping influence of the South is visible in the international response to the 2008 financial crisis. In the past, financial decisions were made by the major industrial powers alone, as in the 1985 Plaza Accord. This time, a more extensive group, the Group of 20 (G20), which includes the largest developing economies, played a key role. People in the South are also increasingly taking leadership positions in long-established international organizations.[4]

These are just preliminary signs of change in international institutions and of the possibility that the new actors in the South may help resume efforts to provide better global public goods. Indeed, the rise of the South adds to the urgency with which governments and international organizations will need to confront challenges that are likely to loom large in the future: equity in opportunities, civic engagement in governance, environmental sustainability and the demographic bulge, to name a few. The next sections elaborate on specific features of the rise of the South.

FIGURE 1

Acceleration of growth on the HDI

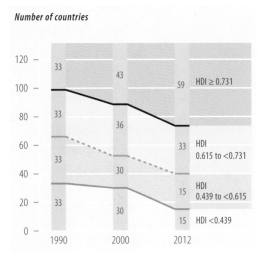

Number of countries

Note: Thresholds are the 25th, 50th and 75th percentiles of HDI values for 132 countries in 1990.
Source: HDRO.

FIGURE 2

More than 40 countries of the South had greater gains on the HDI between 1990 and 2012 than would have been predicted from their previous performance on the HDI

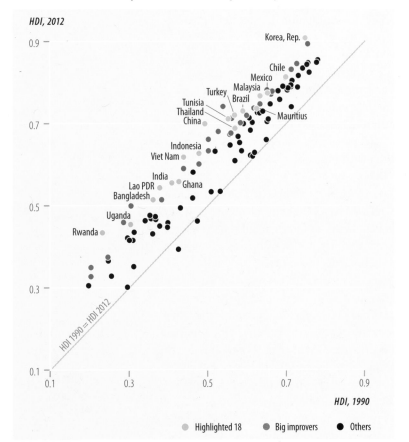

Note: Countries above the 45 degree line had a higher HDI value in 2012 than in 1990. Blue and grey markers indicate countries with significantly larger than predicted increases in HDI value between 1990 and 2012 given their HDI value in 1990. These countries were identified based on residuals obtained from a regression of the change in log of HDI between 2012 and 1990 on the log of HDI in 1990. Countries that are labelled are a selected group of rapid HDI improvers that are discussed in greater detail in chapter 3.
Source: HDRO calculations.

Broad-based progress

The 21st century transformation of the South has been accompanied by major advances in public health, education, transportation, telecommunications and civic engagement in national governance. The human development consequences have been profound: the proportion of people living in extreme poverty fell from 43.1% in 1990 to 22.4% in 2008; more than 500 million people have been lifted out of poverty in China alone.[5]

Countries at low levels of human development accelerated their achievements in health, education and income more in the past decade than in the preceding one. The number of countries with a Human Development Index (HDI) value below the 25th percentile in 1990 dropped from 33 to 30 between 1990 and 2000 and was halved from 30 to 15 between 2000 and 2012 (figure 1). At the upper end of the distribution, the number of countries with an HDI value above the 75th percentile rose from 33 to 43 between 1990 and 2000 and from 43 to 59 between 2000 and 2012. The picture is more mixed in the middle quartiles of the HDI. Overall, no country had a lower HDI value in 2012 than in 2000, in contrast to the prior decade, when 18 countries had a lower HDI value in 2000 than in 1990.

Between 1990 and 2012, almost all countries improved their human development status. Of 132 countries with a complete data series, only 2 had a lower HDI value in 2012 than in 1990 (Lesotho and Zimbabwe). Progress was particularly rapid in more than 40 countries of the South, whose increases in HDI value were significantly larger than predicted for countries that were at a similar level of HDI value in 1990.[6] This includes countries as diverse as Ghana, Rwanda and Uganda in Sub-Saharan Africa; Bangladesh and India in South Asia; Tunisia in the Arab States; China, Lao PDR and Viet Nam in East Asia and the Pacific; and Brazil, Chile and Mexico in Latin America and the Caribbean (figure 2).

Global rebalancing

For the first time in 150 years, the combined output of the developing world's three leading economies—Brazil, China and India—is about equal to the combined GDP of the long-standing industrial powers of the North—Canada, France, Germany, Italy, the United Kingdom and the United States.[7] This represents a dramatic rebalancing of global economic power. In 1950, Brazil, China and India together accounted for only 10% of the world economy, while the six traditional economic leaders of the North accounted for roughly half. According to projections in this Report, by 2050 Brazil China and India will together account for 40% of global output (figure 3), far surpassing the projected combined production of today's Group of Seven bloc.[8]

Today, the South as a whole produces about half of world economic output, up from about a third in 1990. The combined GDP of eight major developing countries alone—Argentina, Brazil, China, India, Indonesia, Mexico, South Africa and Turkey—now equals the GDP of the United States, still by far the world's biggest national economy.[9] As recently as 2005, the combined economic weight of those eight

countries was barely half that of the United States.

This major increase in share of economic output would not mean much in human development terms, however, if it had not been accompanied by an unprecedented reduction in deprivation and expansion of human capabilities. The first Millennium Development Goal of halving the proportion of people living on less than $1.25 a day relative to 1990 has been met three years before the target date. This is primarily because of the success of some of the most populous countries in eradicating extreme poverty: Brazil, China and India have all dramatically reduced the proportion of their people who are income poor—Brazil from 17.2% of the population in 1990 to 6.1% in 2009, China from 60.2% in 1990 to 13.1% in 2008 and India from 49.4% in 1990 to 32.7% in 2010.[10]

Broader development challenges, however, have not diminished. An estimated 1.57 billion people, or more than 30% of the population of the 104 countries studied for this Report, live in multidimensional poverty,[11] a measure of both

Today, the South as a whole produces about half of world economic output, up from about a third in 1990

FIGURE 3

Brazil, China and India combined are projected to account for 40% of global output by 2050, up from 10% in 1950

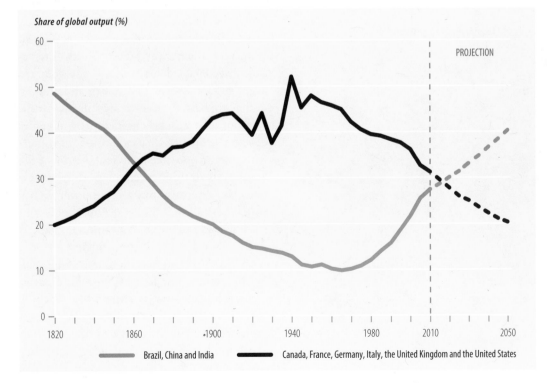

Note: Output is measured in 1990 purchasing power parity dollars.
Source: HDRO interpolation of historical data from Maddison (2010) and projections based on Pardee Center for International Futures (2013).

the number and the intensity of overlapping human deprivations in health, education and standard of living. For many of the rapidly growing countries of the South, the population living in multidimensional poverty exceeds that living in income poverty. And income inequality is on the rise in many countries. Based on calculations for the Inequality-adjusted HDI for 132 countries in 2012, almost a quarter of HDI value, 23%, is lost to inequality. Between 1990 and 2005, Inequality-adjusted HDI trends for 66 countries show that overall inequality declined only marginally, because declining inequality in health and education was offset by rising inequality in income.[12] Latin America, in contrast to overall global trends, has seen income inequality fall since 2000 but still has the most unequal distribution of all regions. Sub-Saharan Africa has the most inequality in health, and South Asia in education.

Massive expansion of the middle class

The middle class in the South is growing rapidly in size, income and expectations.

FIGURE 4

The middle class in the South is projected to continue to grow

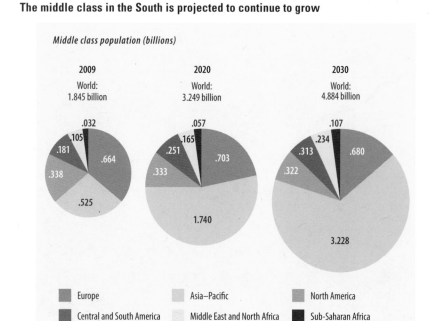

Middle class population (billions)

| 2009 | 2020 | 2030 |
| World: 1.845 billion | World: 3.249 billion | World: 4.884 billion |

Legend:
- Europe
- Central and South America
- Asia–Pacific
- Middle East and North Africa
- North America
- Sub-Saharan Africa

Note: The middle class includes people earning or spending $10–$100 a day (in 2005 purchasing power parity terms).
Source: Brookings Institution 2012.

Between 1990 and 2010, the South's share of the global middle class population expanded from 26% to 58%. By 2030, more than 80% of the world's middle class is projected to be residing in the South and to account for 70% of total consumption expenditure.[13] The Asia–Pacific Region will host about two-thirds of the world's middle class by 2030, Central and South America about 10% and Sub-Saharan Africa 2% (figure 4). Within Asia, China and India will account for more than 75% of the middle class as well as its share of total consumption. Another estimate is that by 2025, annual consumption in emerging market economies will rise to $30 trillion, from $12 trillion in 2010, with the South home to three-fifths of the 1 billion households earning more than $20,000 a year.[14] The continued expansion of the middle class is certain to have a profound impact on the world economy.

The sheer number of people in the South— the billions of consumers and citizens— multiplies the global human development consequences of actions by governments, companies and international institutions in the South. The South is now emerging alongside the North as a breeding ground for technical innovation and creative entrepreneurship. In North–South trade the newly industrializing economies have built capabilities to efficiently manufacture complex products for developed country markets. But South–South interactions have enabled companies in the South to adapt and innovate with products and processes that are better suited to local needs. This is creating new business models, as companies develop products that can reach customers with lower disposable incomes. The rise of the South is also diffusing technology through new models of extensive coverage with low margins, which serve lower income households and reach a large number of consumers in markets that have weak support infrastructure.

The world is also becoming more educated. Assuming a robust increase in school enrolment rates, the share of the world's people older than 15 who lack formal schooling is projected to shrink from 12% in 2010 to 3% in 2050, and the share with secondary or tertiary education will climb from 44% in 2010 to 64% in 2050. Furthermore, the digital divide is rapidly narrowing, giving people from everywhere comparable access to information, especially through increasingly affordable mobile broadband Internet.

The rapid expansion in the educated population in much of the South adds to the urgency of job creation on a mass scale. Countries of the South that experience low dependency rates in the future can create a "demographic dividend" only if the increase in the labour force is matched by equally rapid expansion of employment opportunities. If enough decent jobs are not available to meet this demographic demand, the consequences are likely to include rising civil unrest, as demonstrated by the youth-led insurrections of the Arab Spring.

Unprecedented connectedness

Trade, travel and telecommunication exchanges are expanding worldwide at an unprecedented pace. People are moving between countries in numbers never seen before, as business professionals, as tourists and as migrants. In 2010, first-generation immigrants accounted for nearly 3% of the world's population, or more than 215 million people—a three-fold increase since 1960.[15] Nearly half of remittances sent home by emigrants from the South come from workers living in other developing countries.

Countries of the South are also hosting more tourists than ever from other developing countries: by 2020, there will be nearly 1.6 billion tourist arrivals globally, with 75% of them expected to be intraregional. The share of South–South trade in world commerce has more than tripled over the past three decades to 25%; South–South foreign investment now accounts for 30%–60% of all outside investment in the least developed countries.[16]

There has been an exponential rise in the number of people in the South with access to the world wide web (Internet). The takeoff has been especially notable in the past decade (figure 5). Between 2000 and 2010, average annual growth in Internet use surpassed 30% in around 60 developing countries with a population of 1 million or more. In September 2012, the online social networking website Facebook recorded 1 billion monthly active users, with 140.3 billion connections among "friends"; four of the five countries with the greatest number of Facebook users are in the South: Brazil, India, Indonesia and Mexico.[17]

Interdependence in commerce is allowing more people to participate in the global marketplace, from Ugandan banana exporters to shrimp farmers on the Mekong River. The global trade to GDP ratio, a conventional measure of trade integration, reached 22% in 1913, a dramatic increase over the estimated

The rapid expansion of educated people in much of the South adds to the urgency of job creation on a mass scale

FIGURE 5

The exponential rise in Internet use in the South has been most notable over the past decade

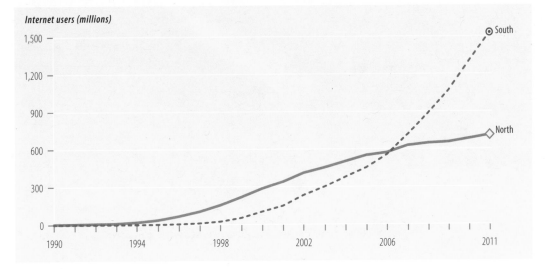

Source: World Bank 2012a.

2% in 1800.[18] Today the ratio exceeds 56%.[19] At least 15 developing countries have substantial trading relationships with more than 100 trade partners as both exporters and importers, up from about 6 in 1996 (figure 6). The South now accounts for half of global trade flows, up from barely a quarter 30 years ago. These increasing trade connections are deepening even faster "horizontally", on a South–South basis, than on the traditional North–South axis.

A substantial share of South–South trade continues to be driven by demand in the North, but the opposite is also true: developing countries are major importers from the North. Since 2007, for example, US exports to established partners in the Organisation for Economic Co-operation and Development (OECD) have risen 20%, but US exports to

Latin America and the Caribbean and China have risen more than 50%. The South needs the North, but, increasingly, the North also needs the South.

Countries of the South are also emerging as natural hubs for absorbing technologies and developing new products. There is now greater potential for human development thanks to technology transfer from the South. Technology transfer from the North often requires costly adaptation due to differences in absorptive capacity. Technological transfer from the South has been more amenable to direct adoption.[20] And technological adaptation by the South has also led to new kinds of innovation with immediate human development benefits. Take the uses to which Africans are putting affordable Asian-built

FIGURE 6

At least 15 developing countries have substantial trading relationships with more than 100 trade partners as both exporters and importers

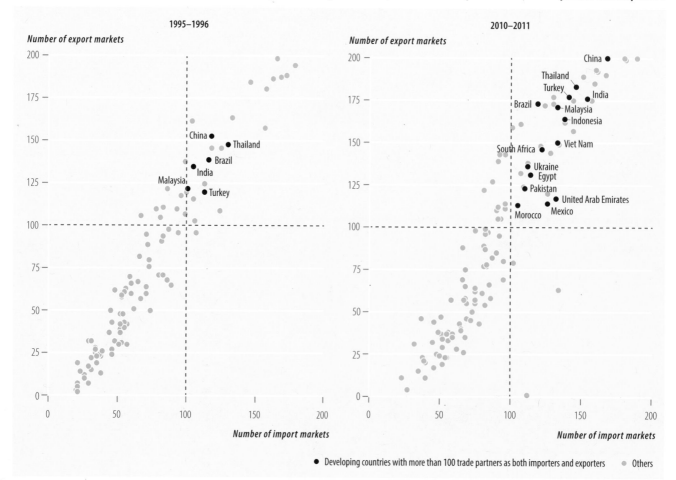

Note: Values are averages for 1995 and 1996 and for 2010 and 2011. Includes only countries with bilateral trade exceeding $1.5 million in 1995–1996 and $2 million in 2010–2011.
Source: UNSD 2012.

mobile phones: cellular banking is cheaper and easier than opening a traditional bank account, farmers can obtain weather reports and check grain prices and entrepreneurs can provide business services through mobile phone kiosks. These and other transformations multiply the possibilities of what people can do with technology: participating in decisions that affect their lives; gaining quick and low-cost access to information; producing cheaper, often generic medicines, better seeds and new crop varieties; and generating new employment and export opportunities. These new technologies are connecting people in formerly isolated and marginalized rural communities and in poor urban neighbourhoods. They also give them access to valuable tools, resources and information and enable them to more actively participate in the wider national and even global society.

Pragmatic development policies

The rise of the South spans diverse country experiences, showing that there are multiple ways to achieve and sustain human development. Countries were pragmatic in adopting policies suited to their unique circumstances: for example, between 1979 and 1989, no fewer than 40% of China's national regulations were deemed experimental.[21] There were broadly shared common approaches as well. Most fast-developing countries of the South opened up to foreign trade, investment and technologies. But that opening alone did not guarantee success. They also invested in their own human development capabilities, strengthened domestic institutions and built new areas of comparative advantage. The critical combination of external openness with internal preparedness allowed countries to prosper in the global marketplace, with positive human development outcomes for the population at large.

Active government leadership was crucial in accelerating economic progress and minimizing social conflict. Growth created the needed fiscal space for investment in health and education and paved the way for a virtuous synergy between economic and social policy. Well known innovative programmes in Brazil, India and Mexico—conditional cash transfer programmes and rural employment guarantee programmes—exemplify active interest in fostering a more equitable distribution of economic and social opportunities. China has also stressed the importance of such an approach in its strategic pursuit of a "harmonious society". Elements of these programmes have been emulated by many other countries in the South.

A common emphasis of these social initiatives has been to promote equity and social integration, aspects that were underappreciated in past development models but are proving to be essential elements of any sustainable path for human progress. Ruling elites are increasingly recognizing that social and economic progress can profoundly influence their own legitimacy. Investments in social welfare and public goods have become building blocks for long-term development. These exemplary initiatives—which combine health, education and economic policies in a broader agenda of equity, empowerment and participation—highlight the importance of supporting social justice not only on moral grounds, but also as a crucial means of advancing human development.

New partners for development

The South is now in a position to influence, even reshape, old models of development cooperation with augmented resources and home-grown lessons, but it also exerts new competitive pressures on other aspects of bilateral cooperation. The rise of the South is spurring innovation in bilateral partnership and regional cooperation, resulting in greater options within the South for concessional finance, infrastructural investment and technology transfer. The growing assistance from the South is often without explicit conditions on economic policy or approaches to governance. The development emphasis on improved infrastructure, for example, has been rediscovered because of the domestic experience and lessons of some emerging economies. Over the past decade, nearly half of financing for infrastructure in Sub-Saharan Africa was provided by governments and regional funds from elsewhere in the South.[22]

Furthermore, the extraordinary increase in capital accumulation in the fastest growing economies of the South—exemplified most

The South is now in a position to influence old models of development cooperation with augmented resources and home-grown lessons, but it also exerts new competitive pressures on other aspects of bilateral cooperation notably by the surge in foreign exchange reserves—represents a largely untapped store of development capital. Three-quarters of the increase in foreign exchange reserves between 2000 and 2011 was accumulated by countries of the South, partly as self-insurance against future financial downturns and crises (figure 7).

As early as 1995, the United Nations Development Programme identified 23 developing countries as being pivotal to South–South cooperation. Over the past decade, those countries have accelerated their engagement with other developing countries.[23] Outside the OECD, Brazil, China and India are the three largest donors.[24] Other countries such as Malaysia, Thailand and Turkey are also important in regional development. New development partnerships, fashioned on "win-win" for all parties, have supported development efforts and opened opportunities for bilateral trade and investment exchanges, sustaining the rise of the South. In the process, international regimes are realigning, and international organizations are reorienting to the shifts in global economic power due to the rise of the South.

*   *   *

This Report examines in greater detail many aspects of the rise of the South and their implications for human development. Chapter 1 takes stock of the current status of human development globally and regionally, with an emphasis on trends, challenges and advances in such key interrelated areas as poverty, inequality, social integration and human security. Chapter 2 shows how countries of the South are emerging as significant players in the world economy, becoming both drivers of growth and catalysts for change in other developing

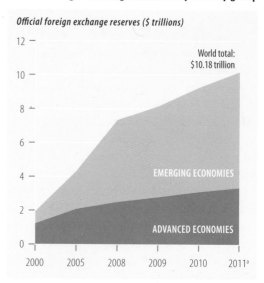

FIGURE 7

Official foreign exchange reserves by country group

Official foreign exchange reserves ($ trillions)

World total: $10.18 trillion

EMERGING ECONOMIES

ADVANCED ECONOMIES

a. Preliminary third-quarter data.
Note: The classification of countries follows that used by the International Monetary Fund (IMF); it includes 34 advanced economies and 110 emerging and developing economies that report to the IMF's Currency Composition of Official Foreign Reserves database.
Source: Grabel 2013.

countries, and identifies some of the emerging challenges. Chapter 3 looks at the policies and strategies that have underpinned progress in some of the more successful countries of the South. Chapter 4 asks two basic questions: can this progress be sustained, and what are likely to be the future challenges to sustaining human development? Chapter 5 looks at prospects for policies and principles for a new framework of global and regional governance that fully represents and responds to the rise of the South in the long-term interests of the South and North alike. As the Report shows, the increasingly complex challenges of the 21st century require new partnerships and new approaches that reflect the realities of this rapidly changing world.

"The political problem of mankind is to combine three things: Economic Efficiency, Social Justice and Individual Liberty."

John Maynard Keynes

1.

The state of human development

From Brazil to South Africa to India to China, the largest developing countries have become major drivers of the global economy. In 2012, however, even the most vigorous economies of the South began to be affected by the financial problems of the North. Struggling to emerge from a debt crisis and large budget deficits, many developed countries are imposing severe austerity programmes that are not only causing hardship for their own citizens, but are also undermining the human development prospects of millions of other people across the world.

The first *Human Development Report* in 1990 laid out a vision of economic and social progress that is fundamentally about people enlarging their choices and capabilities. Since then, there has been substantial progress: many developing economies continue to grow rapidly and raise standards of human development. The rise of the South is a feature of a rapidly changing world. The South now accounts for almost a third of world output[1] and consumption.[2] Without the robust growth in these economies, led by China and India, the global economic recession would have been deeper.[3]

Nevertheless, there are signs of contagion, with real concern that in an interconnected world the crisis in the North may slow developing countries' progress. In industrialized countries, with some notable exceptions, governments are introducing harsh austerity measures that reduce the government's welfare role and cut back on spending and public services,[4] leading to hardship and exacerbating economic contractions. Living standards are declining for many people in the developed world. Several countries have seen major street demonstrations and general disillusionment with politicians and economic management as a result.

The world has known similar crises: in Europe and the United States in the 1930s, in Latin America in the 1980s and in Asia in the 1990s. But this time around, well into the second decade of the 21st century, the crisis is again happening in the heart of Europe.

Governments are imposing austerity programmes because of a legitimate concern about the sustainability of sovereign debt. But there is a risk that short-term measures will cause long-term damage, eroding the human development and social welfare foundations that enable economies to grow, democracies to flourish and

societies to be less unequal and less vulnerable to shocks.[5]

There is also evidence that deploying drastic austerity programmes too quickly can deepen and prolong recessions. Fiscal consolidation has already had contractionary effects on private domestic demand and gross domestic product (GDP)[6] while weakening economic conditions and increasing unemployment.[7] Rollbacks of health, education and other public services are likely to impair the health of the population, the quality of the labour force and the state of scientific research and innovation for years to come (box 1.1). This could put progress in human development on a lower trajectory for some time (box 1.2). Moreover, economic stagnation reduces the tax revenues that governments need to finance social services and public goods.

Much of this damage is avoidable. Historical evidence indicates that the best time to cut deficits is after economic growth has taken off.[8] As John Maynard Keynes put it succinctly nearly 75 years ago, "The boom, not the slump, is the right time for austerity."[9]

It is also vital to consider not just the quantity of public expenditure, but also its composition and how it can be changed. According to the International Labour Organization, a fiscally neutral change in the composition of government revenues and expenditures designed to foster employment and promote human development could create 1.8–2.1 million jobs in 33 advanced economies over the next year or two.[10]

While countries have different degrees of freedom to adjust their spending priorities, for many there is ample scope for reprioritization. For instance, military spending worldwide exceeded $1.4 trillion in 2010, more than the GDP of the world's 50 poorest countries

BOX 1.1

Fairness, macroeconomics and human development

The rising income inequality in the United States and some European countries highlights fairness in how incomes are distributed and who benefits from growth. These concerns are entering the mainstream political discourse in developed countries, though with limited impact on policies so far. Unemployment in developed countries is at its highest level in years, and a large share of the workforce has had no significant increase in real wages over the last few decades, while the richest deciles have seen a substantial increase in income. Increasing inequality has been accompanied by demands by many of the better-off for smaller government and fiscal restraint: the well-off have not only benefited disproportionately from earlier growth, but also appear committed to protecting their gains. It is surprising that in democracies, despite considerable pressure from civil society, government agendas are dominated by austerity programmes rather than social protection programmes.

The call for austerity measures is not limited to countries in the euro area. The United Kingdom plans to reduce public investment by about 2% of GDP under the current austerity programme. This call for austerity comes when public investment is at a historic low. For instance, net public investment in the United Kingdom for fiscal year 2011/2012 is less than 2% of GDP. A continued push for reduced government and social expenditures may well worsen the prospects for recovery and growth.

Macroeconomic policies can have large consequences for human development. Cutting social spending to reduce public debt can have long-term effects. If economies keep contracting, successive rounds of debt reduction will do little to further debt sustainability. Cutting spending reduces aggregate demand, which, coupled with high income inequality, makes it challenging to revive the economy and put people back to work. In the quest for full employment, reduced aggregate demand has to be compensated for. In the United States (and other industrialized countries) this was achieved through low interest rates, which, along with new financial instruments and lax regulation, caused a bubble that eventually led to the current financial crisis. Countries in the euro area, constrained in their use of policy instruments, cannot use monetary policies to devalue (or inflate) their way out of a crisis.

Source: Atkinson 2011, 2012; Block 2013; HM Treasury 2010; Nayyar 2012; Sen 2012; Stiglitz 2012.

BOX 1.2

Short-term cuts have long-term consequences: rising fertility rates in Africa

Why did fertility rates rise between 1970 and 1990 in many Sub-Saharan African countries despite falling in every other region? The evolution of fertility rates appears to be associated with social expenditure cuts, particularly in education, made as part of structural adjustment programmes in the 1980s.

Cuts in education not only limit human capabilities, but also affect the age structure of the population years later because of their impact on birth rates. Countries with lower levels of education, especially countries where girls lack secondary education, tend to have higher fertility rates. Almost universally, women with higher levels of education have fewer children. This effect is particularly strong in countries that are early in their demographic transition and still have high overall fertility rates. Education reduces fertility rates by enhancing information, changing the incentives for behaviour and empowering people to better pursue their own preferences.

In the 1980s, Sub-Saharan Africa saw a partial reversal in the progress towards demographic transition, with real expenditure per capita on education falling nearly 50% on average. Between 1980 and 1986, enrolment in primary education dropped from 79% to 73% for the region as a whole (falling in 16 countries and rising in 17). The reduced education expenditures had a negative impact on female education, causing average female combined primary and secondary gross enrolment rates to increase more slowly than in the period before the structural adjustment programmes.

Source: Lutz and KC 2013; Rose 1995.

combined. Even where fiscal consolidation is necessary, it need not involve cuts in welfare services. Consolidation through enhanced efficiency and reduced subsidies on fossil fuels, for instance, could leave social spending relatively unaffected.[11]

The countries of the South have shown greater resilience in the face of the current global economic crisis. After transitory setbacks following the 2008 crisis, African and Latin American countries have resumed their upward trajectories of human development and growth. This is partly because they have been more pragmatic, taking countercyclical measures and postponing debt reduction for more appropriate times. Continuing demand from the South has also helped sustain many developing country exports, offsetting the effects of sluggish economic activity in the North.[12]

At the same time, many developing countries continue to invest in long-term human development. They recognize a clear positive correlation between past public investment in social and physical infrastructure and progress on the Human Development Index (HDI).[13] Governments in the South have also appreciated that sustainable progress must be based on social integration. Brazil and India, for example, have supported aspects of human development underappreciated in past development models by introducing cash transfer programmes and right-to-work programmes.

Overall, over the past few decades, many countries of the South have made substantial strides in HDI performance, not only boosting economic growth and reducing poverty, but also making large gains in health and education (discussed in greater detail later in the chapter). This broad-based achievement is notable because income growth does not necessarily translate into gains in other aspects of human development. Growth may generate resources to invest in health and education, but the link is not automatic. Moreover, growth may have little impact on other important human development priorities such as participation and empowerment.

Now more than ever, indicators are needed to capture these dimensions as well as the environmental sustainability of development pathways.

Progress of nations

Every *Human Development Report* has monitored human progress, notably through the HDI, a composite measure that includes indicators along three dimensions: life expectancy, educational attainment, and command over the resources needed for a decent living. Other indices have delved into inequality, poverty and gender deficits. HDI values for 2012 are presented in statistical table 1.

The HDI in 2012 reveals much progress. Over the past decades, countries across the world have been converging towards higher levels of human development. The pace of progress on the HDI has been fastest in countries in the low and medium human development categories. This is good news. Yet progress requires more than average improvement in HDI value. It will be neither desirable nor sustainable if increases in HDI value are accompanied by rising inequality in income, unsustainable patterns of consumption, high military spending and low social cohesion (box 1.3).

In 2012, the global average HDI value was 0.694; Sub-Saharan Africa had the lowest HDI value (0.475), followed by South Asia (0.558). Among developing regions, Europe and Central Asia had the highest HDI value (0.771), followed by Latin America and the Caribbean (0.741).

There are large differences across HDI groups and regions in the components of the HDI— life expectancy, mean years of schooling and income. Average gross national income (GNI) per capita in very high HDI countries is more than 20 times that in low HDI countries (table 1.1). Life expectancy in very high HDI countries is a third higher than in low HDI countries, while average years of schooling among adults over 25 are nearly three times greater in very high HDI countries than in low HDI countries. However, expected years of schooling, which better reflect changing education opportunities in developing countries, present a much more hopeful picture: the average incoming elementary school student in a low HDI country is expected to complete 8.5 years of school, about equal to the current years of schooling among adults in high HDI countries (8.8 years). Overall, most low HDI countries have achieved or are advancing towards full enrolment in elementary school and more than 50% enrolment in secondary school.

There are large disparities in achievements within HDI groups and regions. One way of assessing disparities within country groups is to compare the ratio of the highest to the lowest HDI values among countries in the group. This ratio is highest in Sub-Saharan Africa, followed by the Arab States, South Asia, and Latin America and the Caribbean. In Sub-Saharan Africa, most of the disparity arises from substantial differences in income per capita (with a ratio of 70.1[14]) and mean years of schooling (with a ratio of 7.8). In South Asia, the disparities also arise primarily from differences in income per capita, with a ratio of 10.7, and mean years of schooling (with a ratio of 4.0). In the Arab States, and to a lesser extent Latin America and the Caribbean, the main driver is differences in income per capita.

Overall, the last decade has seen greater convergence in HDI values, involving accelerated human development among countries with lower HDI values. All HDI groups and

There is a clear positive correlation between past public investment in social and physical infrastructure and progress on the Human Development Index

What is it like to be a human being?

Almost half a century ago, the philosopher Thomas Nagel published a famous paper called "What Is It Like to Be a Bat?" The question I want to ask is: what is it like to be a human being? As it happens, Tom Nagel's insightful paper in *The Philosophical Review* was also really about human beings, and only marginally about bats. Among other points, Nagel expressed deep scepticism about the temptation of observational scientists to identify the experience of being a bat—or similarly, a human being—with the associated physical phenomena in the brain and elsewhere in the body that are within easy reach of outside inspection. The sense of being a bat or a human can hardly be seen as just having certain twitches in the brain and of the body. The complexity of the former cannot be resolved by the easier tractability of the latter (tempting though it may be to do just that).

The cutting edge of the human development approach is also based on a distinction—but of a rather different kind from Nagel's basic epistemological contrast. The approach that Mahbub ul Haq pioneered through the series of *Human Development Reports* which began in 1990 is that between, on the one hand, the difficult problem of assessing the richness of human lives, including the freedoms that human beings have reason to value, and on the other, the much easier exercise of keeping track of incomes and other external resources that persons—or nations—happen to have. Gross domestic product (GDP) is much easier to see and measure than the quality of human life that people have. But human well-being and freedom, and their connection with fairness and justice in the world, cannot be reduced simply to the measurement of GDP and its growth rate, as many people are tempted to do.

The intrinsic complexity of human development is important to acknowledge, partly because we should not be side-tracked into changing the question: that was the central point that moved Mahbub ul Haq's bold initiative to supplement—and to some extent supplant—GDP. But along with that came a more difficult point, which is also an inescapable part of what has come to be called "the human development approach." We may, for the sake of convenience, use many simple indicators of human development, such as the HDI, based on only three variables with a very simple rule for weighting them—but the quest cannot end there. We should not spurn workable and useful shortcuts—the HDI may tell us a lot more about human quality of life than does the GDP—but nor should we be entirely satisfied with the immediate gain captured in these shortcuts in a world of continuous practice. Assessing the quality of life is a much more complex exercise than what can be captured through only one number, no matter how judicious is the selection of variables to be included, and the choice of the procedure of weighting.

The recognition of complexity has other important implications as well. The crucial role of public reasoning, which the present *Human Development Report* particularly emphasizes, arises partly from the recognition of this complexity. Only the wearer may know where the shoe pinches, but pinch-avoiding arrangements cannot be effectively undertaken without giving voice to the people and giving them extensive opportunities for public discussion. The importance of various elements in evaluating well-being and freedom of people can be adequately appreciated and assessed only through persistent dialogue among the population, with an impact on the making of public policy. The political significance of such initiatives as the so-called Arab Spring, and mass movements elsewhere in the world, is matched by the epistemic importance of people expressing themselves, in dialogue with others, on what ails their lives and what injustices they want to remove. There is much to discuss—with each other and with the public servants that make policy.

The dialogic responsibilities, when properly appreciated across the lines of governance, must also include representing the interest of the people who are not here to express their concerns in their own voice. Human development cannot be indifferent to future generations just because they are not here—yet. But human beings do have the capacity to think about others, and their lives, and the art of responsible and accountable politics is to broaden dialogues from narrowly self-centred concerns to the broader social understanding of the importance of the needs and freedoms of people in the future as well as today. This is not a matter of simply including those concerns within one single indicator—for example, by overcrowding the already heavily loaded HDI (which stands, in any case, only for current well-being and freedom)—but it certainly is a matter of making sure that the discussions of human development include those other concerns. The *Human Development Reports* can continue to contribute to this broadening through explication as well as presenting tables of relevant information.

The human development approach is a major advance in the difficult exercise of understanding the successes and deprivations of human lives, and in appreciating the importance of reflection and dialogue, and through that advancing fairness and justice in the world. We may be much like bats in not being readily accessible to the measuring rod of the impatient observational scientist, but we are also capable of thinking and talking about the many-sided nature of our lives and those of others—today and tomorrow—in ways that may not be readily available to bats. Being a human being is both like being a bat and very unlike it.

---

regions saw notable improvement in all HDI components, with faster progress in low and medium HDI countries. East Asia and the Pacific and South Asia saw continuing progress from earlier decades, while Sub-Saharan Africa saw more rapid progress in the last decade. The convergence in HDI values has become more pronounced in the last decade.

One of the principal components of the HDI is life expectancy. In 2012, average life expectancy was 70.1 years, with wide differences across HDI groups: 59.1 years in low HDI countries and 80.1 years in very high HDI countries. Differences across countries are even wider, with a low of 48.1 years in Sierra Leone and a high of 83.6 years in Japan. In Sub-Saharan Africa, life expectancy stagnated at 49.5 years between 1990 and 2000, a result of the HIV and AIDS pandemic. Between 2000 and 2012, however, it increased 5.5 years.

Another important influence on the HDI, and one of the most sensitive indicators of

TABLE 1.1

HDI and components, by region and HDI group, 2012

Region and HDI group	HDI	Life expectancy at birth (years)	Mean years of schooling (years)	Expected years of schooling (years)	Gross national income per capita (2005 PPP $)
Region					
Arab States	0.652	71.0	6.0	10.6	8,317
East Asia and the Pacific	0.683	72.7	7.2	11.8	6,874
Europe and Central Asia	0.771	71.5	10.4	13.7	12,243
Latin America and the Caribbean	0.741	74.7	7.8	13.7	10,300
South Asia	0.558	66.2	4.7	10.2	3,343
Sub-Saharan Africa	0.475	54.9	4.7	9.3	2,010
HDI group					
Very high human development	0.905	80.1	11.5	16.3	33,391
High human development	0.758	73.4	8.8	13.9	11,501
Medium human development	0.640	69.9	6.3	11.4	5,428
Low human development	0.466	59.1	4.2	8.5	1,633
World	0.694	70.1	7.5	11.6	10,184

Note: Data are weighted by population and calculated based on HDI values for 187 countries. PPP is purchasing power parity.
Source: HDRO calculations. See statistical table 1 for detailed data sources.

human well-being, is child survival. In 2010, the global under-five mortality rate was 55 deaths per 1,000 live births, though spread unevenly across HDI groups. Low HDI countries had the highest rate (110 deaths per 1,000 live births), followed by medium HDI countries (42), high HDI countries (18) and very high HDI countries (6). Poor child health can permanently damage a child's cognitive development and later affect labour productivity as an adult.

HDI comparisons are typically made between countries in the North and the South, and on this basis the world is becoming less unequal. Nevertheless, national averages hide large variations in human experience, and wide disparities remain within countries of both the North and the South. The United States, for example, had an HDI value of 0.94 in 2012, ranking it third globally. The HDI value for residents of Latin American origin was close to 0.75, while the HDI value for African-Americans was close to 0.70 in 2010–2011.[15] But the average HDI value for an African-American in Louisiana was 0.47.[16] Similar ethnic disparities in HDI achievement in very high HDI countries can be seen in the Roma populations of southern Europe.

The range in human development is also wide in some developing countries. In Brazil, for example, the highest HDI value in 2000, the most recent year for which subnational data are available, was in São Caetano do Sul in the state of São Paulo (0.92), while the lowest was in Manari in the state of Pernambuco (0.47). China has similar, if less marked, provincial variations, with Shanghai at the top (0.91), and Tibet at the bottom (0.63).[17]

Income and human development

Another essential component of human development and the HDI is command over resources, as measured by income per capita. Between 1990 and 2012, income per capita rose in all four HDI groups, though in varying degrees (figure 1.1). The highest average annual growth in income per capita was recorded in China and Equatorial Guinea, both over 9%. Only 12 countries surpassed 4% growth, while 19 saw income per capita fall.

One of the most striking achievements has been in Sub-Saharan Africa. From 2003 to 2008—the five years preceding the global

HDI comparisons are typically made between countries in the North and the South, and on this basis the world is becoming less unequal

FIGURE 1.1

Income per capita is rising to varying degrees in all four HDI groups

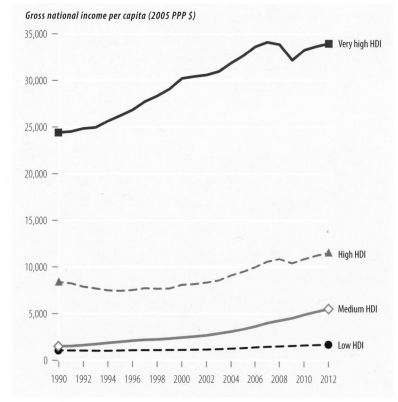

Note: PPP is purchasing power parity.
Source: HDRO calculations based on a panel of the same 161 countries and territories.

FIGURE 1.2

Sub-Saharan Africa has sustained income growth over the last decade

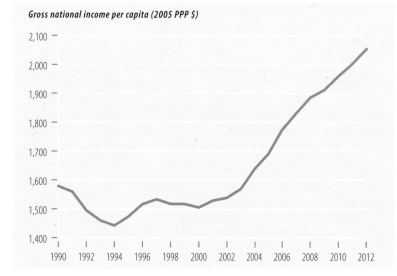

Note: PPP is purchasing power parity.
Source: HDRO calculations.

financial crisis—income per capita in the region grew 5% a year, more than twice the rate of the 1990s (figure 1.2).[18] This upward trend was led by resource-rich countries that benefited from price increases in Africa's main commodity exports—notably, gas, oil, minerals and agricultural products—thanks mostly to strong demand from the South, led by China.

But growth was also widespread in other countries, with strong performance among more diversified economies and agriculture-based economies. Despite commodity price increases, many net commodity-importing countries, such as Ethiopia, Rwanda and Uganda, continued to grow fast. Sub-Saharan African economies were also partly shielded from global shocks by greater regional integration, particularly in East Africa.

As most *Human Development Reports* have underscored, what matters is not only the level of income, but also how that income is used. A society can spend its income on education or on weapons of war. Individuals can spend their income on essential foods or on narcotics. For both societies and individuals, what is decisive is not the process of wealth maximization, but how they choose to convert income into human development. Table 1.2 shows country successes in this respect, as measured by the largest positive difference between GNI per capita and HDI ranks.[19] New Zealand tops the list for very high human development countries, and Cuba tops the list for high human development countries.

Poverty

One of the world's main priorities is to eradicate poverty and hunger. This is the first of the eight Millennium Development Goals, for which the target for 2015 was to halve the proportion of people living on less than $1.25 a day relative to 1990. This goal was achieved three years before that target date, primarily because of the success of some of the most populous countries: Brazil (where the percentage of the population living on less than 2005 PPP $1.25 a day went from 17.2% to 6.1%), China (from 60.2% to 13.1%) and India (from 49.4% to 32.7%).[20] As a result, many fewer people are poor. For example, between 1990 and 2008, China alone lifted a remarkable 510 million people out of poverty.[21]

Poor people do not just suffer from a lack of income. Poverty has multiple dimensions, with deficits in health and education, for example. Moreover, an estimated 10% of the global population is afflicted by some form of disability, potentially limiting their standard of living regardless of income.[22]

In the early and middle 20th century, European countries reduced poverty not only by increasing incomes, but also by providing public goods such as health care and education.[23] When considering relative poverty levels, it is also important to consider the social and political arenas, including whether the poor can "appear in public without shame".[24] Translating income into a decent standard of living depends on a range of assets and capabilities. These are all issues in which the state has an important role facilitating access to health, education, and public and personal safety (box 1.4). How income is converted into well-being, particularly for the poor, also depends on environmental circumstances.[25]

Poverty can be measured more comprehensively using the Multidimensional Poverty Index (MPI), which looks at overlapping deprivations in health, education and standard of living. The MPI is the product of the multidimensional poverty headcount (the share of people who are multidimensionally poor) and the average number of deprivations that each multidimensionally poor household experiences (the intensity of their poverty). Focusing on the intensity of poverty enables the MPI to provide a more complete picture of poverty within a country or a community than is available from headcount measures alone. In the 104 countries covered by the MPI, about 1.56 billion people—or more than 30% of their population—are estimated to live in multidimensional poverty.[26] This exceeds the estimated 1.14 billion people in those countries who live on less than $1.25 a day, although it is below the proportion who live on less than $2 a day.[27] The pattern holds true for all four HDI groups, though the difference is larger in low HDI countries than in medium of high HDI countries (figure 1.3). This also holds true for many of the rapidly growing countries of the South (figure 1.4).

The countries with the highest headcount percentages based on the MPI are in Africa: Ethiopia (87%), Liberia (84%), Mozambique (79%) and Sierra Leone (77%; see statistical table 5). The countries with the highest intensity of poverty (deprivations in at least 33% of weighted indicators) are Ethiopia and Mozambique (about 65% each in 2007–2011), followed by Burkina Faso (64%), Senegal (59%) and Liberia (58%). Despite having a smaller proportion of multidimensional poor (lower headcount ratio) than Liberia does, Mozambique has a higher MPI value (0.512) because it has the highest intensity of deprivation among countries with data.

TABLE 1.2

Top five countries that rank better on the HDI than on gross national income per capita in 2012

HDI group and country	HDI value	Gross national income (GNI) per capita (2005 PPP $)	GNI rank minus HDI rank
Very high human development			
New Zealand	0.919	24,358	26
Ireland	0.916	28,671	19
Australia	0.938	34,340	15
Korea, Rep.	0.909	28,231	15
Israel[a]	0.900	26,244	13
High human development			
Cuba	0.780	5,539	44
Georgia	0.745	5,005	37
Montenegro	0.791	10,471	24
Albania	0.749	7,822	21
Grenada	0.770	9,257	21
Medium human development			
Samoa	0.703	3,928	28
Tonga	0.710	4,153	26
Fiji	0.702	4,087	24
Kyrgyzstan	0.622	2,009	24
Ghana	0.558	1,684	22
Low human development			
Madagascar	0.483	828	28
Togo	0.459	928	16
Kenya	0.519	1,541	15
Zimbabwe	0.397	424	14
Nepal[b]	0.463	1,137	11

a. The difference between GNI and HDI ranks is also 13 for Chile, Estonia and Greece, all very high HDI countries.
b. The difference between GNI and HDI ranks is also 11 for Liberia, a low HDI country.
Source: HDRO calculations. See statistical table 1 for detailed data sources.

BOX 1.4

Subjective indicators of well-being: increased acceptance in thinking and policy

Interest in using subjective data to measure well-being and human progress and to inform public policy has grown in recent years.[1] In the United Kingdom, the government committed itself to explore the use of subjective indicators of well-being, as suggested by Stiglitz, Sen and Fitoussi (2009). Bhutan has integrated the subindicators that constitute the Gross National Happiness Index into its public policy measures. Subjective data can complement but not substitute for objective data.

Kahneman and Krueger (2006) lay the analytical basis for measuring subjective well-being on the fact that people often depart from the standards of the "rational economic agent". Making inconsistent choices, not updating beliefs in the light of new information, desisting from gainful exchanges: all violate the assumption of rationality that underlies the translation of observed behaviour into a theory of revealed preferences in economics. If the assumed link between observed data and actual preferences is tenuous, the case for relying exclusively on objective data is weakened, and there exists a greater case for using subjective data as well.

Stiglitz, Sen and Fitoussi (2009) adopt subjective well-being as one of their three conceptual approaches to measuring quality of life. They point out that the approach has strong links to the utilitarian tradition but also has broader appeal. Subjective measures of quality of life, however, do not have objective counterparts. For instance, there is no observed measure of happiness, whereas inflation can be measured as either actual or perceived inflation. They further note that subjective approaches allow for a distinction between quality of life dimensions and the objective factors that shape them.

Subjective measures are not without problems. They are ordinal in nature and usually are not comparable across countries and cultures or reliable across time. Thus it can be misleading to use subjective indicators such as happiness as the only or main policy criterion. However, these indicators—appropriately measured and carefully used—can be valuable supplements to objective data to inform policy, particularly at the national level.

An important subjective indicator of well-being that can be gleaned from surveys is overall life satisfaction. Data for 149 countries place average life satisfaction globally at 5.3 on a scale of 0–10 (see table), with a low of 2.8 in Togo and a high of 7.8 in Denmark (see statistical table 9). Not surprisingly, life satisfaction tends to be higher in countries with higher human development.

Overall life satisfaction and satisfaction with health care and education

HDI group and region	Overall life satisfaction, 2007–2011[a] (0, least satisfied, 10, most satisfied)	Satisfaction with health care, 2007–2009[a] (% answering "yes")	Satisfaction with education quality, 2011 (% answering "yes")
HDI group			
Very high human development	6.7	61.9	61.3
High human development	5.9	55.2[b]	58.0
Medium human development	4.9	68.7[b]	69.2
Low human development	4.5	50.0	56.5
Region			
Arab States	4.8	54.3[b]	50.0
East Asia and the Pacific	5.1[b]	79.5[b]	68.2[b]
Europe and Central Asia	5.3	44.8	51.8
Latin America and the Caribbean	6.5	56.7	61.4[b]
South Asia	4.7	64.8	73.3
Sub-Saharan Africa	4.4	50.1[b]	52.0
World	5.3	61.0[b]	64.2

a. Data refer to the most recent year available during the period specified.
b. Value is not displayed in the statistical tables because data are not available for at least half the countries covering at least two-thirds of the population of the group.
Source: HDRO calculations based on Gallup (2012).

Other important subjective indicators of human well-being are satisfaction with the quality of health care and education. Survey results indicate that high-quality health care and education can be delivered at a wide range of income and human development levels. Average global satisfaction with health care quality was 61%, with a low of 19% in Ethiopia and a high of 90% in Luxembourg (see statistical table 7). Average global satisfaction with education quality was 64%, with a low of 35% in Mali and a high of 94% in Cambodia (see statistical table 8).

In South Asia, 65% of respondents indicated satisfaction with health care quality, with Pakistan at 41% and Sri Lanka at 83%, the latter showing that even at comparatively low levels of income it is possible to reinforce social perceptions about community and the state. By contrast, health care satisfaction is 45% in Europe and Central Asia.

1. Dolan, Layard and Metcalfe 2011. Krueger and Schkade (2008) note that over 2000–2006, 157 papers and numerous books were published in the economics literature using data on life satisfaction or subjective well-being.
Source: Kahneman and Krueger 2006; Stiglitz, Sen and Fitoussi 2009; Dolan, Layard and Metcalfe 2011; Stewart 2013.

In South Asia, the highest MPI value is in Bangladesh (0.292 with data for 2007), followed by Pakistan (0.264 with data for 2007) and Nepal (0.217 with data for 2011). The proportion of the population living in multidimensional poverty is 58% in Bangladesh, 49% in Pakistan and 44% in Nepal, and the intensity of deprivation is 50% in Bangladesh, 53% in Pakistan and 49% in Nepal. Although a larger proportion of the population (headcount) lives in multidimensional poverty in Bangladesh than in Pakistan, the intensity of deprivation is higher in Pakistan. Moreover, in Bangladesh and Nepal, the living standards dimension contributes more than the health and education dimensions, but in Pakistan, the health dimension contributes more than the other two dimensions.

Equity and human development

An essential part of human development is equity. Every person has the right to live a fulfilling life according to his or her own values and aspirations. No one should be doomed to a short life or a miserable one because he or she happens to be from the "wrong" class or country, the "wrong" ethnic group or race or the "wrong" sex.

Inequality

Inequality reduces the pace of human development and in some cases may even prevent it entirely. This is most marked for inequality in health and education and less so for inequality in income, where the effects are more substantial in high and very high HDI countries. An analysis of 132 developed and developing countries for this Report finds an inverse relationship between inequality and human development (box 1.5), reinforcing the conclusions of several studies of developed countries.[28]

The effects of inequality on human development can be captured by the Inequality-adjusted Human Development Index (IHDI), which examines the average level of human development and its distribution along the dimensions of life expectancy, educational attainment and command over the resources needed for a decent living. Where there is no inequality, the IHDI equals the HDI. A difference between the two

FIGURE 1.3

The lower the HDI value, the larger the gap between income poverty and multidimensional poverty

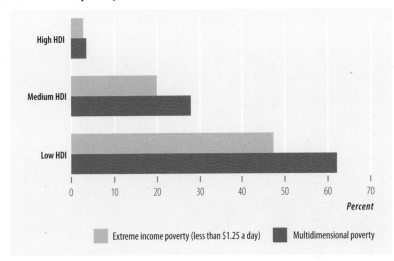

Percent

Extreme income poverty (less than $1.25 a day)   Multidimensional poverty

Note: Data refer to 2002–2011. The population-weighted averages are based on 22 countries for the high HDI group and 36 countries each for the medium and low HDI groups.
Source: HDRO calculations.

denotes inequality; the greater the difference, the greater the inequality.[29]

Based on IHDI calculations for 132 countries in 2012, almost a quarter of HDI value, or 23% is lost to inequality (see statistical table 3). Low HDI countries suffer most because they tend to have greater inequality in more dimensions. Low HDI countries lose a third of HDI value to inequality, whereas very high HDI countries lose only 11%.

Globally, there have been much greater reductions in inequality in health and education in the last two decades than in income.[30] This is partly because of the measures used—life expectancy and mean years of schooling have upper bounds to which all countries eventually converge. But for income, there is no upper limit. Virtually all studies agree that global income inequality is high, though there is no consensus on recent trends.[31] One study that integrated the income distribution of 138 countries over 1970–2000 found that although mean income per capita has risen, inequality has not.[32] Other studies conclude the opposite.[33] Still others find no change at all.[34]

IHDI trends for 66 countries over 1990–2005 show that overall inequality declined marginally due to declines in health and education inequality being offset by increases in income inequality (figure 1.5). Most

No one should be doomed to a short life or a miserable one because he or she happens to be from the "wrong" class or country, the "wrong" ethnic group or race or the "wrong" sex

FIGURE 1.4

There is notable variation among countries in the gap between income poverty and multidimensional poverty

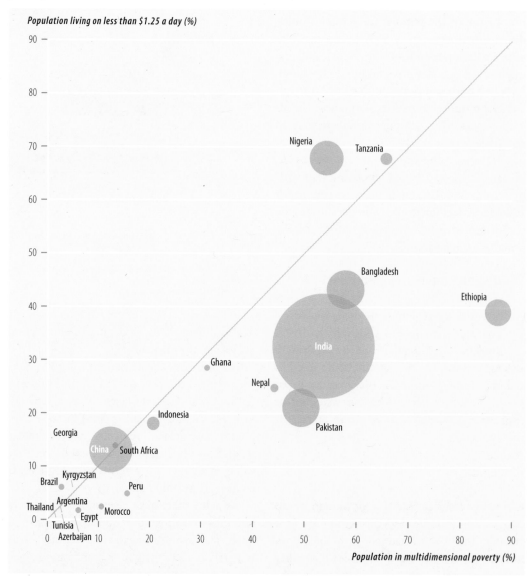

Population living on less than $1.25 a day (%)

Population in multidimensional poverty (%)

Note: Data refer to 2002–2011. Bubble size is proportional to the number of people in multidimensional poverty. Diagonal line indicates where population living on less than $1.25 a day equals population in multidimensional poverty.
Source: HDRO calculations.

regions show rising inequality in income and declining inequality in health and education (figure 1.6). Latin America has seen income inequality fall since 2000, but it still has the most unequal distribution of all regions. Sub-Saharan Africa has the most inequality in health, while South Asia has the most inequality in education.

The world has made much progress in reducing inequality in educational attainment in both enrolment ratios and expected years of schooling over 1990–2010, particularly in

Europe and Central Asia (loss due to inequality in education declined almost 68%), East Asia and the Pacific (34%) and Latin America and the Caribbean (32%). In both developed and developing countries, the average enrolment ratio for primary education is nearly 100%. And more children are finishing school.

Declines in inequality in both health and education may reflect corresponding government priorities and innovations in social policy. There is also a link between health and education. Better education for women, for example, tends to result in better health outcomes for them and for the next generation. Thus life expectancy and educational attainment may move in tandem. Most inequality in education today reflects disparities in quality (box 1.6): many developing countries have dual-track systems, with the well-off attending good schools and universities, mostly privately funded, and the poor attending inadequate, mostly publicly funded facilities.[35]

Rising inequality, especially between groups, can lead to social instability, undermining long-term human development progress. Persistence of inequality often results in a lack of intergenerational social mobility, which can also lead to social unrest.

The rise in income inequality to some extent reflects a failure of national fiscal, and particularly taxation, systems. This can be offset by social protection. In Latin America, for example, income inequality has declined as a result of cash transfer programmes.

Gender and women's status

Gender equality is both a core concern and an essential part of human development. All too often, women are discriminated against in health, education and the labour market, which restricts their freedoms. The extent of discrimination can be measured through the Gender Inequality Index (GII), which captures the loss of achievement due to gender inequality in three dimensions: reproductive health, empowerment and labour market participation. The higher the GII value, the greater the discrimination. Based on 2012 data for 148 countries, the GII shows large variations across countries, ranging from 0.045 (in Netherlands) to 0.747 (in Yemen), with an average of 0.463 (see statistical table 4).

High gender disparities persist in South Asia (0.568), Sub-Saharan Africa (0.577) and the Arab States (0.555). In South Asia, the three driving factors are low female representation in parliament (18.5%), gender imbalances in educational achievement (28% of women have completed at least secondary education, compared with 50% of men) and low labour force participation (31% of women are in the labour force, compared with 81% of men).

BOX 1.5

Inequality holds back human development

HDRO research using Human Development Index (HDI) data yields robust findings of an inverse relationship between inequality and subsequent improvement in human development, driven mostly by inequality in health and education rather than in income.

Using data on 132 countries for 2012, regression analysis showed the effects of multidimensional inequality (measured as the loss in the Inequality-adjusted Human Development Index relative to the HDI) on the HDI and each of its components (health, education and income) due to four explanatory variables: overall inequality in human development, inequality in life expectancy, inequality in educational attainment and inequality in income per capita. A different regression was used for each explanatory variable, and all regressions included dummy variables to control for the level of human development (low, medium, high and very high). Overall inequality in human development, inequality in life expectancy and inequality in educational attainment showed a highly statistically significant (at the 1% level) negative correlation, but inequality in income per capita showed no correlation. Results were robust to different specifications, including grouping countries with low and medium human development on the one side and countries with high and very high human development on the other.

Source: HDRO.

FIGURE 1.5

Losses due to inequality in HDI and its components

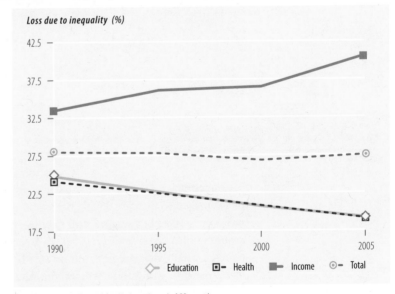

Note: Based on a population-weighted balanced panel of 66 countries.
Source: HDRO calculations using data from Milanović (2010).

Between 2000 and 2012, progress in reducing the GII value has been virtually universal, but uneven.[36] Countries in the very high human development group outperform those in other human development groups and demonstrate greater parity between women and men in educational attainment and labour market participation. Even in this group, however, several countries have huge gender gaps in

FIGURE 1.6

Most regions show declining inequality in health and education and rising inequality in income

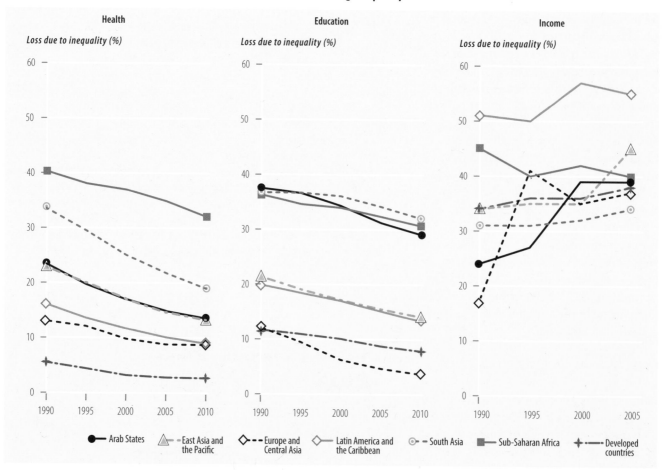

Note: Based on a population-weighted balanced panel of 182 countries for loss due to health inequality, 144 countries for loss due to education inequality and 66 countries for loss due to income inequality. Data on income inequality from Milanović (2010) are available through 2005.
Source: HDRO calculations using health data from United Nations Department of Economic and Social Affairs life tables, education data from Barro and Lee (2010) and income inequality data from Milanović (2010).

parliamentary representation. Italy, for example, managed to increase female representation more than 50%, but women still occupy only around a fifth of all seats (20.7%). In Ireland, female parliamentary representation is still below 20% while in Rwanda, women outnumber men in parliamentary representation (52% compared with 48%).

Though many countries in Sub-Saharan Africa showed improvement in their GII value between 2000 and 2012, they still perform worse than countries in other regions, mainly because of higher maternal mortality ratios and adolescent fertility rates and huge gaps in educational attainment.

One of the most disturbing trends concerns the sex ratio at birth, which is deteriorating in some fast-growing countries. The

natural ratio for children ages 0–4 is 1.05 (or 105 boys to 100 girls). But in the 175 countries for which 2012 data are available, the average was 1.07, and 13 countries had a ratio of 1.08–1.18.[37]

In some countries, sex-selective abortion and infanticide are artificially altering the demographic landscape, leading to a shortage of girls and women. This is not just a concern for gender justice and equality; it also has major implications for democracy and could lead to social violence.

The high male sex ratio at birth reflects women's status in society, entrenched patriarchal mores and prejudices, which are an aspect of deep-rooted sociocultural beliefs, the changing aspirations of urban and rural societies, and the dowry system in some countries.[38] In recent years, the problem has been exacerbated by the spread and misuse of ultrasound technologies that enable parents to exercise age-old preferences for boys. The key driver, however, is the combination of patriarchal mores and greater economic value of boys in the presence of a dowry system. In absence of the latter—for instance, in African countries—patriarchal prejudices alone do not manifest in high male sex ratio at birth.

Redressing this imbalance will involve changing many social norms, including those that affect the economic incentives of the household to have boys rather than girls. This would include effectively ending the exploitative dowry system,[39] generating greater economic opportunities for women, creating conditions for women to have greater control over their lives and enhancing their political participation and decisionmaking within households.

It has often been argued that improving education for women helps raise their levels of health and nutrition and reduces fertility rates.[40] Thus, in addition to its intrinsic value in expanding women's choices, education also has an instrumental value in enhancing health and fertility outcomes of women and children. In this respect, low and medium HDI countries still have some way to go. There was also a gender imbalance among the uneducated population in high and very high HDI countries in 1970–2010, although there was substantially more gender balance at all education levels in these countries for girls and young women currently of school attendance age.

Important as education and job creation for women are, they are not enough. Standard policies to enhance women's income do not take into account gender differences within households, women's greater burden of unpaid work and gender division of work as per cultural norms. Policies based on economic theory that does not take these factors into account may have adverse impacts on women, even though they create economic prosperity.[41] Key to improving gender equity are political and social reforms that enhance women's human rights, including freedom, dignity, participation, autonomy and collective agency.[42]

BOX 1.6

Education quality: achievement on the Programme for International Student Assessment

The education component of the Human Development Index has two measures: mean years of schooling and expected years of schooling. But even more than years of schooling, quality of education is a key factor in expanding human capabilities (see figure).

The Organisation for Economic Co-operation and Development's Programme for International Student Assessment (PISA) collects internationally compatible data on the educational attainment of students and allows for cross-country comparison of average learning scores, share of low-performing schools and consistency of quality outcomes. For example, the advantages of a highly educated labour force, which countries such as the United States have traditionally had, appear to be eroding as young cohorts in other countries (such as Ireland, Japan and the Republic of Korea) reach and surpass the qualifications found in the United States.

In the most recent PISA, conducted in 63 countries and territories in 2009, many countries showed impressive strides in quality of learning outcomes. Students from Shanghai, China, outperformed students from 62 countries in reading, mathematics and science skills. They were followed by students from the Republic of Korea, Finland and Hong Kong, China (SAR) in reading; Singapore, Hong Kong, China (SAR) and the Republic of Korea in mathematics; and Finland, Hong Kong, China (SAR) and Singapore in science. The United States performed below average in mathematics, sharing 29th place with Ireland and Portugal; slightly above average in science, in 21st place; and above average in reading, sharing 15th place with Iceland and Poland. Brazil, Chile, Indonesia and Peru have seen impressive gains, catching up from very low levels of performance. Investments by some countries in education quality will likely bring future payoffs in a more knowledge-driven globalized world.

Programme for International Student Assessment scores in reading positively correlate with HDI values

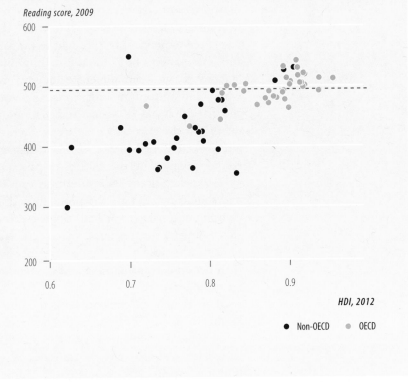

Source: HDI values, HDRO calculations; Programme for International Student Assessment scores, OECD (2010b).

Intergenerational equity and sustainability

When one crisis follows another, it is easy to lose perspective about important long-term consequences of current actions. It is thus important to bear in mind that today's choices can have a large and decisive influence on the choices available for decades in the future. Sustainable human development is about understanding the links between temporal choices of different generations and about assigning rights to both present and future generations.

Clearly a balance is needed. Enhancing people's capabilities now—especially the capabilities of those who are poor or live with multiple deprivations—is vital as a matter of basic rights and part of the universalism of life claims.[43] Moreover, poverty and misery today have negative consequences for the future. The objective should thus be both intragenerational and intergenerational equity.

Investing in people today requires a prudent balance between debts incurred today and the obligations they impose on future generations. As the 1994 *Human Development Report* underscores, "All postponed debts mortgage sustainability, whether economic debts, social debts or ecological debts."[44] The recent economic crisis has brought to the fore the sustainability of economic debt, public and private, when economies are not growing, while tending to draw attention away from the critical issues of social and ecological debts. On the environmental front, there is already extensive evidence of severe damage to ecosystems from the choices of past and current generations. Poor countries cannot and should not imitate the production and consumption patterns of rich countries. And rich countries must reduce their ecological footprint because from a global perspective their per capita consumption and production are not sustainable.

Of particular concern now are the global challenges of climate change and fragile ecosystems. An influential study concluded that "Humanity has already transgressed at least three planetary boundaries,"[45] a point repeated in the 2012 Report of the UN Secretary General's High Level Panel on Global Sustainability.[46] Few countries are following an ecologically sustainable path now, underscoring the need for technological innovations and shifts in consumption that can facilitate movement towards sustainable human development.[47]

Figure 1.7 plots the ecological footprint of consumption of 151 countries against their HDI value in 2012.[48] Very few countries have both a high HDI value and an ecological footprint below the world average biocapacity (1.79 global hectares per capita in 2008). This does not bode well for the world. Over time, the situation is becoming more dire. While some high HDI countries have an ecological footprint below the world average, their footprints have been increasing over time.

People care not only about the choices open to them, but also about how those choices are secured, by whom and at whose expense. Progress in human development achieved sustainably is superior to gains made at the cost of future generations. Indeed, a proper accounting system for sustainable human development would include both future human development and current achievements.

Better ways to monitor environmental sustainability are also needed. The 2012 UN Conference on Sustainable Development called for measures that address the connections between present and future sets of choices. Such measures should monitor the accumulation of economic and environmental debt based on the premise that every citizen on the planet, whether alive or not yet born, has an equal right to live a comfortable, fulfilling life. These measures should also highlight planetary boundaries or "tipping points", recognizing that climate change, for example, already imposes substantial costs, with the brunt of them borne by poor countries and poor communities.

Social integration

Human development involves expanding individual capabilities. Yet individuals are also bound up with others. Thus, how individuals relate to each other is important in building cohesive and enduring societies. Integrating different groups can be as critical for well-being

> Progress in human development achieved sustainably is superior to gains made at the cost of future generations

FIGURE 1.7

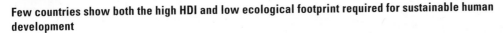

Few countries show both the high HDI and low ecological footprint required for sustainable human development

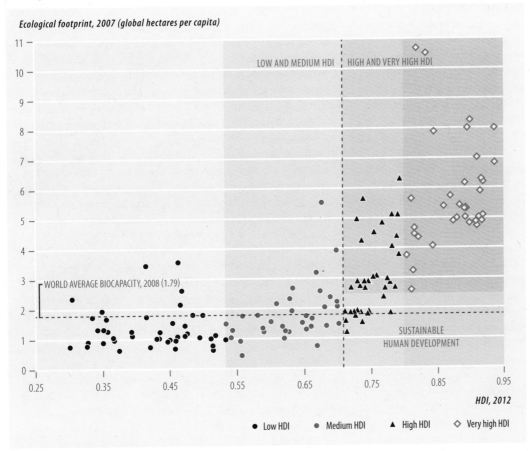

Note: Ecological footprint is a measure of the biocapacity of the earth and the demand on biocapacity. It depends on the average productivity of biologically productive land and water in a given year.
Source: HDRO calculations and Global Footprint Network (2011).

and social stability as economic success. Inequity and exclusion are social injustices that fundamentally weaken human freedoms.

An integrated society relies on effective social institutions that enable people to act collectively, enhancing trust and solidarity between groups. These institutions include formal nongovernmental organizations, informal associations and cooperatives, as well as norms and rules of behaviour. They influence individual human development outcomes, social cohesion and social stability. To differentiate them from individual capabilities, the functioning of these institutions and their impact on people can be described as "social competencies" (box 1.7). The extent to which social competencies foster more-cohesive societies can be assessed by their

success at achieving social inclusion and social stability.

Some developing countries have sought to address social exclusion by distributing the benefits of growth more evenly in a refinement of the growth with redistribution strategy. But this commodity-centric view of inclusive growth does little to end the economic and social discrimination that often has long-standing historical and cultural roots. Such discrimination may be widespread even in countries with high income per capita. Clearly income growth alone cannot achieve social cohesion; active policies are needed.

The impact of inequity can persist over generations. For instance, a study of eight developed countries found that more-unequal countries usually had lower social mobility.[49] In

BOX 1.7

Social competencies: human development beyond the individual

Individuals cannot flourish alone; indeed, they cannot function alone. The human development approach, however, has been essentially individualistic, assuming that development is the expansion of individuals' capabilities or freedoms. Yet there are aspects of societies that affect individuals but cannot be assessed at the individual level because they are based on relationships, such as how well families or communities function, summarized for society as a whole in the ideas of social cohesion and social inclusion. Individuals are bound up with others. Social institutions affect individuals' identities and choices. Being a member of a healthy society is an essential part of a thriving existence.

So one task of the human development approach is to explore the nature of social institutions that are favourable for human flourishing. Development then has to be assessed not only for the short-run impact on individual capabilities, but also for whether society evolves in a way that supports human flourishing. Social conditions affect not only the outcomes of individuals in a particular society today, but also those of future generations.

Social institutions are all institutions in which people act collectively (that is, they involve more than one person), other than profit-making market institutions and the state. They include formal nongovernmental organizations, informal associations, cooperatives, producer associations, neighbourhood associations, sports clubs, savings associations and many more. They also consist of norms and rules of behaviour affecting human development outcomes. For example, attitudes towards employment affect material well-being, and norms of hierarchy and discrimination affect inequality, discrimination, empowerment, political freedom and so on. To describe what those institutions can be and do, and to understand how they affect individuals, we can use the term *social competencies*.

Central to the human development perspective is that societal norms affect people's choices and behaviours towards others, thus influencing outcomes in the whole community. Community norms and behaviours can constrain choice in deleterious ways from a human development perspective—for example, ostracizing, or in extreme cases killing, those who make choices that contravene social rules. Families trapped in poverty by informal norms that support early marriage and dowry requirements might reject changes to such entrenched social norms. Social institutions change over time, and those changes may be accompanied by social tension if they hamper the interests of some groups while favouring others.

Policy change is the outcome of a political struggle in which different groups (and individuals) support or oppose particular changes. In this struggle, unorganized individuals are generally powerless, but by joining together they can acquire power collectively. Social action favouring human development (such as policies to extend education, progressive taxation and minimum wages) happens not spontaneously, but because of groups that are effective in supporting change, such as producer groups, worker associations, social movements and political parties. These organizations are especially crucial for poorer people, as demonstrated by a group of sex workers in Kolkata, India, and women in a squatter community in Cape Town, South Africa, who improved their conditions and self-respect by joining together and exerting collective pressure.

Societies vary widely in the number, functions, effectiveness and consequences of their social competencies. Institutions and norms can be classified as human development–promoting, human development–neutral and human development–undermining. It is fundamental to identify and encourage those that promote valuable capabilities and relationships among and between individuals and institutions. Some social institutions (including norms) can support human development in some respects but not in others: for example, strong family bonds can provide individuals with support during upheavals, but may constrain individual choices and opportunities.

Broadly speaking, institutions that promote social cohesion and human development show low levels of disparity across groups (for example, ethnic, religious or gender groups) and high levels of interaction and trust among people and across groups, which results in solidarity and the absence of violent conflict. It is not a coincidence that 5 of the 10 most peaceful countries in the world in 2012, according to the Global Peace Index, are also among the most equal societies as measured by loss in Human Development Index value due to inequality. They are also characterized by the absence of discrimination and low levels of marginalization. In some instances antidiscriminatory measures can ease the burden of marginalization and partially mitigate the worst effects of exclusion. For instance, US law mandating that hospital emergency rooms offer treatment to all patients regardless of their ability to pay partly mitigates the impact of an expensive health care system with limited coverage, while affirmative action in a range of countries (including Brazil, Malaysia, South Africa and the United States) has improved the situation of deprived groups and contributed to social stability.

The study of social institutions and social competencies must form an essential part of the human development approach—including the formation of groups; interactions between groups and individuals; incentives and constraints to collective action; the relationship among groups, politics and policy outcomes; the role of norms in influencing behaviours; and how norms are formed and changed.

Source: Stewart 2013; Institute for Economics and Peace 2012.

---

the United Kingdom in particular, as inequality rose, intergenerational mobility declined.

The 2010 *Latin America and the Caribbean Human Development Report* highlighted the link between the lack of social mobility and persistent inequality.[50] In Brazil, at least a quarter of inequality in earnings is associated with household circumstances, such as parents' educational attainment, race or ethnicity, or place of birth.[51] Such persistence of income distribution patterns across generations is also evident in Chile and Mexico, although Mexico has seen increased intergenerational mobility in recent years.[52] Generally, Latin America suffers from low social mobility, stifling opportunities for individuals at the bottom of the income distribution for whom performance in society is determined largely by background characteristics beyond their control. The problem is particularly intractable in heterogeneous societies, as members of deprived groups find it particularly difficult to progress.

Inequity and exclusion endure when the excluded and those at the lower ends of the distribution lack the political voice to seek redress. More-equal and more-just societies, essential for satisfactory and sustainable human progress, thus require greater voice and political participation and more-accountable governments (box 1.8).

Even in the European Union, where a large part of the population has seen rising prosperity, some groups have been left behind. The Roma, for example, have been part of European civilization for more than a thousand years. With an estimated 7–9 million people, they are Europe's biggest ethnic minority, present in all 27 EU member states. Most are EU citizens but continue to suffer discrimination and social exclusion. As two regional *Human Development Reports* have revealed, the Roma are often trapped in a vicious cycle of social exclusion that has persisted generation after generation.[53]

The presence of inequalities can adversely affect social interactions and restrict freedom

> The presence of inequalities can adversely affect social interactions and restrict freedom of choice

---

BOX 1.8

Poverty's structural dimensions

The traditional agendas for reducing poverty recognize but inadequately address its structural sources. Contemporary interventions to promote inclusive growth have tended to focus on the outcomes of development through expanding and strengthening social safety nets. While such public initiatives are to be encouraged, they address the symptoms of poverty, not its sources.

The results of such restrictive interventions are reduction of income poverty to varying degrees and some improvement in human development. But across much of the South, income inequalities have increased, social disparities have widened and injustice remains pervasive, while the structural sources of poverty remain intact. Any credible agenda to end poverty must correct the structural injustices that perpetuate it.

Unequal access to assets

Inequitable access to wealth and knowledge disempowers the excluded from competing in the marketplace. Rural poverty, for example, originates in insufficient access to land and water for less privileged segments of rural society. Land ownership has been not only a source of economic privilege, but also a source of social and political authority. The prevailing structures of land ownership remain inimical to a functioning democratic order. Similarly, lack of access to capital and property perpetuates urban poverty.

Unequal participation in the market

With the prevailing property structures of society, the resource-poor remain excluded from more-dynamic market sectors. The main agents of production tend to be the urban elite, who own the corporate assets that power faster growing economic sectors. By contrast, the excluded partake only as primary producers and wage earners, at the lowest end of the production and marketing chains, leaving them with little opportunity to share in market economy opportunities for adding value to their labour.

Capital markets have failed to provide sufficient credit to the excluded, even though they have demonstrated their creditworthiness through low default rates in the microcredit market. And formal capital markets have

not provided financial instruments to attract the savings of the excluded and transform them into investment assets in the faster growing corporate sector.

Unjust governance

This inequitable and unjust social and economic universe can be compounded by unjust governance. Often the excluded remain voiceless in the institutions of governance and thus underserved by public institutions. The institutions of democracy remain unresponsive to the needs of the excluded, both in the design of policy agendas and in the selection of electoral candidates. Representative institutions thus tend to be monopolized by the affluent and socially powerful, who then use office to enhance their wealth and perpetuate their hold over power.

Promoting structural change

To correct these structural injustices, policy agendas need to be made more inclusive by strengthening the capacity of the excluded to participate on more equitable terms in the market economy and the democratic polity. Such agendas should reposition the excluded within the processes of production, distribution and governance. The production process needs to graduate the excluded from living out their lives exclusively as wage earners and tenant farmers by investing them with the capacity to become owners of productive assets. The distribution process must elevate the excluded beyond their inherited role as primary producers by enabling them to move upmarket through greater opportunities to share in adding value through collective action. Access to assets and markets must be backed by equitable access to quality health care and education, integral to empowering the excluded.

The governance process must increase the active participation of the excluded in representative institutions, which is crucial to enhancing their voice in decisionmaking and providing access to the institutions of governance.

Source: Sobhan, R. 2010. *Challenging the Injustice of Poverty.*

TABLE 1.3

Inequality and satisfaction with freedom of choice and community

HDI group and region	Overall loss in HDI value due to inequality, 2012 (%)	Satisfaction with freedom of choice, 2007–2011[a] (% satisfied)	Satisfaction with community,[b] 2007–2011[a] (% answering yes)
HDI group			
Very high human development	10.8	81.5	85.9
High human development	20.6	66.3	76.4
Medium human development	24.2	77.8	79.9
Low human development	33.5	61.8	72.2
Region			
Arab States	25.4	54.6	67.6
East Asia and the Pacific	21.3	78.7[c]	80.1[c]
Europe and Central Asia	12.9	58.5	76.5
Latin America and the Caribbean	25.7	77.9	79.0
South Asia	29.1	72.9	83.2
Sub-Saharan Africa	35.0	69.1	65.2
World	23.3	73.9	79.0

a. Data refer to the most recent year available during the period specified.
b. Based on the Gallup survey question on overall satisfaction with city.
c. Value is not displayed in the statistical tables because data are not available for at least half the countries covering at least two-thirds of the population of the group.
Source: Overall loss in HDI value due to inequality, HDRO calculations based on the Inequality-Adjusted HDI; satisfaction with freedom of choice and community, HDRO calculations based on Gallup (2012).

of choice. Subjective data can provide an insight into the state of social integration within a country or community. Evidence suggests a small negative correlation between losses due to inequality and satisfaction with freedom of choice and with the community. Evidence also suggests that people in countries with a high HDI value are generally more satisfied with their freedom of choice and with the community. Exploring these associations can offer important policy lessons for countries (table 1.3).

Human security

The 1994 *Human Development Report* argued that the concept of security must shift from the idea of a militaristic safeguarding of state borders to the reduction of insecurity in people's daily lives (or human insecurity).[54] In every society, human security is undermined by a variety of threats, including hunger, disease, crime, unemployment, human rights violations

and environmental challenges. The intensity of these threats differs across the world, but human security remains a universal quest for freedom from want and fear.

Consider economic insecurity. In the countries of the North, millions of young people are now unable to find work. And in the South, millions of farmers have been unable to earn a decent livelihood and forced to migrate, with many adverse effects, particularly for women. Closely related to insecurity in livelihoods is insecurity in food and nutrition. Many developing country households faced with high food prices cannot afford two square meals a day, undermining progress in child nutrition. Another major cause of impoverishment in many countries, rich and poor, is unequal access to affordable health care. Ill health in the household (especially of the head of the household) is one of the most common sources of impoverishment, as earnings are lost and medical expenses are incurred.

Perspectives on security need to shift from a misplaced emphasis on military strength to a well rounded, people-centred view. Progress in this shift can be gleaned in part from statistics on crime, particularly homicides, and military spending.

Crime

Freedom from fear should be reflected in low crime rates, specifically low homicide rates. A few studies have also used homicide rates to assess civic engagement and trust.[55] The 2012 *Caribbean Human Development Report*, for example, argues that violent crime erodes confidence in future development prospects, reduces the competitiveness of industries and services by imposing burdensome security costs and damages the investment climate. Crime may also lead to a brain drain from the country or affected community. And diverting resources to control crime reduces the funds available to invest in health care and education, thus slowing social integration and dampening development.[56]

In recent years, the global average homicide rate for 189 countries with data was 6.9 per 100,000 people,[57] with a low of 0 in Monaco and a high of 91.6 in Honduras

MAP 1.1

There is a small negative connotation between homicide rates and HDI values

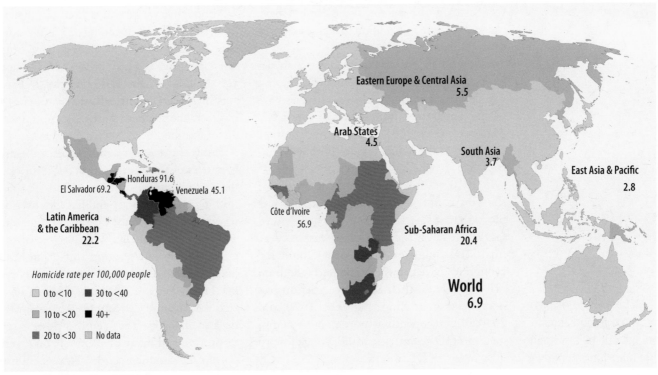

Source: HDRO calculations based on UNODC 2012.

(see statistical table 9). There is a small negative correlation between homicide rate and HDI value, with low HDI countries at 14.6 per 100,000 people, high HDI countries at 13.0 and very high HDI countries at 2.1. Homicide rates are highest in Latin America and the Caribbean (22.2 per 100,000 people), followed by Sub-Saharan Africa (20.4), Europe and Central Asia (5.5), the Arab States (4.5), South Asia (3.7) and East Asia and the Pacific (2.8).

It can also be instructive to look at the homicide rates for cities. Contrary to popular perception, crime is not generally higher in poorer cities. Amartya Sen notes that Kolkata "is not only one of the poorest cities in India, and indeed in the world, but it also has the lowest violent crime rate of all Indian cities."[58] This is also true for homicide: Kolkata's average incidence of murder, 0.3 per 100,000 people, is lower than in much more affluent London (2.4) and New York (5.0).[59]

Sen argues that Kolkata has benefited from its long history as a "mixed" city, without ethnic or income separation between neighbourhoods.

For several decades, the city has also had a system of basic public services, including government hospitals, schools, colleges and a low-cost public transport system, which have dampened the impacts of economic and social exclusion. In local trains, poor vendors commonly travel side by side with wage labourers and white-collar workers.

But when people do not have access to services, they may be more prone to crime. A UK study of reoffending criminals, for example, noted that many prisoners are victims of a lifetime of social exclusion[60] and are effectively excluded from access to basic services.[61]

Military spending

Since the end of the Cold War, there has been no overall intensification of militarization, measured by military expenditure as a proportion of GDP, partly because of changes in the threats to national security. While interstate conflicts appear to be on the decline since the early 1990s, the number of intrastate conflicts has increased since the mid-20th century.

Today the majority of security threats come not from other countries but from insurgencies, terrorism and other civil conflicts.[62] Conflicts in the post–Cold War era have claimed more than 5 million casualties, 95% of them civilians.[63]

In South Asia, for example, all nine countries have experienced internal conflict in the last two decades, and the resulting casualties have outnumbered those from interstate conflicts.[64] Moreover, since 2001, more of the conflicts have been in the poorer regions of those countries than elsewhere.[65]

In 2010, military spending worldwide for the 104 countries with data available was more than $1.4 trillion, or 2.6% of world GDP. Most of the spending was by very high HDI countries. But as other countries' economies have grown, particularly medium HDI countries, their military expenditures have been increasing. Between 1990 and 2010, military spending more than tripled in medium HDI countries, while rising close to 50% in low HDI countries and 22% in very high HDI countries and falling almost 47% in high HDI countries. Nevertheless, in the three HDI groups where total military expenditure grew, the increase was slower than GDP growth. These aggregates hide considerable diversity. Europe and Central Asia saw military spending decline 69% between 1990 and 2010, while South Asia, East Asia and the Pacific, and the Arab States saw it rise 43%–388%.[66]

Although development is often accompanied by a rise in military spending, this is not always the case (figure 1.8). The highest shares of military spending as a proportion of GDP are in very high and high HDI countries, but some very high HDI countries have a share below 1% of GDP, among them Austria, Iceland, Ireland and Luxembourg.

This is of particular significance for the rising countries of the South. Costa Rica, for example, has not had an army since 1948.[67] It spends nothing on the military and has thus been able to earmark more funds for social programmes and social investments.[68] In 2009, it invested 6.3% of GDP in education and 7% in health. Such choices contributed to its progress on the HDI from 0.621 in 1980 to 0.773 in 2012.

Today, around 20 countries have small or no armed forces. They tend to possess small territories, and many of them rely on external powers for national security. Not all countries have the preconditions for complete demilitarization, but most have scope for substantial slowing in their military spending. Particularly with respect to internal conflicts, India has shown that while policing may be more effective in curbing violence in the short term, redistribution and overall development are better strategies to prevent and contain civil unrest in the medium term.[69]

*   *   *

This analysis of the state of human development is positive and hopeful. Yet much work remains. Almost every country has challenges to overcome and opportunities for further progress. Of particular concern is that some developed countries, in response to the debt crisis, are pursuing austerity policies that could foreclose or reduce future choices and options for people in the South.

The only viable path to higher human development is through active investment in enhancing capabilities and enlarging opportunities. As the 1991 *Human Development Report* noted, "People who are healthier, confident, and skilled will be in a much better position to cope with a fast-changing environment and meet the

> Not all countries have the preconditions for complete demilitarization, but most have scope for substantial slowing in their military spending

FIGURE 1.8

Development is not always accompanied by a rise in military spending

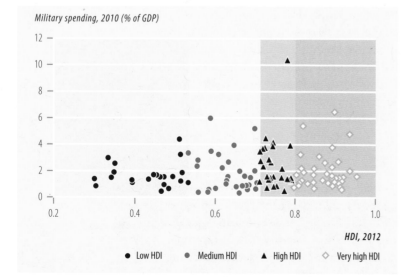

Source: Military expenditure, Stockholm International Peace Research Institute; HDI, HDRO calculations.

technological and competitive demands of the international marketplace."[70]

The next chapter documents the extent to which many countries of the South have been able to follow this route, as well as the global impact they are having. Later chapters will consider how they have done this and examine the implication of the rise of the South for international governance and for reshaping global power relations.

"When the music changes,
so does the dance."

African proverb

"I do not want my house to be
walled in on all sides and my
windows to be stuffed. I want
the cultures of all the lands to
be blown about my house as
freely as possible. But I refuse
to be blown off my feet by any."

Mahatma Gandhi

2.

A more global South

A striking feature of the world scene in recent years is the transformation of many developing countries into dynamic economies that are doing well in economic growth and trade and progressing rapidly on human development. During these uncertain times, they are collectively bolstering world economic growth, lifting other developing economies, reducing poverty and increasing wealth on a grand scale. They still face formidable challenges and are home to many of the world's poor.[1] But they have demonstrated how pragmatic policies and a strong focus on human development can release the opportunities latent in their economies, facilitated by globalization.

The rise of the South is noteworthy for its diversity. This wave of developing countries encompasses countries with very different endowments, social structures, geography and history: for example, Algeria and Argentina, Brazil and Bangladesh, China and Chile, Ghana and Guyana, India and Indonesia, and Malaysia and Mozambique. These countries demonstrate that rapid people-centred development can take root in a wide range of contexts. And their experiences and knowhow are an expanding source of best practice that should enable other developing countries to catch up.

The rapidly expanding connections between these countries are also leading to a more balanced form of globalization. New trade routes are flourishing: countries as diverse as Morocco, South Africa, Thailand, Turkey and Viet Nam each have substantial export and import relationships with more than 100 economies.[2] New and improved technologies, adapted to local conditions, are boosting people's productivity and enabling production to be shared across borders.

And all this is happening as people and continents are connected on a previously unimaginable scale. More than 2 billion people use the Internet, and every year more than 1 billion people travel internationally.[3]

This transformation is affecting the dynamics of regional and global relationships. The leading countries of the South played a crucial role in responding to the 2008 financial crisis. Dialogue is intensifying on the appropriate provisioning of global public goods, such as curbing climate change, developing rules for stable financial markets, advancing multilateral trade negotiations and agreeing on mechanisms to finance and produce green technologies. It may seem that increasing the number of participants will make it more difficult to arrive at a global consensus. But the rise of the South could help break stalemates on some of today's global issues and lead to more development-friendly global agreements.

Rebalancing: a more global world, a more global South

Global production is rebalancing in ways not seen for 150 years. Growth in the cross-border movement of goods, services, people and ideas has been remarkable. In 1800, trade accounted for 2% of world output.[4] The proportion remained small right after the Second World War, and by 1960 it was still less than 25%. By 2011, however, trade accounted for nearly 60% of global output.[5] The expansion it represents is widely distributed, with at least 89 developing countries increasing their trade to output ratio over the past two decades (box 2.1).[6]

Today, as a result of reduced trade barriers and lower transport costs, the production of manufactures is fragmented across borders, with many countries trading intermediate goods.[7] And changes in information technology have made services increasingly tradable. The result has been a remarkable rise in intraindustry and intrafirm trade.

Developing countries, particularly in Asia, have ridden these shifts to great advantage. Between 1980 and 2010, they increased their share of world merchandise trade from about 25% to 47%[8] and their share of world output from 33% to 45%. Today, developing countries account for a third of value added in world production of manufactured goods.[9] Between 1990 and 2010, the merchandise exports of eight developing country members of the Group of 20 (G20) increased 15-fold, from about

BOX 2.1

The South's integration with the world economy and human development

In a sample of 107 developing countries over 1990–2010, about 87% can be considered globally integrated: they increased their trade to output ratio, have many substantial trading partnerships1 and maintain a high trade to output ratio relative to countries at comparable income levels.[2] All these developing countries are also much more connected to the world and with each other: Internet use has expanded dramatically, with the median annual growth in the number of users exceeding 30% between 2000 and 2010.

While not all globally integrated developing countries have made rapid gains in Human Development Index (HDI) value, the converse is true. Almost all developing countries that made the most improvement in HDI value relative to their peers between 1990 and 2012 (at least 45 in the sample here) have integrated more with the world economy over the past two decades; their average increase in trade to output ratio is about 13 percentage points greater than that of the group of developing countries with more modest improvement in HDI value. This is consistent with earlier findings that countries tend to open more as they develop.[3]

The increasingly integrated countries with major improvement in HDI value include not only the large ones that dominate the headlines, but also dozens of smaller and least developed countries. Thus they constitute a larger and more varied group than the emerging market economies often designated by acronyms, such as BRICS (Brazil, Russian Federation, India, China and South Africa), IBSA (India, Brazil and South Africa), CIVETS (Colombia, Indonesia, Viet Nam, Egypt, Turkey and South Africa) and MIST (Mexico, Indonesia, South Korea [Republic of Korea] and Turkey).

The figure below plots improvement in HDI value[4] against the change in trade to output ratio, an indicator of the depth of participation in global markets. More than four-fifths of these developing countries increased their trade to output ratio between 1990 and 2012. Among the exceptions in the subgroup that also made substantial improvement in HDI value are Indonesia, Pakistan and Venezuela, three large countries that are considered global players in world markets, exporting or importing from at least 80 economies. Two smaller countries whose trade to output ratio declined (Mauritius and Panama) continue to trade at levels much higher than would be expected for countries at comparable income levels. All countries that had substantial improvement in HDI value and increased their trade to output ratio between 1990 and 2012 are highlighted in the upper right quadrant of the figure. Countries in the lower right quadrant (including Kenya, the Philippines and South Africa) increased their trade to output ratio but made modest improvement in HDI value.

Human progress and trade expansion in the South

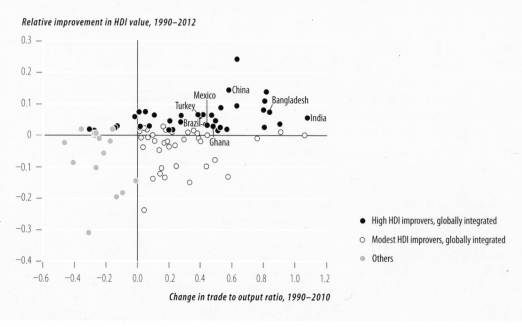

1. Bilateral trade exceeding $2 million in 2010–2011.
2. Based on results from a cross-country regression of trade to GDP ratio on income per capita that controls for population and landlockedness.
3. See Rodrik (2001).
4. Relative HDI improvement is measured by residuals from a regression of the change in the log of HDI value between 1990 and 2012 on the log of initial HDI value in 1990. Five countries with black dots in the upper left quadrant made substantial improvement in HDI value but reduced their trade to output ratio between 1990 and 2010, though they either maintained a large number of substantial trading ties globally or traded more than predicted for countries at comparable levels of income per capita. Countries with open circles in the upper right and lower right quadrants had modest relative improvement in HDI value between 1990 and 2012 but increased their trade to output ratio or maintained a large number of substantial trading ties.
Source: HDRO calculations; trade to output ratios from World Bank (2012a).

$200 billion to $3 trillion.[10] But trade has also increased for many other countries. In 2010, merchandise exports per capita from Sub-Saharan Africa were more than twice those from India.[11]

In 1995–1996 Thailand had around 10 trading partners to which it exported more than $1 billion in goods each; just 15 years later it had three times as many, spread across the globe (map 2.1).[12]

MAP 2.1

Thailand's export expansion, 1995–2011

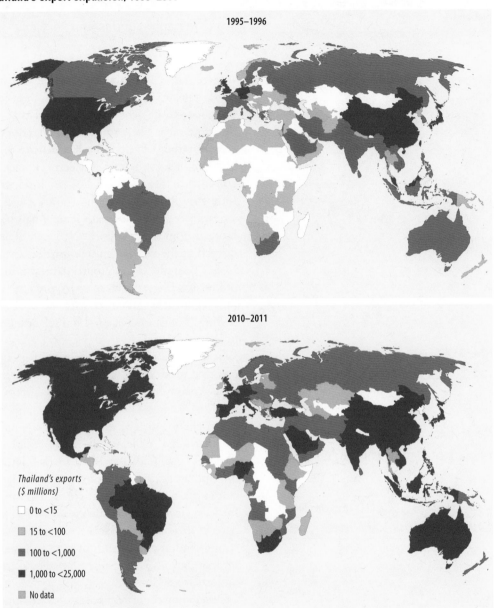

1995–1996

2010–2011

Thailand's exports
($ millions)

☐ 0 to <15

▨ 15 to <100

▨ 100 to <1,000

■ 1,000 to <25,000

▨ No data

Note: Data are averages for 1995 and 1996 and for 2010 and 2011.
Source: UNSD 2012.

Global rebalancing has been accompanied by an unprecedented linking of developing regions. Between 1980 and 2011, South–South trade as a share of world merchandise trade rose from 8.1% to 26.7%, with growth particularly remarkable in the 2000s (figure 2.1). Over the same period, the share of North–North trade declined from about 46% to less than 30%. These trends hold even when exports and imports of natural resources are excluded.[13] South–South trade has been an important growth stimulus during the recent economic downturn. Countries of the South are exporting more merchandise (and manufactures) to each other than to countries of the North, and those exports are more intensive in skills and technology.[14]

Sub-Saharan Africa has become a major new source and destination for South–South trade. Between 1992 and 2011, China's trade with Sub-Saharan Africa rose from $1 billion to more than $140 billion. Indian companies are investing in African industries ranging from infrastructure to hospitality and

FIGURE 2.1

As a share of world merchandise trade, South–South trade more than tripled over 1980–2011, while North–North trade declined

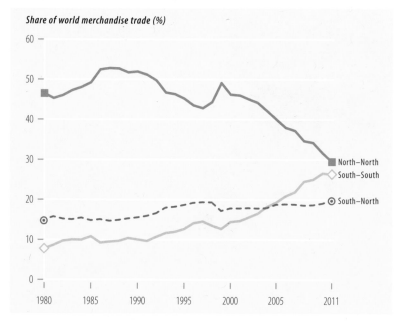

Share of world merchandise trade (%)

North–North
South–South
South–North

1980   1985   1990   1995   2000   2005   2011

Note: North in 1980 refers to Australia, Canada, Japan, New Zealand, the United States and Western Europe.
Source: HDRO calculations based on UNSD (2012).

TABLE 2.1

Least developed countries' trade with China, 2000–2001 and 2010–2011 ($ millions at current exchange rates)

Sector	Imports from China		Exports to China	
	2000–2001	2010–2011	2000–2001	2010–2011
Agricultural raw materials	16	105	243	1,965
Food and beverages	164	1,089	378	841
Fuel, ores and metals	42	323	3,126	44,244
Chemicals	232	2,178	1	93
Textiles and leather	1,323	8,974	14	138
Iron and steel	61	1,642	0	1
Other material-based manufactures	236	3,132	44	540
Industrial machinery	400	4,415	1	1
Electronics	382	3,806	3	7
Road vehicles and equipment	266	6,691	0	1
Apparel and footwear	266	2,577	4	129
Professional equipment and fixtures	147	2,291	1	34

Note: Export values are averaged for 2000 and 2001 and for 2010 and 2011 and rounded to the nearest whole number, as reported by China; import values include cost, insurance and freight.
Source: HDRO calculations based on UNSD (2012).

telecommunications, while Brazilian firms are some of the largest employers in Angola.[15]

Trade in capital goods and services

South–South trade offers developing countries access to affordable capital goods that are often more appropriate to their needs than are capital goods from richer countries and that are therefore more likely to be acquired, adopted and imitated.[16] Even India has benefited. In 2010, capital goods such as electrical machinery, nuclear reactors and boilers dominated India's imports from China (60%) and cost an estimated 30% less than if they had been sourced from richer countries.[17] This still does not reflect the full dynamism of such exchanges. For example, China's fourth-largest turbine producer, Mingyang, recently acquired 55% of India's Global Wind Power, with the aim of installing 2.5 gigawatts of wind and solar capacity in India.[18]

In 2010–2011, crucial inputs for augmenting productive capacity and infrastructure—road vehicles and equipment, industrial machinery, professional equipment and fixtures, chemicals, and iron and steel—made up nearly half of least developed countries' imports from China (table 2.1). The largest import category was textiles and leather, including yarn and fabric that are used as inputs for least developed countries' exports of apparel to markets in the North. Consumer electronics and apparel and footwear accounted for less than 20% of least developed countries' imports from China.

Developing countries have also seized opportunities for trade in services. Advances in information technology have facilitated services trade at different skill levels: lower skill work, as in call centres and data entry; medium-skill work, as in back office accounting, programming, ticketing and billing; and high-skill work, as in architectural design, digital animation, medical tests and software development. This trend is expected to intensify as developing countries take advantage of the benefits of scale from servicing their own expanding consumer markets.

One of the largest internationally traded services is tourism, which accounts for as much as 30% of world exports of commercial services.[19] Tourists spent roughly $1 trillion in 2010; China was among the most popular destinations (more than 57 million arrivals), along with Egypt, Malaysia, Mexico, Thailand and Turkey. The UN World Tourism Organization projects that by 2020, three-fourths of more than 1.5 billion tourist arrivals will occur within the same geographic region.

Foreign direct investment

The increase in output and trade in many developing countries has been assisted by large inflows of foreign direct investment (FDI): between 1980 and 2010, the countries of the South increased their share of global FDI from 20% to 50%.[20] FDI flows into developing countries have been a forerunner of outward FDI from developing countries. The growth rate of the South's FDI inflows and outflows rose rapidly in the 1990s and early to mid-2000s (figure 2.2). FDI from the South destined for other countries in the South grew 20% a year over 1996–2009.[21]

FIGURE 2.2

Foreign direct investment flows to and from the South have veered sharply upward since the 1990s

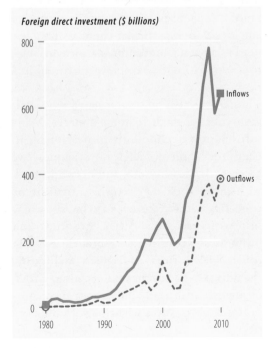

Foreign direct investment ($ billions)

Inflows

Outflows

Note: Data are for developing and transitional economies as defined by the United Nations Conference on Trade and Development. Data are converted to US dollars at current exchange rates.
Source: HDRO calculations based on UNCTAD (2011a).

In many least developed countries, a sizeable share of inward FDI now originates in other developing countries, especially from the fast-growing multinational corporations based in the South.

These investments generally involve links with local firms and transfers of technology that make intensive use of labour and local content. There is some evidence of a strong regional dimension to South–South FDI, with most investments in countries in the same region, often to neighbours and to countries with shared languages.[22] The biggest outward investor from the South is China, with an investment stock of $1.2 trillion.[23]

In 1990, companies in the South made up only 4% of the Fortune Global 500 ranking of the world's biggest corporations; in 2011, their share was 22%. Today, one in four transnational corporations is based in the South. Though the enterprises may be smaller, they are numerous: there are now more Korean than Japanese multinational companies, and more Chinese ones than US ones. Enterprises from the South are going global earlier than firms from developed countries did at a similar stage of development.[24] They are augmenting their competitiveness by acquiring strategic assets such as brands, technology and distribution networks (box 2.2).

Production networks

The increase in trade and investment by multinational corporations and others has been linked to the expansion of international production networks, especially in Asia. Likened to a third industrial revolution,[25] these networks split production processes into multiple steps that cross national borders. As a result, developing countries have been able to diversify their industrial structures and participate in complex production processes. Developing countries engage initially in the labour-intensive segments, typically in product assembly, and then graduate to component fabrication and equipment manufacture. Meanwhile, the less complex production relocates to less advanced neighbouring economies. At the same time, these manufacturing plants create demand for domestic firms to supply inputs and producer

The increase in trade and investment by multinational corporations and others can be likened to a third industrial revolution

BOX 2.2

Acquisitions by the South of brands in the North

In 2011, 61 of the world's biggest corporations on the Fortune 500 list were Chinese, 8 were Indian and 7 Brazilian. Just five years earlier, China had 16 on the list, India 5 and Brazil 3. The South is going global through outward investment using mergers and acquisitions. The acquisition of venerated brands from the North by companies in lower and upper middle-income countries is a portent of the rise of the South. In 2005, the Chinese company Lenovo bought IBM's laptop division for $1.25 billion and took over $500 million of its debt. In 2010, Zhejiang Geely purchased the Swedish car company Volvo. In 2011 alone, Chinese firms spent $42.9 billion on an eclectic mix of more than 200 acquisitions: Sany Heavy Industry Co. acquired Putzmeister, Germany's largest concrete pump maker; Liugong Machinery Co. Ltd. purchased the Polish construction equipment manufacturer Huta Stalowa Wola; and Shandong Heavy Industry Group bought a 75% stake in Italy's Ferretti Group, a luxury yacht maker.

India's Tata Group acquired the Anglo-Dutch steel firm Corus for $13.3 billion in 2007 and Jaguar Land Rover for $2.6 billion in 2008. The Aditya Birla Group bought US aluminium firm Novelis in 2007 and Columbian Chemicals in 2011. Mahindra and Mahindra acquired Sangyong, a bankrupt Korean carmaker. Brazil's food companies have also been active: in 2007,

JBS Friboi bought Swift, a US rival, to ease its entry into the United States. In 2011, Turkish companies made 25 deals worth nearly $3 billion. One of Turkey's famous acquisitions is Godiva, a Belgian chocolate manufacturer, bought for $850 million by Yildiz Holding. There are scores of lesser known purchases of smaller brands from the North by companies in Southeast Asia and the Arab States. (Many big purchases are also South–South. In 2010, India's Bharti Airtel acquired the African operations of Zain for $10.7 billion, and China spent $9.8 billion in 27 deals across Brazil, India, the Russian Federation and South Africa.)

South–North acquisitions are often interpreted in patriotic terms. Whether the deals help short-run profitability and value creation is unclear. In the long run, however, the strategic motives (outside the resource sector) appear to be about acquiring proprietary knowledge, skills and competencies that will help companies expand abroad and at home. Acquiring an established, albeit struggling, brand from the North gives companies from the South a foothold in mature markets. The acquiring companies lower their cost base by diversifying and globalizing supply chains and gain the technology and tacit knowhow (such as risk management or credit rating in the case of financial institutions) to enhance operating capabilities.

Source: HDRO; *China Daily* 2012; *The Economist* 2011a,b, 2012a; Deloitte 2012a,b; Luedi 2008.

---

services. In this way, opportunities to participate in international production have widened for new entrants—as for Malaysia in the 1970s, Thailand in the 1980s, China in the 1990s and Viet Nam today.

The North has played an important role in this rise of the South, just as the South is contributing to the North's recovery from the economic slowdown (box 2.3). International production networks have been driven mainly by final demand in the North. The surge in integrated production networks within Asia alone resulted in a high-technology export boom of nearly $320 billion between 1995 and 2005.[26]

Personal networks

Many transnational opportunities in both trade and investment arise through personal connections, often between international migrants and their countries of origin. In 2010, an estimated 3% of the world's people (215 million) were first-generation immigrants,[27] and close to half of them lived in developing countries.[28] Almost 80% of South–South migration takes place between bordering countries.[29]

Migrant diasporas are a huge source of foreign exchange. In 2005, South–South

remittances were estimated at 30%–45% of worldwide remittances.[30] Diasporas are also a source of information about market opportunities. Diasporas can be associated with increased bilateral trade and FDI.[31] For example, US multinational firms with a high proportion of employees from particular countries have less need to rely on joint-venture partners in countries with which their employees have cultural ties.[32]

Links can also be strengthened when migrants return to their home country. Many information technology professionals in California's Silicon Valley, for example, have taken their ideas, capital and networks back with them when they return to their home countries. Other returnees are building new infrastructure, universities, hospitals and businesses. Returning entrepreneurs stay in touch with former colleagues, facilitating the diffusion of business information. Cross-border scientific collaboration also disproportionately involves scientists with diaspora ties.[33]

Other flows of information are made possible by the widening penetration of the Internet and new social media. Between 2000 and 2010, average annual growth in Internet use

BOX 2.3

Ties that bind: the mutual dependence of North and South

A substantial share of South–South trade, especially in manufactured parts and components, is driven by demand in the North. This makes the countries of the South sensitive to shocks in the North. After the 2008 global financial crisis, for instance, exports from Southeast Asia to Japan, the European Union and the United States fell about 20% between 2008 and 2009. The percentage drop in China's exports to these economies was also in double digits.

The North is also increasingly relying on the South to power its own rebound. Since 2007, US exports to China and Latin America and the Caribbean have grown two and a half times faster than US exports to traditional markets in the North. Helped by a weak dollar and increasing purchasing power in the South, expansion of US exports involved not only traditional sectors such as aircraft, machinery, software and Hollywood movies, but also new, high-value services such as architecture, engineering and finance. Behind Shanghai's booming architectural wonders (including Shanghai Towers, which will be the country's tallest building in 2015) are US designers and structural engineers, who are drawing an ever-increasing share of fees and royalties from services exported to Brazil, China and India.

Furthermore, a growing "app economy" supported by such companies as Apple, Facebook and Google employs more than 300,000 people whose creations are easily exported across borders. Zynga, a large company that makes online games and mobile applications, recorded $1.1 billion in revenue in 2011, a third of it from players outside the United States. The impact of a growing consumer class in the South is felt not only in services, but also in manufacturing and commodities. A third of US exports are now accounted for by firms employing fewer than 500 people; through new techniques, such as three-dimensional printing, many are recapturing markets once lost to imports. Emerging markets have also revived the US role as a commodity producer (of grains, for example). These shifting trade patterns suggest that a slowdown in the South would halt growth in the newly dynamic exports from the North, just as the recession in the North hit the South.

Source: HDRO; *The Economist* 2012b.

was exceptionally high in around 60 developing countries (figure 2.3).[34] Of the 10 countries with the most users of popular social networking sites such as Facebook, 6 are in the South.[35] While these rates reflect in part the low base in 2000, the spread and adoption of new media have revolutionized many sectors across diverse countries (box 2.4).

Impetus from human development

Successful performance in trade, investment and international production also depends on rising levels of human development, as illustrated by the association between high export earnings per capita and achievement in education and health (figure 2.4). The more successful countries in the upper right quadrant of the figure also tend to have better economic opportunities for women. Increased trade draws new workers, often women, into the labour market, expanding their choices. These new workers do not always benefit from good working conditions; efforts to keep costs low can put pressure on wages and work environments. Some governments may be reluctant to expand worker rights, if they believe it would raise production costs and reduce competitiveness (box 2.5).[36]

The capacity of people and institutions also affects the benefits from FDI. Host countries need to invest in the capacity of their people to identify, assimilate and develop the useful knowledge embedded in foreign capital and ideas.[37] Indeed, an educated and healthy workforce is often a key factor in influencing the decision of foreign investors on where to locate. This positive association between FDI inflows and achievements in health and education is evident for a sample of 137 countries (figure 2.5).[38]

This relationship between a skilled populace and inward foreign investment tends to be mutually reinforcing. But there are outliers. FDI could still flow to countries with modest achievements in human development if they are exceptionally well endowed in natural resources. Between 2003 and 2009, for instance, many resource-rich African countries where FDI contributed substantially to economic growth saw some of the lowest nonincome Human Development Index (HDI) values.[39] However, the impact on development is limited when such investments are confined to enclaves and delinked from the rest of the economy. Spillover benefits from FDI are unlikely to be widespread if there is no sustained investment in people's capabilities. In this regard, relatively

Host countries need to invest in the capacity of their people to identify and use the knowledge embedded in foreign capital and ideas

FIGURE 2.3

Between 2000 and 2010, Internet use grew more than 30% a year in around 60 developing countries

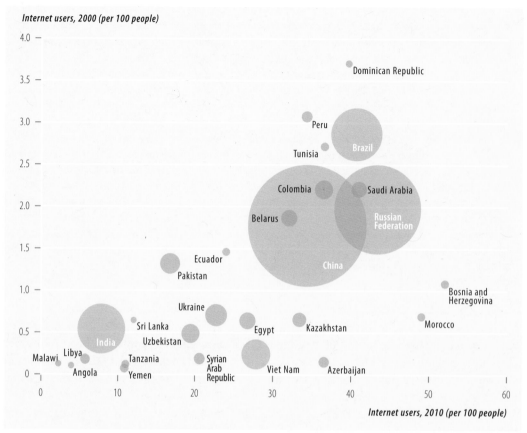

Internet users, 2000 (per 100 people)

Internet users, 2010 (per 100 people)

Note: Bubble size is proportional to total Internet subscriptions in 2010 (320,000 in Angola and 6.7 million in Viet Nam, for reference). Only developing countries exceeding the 75th percentile of compound annual growth in Internet users are shown.
Source: ITU 2012; World Bank 2012a.

Human development is vital for participating in global supply chains; an abundance of low-wage and low-skill labour is not enough

resource-poor Ethiopia and Tanzania are noteworthy for their large increase in nonincome HDI value between 2000 and 2010 and for their above-average FDI over the same period.

Human development is also vital for participating in global supply chains. Contrary to popular perception, an abundance of low-wage and low-skill labour is not enough. Even assembling components made elsewhere can be complex, requiring individual skills and social competencies to coordinate and organize on a large scale. People can learn such skills with appropriate education, training and policy support. Basic human capabilities are also crucial.[40] China, Malaysia, the Philippines and Thailand in East Asia; Brazil, Costa Rica and Mexico in Latin America and the Caribbean; and Morocco and Tunisia in the Arab States have some of the highest trade shares in parts

and components. Widespread benefits accrue only when activities are scaled up (box 2.6). However, it should also be noted that in trade of parts and components, the share of value added by any one country is generally low. In countries where production takes place almost entirely in enclaves connected to overseas supply chains, with limited ties to the domestic economy, the benefits to the rest of the economy are limited.[41]

Helping other countries catch up

All developing countries are not yet participating fully in the rise of the South. The pace of change is slower, for instance, in the majority of the 49 least developed countries, especially those that are landlocked or far from world markets. Nevertheless, many of these countries have also begun to benefit from South–South

BOX 2.4

Mobile phones and the Palapa Ring: connecting Indonesia

Indonesia used telecommunications technology to connect its large cluster of far-flung islands and to open the country to the outside world in ways unimaginable a generation ago. This transformation was not spontaneous: it required extensive private and public investment and prescient policy guidance from the state-run information and communications technology council, Dewan Teknologi Informasi dan Komunikasi Nasional (DETIKNAS). With a diverse population stretched across a vast archipelago of nearly a thousand inhabited islands, Indonesia faced formidable obstacles in its transition to the digital age. Communications between islands was limited. Landline telephones were few, available to most ordinary Indonesians only in major cities and at high cost.

By 2010, however, 220 million mobile phones were registered in a country of 240 million people. An estimated 85% of adults owned phones, as state encouragement and market competition slashed the prices of handsets and phone service alike. The number of Indonesian Internet users has also grown exponentially. As recently as 2008, just an estimated 13 million had regular Internet access. By late 2011, more than 55 million people did, according to industry surveys. The majority of young Indonesians in urban areas now enjoy Internet access, mostly through mobile phones, but also through the country's 260,000 Internet cafes (*warnets*).

Through DETIKNAS the government has made Internet access a national priority, building what it calls a Palapa Ring of fibre-optic cables throughout the archipelago. It is closing in on its goal of wiring schools in a thousand remote rural villages with Internet service and has introduced e-budgeting and e-procurement systems for its own business operations. Perhaps most striking is the explosion of social media. In July 2012, there were 7.4 million registered Facebook users in greater Jakarta alone—the second most of any city in the world, after Bangkok's 8.7 million. In all of Indonesia, there were 44 million Facebook accounts—almost as many as India's 49 million. Indonesia has become a country where cabinet ministers send daily tweets to constituents. It has the third most Twitter subscribers in the world, and environmentalists use online databases and Google Earth mapping tools to publicize deforestation.

The human development benefits of this digital revolution are apparent, Indonesian analysts say, with mobile phones giving rural communities access to public health information, banking services and agricultural market information. Civic engagement has benefited, with online public information services expanding since the 2010 passage of a far-ranging access to information law. The economy is profiting too. A December 2011 study by Deloitte Access Economics calculated that the Internet economy already accounts for 1.6% of Indonesia's GDP, greater than the value of natural gas exports and comparable to the share in Brazil (1.5%) and the Russian Federation (1.6%), though still less than in China (2.6%) and India (3.2%). Deloitte projects an increase to at least 2.5% of GDP in five years, a substantial contributor to Indonesia's International Monetary Fund–predicted annual GDP growth rate of 6%–7% through 2016.

Source: Karimuddin 2011; Deloitte 2011.

---

trade, investment, finance and technology transfer.

A recent study of trends over 1988–2007 finds positive growth spillovers from China to other developing countries, particularly close trading partners.[42] These benefits have to some extent offset slackening demand from developed countries. Growth in low-income countries would have been an estimated 0.3–1.1 percentage points lower in 2007–2010 had growth fallen at the same rate in China and India as in developed economies.[43] FDI from a single source country, China, was credited with contributing substantially to growth rates in several African countries, including in 2008–2009 when other growth impulses were dissipating. Between 2003 and 2009, the estimated contribution to growth from Chinese FDI ranged from 0.04 percentage point in South Africa to 1.9 percentage points in Zambia. The contribution was also high in the Democratic Republic of the Congo (1.0 percentage point), Nigeria (0.9), Madagascar (0.5), Niger (0.5) and Sudan (0.3).[44]

Commodity producers in Sub-Saharan Africa and elsewhere have benefited from a prolonged commodity boom arising in East and South Asia. Cheap imports also increase the purchasing power of low-income consumers and the competitiveness of export-oriented producers. Some African countries may, however, be hampered by the enclave character of extractive industries, which reduces the potential gains from South–South trade and exposes economies to the risk of Dutch disease. Nevertheless, the primary sector can generate sizeable backward and forward links, as Brazil, Chile, Indonesia, Malaysia, and Trinidad and Tobago have shown. Possibilities include agroindustry and logistics infrastructure, as well as demand for services (in food processing and distribution, construction, repair and maintenance), all of which create jobs, income and learning and can enable entrepreneurs to begin new cycles of innovation and investment.

Several encouraging signs are evident. The more recent investments from East and

FIGURE 2.4

Export earnings per capita and human development are highly correlated

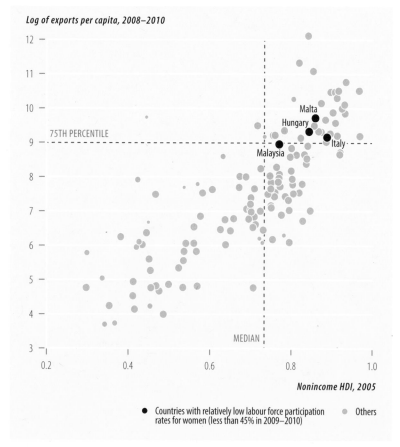

Log of exports per capita, 2008–2010

75TH PERCENTILE

Malta
Hungary
Italy
Malaysia

MEDIAN

Nonincome HDI, 2005

● Countries with relatively low labour force participation rates for women (less than 45% in 2009–2010)　　● Others

Note: Bubble size is proportional to the share of the nonprimary sector in output.
Source: HDRO calculations and World Bank (2012a).

South Asia in the African commodity sector show fewer enclave characteristics. And many governments in the South are being more pragmatic. While adopting sound macroeconomic policies, strengthening institutions and becoming more open, they are actively engaging in industrial policy and promoting entrepreneurship, education, skill formation and technology upgrading. While supporting industrial clusters and economic zones and expanding regional trade and investment, they are also creating finance and credit facilities for small and medium-size enterprises. Sound macroeconomic policy helps manage the risks of large foreign exchange inflows, while smart industrial policy strenghtens domestic links and enhances market multipliers.

Many countries have also benefited from technology transfer and FDI into sectors that contribute to human development. Indian firms, for example, are supplying affordable medicines, medical equipment, and information and communications technology products and services to countries in Africa. Brazilian and South African companies are doing the same in their regional markets. Asian FDI in Africa has also expanded utility and telecommunications infrastructure.

Rising competitive pressures

Nevertheless, exports from larger countries can also have disadvantages. Large countries generate competitive pressures in smaller countries that can stifle economic diversification and industrialization. Examples span the electrical industry in Zambia, clothing in Kenya and Senegal and textiles in South Africa.[45] Clothing exports from Africa would struggle to retain their trade share in major markets without the trade preferences and liberal rules of origin available through the US African Growth and Opportunity Act and the EU Everything But Arms initiative.[46]

Even larger countries are not immune from competitive pressures. Chinese exports affect Brazilian manufacturing through imports of cheaper manufactures and indirectly through competition in third markets.[47] As an indirect response, in September 2011, Brazil formally submitted a proposal to the World Trade Organization to examine trade remedies for redressing currency fluctuations that lead to import surges.[48] India has long sought reciprocal market access for its automobiles in China.

To check the adverse consequence of rising exports on some of its partners, China is providing preferential loans and setting up training programmes to modernize the garment and textile sectors in African countries.[49] China has encouraged its mature industries such as leather to move closer to the supply chain in Africa and its modern firms in telecommunications, pharmaceuticals, electronics and construction to enter joint ventures with African businesses.[50]

Moreover, there are instances where competitive jolts have been followed by industrial revival. Ethiopia's footwear industry, for example, was initially displaced by cheap East Asian imports, resulting in large-scale layoffs

BOX 2.5

Decent work in a competitive world

The availability of decent, well paying jobs is economically empowering, especially for women. Yet today's competitive global environment pressures workers to do more in less time for a lower wage. From both a human development and a business perspective, competitiveness is best achieved by raising labour productivity. Competitiveness squeezed out through lower wages and longer working hours is not sustainable. Labour flexibility should not mean adhering to practices that compromise decent working conditions. At least 150 countries have signed on to core International Labour Organization conventions on such matters as freedom of association and discrimination in the workplace. Labour laws on minimum wage, employment protection, working hours, social security and forms of contracts all aim to reduce inequality, insecurity and social conflict; they also provide incentives for businesses to pursue high-road management strategies. The view that more regulation is always bad for business has been discredited. One of the World Bank Group's core Doing Business indicators on employing workers, which ranked countries on the leniency of measures related to hiring and firing workers, was discontinued because it falsely implied that fewer regulations were always preferable.

International retailers and sourcing agents have a responsibility to ensure that working conditions in the firms they source inputs from comply with international standards. Consider the recent case of one of the world's most valuable companies, Apple, and its contractor, Foxconn. After a series of media exposés that documented terrible labour conditions in Foxconn factories, Apple asked a monitoring group, the Fair Labor Association, to investigate. When the association published its findings of low pay, long hours and hazardous working conditions, Foxconn agreed to substantial reforms, eventually reducing the average workweek to 49 hours as required by Chinese law. As China's largest private sector employer, Foxconn had the power to directly improve and indirectly influence the working conditions of millions of people. Notable in this episode was that public opinion in a country of the North (US media and advocacy groups) pressured a corporation headquartered in that country to nudge a partner in a country of the South to uphold that country's own labour standards. This outcome was possible only in an era when trade, business practices and ethics and the universality of basic human rights are coalescing into a global norm.

Source: HDRO; Berg and Cazes 2007; Duhigg and Greenhouse 2012; Heller 2013.

and business closures, especially in the lower end of the market traditionally catered to by Ethiopian microenterprises. But the industry soon rebounded, even finding its way into the international market.[51] One survey found that 78 of the 96 Ethiopian firms that reported in 2006 being hit hard by import competition had adjusted and become competitive within a few years. Nigeria's plastics industry experienced a similar revival.[52]

Another concern is that the current patterns of demand from other countries in the South could accentuate the chronic specialization by many African economies in primary commodities. The experience of the least developed countries, 33 of which are in Africa, seems to bear out this concern (see table 2.1). In 2011, agricultural raw materials and fuel, metals and ores made up more than 96% of least developed countries' exports to China. Total exports of manufactures by least developed countries to China were less than $1 billion; manufactured imports from China exceeded $38 billion.

Over the longer term, however, South–South cooperation could undo this pattern by fostering sequential investments outside natural resource industries in agriculture and manufacturing, as well as in services such as finance

FIGURE 2.5

Current foreign direct investment is positively associated with achievements in health and education in previous years

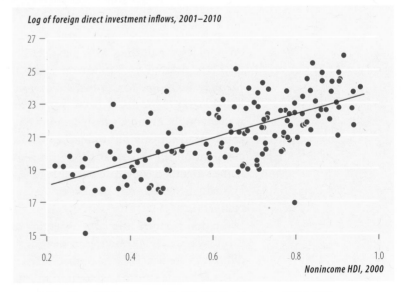

Log of foreign direct investment inflows, 2001–2010

Nonincome HDI, 2000

Note: Inward FDI (in millions of US dollars) is averaged for 2001–2010. Nigeria's nonincome HDI is for 2005.
Source: HDRO calculations and UNCTAD (2011a).

and telecommunications. In Africa, after years of neglect by governments and traditional donors, infrastructure has again become a priority, drawing on the experiences and support of the region's new development partners. Some

BOX 2.6

Final assembly is about more than low wages

The iPhone and iPad, two popular technology products, are assembled in a firm in Shenzen, China, and sold worldwide at retail prices in the hundreds of dollars. The value of labour performed in China, at under $10, accounts for less than 2% of the cost of an iPad, while just 3.6% of the wholesale cost of an iPhone went to Chinese workers. The rest of the value is earned by suppliers of parts and components headquartered in Germany, Japan, the Republic of Korea and the United States. Korean firms LG and Samsung make the display and memory chips; Apple retains the product design, software development and marketing functions in the United States; and the assembly firm is owned by a company from Taiwan Province of China.

The low share of value captured by workers in China could give the impression that assembly does not require much sophistication. This is misleading. While Asia is attractive because of cheaper wages, especially for semiskilled workers, a more important challenge for technology companies is managing global supply chains that involve procuring parts and components from hundreds of companies. This requires a rare combination of industrial skills, flexibility, speed and diligence at both the individual and collective levels. For instance, an Apple executive told *The New York Times* that "the US has stopped producing people with the skills we need."

Consider this incident from mid-2007, when Apple hastily redesigned the glass for the iPhone's screen. The first delivery of a new load of strengthened, scratch-free glass arrived at a Foxconn plant in the middle of the night, and work started immediately. Within three months, Apple had sold a million iPhones. It took 15 days to hire 8,700 industrial engineers to oversee the 200,000 assembly-line workers eventually involved in manufacturing iPhones. Apple's internal estimate was that a similar feat in the United States would have taken nine months.

Source: HDRO; Kraemer, Linden and Dedrick 2011; Xing and Detert 2010; Duhigg and Bradsher 2012.

---

countries have even resorted to unique credit arrangements to fund infrastructure, backed by supplies of commodities.[53]

Neither the complementary nor the competitive perspective is sufficient to explain South–South interactions. Because a competitive role today may easily turn into a complementary role tomorrow, these labels should not be applied rigidly. Moving from competition to cooperation seems to depend on policies for dealing with new challenges. More pessimistic pronouncements that there is no hope for industrialization in Sub-Saharan Africa have been overtaken by realities on the ground, which demonstrate an ability to advance despite or maybe because of competition. In this regard, African writers such as Dambisa Moyo are positive about the mutually beneficial role of new actors in the continent.[54]

The shift from traditional to emerging markets is also affecting countries in ways that are difficult to predict. Take the timber industry in Africa, which has reoriented itself from serving a predominantly European market towards China.[55] In sheer volume China is the most important market, which is good for focusing business on it. The set of technical standards that China requires of exporters, however, is less onerous than those the European Union requires. Standards range from product specifications to accreditation from third-party certification schemes for forest sustainability and health regulations governing formaldehyde emissions. There is no evidence so far that the shift towards emerging markets is being accompanied by a ratcheting up of the technical standards they require, which would have required upgrading workers' skills and capabilities.[56]

Innovation and entrepreneurship in the South

In North–South trade, the newly industrializing economies developed capabilities for efficiently manufacturing complex products for developed country markets. But South–South interactions have enabled companies in the South to adapt and innovate in ways that are more suited to developing countries. This includes new business models whereby companies develop products for a large number of low-income customers, often with low margins.

Countries of the South are also natural locations for experimentation in new technologies and products, such as those based on the global system for mobile (GSM) communications standard. Under the 2005 GSM Emerging Markets Initiative, manufacturers slashed the price of mobile handsets by more than half and expanded the GSM subscriber base by 100 million connections a year. This in turn stimulated investment: in 2007, mobile operators, including South Africa's MTN and Kuwait's Zain, announced a five-year plan to invest an additional $50 billion in Sub-Saharan Africa to improve mobile coverage and expand it to 90% of the population. Indeed, the spectacular increase in phone connectivity in Africa has been driven almost entirely by companies based in India, South Africa and the United Arab Emirates.[57]

Mobile phone manufacturers have also re-engineered products for the needs of lower income consumers. For example, in 2004, TI India, a research and development centre of Texas Instruments in Bengaluru, designed a single-chip prototype for use in high-quality, low-cost mobile phones. In 2005, Nokia, in cooperation with TI, began to market the Indian-made one-chip handsets in India and Africa, selling more than 20 million units. Single-chip designs have also emerged for other devices, including affordable digital display monitors and medical ultrasound machines. Intel has developed a handheld device for rural banking, and Wipro has marketed a low-power desktop computer for basic Internet connectivity. And in 2008, Tata announced the ultra-low-cost Nano car, exportable in kits for assembly by local technicians.

Technology diffusion through South–South investment is also unleashing entrepreneurial spirit, particularly in Africa. People are often self-organizing, creating buyer–seller relationships and becoming entrepreneurs to fill unmet needs in spontaneously sprouting markets. This is evident in the uses to which Africans are putting affordable Asian-built mobile phones: cellular banking, for example, is cheaper and easier than opening a bank account; farmers can obtain weather reports and check produce prices; and entrepreneurs can provide business services through mobile phone kiosks. The use of mobile phones in Niger has improved the performance of the grain market, and Ugandan farmers are using mobile phones to obtain higher prices for their bananas.

These and other transformations multiply the possibilities of what people can do with technology: participating in decisions that affect their lives; gaining quick and low-cost

access to knowledge; producing cheaper, often generic medicines, better seeds and new crop varieties; and generating new employment and export opportunities. These possibilities cut across income classes, reaching down to the grassroots.

To respond to the changing needs of middle class consumers, companies doing well in the South tend to be long-term risk-takers and agile in adapting and innovating products for local buyers. Consumers in the South tend to be younger, are often first-time shoppers for modern appliances with distinct in-store habits and are usually more receptive to branding. Companies in emerging market economies have the advantage of different management approaches from those dominant in the North: majority shareholders have greater power and redeploy resources more speedily than those in companies in the North.[58]

Some of these developments are based on interactions among research and development institutions, businesses and community stakeholders. In such ways, innovation and its benefits spread, spawning faster change. There is greater appreciation of a broader role for the state in stimulating research and development and in nurturing synergies stemming from cooperation among private, university and public research institutions. For example, many African countries have emulated the early success of Mauritius in attracting East Asian FDI by creating export processing zones. Malaysia's investment promotion policies have also been widely copied.

Increasingly, the most important engine of growth for countries of the South is likely to be their domestic market. The middle class is growing in size and income. By 2030, 80% of the world's middle class is projected to live in the South. Countries in South Asia and East Asia and the Pacific will alone account for 60% of the middle class population and 45% of total consumption expenditure.[59] Another estimate is that by 2025, a majority of the 1 billion households earning more than $20,000 a year will live in the South.[60]

Since 2008, Chinese, Indian and Turkish apparel firms have shifted production from shrinking global markets to expanding domestic markets. Greater reliance on domestic markets will boost internal dynamism and

Companies doing well in the South tend to be long-term risk-takers and agile in adapting and innovating products for local buyers contribute to more-inclusive growth. Given current trends, African consumers will continue to benefit from increased imports of affordable products. Flourishing local markets are likely to breed local entrepreneurs and attract more investment in extractive industries as well as in infrastructure, telecommunications, finance, tourism and manufacturing—particularly light manufacturing industries in which African countries have latent comparative advantage. In this scenario, which has already begun to play out in the past decade and in other regions, host economies undergo structural change, and indigenous industry responds to competitive pressure from imports and investment inflows by upgrading production. But the process is proving difficult in countries where technological capabilities and infrastructure are less well developed.

Such expansion of domestic markets will be hampered by substantial pockets of deprivation and lagging regions within large developing countries. Although South Asia, for example, reduced the proportion of the population living on less than $1.25 a day (in 2005 purchasing power parity terms) from 61% in 1981 to 36% in 2008, more than half a billion people there remained extremely poor.[61]

These disparities undermine the sustainability of progress because they create social and political tensions. In India, the Maoist rebels are active in a large swathe of the country's hinterlands; in neighbouring Nepal, Maoists evolved from an ill-equipped militia to become the country's largest political party within 12 years.

New forms of cooperation

Many developing countries are emerging as growth poles and drivers of connectivity and new relationships, opening up opportunities for less developed countries of the South to catch up and leading to a more balanced world. Instead of having a centre of industrialized countries and periphery of less developed countries, there is now a more complex and dynamic environment. Countries of the South are reshaping global rules and practices in trade, finance and intellectual property and establishing new arrangements, institutions and partnerships.

Development assistance

The rise of the South is influencing development cooperation bilaterally, regionally and globally. Bilaterally, countries are innovating through partnerships that bundle investment, trade, technology, concessional finance and technical assistance. Regionally, trade and monetary arrangements are proliferating in all developing regions, and there are pioneering efforts to deliver regional public goods. Globally, developing countries are participating actively in multilateral forums—the G20, the Bretton Woods institutions and others—and giving impetus to reforms in global rules and practices.

A rising number of developing countries provide aid bilaterally and through regional development funds. Often, this involves entwining conventional development assistance with trade, loans, technology sharing and direct investments that promote economic growth with some degree of self-reliance. Countries of the South provide grant aid on a smaller scale than traditional donors do but also give other forms of assistance, often without explicit conditions on economic policy or approaches to governance.[62] In project-based lending, they may not always have been very transparent, but they do give greater priority to the needs identified by receiving countries, ensuring a high degree of national ownership (table 2.2).

Brazil, China and India are important providers of development assistance, which is substantial for countries in Sub-Saharan

TABLE 2.2

Different models of development partnerships

Paris Declaration principle	Traditional donors	New development partners
Ownership	National development strategies outline priorities for donors	National leadership articulates need for specific projects
Harmonization	Shared arrangements to minimize burden on recipients	Fewer bureaucratic procedures to minimize burden on recipients
Managing for results	Recipient-led performance assessment practices	Focus on delivering aid quickly and at low cost
Mutual accountability	Greater accountability through targets and indicators	Mutual respect of sovereignty; policy conditionality eschewed

Source: Adapted from Park (2011).

Africa.[63] Brazil has transplanted its successful school grant programme and its programme for fighting illiteracy to its African partners. In 2011, it had 53 bilateral health agreements with 22 African countries.[64] China has complemented its investment flows and trade arrangements with finance and technical assistance for building hard infrastructure. In July 2012, China pledged to double concessional loans to $20 billion over the next three years.[65] The Export-Import Bank of India has extended $2.9 billion in lines of credit to Sub-Saharan African countries and has pledged to provide an additional $5 billion over the next five years.[66] Between 2001 and 2008, countries and institutions from the South met 47% of official infrastructure financing for Sub-Saharan Africa.[67]

The new development partners from the South follow their own model of bilateral cooperation (box 2.7). The scale of their financial assistance, combined with their approach to conditionality, can enhance policy autonomy in less developed countries.[68] Less developed countries can now look to more emerging partners for development support.[69] This expands their choices, as foreign powers compete for influence, access to local consumers and favourable investment terms.

The regional development assistance architecture is also evolving through the regional development banks: the African Development Bank, the Asian Development Bank and the Inter-American Development Bank. In 2009, playing a countercyclical role, the regional development banks together provided 18.4% ($3.4 billion) of the aid provided by all multilateral institutions, a 42% increase over 2005. Development assistance from the Arab States has also made important contributions, reaching $6 billion in 2008.[70] Some of the largest financiers of infrastructure in Sub-Saharan Africa between 2001 and 2008 were regional banks and funds based in Arab States.[71] Development assistance from regional development banks may become more important to low-income countries in the coming years (as may South–South development assistance) if policymakers in wealthy countries curtail aid commitments because of domestic economic and political challenges.[72]

BOX 2.7

Brazil, China and India at work in Zambia

The model of bilateral cooperation being practiced by new development partners from the South has been changing rapidly. Until recently, the contribution of the new partners to Zambia's overall development finance was small. Of the total $3 billion in grants and loans that Zambia received between 2006 and 2009, disbursements by Brazil, China and India made up less than 3%.

In November 2009, China and Zambia announced that China would extend a $1 billion concessional loan, in tranches, to Zambia for the development of small and medium-size enterprises. This is the equivalent of 40% of Zambia's total public external debt stock. In 2010, the Export-Import Bank of China extended a $57.8 million loan to Zambia to procure nine mobile hospitals. Also in 2010, India announced a line of credit of $75 million, followed by another line of credit of $50 million, to finance a hydroelectric power project. Brazil has invested heavily in mining equipment at the Konkola Copper Mines in the Northwestern province of Zambia (managed by an Indian company). The large Brazilian mining company, Vale, is in a joint venture with the South African company Rainbow in copper prospecting and mining in Zambia, with an initial investment of about $400 million. Brazil and Zambia have also signed technical cooperation agreements covering livestock and health.

Source: HDRO; Kragelund 2013.

Development partners in the South have not sought to engage with or overturn the rules of multilateral development assistance. But they have indirectly introduced competitive pressures for traditional donors and encouraged them to pay greater attention to the needs and concerns of developing countries. In contrast to many traditional donors' focus on social sectors, new partners have in recent years invested heavily in new infrastructure across low-income countries—resulting in, for instance, a 35% improvement in electricity supply, a 10% increase in rail capacity and reduced price of telecommunications services.[73]

Trade and financial agreements

Africa, Asia and Latin America have seen an expansion of trade agreements—bilateral, subregional and regional. In South Asia, these regional agreements have trumped political differences. In East Africa, greater regional integration has helped shield economies from global shocks.[74] There is scope to strengthen regional integration through practical measures such as streamlining transit, transport and customs procedures and harmonizing national regulatory schemes. There is also scope to lower tariffs on South–South trade in final products,

There is much scope to strengthen regional integration through practical measures such as streamlining transit and transport procedures

FIGURE 2.6

Emerging market economies have amassed large foreign exchange reserves since 1995

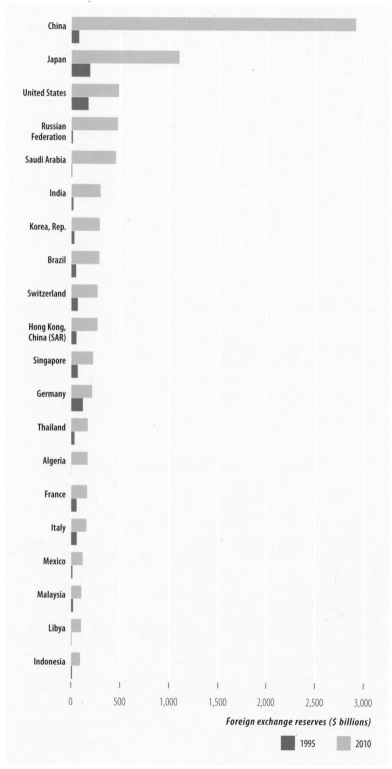

Foreign exchange reserves ($ billions)

■ 1995   ■ 2010

Note: Includes holdings of gold.
Source: World Bank 2012a.

which are higher than those on North–South trade.[75]

In the aftermath of the 1997 Asian financial crisis, several countries of the South developed new monetary arrangements, which are transforming the financial architecture and creating space for countries to craft home-grown policies. The new lending arrangements emphasize pragmatism over ideology and conditionality.

In addition, the global financial architecture is being shaped by the rising South's vast financial reserves. A number of countries, not just Brazil, China and India, but also Indonesia, the Republic of Korea, Malaysia, Mexico, Thailand and others have amassed pools of foreign exchange reserves as self-insurance against future financial downturns and crises (figure 2.6). Between 2000 and the third quarter of 2011, global foreign exchange reserves rose from $1.9 trillion to $10.1 trillion, with a dominant share of the increase accumulated by emerging and developing countries, whose reserves totalled $6.8 trillion.[76] Some of these countries used their reserves to stimulate growth in the aftermath of the 2008 global financial crisis. In a reversal of roles, these funds have been sought by the International Monetary Fund for assistance with the financial crisis in Europe.

Developing countries with large reserve holdings generally transfer part of these to sovereign wealth funds. According to data by the Sovereign Wealth Fund Institute, these funds had an estimated $4.3 trillion in assets at the end of 2010, with $3.5 trillion held by developing and emerging economies and $800 billion in East Asia alone.[77] As of March 2011, developing and emerging economies held 41 sovereign wealth funds, 10 with assets of $100–$627 billion.

Large foreign exchange reserves and sovereign wealth funds are not the most efficient insurance against financial shocks. This unprecedented accumulation of foreign exchange has opportunity costs both for the countries holding the reserves and for other developing countries.[78] The resources could be deployed in more productive ways to support the provision of public goods, to provide capital to projects that enhance productive capacities and economic and human development and to promote regional and subregional financial stability by increasing the resource pools of regional institutions.

Overall, the rise of the South is infusing new patterns of resource accumulation into the global financial system and building a denser, multilayered and more heterogeneous financial architecture for the South. These arrangements sometimes substitute for the Bretton Woods institutions, but in most cases, the emerging institutions and arrangements complement the global financial architecture. The changing financial landscape in the South has the potential to promote financial stability and resilience, support the development of long-run productive capacities, advance aims consistent with human development and expand national policy space. Moreover, emerging economies are having a transformative effect by pressing the Bretton Woods institutions to respond to concerns about representation, governance principles and the use of conditionalities.

The G20 has expanded its participation in such key global financial governance institutions as the Financial Stability Board, tasked with ensuring greater accountability in institutions that set international financial standards. Likewise, all G20 countries, among others, are now represented in the Basel Committee on Banking Supervision and the International Organization of Securities Commissions. The South is also gaining influence in the International Monetary Fund, where China has filled a newly created deputy managing director post and stands to become the third largest shareholder.[79] At the World Bank, the voting power of developing and transition economies rose 3.13 percentage points in 2010, reaching 47.19%.[80]

Migration policy

Regional organizations such as the Association of Southeast Asian Nations, the African Union and the Common Market of the South have added migration to their agendas. Some of this activity is through regional consultations, which are informal, nonbinding processes dedicated to finding common ground among countries. Many of these processes are interregional and straddle origin and destination regions in ways intended to enable capacity building, technical standardization and agreements on issues such as readmissions. They have lowered barriers to communication and provided a venue for countries to come together, understand each other's perspectives and identify common solutions.

These dialogues can be credited with paving the way for subsequent successful efforts on migration, most ambitiously the Berne Initiative 2001–2005, the 2006 High Level Dialogue on Migration and Development hosted by the UN General Assembly and the subsequent creation of the Global Forum on Migration and Development.[81] As the 2009 *Human Development Report* recommended, such efforts could improve outcomes for migrants and destination communities by liberalizing and simplifying channels that allow people to seek work abroad, ensuring basic rights for migrants, reducing transaction costs associated with migration, enabling benefits from internal mobility and making mobility an integral part of national development strategies.[82]

Environmental protection

The UN Conference on Sustainable Development in Rio de Janeiro demonstrated the promise of regional arrangements, as governments from the South showed how they are coming together to manage the resources they share. One initiative, negotiated by governments from the Asia–Pacific region, will protect the Coral Triangle, the world's richest coral reef that stretches from Malaysia and Indonesia to the Solomon Islands and provides food and livelihoods to more than 100 million people. In the Congo River Basin, countries are working together against the illegal timber trade to conserve the world's second largest rainforest.[83] At Rio+20, a group of regional development banks announced a $175 billion initiative to promote public transportation and bicycle lanes in some of the world's largest cities.[84]

The rise of the South is also reflected in an array of bilateral arrangements to tackle climate change. With climate-related natural disasters and rising sea levels threatening to undermine human development progress,

With climate-related natural disasters and rising sea levels threatening to undermine human development progress, countries recognize that they have little choice but to formulate policies on adapting to climate change now and mitigating climate change for the future countries recognize that they have little choice but to formulate policies on adapting to climate change now and mitigating climate change for the future. Countries are, for example, agreeing to cooperate on technology development and to establish region-specific carbon markets. A partnership between China and the United Kingdom will test advanced coal combustion technologies, while India and the United States have forged a partnership to develop nuclear energy in India.[85]

Countries in the South are also developing and sharing new climate-friendly technologies. China, the fourth largest producer of wind energy in 2008, is the world's largest producer of solar panels and wind turbines.[86] In 2011, India's National Solar Mission helped spur a 62% increase in investment in solar energy to $12 billion, the fastest investment expansion of any large renewables market. Brazil made an 8% increase in investment in renewable energy technology to $7 billion.[87]

Regional, bilateral and national initiatives in the South to mitigate climate change and protect environmental resources are positive steps. But climate change and the environment are inherently global issues that require global resolution through multilateral agreements. The cooperation and participation of rising economies of the South in such agreements are vital to their success. Regional collaboration and agreement may be a step in this direction, indicating genuine interest in tackling the climate challenge.

Sustaining progress in uncertain times

The rise of the South was facilitated by a historic global expansion of trade and investment. More than 100 developing countries recorded growth in income per capita of more than 3% in 2007. Recently, the economic slowdown in developed countries has nudged the South to look towards regional demand.[88] Already, developing countries trade more among themselves than with the North, and this trend can go much further. South–South trade blocs remain riddled with nontariff barriers that constrict the scale of trade possibilities. Large foreign exchange reserves remain idle when

there are higher returns and more-secure opportunities for South–South investment. There is potential to expand development partnerships and regional and interregional cooperation.

The rise of the South has underpinned rapid economic growth in Sub-Saharan Africa and enhanced opportunities there for human development progress. Many of the fastest growing economies in this century rank low on human development. While some have made progress on nonincome indicators, others have not.

Governments should seize the growth momentum and embrace policies that convert rising incomes into human development. Policies that build human capabilities and domestic productive capacity will enable countries to avoid "the commodities trap" and diversify economic activity. South–South cooperation can help bring out the learning and diffusion potential in trading, investing and partnering in all industries, even commodities. South–South partnerships can facilitate industrial diversification through FDI and joint ventures, technology sharing through peer learning, and provision of affordable products and innovative uses that meet the needs of the emerging entrepreneurial class. This cooperation is already happening and can be scaled up substantially in the years ahead.

All said, the rise of the South has been dramatic but is still in its early stages. The breadth of social, economic, technological and entrepreneurial connectedness among developing countries today is unprecedented. The daily headlines may carry dismal messages about world events. But interspersed among these discouraging notes are frequent snippets reporting on entrepreneurial ventures and common-sense applications of new technologies by enterprising people in unexpected places.

Multiply each story by the number of people in developing countries and the cumulative potential for a rising South across all regions is astounding. Chapter 3 explores this potential by identifying some of the core drivers that have enabled leading countries of the South to make rapid progress, offering inspiration to other countries that might follow.

Developing countries trade more among themselves than with the North, and this trend can go much further

Global prospects are uncertain, and the economic downturn in the North is adversely affecting the South. With the right reforms, however, including a shift in policy orientation,[89] the promise of sustained human progress is stronger as a result of the shift within the world economy brought about by the rise of the South.

"We cannot expect that
all nations will adopt like
systems, for conformity is
the jailer of freedom and
the enemy of growth."

John F. Kennedy

"Wisdom lies neither in fixity
nor in change, but in the
dialectic between the two."

Octavio Paz

3.

Drivers of development transformation

How have so many countries in the South transformed their human development prospects? Given their social and political diversity and their contrasting natural resource endowments, their trajectories have often diverged. Yet some underlying themes have been consistent. This chapter looks at the experience of some of the more successful countries and at three of their common drivers: their proactive developmental states, their capacity to tap into global markets and their focus on social policy innovation.

Many countries have made substantial progress over the past two decades: the rise of the South has been fairly broad-based. Nevertheless, several high achievers have not only boosted national income, but also had better than average performance on social indicators in areas such as health and education. One way to identify high achievers is to look at countries with positive income growth and good performance on measures of health and education relative to other countries at comparable levels of development. These high achievers include some of the largest countries—Brazil, China and India—as well as smaller countries, such as Bangladesh, Chile, Ghana, Indonesia, the Republic of Korea, Malaysia, Mauritius, Mexico, Thailand, Tunisia, Turkey, Uganda and Viet Nam (figure 3.1).

This chapter analyses the performance of a set of countries that, since 1990, have substantially improved both income growth and the noncome dimensions of human development, namely health and education. Some countries were more successful in one aspect than the other: Brazil and Turkey did better on the noncome dimensions of the Human Development Index (HDI), whereas China's performance over 1990–2010 was dominated by growth in income (in part because when reforms began in the late 1970s, China's achievements in health and education were already high).[1] Furthermore, as mentioned in chapter 1, the group of countries whose improvements on the HDI stood out relative to the performance of peers between 1990 and 2012 includes least developed countries, such as Lao PDR, Mali, Mozambique, Rwanda and Uganda.

Another way of identifying high achievers in human development is to look for countries that have been more successful in closing the "human development gap," as measured by the reduction in their HDI shortfall (the distance from the maximum HDI score).[2] Table 3.1 lists 26 countries that were among either the top 15 developing countries that registered the largest reduction in HDI shortfall over 1990–2012[3] or the top 15 that registered the highest rates of annual growth in income per capita during the same period.

The first set of countries successfully supplemented fast economic growth with social policies that benefit society more broadly, especially the poor. China, for instance, reduced its HDI shortfall more than all other countries

FIGURE 3.1

Some countries have performed well on both the noncome and the income dimensions of the HDI

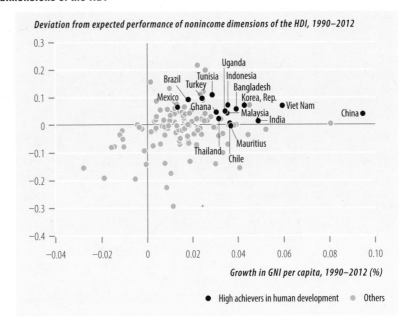

Note: Based on a balanced panel of 96 countries.
Source: HDRO calculations.

TABLE 3.1

Selected developing countries that registered large reductions in HDI shortfall or high rates of growth in gross national income per capita, 1990–2012

Country	HDI (value)		Reduction in HDI shortfall[a]		Average annual growth in gross national income per capita	
			(%)	Rank	(%)	Rank
	1990	2012	1990–2012		1990–2012	
Korea, Rep.	0.749	0.909	63.6	1	4.2	8
Iran, Islamic Rep.	0.540	0.742	43.9	2	2.5	32
China	0.495	0.699	40.5	3	9.4	1
Chile	0.702	0.819	39.4	4	3.8	13
Saudi Arabia	0.653	0.782	37.3	5	0.4	77
Argentina	0.701	0.811	36.9	6	3.5	18
Malaysia	0.635	0.769	36.6	7	3.6	17
Tunisia	0.553	0.712	35.6	8	2.9	29
Turkey	0.569	0.722	35.5	9	2.5	33
Qatar	0.743	0.834	35.3	10	3.2	22
Mexico	0.654	0.775	35.0	11	1.3	58
Algeria	0.562	0.713	34.4	12	1.0	69
Panama	0.666	0.780	34.3	13	3.9	11
Brazil	0.590	0.730	34.1	14	1.7	50
Brunei Darussalam	0.782	0.855	33.4	15	−0.4	87
Viet Nam	0.439	0.617	31.8	21	5.9	3
Mauritius	0.626	0.737	29.8	25	3.6	14
Dominican Republic	0.584	0.702	28.3	28	3.9	12
Myanmar	0.305	0.498	27.8	30	7.9	2
Sri Lanka	0.608	0.715	27.3	31	4.4	7
Guyana	0.502	0.636	26.7	36	5.3	4
Lao PDR	0.379	0.543	26.5	39	4.4	6
India	0.410	0.554	24.5	45	4.7	5
Bangladesh	0.361	0.515	24.1	47	3.9	10
Trinidad and Tobago	0.685	0.760	23.9	49	3.6	15
Mozambique	0.202	0.327	15.6	72	4.1	9

a. Reduction in the distance from the maximum HDI score.
Note: Based on a balanced panel of 96 developing countries.
Source: HDRO calculations.

reduction in HDI shortfall despite years of internal conflict.[4]

India's economic performance has also been impressive, averaging nearly 5% income growth a year over 1990–2012. Nevertheless, India's per capita income is still low, around $3,400 in 2012; to improve living standards, it will need further growth, since it is difficult to achieve much poverty reduction through redistribution alone at low income. India's performance in accelerating human development, however, is less impressive than its growth performance. Indeed, Bangladesh, with much slower economic growth and half India's per capita income, does nearly as well—and better on some indicators.

Among the top 15 countries in reducing HDI shortfall are Algeria, Brazil and Mexico, even though their growth in income per capita averaged only 1%–2% a year over 1990–2012. Their experience points to the second broad strategy that has paid human development dividends: giving primacy to state investment in people's capabilities—especially their health, education and nutrition—and making their societies more resilient to economic, environmental and other threats and shocks.

There is a lesson here: countries cannot rely on growth alone. As the 1993 and 1996 *Human Development Reports* argued, the link between growth and human development is not automatic.[5] It needs to be forged through pro-poor policies by concurrently investing in health and education, expanding decent jobs, preventing the depletion and overexploitation of natural resources, ensuring gender balance and equitable income distribution and avoiding unnecessary displacement of communities.

This is not to say that economic growth does not matter. Poor countries with many poor people need higher incomes. At the national level, faster growth can enable countries to reduce debts and deficits and generate additional public revenues to step up investment in basic goods and services, especially in health and education. And at the household level, income growth helps meet basic needs, improve living standards and enhance quality of life.

Nevertheless, higher income does not necessarily produce a corresponding improvement in

except Iran and the Republic of Korea. The Republic of Korea, despite lower economic growth than China, had the biggest gains in HDI value. Viet Nam also fared well, ranking third in income growth and among the top 20 in HDI improvement. Sri Lanka, too, has had high income growth as well as a notable human well-being. Populations in large cities, for example, typically report high income per capita, but they also have high levels of crime, pollution and traffic congestion. In rural areas, farming households may see income grow while lacking a village school or health centre. Initial conditions have considerable influence on the pace of countries' current and future development. Nonetheless, they are not the only things that matter (box 3.1).

In fact, the links between economic growth and human development have snapped several times. The 1996 *Human Development Report* identified six unwelcome types of growth: jobless growth, which does not increase employment opportunities; ruthless growth, which is accompanied by rising inequality; voiceless growth, which denies the participation of the most vulnerable communities; rootless growth, which uses inappropriate models transplanted from elsewhere; and futureless growth, which is based on unbridled exploitation of environmental resources.[6]

What accounts for the superior generation of growth and its conversion into human development? What are the policy lessons from the diverse human development experiences of these countries? Indeed, what are the drivers of transformation? This chapter identifies three:

- A proactive developmental state.
- Tapping of global markets.
- Determined social policy innovation.

These drivers are not derived from abstract conceptions of how development should work; rather, they are demonstrated by the transformational development experiences of many countries in the South. Indeed, they challenge preconceived and prescriptive approaches: on the one hand, they set aside a number of collectivist, centrally managed precepts; on the other hand, they diverge from the unfettered liberalization espoused by the Washington Consensus.

These drivers suggest an evolution towards a new approach, in which the state is a necessary catalyst that pragmatically adjusts its policies and actions in line with new realities and the challenges of global markets. This new perspective recognizes that development does not happen automatically and that transformation cannot be left to markets alone. Instead, the

This chapter identifies three drivers of transformation: a proactive developmental state, tapping of global markets and determined social policy innovation

BOX 3.1

History and initial conditions matter, but they are not destiny

"Initial conditions" have profound impacts, as certain characteristics are not only difficult to change, but also often perpetuated by institutions and policies. In societies that began with high inequality, elites can establish a legal framework that locks in their influence, which in turn enables them to maintain high inequality to their benefit. Take, for example, the Americas, where three distinct types of colonies took shape in the 1700s, depending on the initial conditions of soil, climate and native inhabitancy.

In the Caribbean, soil and climate made colonies suited for the production of large-scale lucrative commodities. The distribution of wealth and human capital was extremely unequal, advantaging the elite who could assemble large companies of slaves. In Spanish America, abundant in minerals and natives, authorities distributed land resources to the Spanish colonists. Elites served the Spanish crown and maintained their status after independence. Income inequality persisted across racial lines, with ownership of large tracts of land being a requirement for citizenship. In Peru today, as in many other countries, severe horizontal inequalities persist between indigenous populations and those of European descent. In the northern parts of the Americas the native population was not abundant, and soil and climate did not lend themselves to economies of scale. Thus, there was reliance on labourers of European descent with high human capital and more equal distribution of wealth. Because of abundant land and low capital requirements, most adult men operated as independent proprietors.

Haiti today is the poorest country in the Western Hemisphere. On the eve of its revolution in 1790, it was probably the richest country in the New World. Similarly, after the Seven Years War between the British and the French (1756–1763), the British debated whether to take Canada or Guadeloupe as reparation. Several centuries later the former proved to be more successful than other economies in the hemisphere.

Yet history and initial conditions are not insurmountable barriers. About half the progress in development, measured by the HDI, over the past 30 years is unexplained by the initial HDI value in 1980. Countries that start at a similar level—such as India and Pakistan, Chile and Venezuela, Malaysia and the Philippines, or Liberia and Senegal—have ended up with different outcomes. As the 2010 *Human Development Report* argued, if countries with similar starting points go on divergent development paths, but average global achievements have not changed, we can infer that it is national forces policies, institutions, social context and idiosyncratic shocks that drive national development outcomes. No country remains a prisoner of history for long if it wants to break out.

Source: Engerman and Sokoloff 2002; Hoff 2003; Thorp and Paredes 2011; UNDP 2010a.

state needs to mobilize society through policies and institutions that advance economic and social development.

However, this is not a universal prescription. The way these three elements are translated into policies is context-specific, depending on country characteristics, government capacities and relationships with the rest of the world.

Driver 1: a proactive developmental state

Development is about changing a society to enhance people's well-being across generations—enlarging their choices in health, education and income and expanding their freedoms and opportunities for meaningful participation in society.

A common feature of countries that have brought about such transformations is a strong, proactive state—also referred to as a "developmental state". The term refers to a state with an activist government and often an apolitical elite that sees rapid economic development as their primary aim. Some countries go further and add an additional feature: a bureaucracy with the power and authority to plan and implement policies. High growth rates and improved living standards in turn provide the state apparatus and the ruling elites their legitimacy.[7]

In some notable cases, development progress is guided by a long-term vision, shared norms and values, and rules and institutions that build trust and cohesion. Further, viewing development as transformation demands consideration of these intangible factors as well as an understanding of how they affect the organization of society and interact with individual policies and reforms.

Country ownership of development strategy, strong bureaucratic capacities and appropriate policies are essential elements that together shape the transformation process.[8] Policies must be aimed at facilitating transformation by identifying barriers to and potential catalysts of changes. In this process, institutions, societies and individuals need to set their own objectives and identify the strategies and policies that can achieve them. Although not pursued everywhere, broad

participation of people, in the sense that they are being listened to, that their views are taken into account in decisionmaking and that they are actively involved in setting the agenda, is conducive to sustainable long-term development—as is consistent political leadership backed by strong technocratic teams that can ensure institutional memory and continuity of policy (box 3.2).[9]

There is no simple recipe for connecting human development and economic growth or for accelerating growth.[10] One study using cross-country data for 1950–2005 found that the vast majority of takeoffs in growth are not generated by substantial economic reforms and that most substantial economic reforms do not yield takeoffs in growth.[11] Successful countries have grown fast by gradually removing binding constraints to progress, not by implementing a long list of policies and reforms. The state has a critical role in that. Countries that have succeeded in igniting sustained growth, have faced different sets of challenges and adopted varying policies on market regulation, export promotion, industrial development and technological adaptation and progress.[12] When a country is already growing fast, the challenge is to remove or anticipate future constraints as they become actually or potentially binding. Positive terms of trade shocks, like the recent commodity boom as a result of the rise of the South, can help begin growth acceleration but not sustain it. However, focused economic and institutional reforms appear to have statistically and quantitatively significant impacts on how sustained growth accelerations are.[13]

In many high-performing developing countries, the state operates differently from the conventional welfare state, which aims to correct market failures and build social safety nets while promoting market-led growth. Instead, developmental states have been proactive: initiating and monitoring transformations in people's lives.[14] Rather than merely being market-friendly, these states have been development-friendly. Those with strong, innovative social programmes are often also people-friendly—a necessary progression in the move from a focus on growth to human development.

A common feature of countries that have brought about transformational development is a strong, proactive state —also referred to as a "developmental state"

BOX 3.2

What is a developmental state? Need it be authoritarian?

The recent literature on developmental states has grown out of the experiences of the East Asian "miracle" economies: Japan before the Second World War and Hong Kong, China (SAR), the Republic of Korea, Singapore and Taiwan Province of China in the second half of the 20th century. Recently, China and Viet Nam (as well as Cambodia and Lao PDR) can be seen as developmental states. Common traits include promoting economic development by explicitly favouring certain sectors; commanding competent bureaucracies; placing robust, competent public institutions at the centre of development strategies; clearly articulating social and economic goals; and deriving political legitimacy from their record in development.

That some East Asian developmental states were not democracies has prompted many to think that the developmental state model is also autocratic. But evidence of the relationship between authoritarianism and development is mixed. Democratic countries such as Japan and the United States have functioned as developmental states. After the Second World War France initiated planning by the Planning Commission, with sectoral industrial policy led by elite bureaucrats and the aggressive use of state-owned enterprises. Since the 1950s, the Scandinavian countries have also acted as a type of developmental state, where political legitimacy is derived from the welfare state and full employment rather than from rapid growth. The Swedish state developed strategic sectors through public-private partnerships (iron and steel, railways, telegraphs and telephone, and hydroelectric power). It also provided targeted protection to support the emergence of heavy industries, promoting research and development. Its welfare policy was closely integrated with strategies to promote structural change towards high-productivity sectors.

The United States has a long history of being a developmental state, going back to the early days of the republic. Alexander Hamilton, the first US treasury secretary, is widely considered the father and inventor of the infant industry argument. Between 1830 and 1945, the United States had some of the highest trade barriers in the world. In the same period it invested heavily in infrastructure (Pacific railways, Midwestern canals and agricultural infrastructure), higher education, and research and development. Even after the Second World War, when the United States had attained industrial supremacy, and despite the rise of market fundamentalism, the developmental state survived.

Block (2008) argues that the state has focused on translating cutting-edge technological research into commercial use through cooperation among a network of people with high levels of technological expertise situated in state agencies, industries, universities and research institutions. Developmentalism has lived in the shadows of US policy because acknowledging the state's central role in promoting technological change is inconsistent with the claim that the private sector should be left alone to respond to market signals autonomously. Yet, although limited in scope due to a lack of legitimacy, unstable funding and other limitations caused by its "hidden" nature, the US developmental state has been quite successful. In many sectors, the United States has developed international competitiveness through public funding for research and development and through public procurement for defence (computers, aircraft, Internet) and health (drugs, genetic engineering).

Source: Evans 2010; Chang 2010; Edigheji 2010; Block 2008.

Another characteristic of developmental states is their pursuit of industrial policies to redress coordination problems and externalities by "managing" comparative advantage.[15] For example, the state may foster industries believed to have a latent comparative advantage or seek to elevate those that are stuck in static comparative advantage. As a result, several industries that benefited from tariff protection subsequently succeeded in world markets.[16] Nonetheless, it can be difficult to attribute the success or failure of a particular industry to specific trade policies because government interventions are guided by multiple motives, from revenue generation to protection of special interests.

Evidence across industries from studies of the benefits of industry protection is ambiguous. However, there is a distinction between the general desirability of "soft" industrial policies, such as improving infrastructure and technological adoption, and "hard" industrial policies, such as direct taxes and subsidy interventions favouring specific industries, whose efficacy depends on country circumstances. There is no global prescription, though: what worked in East Asia may not work in Latin America.

- *Japan.* Japan has long acted as a developmental state. By the 1870s, it had a group of "well-educated, patriotic businessmen and merchants and government that were focused on economic modernization".[17] Many subsequent reforms created the infrastructure of a modern country, including a unified currency, railroads, public education and banking laws. The government built and operated state-owned plants in industries ranging from cotton to shipbuilding. It also encouraged domestic production by raising import tariffs on many industrial products. Since the end of the Second World War, Japan has undergone a fundamental transformation from aid recipient to donor (box 3.3).
- *Republic of Korea.* Between 1960 and 1980, the Republic of Korea had significant

One characteristic of developmental states is their pursuit of industrial policies to redress coordination problems and externalities by "managing" comparative advantage

> More important than getting prices right, a developmental state must get policy priorities right. They should be people-centred, promoting opportunities while protecting against downside risks

success. After 1961, the government achieved a position of dominance over its business class through a series of reforms, including measures that increased the institutional coherence of the state, such as the creation of the Economic Planning Board, but centred on control over finance. It also avoided the capture of state policies on subsidies. Subsequently, it was able to guide a shift from import substitution to export promotion.[18]

Other rising countries of the South have pursued similar policies. Governments have partnered with the private sector to develop comparative advantage in the most promising sectors while ensuring effective macroeconomic management and promoting innovation. They have also paid special attention to expanding social opportunities by setting policy priorities, nurturing selected industries, fostering state-market complementarities, committing to long-term reforms, having strong political leadership, learning by doing and boosting public investment.

Setting policy priorities

More important than getting prices right, a developmental state must get policy priorities right. They should be people-centred, promoting opportunities while protecting against

downside risks. Getting policies and policy priorities right raises the equally important issue of getting policymaking right. Governing institutions and policies are profoundly and inextricably linked; one cannot succeed without the other. It is thus important to have policy processes managed by committed people in effective and responsive government structures. Policies also change at different stages of development: at early stages, for example, many countries prioritize job creation and poverty reduction.

- *Indonesia.* From the mid-1970s, supported by revenues from newfound oil wealth, Indonesia complemented import-substituting industrialization with a major thrust in agriculture and rural development (see box 3.4 for the transformative potential of strategic investments in agriculture). This strategy of balanced growth increased the demand for labour, thus reducing unemployment and increasing real wages.[19] Then in the mid-1980s, as oil income began to decline, Indonesia shifted from import substitution to outward-oriented industrialization, drawing in surplus labour from agriculture to work in manufacturing, which offered higher wages. By the early 1990s, when the supply of surplus labour had been exhausted, poverty reduction continued primarily through wage increases.

BOX 3.3   *Akihiko Tanaka, President, Japan International Cooperation Agency*

Japan and triangular cooperation

Bolstered by the remarkable economic performance of emerging countries, South–South cooperation and triangular cooperation have grown rapidly in recent years. They have outgrown their traditional role as complements to North–South cooperation and are now an indispensable source of knowledge sharing and innovation for many developing countries.

There are four virtues and merits of South–South and triangular cooperation: the benefits accrued from sharing knowledge and experience among peers to find more effective solutions; sharing appropriate technology and experience that can promote convergence with North–South cooperation goals; respecting real ownership, with the South in the driver's seat; and developing countries' rapidly emerging as new donors.

As early as 1975, Japan recognized the value of South–South and triangular cooperation and began a large-scale triangular training programme. Japan had experienced a development trajectory similar to that of some emerging countries today, having first been a net foreign aid recipient then playing a dual role as aid recipient and emerging donor for a

number of years before finally becoming only a donor as the first Asian member of the Organisation for Economic Co-operation and Development in 1964.

This development pathway led Japan to believe that sharing development experience, knowledge and appropriate technology among developing countries can play a very useful role in development cooperation and thus warranted donor support.

A prime example is the cooperation among Brazil, Japan and Mozambique. Japan helped Brazil develop its own tropical savannah region, known as the Cerrado, making it a leading producer of soybeans and other agricultural products. The two countries now extend collaborative support to Mozambique to develop that country's vast savannah.

An emerging challenge now is to scale up South–South and triangular cooperation as a central approach in development cooperation, while avoiding excessive aid fragmentation among an increasing number of development actors.

BOX 3.4

Investing in agriculture

Strategic investments in the agricultural sector can have transformative effects. Higher crop yields not only lead to improved livelihoods for farmers, they also increase demand for goods and services in rural areas, giving rise to new opportunities for economic development. They may also lead to lower food prices, reducing the share of food in household expenditures and creating markets for other sectors of the economy.

Agricultural research is a public good and tends to be underprovided by the private sector. Consequently, governments can make useful contributions in this area. Recent studies on several African, Asian and Latin American countries show that increased public spending on agriculture is particularly good for promoting growth. Disaggregating agricultural expenditure into research and nonresearch spending shows that research spending is especially effective. Provision of other public goods, such as agricultural extension services and irrigation systems, is also beneficial.

China has the world's largest agricultural research and development system in the world. Its research is based at the Chinese Academy of Agricultural Sciences, universities and the Chinese Academy of Science, which together comprise of more than 1,100 research institutions. China is becoming a leader in South–South cooperation with African countries, many of which are now benefiting from its research.

Agricultural technology has also been a strength of Brazil, where an estimated 41% of 2006 agricultural research spending in Latin America occurred. The System for Agricultural Research and Innovation has contributed greatly to the nearly fourfold growth in agricultural efficiency per worker. The Brazil Agricultural Research Corporation, a state-owned enterprise, has been instrumental in increasing the land area used for cultivation. Similarly, many of Brazil's agricultural programmes were developed with sustainability in mind. For example, to qualify for price support and credit programmes, farmers must respect zoning laws. Another programme, Moderagro, provides farmers with credit to improve agricultural practices and preserve natural resources, Produsa provides credit for planting on agricultural land that has degraded soil and Propflora uses credit to encourage the planting of forests (particularly palm oil).

Source: OECD 2006, 2011a; Fan and Saurkar 2006; Fan, Nestorova and Olofinbiyi 2010; Stads and Beintema 2009; World Bank 2012a.

Each phase thus involved a people-centred approach in which the growth strategy was modified in response to changing conditions.

Enhancing public investment

Traditional economic and social policy thinking, as emphasized by the "Washington Consensus", focused on getting economic fundamentals right as a precondition for economic growth, arguing that other human development improvements would follow. A human development approach, on the other hand, demands that improvement in poor people's lives not be postponed. Thus, people-friendly developmental states are those that expand a number of basic social services (box 3.5).[20] In this view, investing in people's capabilities—through health, education and other public services—is not an appendage of the growth process but an integral part of it.

In addition to the levels of public expenditures, their composition and the efficiency with which they are delivered, all taken together, influence the effective delivery of public services and expansion of capabilities. The effectiveness of public expenditure differs across countries. A global cross-country analysis shows a positive correlation between previous public expenditure per capita on health and education and current human development achievement (figure 3.2). Also, higher previous public spending per capita on health is associated with better child survival and lower under-five child mortality rates (figure 3.3). Such outcomes naturally depend on a country's stage of development and on how well the money is spent. Countries should put in place checks and balances to prevent reckless borrowing sprees and wasteful spending.

There has been much debate about whether public investment crowds in or crowds out private investment. Both outcomes are possible because of the many different uses of public capital in developing countries. From the lower levels of health, education and infrastructure development in South Asia and Sub-Saharan Africa than in the high-performing countries of East and Southeast Asia, it is reasonable to infer that public investment, as well as its composition, performs a critical role.

- *Bangladesh.* Bangladesh has sustained growth in part by increasing the rate of public investment over time while avoiding the fiscal deficits that have plagued the rest of the region.

Investing in people's capabilities—through health, education and other public services—is not an appendage of the growth process but an integral part of it

BOX 3.5

Eastern Europe and Central Asia: where North meets South

Connecting the North and the rising South is the transforming East. Eastern Europe and Central Asia accounts for 5% of world population and output. Its experience in managing a rapid transition from centrally planned to market economies holds useful policy lessons for developing countries elsewhere. The first phase of the transformation began with a sharp drop in living standards and human development. While each country managed a subsequent recovery under varying political and economic conditions, the overall experience underscores the importance of social inclusion and a responsible role of the state.

The 2011 *Regional Human Development Report for Europe and the Commonwealth of Independent States* showed a negative correlation between Human Development Index values and measures of social exclusion in Eastern Europe and Central Asia. It noted that economic variables accounted for less than a third of the risks contributing to individual exclusion. Labour informality, corruption and lengthy procedures for business startups were associated with high social exclusion. By contrast, because employment facilitates inclusion, functional and accessible labour market institutions were found to be important. A major lesson from two decades of transition is that the state has a critical role in creating an environment

for inclusive growth and societies. Abruptly abandoning areas of responsibility by the state or insisting on rapid privatization of all state-owned companies may prove very costly for societies in the long run. Yet at the same time, retaining these responsibilities does not mean keeping the earlier structures intact. On the contrary, reforms to strengthen national institutions' transparency and accountability and to limit the scope of corruption are necessary to improve the quality of governance and efficiency of governments.

Many countries of the region are now active members of the European Union. They, together with Croatia, Kazakhstan, the Russian Federation and Turkey, have also become emerging donors, with aid disbursements exceeding $4 billion in 2011. The emerging donors are also active in bilateral or trilateral exchange of knowledge with countries with common heritage or beyond. In recent years Romania has shared its experience conducting elections with Egypt and Tunisia, Poland has helped Iraq with small and medium-size enterprise development, the Czech Republic has cooperated with Azerbaijan on environmental impact assessments and Slovakia has assisted Moldova and Montenegro in public finance management.

Source: HDRO; UNDP 2011b.

- *India.* India increased central government spending on social services and rural development from 13.4% in 2006–2007 to 18.5% in 2011–2012.[21] And social services as a proportion of total expenditure rose from 21.6% in 2006–2007 to 24.1% in 2009–2010 and to 25% in 2011–2012.

Nurturing selected industries

Governments can encourage a market-disciplined private sector by adopting a dynamic view of comparative advantage, nurturing sectors that would not otherwise emerge due to incomplete markets.[22] Although this poses some political risks of rent seeking and cronyism, it has enabled several countries of the South to turn industries previously derided as inefficient and unable to withstand foreign competition into early drivers of export success once their economies became more open.

- *India.* For decades after independence in 1947, India followed a strategy of state-led, import-substituting industrialization. It inhibited the private sector while bestowing wide powers on technocrats who

controlled trade and investment, creating a system that became increasingly laden with bureaucratic intricacies (the "licence Raj").[23] During these years, however, there was a deliberate policy to build human capabilities and invest in world-class tertiary education, though perhaps neglecting primary education. Following the reforms of the 1990s, these investments paid off when India was unexpectedly able to capitalize on its stock of skilled workers in emergent information technology–enabled industries, which by 2011–2012 were generating $70 billion in export earnings. Another industry built during the inward-looking years is pharmaceuticals. India granted patents only to processes, not to products, which encouraged firms to reverse engineer and become world leaders in generic drugs.[24] Similar tales of capacity building can be told for India's automobile, chemical and service industries, now vigorously tapping into world markets.

- *Brazil.* For long stretches, Brazil also experimented with inward-oriented economic strategies. During these periods, individual firms that benefited from large

A dynamic view of comparative advantage has enabled several countries to turn inefficient industries unable to withstand foreign competition into drivers of export success once their economies became more open domestic markets were not encouraged to export and compete globally. But when they did so, they were able to rely on capacities built up over decades. Embraer, for example, is now the world's leading producer of regional jet commercial aircraft of up to 120 seats.[25] The country's steel and shoe industries also grew under public ownership, with research and development augmenting capabilities for domestic innovation.

Prioritizing job creation

Pragmatic policies aimed at creating secure and remunerative jobs are likely to strengthen the link between economic growth and human development. Evidence from Asia suggests that countries with simultaneously high rates of growth and poverty reduction also rapidly expanded employment. This was true for Malaysia and Thailand in the 1970s, China and Indonesia in the 1980s and India and Viet Nam in the 1990s.[26] The first generation of fast-growing Asian economies—Hong Kong, China (SAR), Republic of Korea, Singapore and Taiwan Province of China— expanded employment 2%–6% a year before the 1990s, while raising productivity and wages. Such patterns of growth were often led by small-scale agriculture as in Taiwan Province of China and by labour-intensive export-oriented manufacturing in Hong Kong, China (SAR), the Republic of Korea and Singapore.[27]

The success of some Asian countries— such as the Republic of Korea and later Thailand—holds lessons for less developed economies, especially in Sub-Saharan Africa, because they created jobs two to three times faster when they were at a comparable level of development. For example, over the past 10 years, Africa's labour force expanded by 91 million people but added only 37 million jobs in wage-paying sectors.[28] With proactive government policies in labour-intensive subsectors of manufacturing and agriculture, as well as retail, hospitality and construction, Africa is projected to create up to 72 million jobs by 2020, an additional 18 million jobs over present growth levels.[29] Such policies, however, require not only investing in young people's education and training, but also

FIGURE 3.2

Current HDI values and previous public expenditures are positively correlated . . .

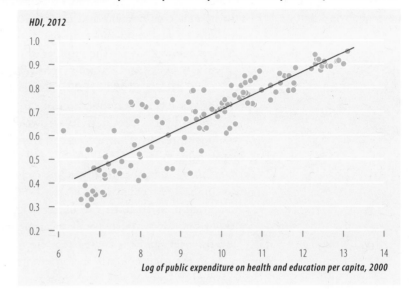

Source: HDRO calculations and World Bank (2012a).

FIGURE 3.3

. . . as are current child survival and previous public expenditure on health

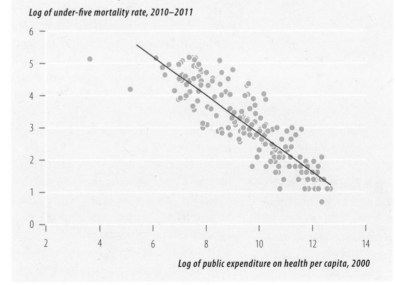

Source: HDRO calculations based on World Bank (2012a).

improving infrastructure aimed at economic diversification and removing obstacles to private entrepreneurship, such as lack of finance and onerous regulations.[30]

- *Mauritius.* The possibilities of labour-intensive growth are higher when countries are at a lower level of industrialization. Analysing the performance of Mauritius over two decades, one study finds that during the first decade (1982–1990), 80% of annual economic growth was accounted for by new employment and capital accumulation.[31] Unemployment dropped from 20% to below 3%, with the number of jobs growing 5.2% a year. Economic growth in the next decade (1991–1999), however, was driven less by accumulation of capital and more by the productivity growth of workers, a result of investment in human capabilities.[32]

- *Bangladesh.* The more rapid decline in poverty in the 1990s compared with the 1980s[33] was attributed to both the expansion of labour-intensive exports (such as garments and fisheries) and the increase in employment in the rural nonfarm sector (comprising small and cottage industries, construction and other nontradable services). The stimulus, however, came less from productivity improvements within this sector than from rising demand facilitated by an increase in crop production, an inflow of remittances and growing exports.[34]

- *Rwanda.* Expansion in jobs does not always have to come from export-oriented manufacturing. In Rwanda, jobs in tourism services have increased over the past decade. The sector now sees export earnings that exceed those from coffee and tea and employs nearly 75,000 people.[35]

- *Uganda.* Like Rwanda's, Uganda's high growth during the 1990s was poverty alleviating because of income growth in agriculture through large scale absorption of labour, especially in the cash crops sector that was buoyed by world prices and improvement in agriculture's terms of trade.[36]

- *Thailand.* Developing countries endowed with arable land can continue to create stable jobs in agriculture, even though its share in total output typically declines over time. This is the case in Thailand, whose employment pattern of the 1960s is comparable to that of many Sub-Saharan African countries today. While Thailand has since become a manufacturing powerhouse, millions of stable jobs continue to be created in nonmanufacturing sectors such as retail, hospitality and construction, as well as in commercial farming: the number of

stable jobs in agriculture increased from 519,000 in 1960 to nearly 3 million in 2008. Overall, in the 1990s alone, Thailand increased its share of stable jobs by 11 percentage points (as Brazil did between 1970 and 1988).[37]

- *Indonesia.* Indonesia before the 1997 Asian financial crisis stood out for pursuing growth that had a high labour intensity. Real wages increased at an average annual rate of 5% for two decades preceding the crisis. Between 1990 and 1996 alone, formal nonagricultural employment increased from 28.1% of the workforce to 37.9% and the share of workforce in agriculture declined from 55.1% to 43.5%.[38] Post-crisis, when some of the development gains were reversed, the proportionate increase in poverty was lowest for agricultural workers.[39]

As these examples suggest, patterns of growth are rarely consistently pro-poor over consecutive decades. This is because developmental transformation is synonymous with the change in the structure of production and sectors differ in their capacities to create jobs. Skilled and unskilled jobs, for example, require a different mix of complementary inputs, such as formal education and industry-specific training. The larger point is that human development–oriented policies require both growth and an equitable expansion of opportunities. Developmental states, therefore, have to be conscious that the nature of growth (and the intensity of labour use in sectors that drive growth) evolves as the economy transforms, and they need then to respond with matching investments in people's skills.

Fostering state–market complementarities

Both markets and governments can fail, but there are synergies when they work together. Development progress cannot be left to markets alone. Some markets not only fail to function, but may not exist at all at early stages of development. Most successful developmental states have introduced industrial and related policies that enhance the private sector's potential to contribute to human development, especially by creating jobs in new sectors.

States have to be conscious that the nature of growth (and the intensity of labour use in sectors that drive growth) evolves as the economy transforms, and to respond with matching investments in people's skills

- *Turkey.* The state created favourable economic conditions that encouraged construction and the manufacture of furniture, textiles, food and automobiles—all industries with a high capacity to absorb labour. Turkey's export basket has since moved towards products that involve more processing, higher technology content and the use of skilled labour.[40]
- *Tunisia.* Since the early 1970s, Tunisia has relied on financial and fiscal incentives to attract foreign and domestic capital to export-oriented industries, particularly for garment production.[41] Various forms of business–government relations have enhanced industrial upgrading and promoted industry clusters. Today, Tunisia is among the top five exporters of apparel to the European Union.[42] It also has the potential to export health services by providing treatment to visitors from neighbouring countries, to a value equivalent to a quarter of Tunisia's private health sector output.[43]
- *Chile.* After returning to democracy in the 1990s, Chile encouraged investment and technological upgrading in sectors where the country had an intrinsic comparative advantage. It subsidized the formation and operation of innovation-based consortia between private firms and universities and engaged in other innovation-promoting activities.[44]

Committing to long-term development and reform

Achieving enduring transformation is a long-term process that requires countries to chart a consistent and balanced approach to development. Some technical or managerial solutions may appear to be attractive quick fixes, but they are generally inadequate.
- *China.* Since market-oriented reforms in the late 1970s, China has experienced a "complex and interlocking set of changes: from a command to a market economy; from rural to urban; from agriculture to manufacturing and services; from informal to formal economic activities; from a fragmented set of fairly self-sufficient provincial economies to a more integrated economy; and from an economy that was fairly shut off from the world to a powerhouse of international trade".[45] The scale of these changes required a committed state pursuing a long-term vision to build the necessary institutions and capacities. The leadership deliberately replaced the old guard, who might have been expected to resist change, with a younger, more open and better educated government bureaucracy. By 1988, a remarkable 90% of officials above the county level had been appointed since 1982.[46] Capacity upgrading is still a priority, and the education levels of officials have risen continuously. The Chinese bureaucracy has been designed with a strong results orientation, linking career development to the achievement of central objectives of modernization and economic progress.[47]

People-friendly developmental states need strong political leadership committed to equity and sustainability. Effective leadership aligns the long-term goals of policymakers and enables constituencies to appreciate the state's work in fostering individual capabilities and social integration for human development. This requires a balanced approach to development and an ability to convert crises into opportunities for introducing broad-based economic reforms.
- *Brazil.* By the time the Brazilian transformation to a developmental state began (around 1994), the government had implemented macroeconomic reforms to control hyperinflation through the Real Plan and concluded the trade liberalization that had begun in 1988 with tariff reductions and the removal of other restrictions.[48] Trade openness and prudent monetary and fiscal policy followed, as did innovative social programmes that reduced poverty and income inequality.

In large and complex societies, the outcome of any particular policy is inevitably uncertain. Developmental states need to be pragmatic and test a range of different approaches.
- *China.* China's reform and opening resulted from an explicit choice in the late 1970s to relax constraints on people's participation in economic decisions. But the institutional innovations that went on to underpin China's transformation resembled Deng Xiaoping's approach to "crossing the river

People-friendly developmental states need strong political leadership committed to equity and sustainability by feeling the stones".[49] Between 1979 and 1989, no fewer than 40% of China's national regulations were deemed experimental. The first set of agrarian reforms permitted farmers to lease land, submit a share of produce at fixed prices to the state and sell the surplus. Next came the expansion of the township and village enterprises.[50] The gradual approach reflected the pragmatism of Chinese leaders. Another reason for this pragmatism was the perception that the transition was impossible to plan, compounded by disillusionment with the whole planning system.

Driver 2: tapping of global markets

A common element of the fast-developing countries of the South has been to strengthen the capabilities of people and the competencies of firms while embracing global markets. This has enabled them to source intermediate inputs and capital goods at competitive world prices, adopt foreign knowhow and technology and use them to sell to global markets.[51] All newly industrializing countries have pursued a strategy of "importing what the rest of the world knows and exporting what it wants".[52] Indeed, few countries have developed successfully by shunning international trade or long-term capital flows; very few have sustained growth without increasing their trade to output ratio, and there is no evidence that in the post-war period inward-looking economies have systematically developed faster than those that have been more open.[53]

This experience does not mean, however, that countries can ignite growth simply by dismantling trade and investment barriers. Some influential cross-national studies in the 1990s purported to show that rapidly opening up would automatically lead to high economic growth. But these were subsequently found to have significant methodological limitations.[54] In particular, growth cannot be sufficiently explained by average tariff and nontariff barriers.[55]

Actual development experiences from the South have demonstrated a more nuanced consensus.[56] In this view, successful and sustained progress is more likely to be the result of gradual and sequenced integration with the world economy, according to national circumstances, and accompanied by investment in people, institutions and infrastructure.[57] Country studies confirm that what is needed is a package that involves the interaction of reforms in trade, exchange rates, and fiscal, monetary and institutional policies.[58] A recent study finds that more decisive benefits come from trade liberalization embedded in broader reforms: in the post-liberalization period between 1950 and 1998, the countries that were considered to have implemented such policies posted growth rates that were 1.5 percentage points higher, investment rates that were 1.5–2 percentage points higher and trade to output ratios that were 5 percentage points higher.[59]

As countries develop, they tend to dismantle trade barriers and become more open.[60] HDRO analysis of the association between the change in trade openness and relative improvement in HDI value between 1990 and 2010 supports this conclusion (see box 2.1 in chapter 2). Not all countries that increased trade openness made big improvements in HDI value relative to their peers. But those that did make big improvements in HDI value typically increased their trade to output ratio or established a global network of trade links of substantial bilateral value. In a sample of 95 developing countries and transitional economies, the average increase in trade to output ratio of countries considered to be rapid improvers on the HDI between 1990 and 2012 was about 13 percentage points higher than that of more modest improvers.

As discussed in box 2.1 in chapter 2, almost all countries with substantial improvement in HDI value over the past two decades have also become more integrated with the world economy. Table 3.2 reconfirms this for a selected group of high human development–achieving countries discussed in this chapter, which have vigorously tapped opportunities presented by globalization by expanding their share of exports in world markets between 1990 and 2010. The only exception in this group is Mauritius, one of the first countries in the South to pursue an export-oriented development strategy, whose share in world exports peaked in 2001.[61] As the more populous countries deepen their

As countries develop, they tend to dismantle trade barriers and become more open integration with the world economy, they have accelerated their structural diversification in manufacturing and services and boosted agricultural productivity, helping lift hundreds of millions of people out of poverty in a few decades.

Gradual and sequenced integration

Rather than opening suddenly to world markets, some of the more successful countries have opened gradually, as the situation demanded.

- *China.* A rapid opening up in China would have shut down state enterprises without creating new industrial activities, so the state reformed gradually. To attract foreign direct investment (FDI), create jobs and promote exports, the state established special economic zones, often in less built-up areas.[62] At the same time, China increased the competencies of its workers and firms by requiring foreign firms to enter joint ventures, transfer technology or meet high requirements for domestic content. By the early 1990s, China was ready to expand its external interactions, building on investments in health and education during the 1960s and 1970s and on the newly acquired competencies of farmers and firms. Between 1993 and 1996, China was already the destination of more than 10% of worldwide FDI inflows.[63] Its trade to GDP ratio nearly doubled, from 21.7% in 1980 to about 42% in 1993–1994. By 2011, China had completed 10 years of membership in the World Trade Organization and overtaken Germany as the second-largest exporter of goods and services.[64]

- *India.* Domestic reforms began in India in the mid-1980s and expanded after the 1990–1991 external payments crisis. Before the reforms, India had import quotas and high tariffs on manufactured goods and banned imports of manufactured consumer products.[65] Early reforms focused on dismantling the systems of licences for industrial activity and ending restrictions on investment.[66] Quantitative restrictions on manufactured capital goods were ended in 1993. Tariffs on manufactured goods were reduced quickly from 76.3% in 1990 to 42.9% in 1992, but further cuts were spread

TABLE 3.2

Share of world exports of goods and services of high achievers in human development, 1985–1990 and 2005–2010 (%)

Country	1985–1990	2000–2010
Bangladesh	0.042	0.089
Brazil	0.946	1.123
Chile	0.232	0.420
China	1.267	8.132
Ghana	0.029	0.041
India	0.519	1.609
Indonesia	0.624	0.803
Malaysia	0.685	1.197
Mauritius	0.038	0.027
Thailand	0.565	1.095
Tunisia	0.116	0.118
Turkey	0.449	0.852

Note: Values are averages for 1985–1990 and for 2005–2010.
Source: World Bank 2012a.

over the next two decades to reach about 8% in 2009. Restrictions on manufactured consumer products were gradually lifted and phased out by 2001, 10 years after the reforms began.[67] In 2010, India's trade to output ratio was 46.3%, up from only 15.7% in 1990. FDI also reached a peak of 3.6% of GDP in 2008, up from less than 0.1% in 1990.[68]

Building up industrial competencies for global markets

Several countries have built up industrial competencies under periods of import substitution that they have subsequently used to supply overseas markets.

- *Turkey.* Trade performance after the 1980s rested on production capacities built in the pre-1980 era of import-substituting industrialization in Turkey.[69] Between 1990 and 2010, its trade to GDP ratio rose from 32% to 48%, a substantial jump for a middle-income country with a large domestic market. In 2011, the top exports—automobiles, iron and steel, and household appliances and consumer electronics—were all from industries that had grown under trade protection.

Several countries have built up industrial competencies under periods of import substitution that they have subsequently used to supply overseas markets

- *Republic of Korea.* When the Republic of Korea and some of the other East Asian economies went through a phase of moderate import substitution for consumer goods, they did not protect domestic producers of capital goods.[70] Even when they were ambivalent about FDI in the 1980s, they chose to import technology under licensing agreements and to develop links with multinational firms. The goal was to build indigenous capabilities for the long haul by borrowing and assimilating foreign technologies.

- *Thailand.* Thailand's manufacturing prowess continues to strengthen through the country's participation in international production networks. In 2009–2010, its exports of parts and components—notably in the automotive and electronics industries—were valued at $48 billion, a quarter of its merchandise exports. The government is keen to establish Thailand as the "Detroit of Asia", not only a cluster for logistics, but also a high-tech hub that forges research collaboration among firms, universities and the public sector.[71]

- *Malaysia.* Malaysia's pre-eminence in the electronics industry began in the early days of the international division of labour, with its courting of multinational companies from countries in the North. Free trade zones, established primarily for manufacturing electronic goods,[72] helped the country develop rapidly between the 1970s and the 1990s. Today, however, Malaysia's economy is seen to be in a "middle-income trap", no longer able to compete with low-cost production in neighbouring countries and lacking the skills for high-end tasks in global production networks.[73] The government's own advisory council is concerned that a slowdown in FDI inflows could affect the prospects for graduating to high-income status.[74] Malaysia's good record in secondary education does not seem to have produced a strong enough base for an innovation-driven economy: Malaysia's future progress is hampered by inadequate research and development capacity and a lack of design and process engineers and technical and production workers.[75]

- *Indonesia.* In the 1990s, to avoid the high costs associated with aspects of protection, Indonesia and some other East Asian countries established export processing zones, bonded warehouses and duty drawback systems—all requiring a competent bureaucracy. When countries felt they lacked that capacity, they resorted to unconventional approaches. For a period Indonesia even privatized its customs administration.[76] Having weathered the Asian financial crisis in 1997, Indonesia today stands out for effectively managing its commodity exports.[77]

Piggybacking on niche products

One option for smaller economies is to tap into world markets for niche products. The choice of successful products is not accidental; it is often the result of years of state support and facilitation that build on existing competencies or the creation of new ones.

- *Chile.* With active support from the state, Chilean firms have had major success in expanding exports of processed agricultural food and beverages and forestry and fish products. For example, in the 1960s, there was substantial public research and development in the cultivation of grapes for wine production. There has also been a long history of subsidized plantations in forestry, and the state has made major efforts to turn the wood, pulp and paper, and furniture cluster into a major export industry.[78] Similar support from a nonprofit corporation, Fundación Chile, has helped make the country's commercial salmon cultivation one of the most prolific in the world.[79]

- *Bangladesh.* Bangladesh took advantage of market distortions in world apparel trade.[80] But without the initiative of its entrepreneurs, it could easily have squandered the opportunity. In 1978, the Desh Company signed a five-year collaboration agreement with Daewoo, a Korean company, that connected Bangladesh to international standards and a network of apparel buyers. Daewoo trained Desh employees in production and marketing in the Republic of Korea. Within a year, 115 of the 130 trainees had left Desh to start their own garment export firms.[81] By 2010, Bangladesh's share of world apparel exports had increased to about 4.8%, from about 0.8% in 1990.[82]

- *Mauritius.* With limited arable land, an expanding population and overreliance on one commodity (sugar), Mauritius had to seek a larger, overseas market. Asian garment exporters, constrained by quotas, were attracted to the country. Until the 1990s, Mauritius was one of the most protected economies, but it provided duty-free access to imported inputs, tax incentives and flexible labour market conditions, including supporting the entry of women into labour-intensive jobs in the export processing zones.[83]

- *Ghana.* Cocoa has been at the heart of Ghana's economy for decades. In the 1970s and early 1980s, however, the sector faced near-collapse. Ghana restored its international competitiveness with reforms begun in 1983, especially by devaluing the currency, increasing the capacity of the private sector in procurement and marketing, and giving farmers a much higher share of prices received. Between 1983 and 2006, the country doubled its production of cocoa per hectare, and today the sector supports the livelihoods of 700,000 people.[84] Over the past 10 years, Ghana has also diversified into services, with the telecom sector growing fast and augmenting the capacity of farmers to connect to sources of market information. A recent survey found that around 61% of cocoa farmers owned mobile phones.[85]

A common thread that runs through the economies that have had meaningful engagement with the world is their investment in people. Tariff reform, at home or in partner countries, may provide an unexpected opening into export markets; some countries may enjoy resource windfalls or ride a wave of short-term success by mimicking others. However, the lesson is that development cannot be sustained without adequate investment in people's skills to constantly upgrade the quality of products and production techniques. The countries discussed here began from diverse initial conditions and have become adept at tailoring nurtured domestic strengths to reap external opportunities presented by world markets.

Driver 3: determined social policy innovation

Evidence shows that substantial public investment—effectively deployed not just in infrastructure, but also in health and education—is key to achieving and sustaining human development. Development strategies cannot succeed without a commitment to equality of opportunity, giving everyone a fair chance to enjoy the fruits of growth. Indeed, there is strong multicountry evidence that promoting higher human development levels helps accelerate economic growth.[86]

A good test of a government's commitment to equality of opportunity is its determination to provide education, particularly to girls. Countries that have sustained high long-term growth have generally put considerable effort into educating their citizens and deepening human capital.[87] Investing in education is important for improving cognitive skills, as measured by the performance of students on mathematics and science tests.[88] However, the benefits derive from investment not so much in the production of specialist skills but in "education for all".[89] Similarly, improvements in public health help growth by boosting labour productivity.[90]

Growth accompanied by high or rising inequality generally involves slower advances in human development, poor social cohesion and slow reduction in poverty. Moreover, it is usually considered unsustainable.[91] Thus the aim should be to create virtuous cycles in which growth and social policies reinforce each other. Growth has frequently been much more effective at reducing poverty in countries with low income inequality than in countries with high income inequality. Growth is also less effective in reducing poverty when the distribution of income worsens over time.[92]

The exceptions seem to be China and Brazil. Over the last 30 years, as a result of very high rates of growth, China has reduced poverty despite increasing income inequality. Similarly, in the early 2000s, Brazil used targeted policies to reduce poverty despite high income inequality—though income distribution became more equal over this period.

Promoting equality—especially equality across groups, known as horizontal

Development strategies cannot succeed without a commitment to equality of opportunity, giving everyone a fair chance to enjoy the fruits of growth equality—also helps reduce social conflict. The sharpest contractions in growth after 1975 occurred in countries with divided societies (as measured by indicators of inequality and ethnic fragmentation). They also suffered from weak institutions for conflict management, with poor quality government institutions that had less capacity to ensure the rule of law, democratic rights and social safety nets.[93]

Education, health care, social protections, legal empowerment and social organization all enable poor people to participate in growth. But even these basic policy instruments may not empower disenfranchised groups. Poor people on the fringes of society struggle to voice their concerns, and governments do not always evaluate whether services intended to reach everyone actually do.[94] Often, problems are exacerbated by external shocks, but in many cases policies are implemented where local institutional capacity and community involvement are low.

- *Uganda.* In post-conflict Uganda, a series of macroeconomic reforms, from the loosening of price control and exchange rates to changes in state-owned enterprises and the civil service, paved the way for a wide-ranging poverty reduction plan in 1997. Uganda went on to become one of the few Sub-Saharan African countries to have halved extreme poverty before the Millennium Development Goal deadline of 2015, from 56.4% in 1992–1993 to 24.5% in 2009–2010. However, increasing income inequality has slowed the pace of poverty reduction.[95] On balance, the economic success of these efforts show that programmes are more effective when the national leadership is committed to reducing poverty, notably by enhancing the consistency of goals and approaches across government agencies.[96] In turn, such progress can have a profound influence on the legitimacy of leaders and their governments.

Promoting inclusion

All countries have, to a greater or lesser extent, multireligious, multicultural, pluralistic societies, and different groups generally have different levels of human development. Even in advanced countries, there is persistent discrimination against certain ethnic groups in labour markets.[97] Nonmarket discrimination can be equally severe and destabilizing. Moreover, historical discrimination has long-lasting effects. Ensuring nondiscrimination and equal treatment, including providing special programmes for disadvantaged groups, is becoming increasingly critical for political and social stability.

In the South, too, different levels of achievement often have historical or colonial origins—for instance, in India, between upper and lower castes, and in Malaysia, among Bumiputras (Malays), Chinese and Indians. Economic prosperity alone cannot end group discrimination that leads to horizontal inequality. To bridge inequalities and correct historical disadvantages, both India and Malaysia have adopted deliberate policy interventions, such as affirmative action.

Providing basic social services

States can underpin long-term economic growth by providing public services that contribute to a healthy, educated labour force. Such measures also help build national stability, reducing the likelihood of political unrest and strengthening the legitimacy of governments.

Developing countries sometimes receive policy advice urging them to view public expenditures on basic services as luxuries they cannot afford. Over the long term, however, these investments pay off. Although not all services need be publicly provided, a minimum universal level of basic health, education and social security needs to be established to ensure that all citizens have secure access to the basic requirements of human development, whether from public or private providers. Compulsory public primary and secondary education has contributed decisively to human development in Europe and in some developing countries, such as Costa Rica.

Access to high-quality education

Growth in HDI value is associated with growth in public spending on education. On average, countries with higher government expenditures on health and education have experienced high growth in human development, although local variations may remain.

- *Indonesia.* During Indonesia's economic boom years (from 1973 onwards), the government funded the construction of schools for basic education through development programmes, and in the following decade public expenditure on education more than doubled.
- *India.* Following the constitutional amendment to make education a fundamental right for every child, India has taken progressive steps towards ending discrimination in its school system (box 3.6).
- *Ghana.* One of the earliest initiatives in independent Ghana was the 1951 Accelerated Development Plan for Education, which aimed at a massive expansion of primary and middle school education. The 1961 Education Act removed fees for elementary education so that households had to pay only a modest amount for textbooks. Enrolment in public elementary schools doubled over the next six years. Between 1966 and 1970, the public discourse on education moved from access to quality. In the early 1970s,

the focus came back to access, this time for secondary education. The next major round of reforms took place in 1987. The most significant aspect of the curriculum reform was to provide children with literacy in three languages—two Ghanaian languages and English—as well as modern farming skills, vocational skills and practical mathematics skills.

- *Mauritius.* The government of Mauritius developed a national consensus on providing high-quality primary, secondary and tertiary schooling free of charge.
- *Bangladesh.* The Ministry of Primary and Mass Education was established in 1992 with the goal of universalizing primary education and eliminating gender and poverty gaps in primary education in Bangladesh. Demand-side interventions, such as the Female Secondary School Assistance Program and the Food for Education programme, broadened coverage, particularly for girls.
- *China.* In 1986, China's National People's Congress passed a law proclaiming the compulsory provision of nine-year basic education regardless of gender, ethnicity or race. From 1990 to 2000, the average years

BOX 3.6

India's Supreme Court issues a progressive verdict mandating seats for disadvantaged children in private schools

Most schools in developing countries are government run, but demand for private schools is expanding in response to the failures of public schools: bad infrastructure, overcrowded classrooms, poor access, teacher shortages and absenteeism. Parents with enough money send their children to private schools, creating a society in many countries divided between public and private school students.

India has made education free and compulsory for children ages 6–14. The vast majority of children are enrolled in government schools, especially in rural areas. But most children from elite households—the rich, the political class, government employees and the growing middle class—are sent to private schools. In many instances, boys are sent to private schools, and girls to free government schools.

To reduce these trends towards segregation, India passed the Right of Children to Free and Compulsory Education Act in 2009. It requires private schools to admit at least 25% of students from socially disadvantaged and low-income households. In turn, private schools are reimbursed for either their tuition charge or the expenditure per student in government schools, whichever is lower. The act was based on the following rationales:

schools must be sites for social integration, private schools do not exist independently of the state that provides them land and other amenities, the social obligation of private schools cannot be waived by contending that only children whose parents pay their fees have a right to be in these schools and the requirement to admit at least 25% of students from disadvantaged groups is fair given that these groups constitute around 25% of the population.

In a landmark judgement on 12 April 2012, the Supreme Court of India upheld the constitutional validity of the act, making two points in support of its decision. First, since the act obligates the state to provide free and compulsory education to all children ages 6–14, the state has the freedom to decide whether it shall fulfil its obligation through its own schools, aided schools or unaided schools. The 2009 act is "child-centric" and not "institution-centric". Second, the right to education "envisages a reciprocal agreement between the state and the parents, and it places an affirmative burden on all stakeholders in our civil society." Private, unaided schools supplement the primary obligation of the state to provide free and compulsory education to the specified category of students.

Source: Government of India 2009; Supreme Court of India 2012.

of schooling for people ages 15 and older in rural areas rose from 4.7 years to 6.8.

- *Uganda*. School fees for primary education were abolished in Uganda in 1997 with the aim of universalizing primary education. Initially this strained the education infrastructure.[98] To improve quality, the Ministry of Education emphasized five areas: curriculum development, basic learning materials, teacher training, language of instruction and quality standards. The early drops in quality and completion rates have since been reversed, and the gains have been solidified and extended.

- *Brazil*. State-led investments in education have dramatically improved development outcomes in Brazil. The transformation of education started with the equalization of funding across regions, states and municipalities. The national Development Fund for Primary Education, created in 1996, guaranteed national minimum spending per student in primary education, increasing the resources for primary students in the Northeast, North and Centre West states, particularly in municipally run schools. Funding "followed the student", providing a significant incentive for school systems to expand enrolment. Similarly, states were required to share resources across municipalities so that all state and municipal schools could reach the per student spending threshold. As a result of this investment, Brazil's math scores on the Programme for International Student Assessment rose 52 points between 2000 and 2009, the third-largest leap on record.

Access to high-quality health care

Advancing health requires more than high-quality health services. Many countries are discovering that they need simultaneous interventions on multiple fronts

Advancing health requires more than high-quality health services. Previous *Human Development Reports* have shown that human poverty is multidimensional. Many countries are discovering that they need simultaneous interventions on multiple fronts. Algeria, Morocco and Tunisia, for example, have seen striking gains in life expectancy in the last 40 years. Possible explanations include improvements in health and drug technology, widespread vaccinations, information technology advances, better access to improved water and sanitation, increased energy provision, and public and private investments in health.

- *Bangladesh*. To improve child survival rates, Bangladesh has taken a multisectoral approach: expanding education and employment opportunities for women; improving women's social status; increasing political participation, social mobilization and community participation; disseminating public health knowledge; and providing effective, community-based essential health services (box 3.7).

Health service provision has been heavily skewed towards the better-off, who have been more likely to have good access to the public services and pay for private ones. Those with greatest access to health care have been workers in the formal sector, who have partly financed their needs with annual contributions. Workers in the informal sector are more difficult to provide for. In India, for example, there are no clearly identified regular employers who can contribute on behalf of the estimated 93% of the workforce in the informal sector.[99]

Everyone should be entitled to the same quality of health care, and several countries have attempted to provide and finance universal health coverage. Some have done so through public health services targeted to the poor. This is neither desirable nor efficient, generally resulting in a health care system in which poor people receive inferior quality services, often in public facilities, while the nonpoor get better health care services from the private sector. Health services targeted to the poor generally remain underfunded partly because the more powerful people who are not poor have no stake in making the system better. Also, special insurance schemes for the poor miss the advantages of pooling risks across the whole population and are thus likely to become financially unviable, often diverting resources from preventive and primary care to more-expensive tertiary care.

Governments also attempt to finance health care through user fees. However, there is near unanimous consensus now that such fees have adverse consequences, especially for the poor. They discourage the poor from using services and generally mobilize little in terms of resources.[100]

BOX 3.7

Bangladesh makes dramatic advances in child survival

In 1990, the infant mortality rate in Bangladesh, 97 deaths per 1,000 live births, was 16% higher than India's 81. By 2004, the situation was reversed, with Bangladesh's infant mortality rate (38) 21% lower than India's (48). Three main factors seem to explain the dramatic improvements.

First, economic empowerment of women through employment in the garment industry and access to microcredit transformed their situation. The vast majority of women in the garment industry are migrants from rural areas. This unprecedented employment opportunity for young women has narrowed gender gaps in employment and income. The spread of microcredit has also aided women's empowerment. Grameen Bank alone has disbursed $8.74 billion to 8 million borrowers, 95% of them women. According to recent estimates, these small loans have enabled more than half of borrowers' households to cross the poverty line, and new economic opportunities have opened up as a result of easier access to microcredit. Postponed marriage and motherhood are direct consequences of women's empowerment, as are the effects on child survival.

Second, social and political empowerment of women has occurred through regular meetings of women's groups organized by nongovernmental organizations. For example, the Grameen system has familiarized borrowers with election processes, since members participate in annual elections for chairperson and secretaries, centre-chiefs and deputy centre-chiefs, as well as board member elections every three years. This experience has prepared many women to run for public office. Women have also been socially empowered through participation in the banks. A recent analysis suggests much better knowledge about health among participants in credit forums than among nonparticipants.

Third, the higher participation of girls in formal education has been enhanced by nongovernmental organizations. Informal schools run by the nongovernmental organization BRAC offer four years of accelerated primary schooling to adolescents who have never attended school, and the schools have retention rates over 94%. After graduation, students can join the formal schooling system, which most do. Monthly reproductive health sessions are integrated into the regular school curriculum and include such topics as adolescence, reproduction and menstruation, marriage and pregnancy, family planning and contraception, smoking and substance abuse, and gender issues. Today, girls' enrolment in schools exceeds that of boys (15 years ago, only 40% of school attendees were girls).

Women's empowerment has gone hand-in-hand with substantial improvements in health services and promotion. With injectable contraceptives, contraceptive use has surged. Nearly 53% of women ages 15–40 now use contraceptives, often through services provided by community outreach workers. BRAC also provided community-based instruction to more than 13 million women about rehydration for children suffering from diarrhoea. Today Bangladesh has the world's highest rate of oral rehydration use, and diarrhoea no longer figures as a major killer of children. Almost 95% of children in Bangladesh are fully immunized against tuberculosis, compared with only 73% in India. Even adult tuberculosis cases fare better in Bangladesh, with BRAC-sponsored community volunteers treating more than 90% of cases, while India struggles to reach 70% through the formal health system.

Source: BRAC n.d.; Grameen Bank n.d.; World Bank 2012a.

The lesson from global experience is that the main source of financing for universal health care should be taxation. Most countries in Southeast Asia, for example, have embraced the idea. Governments have sought to reduce private out-of-pocket spending, increase pooled health finance and improve the reach and quality of health services, although coverage varies.[101] Identifying and reaching poor people remain challenges, and resource-poor developing countries such as Lao PDR and Viet Nam have relied heavily on donor-supported health equity funds.

- *Thailand*. Thailand's 2002 National Health Security Act stipulated that every citizen should have comprehensive medical care. By 2009, 76% of the population, about 48 million people, were registered in the Universal Health Coverage Scheme, which provides free inpatient and outpatient treatment, maternity care, dental care and emergency care. The scheme is fully financed by the government, with a budget in 2011 of $34 million—$70 for each insured person—which accounts for 5.9% of the national budget.[102]

- *Mexico*. In 2003, the Mexican state approved Seguro Popular, a public insurance scheme that provides access to comprehensive health care for poor households formerly excluded from traditional social security. Public resources for health have increased and are being distributed more fairly. Access to and use of health care services have expanded. Financial protection indicators have improved. By the end of 2007, 20 million poor people were benefiting from the scheme.[103] Mexico is a leader in moving rapidly towards universal health coverage by adopting an innovative financing mechanism.

- *Rwanda*. Access to health services has been expanded in Rwanda by introducing community-based health insurance. Health care providers were given incentives by linking resources to performance. As a result, health care became more affordable in rural areas. And there were visible improvements in health outcomes. Under-five mortality fell from 196 deaths per 1,000 live births in 2000 to 103 in 2007, and the maternal mortality ratio declined more than 12% a year over 2000–2008. Rwanda is on track to reach the Millennium Development Goal for maternal health.

One concern in a number of countries is the emergence of dual-track services. Even if public provision is universal in principle, quality and access may be poor, driving people towards expensive private providers.

- *China*. Much of China's health care success took place between 1950 and 1980, when the government established a three-level system of village clinics, township health centres and county hospitals in rural areas and health centres and district hospitals in urban areas. Since the 1980s, however, the health sector has been driven by a fee-for-service model. As a result, while China's overall health status has continued to improve, disparities have grown between the eastern and western provinces and between rural and urban areas. In many parts of the country quality health care has become unaffordable for the poor.

- *Chile*. Before 1980, Chile's health system was publicly financed through social security and public funds. After health reform in 1981, however, risk insurance was introduced, and market mechanisms began to regulate levels of protection. By 2006, a dual system of coverage was in place. The National Health Care Fund, funded by federal government tax revenues and by premiums from beneficiaries, covered 69% of the population, but its resource constraints have prevented it from ensuring timely and quality services. Private health insurance companies covered 17% of the population. The National Health Care Fund offers a universal health plan. This dual system has been criticized because it leaves low-income and high-risk populations to be treated mainly in the public system, which is poorly resourced and thus tends to provide lower quality service. In 2004, aware of the risks,

the state introduced El Plan de Acceso Universal de Garantías Explícitas, which guarantees a medical benefits package consisting of a prioritized list of diagnoses and treatment for 56 health conditions, as well as universal coverage for all citizens.

Providing universal health care and at least nine years of compulsory education requires strong state commitment, involvement and consistency over time. The challenge for countries in the South is to ensure equity in access to health and education services and basic quality standards to prevent a dual-track service industry that provides low-quality public services (or none at all) to the poor and higher quality private services to the rich.

Universal public health and education policies can be designed and implemented without sacrificing quality for the sake of greater coverage. Poor people have no alternatives to a public system, while wealthier people can pay for private services. Such dynamics entrench inequalities, reduce social integration and undermine sustainable human development. New programmes, such as those in China, Mexico and Thailand, illustrate the possibilities of ensuring that basic services are universal and of reasonable quality. When financial resources are adequately provided, publicly provided services need not be inferior to private services.

Increasing social cohesion by broadening development

Transforming development requires that all citizens feel vested in the broader goals of society, showing respect and compassion for others and a commitment to building social cohesion. This requires that states and citizens understand that human development is about more than just enhancing individual capabilities. Individual capabilities are embedded in a broader social system whose health requires enhanced social competencies (see box 1.7 in chapter 1).

More effective social protection systems are also needed to help individuals and communities manage risks to their welfare. Globalization has contributed to the dismantling of some aspects of social protection and social insurance, especially for systems relying on universal

> Universal public health and education policies can be designed and implemented without sacrificing quality for the sake of greater coverage

coverage and large government expenditures. At the same time, it has increased the need for social protection, as fluctuations in economic activity become more frequent. Thus, social policies become as important as economic policies in advancing human development. In fact, social and economic policies can hardly be disentangled because their goals and instruments are analogous.[104]

In many parts of the South, states have introduced and provided social protection programmes to integrate poor people into the new economy. Cash transfer programmes have been particularly important in reducing poverty and improving income inequality through redistribution. But transfers cannot substitute for public provision of essential goods and services (box 3.8). At best, they can supplement resources of the poor. Offering cash so that households can buy health care of their choice is unlikely to work where high-quality health care is in short supply. Similarly, giving cash to households so that they can choose their school is unlikely to help the poor if few schools offer high-quality education. Nor can cash transfers substitute for incomes earned through decent work.

- *India*. India's National Rural Employment Guarantee Scheme provides up to 100 days of unskilled manual labour to eligible rural poor at the statutory minimum agricultural labour wage. This initiative is promising because it provides access to income and some insurance for the poor against the vagaries of seasonal work and affords individuals the self-respect and empowerment associated with work.[105] In addition, it aims to help build economies in rural areas by developing infrastructure. The scheme has innovative design features such as social audits and advanced monitoring and information systems.

> Cash transfer programmes—important in reducing poverty and improving income inequality—cannot substitute for public provision of essential goods and services

BOX 3.8

Cevdet Yılmaz, Minister of Development, Turkey

Strengthening social protection in Turkey

As recently as 2002, an estimated 30% of Turkey's people lived below the government's poverty threshold of $4.30 a day. Government spending on social protection accounted for just 12% of GDP, less than half the EU average of 25%. And expenditures on social assistance for the poor accounted for only 0.5% of GDP, prompting criticism that Turkey's social support systems were both fragmented and insufficient.

Over the past decade, however, Turkey's strong economic performance, pro-poor approach to social policies and targeted assistance with greater resources have helped accelerate poverty reduction. Key policy changes include systematic strengthening of social assistance programmes, conditional cash transfers, social security reforms and an ambitious transformation of the national public health system. Under the conditional cash transfer programme alone, launched in 2003, more than 1 million children have received health care support, and about 2.2 million have benefited from education aid. School children have received more than 1.3 billion textbooks since 2003 under a new free schoolbook programme, and nearly 1 million now get free transportation to school.

As a result of these and other initiatives, the share of the population living on less than $4.30 a day fell sharply, to 3.7% in 2010, and the share of GDP devoted to poverty assistance and related social services nearly tripled, to 1.2%.

The share of social expenditures in Turkey's GDP is still less than the EU average, and social assistance schemes have not yet had the desired impact on poverty rates. To increase their effectiveness, the government is working on new methods of poverty measurement and social protection, new approaches to in-kind and cash assistance, stronger links to job opportunities and continuing consultations with targeted communities and households.

Similarly, the expansion and modernization of health services have had a direct, measurable impact on public health. Health insurance is now available to the entire population. Under the Health Transformation Programme launched in 2003, family practitioners were assigned to families to strengthen basic health services, with primary and emergency health care provided free of charge. The results have been swift and encouraging. For the first time, almost all children are getting free regular vaccinations. Seven million schoolchildren get free milk every day. Iron and vitamin D supplements are provided without charge to mothers and children. Infant mortality rates have fallen sharply, to 10 per 1,000 live births in 2010, down from 29 in 2003, according to government figures. This two-thirds drop greatly exceeds the reduction targeted under the Millennium Development Goals.

Pro-child policies go beyond health care and education, to broader assistance for their home communities. The government started a new Social Support Program in 2008 to develop social cohesion and ensure social integration, particularly in the less-developed eastern regions of the country. Its projects aim to increase participation in national economic and social life by disadvantaged people marginalized by poverty and social exclusion. The goals of the programme's several thousand projects to date go beyond job creation in these lower income regions to include support for young people and women to express themselves through cultural, artistic and athletic accomplishments.

More important, though, is what these improvements already mean to the lives of ordinary Turkish families. Throughout the country, parents and children alike can now look forward to healthier, more secure, more fulfilling lives—the underlying goal and core principle of human development.

- *China.* The Minimum Livelihood Guarantee Scheme is the Chinese government's main response to the new challenges of social protection brought about by increasing privatization and engagement with the global market. It guarantees a minimum income in urban areas by filling the gap between actual income and a locally set poverty line. So, despite increasing income inequality in China, there is potential for redistributive policies to reduce poverty and enhance food security. In addition, extending equal rights to migrants in cities can have a decisive impact on their ability to access comparable social services.
- *Brazil.* Despite slower economic growth than in China and India, Brazil has reduced inequality by introducing a poverty reduction programme, extending education and raising the minimum wage. Its conditional cash transfer programme Bolsa Escola, launched in 2001, followed the conceptual foundation of others in Latin America, such as Mexico's Progresa (now called Oportunidades; box 3.9). In 2003 Bolsa Escola was expanded to Bolsa Familia by folding several other cash and in-kind transfer programmes into a

unified targeting system under streamlined administration. By 2009, Bolsa Familia covered more than 12 million households across the country, or 97.3% of the target population. These programmes have also broken ground in terms of programme administration and female empowerment by developing innovative distribution channels, such as ATM cards for low-income mothers without bank accounts. The result has been substantial declines in poverty and extreme poverty and reduced inequality.[106]
- *Chile.* In response to findings that state subsidies were not reaching the extreme poor, Chile Solidario was launched in 2002 to reach the extreme poor with a combination of aid and skill development. Focusing on household assistance, it takes the view that extreme poverty is multidimensional, extending beyond low income to include other deprivations in basic capabilities such as health and education. Furthermore, poverty reduction requires the mitigation of vulnerability to common events, such as sickness, accidents and unemployment. Together with other social policies, the programme has increased

BOX 3.9

Conditional cash transfer programmes and Mexico's Oportunidades

Conditional cash transfer programmes are designed to increase beneficiaries' incomes and their access to health and education by making transfers conditional on requirements such as visits to health clinics and school attendance. They target certain beneficiaries (typically individuals from low-income or disadvantaged households) and provide support in cash instead of as in-kind benefits, with the transfers conditional on activities related to health and education. Moreover, the programmes can be designed to allow rigorous impact evaluation. For instance, the Tekopora programme in Paraguay has been shown to have positive impacts on nutrition, health, education and poverty reduction without having negative impacts on labour supply.

Mexico's Oportunidades is a conditional cash transfer programme targeted to poor households conditional on children's school attendance and medical checkups and parents' attendance at community meetings where information is provided on personal health and hygiene. The programme is designed to break the intergenerational transmission of poverty. Originally called Progresa, it aims to alleviate current and future poverty by giving parents financial incentives (cash) to invest in the health and education of their children. The programme, which started in 1997, is one of the largest conditional cash transfer programmes in the world, distributing about $3 billion to some 5 million beneficiary households in 2012.

Oportunidades transfers, given bimonthly to female heads of household, have two parts. The first, received by all beneficiary households, is a fixed food stipend, conditional on family members obtaining preventive medical care, and is intended to help families spend on more and better nutrition. The second comes in the form of education scholarships and is conditional on children attending school a minimum of 85% of the time and not repeating a grade more than twice. The education stipend provided for each child under age 18 enrolled in school between the third grade of primary school and the third (last) grade of junior high varies by grade and gender. It rises substantially after graduation from primary school and is higher for girls than for boys during secondary and tertiary school. Beneficiary children also receive money for school supplies once a year.

Conditional cash transfer programmes cost less than traditional in-kind social assistance interventions. Brazil's Bolsa Familia and Mexico's Oportunidades, the two largest programmes in Latin America, cost less than 1% of GDP. In some cases they have been perceived as tools to provide access to universal basic rights such as health and education, but in others they have led to the exclusion of some localities due to the inadequate supply of services.

Source: Hailu and Veras Soares 2008; Ribas, Veras Soares and Hirata 2008.

the take-up of health and education services during boom times, while playing a counter-cyclical role in economic downturns by providing a much needed safety net to the poor.

The rising South is thus developing a broader social and poverty reduction agenda in which policies to address inequalities, institutional failures, social barriers and personal vulnerabilities are as central as promoting economic growth. This follows from an increased understanding that social challenges extend beyond income poverty; they also include lack of access to education, poor health, social inequality and limited social integration (box 3.10).

*　　　　*　　　　*

An agenda for development transformation that promotes human development is multifaceted. It expands people's assets by universalizing access to basic social services; extending credit to the population, especially the poor;

protecting common resources; and introducing land reform where relevant. It improves the functioning of state and social institutions to promote equitable growth where the benefits are widespread. It prioritizes rapid growth in employment and works to ensure that jobs are of high quality. It reduces bureaucratic and social constraints on economic action and social mobility. It holds leadership accountable. It involves communities in setting budget priorities and disseminating information. And it focuses on social priorities.

Many countries of the South have demonstrated what can be achieved through a developmental state. But even in higher achieving countries, continuing success is not guaranteed. Countries across the world are facing a series of challenges, from rising inequality to spreading environmental degradation. The next chapter addresses these threats and considers what is needed to sustain future progress in human development.

> A broader social and poverty reduction agenda is needed in which policies to address inequalities, institutional failures, social barriers and personal vulnerabilities are as central as promoting economic growth

---

BOX 3.10   *Michael Bloomberg, Mayor, New York City*

Why New York City looked South for antipoverty policy advice

In New York City, we are working to better the lives of our residents in many ways. We continue to improve the quality of education in our schools. We have improved New Yorkers' health by reducing smoking and obesity. And we have enhanced the city's landscape by adding bike lanes and planting hundreds of thousands of trees.

We have also sought to reduce poverty by finding new and better ways to build self-sufficiency and prepare our young people for bright futures. To lead this effort, we established the Center for Economic Opportunity. Its mission is to identify strategies to help break the cycle of poverty through innovative education, health and employment initiatives.

Over the last six years, the centre has launched more than 50 pilot programmes in partnership with city agencies and hundreds of community-based organizations. It has developed a customized evaluation strategy for each of these pilots, monitoring their performance, comparing outcomes and determining which strategies are most successful at reducing poverty and expanding opportunity. Successful programmes are sustained with new public and private funds. Unsuccessful programmes are discontinued, and resources reinvested in new strategies. The centre's findings are then shared across government agencies, with policymakers, with nonprofit partners and private donors and with colleagues across the country and around the world who are also seeking new ways to break the cycle of poverty.

New York is fortunate to have some of the world's brightest minds working in our businesses and universities, but we recognize there is much to learn from programmes developed elsewhere. That is why the centre began its work by conducting a national and international survey of promising antipoverty strategies.

In 2007, the centre launched Opportunity NYC: Family Rewards, the first conditional cash transfer programme in the United States. Based on similar programmes operating in more than 20 other countries, Family Rewards reduces poverty by providing households with incentives for preventive health care, education and job training. In designing Family Rewards, we drew on lessons from Brazil, Mexico and dozens of other countries. By the end of our three-year pilot, we had learned which programme elements worked in New York City and which did not; information that is now helpful to a new generation of programmes worldwide.

Before we launched Opportunity NYC: Family Rewards, I visited Toluca, Mexico, for a firsthand look at Mexico's successful federal conditional cash transfer programme, Oportunidades. We also participated in a North–South learning exchange hosted by the United Nations. We worked with the Rockefeller Foundation, the World Bank, the Organization of American States and other institutions and international policymakers to exchange experiences on conditional cash transfer programmes in Latin America, as well as in Indonesia, South Africa and Turkey.

Our international learning exchanges are not limited to these cash transfer initiatives; they also include innovative approaches to urban transportation, new education initiatives and other programmes.

No one has a monopoly on good ideas, which is why New York will continue to learn from the best practices of other cities and countries. And as we adapt and evaluate new programmes in our own city, we remain committed to returning the favour and making a lasting difference in communities around the world.

"Each generation will reap what the former generation has sown."

Chinese proverb

"We have to free half of the human race, the women, so that they can help to free the other half."

Emmeline Pankhurst

4.

Sustaining momentum

Much of the news about developing countries in recent decades has been positive, especially their accelerated progress in human development. But what of the future? Can these countries continue to advance human development at the same rapid pace, and can other countries in the South share in the benefits? Yes, with the right policies. These include enhancing equity, enabling voice and participation, confronting environmental pressures and managing demographic change. Policymakers will need to strive for greater policy ambition and to understand the high cost of policy inaction.

Over the next few years, policymakers in developing countries will need to follow an ambitious agenda that responds to difficult global conditions, notably the economic slowdown, which has decreased demand from the North. At the same time, they will need to address their own urgent policy priorities.

Policy priorities for developing countries

Four policy priorities stand out for developing countries over the next few years if they are to continue the gains of recent decades and if the benefits are to extend to countries still lagging behind:

- *Enhancing equity.* Equity and social justice, valuable in their own right, are important for expanding capabilities.[1] Progress in human development is difficult to sustain in the face of growing or persistent inequity.[2] Inequity in specific capabilities—for example, proxied and measured as disparities in health and education outcomes, as well as in income—also impedes progress in human development, though the effects may be less pronounced. At the core of these negative relationships is gender inequality: women's health and education are crucial to addressing demographic and other human development challenges. Although some countries in Latin America and elsewhere have greatly reduced income inequality, not all countries recognize the importance of addressing inequality in health, education and income.[3]
- *Enabling voice and participation.* As education levels rise and access to information and communication technologies spreads, people are demanding more participation in political processes, challenging decisionmakers to be more accountable and expand opportunities for open public discourse. Restricted opportunities for political participation, at a time when unemployment is rising and the economic environment is deteriorating, can fuel civil unrest. Expanded opportunities for political participation, along with greater government accountability in ensuring that basic human needs are met, can foster human freedoms and sustain human development. Strong political participation by the relatively deprived provides an important source of support for pro–human development policy change.
- *Confronting environmental pressures.* Climate change and local stresses on natural resources and ecosystems are increasing pressure on the environment in almost all countries, regardless of their stage of development. Unless action is taken urgently, future progress in human development will be threatened. Building on scenarios developed for *Human Development Report 2011*, this Report argues for aggressive action nationally and internationally to tackle these challenges.
- *Managing demographic change.* In some developing countries, mostly in Sub-Saharan Africa, large cohorts of young people are entering the workforce. In other countries, notably in East Asia, the share of working-age people in the population is falling as the share of elderly rises. New policy interventions are needed to generate sufficient productive employment while meeting the growing demand for social protection.

There will be other challenges to human development, including volatile commodity prices, especially for food and fuel. In an increasingly globalized world, these and other concerns will make for a complex environment with attendant risks, including progress reversals, rising insecurity and greater inequality. Forecasting is difficult in such a complex environment because modelling may miss key variables, such as technological progress, that can dramatically change both production and personal possibilities. Nevertheless, modelling scenarios are helpful for illustrating policy choices and their implications.

Enhancing equity

Greater equity, including between men and women and across groups (religious, racial and others), is not only valuable in itself, but also essential for promoting human development. One of the most powerful instruments for advancing equity and human development is education, which builds people's capacities and expands their freedom of choice. Education boosts people's self-confidence and makes it easier for them to find better jobs, engage in public debate and make demands on government for health care, social security and other entitlements.

Education also has striking benefits for health and mortality (see box 4.1 on differences in education futures in the Republic of Korea and India). Evidence worldwide establishes that

---

BOX 4.1

Why population prospects will likely differ in the Republic of Korea and India

Educational attainment has risen rapidly in the Republic of Korea. In the 1950s a large proportion of school-age children received no formal education. Today, young Korean women are among the best educated women in the world: more than half have completed college. As a consequence, elderly Koreans of the future will be much better educated than elderly Koreans of today (see figure), and because of the positive correlation between education and health, they are also likely to be healthier.

Assuming that enrolment rates (which are high) remain constant, the proportion of the population younger than age 14 will drop from 16% in 2010 to 13% in 2050. There will also be a marked shift in the population's education composition, with the proportion having a tertiary education projected to rise from 26% to 47%.

For India, the picture looks very different. Before 2000, more than half the adult population had no formal education. Despite the recent expansion in basic schooling and impressive growth in the number of better educated Indians (undoubtedly a key factor in India's recent economic growth), the proportion of the adult population with no education will decline only slowly. Partly because of this lower level of education, particularly among women, India's population is projected to grow rapidly, with India surpassing China as the most populous country. Even under an optimistic fast track scenario, which assumes education expansion similar to Korea's, India's education distribution in 2050 will still be highly unequal, with a sizeable group of uneducated (mostly elderly) adults. The rapid expansion in tertiary education under this scenario, however, will build a very well educated young adult labour force.

Comparative population and education futures in the Republic of Korea and India

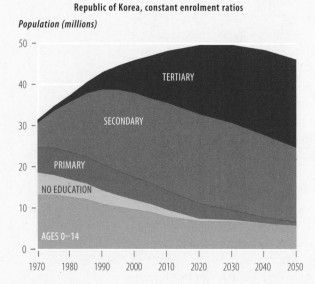

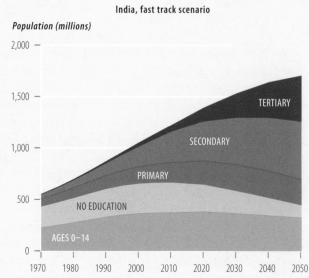

Source: Lutz and KC 2013.

better education of parents, especially of mothers, improves child survival. Moreover, working women and more-educated women (who tend to complete their schooling before bearing children) are likely to have fewer children.[4] Educated women also have healthier children who are more likely to survive (table 4.1), thus reducing the incentive to have a larger family.[5] Educated women also have better access to contraception and use it more effectively.[6]

Drawing on Demographic and Health Surveys and micro-level surveys, research for this Report reinforces these arguments, finding mother's education to be more important to child survival than household income or wealth is. This has profound policy implications, potentially shifting emphasis from efforts to boost household income to measures to improve girls' education.

This relationship can be illustrated by data on child mortality (see table 4.1). Many African countries, most notably Mali and Niger, have a high under-five mortality rate. But in every country, the mortality rate is lower among better educated mothers. In some countries, such as Nigeria, much lower child mortality is associated with primary education; in others, such as Liberia and Uganda, the decisive difference is associated with secondary education.

A modelling exercise conducted for this Report projects the impact of differences in education levels on child mortality over 2010–2050 under two scenarios. The "base case" scenario assumes that current trends in educational attainment at the national level continue without substantial new funding commitments or policy initiatives. Under this assumption, the proportion of each group of children—categorized by age and gender—advancing to the next education level remains constant (see *Technical appendix*).

The "fast track" scenario assumes much more ambitious education policy targets, similar to those achieved in recent decades by the Republic of Korea, for example, with the proportion of schoolchildren advancing to the next education level steadily increasing

> A mother's education is more important to her child's survival than is household income or wealth

TABLE 4.1

Under-five mortality rate and total fertility rate by mother's education level
In selected countries, most recent year available since 2005

Country	Survey year	Under-five mortality rate (per 1,000 live births)				Total fertility rate (births per woman)			
		No education	Primary	Secondary or higher	Overall	No education	Primary	Secondary or higher	Overall
Bangladesh	2007	93	73	52	74	3.0	2.9	2.5	2.7
Egypt	2008	44	38	26	33	3.4	3.2	3.0	3.0
Ethiopia	2005	139	111	54	132	6.1	5.1	2.0	5.4
Ghana	2008	103	88	67	85	6.0	4.9	3.0	4.0
India	2005/2006	106	78	49	85	3.6	2.6	2.1	2.7
Indonesia	2007	94	60	38	51	2.4	2.8	2.6	2.6
Liberia	2009	164	162	131	158	7.1	6.2	3.9	5.9
Mali	2006	223	176	102	215	7.0	6.3	3.8	6.6
Niger	2006	222	209	92	218	7.2	7.0	4.8	7.0
Nigeria	2008	210	159	107	171	7.3	6.5	4.2	5.7
Rwanda	2007/2008	174	127	43	135	6.1	5.7	3.8	5.5
Uganda	2006	164	145	91	144	7.7	7.2	4.4	6.7
Zambia	2007	144	146	105	137	8.2	7.1	3.9	6.2

Note: Data refer to the period 10 years before the survey year.
Source: Lutz and KC 2013.

over the years. The results from the fast track scenario show substantially fewer child deaths as mother's level of schooling rises. The model also shows that a greater emphasis on progress in education would substantially and continually reduce child deaths in all countries and regions, as a direct result of improvements in girls' education (table 4.2).

India has the most projected child deaths over 2010–2015, almost 7.9 million, accounting for about half the deaths among children under age 5 in Asia.[7] In the final projection period, 2045–2050, nearly 6.1 million children are projected to die under the base case scenario but just half that many (3.1 million) under the fast track scenario.

China has more people than India but is projected to have less than a quarter (1.7 million) the number of child deaths over 2010–2015. And due to China's advances in education, projections look optimistic under both scenarios. If China follows the fast track scenario, as

seems likely, child deaths will decline to about half a million by 2045–2050, less than a third of the current level.

Projections are less optimistic for some other countries. Under the base case scenario, child deaths in Kenya, for example, would rise from about 582,000 in 2010–2015 to about 1.6 million in 2045–2050. Under the fast track scenario, the number of deaths over 2045–2050 would drop to 371,000, much better, but not far below the level in 2010–2015.

The projected declines in child deaths reflect the combined effects of better educated women having fewer children and of fewer of those children dying. The projections also show that policy interventions have a greater impact where education outcomes are initially weaker.

These results underscore the importance of reducing gender inequality, especially in education and in low Human Development

TABLE 4.2

Projected number of deaths of children under age 5, by education scenario, 2010–2015, 2025–2030 and 2045–2050 (thousands)

Country or region	2010–2015 Base case	2025–2030 Base case	2025–2030 Fast track	2045–2050 Base case	2045–2050 Fast track
Country					
Brazil	328	224	177	161	102
China	1,716	897	871	625	526
India	7,872	6,707	4,806	6,096	3,064
Kenya	582	920	482	1,552	371
Korea, Rep.	9	8	9	7	7
Mali	488	519	318	541	150
Pakistan	1,927	1,641	1,225	1,676	773
South Africa	288	198	165	134	93
Region					
Africa	16,552	18,964	12,095	24,185	7,495
Asia	15,029	11,715	8,924	10,561	5,681
Europe	276	209	204	196	187
Latin America and the Caribbean	1,192	963	704	950	413
North America	162	160	155	165	152
Oceania	11	11	11	12	10

Note: See *Technical appendix* at the end of this Report for a discussion of the base case and fast track scenarios.
Source: Lutz and KC 2013.

Index (HDI) countries. Gender inequality is especially tragic not only because it excludes women from basic social opportunities, but also because it gravely imperils the life prospects of future generations.

Enabling voice and participation

In the 1995 *Human Development Report*, Mahbub ul Haq highlighted that unless people can participate meaningfully in the events and processes that shape their lives, national human development paths will be neither desirable nor sustainable.

Equitable and sustainable human development requires systems of public discourse that encourage citizens to participate in the political process by expressing their views and voicing their concerns. People should be able to influence policymaking and results, and young people should be able to look forward to greater economic opportunities and political accountability. Exclusion from this process limits people's ability to communicate their concerns and needs and can perpetuate injustices.

Autocratic regimes impose restrictions that directly counter human development by restraining essential freedoms. But even in democracies, poor people and poor groups often have limited access to information, voice or public participation. Poor people need to work together to effectively exercise their political voice. Yet in many countries, organizations representing the poor are not supported but discouraged. Democracies can also extend accountability from what is often a narrow constituency of elites to all citizens, particularly those who have been underrepresented in public discourse, such as women, youth and the poor.

Governments that do not respond to citizens' needs or widen opportunities for political participation risk losing their legitimacy. Dissatisfaction is on the rise in the North and the South as people call for more opportunities to voice their concerns and influence policy, especially on basic social protection. According to a recent International Labour Organization report, government dissatisfaction, measured by the Social Unrest Index, rose in 57 of 106 countries from 2010 to 2011. The largest increases were in countries of the North, followed by those in the Arab States and Sub-Saharan Africa.[9]

People in the North have been protesting against austerity measures and reductions in public spending and jobs, as in France, Greece, Italy, Spain and the United Kingdom. Citizens have challenged governments to address the social consequences of their policies, pointing out that the burden of austerity is being borne disproportionately by the poor and socially disadvantaged.[10] Other focuses of unrest have included food prices, unemployment and pollution:

- *Rising food prices.* Riots in response to high food prices in 2008 challenged stability in more than 30 countries in Africa and the Arab States.[11]
- *Unemployment and low wages.* Workers are demanding that governments respond to their needs. The unemployed are voicing their dissatisfaction in many countries.[12] In Viet Nam strikes doubled in 2011 as workers struggled to gain higher wages in the face of inflation.[13]
- *Environmental pollution.* Mass protests against environmental pollution are also widespread. Protesters in Shanghai, China, for example, fought a proposed wastewater pipeline,[14] and in Malaysia local residents have been opposing the construction of a rare earth metal refinery in their neighbourhood.[15]

Among the most active protesters are youth, in part a response to job shortages and limited employment opportunities for educated young people. In a sample of 48 countries, youth unemployment was more than 20% in 2011, well above the 9.6% overall rate.[16] Youth discontent in response to rising unemployment is even more likely in areas with an educated population.[17] Education alters people's expectations of government and instils the political skills and resources needed to challenge government decisions. This is not to say that the educated have greater rights. But unless governments give greater priority to job creation, they are likely to face increasing youth dissatisfaction as education coverage expands (figure 4.1).[18]

At the same time, mobile broadband Internet and other modern technologies are opening

Dissatisfaction is on the rise as people call for more opportunities to voice their concerns and influence policy, especially on basic social protection

FIGURE 4.1

Under the fast track scenario, education outcomes are enhanced

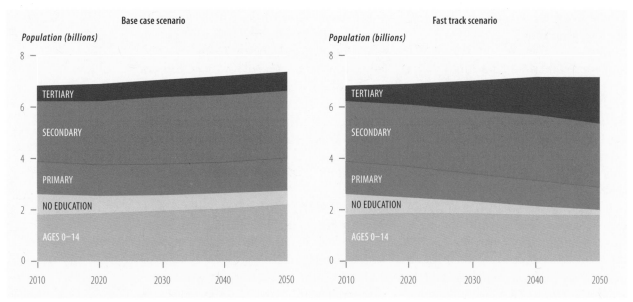

Note: See *Technical appendix* for a discussion of the base case and fast track scenarios.
Source: HDRO calculations based on Lutz and KC (2013).

> Participation and
> inclusivity, valuable in their
> own right, also improve
> the quality of policies and
> their implementation and
> reduce the probability
> of future upheaval

new channels through which citizens, particularly young people, can demand accountability. They are also enabling people in different countries to share values and experiences, bringing them closer together.

The Internet and social media, as "low-cost aggregators" of public opinion, are amplifying people's voices. In China, for example, the post-1990 generation is highly educated, politically aware and outspoken on social media.[19] Less than a week after the July 2011 high-speed train accident in Wenzhou, China's two major microblogs (*weibos*) had distributed some 26 million messages commenting on the accident and expressing concerns about safety.[20]

Social movements and media draw attention to specific issues, but this does not always result in political transformations that benefit the broader society. In India, for example, the Anna Hazare movement against corruption created pressure for change. Critics, however, point out that such movements can favour policies that may not be supported by the wider electorate. Thus, it is important to institutionalize participatory processes that can adjust the political balance by providing a platform for excluded citizens to demand accountability and redress of inequities, ranging from

systemic discrimination to unfair and unjust exclusion.[21]

Participation and inclusivity, valuable in their own right, also improve the quality of policies and their implementation and reduce the probability of future upheaval. Failure to build an accountable and responsive polity may foment discontent and civil strife. This can derail human development. History is replete with popular rebellions against unresponsive governments, as unrest deters investment and impedes growth and governments divert resources to maintaining law and order.

In recent years, countries in both the North and the South have faced escalating crises of legitimacy that have pitted citizens against their institutions. Millions of people in the Arab States have risen to demand opportunities, respect and dignity as well as fuller citizenship and a new social contract with those who govern in their name. As a result, Egypt, Libya and Tunisia have seen autocratic governments deposed, Yemen has embarked on an internationally brokered political transition, Jordan and Morocco have undertaken political reforms and Syrian Arab Republic is in the throes of civil war.

One way to foster peaceful change is to allow civil society to mature through open practice. Even under autocratic governments, Egypt and Tunisia, for example, had fairly well developed associational structures and self-disciplined political opposition movements. By contrast, Libya lacked such experience, which contributed to an all-out civil war. Building political cohesion after conflict is difficult in countries that lack a tradition of civic participation. Diverse experiences show that changes in political regimes do not automatically enhance voice, participation, inclusion or accountability or make states work more effectively.

Accountability and inclusion are vital not only in the political sphere, but also in economic and social areas, through promoting job creation and social inclusion, especially in societies with a large and growing educated population. This requires effective mediating institutions; otherwise, modernization can be destabilizing.[22] This is not to suggest that people should be educated only if there are jobs for them—in the human development paradigm, access to knowledge and education is an end in itself—but recent social upheavals show that a mismatch between education and economic opportunity can lead to alienation and despair, especially among young people.

Of the 20 countries with the largest increases in mean years of schooling over 1980–2010, 8 were in the Arab States (figure 4.2). In most of these countries, employment opportunities failed to keep pace with educational attainment. Most countries that were part of the recent unrest in the Arab States are in the lower right quadrant of figure 4.2, because they had major gains in educational attainment but below-median employment to population ratios.[23]

It is hard to predict when societies will reach a tipping point. Many factors precipitate demands for change. When educated

> Accountability and inclusion are vital not only in the political sphere, but also in economic and social areas, through promoting job creation and social inclusion

FIGURE 4.2

In most countries, employment opportunities have not kept pace with educational attainment

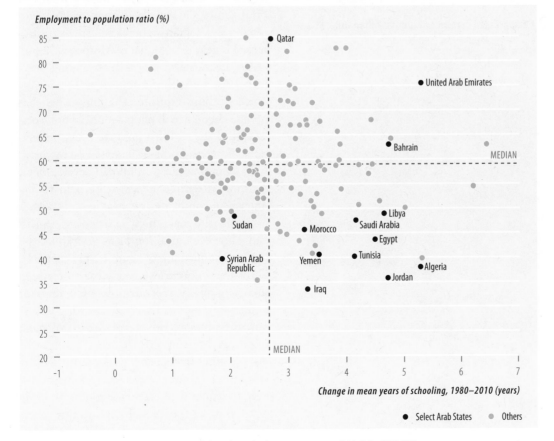

Note: Analysis covers 141 countries. Employment to population ratios are for the most recent year available during 2006–2010.
Source: Adapted from Campante and Chor (2012) using updated data.

young people cannot find work, they tend to feel aggrieved. Average years of schooling have risen over the past 30 years in all countries with data available.[24] Yet grievances alone do not trigger upheavals. The public can be angry, but if people believe that the cost in time and effort to engage in political action outweighs the likelihood of real change, they may not act.[25] Mass protests, especially by educated people, tend to erupt when bleak prospects for economic opportunities lower the opportunity cost of engaging in political activity. These "effort-intensive forms of political participation"[26] are then easily coordinated through new forms of mass communication.

Around the world people are calling on governments to become more accountable to citizens and to expand public opportunities to influence policymaking. Such transformations have taken place in the past. For example, Karl Polanyi documented the Great Transformation of 1944, where governments in the North responded to demands from civil society and labour unions to regulate the market and extend social protection so that the market served society rather than society being subservient to the market.[27] Many governments introduced regulations to constrain the activities of firms and improve working conditions and extended social services and social protection. Governments also assumed power over macroeconomic policy and introduced some restrictions on international trade. The time may be right again for a transformation, appropriate for 21st century concerns and conditions.[28]

Confronting environmental pressures

A major challenge for the world is to reduce greenhouse gas emissions. While it might seem that carbon productivity (GDP per unit of carbon dioxide) would rise with human development, the correlation is quite weak (figure 4.3). At each HDI level, some countries have greater carbon productivity than others.

Consider medium HDI Guatemala and Morocco, countries with nearly identical HDI values. Guatemala's carbon productivity ($5.00 per kilogram in purchasing power parity terms) is nearly twice that of Morocco ($2.60). Differences can be just as great among provinces or states within countries, as in China.[29] These findings reinforce the arguments that progress in human development need not worsen carbon use and that improved environmental policy can accompany human development.

To sustain progress in human development, far more attention needs to be paid to the impact human beings are having on the environment. The goal is high human development and a low ecological footprint per capita (the lower right quadrant of figure 1.7 in chapter 1). Only a few countries come close to creating such a globally reproducible high level of human development without exerting unsustainable pressure on the planet's ecological resources. Meeting this challenge on a global scale requires that all countries adjust their development pathway: developed countries will need to reduce their ecological footprint, while developing countries will need to raise their HDI value without increasing their ecological footprint. Innovative clean technologies will pay an important part in this.

> Around the world people are calling on governments to become more accountable to citizens and to expand public opportunities to influence policymaking

FIGURE 4.3

At each HDI level, some countries have greater carbon productivity than others

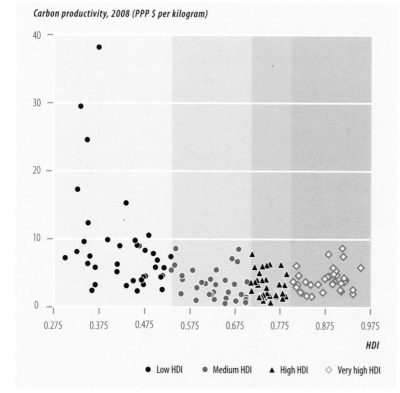

Carbon productivity, 2008 (PPP $ per kilogram)

● Low HDI ● Medium HDI ▲ High HDI ◇ Very high HDI

Note: Carbon productivity is GDP per unit of carbon dioxide. PPP is purchasing power parity.
Source: HDRO calculations based on World Bank (2012a).

While environmental threats such as climate change, deforestation, air and water pollution, and natural disasters affect everyone, they hurt poor countries and poor communities most. Climate change is already exacerbating chronic environmental threats, and ecosystem losses are constraining livelihood opportunities, especially for poor people. A clean and safe environment should be seen as a right, not a privilege. The 2011 *Human Development Report* highlighted that equity and sustainability are inextricably linked. Sustainable societies need policies and structural changes that align human development and climate change goals through low-emission, climate-resilient strategies and innovative public-private financing mechanisms.[30]

Most disadvantaged people contribute little to global environmental deterioration, but they often bear the brunt of its impacts.[31] For example, although low HDI countries contribute the least to global climate change, they are likely to experience the greatest loss in annual rainfall and the sharpest increases in its variability, with dire implications for agricultural production and livelihoods. The magnitude of such losses highlights the urgency of adopting coping measures to increase people's resilience to global climate change.[32]

Natural disasters, which are increasing in frequency and intensity, cause enormous economic damage and loss of human capabilities. In 2011 alone, natural disasters accompanying earthquakes (tsunamis, landslides and ground settlements) resulted in more than 20,000 deaths and damages totalling $365 billion, including loss of homes for about a million people.[33] The impact has been severe for small island developing states, some of which have incurred losses of 1% of GDP—and some as much as 8% or even multiples of their GDP. St. Lucia, for example, lost almost four times its GDP in 1988 from Hurricane Gilbert, and Granada lost twice its GDP in 2004 from Hurricane Ivan.[34]

The 2011 *Human Development Report* examined several environmental scenarios. The "environmental challenge" scenario factored in the anticipated adverse effects of global warming on agricultural production, access to clean water and improved sanitation, and pollution. Under this scenario, the average global HDI value would be 8% lower by 2050 than under the "base case" scenario, which assumes a continuation but not a worsening of current environmental trends. Most dramatically, the average regional HDI value in both South Asia and Sub-Saharan Africa would be 12% lower under the environmental challenge scenario than under the base case scenario. Under a more severe "environmental disaster" scenario, the global HDI value in 2050 would fall 15% below that under the baseline scenario—22% below in South Asia and 24% below in Sub-Saharan Africa, effectively halting or even reversing decades of human development progress in both regions.

This Report looks more specifically at the impact of these environmental scenarios on the number of people living in extreme income poverty (figure 4.4). Some 3.1 billion more people would live in extreme income poverty in 2050 under the environmental disaster scenario than under the accelerated progress scenario (table 4.3). Under the base case scenario, by contrast, the number of people in extreme income poverty worldwide would decline by 2050.

Some 2.7 billion more people would live in extreme income poverty under the environmental disaster scenario than under the base case scenario, a consequence of two interrelated factors. First, the model shows an increase of 1.9 billion people in extreme income poverty due to environmental degradation. Second, environmental calamities would keep some 800 million poor people from rising out of extreme income poverty, as they would otherwise have done under the base case scenario (see *Technical appendix*).

These outcomes underscore a central message of this Report: environmental threats are among the most grave impediments to lifting human development, and their consequences for poverty are likely to be high. The longer action is delayed, the higher the cost will be.

Managing demographic change

Between 1970 and 2011, the world population swelled from 3.6 billion to 7 billion. Development prospects are influenced by the age structure of the population, as well as its size.[35] Declining fertility rates and shifts in

Some 3.1 billion more people would live in extreme income poverty in 2050 under an environmental disaster scenario than under the accelerated progress scenario

FIGURE 4.4

Different environmental scenarios have different impacts on extreme poverty

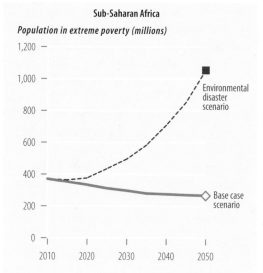

Sub-Saharan Africa
Population in extreme poverty (millions)

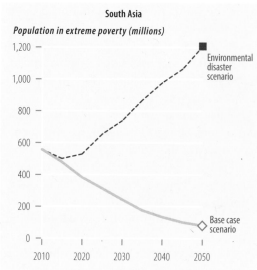

South Asia
Population in extreme poverty (millions)

Note: Extreme poverty is defined as $1.25 a day in purchasing power parity terms. See *Technical appendix* for a discussion of the base case and fast track scenarios.
Source: HDRO calculations based on Pardee Center for International Futures (2013).

TABLE 4.3

Population in extreme poverty under the environmental disaster scenario, by region, 2010–2050 (millions)

Region	2010	2020	2030	2040	2050	Increase, 2010–2050	Difference From base case scenario, 2050	Difference From accelerated progress scenario, 2050
Arab States	25	25	39	73	145	120	128	144
East Asia and the Pacific	211	142	211	363	530	319	501	522
Europe and Central Asia	14	6	17	32	45	30	41	44
Latin America and the Caribbean	34	50	90	138	167	134	135	155
South Asia	557	530	738	978	1,207	650	1,126	1,194
Sub-Saharan Africa	371	377	496	709	1,055	685	788	995
World	**1,212**	**1,129**	**1,592**	**2,293**	**3,150**	**1,938**	**2,720**	**3,054**

Note: Extreme poverty is defined as $1.25 a day in purchasing power parity terms. See *Technical appendix* for a discussion of the base case and fast track scenarios.
Source: HDRO calculations based on Pardee Center for International Futures (2013).

age structure can have considerable effects on economic growth.[36] Over 1970–2010, the dependency ratio (the ratio of younger and older people to the working-age population ages 15–64) declined sharply in most regions—most dramatically in East Asia and the Pacific, where it dropped 39.5%, followed by Latin America and the Caribbean and the Arab States, where it fell 34%.

Over 2010–2050, however, dependency ratios are likely to rise in medium, high and very high HDI countries, particularly in developed countries and in East Asia and the Pacific. In poorer regions, such as South Asia and Sub-Saharan Africa, dependency ratios will continue to fall, but more slowly.

Changing demography will profoundly affect most countries in the South in coming decades, but in very different ways. Some poorer countries will benefit from a demographic dividend as the share of the population in the workforce rises.[37] Richer regions of the South, however, will confront the challenge of rising dependency ratios, with ageing populations and full school enrolment mirrored by a decline in the number of people earning incomes.

In the long term, both demographic challenges can be mitigated by raising educational achievement. First, education accelerates reductions in fertility rates where they are still high. Second, education can boost labour productivity in richer countries with smaller workforces. At the same time, governments will need to foster job creation more actively to expand opportunities for productive employment for younger and older workers alike.

The failure of economic opportunity and productivity to keep pace with these demographic changes can not only keep countries from benefiting from the demographic dividend, it can also threaten social stability, as seen in many countries in recent years.

Modelling demography and education

Demographic trends are not deterministic, however. They can be influenced, at least indirectly, by education policies and sometimes by migration policies.[38] Effective policy options can be identified by modelling demographic and education trends.[39] Two scenarios for 2010–2050 illustrate the impact of different policy responses: the base case scenario, in which enrolment ratios remain constant at each level of education, and a fast track scenario, in which countries with the lowest initial education levels embrace ambitious education targets.[40]

The dependency ratio is an increasingly critical concern. A high dependency ratio can impoverish a country and lead to reversals in human development. The base case scenario projects a 9.7 percentage point decline in the dependency ratio over 2010–2050 for low HDI countries, a 9 percentage point increase for medium HDI countries, a 15.2 percentage point increase for high HDI countries and a 28.7 percentage point increase for very high

HDI countries (figure 4.5). Under the fast track scenario, the dependency ratio for low HDI countries drops 21.1 percentage points over 2010–2050, more than twice the decrease under the base case scenario. The dependency ratio rises more slowly under the fast track scenario than under the base case scenario for medium HDI countries (6.1 percentage points) and high HDI countries (4.9 percentage points); however, this rise is less pronounced for very high HDI countries.

Under the base case scenario, the share of the elderly in the population rises for all HDI groups: 3.9 percentage points for low HDI countries, 17.7 percentage points for medium HDI countries, 20.2 percentage points for high HDI countries and 22.3 percentage points for very high HDI countries.[41] Over 2010–2050, the share of the young population is projected to fall in all HDI groups. For low HDI countries, the dependency ratio will decrease because the decline in the share of the young population is greater than the rise in the share of the elderly population.

In the Arab States, South Asia and Sub-Saharan Africa, the dependency ratio is projected to decline under the base case scenario and even faster under the fast track scenario. In Sub-Saharan Africa, for example, the dependency ratio falls 11.8 percentage points under the base case scenario and 25.7 percentage points under the fast track scenario.

In East Asia and the Pacific, Europe and Central Asia, and Latin America and the Caribbean, the dependency ratio is projected to increase. East Asia and the Pacific will see a striking increase in the share of the elderly—up 25.8 percentage points, which is an even greater rise than in very high HDI countries.

Brazil and Chile demonstrate the potential for ambitious education policies to alter dependency ratios. In Brazil, the dependency ratio rises 15.6 percentage points under the base case scenario but only 10.8 percentage points under the fast track scenario (table 4.4). Chile would see a similar increase, 20.2 percentage points and 17.3 percentage points.

The challenges differ considerably by country under the two scenarios. Under the base case scenario, China would experience a more rapid increase (27.3 percentage points) than, say, Thailand (23.9 percentage points) or Indonesia

Demographic trends are not deterministic. They can be influenced by education policies and sometimes by migration policies

FIGURE 4.5

Education policies can alter dependency ratios

Note: See *Technical appendix* for a discussion of the base case and fast track scenarios.
Source: HDRO calculations based on Lutz and KC (2013).

(8.7 percentage points), countries where even a more ambitious education policy would have only a limited impact on dependency ratios because education levels are already high.

Countries can respond to a declining labour force in various ways. They can reduce unemployment, promote labour productivity and foster greater labour force participation, particularly among women and older workers. They can also outsource work to offshore production and attract international migrants.[42]

Without proper policy measures, demographic dynamics can increase inequality in the short run, given that differences in the speed of the demographic transition across households give richer households an initial advantage. Declining fertility rates and shifts in age structures can affect economic growth.[43] Reinforcing the cross-country analysis conducted for this Report, a recent study finds that youth dependency ratios tend to be higher for poor households and lower for wealthier ones, especially in Latin America and Sub-Saharan Africa, and that differences in youth dependency ratios between rich and poor dissipate over time.[44] During demographic transitions,

TABLE 4.4

Trends in dependency ratios, selected countries, 1970–2050

Country	1970	1980	1990	2000	2010	Scenario	2020	2030	2040	2050
Bangladesh	0.929	0.946	0.859	0.704	0.560	Base case	0.462	0.434	0.433	0.481
						Fast track	0.457	0.422	0.418	0.465
Brazil	0.846	0.724	0.656	0.540	0.480	Base case	0.443	0.484	0.540	0.637
						Fast track	0.437	0.460	0.499	0.589
Chile	0.811	0.629	0.564	0.540	0.457	Base case	0.471	0.549	0.609	0.659
						Fast track	0.467	0.531	0.582	0.630
China	0.773	0.685	0.514	0.481	0.382	Base case	0.408	0.450	0.587	0.655
						Fast track	0.404	0.434	0.562	0.628
Ghana	0.934	0.946	0.887	0.799	0.736	Base case	0.704	0.656	0.643	0.645
						Fast track	0.686	0.595	0.548	0.532
India	0.796	0.759	0.717	0.638	0.551	Base case	0.518	0.496	0.491	0.511
						Fast track	0.510	0.474	0.463	0.480
Indonesia	0.868	0.807	0.673	0.547	0.483	Base case	0.452	0.457	0.504	0.571
						Fast track	0.451	0.454	0.501	0.567
Thailand	0.904	0.756	0.532	0.447	0.417	Base case	0.426	0.488	0.576	0.656
						Fast track	0.425	0.484	0.570	0.650
Turkey	0.850	0.787	0.671	0.560	0.478	Base case	0.458	0.467	0.504	0.585
						Fast track	0.450	0.443	0.473	0.547

Source: HDRO calculations based on Lutz and KC (2013). See *Technical appendix* for a discussion of the base case and fast track scenarios.

the wealthiest people tend to lead the decline in fertility, producing a short-term increase in income inequality as they capture the benefits of demographic change first. Then the middle class catches up as its members educate daughters and plan families, followed by the poor. Eventually fertility is lower across all income groups, and the economic benefits of the demographic dividend are spread more evenly.[45] This is consistent with previous studies for Latin America and Africa.[46]

This short-term rise in inequality is not inevitable, however, and can be influenced by public policies, especially in education and reproductive health, that enable the benefits of the demographic transition to reach all income groups at the same time. Consider the three countries with the largest declines in child dependency ratios: Côte d'Ivoire (with a GDP per capita in 2011 of $1,800), Namibia ($6,800) and Peru ($10,300). In Côte d'Ivoire, the dependency ratio fell most among the rich

and least among the poor; in Namibia, it fell most in the middle of the income range; and in Peru, it fell across the board in roughly equal amounts.[47] See box 4.2 for a discussion of the distribution of the benefits of the demographic dividend in China and Ghana.

In 13 of 18 countries with a declining dependency ratio and rising female education over 1970–2010, rising labour productivity over 1980–2008 and falling unemployment over 2005–2010, the female labour participation rate grew faster than the overall labour participation rate over 2000–2004 to 2005–2010, indicating greater gender balance in the labour market. Employment, however, did not necessarily become easier as education levels rose. Indeed, in some countries, the labour market situation became tighter for better educated female workers. Additional policy measures are needed to promote labour market conditions that offer productive opportunities for a more qualified and expanded labour force.

BOX 4.2

China and Ghana: who benefits from the demographic dividend?

The global trend towards slower population growth and population ageing is driven partly by China, the world's most populous country, which is going through a demographic transition. For Sub-Saharan Africa, a fast track education policy with incremental enrolment gains could accelerate the demographic transition and generate a demographic dividend for the region. The cases of China and Ghana illustrate what can happen.

China

In 1970, youth constituted the largest share of China's population, resulting in a high dependency ratio of 0.770, with 1.08 boys for each girl among infants ages 0–4 (figure 1). By 2010, China's population pyramid looked completely different. As fertility rates fell, the share of the working-age population rose faster than the share of the youth population, lowering the dependency ratio to 0.382. The gender imbalance became more pronounced among infants, with 1.18 boys for each girl. The productive-age population (ages 35–50), currently the largest population share, will reach retirement in 15–25 years. By 2030, China will thus face the challenge of an ageing population, putting more pressure on the social sector and raising the dependency ratio. At retirement, this cohort will have a higher educational attainment than its predecessors 40 years ago.

Under the fast track scenario, with strong education policies, the age structure of China's population in 2050 will be transformed, with the population ages 60–64 becoming the largest cohort. The education level of the working-age group will rise considerably, contributing to a more productive workforce. A more skilled and productive workforce could offset some of the negative effects of a high dependency ratio and a large share of older people. In this scenario, the ratio of boys to girls will fall to 1.06, close to the global average.

Ghana

In 1970, Ghana had a population of 8.7 million. The largest share of the population was young people, resulting in a high dependency ratio (0.934). The share of the population without formal education was also high, especially among women. By 2010, Ghana's population had nearly tripled, to 24.4 million. Its age structure had changed little, although improvements in life expectancy rounded out the middle of the pyramid. The youth population, though smaller than in 1970, remained large, and the dependency ratio was still high, at 0.736. Education levels, however, had improved considerably, and the share of people with primary and secondary education had increased.

Ghana's prospects for 2050 differ markedly under the two education policy scenarios. In the base case, which assumes constant enrolment ratios over 2010–2050, Ghana's population pyramid would remain triangular, with a large share of young people and a high dependency ratio (0.645; figure 2). The population is projected to reach 65.6 million in the base case scenario, but just 48.2 million in the fast track scenario.

Under the fast track scenario, the demographic outlook would change considerably as falling fertility rates lower the dependency ratio to 0.532, mainly because of the decrease of the youth as a share of Ghana's total population. The share of working-age people with no education would also fall, implying a rise in productivity and improved capacity for benefiting from the demographic dividend, provided that job creation matches the labour supply of these new cohorts.

Figure 1 Demographic prospects for China

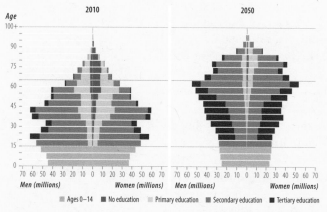

Figure 2 Demographic prospects for Ghana

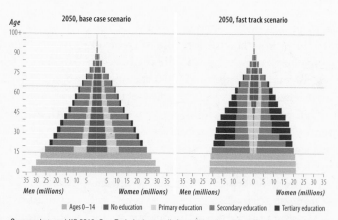

Source: Lutz and KC 2013. See *Technical appendix* for a discussion of the base case and fast track scenarios.

Source: Lutz and KC 2013. See *Technical appendix* for a discussion of the base case and fast track scenarios.

Impact of the rate of population ageing

Populations are ageing faster than in the past, as fertility rates decline and life expectancy rises.[48] For example, for the share of the elderly population to double from 7% to 14% took more than a century (from 1865 to 1980) in France, 85 years in Sweden, 83 in Australia and 69 in the United States. Ageing is progressing faster still in developing countries. In eight of a sample of nine developing countries, the share of the elderly population is projected to reach 14% in 30 years or less (figure 4.6). The only exception is Ghana, where it is expected to take 50 years or more.

The rate of population ageing matters because if developing countries are still poor after the demographic transition, they will struggle to meet the needs of an older population. Many developing countries have only a brief window of opportunity to reap the full benefits of the demographic dividend of a larger working-age population.[49]

The need for ambitious policies

To accelerate and sustain development progress, countries need to adopt ambitious policies that expand women's education and that have cross-cutting benefits for human development. Timing is critical. Countries that act promptly to take advantage of the demographic dividend and avoid further environmental damage can reap substantial gains. Countries that do not could face high costs that would be compounded over time.

The importance of bold, prompt policy action can be demonstrated through two more scenarios that show the impact of different policy measures on projected HDI and its components in 2050. The base case scenario assumes continuity with historical trends and policies in recent decades. The accelerated progress scenario sets some of the choices and targets along 12 policy dimensions for aggressive but reasonable interventions to reduce poverty, expand infrastructure and improve governance. Examples of ambitious targets are a doubling of lending by international financial institutions over 10 years, a 50% increase in migration over 20 years,[50] a 20% increase in health spending over 10 years, a 20% expansion in infrastructure over 30 years and a 20% improvement in governance over 10 years.

The projections of the base case scenario are fairly optimistic in that they carry forward the momentum of advances over recent decades, including dramatic improvements in human development. Countries do much better under the accelerated progress scenario, with progress most rapid in low HDI countries (figure 4.7). Aggregate HDI rises 52% in Sub-Saharan Africa (from 0.402 to 0.612) and 36% in South Asia (from 0.527 to 0.714). Low HDI

FIGURE 4.6

Populations are ageing more rapidly in developing countries

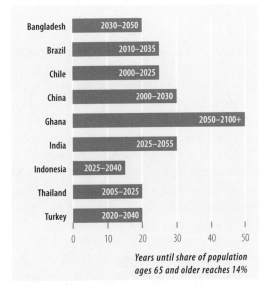

Years until share of population ages 65 and older reaches 14%

Source: HDRO calculations based on Lutz and KC (2013). See *Technical appendix* for a discussion of the base case and fast track scenarios.

FIGURE 4.7

Human development prospects for 2050 are greater under the accelerated progress scenario, especially for low HDI countries

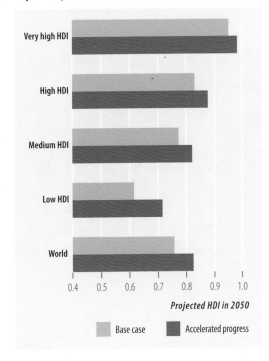

Projected HDI in 2050

Base case   Accelerated progress

Note: See *Technical appendix* for a definition of the base case and accelerated progress scenarios.
Source: HDRO calculations based on Pardee Center for International Futures (2013).

countries thus converge towards the levels of human development achieved by high and very high HDI countries.

Ambitious, fully integrated policies can thus provide strong leverage for advancing human development (figure 4.8). The effects are strongest for Sub-Saharan Africa and South Asia, followed by the Arab States and Latin America and the Caribbean. The impacts are weaker in Europe and Central Asia and in East Asia and the Pacific.

Across all regions, the greatest impacts result from policy interventions in health and education. In Sub-Saharan Africa, for example, ambitious policies raise HDI value in 2050 from 0.612 under the base case scenario to 0.651. In most regions, improving governance has the next greatest impact through progress on reducing corruption, strengthening democratic institutions and empowering women. In South Asia and Sub-Saharan Africa, however, infrastructure investment is even more important.

The two scenarios show notable differences in the individual dimensions of the HDI. In Sub-Saharan Africa, life expectancy rises from 53.7 years in 2010 to 69.4 in 2050 under the base case scenario, partly in response to sustained progress against HIV/AIDS and other communicable diseases, but to 72.9 under the accelerated progress scenario. Over the same period, the average years of formal education in Sub-Saharan Africa are projected to rise from 4.3 to 6.7 under the base case scenario, but to 8.1 under the accelerated progress scenario.

The gains under the accelerated progress scenario are even larger for GDP per capita (figure 4.9). This is true for all HDI groups, where differences across scenarios are considerable in both cases. Globally, GDP per capita would rise from $8,770 in 2010 to $17,873 in 2050 under the base case scenario and to $27,995 under the accelerated progress scenario. The largest differential gains would be in Sub-Saharan Africa and South Asia. In Sub-Saharan Africa, GDP per capita would rise from $1,769 in 2010 to $5,730 in 2050 under the base case scenario and to an impressive $13,210 under the accelerated progress scenario—more than double the level under the base case scenario. Under the accelerated progress scenario, South Asia would see a stunning rise from $2,871 to $23,661.

The differential rise in income directly influences poverty reduction. Under the base case scenario, income poverty almost disappears in China but decreases only marginally in Sub-Saharan Africa, as the population continues to grow, and remains high in India, which would still have more than 130 million poor people in 2030. Under the accelerated progress scenario, the number of poor people falls much more rapidly, nearly disappearing in some countries and regions (table 4.5).

Substantially reducing poverty by 2050 depends on ambitious policy measures. Failing to act boldly to avert the environmental disaster scenario, for instance, would severely inhibit poverty reduction.

Seizing the moment

Greater progress in human development is both possible and imperative. But accelerating

FIGURE 4.8

Human development outcomes through 2050 improve more under the accelerated progress scenario

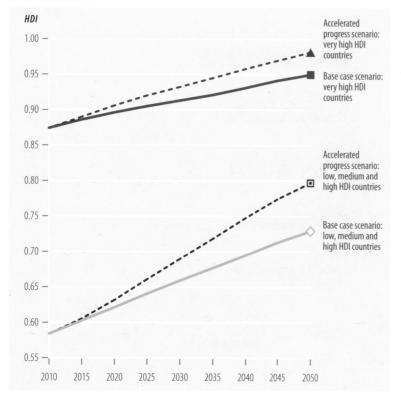

Note: See *Technical appendix* for a definition of the base case and accelerated progress scenarios.
Source: HDRO calculations based on Pardee Center for International Futures (2013).

progress will require coordinated policy measures across development fronts. One of the most important of these is equity, because more-equitable societies fare better in most aspects of well-being and are more sustainable. Another is reducing child mortality: rapid progress is possible in all countries through education, particularly of women.

Policies also need to consider other forces that will influence development, especially people's meaningful participation in the processes that shape their lives. Demand for participation grows as people become more educated and more connected. Other major issues are environmental and demographic change; countries need to act during brief windows of opportunity to avoid high costs in forgone human development.

Most of the opportunities for sustaining and even accelerating the momentum in human development lie in the hands of national governments. In an increasingly globalized world, however, governments do not act alone. The final chapter considers the complex web of international arrangements with which national governments need to engage and how regional and global institutions can work more effectively for sustainable human development.

FIGURE 4.9

Advances in GDP per capita through 2050 are especially strong under the accelerated progress scenario

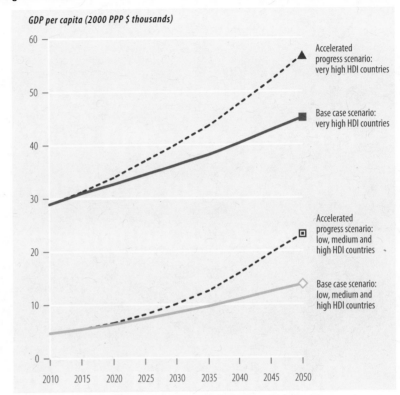

Note: See *Technical appendix* for a definition of the base case and accelerated progress scenarios.
Source: HDRO calculations based on Pardee Center for International Futures (2013).

TABLE 4.5

Number of people in extreme poverty by region and selected countries, base case and accelerated progress scenarios, 2010–2050 (millions)

Region or country	2010	2020	2030	2040	2050, base case	2050, accelerated progress
Arab States	25	19	17	16	17	1
East Asia and the Pacific	211	74	42	29	29	9
China	94	13	5	1	1	0
Europe and Central Asia	14	2	3	3	4	1
Latin America and the Caribbean	34	29	26	27	32	13
South Asia	557	382	243	135	81	13
India	416	270	134	53	21	2
Sub-Saharan Africa	371	333	297	275	267	60
World	1,212	841	627	485	430	96

Note: Extreme poverty is defined as $1.25 a day in purchasing power parity terms. See *Technical appendix* for a discussion of the base case and fast track scenarios.
Source: HDRO calculations based on Pardee Center for International Futures (2013).

"Let us join hands to try to create a peaceful world where we can sleep in security and wake in happiness."

Aung San Suu Kyi

"The forces that unite us are intrinsic and greater than the superimposed influences that keep us apart."

Kwame Nkrumah

5.

Governance and partnerships for a new era

Today's systems for international development and global governance are a mosaic of old structures and new arrangements. The rise of the South will make these systems more diverse: international cooperation is likely to involve an even more complex web of bilateral, regional and global processes. All these structures, however, will need to work better in concert—particularly for the provision of public goods. Duplication of effort and failure to agree on common norms and goals are not just inefficient, but potentially counterproductive, setting back human progress. It is vital to strengthen both global and regional organizations while extending representation and accountability to a wider group of states and stakeholders to reflect the emergence of these new forces. This chapter considers options and offers conclusions for this new era of partnership.

Countries of the South have been developing rapidly, and many are much more actively engaged on the world stage. They have been pursuing their individual and collective interests through a variety of channels, particularly regional arrangements and bilateral partnerships that permit them to engage on issues of their choosing, often very much on their own terms. Brazil, China, India and other emerging economies have forged deeper and stronger economic relations with their neighbours and across the developing world: they are rapidly expanding their global markets and production; they have presented innovative complements to the Bretton Woods financing institutions; they are increasingly influential in global regulation of trade, money and finance; and they are influencing culture, science, the environment, peace and security.

The new arrangements promoted by the South and the resulting pluralism are challenging existing institutions and processes in the traditional domains of multilateralism—finance, trade, investment and health—sometimes directly and sometimes indirectly through alternative regional and subregional systems. Global and regional governance is becoming a multifaceted combination of new arrangements and old structures that need collective nurturing in multiple ways. Reforms in global institutions must be complemented by stronger cooperation with regional institutions—and in some cases broader mandates for those regional institutions. The accountability of organizations must be extended to a wider group of countries, as well as to a wider group of stakeholders. In some

respects, progress has become more difficult. Country groups are in flux, their coordination mechanisms have become increasingly unwieldy and in many cases deliberations among groups have come to a near standstill.[1] The growing diversity of voices in international governance thus brings both opportunities and challenges for human development.

At the same time, there are signs of a more diverse global civil society.[2] New voices from the South are calling for more accountability and broader representation. Civil society organizations have already influenced global transparency and rule setting on aid, debt, human rights, health and climate change. Civil society networks can now take advantage of new media and new communications technologies that make it easier to establish links between local and transnational activists and allow people to share ideas and concerns and to generate collective perspectives in a global public sphere.

In an interconnected world, every country's actions have implications for its neighbours and, ultimately, for people everywhere, today and in the future. Responsible sovereignty requires carefully and conscientiously taking into account the global and regional consequences of national behaviour.

Some major challenges can be addressed constructively at the regional or bilateral level, including regional trade and security issues. But these issues also require longer term international solutions. The continuing impasse in negotiations at the Doha World Trade Organization (WTO) round impedes progress towards agricultural self-sufficiency and the eradication of poverty and hunger in Africa and elsewhere in the developing world. Other urgent issues such as climate change can be resolved only globally, and failing to act on them collectively today will make them even more acute and costly in the future.

A new global view of public goods

Areas of global international concern meriting urgent attention include trade, migration, climate change and development. Each area, along with its governance, has been significantly altered by the rise of the South

This changing world has profound implications for the provision of public goods such as clean air and other shared resources that the market alone produces or allocates insufficiently or not at all and for which state mechanisms are essential.[3] Desirable global public goods include a stable climate and a healthy global commons. They require rules for more stable financial markets, progress on trade reforms (such as those involved in the Doha round of trade negotiations) and mechanisms to finance and produce green technologies.

To that end, we need to rethink what is public and what is private, what is best provided unilaterally and what multilaterally, and, importantly, when taking collective action, what our respective responsibilities are. Public provision of goods is important at the national and global levels, but coexistence of the public and the private is inevitable (box 5.1). For example, in responding to climate change and the depletion of natural resources such as coal, oil and water, governments have partnered with the private sector to invest in research and development for alternative sources of energy.

Areas of global international concern meriting urgent attention and cooperation include trade, migration, climate change and development. Each area, along with its governance, has been significantly altered by the rise of the South. At the same time, the new position of the South presents opportunities for agreement and improved cooperation.

Trade

Countries throughout the South would benefit from the completion of the far-reaching international trade agreements envisioned by the Doha development round of the WTO. However, the Doha round remains stalled while an increasingly complex web of bilateral

---

BOX 5.1

The shifting line between public and private in transportation

Whether mass transportation is provided publicly or privately has an important bearing on shared development goals of sustainability and affordable access. A society more concerned with equitable outcomes is more likely to provide greater amounts of public transportation. Cost savings from economies of scale are passed on to the public in the form of relatively cheap access to public transportation. In more egalitarian societies, low-earning groups, including students, the elderly and the disabled, are likely to receive further discounts and subsidies. The idea is to reduce the excludability of transportation services.

Mass public transport can minimize the congestion and carbon emissions from vehicles traditionally associated with private transportation. When a sizeable public transportation system already exists, it can be more amenable to the quick introduction of greener technologies. For example, New Delhi mandates the use of compressed natural gas in public buses, a much greener fuel than gasoline (the buses are run by both the public and the private sectors).

Environmentally conscious societies tend to incentivize the use of public over private transport through congestion and carbon taxes on private vehicles, as in London, Milan and Singapore (and considered by San Francisco). Making public transportation affordable is not the only challenge. Because more-affluent people generally prefer private transport, the answer is to make public transport less of an inferior good by ensuring safety, efficiency and reliability.

Public-private partnerships could be one way forward. They tend to result in more efficient construction and operation of projects. The public partner safeguards property rights, provides the regulatory framework and sometimes uses subsidies to meet the gap between private and social returns.

Most railway projects in Latin America and the Caribbean have been implemented through public-private partnerships. India has one of the most rapidly expanding public-private partnership programmes in transport; between 1995 and 2006, about 230 public-private partnership projects costing $15.8 billion were implemented. China has extensively used the build-operate-transfer model of public-private partnerships for toll roads and other infrastructure, especially since the 2000s.

Spurred by increasing gas prices, private companies are likely to conduct research on greener fuels and technologies on their own account. However, public funding and incentives are also required to ensure socially optimal levels of research into greener fuels and technologies. Indeed, green technological breakthroughs are one of the most essential global public goods and must remain in the public domain.

Source: World Bank 2003, n.d.; Cheng, Hu and Zhao 2009.

and regional trade arrangements has developed. These arrangements, involving fewer and sometimes more-homogeneous players, can align interests and realize mutual gains for those engaged, without the deadlock encountered at the multilateral level.

Subregional trade and investment groups, such as the Economic Community of West Africa States and the Common Market of the South, have facilitated greater economic interaction and policy cooperation in other areas as well, from security to water resource management. These bilateral and regional arrangements offer opportunities for further South–South economic integration and provide a training ground for building competitive strengths.[4]

Still, despite the benefits of bilateral and regional trade agreements, without better global trade rules and coordinating mechanisms there are considerable efficiency costs. While encouraging freer trade among members, trading blocs tend to erect barriers to free trade with each other, ultimately reducing global welfare.[5] Other efficiency losses can result from the increased market power that countries gain by consolidating into trading blocs.[6] As research for this Report has shown, freer and fairer trade rules can accelerate human development when coupled with sustained public investment in human capabilities—including health, education and other social services—and essential infrastructure—such as modern transportation and telecommunications links.

Many aspects of a freer, nondiscriminatory trade regime are best overseen by a stronger, reinvigorated set of multilateral agreements, but since regionalism may be here to stay, one way forward is to gradually "multilateralize regionalism". This would involve the WTO's initiating "soft-law" ideas, such as the negotiation of voluntary best-practice guidelines for new regional trade agreements and modifications of existing ones: the WTO could, for example, organize a hierarchy of guidelines for North–North, North–South and South–South regional trade agreements.[7]

Migration

In 2010, at least 25 economies of the South reported remittance inflows from migrants exceeding 10% of GDP. Yet governance of migration is largely unilateral, by destination countries or bilateral. There are few mechanisms for multilateral coordination.[8] Real human development concerns are at stake, most importantly, the rights of migrants. While remittances provide income for poor households, social upheaval and disruption also come with large-scale migration. Multilateral mechanisms could liberalize and simplify channels that allow people to seek work abroad, ensure basic rights for migrants, reduce transaction costs associated with migration and improve outcomes for migrants and destination communities alike.[9]

With the rise of the South, migration patterns are changing. Nearly half of remittances sent home to countries in the South come from emigrant workers in other developing countries. In recent years, regional organizations and economic integration processes have added migration to their agendas. These include the Association of Southeast Asian Nations, the African Union, the Common Market of the South and the Southern African Development Community.[10] In 2012, the Global Forum on Migration and Development held discussions on South–South migration for the first time.

While the governance of migration is not inevitably or exclusively a multilateral issue, international coordination mechanisms could provide a supporting framework for the emerging networks of regional and bilateral agreements. The beneficial impact of these dialogues could be multiplied by global initiatives on migration issues.

With the continuing growth in annual international migration—from an estimated 70 million four decades ago to more than 200 million today, originating largely from the South—there is a growing need for rules to protect the rights of migrants and provide agreed international norms for the flow of immigrants between source and host countries.[11] Such rules would benefit all parties, in both economic and social terms, while the costs of inaction will continue to mount. These costs are not solely or even primarily financial: they include the profound human costs of forcibly prolonged family separation, all-too-common mistreatment in the workplace and the unnecessary and indefensible degradation of human

With the rise of the South, migration patterns are changing. Nearly half of remittances sent home to countries in the South come from emigrant workers in other developing countries dignity when foreign resident workers are not accorded basic legal rights.

Climate change

Climate change is perhaps the most widely recognized issue that requires global cooperation through multilateral agreements. The South is going beyond bilateral approaches by incorporating ways to tackle climate change into national development strategies. China has pledged to reduce its carbon intensity (carbon dioxide emissions per unit of GDP) 40%–45% from 2005 levels by 2020.[12] In 2010, India announced voluntary targeted reductions of 20%–25% in carbon intensity.[13] Korean lawmakers approved a national emissions trading programme in March 2012 to reduce emissions from factories and power plants.[14] At the UN Conference on Sustainable Development in Rio de Janeiro in 2012, Mozambique announced a new Green Economy Roadmap. And Mexico recently enacted the world's first comprehensive climate change law, aiming to cut emissions and build the renewable energy sector.[15]

Addressing climate change requires true multilateralism. For example, to reduce global greenhouse emissions by the amount required, the North and the South have to reach a mutually acceptable and fair agreement on how to share responsibilities while ensuring that the legitimate development aspirations of the South can be met.

The 2012 UN Conference on Sustainable Development in Rio de Janeiro created opportunities for collaboration and alliances among groups of rich and poor; public and private; and civil, corporate and state bodies. For example, Unilever, Coca-Cola and Walmart were among 20 large multinational corporations that committed, through the Consumer Goods Forum, to eliminating deforestation from their supply chains.[16] Microsoft promised to go carbon-neutral by 2012. And FEMSA, the Latin American soft drink bottler, said it would obtain 85% of its energy needs in Mexico from renewable resources.[17] Despite many promising initiatives though, a wide gap remains between the emissions reductions needed, on the one hand, and the modest reductions promised, on the other.

> Addressing climate change requires true multilateralism

Development cooperation

An essential component of more-inclusive international governance should be more-inclusive and more-effective forms of development cooperation. Developing countries are increasingly providing development assistance and investment bilaterally and regionally, through new financing arrangements and technological cooperation that offer alternatives to or complement the approaches of traditional donors and strengthen choices for aid recipients.

In 2011, developing countries and civil society organizations endorsed the Busan Partnership for Effective Development Cooperation at the 4th High Level Forum on Aid Effectiveness in Busan, Republic of Korea. Ownership, focus on results, inclusive development partnerships, mutual accountability and transparency were selected as the underlying pillars for a new global monitoring framework. Stronger emphasis was placed on country systems as the way of doing business, coupled with a demand on behalf of partner countries to explain any deviance. Traditional Organisation for Economic Co-operation and Development (OECD) donors recognized that a different governance structure would be needed to support a broader partnership and accommodate emerging economies.[18] Based on the core principles of national ownership and capacity, this partnership would establish an international governing mechanism and indicators for assessing progress.

Along with traditional donors, new development partners, including Brazil, China and India, endorsed the principles of national ownership and capacity building. However, the Busan Declaration noted that these partners have domestic development challenges of their own and have their established methods of foreign cooperation. This was reflected in the text of the declaration, which stated that for these countries the "principles, commitments and actions agreed in Busan shall be the reference for south-south partnerships on a voluntary basis".[19] Moving forward, the OECD's Development Assistance Committee and the United Nations Development Programme are to jointly support the new Global Partnership for Effective Development Cooperation through the UN Development Cooperation Forum. Despite signatories' commitment to transparency, the outcome document does not contain any other time-bound measurable commitments or targets to which citizens can hold them to account.

The post-Busan architecture has yet to take shape. But some intermediate priorities have surfaced. One is for traditional donors to meet their commitments from the 2005 Group of Eight Gleneagles summit to increase aid and to deliver on better coordination and alignment.[20] Traditional donors can also work with emerging donors, who can contribute knowledge and experience from a developing country perspective. The United Nations, with its universal membership, is well positioned to engage partners from the South in such trilateral development cooperation through the UN Development Cooperation Forum. One of the main tasks is to achieve better alignment between North–South and South–South development cooperation and global norms.

The Busan agreement marks a first step in reshaping development cooperation so that it can be more effective and better harness the potential of emerging countries. As with other global public goods, once common understanding is reached at the global level, operationalizing the principles can in most cases be decentralized to national governments using the agreed common policy frameworks. Take the Millennium Declaration of September 2000 and the global agreement on the Millennium Development Goals that eventually emerged. Agreement on these goals gave impetus to a wide range of activities and institutions by highlighting a simple truth: enhancing the capabilities of people and advancing the development of all societies are important global public goods.[21] The actual progress in the achievement of these goals has been very much at the country level, through national initiatives and ownership.

Better representation for the South

The current institutions and principles for international governance require rethinking or at least recalibrating to accommodate the growing diversity in voice and power and to sustain long-term development progress. Many were designed, long before the rise of the South, for a post–Second World War order that does not match contemporary reality.

As a consequence, these institutions greatly underrepresent the South. Voting quotas in the Bretton Woods institutions are weighted towards countries in the North, despite changing global economic realities. For example, China, which is the world's second largest economy and holds more than $3 trillion in foreign reserves, has had a smaller voting share in the World Bank than both France and the United Kingdom.

Similarly, the United Nations Security Council makes decisions on global peace and security with a permanent membership that reflects the geopolitical structure of 1945. At the 2012 United Nations General Assembly meeting in New York, several heads of government from the South again voiced their long-standing demands for permanent seats on the council for Africa, Latin America and such unrepresented developing country powers as India.[22]

The major international institutions need to be more representative, transparent and accountable. The Bretton Woods institutions, the regional development banks and even the UN system all risk diminishing relevance if they fail to represent all member states and their people adequately. These bodies need to respect and draw constructively on the experiences of both the South and the North and to aim for equitable and sustainable outcomes for present and future generations.

At the same time, the rising South has to assume more responsibility on the global stage, in line with its increasing economic power and political clout, including by contributing more resources to multilateral organizations.[23] The South has to take larger leadership roles at both the regional and global levels. Greater transparency and accountability in global institutions, while desirable in and of themselves, will facilitate more such participation by the South.

There have been some positive moves in this direction. Developing countries are already playing a greater role in the Bretton Woods institutions and in global dialogues through the summits for Group of 20 (G20) heads of state. The OECD has opened membership to some

Current institutions and principles for international governance require rethinking to accommodate the growing diversity in voice and power and to sustain long-term development progress developing countries. Developed countries should welcome these changes, as the success of the South extends benefits to the North and advances the prosperity of all.

Indeed, some intergovernmental processes would be invigorated by greater participation from the South, which can bring substantial financial, technological and human resources. Emerging economies could lead in achieving the Millennium Development Goals, innovating in climate change mitigation and concluding the Doha development round.

Global organizations that are more representative of the world's countries would in principle be accountable to the world's people through national governments. However, state mediation alone is inadequate. International governance is increasingly influenced by a multitude of voices and actors through global movements and transnational activist networks. Indeed, this has been the thrust of antiglobalization movements, sometimes self-described as "global democracy" movements, which cut across a range of issues, articulate diverse concerns and embrace an almost endless variety of political messages but share the basic concern of making transnational power and governance accountable to civil society.

To this end, today's multilateral institutions are encouraged to recalibrate their representation and guiding principles, in areas such as:

- *Voice.* Matching the circles of stakeholders and decisionmakers so that all have an effective voice in global matters that concern them.
- *Public goods.* Building bridges across organizational lines to facilitate the multilevel, multisector, multiactor production that many global public goods require.
- *Leadership.* Encouraging global leaders, state and nonstate, individually or collectively, to exercise leadership to assist the international community on issues that are caught in global policy stalemates and problems that are reaching crisis proportions.
- *Convening.* Realigning existing organizations to reflect changing global economic and political realities, and vesting them with the authority and expertise to effectively mediate among different stakeholders.
- *Information and resources.* Helping poorer countries in the South participate more

effectively in global governance through better access to information, technical assistance and finance.
- *Citizen participation.* Drawing on the wealth of ideas and views emerging from citizen networks and from participants previously sidelined from the global discourse.

International organizations are becoming more inclusive and sensitive to the requirements of a rapidly changing world. The United Nations Economic and Social Council, for example, has established the Development Cooperation Forum to promote more broad-based discussion of development assistance. There is scope for renewed multilateralism. However, there have been only modest governance reforms at the International Monetary Fund (IMF) and the World Bank. The United Nations Security Council's core structure remains unchanged, despite decades of debate. More-determined reform is needed for multilateral institutions to facilitate cross-national collaboration on stalemated global issues in ways viewed as fair and just by all countries.

Global civil society

International governance institutions can be held to account not just by member states, but also by global civil society, which can shape the exercise of power and act as a countervailing force to states and markets. All kinds of voluntary associations—including nongovernmental organizations, social movements, advocacy groups, unions and community groups—have used channels of influence such as elections, lobbying, media and public campaigns to become drivers of social change within many leading countries of the South—including Brazil, Egypt, India and South Africa. In the Indian state of Kerala a rich history of civic engagement influenced the government to prioritize extensive social rights and equity-promoting public policies. In Brazil, the Sanitarista movement of health care professionals played a central role in developing the country's public health care system and expanding services to the poor.[24]

National civil society groups are increasingly using their experience engaging with national governments to open up independent networks of North–South and South–South dialogues outside traditional official international governance channels. These transnational networks are laying the groundwork for an emerging global civil society that is pushing for action on issues ranging from climate change to migration policy to human rights.

The potential for global civil society to influence decisionmaking on critical global issues has been greatly magnified by the Internet revolution, which enables hyperconnectivity of disparate groups and offers platforms for citizens' ideas and concerns to spread rapidly around the globe. People can speak to people, and communities of scientists and other professionals can share ideas, unmediated by state power or markets. This new ease of global communication is fuelling creative partnerships, empowering individuals and social organizations, leading to new forms of solidarity and allowing people to interact and express their values internationally.

The recent uprisings in several Arab States countries, the culmination of complex historical developments, have shown that social media is a force that world leaders and global institutions ignore at their peril. The rapid spread and wide response to the video *Kony 2012,* about indicted war criminal Joseph Kony of the Lord's Resistance Army, showed that social media can engage many millions of people in discussion of important issues within days.[25] There may be disagreement over the legitimacy of particular concerns and platforms, but the rapid sharing of information across social networks clearly sways public opinion on issues that matter to the global citizenry and ultimately influences international governance.

Indeed, one of the most valuable tools of global civil society is the ability to diffuse new norms that transform the behaviour of state and private actors. By taking up and framing issues and pressuring states, civil society networks can put new issues on the table and influence government and international action towards new treaties, stronger enforcement mechanisms and even direct intervention. Classic examples of civil society influence on global norms include the global diffusion of the women's suffrage movement, the antislavery movement and the Red Cross movement that led to the production of the Geneva conventions and the International Federation of the Red Cross and Red Crescent Societies. More recently, global civil society networks have been influential in institutionalizing anti–land mine legislation, more open access to AIDS medicines and campaigns opposing violence against women.

While global civil society holds much potential for influencing international governance norms and decisionmaking, the likely contribution of civil society organizations and transnational networks should be kept in perspective. Higher levels of resourcing lead the international nongovernmental organizations of the North to wield disproportionate influence in the global civil society space.[26] The international human rights regime, for example, often emphasizes civil and political rights, which are of particular concern to civil society in Eastern Europe, rather than social rights, which figure much more centrally in the demands of popular movements in the South. Limitations on civic space as well as other constraints can affect the capacity of civil society organizations to function.[27] A further consideration is one of transparency, as it can be unclear how autonomous civil society groups are from state and market forces. When civil society organizations become extensions of state power, economic influence or traditional authority, civil society activity may magnify rather than reduce inequalities and instability.[28]

The future legitimacy of international governance will depend on the capabilities of institutions to engage with citizen networks and communities—understanding their concerns and borrowing from their ideas and approaches to find direction for their own efforts and energies. Such engagement will maximize the legitimacy of their actions and ensure accountability to the citizens of member states (box 5.2). The idea of ecological citizenship, for example, may be a promising way to construct from the ground up global public opinion on the provisioning of global public goods.[29]

To be effective, international organizations need to form productive partnerships with social media communities and nongovernmental organizations in the South and North alike. They should engage with citizen groups to support policy changes and a transition towards more-equitable principles and institutions of

Global civil society has the ability to diffuse new norms that transform the behaviour of state and private actors

BOX 5.2   *Jo Leinen, Member of the European Parliament*

A world parliament for global democracy?

Legitimacy and representativeness of the world's people in global decision-making are imperative for the governance of global issues, but global decisionmaking bodies have no institutional mechanisms for effective and influential citizen participation. At a time when intergovernmental decision-making has shown its limits, the quest for equity and sustainability and the urgency of addressing defining challenges for our planet require the engagement of the global citizenship.

A world parliament would complement the United Nations General Assembly—either formally integrated in the UN system or instituted as a separate body. This idea is not new, but as it matures, it is receiving increasing support from civil society actors and regional parliaments (including the European, Latin American and African Parliaments) and was recently highlighted in the Manifesto for Global Democracy put forward by a multinational group of intellectuals.[1]

A world parliament would be composed of delegates from national parliaments, representing multiple political parties from each country. Since the great majority of national parliaments are democratically elected, such

a body would have a high level of representativeness and political accountability. A world parliament would serve as a link between national policymaking and global decisionmaking, providing incentives for national parliaments and governments to consider the implications of decisions beyond national borders and instilling national parliaments with knowledge and experience on governing global issues.

This assembly could have one extended annual session, during which it would issue recommendations and add agenda items to the UN General Assembly and, by a qualified majority, submit agenda items to the UN Security Council for debate and decisions. The deliberations would possess a high moral and political authority, although the final decisionmaking power would remain with national governments. The composition of each national delegation could be determined either by national parliaments or through special elections allowing citizens to choose representatives for the world parliament. Delegation size would be proportional to a country's population, an approach considerably different from international bodies where voting quotas are based on monetary contributions.

1. Beeston 2012.

---

international governance. The World Health Organization, for example, has had to manage state interests carefully and adjust to the emphasis on privatizing health services that became dominant in the 1980s. Its core commitments to public health and its ties to civil society, however, have enabled it to continue to pursue policies that emphasize a rights-based approach to health.[30]

Towards coherent pluralism

The challenge facing the multilateral system in response to the rise of the South is not a false choice between globalism and regionalism or between older structures devised and managed by the traditional powers of the North and newer arrangements responding to the needs of the developing world. Rather, it is integrating, coordinating and in some cases reforming these institutions so that they can all work more effectively together. Diversity and flexibility in global governance mechanisms can be net positives for the international system but cannot substitute for the global pursuit of solutions to problems that are inherently global in nature. Policymakers working both regionally and internationally should strive towards a more coherent pluralism in multilateral governance,

with shared norms and goals supporting varied yet complementary regional and global development initiatives.

Recent experience in much of the South has shown that some public goods can be effectively provided at the regional level. As noted in chapter 2, regional institutions can sometimes respond to regional needs faster and more efficiently than can global forums—for example, programmes for eradicating endemic diseases, protecting shared ecosystems and removing barriers to intraregional commerce. In such cases, it makes sense for like-minded neighbouring states to address these challenges cooperatively while pursuing global responses to these issues where needed.

Increasing regional cooperation can also have disadvantages—adding further complexity to an already diverse array of multilateral institutions, with all the attendant risks of exclusion, duplication and interagency competition. In many areas, regional institutions have the potential to complement global structures, even if that kind of coordination seems rare or inadequately synchronized today.

Global governance arrangements must respect the mixed strategies that countries are choosing. It is clear that developing and emerging economies are choosing to cooperate in different ways—bilaterally, regionally and

The challenge facing the multilateral system is not a false choice between older structures devised by the North and newer arrangements responding to the needs of the developing world. It is integrating, coordinating and in some cases reforming these institutions so that they can work more effectively together internationally. Over time, as new sets of challenges have emerged, countries have created new forms of governance to deal with these. In finance, for example, countries want to diversify their exposure and their "insurance policies". They seek to use a mixture of national reserves, bilateral credit lines, regional arrangements and the IMF. The international regime needs to be pluralist while ensuring that cooperation at the regional and subregional levels is consistent with mechanisms and policies at the international level.

The ultimate purpose of this "coherent pluralism" is to ensure that institutions at all levels work in a coordinated fashion to provide global public goods. The complementarity not just between global and regional institutions, but also across public, private and civil society organizations, has the potential to be constructive, even if it may appear fledgling and inadequate at present. Where new arrangements and new partnerships arise to meet the gaps left by old arrangements, they should be encouraged, avoiding duplication to the greatest extent possible. New arrangements at all levels must work in concert with each other and in step with existing multilateral organizations, aligning interests and sharing responsibilities.

While pluralism and greater diversity are welcome developments, duplication and inefficiency occur among the plethora of new organizations. Moving towards a coherent structure, some organizations will survive, and others will be deemed redundant.

The governance of global public goods for sustained progress in human development requires effective multilateralism. International institutions can also provide guidance on human rights and other universal principles and arbitrate in such areas as public international law. However, multilateralism will need to be more flexible to deal with new challenges and geopolitical realities. In a coherent pluralistic system, international institutions can serve as coordinating bodies, playing a catalytic or convening role for all stakeholders. To do this, they need the mandate and sufficient expertise and resources to mediate and facilitate, to analyse and respond to often divergent interests and to propose workable and mutually beneficial outcomes. To fully engage the South, many international organizations need updating

and transforming. The South in turn is more likely to use and fully support multilateral institutions that are seen to be acting as much in the interests of the South as in the interests of developed countries.

Financial architecture: redesign for the rising South

The rise of the South is creating new patterns of resource accumulation, potentially leading to a denser, multilayered and more heterogeneous financial architecture. This could promote financial stability and resilience, support long-run productive capacities, advance human development and enlarge national policy space.

In some cases, these emerging institutions and arrangements could substitute for some of the functions of the Bretton Woods institutions, but in most cases, they complement the existing global financial architecture. Moreover, emerging institutions may prove transformative by prodding the Bretton Woods institutions to respond to concerns about representation, governance principles and conditionalities.

The South has already developed several alternative institutions and approaches, including regional monetary and support arrangements:
- The Chiang Mai Initiative emerged in the wake of the 1997 Asian financial crisis, taking the form of a series of swap arrangements among Asian countries. It evolved into the Chiang Mai Initiative Multilateralization, which allows members to draw on the multilateral swap facility to address balance of payments and short-term liquidity difficulties.
- The Arab Monetary Fund, founded in 1976 by the 22 member countries of the League of Arab States, has some $2.7 billion to support emergency financing for member countries as well as broader monetary cooperation. There is also an aspiration for a unified Arab currency.[31]
- The Reserve Bank of India recently announced a $2 billion swap facility for members of the South Asian Association for Regional Cooperation.[32]
- The Latin American Reserve Fund, with a capitalization of about $2.3 billion, offers balance of payments support to members. It also guarantees third-party loans and

The ultimate purpose of "coherent pluralism" is to ensure that institutions at all levels work in a coordinated fashion to provide global public goods facilitates reserve investments and regional coordination of monetary policies. Its potential is limited by its incomplete regional membership; Brazil, the region's largest economy, does not participate.[33]

- The Andean Development Corporation is gaining attention due to its fourfold growth in lending over 1991–2007 and almost exclusive ownership by members, nearly all of which are developing countries (except Portugal and Spain).[34]

Such regional arrangements, however, do not necessarily reduce the role of the IMF. Large disbursements from the funds can require borrowing countries to be under IMF surveillance programmes, as with the Chiang Mai Initiative Multilateralization (box 5.3).

The evolving regional financial architecture fostered by countries of the South offers renewed space for policies that emphasize pragmatism rather than ideology and ensures that conditionality is narrow and appropriate to the country (box 5.4).[35] Regional institutions that lend closer to home are also more likely to design programmes that are more sensitive to political concerns and economically appropriate, with light-touch surveillance and less emphasis on conditionality.

Some institutions, such as the nascent Bank of the South,[36] renounce conditionality altogether. Others, including the Chiang Mai Initiative Multilateralization and the Arab Monetary Fund, use conditionality only in specific circumstances, and it remains a point of discussion among members. Still others, such as the Latin American Reserve Fund, apply surveillance but do not use the IMF's top-down approach and instead collaborate with borrowing governments.

Regional trade agreements

Regional and subregional trade arrangements have expanded and deepened in Africa, Asia and Latin America, even as the Doha round of global trade negotiations has stalled. Agreements that open up South–South trade hold enormous potential, with benefits at least as large as those providing greater access to markets in the North. OECD estimates

---

BOX 5.3

Regional finance in Asia: Chiang Mai Initiative Multilateralization and the Asian Development Bank

The current financial crisis has been a powerful impetus for expanding the scope of the Chiang Mai Initiative, a regional agreement among the Association of Southeast Asian Nations, plus China, Japan and the Republic of Korea (ASEAN+3). In early 2009, the initiative was multilateralized and renamed the Chiang Mai Initiative Multilateralization. At that time, disbursements of more than 20% of the credits available to a country required that the borrowing country be under an International Monetary Fund (IMF) surveillance programme to address the difficult task of devising and implementing regional surveillance.

ASEAN+3 members have continued to deepen the Chiang Mai Initiative Multilateralization. In May 2012, the size of the currency swap pool was doubled to $240 billion. For 2012–2013, the need to be under an IMF programme does not become operative until the swap drawn equals 30% of the maximum for the country (40% in 2014, pending the outcome of current discussions). The maturity of both the IMF-linked and the delinked swaps were lengthened. And for the first time, a precautionary credit line facility was introduced, allowing members to draw on swaps governed by a formula based on country size. (The Asian Bond Market Initiative was also expanded in May 2012.)

The ASEAN+3 Macroeconomic Research Office opened on 30 January 2012 to conduct IMF Article IV–type monitoring of members. It describes itself as the "regional surveillance unit of the Chiang Mai Initiative Multilateralization". Its purposes are to monitor and analyse regional economies and to contribute to the early detection of risks, implementation of remedial actions and effective decisionmaking by the initiative. Some observers have noted the tensions over the mandate and the continuing reluctance in Asia to criticize the policies of regional neighbours and thus the obstacles to conducting firm surveillance.

Prior to the global financial crisis, the Asian Development Bank (ADB) was already lending more in the region than the World Bank was. The crisis accelerated this trend. In some cases, the ADB responded more quickly and with larger loans than the IMF and the World Bank did, and it introduced new types of temporary rapid financing programmes and countercyclical lending facilities to support developing and low-income countries. In April 2009, Indonesia proposed that a portion of the IMF's new financing be devolved to the ADB. With Group of 20 backing, the ADB introduced the Countercyclical Support Facility to provide up to $3 billion to economies in Asia affected by the crisis.

Between 2008 and 2009, the ADB's lending commitments grew 42% and its disbursements 33%. Other regional development banks quickly followed the ADB's example and were granted a portion of the new funds committed to the IMF to establish new regional lending facilities to promote rapid countercyclical support within their region.

Source: Woods 2010; Chin 2010, 2012; Ocampo and others 2010; ADB 2009; Ciorciari 2011; AMRO 2012.

a welfare gain for the South of $59 billion if South–South tariffs were lowered to that of North–South levels.[37] Even within Africa, given appropriate institutional arrangements for more open agricultural trade, there is huge potential for increasing the trade of the region's many and diverse crops.

An example of a successful regional arrangement is the Sao Paulo Round in 2010, in which 22 developing countries agreed to reduce tariffs at least 20% on about 70% of the trade among themselves. The reductions were negotiated within the 1989 framework of the Global System of Trade Preferences, established to take advantage of the enabling clause within the agreements of the WTO, which allows developing countries to provide concessions to each other without jeopardizing their most favoured nation obligations.

Bilateral arrangements can facilitate trade flows when multilateral negotiations stall. Other options such as preferential trade arrangements for furthering the goal of freer, nondiscriminatory trade could be overseen by a global multilateral institution like the WTO or by regional bodies.

Take, for example, negotiations aimed at reducing the massive production and export subsidies in agriculture given mainly by developed countries. Those subsidies distort world trade and expose farmers in developing countries to unfair competition. However, this issue is almost impossible to settle satisfactorily in a bilateral or regional setting; it requires

BOX 5.4   *Enrique Garcia, President, CAF*

CAF: a Latin American development bank

When established in 1970, the multilateral bank CAF had five Andean country members (Bolivia, Colombia, Ecuador, Peru and Venezuela). Today, its shareholders include 18 countries from Latin America, the Caribbean and Europe as well as 14 private banks, and it obtains most of its funding in global financial markets. CAF promotes sustainable development and regional integration through credit operations, grants and technical support and offers financial structuring to public and private sector projects in Latin America. Its headquarters are in Caracas, and it has offices in Asuncion, Bogota, Brasilia, Buenos Aires, La Paz, Lima, Madrid, Montevideo, Quito and Panama City. Over the last decade, Latin America has experienced rapid economic growth thanks to a favourable external environment, which has resulted in higher commodity prices, a stable macroeconomic environment and greater domestic demand due to poverty reduction and higher income. CAF has helped its member countries take advantage of these favourable economic conditions through a comprehensive development agenda that includes projects and programmes designed to support the region's productive transformation and its competitive participation in the global economy, to improve the quality of institutions and to promote environmental conservation. CAF has provided substantial financing at times when markets were "dry" and other international financial institutions were imposing stringent conditions on their financing.

Among the reasons for CAF's success in the region are its Latin American essence, the strong political and financial commitment of its member countries, the maintenance of prudent financial policies (especially in times of economic stress) and its policy of nonconditionality. Today, CAF is one of the main sources of multilateral financing for infrastructure and energy in the region, with approvals of more than $10 billion at the end of 2011, or some 30% of total multilateral lending for Latin America (compared with and $12.4 billion for the Inter-American Development Bank and $13.9 billion for the World Bank; see Ocampo and Titelman 2012). CAF's countercyclical role in times of economic turbulence in international markets and its support to shareholders when financing has become scarce have been especially valuable. In addition to channelling funds from international markets to the region, directed mainly to infrastructure projects, CAF, together with its member countries, has designed and implemented an ambitious agenda of programmes and projects supported by grants aimed at tackling some of Latin America's major obstacles to growth.

CAF borrows in international capital markets through a funding strategy that aims to diversify sources of financing to mitigate interest rate and currency risks while matching the average maturity of its assets and liabilities to maintain sufficient liquidity in its portfolio. CAF obtained its first credit ratings in 1993 from the three main rating agencies, and its ratings have steadily improved, even during economic crises in the region. CAF is now the highest rated frequent bond issuer in Latin America. Since 1993 CAF has borrowed more than $13.9 billion through 87 bond issues in the most important international capital markets in the Asia, Europe Latin America and the United States. Prudent financial policies have made CAF a profitable institution that reinvests, through grants and technical cooperation, in programmes and projects to support its member countries.

CAF's performance has been distinguished due to capacity to adapt to a changing and challenging environment. Of particular importance has been its governance structure. Since its foundation, CAF's shareholders have given the institution the autonomy to design and implement operational policies without political pressure. Member countries have always supported the institution. Never in CAF's history has a member country defaulted on its obligation, even during economic crises. With an ownership that is almost entirely Latin American (Portugal and Spain are minority shareholders due to their historical ties to the region), CAF has avoided the conflicts that have arisen in other multilateral institutions where donors' and recipients' aims are not always aligned. In this regard, CAF is recognized as an institution run by and for Latin America, providing a useful example of pragmatic financial integration.

multilateral disciplines that can be negotiated only at the WTO. Most countries accept the necessity of a strong multilateral body to referee the rules of world trade while knowing that regionalism is here to stay; one way forward is to gradually "multilateralize regionalism".[38]

Responsible sovereignty

While most governments support the principles of multilateralism, they are also understandably concerned with preserving national sovereignty. Overly strict adherence to the primacy of national sovereignty can encourage cross-border rivalries and zero-sum thinking. Countries on their own are less able to defend themselves from the contagion effects of financial crises or the ill effects of global warming. National action does not ensure that a country's citizens have access to global public goods. Some governments are unable to sufficiently protect the human rights of their citizenry. A better strategy is responsible sovereignty—that is, taking the long-term interests of the world as a whole into account when formulating national policy.

Most global public goods depend on the effective management of cross-border consequences and an adequate provision of national and regional public goods, and thus on national institutional capacity and a willingness to cooperate regionally and globally. Countries must take into account their respective international responsibilities in providing public goods and avoid undermining the collective welfare and the well-being of other countries, such as through pollution or other abuses of the global or regional commons. Responsible sovereignty includes taking steps towards collective endeavours—such as trade liberalization and climate change mitigation—that, if designed effectively, could greatly enhance global collective welfare.

In a highly interconnected world, effective national decisionmaking cannot be carried out in isolation from regional and global policies. National policies have regional and global consequences; examples include protectionist national responses to international economic downturns and the failure to regulate overfishing and ocean pollution. At the same time,

regional and global policies provide a context for national policymaking. Countries and regional and multilateral organizations must come together and align national policies towards common international goals. In an increasingly globalized and interconnected world, this is a matter of enlightened self-interest: decisions taken at the national level today can affect people in all countries for generations to come.

If national leaders are unable to look beyond narrowly conceived immediate national interests, the potential gains from cooperation will be lost, and the costs of inaction will mount. National policies will undermine rather than reinforce and complement each other. Examples include public spending and stimulus policies in the wake of the global financial crisis: coordination by central banks around the world to lower interest rates in concert helped avert further deepening of the worldwide recession.

The South, due to its rising economic stature and political influence, is an increasingly important partner in global decisionmaking. The rise of the South, accompanied by stronger cross-border links, makes decisionmaking more interdependent than ever. The North and the South must find common ground for meaningful progress on today's pressing global problems.

Responsible sovereignty also requires that states honour agreed universal human rights and obligations towards people residing in their territories and ensure their security and safety. The Responsibility to Protect initiative, for example, is an attempt to develop a new international security and human rights norm that can address the international community's failures to prevent and stop genocides, war crimes, ethnic cleansing and crimes against humanity. In this view, sovereignty is seen not just as a right, but also as a responsibility. While a positive step towards establishing guiding principles on global governance in human security, the initiative lacks procedures to ensure that the principles are upheld.[39] There are no agreed thresholds of violations or atrocities that would automatically activate international interventions. This mismatch between principles and procedures highlights the importance of building capacities into

> Responsible sovereignty takes the long-term interests of the world as a whole into account when formulating national policy

international governance systems to hold governments and political systems accountable to the people they represent. Without binding mechanisms for holding states accountable to their citizens, the legitimacy of institutions such as the United Nations Security Council is brought into question. But agreement on a principle of responsible and mutually supportive sovereignty will be forthcoming only if the preconditions of global fairness and justice are met.

New institutions, new mechanisms

The rise of the South presents opportunities for innovative new structures for development partnerships and new approaches to development policy, both globally and regionally. The substantial foreign reserves accumulated by the leading economies of the South could be leveraged for development financing in less developed countries, for example. New mechanisms for aid, trade and technology exchange within regions of the developing world can usefully parallel and complement existing arrangements. The countries of the South themselves could take greater leadership roles in the global policy dialogue about the most urgent international development needs and about the most effective ways to meet these 21st century challenges.

Infrastructure development banks

The rise of the South is also creating new possibilities for financing equitable and sustainable human development. Brazil, China, India, the Russian Federation and South Africa, for example, have proposed a BRICS Development Bank that would draw upon their considerable reserves to finance projects in developing countries.[40] Like the European Bank for Reconstruction and Development, such a bank could offer a range of instruments, including loans, equity and guarantees. In addition to financing productive projects, this flow of resources would also assist with global financial rebalancing.

An important use for such reserves would be building infrastructure. To meet urgent needs, infrastructure spending in developing countries must reach \$1.8–\$2.3 trillion a year by 2020, or about 6%–8% of GDP, compared with current levels of \$0.8–\$0.9 trillion a year, or about 3% of GDP.[41] One means of enabling and facilitating such investments would be through a development bank for infrastructure and sustainable development. That could bolster developing country borrowing to finance economically productive infrastructure.

Because borrowers need to be concerned about debt sustainability, efforts are required to go beyond domestic government borrowing by leveraging other forms of financial assistance. A new institution could crowd in the right type of capital through guarantees and other instruments.[42] New institutions will be more effective if they work in concert with existing regional and global institutions, filling gaps in funding and investment.

Chapter 4 presented an accelerated progress scenario that set ambitious targets for raising the Human Development Index (HDI) value in all regions by 2050 through a series of public spending initiatives. This scenario assumes about 20% improvement in infrastructure by 2050, universal access to electricity by 2030, elimination of solid fuels as the primary source for heating and cooking in the home by 2030, renewable energy production 50% above the base case by 2050 and universal access to mobile telephone and broadband by 2030. The largest projected increases in HDI value under this scenario are in Sub-Saharan Africa (65%) and South Asia (47%; figure 5.1). Current average public investment in Sub-Saharan Africa and South Asia is around 7.7% of GDP.[43]

Allocating a small fraction of the international reserves of the nine G20 countries of the South could provide substantial additional resources for public investment in infrastructure in Sub-Saharan Africa and South Asia (figure 5.2). Depending on the share of reserves allocated, public investment would rise 17.6%–52.8%. In fact, allocating just 3% of liquid international reserves of the nine G20 countries of the South would increase the share of public investment in these countries 4.1%–11.7% of GDP, close to the average level of public investment for all developing countries.[44]

For reserve-holding countries and their sovereign wealth funds, investing in developing

The rise of the South presents opportunities for innovative new structures for development partnerships and new approaches to development policy, both globally and regionally

FIGURE 5.1

Under the accelerated progress scenario, the largest projected increases in the Human Development Index are in Sub-Saharan Africa and South Asia

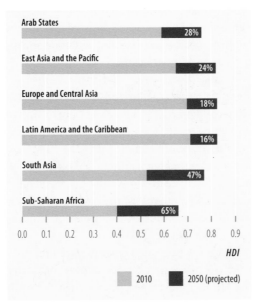

Note: See chapter 4 for discussion of the accelerated progress scenario.
Source: HDRO calculations based on Pardee Center for International Futures 2013.

FIGURE 5.2

Allocating a small fraction of the international reserves of the nine G20 countries of the South could provide substantial additional resources for public investment in infrastructure in Sub-Saharan Africa and South Asia

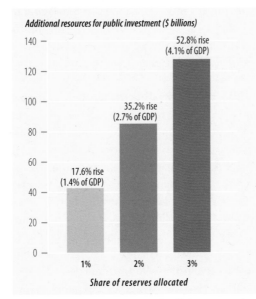

Note: Numbers in parentheses are the increase in public investment as a share of GDP.
Source: HDRO calculations based on World Bank (2012a).

countries is financially attractive, allowing them to diversify while gaining higher profits without added risks.[45] Sovereign wealth funds have long investment horizons and low risk of redemption, enabling them to make long-term investments. Since many give priority to social over private returns, they can also take socially responsible positions. For example, Norway has applied global sustainability criteria to its sovereign wealth fund investments through the Norges Bank Investment Management, committing to the UN Global Compact Norms and investing in initiatives to reduce deforestation in Guyana, Indonesia and Tanzania.[46] The governance challenge is to operationalize socially responsible investment, define suitable benchmarks and provide sovereign wealth funds easier access to investments with a high human development impact.[47]

Institutions from the South, ranging from the BRICS Bank to the Chiang Mai Initiative Multilateralization to the African Union, have considerable potential to influence international governance. Collective action requires a shared vision. The premise for this vision cannot be taken for granted. The proliferation of regional and other arrangements shows that governments recognize the benefits of, and have a commitment to, collective development.

A new South Commission?

In 1987, leaders of the Non-Aligned Movement established the South Commission to explore policy options and areas for cooperation for the countries of the South. Its final report in 1990, *The Challenge to the South*, produced under the leadership of Julius Nyerere, then-president of Tanzania, and the economist Manmohan Singh, future prime minister of India, was a seminal and prescient analysis.[48] It identified climate change as a priority and underscored challenges that stubbornly persist today, such as poverty, social exclusion and the widening gap between rich and poor.[49] Equally important, the South Commission looked closely at the then-emerging possibilities of greater South–South cooperation in aid, trade and other aspects of international policymaking.

The world and the South have been thoroughly transformed over the past two decades. The South of the 21st century is led by fast-growing economies with trillions of dollars of foreign exchange reserves and trillions more to invest outside their borders. Businesses from the South number among the world's largest. The possibilities for collective action have never been greater; however, agreement on this cannot be taken for granted. The institutions for South–South cooperation—the Group of 77, the Non-Aligned Movement and South Summits—were forged in the crucible of decolonization, which created strong political, economic, social, and cultural bonds among the emerging countries of the developing world. That formative experience is increasingly distant from the current generation, and the commitment to South solidarity common to their elders is in many cases now giving way to the pursuit of national interests.

The new realities of the 21st century require a fresh look at these issues and at institutions led by the countries of the South themselves. A new South Commission, building on the legacy of the first commission but reflecting the strengths and needs of the South today, could provide a fresh vision, based on recognition of how the diversity of the South can be a force for a new kind of solidarity, aimed at accelerating human development progress for decades to come. The economic links within the South and the mutual benefits of cooperation are likely to provide further incentives to establish such a body.

Conclusions: partners in a new era

The rise of the South has to some extent caught the world by surprise. The previous, if unspoken, assumption was that developing countries would steadily approach the standards of human development in industrialized countries ("convergence") but that the industrialized countries would remain in a strong, leading position. In many respects, that is still the case: average HDI values are substantially lower in many countries of the South. What has caught the world unawares, however, is that even at lower levels of human development, the countries of the South are now weighty players on the global stage, with the financial resources and political clout to sway international decisionmaking.

This was already evident during the early years of the 21st century, as China and other emerging economies accumulated vast reserves, which they held as US Treasury bonds, effectively propping up the US dollar. But the situation came into sharper relief after 2008, following the banking crisis and subsequent economic shocks that pushed some of the richer countries into recession and threatened the survival of one of the world's major currencies. Now the countries of the North are looking to those of the South to keep the global economy moving forward.

In practice, each group of countries needs the other more than ever. The North needs the most vigorous countries of the South to sustain demand for exported goods and services, especially as a number of their own economies and societies are weakened by fierce austerity programmes. The South needs the North not only as a mature market, but also as a source of innovation and complex technologies.

The rise of the South demonstrates that the world has become more diffuse and cross-connected. One consequence is that rather than looking to the North for inspiration, developing countries are looking to their peers in the South for appropriate development models. Here, rather than seeing a sterile menu of ideological options, they can examine what has worked, under what circumstances, and choose the most appropriate tools. Chapter 3 provided examples of programmes and policies that have worked to improve human development in emerging economies of the South, from investments in public health and education to conditional cash transfer programmes. Such examples can inspire similar policies in other countries, but with understandings of specific national conditions, institutions and needs.

This Report has summarized some of the most effective drivers of development: a proactive developmental state, the capacity to tap into global markets and the promotion of social inclusion and broad-based human development. Within each of these there are multiple options but no universal solutions.

Rather than looking to the North for inspiration, developing countries are looking to their peers in the South for appropriate development models

What worked in one country might have stood little chance in another.

Nevertheless, the most successful countries have demonstrated that innovative and sometimes counterintuitive options can work. Paying parents to take their children to health clinics may seem unnecessary, but as the case of Mexico illustrates, it can work to improve children's health; its conditional cash transfer programmes have sparked interest around the world. Similarly, using a mobile phone for banking made eminent sense in Kenya and the Philippines to people who had never had a personal bank account before and often lived nowhere near a bank office.

The countries of the South have thus been using their own ideas and energy to create a new momentum for human development. In a complex global political, economic and social environment, however, this dynamism may still not yield sustainable outcomes. Already there are signs of rising inequality and frustrated expectations that could lead to violent social strife. And there are serious concerns that over-exploitation of global resources combined with the effects of climate change could wreck the earth for future generations.

Good policymaking requires greater focus on enhancing social capacities, not just individual capabilities

That is why this Report has also focused on what is needed to ensure that human development proceeds in ways that are both productive and sustainable. This includes measures aimed at enhancing equity, enabling voice and participation, confronting environmental pressures and managing demographic change.

Addressing these issues will demand considerable skill and commitment from national governments and civil society. As this chapter has argued, it will also demand much more fruitful global cooperation as national governments, international organizations and a nascent global civil society feel their way towards new models of mutual understanding and cooperation. Some of these will involve refashioning existing institutions to accommodate a new global power balance. Others may take any number of new institutional forms.

Through all this, the fundamental principles of human development endure. As ever, the aim is to expand the choices and capabilities for everyone, wherever they live. Many countries of the South have already demonstrated what can

be done, but they have gone only part of the way. For the years ahead, this Report suggests five broad conclusions.

Rising economic strength in the South must be matched by a full commitment to human development

Investments in human development are justified not only on moral grounds, but also because good health, education and social welfare are key to success in a more competitive and dynamic world economy. In particular, these investments should target the poor—connecting them to markets and increasing their livelihood opportunities. Poverty is an injustice that can and should be remedied by determined action. There are sufficient global resources to achieve that goal, if they are directed towards that purpose.

Good policymaking also requires greater focus on enhancing social capacities, not just individual capabilities. Individuals function within social institutions that can limit or enhance their development potential. Policies that change social norms that limited human potential, such as new legal strictures against early marriages or dowry requirements, can open up additional opportunities for individuals to reach their full potential.

As this Report highlights, one consequence of the rise of the South is that most countries now have growing policy and fiscal space to set bold targets—to eliminate poverty, push for full employment commitments and innovate towards low-carbon pathways. More countries are unencumbered by conditionalities often attached to international aid and resource transfers, and the recent rise in commodity prices has reversed the long decline in terms of trade faced by many primary goods producers.[50] This provides a cushion of resources that can be managed in ways that enhance national human development by governments committed to avoiding the "resource curse".

Projections presented in chapter 4 reinforce this point. They show that with strong commitment to human development and prudent macroeconomic policies, it is possible to reduce poverty dramatically in Sub-Saharan Africa—a region where baseline scenarios show a likely future increase in the number of poor people because population growth outpaces economic growth.

Less developed countries can learn and benefit from the success of emerging economies in the South

The unprecedented accumulation of financial reserves and sovereign wealth funds in the South ($6.8 trillion) as well as the North ($3.3 trillion) provides an opportunity to accelerate broad-based progress. Even a small portion of these funds dedicated to human development and poverty eradication could have a large effect. As mentioned, public investment in South Asia and Sub-Saharan Africa could increase to 11.7% of GDP using just 3% of international reserves from some of the largest economies in the South.

At the same time, South–South trade and investment flows can leverage foreign markets in new ways, such as participating in regional and global value chains to facilitate the spread of ideas and technologies. Burgeoning South–South trade and investment in particular can lay the basis for shifting manufacturing capacity to other less developed regions and countries. Recent Chinese and Indian joint ventures and startup manufacturing investments in Africa serve as a prelude to a much expanded force that this potential represents. To harness the full extent of this potential, new and innovative institutions may be called for. International production networks provide opportunities to speed up the development process by allowing countries to leap-frog to more sophisticated production nodes while offering the double benefit of protection against the vagaries of foreign exchange fluctuations.

South–South development cooperation and technology transfer hold immense potential to support human development. Technology transfers from the North require costly adaptation due to differences in absorptive capacity, but technological transfers within the South are more likely to need little adaptation and to involve more-appropriate technologies and products. Growing markets in developing countries provide companies in the South an opportunity to mass market innovative and affordable versions of standard products, including food, clothing, appliances and motor vehicles. Importantly, the sharp drop in the price of capital goods as a result of intense global competition led by China and India could accelerate the creation of manufacturing production capacities in many developing countries. Such production can be adapted to the income levels and tastes of local consumers. This dynamic has the potential to provide the poor access to consumer goods, while innovators create jobs and develop producer capabilities.

New institutions and new partnerships can facilitate regional integration and South–South relationships

New institutions and partnerships can help countries share knowledge, experiences and technology.

In finance and aid, the South is already actively establishing regional governance institutions. Regional alternatives to the IMF, such as the Chiang Mai Initiative Multilateralization and the Latin American Reserve Fund, have freed up policy space for countries to protect national priorities while also addressing balance-of-payments problems and short-term liquidity issues.

The foundations exist for strong regional institutions, but more can be done to accelerate and deepen these relationships and ensure inclusiveness. As wealthy countries have curtailed aid to address domestic issues, regional development banks and bilateral aid relationships provide additional resources for development projects. These new aid mechanisms also tend to emphasize pragmatism over ideology. Infrastructure development banks, for example, offer new possibilities for development finance. Brazil, China, India, the Russian Federation and South Africa have proposed a development bank to mobilize their considerable reserves to finance projects across developing countries. Building infrastructure would be an important use of such reserves.

Trade with other developing countries now accounts for a majority of merchandise and manufactures exports from developing countries, and these exports are increasingly skill- and technology-intensive. Stronger institutions are now needed to facilitate these South–South trade and investment links. Expanded

The foundations exist for strong regional institutions, but more can be done to accelerate and deepen these relationships and ensure inclusiveness

South–South trade and investment can reduce vulnerability to economic downturns in the North and provide opportunities to leverage foreign markets in new ways.

Regional trade and investment relationships can also be strengthened by streamlining transit, transport and customs procedures; harmonizing regulatory schemes; investing in regional transport infrastructure; and lowering tariffs on South–South trade in final products. Lowering such tariffs could yield collective gains of an estimated $59 billion for the economies of the South.[51]

A new South Commission for the early 21st century could help bring a fresh vision of how the strength and diversity of the South can be a global force for development solidarity. The key elements are there: different endowments provide a basis for expanded exchange, diverse experiences are ripe for sharing, new cross-border partnerships can compete in world markets and, above all, the recognition and implementation of win-win strategies can motivate new forms of South–South cooperation.

Greater representation for the South and civil society can accelerate progress on major global challenges

The rise of the South is leading to a greater diversity of voice on the world stage. This represents an opportunity to build governance institutions that fully represent all constituencies that would make productive use of this diversity in finding solutions to world problems.

New guiding principles for international organizations are needed that incorporate the experience of the South. The G20 incorporates their experience, but the countries of the South also need more-equitable representation in the Bretton Woods institutions, the United Nations and other international bodies.

Active civil society and social movements, both national and transnational, are using the media to amplify their calls for just and fair governance. The spread of movements and increasing platforms for vocalizing key messages and demands challenge governance institutions to adapt more-democratic and more-inclusive principles. More generally, a fair and less unequal world requires space for a multiplicity of voices and a system of public discourse.

A fair and less unequal world requires space for a multiplicity of voices and a system of public discourse

The rise of the South presents new opportunities for generating a greater supply of public goods

A sustainable world requires both better governance and a greater availability of global public goods. Global issues today are increasing in number and urgency, from mitigation of climate change and international economic and financial instability to the fight against terrorism and nuclear proliferation. They require a global response. Yet in many areas, international cooperation continues to be slow—and at times dangerously hesitant. The rise of the South presents new opportunities for providing global public goods more effectively and for unlocking today's many stalemated global issues.

"Publicness" and "privateness" are in most cases not innate properties of a public good but social constructs. As such, they represent a policy choice. National governments can step in when there is underprovision at the national level, but when global challenges arise, international cooperation is necessary and can happen only by voluntary action of many governments. Given the many pressing challenges, progress in determining what is public and what is private will require strong, committed, personal and institutional leadership.

*   *   *

The rise of the South is fundamentally the story of the fast-paced transformation of the developing world and its profound impact on diverse facets of human development. Global discussions of this phenomenon so far have focused almost exclusively on economic growth in the biggest developing countries. This Report uses a human development lens to cast a wider net and show that the impacts are widespread in terms of the large number of developing countries involved and the intertwining of ever-growing global challenges and possibilities—from environmental sustainability and equity to poverty eradication and the reform of global institutions. The changes are occurring at unprecedented speed and scale, propelled by interaction with the wider world through trade, travel and telecommunications in ways that were not possible before.

The fast-developing countries chose their own distinct development pathways. Yet they share important characteristics, including effective leadership from governments, open engagement with the world economy and innovative social policies addressing domestic human development needs. They also face many of the same challenges, from social inequalities to environmental risks. And they have developed their own domestic policy approaches with increasing autonomy, for their own sovereign national reasons, without the strictures of enforced conditionality or imposed external models.

The South's progress is propelled by interconnections with developed countries and increasingly with the developing world. In fact, economic exchanges are expanding faster "horizontally"—on a South–South basis—than on the traditional North–South axis. People are sharing ideas and experiences through new communications channels and seeking greater accountability from governments and international institutions alike. The South as a whole is driving global economic growth and societal change for the first time in centuries. The South still needs the North, but, increasingly, the North also needs the South.

Notes

Overview

1   Atsmon and others 2012.
2   Samake and Yang 2011.
3   The demographic dividend is considered a window of opportunity for additional economic growth when the proportion of the working-age population increases. As fertility levels fall in a demographic transition, the number of children declines while the working-age population increases, lowering the dependency ratio. A country can reap the benefits of increased productive capacity associated with the lower proportion of dependents. As fertility levels continue to decline, however, dependency ratios eventually rise with the increase in retired workers.

Introduction

1   According to World Bank (2012a), the average GDP growth rate in 2009 for high-income members of the Organisation for Economic Co-operation and Development was −3.9%, compared with 7.5% in East Asia and Pacific, 7.4% in South Asia, 3.6% in the Middle East and North Africa and 2.1% in Sub-Saharan Africa.
2   According to Maddison (2010), GDP per capita (in international dollars) rose from $1,250 in 1700 to $2,330 in 1850 in the United Kingdom and from $1,257 in 1820 to $2,445 in 1870 in the United States.
3   Atsmon and others 2012.
4   In addition to increased voting shares and senior appointments at the International Monetary Fund and the World Bank, in recent years, the South has held leadership positions at the International Labour Organization, the World Health Organization, the World Trade Organization and the World Intellectual Property Organization.
5   Chen and Ravallion (2012) using the $1.25 a day poverty line.
6   For example, in 1990, Uganda's HDI (0.306) was comparable to that of Benin, Central African Republic and Gambia. By 2012, Uganda's HDI had increased to 0.456, a substantial improvement compared with its peers (and statistically significant at the 95% level). Benin's increased from 0.314 to 0.436, Central African Republic's from 0.312 to 0.352 and Gambia's from 0.323 to 0.439.

7   In purchasing power parity terms, the standard GDP and GNI calculus in *Human Development Reports*.
8   Japan is not included in the long-term historical comparison between the other Group of Seven economies and Brazil, China and India because it did not industrialize until late in the 19th century and did not emerge as a major world economic power until the second half of the 20th century.
9   In current US dollars.
10 Proportion of the population living on less than $1.25 a day (in 2005 purchasing power parity terms), according to World Bank (2012a).
11 Estimates refer to years between 2002 and 2011.
12 The measures used—life expectancy and mean years of schooling—have upper bounds towards which developing countries tend to eventually converge. There is no upper threshold of convergence for income.
13 HDRO calculations based on Brookings Institution (2012). The middle class includes people earning or spending $10–$100 a day in 2005 purchasing power parity terms.
14 Dobbs and others 2012. Ali and Dadush (2012), using car ownership as a proxy for the middle class, suggest that there are up to 600 million people in the middle class in the developing G20 countries, about 50% more than previous estimates by Milanović and Yitzhaki (2002), who counted people earning $10–$50 a day in purchasing power parity terms as belonging to the middle class.
15 UNDP 2009; World Bank 2010a.
16 UNCTAD 2010.
17 Zuckerberg 2012.
18 Estevadeordal, Frantz and Taylor (2003); the trade to GDP ratio is the sum of exports and imports of goods and services divided by total output.
19 The current trade ratio is a five-year average from 2006 to 2010, obtained from World Bank (2012a).
20 Hamdani 2013.
21 Heilmann 2008.
22 United Nations 2012a.
23 United Nations 2012a.
24 Based on data between 2005 and 2008 from Kharas, Makino and Jung (2011) and extrapolation thereafter.

Chapter 1

1   This is in nominal terms. In purchasing power parity terms, the share is about 46%.

2   IMF 2011b.
3   Iley and Lewis (2011); see also IMF (2011b).
4   HDRO calculations based on data on general government expenditure on social protection from the Organisation for Economic Co-operation and Development show that some industrialized countries, including Australia, Austria, Denmark and Norway, increased expenditure on social protection between 2007 and 2010.
5   For some countries confronting high debt levels (such as Greece, Italy and Japan), the subprime crisis spiralled into a sovereign debt crisis, leaving little fiscal space to postpone fiscal consolidation. Holland and Portes (2012) suggest that, while in normal times fiscal consolidation would lower debt to GDP ratios, under current circumstances, in the European Union, it will likely lead to higher debt to GDP ratios in the region in 2013, with the exception of Ireland.
6   Guajardo, Leigh and Pescatori 2011.
7   ILO 2012.
8   Sen 2012.
9   Keynes 1937.
10 ILO 2012.
11 Throughout the crisis, the solutions implemented (such as fiscal consolidation and easy monetary policies) have been criticized for reaching their limits, for their secondary effects and for their transitory nature. In some countries, the solutions have caused the economy to contract, and in others, they have pushed short-term interest rates in key money markets close to zero. These policies run the risk of creating new asset bubbles and exporting inflationary pressures to countries in the South. See Naqvi and Acharya (2012 , pp. 11–12) for more detail.
12 IMF (2011b, p. 29) points out that "emerging and developing economies account for about half of global output and two-thirds of global growth in purchasing power parity (PPP) terms." Moreover, it argues that although the share of emerging and developing countries' consumption (measured as consumption in constant US dollars, not as GDP in purchasing power parity terms) does not make up for the lower consumption contribution of advanced economies on their own, it is large enough to rebalance when combined with US (or European) consumption.

13 HDRO calculations show that countries as disparate as China and the United States have benefited in the long term from government investment in health and education (see chapter 3 for more details).
14 Given by the ratio of GNI per capita for Seychelles ($22,615) and the Democratic Republic of Congo ($319).
15 HDRO calculations based on Burd-Sharp and Lewis (2010).
16 These disparities are of a similar order of magnitude as the disparity between the HDI values of, say, Mexico (0.78) or Ecuador (0.72) on the one hand, and Nigeria, Senegal or Mauritania (0.47), on the other. Subnational HDI values are not directly comparable with national HDI values because they consist of different indicators and are for different years.
17 These disparities are of a similar order of magnitude as the disparity between the HDI values of Belgium (0.90), on the one hand, and Honduras or Kiribati (0.63), on the other.
18 Based on a balanced panel comparison and data from World Bank (2012a).
19 Since income is a flow variable and education and health outcomes are stock variables, sometimes a positive difference between GNI per capita and HDI rank can emerge when a country has built up its development achievements but its income falls in the short term (as in Zimbabwe).
20 United Nations 2012a.
21 World Bank 2012a.
22 United Nations Enable 2012.
23 Sen 2007.
24 Smith 1776.
25 UNDP 2011a.
26 Estimates refer to years between 2002 and 2011.
27 World Bank 2012b.
28 See, for example, Wilkinson and Pickett (2009).
29 Inequality in the HDI components is measured by the Atkinson inequality index, which takes into account inequality in distribution within and across groups consistently. In addition, it puts more weight on the lower end of the distribution, thus accounting for child mortality, illiteracy and income poverty better than the Gini coefficient.
30 OECD (2011b) shows that in the context of Organisation for Economic Co-operation and Development

countries, the provision of health care, education and acceptable living standards have important direct and indirect redistributive effects, especially among population groups at high risk of poverty. Among a range of public services, health and education contribute by far the most to reducing inequality.

31 Anand and Segal 2008.

32 Sala-i-Martin 2006. He uses population-weighted GDP per capita to calculate the mean of country-level distributions and obtains the dispersion around each mean from micro surveys. After estimating a distribution of income for each country and year, he constructs the world distribution of income by integrating all country distributions.

33 Milanović 2009.

34 Bourguignon and Morrisson 2002.

35 The Supreme Court in India recently upheld a government mandate that private schools offer a quarter of their seats to underprivileged children, a measure with the potential to substantially dilute the economic segregation in access to education.

36 Based on 78 countries for which the GII is available.

37 China (1.18), Azerbaijan (1.15), Armenia (1.14), Georgia (1.11), Republic of Korea (1.10), Solomon Islands (1.09), India (1.08), the former Yugoslav Republic of Macedonia (1.08), Montenegro (1.08), Papua New Guinea (1.08), Samoa (1.08), Serbia (1.08) and Suriname (1.08).

38 Dowry here refers to the payment of cash and gifts by a woman's family to her husband's family at the time of the wedding. Many countries have dowry systems that involve small or moderate gifts, but in some countries, such as India, exorbitant amounts can be extracted in dowry from the bride's family during marriages.

39 For instance, the Dowry Prohibition Act of 1961 makes giving or receiving dowry illegal in India. However, the practice continues, sporadically fuelling both female feticide and dowry deaths of new brides.

40 Cleland 2002; Drèze and Murthi 1999; Martin and Juarez 1995.

41 Elson 2002.

42 Fukuda-Parr 2003.

43 As indicated in the 1994 *Human Development Report* (UNDP 1994), the universalism of life claims advocates equality of opportunity, not equality of income—though in a civilized society a basic minimum income should be guaranteed to everyone.

44 UNDP 1994, p. 18.

45 Rockström and others 2009, p. 32.

46 United Nations Secretary-General's High Level Panel on Global Sustainability 2012.

47 Global Footprint Network 2011.

48 The ecological footprint is a measure of humanity's demand on nature that takes into account the quantity of land and water area that a country uses to provide all it takes from nature, including areas used to produce the resource it consumes, the space for accommodating its buildings and roads, and the ecosystems for absorbing its waste emissions such as carbon dioxide (Global Footprint Network 2011).

49 Blanden and others (2005); Wilkinson and Pickett (2012).

50 UNDP 2010b.

51 Bourguignon, Ferreira and Menéndez 2007.

52 De Hoyos, Martinez de la Calle and Székely 2009.

53 Ivanov and others 2003; Ivanov and others 2006.

54 UNDP 1994.

55 Rosenfeld, Messner and Baumer (2001) hypothesized that civic engagement and trust, core elements of social integration, are associated with strong social organization and therefore are indicators of low criminal violence.

56 UNDP 2012.

57 Data refer to the most recent year available between 2005 and 2012. Homicide data suffer from reporting errors in the Supplementary Homicide Reports and inconsistency among reporting systems at the country level, among other problems.

58 Sen 2007, p. 106.

59 The average incidence of murder is 2.7 per 100,000 people across all Indian cities and 2.9 in Delhi. In comparison, the incidence is 2.4 in London, 5.0 in New York, 8.8 in Los Angeles, 21.5 in Johannesburg, 24.0 in São Paulo and an astonishing 34.9 in Rio de Janeiro.

60 United Kingdom, Office of the Deputy Prime Minister, Social Exclusion Unit 2002. Many prisoners have been socially excluded all their lives. Relative to the general population, prisoners are much more likely to have been in state care as a child (13 times), to be unemployed (13 times), to have had a family member convicted of a criminal offence (2.5 times) and to be HIV positive (15 times).

61 Many prisoners were effectively excluded from access to services. An estimated 50% of prisoners had no physician before coming into custody; prisoners are more than 20 times more likely than the general population to have been excluded from

school; and in at least one instance, although 70% of those entering the prison had a drug misuse problem, 80% of them had never received any drug treatment services (United Kingdom, Office of the Deputy Prime Minister, Social Exclusion Unit 2002).

62 Pinker 2011; Center for Systemic Peace 2012.

63 Branczik 2004.

64 Dahal and others 2003.

65 Iyer 2009.

66 Since a large number of participants in internal conflicts are nonstate actors, there are no official records of their expenditure on armaments. Data on military expenditure refer to expenditure by governments alone and not expenditure by nonstate actors.

67 Bird 1981.

68 Green 2010.

69 Justino 2008.

70 UNDP 1991, p. 37.

Chapter 2

1 Three-quarters of the 1.6 billion people who are multidimensionally poor live in middle-income countries of the South.

2 HDRO calculations based on UNSD (2012).

3 Internet-related data are from World Bank (2012a); tourism data are from UNWTO (2011).

4 Estevadeordal, Frantz and Taylor 2003.

5 World Bank (2012a). These ratios are based on gross values, not value added in exports and imports, for which globally comparable data are not yet available. The World Trade Organization (WTO) has an ongoing initiative, Made in the World, to measure and analyse trade in value added.

6 Based on a balanced panel of 127 developing countries. Based on HDRO calculations, when the trade to output ratio is adjusted to cover only trade with the South, 141 of 144 economies (for which data are available) increased trade with the South between 1990–1991 and 2010–2011 (the exceptions were the small economies of Dominica, the Maldives and Tuvalu); in contrast, 92 decreased trade with the North.

7 World Bank (2008). Contrary to popular perception, real prices of air and maritime transport have not changed much since the 1970s, but the decreasing weight to value ratio of international shipments and the growing use of air transport have favoured time-sensitive goods such as fashion, processed food and electronics.

8 HDRO calculations based on UNSD (2012).

9 World Bank 2012a.

10 The eight countries are Argentina, Brazil, China, India, Indonesia, Mexico, South Africa and Turkey. However, the least developed countries saw only about an eightfold increase, from less than $20 billion to $150 billion.

11 When service exports are added to merchandise exports, the difference in export earnings per capita between Sub-Saharan Africa and India narrows from $221 to $130. Smaller countries tend to engage more in international trade than larger ones such as India, whose intranational trade is high. Furthermore, African exports are dominated by commodities whose prices increased in the 2000s.

12 Based on 2011 nominal values adjusted to be comparable to 1996 values.

13 Removing fuel, metals and ores from aggregate trade statistics means that the share of South–South trade in world trade rose from 6.3% in 1980 to 26.1% in 2011 and that the share of North–North trade declined from 50.6% in 1980 to 31.4% in 2011.

14 The traditional classification of goods as high or low technology has become less meaningful as trade in parts and components has increased.

15 Romero 2012.

16 AfDB and others 2011.

17 Gupta and Wang 2012.

18 Hook and Clark 2012.

19 Tourism-related statistics in this paragraph draw on UNWTO (2011).

20 Based on United Nations Conference on Trade and Development data. Its category of developing economies, which includes Hong Kong, China (SAR), the Republic of Korea, Singapore and Taiwan Province of China but excludes Commonwealth of Independent States countries, accounted for 5.3% of overall FDI inflows in 1990–1991 and 8% in 2009–2010.

21 UNCTAD 2011b.

22 Furthermore, South–South FDI is less deterred by differences in institutional quality between host and receiving countries. By similar logic, employment of local personnel and lower overhead costs are likely to make South–South FDI more resilient to local crises. Because the motives for investing and selecting sectors often differ, South–South FDI does not necessarily displace North–South FDI; it can even attract more of it (Bera and Gupta 2009; Aleksynska and Havrylchyk 2011).

23 This figure is for 2010 and includes Hong Kong, China (SAR).

24 The evidence in this paragraph draws on Hamdani (2013).

25 Blinder 2006.

26 UNIDO 2009.

27 UNDP 2009; World Bank 2010a.

28 These HDRO calculations are based on the bilateral migration matrix in World Bank (2010a).

29 Ratha and Shaw 2007.

30 As explained in World Bank (2006), estimates of South–South remittances depend on which explanatory variable is used to apportion the aggregate remittance received by each country among the destination countries of its migrant nationals. The estimate of South–South remittances is higher (30%) when flows are a function of migrant stock and lower (18%) when they are a function of migrant stock plus average incomes of host and sending countries. The upper limit of 45% is obtained when Saudi Arabia is counted as a developing country.

31 See Felbermayr and Jung (2009) and other citations in Kugler and Rapoport (2011).

32 Foley and Kerr 2011.

33 See The Economist (2011a) and works cited therein.

34 HDRO calculation based on data for 144 countries from World Bank (2012a) and ITU (2012).

35 socialbakers.com 2012. A more recent update by Zuckerberg (2012) is that there are now 1 billion active monthly users of Facebook, with the largest number of users located in Brazil, India, Indonesia, Mexico and the United States.

36 The labour force consists of employed people and unemployed people actively seeking employment.

37 Fu 2008.

38 When the sample excludes developed countries, the correlation coefficient remains statistically significant but drops from 0.66 to 0.48.

39 See Whalley and Weisbrod (2011) for estimates of the contribution to annual growth rates attributed to inward Chinese FDI in resource-rich countries such as Angola, Democratic Republic of Congo, Niger, Nigeria, Sudan and Zambia. Average FDI inflow into these six countries nearly quadrupled from $2.4 billion in 1990–2000 to $9 billion in 2001–2011, according to UNCTAD (2011a).

40 Jones and Kierzkowski 2001.

41 Vos 2010.

42 IMF 2011a.

43 Samake and Yang 2011.

44 Whalley and Weisbrod 2011.

45 Hazard and others 2009; Kamau, McCormick and Pinaud 2009; Kaplinsky 2008.

46 See Kamau, McCormick and Pinaud (2009) for the Kenyan case; Kaplinsky and Morris (2009).

47 Jenkins and Barbosa 2012.

48 ICTSD 2011.

49 Davies 2011.

50 Bräutigam 2009.

51 Sonobe, Akoten and Otsuka 2009.

52 Bräutigam 2009.

53 United Nations 2012b.

54 Moyo 2012.

55 According to Hiemstra-van der Horst (2011), China now accounts for a third of the world furniture market.

56 Kaplinsky, Terheggen and Tijaja 2011.

57 United Nations 2012b.

58 These points draw on Dobbs and others (2012); surveys found that positive product recommendations from friends and family were, for example, three times as important for consumers in Egypt than in the United Kingdom or the United States.

59 HDRO calculations based on Brookings Institution (2012).

60 Dobbs and others 2012.

61 World Bank 2012a.

62 In 2008, South–South aid amounted to $15.3 billion—about 10% of total aid flows (UNDESA 2010).

63 Based on data for 2005 and 2008 in Kharas, Making and Jung (2011) and extrapolated for later years.

64 Kragelund 2013.

65 United Nations 2012b.

66 Its wide-ranging technical assistance initiatives include, among others, broadband connectivity of African health and education institutions with centres in India and bringing some 1,600 young Africans to study in India each year (United Nations 2012b).

67 United Nations 2012b.

68 The larger developing countries have had long-standing, if modest, development assistance programmes to Africa. India's Technical and Economic Cooperation Programme was launched in 1964. The Brazilian Cooperation Agency was established in 1987. China's cooperation with Africa has an even longer history, though it is now formalized in the Forum on China–Africa Cooperation, established in 2000 (Kragelund 2013).

69 Bremmer 2012.

70 World Bank 2010c.

71 According to United Nations (2012b), they were the Islamic Development Bank, the Kuwait Fund for Arab Economic Development, the Arab Fund for Economic and Social Development, the Arab Bank for Economic Development in Africa, the Saudi Fund for Development and the Abu Dhabi Fund for Development.

72 These regional institutions have tended to draw their policy inspiration from the Bretton Woods institutions. Neither the Asian Development Bank nor the Inter-American Development Bank, under their prevailing charters, is empowered to modify their ownership structure in any substantial way. The United States retains veto power over changes in the capital base, which has narrowed the policy space in the two organizations. If, for example, the Asian Development Bank were to be reconstructed as a fully Asian entity that retained the flexibility to establish its own policy space, it would need to reconstitute its ownership structure by assigning much larger contributions and voting rights to countries such as China, India and the Republic of Korea (Sobhan 2013).

73 Mwase and Yang 2012.

74 Zuzana and Ndikumana forthcoming.

75 Developing countries could gain an estimated $59 billion from lowering South–South tariffs to North–South levels (OECD 2010a).

76 Grabel 2013.

77 Grabel 2013.

78 Opportunity costs capture the benefits that can be obtained from alternative uses of these resources. See Rodrik (2006) and IMF (2011b).

79 China has the fifth largest voting share, but an agreement reached in 2010 by the Board of Governors, if implemented, will make China the third largest voteholder (IMF 2010).

80 World Bank 2010d.

81 Hansen 2010.

82 UNDP 2009.

83 Leape 2012.

84 Romero and Broder 2012.

85 Keohane and Victor 2010.

86 Li 2010; Bradsher 2010.

87 REN21 2012.

88 See Jacob (2012); Chinese infrastructure companies in Africa are, for instance, boosting demand for heavy machinery and other capital imports.

89 Akyuz (2012) argues that large countries need to change course. Developing countries benefited unusually in the 2000s from the unsustainable consumption patterns in advanced economies; since the global financial crisis, developing countries have relied more on domestic demand.

Chapter 3

1 Life expectancy, for example, had nearly doubled from 35 years in 1949 to 67.9 in 1981 (UNDP 2008).

2 One caveat is that the identification of rapid improvers on the HDI through this method is biased towards countries with high HDI values. But identifying rapid improvers by calculating simple percentage improvement on the HDI provides a bias towards countries with low HDI values. Neither method is completely satisfactory (Ranis and Stewart 2005).

3 Excluded from this list are all developed economies in 1990 as well as Hong Kong, China (SAR), Israel, Singapore and countries from Central and Eastern Europe that have joined the European Union. This gives a balanced panel of 96 countries between 1990 and 2012.

4 The internal armed conflict also meant that national statistics often excluded the northeast of the country.

5 UNDP 1993, 1996.

6 UNDP 1996.

7 Abe 2006.

8 For elaboration of the concepts of ownership and capacity for development, see Fukuda-Parr, Lopes and Malik (2002).

9 See Commission on Growth and Development (2008).

10 For example, Rodrik (2004) emphasized that no short list of evident policy reforms can be applied to yield growth in developing countries.

11 Hausmann, Pritchett and Rodrik 2005.

12 Serra and Stiglitz 2008.

13 Hausmann, Rodrik and Velasco 2005.

14 Arrighi (2007) argues that self-regulating markets are not the means to development and that governments must play a leading role in organizing market exchange and divisions of labour.

15 A country is said to have comparative advantage in an economic activity if it can undertake that activity at a lower opportunity cost than another country can.

16 See Harrison and Rodriguez-Clare (2010) for single-industry, cross-industry and cross-country evidence on infant industry protection and other forms of industrial policy. Succeeding in world markets is just one criterion ("Mill" test) for justifying government support. Such success can come at a net welfare cost to the economy and fail the "Bastable" test, which requires the discounted future benefits to compensate for short-term costs of protection. According to Harrison and Rodriguez-Clare (2010), more instances of industrial policy satisfy the Mill test than the Bastable test.

17 Rodrik 2012, p. 9.

18 Chibber 1999.

19 Osmani 2005.

20 Ranis and Stewart 2005.

21 India Ministry of Finance 2012.

22 Rodrik 2005.

23 See Das (2000) and DeLong (2004).

24 UNCTAD 2003.

25 Done 2011. Between 1996 and 2005 Embraer delivered 710 regional jets around the world (Baer 2008).

26 Pasha and Palanivel 2004.

27 UNDP 1993, 1996.

28 Fine and others (2012), whose classification of Africa includes North Africa as well as Sub-Saharan Africa.

29 Fine and others 2012.

30 AfDB and others 2012.

31 Subramanian and Roy 2001.

32 Chuhan-Pole and Angwafo 2011.

33 The headcount poverty rate fell from 52% in 1983–1984 to 50% in 1991–1992; by 2000, it had dropped to 40% (Osmani and others 2006).

34 Khan 2005.

35 Nielsen and Spenceley 2011.

36 Kabananukye and others 2004.

37 The figures for Thailand and Brazil in this paragraph draw on Fine and others (2012).

38 Islam (2002) discussed in Khan (2005).

39 Khan 2005.

40 Kaminski and Ng 2006.

41 Ayadi and others 2005.

42 Cammett 2007.

43 Lautier 2008.

44 Agosin 1997.

45 Hussain and Stern 2006, p. 14.

46 Malik 2006.

47 Howell 2004.

48 Ravallion 2009.

49 Malik 2012.

50 Rodrik 2011.

51 For faster economic growth, accessing world markets alone is not enough: the sophistication of exports matters equally, for which constant upgrading with the aid of foreign knowhow is key (see Hausmann, Hwang and Rodrik 2007).

52 Commission on Growth and Development (2008, p. 22).

53 Rodrik 2001.

54 See Rodriguez and Rodrik (2001) for a critique of four influential works in this vein: Dollar (1992), Sachs and Warner (1995), Edwards (1998) and Frankel and Romer (1999).

55 Winters 2004.

56 The case for the use of in-depth country-specific case studies to understand and evaluate policy regimes is best articulated by Bhagwati and Srinivasan (2001). They note that even if the theoretical, data and methodological weaknesses inherent in most cross-country regressions were ignored, cross-country results indicate only average effects, masking differences in individual country responses.

57 Rodrik 2001.

58 See Baldwin (2004) and references therein to notable country case studies.

59 Wacziarg and Welch 2008.

60 Rodrik 2011.

61 Mauritius embraced global markets early in the 1970s by fully using trade preferences and quotas, notably to export sugar and clothing. In the 2000s, with the termination of quotas that governed world trade in textiles and clothing and the reduction of EU sugar protocol prices, Mauritius sought to diversify more into light manufacturing and services such as offshore banking and ICT (Zafar 2011).

62 While the state monopolies were abolished early, they were replaced by tariffs, nontariff barriers and import-restricting licences until the mid-1990s. Between 1980 and 2000, China consolidated its industrial base without facing the constraints imposed by the international rules of the World Trade Organization (which it joined in 2001).

63 Between 2008 and 2010, China (excluding Hong Kong, China [SAR]) attracted an average of 7.2% of global FDI inflows (UNCTAD 2011a).

64 China can be viewed as a case that shows the usefulness of a gradual approach. As Arrighi (2007) argues, the steps taken in China's reforms included gradualism, the use of the market as an instrument of governance, the initial reforms occurring in agriculture and then moving to industry and foreign trade, making capitalists compete among themselves.

65 Ahluwalia 2002.

66 OECD 2007.

67 Ahluwalia 2002.

68 World Bank 2012a.

69 Celasun 1994.

70 In addition to import protection, export promotion measures were also used to further industrial development. These included subsidized credit, tax breaks, export processing zones, bonded manufacturing warehouses, duty drawbacks, privatization of customs administration and direct export subsidies.

71 World Bank 2010b. Foreign firms are noticing the strengthening of competencies in Thailand despite political instability in recent years. In 2010, new investment plans were announced by Ford, General Motors, Mazda and Toyota, with new investors such as BMW and Tata also expected to join.

72 See Athukorala (2011) for a detailed study of Penang's rise as an export hub.

73 World Bank 2011a.

74 NEAC 2010.

75 Athukorala and Waglé 2011.

76 Radelet, Sachs and Lee 1997.

77 Sharma 2012.

78 Clapp 1995; Agosin 1997; Rodrik 2004.

79 UNCTAD 2006.

80 World trade in apparel and textiles was governed by quotas for more than 40 years, beginning in the 1960s with the Short Term and Long Term Arrangements Regarding International Trade in Cotton Textiles, followed by the Multi-Fibre Arrangement between 1974 and 1994 and the World Trade Organization Agreement on Textiles and Clothing until 2004. The Multi-Fibre Arrangement in particular forced many successful exporting economies (especially from East Asia) to shift investment to countries less restrained by bilateral quotas. This distorted world trade but benefited such countries as Bangladesh and Mauritius in their efforts to diversify into manufacturing.

81 Kabeer and Mahmud 2004.

82 Based on mirrored trade data from the United Nations Commodity Trade Statistics Database; products belonging to Standard International Trade Classification (Revision 3) Division 84 were classified as apparel exports. Analysis is limited to countries that reported data for apparel exports in each year.

83 Subramanian and Roy 2001.

84 Chuhan-Pole and Angwafo 2011.

85 Ofosu-Asare 2011.

86 Suri and others 2011. In particular, they find that for a one standard deviation decrease in infant mortality rate, over a decade there would be a 2.2 percentage point increase in economic growth. Similarly, a one standard deviation increase in life expectancy over a decade implies a 2.7 percentage point increase in growth, while a one standard deviation increase in secondary enrolment rate over a decade increases growth 1.9 percentage points.

87 Commission on Growth and Development 2008.

88 Hanushek and others (2008) found that across the 50 countries they studied, each additional year of average schooling in a country increased the average 40 year growth rate of GDP about 0.37 percentage point. However, they found that a country whose test score performance was 0.5 standard deviation higher than another country during the 1960s had a growth rate that was, on average, 1 percentage point higher annually over the following 40 year period.

89 To address this question, Hanushek and others (2008) measured the share of students in each country who reach a threshold of basic competency in mathematics and science, as well as the share of students who perform at very high levels.

90 Bloom, Canning and Sevilla (2007) found that a one year increase in a population's life expectancy contributes to a 4% increase in output. Similar positive effects are also associated with improvements in reproductive health. In a study of 97 countries, Bloom and others (2009) found that higher fertility is associated with lower labour force participation of women during their fertile years. On average, each additional child reduces female labour force participation 5–10 percentage points for women ages 20–44.

91 Stern 2003.

92 Cornia 2004.

93 Rodrik 1998.

94 Stern 2003.

95 Ssewanyana, Matovu and Twimukye 2011.

96 Foster and Mijumbi 2002.

97 Bertrand and Mullainathan 2003.

98 Essama-Nssah 2011.

99 Sivananthiran and Venkata Ratnam 2005.

100 Tsounta 2009.

101 Tangcharoensathien and others 2011.

102 UNESCAP 2011.

103 Frenk, Gómez-Dantés and Knaul 2009.

104 Kanbur 2004.

105 Ravallion 2009.

106 Glewwe and Kassouf 2008.

Chapter 4

1 The distinction between equity and equality is linked to the difference between what can be observed and what cannot be. Equity is associated with equal opportunities, which are not observable. Unfortunately, as only outcomes can be observed and measured, the evaluation of whether a society is equitable can only be approximated based on the degree of prevailing inequality.

2 Inequalities across racial, ethnic and religious groups are particularly likely to cause political violence and tend to be extremely persistent unless confronted by comprehensive policies (Stewart 2013).

3 This beneficial trend in Latin America is driven by declining labour income inequality, a closing wage gap between skilled and unskilled workers and conditional cash transfers (see López-Calva and Lustig 2010).

4 Cleland 2002. Martin and Juarez (1995) argue that in some cases, over the short term, education does not necessarily immediately affect reproductive behaviour. See also Hori (2011); Serbessa (2002); Cochrane (1979); Bloom and others (2009); Psacharopoulos and Tzannatos (1992).

5 Taylor, Newman and Kelly 1976.

6 UNDESA 2007; Diamond, Newby and Varle 1999; Population Reference Bureau 2000.

7 This indicator is more commonly reported as deaths per 1,000 live births, or the infant mortality rate,

which is 61.7 deaths per 1,000 live birth per year.

8 UNDP 1995.

9 ILO 2012. The International Labour Organization constructed the index using Gallup survey data.

10 Westaway 2012.

11 Lagi, Bertrand and Bar-Yam 2011. The Food and Agriculture Organization food price index topped 180 in 2008.

12 ILO 2012. According to International Labour Organization estimates based on Gallup data, the majority of people in nearly all regions of the world are not satisfied with the availability of quality jobs. Dissatisfaction is highest in Central and Eastern Europe and Sub-Saharan Africa, followed by the Middle East and North Africa.

13 Bland 2012.

14 Tejada 2012.

15 Gooch 2012.

16 ILO 2012.

17 See, for example, Jenkins and Wallace (1996), who find an association between education and protest involvement, and Dalton, Van Sickle and Weldon (2010), who find a strong positive correlation between education levels and protest involvement across a wide range of developed and developing countries.

18 Between now and 2050, under varying assumptions, the share of the global population older than age 15 that is uneducated is projected to fall to either 3% or 8% depending on the scenario, down from 12% in 2010; the share of the population with secondary or tertiary education will rise to either 50% or 64% depending on the scenario, up from 44% in 2010 (see figure 4.1).

19 Hook 2012.

20 LaFraniere 2011; Wines and LaFraniere 2011.

21 Amartya Sen makes this distinction: unfair exclusion means that some people are kept out or left out; unjust inclusion means that some people are included on deeply unfavourable terms (APRI 2003).

22 Huntington (1968), cited in Campante and Chor (2012).

23 See Campante and Chor (2012).

24 Based on health, education and income attainments in 78 countries over 1980–2011. Unlike mean years of schooling, health and income attainments have been reversed during this period in some countries.

25 Campante and Chor 2012.

26 Campante and Chor 2012, p. 175.

27 Polanyi 1944.

28 FitzGerald, Stewart and Venugopal 2006.

29 For example, Guangdong Province and Liaoning Province have similar HDI values, but Guangdong has more than three times the carbon productivity of Liaoning (UNDP 2010c).

30 UNDP 2011a.

31 See UNDP (2011a) for more detail.

32 The United Nations International Strategy for Disaster Reduction defines *resilience* as "the ability of a system, community or society exposed to hazards to resist, absorb, accommodate to and recover from the effects of a hazard in a timely and efficient manner, including through the preservation and restoration of its essential basic structures and functions" (United Nations Office for Disaster Risk Reduction 2009).

33 Daniell and Vervaeck 2012.

34 IPCC 2012.

35 Each age group in a population faces different needs and behaves differently. Young people (ages 0–14) require investments in health and education. Working-age adults (ages 15–64) require jobs and financial infrastructure to support production and savings. Older adults (ages 65 and older) require health care and retirement income. A country's age structure thus alters its challenges and opportunities.

36 With fewer children to support, parents invest more in their children's education (Becker, Murphy and Tamura 1990; Galor 2006), save more for their retirement (Bloom, Canning and Sevilla 2003), and women increasingly participate in the formal labour market (Bloom and others 2009). As a result, economic growth accelerates, yielding what has been called "the demographic dividend" (Bloom, Canning and Sevilla 2003).

37 A low dependency ratio can generate a demographic dividend, since the increase in the labour force can spur economic growth and greater investment, given the low demand for spending from dependents. (See Abdurazakov, Minsat and Pineda [2013] for a detailed analysis of demographic trends based on projections by Lutz and KC 2013.) But countries can reap these dividends only if they provide productive employment for the large number of new entrants to the labour force.

38 Lutz and KC 2013.

39 A scenario of education level distribution where universal primary education is complemented by broad-based secondary education brings the highest annual economic growth rates for a typical low HDI country with a large share of young people (IIASA 2008). This analysis uses a dataset that disaggregates each country's population by age, sex and educational attainment. Thus, each five-year cohort's population share can be described as having no education, primary education, secondary education or tertiary education. And these attainments can be differentiated by gender. The proportion of the population in each five-year cohort changes with trends in fertility, mortality and migration. The proportion of the young, working-age and elderly populations will thus also change over time.

40 This approach is consistent with that of the Millennium Development Goals and the Education for All initiative. Governing this scenario are several key targets: near universal (99%) primary education by 2015, 50% lower secondary education by 2030 and 90% by 2030, and 60% tertiary education by 2050.

41 HDRO calculations based on Lutz and KC (2013).

42 UNDESA 2007. For developed countries, international migration is unlikely to ease the economic impacts of an ageing population because the volume of migration needed is much larger than is politically feasible. In scenario III of the study, the migration needed to halt the expected increase in the ratio of the elderly over 1995–2050 ranges from an average annual net inflow of 1.1 million people for the United Kingdom and 1.7 million for France to more than 10 million each for Japan and the United States.

43 Becker, Murphy and Tamura 1990; Galor 2006; Bloom, Canning and Sevilla 2003; Bloom and others 2009.

44 Bloom and others 2012. In Sub-Saharan Africa, the youth dependency ratio is 1.07 for the poorest 20% of households but 0.72 for the wealthiest 20%. In Latin America, the ratio is 0.91 for the poorest households and 0.57 for the wealthiest.

45 See *The Economist* (2012b) for a discussion of the main results of the Bloom and others (2012) study.

46 Hausmann and Székely (2001) found that the demographic transition in Latin America accentuated existing inequality trends, with faster and earlier demographic shifts among the wealthiest population groups widening the gap between the rich and the poor. Giroux (2008) found that although fertility differentials associated with education have remained relatively stable in Sub-Saharan African countries as national fertility has fallen, inequality has increased. They show that changes in the education composition of the population have shaped recent variations in reproductive inequality in the region.

47 Bloom and others 2012.

48 World Bank 2011c.

49 In many countries, if the current age of retirement is unchanged, this window will close in a matter of decades. This suggests that important discussions about the retirement age will take place in many countries where the population is ageing quickly.

50 The previous section discussed the role of migration on demographic trends; here the role of migration is more comprehensive, since it is fully integrated into a model in which demographic trends are just one part of several modules used in these projections exercise. See Pardee Center for International Futures (2013).

Chapter 5

1 The Doha round for trade negotiations at the World Trade Organization have been at an impasse since 2008 (Castle and Landler 2008; WTO n.d.). At the United Nations Framework Convention on Climate Change 18th Conference of the Parties in Doha in December 2012, the main legally binding global agreement on climate change, the Kyoto Protocol, was extended until 2020. Countries reiterated that they are determined to adopt, in 2015, a new "protocol, another legal instrument or an agreed outcome with legal force" to come into effect from 2020. However, any agreement on the structure of the new protocol and financing mechanisms was left until next year. (Broder 2012; Harvey 2012)

2 Heller 2013.

3 Global public goods are those that have cross-border consequences. National governments, acting on their own, as well as markets, are unable to produce sufficient quantities of global public goods, and collective intergovernmental action is needed. In a world where trade, financial flows, environmental resources and pollution increasingly transcend national borders, multilateral cooperation for the provision of global public goods becomes crucial for human development (Kaul 2013).

4 While bilateral arrangements can sometimes disadvantage the weaker partner, regional arrangements can help empower poorer regions in their negotiations with richer ones.

5 This is called trade diversion. Lowering of tariff barriers that leads to more trade is called trade creation. See Krugman (1991).

6 See Krugman (1991), who argues further that the net effect on world efficiency is unlikely to be negative

because trading blocs consist of geographical neighbours. Since these countries would be natural trading partners even without special arrangements, the losses from trade diversion are small, while gains from trade creation are large.

7   Multilateralizing regionalism also requires harmonizing a diverse array of trade regulations (such as varying rules of origin for determining local content) and expanding regional agreements to include as many developing country partners as possible. These ideas draw on Baldwin (2007).

8   The International Organization for Migration, not a part of the UN system, has the broadest mandate for migration issues of any international institution. With 146 member states, it has become an increasingly prominent forum for discussions on international migration.

9   UNDP 2009.

10 Hansen 2010.

11 Betts and others 2013.

12 King, Richards and Tyldesley 2011.

13 UNDP 2011a.

14 Han 2012.

15 Leape 2012.

16 Leape 2012.

17 Romero and Broder 2012.

18 Glennie 2011.

19 OECD 2011c.

20 G8 2005.

21 Ocampo 2010.

22 General Assembly addresses by heads of government Sept. 25-Oct.1 (UN News Service www.un.org/news/).

23 At the Group of 20 Summit in Los Cabos in 2012, Brazil, China, India,

the Russian Federation and South Africa announced contributions of $75 billion towards International Monetary Fund resources. These funds come with several conditions. They can be called upon only after existing resources are substantially used. The money was also given in anticipation that "all the reforms agreed upon in 2010 will be fully implemented in a timely manner, including a comprehensive reform of voting power and reform of quota shares" (Chowla 2012).

24 Heller 2013.

25 The video received more than 100 million views and is one of the most "viral" videos of all time.

26 Chandhoke 2009; Heller 2013.

27 This takes many forms—restrictive nongovernmental organization laws, foreign currency and taxation regulations, registration requirements and the like—and is justified by governments on grounds such as national security, accounting failures by nongovernmental organizations, coordination and control, among others. The International Center for Non-profit Law and CIVICUS have consistently been reporting on and analyzing this situation worldwide.

28 Castells 2003; Burawoy 2003.

29 British political theorist Andrew Dobson developed the idea of an "ecological citizenship". Thinking ecologically implies a broad notion of citizenship, one that includes the goal of reducing ecologic footprints. Ecological citizenship goes beyond individual responsibility, since

ecological thinking views citizens as products of and influences on their communities (and their ecosystems) (Revkin 2012).

30 Chorev 2012.

31 Grabel 2013. For a useful summary see also Lamberte and Morgan (2012).

32 Reserve Bank of India 2012.

33 Grabel 2013.

34 Ocampo and Titelman 2009.

35 Grabel 2013.

36 The Bank of the South was founded in 2007 by Venezuelan President Hugo Chavez and officially launched in 2009. Initially envisaged with a very broad mission, by the time of its launch in 2009, its mandate had been narrowed to project finance in the South American region (Chin 2010). Its precise functions and goals are still being debated among member countries.

37 OECD 2010a.

38 Baldwin 2006.

39 See United Nations Security Council (2011), which contains the concept note on responsibility while protecting, as developed by the government of Brazil.

40 India Ministry of External Affairs 2012.

41 Bhattacharya, Romani and Stern 2012.

42 Bhattacharya, Romani and Stern 2012.

43 HDRO calculations based on World Bank (2012a) data on average spending for each country in the region between 2005 and 2010.

44 Based on HDRO calculations using World Bank (2012a) data on international reserves. Given that international reserves play a prominent

role in monetary and exchange rate policy, it may be too ambitious to expect a larger proportion of the reserves to be allocated for other purposes.

45 Some have proposed a global infrastructure initiative whereby rich countries channel investment funds to developing countries, generating a greater return on investment than they could at home (Harding 2012). The same principle applies to investment by emerging economies.

46 Bolton, Samama and Stiglitz 2011. Norway has also offered $1 billion to Brazil for its deforestation efforts, albeit not through its sovereign wealth fund.

47 Public-private partnerships and community-level initiatives can also help broaden the scope and impact of sovereign wealth fund investments.

48 See Hamdani (2013) and South Commission (1990).

49 The South Commission was formally established in 1987, following years of informal discussion among leaders from the South. The report of the South Commission (1990) emphasized that developing countries have many problems and much experience in common. It found that the South is not well organized at the global level and has been unable to effectively mobilize its combined expertise, experience and bargaining power. The report made practical suggestions to be carried out by concerned policymakers.

50 Mwase and Yang 2012.

51 OECD 2010a.

References

Abdurazakov, A., A. Minsat, and J. Pineda. 2013. "Implications of Education Policies in a Country's Demographic Prospects: Detailed Analysis of Demographic Trends Based on Projections by Lutz and KC." Human Development Research Paper. United Nations Development Programme, Human Development Report Office, New York.

Abe, M. 2006. "The Developmental State and Educational Advance in East Asia." *Educate* 6 (1): 6–12.

ADB (Asian Development Bank). 2009. *Annual Report 2009.* Vol. 1. Manila. www.adb.org/documents/adb-annual-report-2009. Accessed 15 May 2012.

AfDB (African Development Bank), OECD (Organisation for Economic Co-operation and Development), UNDP (United Nations Development Programme), and UNECA (United Nations Economic Commission for Africa). 2011. *African Economic Outlook 2011: Africa and Its Emerging Partners.* Paris and Tunis.

———. **2012.** *African Economic Outlook 2012: Promoting Youth Employment.* Paris and Tunis.

Agosin, M. 1997. "Trade and Growth in Chile: Past Performance and Future Prospects." United Nations Economic Commission for Latin America, International Trade Unit, Santiago. www.eclac.org/cgi-bin/getProd.asp?xml=/publicaciones/xml/4/4234/P4234.xml&xsl=/comercio/tpl-i/p9f.xsl&base=/comercio/tpl/top-bottom.xsl. Accessed 15 May 2012.

Ahluwalia, M.S. 2002. "Economic Reforms in India since 1991: Has Gradualism Worked?" *Journal of Economic Perspectives* 16 (3): 67–88.

Akyuz, Y. 2012. "The Staggering Rise of the South." Research Paper 44. South Center, Geneva.

Aleksynska, M., and O. Havrylchyk. 2011. "FDI from the South: The Role of Institutional Distance and Natural Resources." Working Paper 2011-05. Centre D'Études Prospectives et D'Informations Internationales, Paris. www.cepii.fr/anglaisgraph/workpap/pdf/2011/wp2011-05.pdf. Accessed 15 May 2012.

Ali, S., and U. Dadush. 2012. *In Search of the Global Middle Class: A New Index.* Washington, DC: Carnegie Endowment for International Peace. http://carnegieendowment.org/files/middle_class-edited.pdf. Accessed 4 October 2012.

AMRO (ASEAN+3 Macroeconomic Research Office). 2012. "The Joint Statement of the 15th ASEAN+3 Finance Ministers and Central Bank Governors' Meeting." Manila. www.amro-asia.org/wp-content/uploads/2012/05/120503AFMGM+3-JS.pdf. Accessed 31 May 2012.

Anand, S., and P. Segal. 2008. "What Do We Know about Global Income Inequality?" *Journal of Economic Literature* 46: 57–94.

Anderson, L. 2011. "Demystifying the Arab Spring: Parsing the Differences between Tunisia, Egypt, and Libya." *Foreign Affairs* 90 (3): 2–7.

APRI (Asia Pacific Regional Human Development Reports Initiative). 2003. "Potential and Challenges in Human Development Reporting." Report of the UNDP Training Workshop, 24–26 September 2003, Colombo, Sri Lanka. UNDP Asia-Pacific Regional Centre, Bangkok.

Arrighi, G. 2007. "China's Market Economy in the Long Run." In Ho-Fung Hung, ed., *China and the Transformation of Global Capitalism.* Baltimore, MD: Johns Hopkins University Press.

Athukorala, P. 2011. "Production Networks and Trade Patterns in East Asia: Regionalization or Globalization?" *Asian Economic Papers* 10 (1): 65–95.

Athukorala, P., and S. Waglé. 2011. "Foreign Direct Investment in Southeast Asia: Is Malaysia Falling Behind?" *ASEAN Economic Bulletin* 28 (2): 115–33.

Atkinson, A. 2011. "Public Economics after the Idea of Justice." 1st Annual Amartya Sen Lecture, 5 September, The Hague, The Netherlands. www.ethicsandtechnology.eu/images/uploads/1stAnnualAmartyaSenLecture_TonyAtkinson.pdf. Accessed 15 May 2012.

———. **2012.** "Public Economics in an Age of Austerity." Agnar Sandmo Lecture, 12 January, Norwegian School of Economics and Business Administration, Bergen, Norway.

Atsmon, Y., P. Child, R. Dobbs, and L. Narasimhan. 2012. "Winning the $30 Trillion Decathlon: Going for Gold in Emerging Markets." *McKinsey Quarterly*, August. www.mckinseyquarterly.com/Winning_the_30_trillion_decathlon_Going_for_gold_in_emerging_markets_3002. Accessed 15 August 2012.

Ayadi, M., G. Boulila, M. Lahouel, and P. Montigny. 2005. "Pro-Poor Growth in Tunisia." International Development and Strategies, Paris.

Baer, W. 2008. *The Brazilian Economy: Growth and Development.* Boulder, CO: Lynne Rienner Publishers.

Baldwin, R.E. 2004. "Openness and Growth: What's the Empirical Relationship? In R.E. Baldwin and L.A. Winters, eds., *Challenges to Globalization: Analyzing the Economics.* Chicago, IL: University of Chicago Press. www.nber.org/chapters/c9548.pdf. Accessed 6 August 2012.

———. **2006.** "Multilateralizing Regionalism: Spaghetti Bowls as Building Blocks on the Path to Global Free Trade." *World Economy* 29 (11): 1451–1518.

———. **2007.** "Ideas for a WTO Action Plan on Regionalism: Implications for Asia." Post-event Statement. Asian Development Bank Institute Distinguished Speaker Seminar, 26 November, Tokyo. www.adbi.org/event/2366.dance.east.asia.reflections/. Accessed 23 October 2012.

Barro, R.J., and J.-W. Lee. 2010. Educational Attainment Dataset. www.barrolee.com. Accessed 5 May 2012.

Becker, G., K. Murphy, and R. Tamura. 1990. "Human Capital, Fertility, and Economic Growth." *Journal of Political Economy* 98 (5): S12–S37.

Beeston, K. 2012. "Time for Democracy 2.0? The Launch of the Manifesto For A Global Democracy." *Global Policy Journal*, 5 July. www.globalpolicyjournal.com/blog/05/07/2012/time-democracy-20-launch-manifesto-global-democracy. Accessed 28 December 2012.

Bera, S., and S. Gupta. 2009. "South-South FDI vs. North-South FDI: A Comparative Analysis in the Context of India." Working Paper 238. Indian Council of Research in International Economic Relations, New Delhi. www.icrier.org/pdf/WorkingPaper238.pdf. Accessed 15 May 2012.

Berg, J., and S. Cazes. 2007. "The Doing Business Indicators: Measurement Issues and Political Implications." Economic and Labour Market Paper 2007/6. International Labour Organization, Geneva.

Bertrand, M., and S. Mullainathan. 2003. *Are Emily and Greg More Employable than Lakisha and Jamal? A Field Experiment on Labor and Market Discrimination.* Working Paper 9873. Cambridge, MA: National Bureau of Economic Research. www.nber.org/papers/w9873. Accessed 15 May 2012.

Betts, A., J. Prantl, D. Sridhar, and N. Woods. 2013. "Transforming Global Governance for the Twenty-First Century." Human Development Research Paper. United Nations Development Programme, Human Development Report Office, New York. www.spp.nus.edu.sg/docs/HDR-GEG2012-LKYSPP.pdf. Accessed 15 May 2012.

Bhagwati, J., and Srinivasan, T. 2001. "Outward-Orientation and Development: Are Revisionists Right?" In D. Lal and R. Snape, eds., *Trade, Development, and Political Economy.* London: Palgrave.

Bhattacharya, A., M. Romani, and N. Stern. 2012. "Infrastructure for Development: Meeting the Challenge." Centre for Climate Change Economics and Policy, London. www.cccep.ac.uk/Publications/Policy/docs/PP-infrastructure-for-development-meeting-the-challenge.pdf. Accessed 15 May 2012.

Bird, L.A. 1981. *Costa Rica: A Country without an Army.* Bolton, UK: Leeds Northern Friends Peace Board.

Bland, B. 2012. "Vietnam's Factories Grapple with Growing Unrest." *Financial Times*, 19 January. www.ft.com/intl/cms/s/0/67380b5c-427e-11e1-97b1-00144feab49a.html. Accessed 21 December 2012.

Blanden, J., A. Goodman, P. Gregg, and S. Machin. 2005. "Changes in Intergenerational Income Mobility in Britain." In M. Corak, ed., *Generational Income Mobility in North America and Europe.* Cambridge, MA: Cambridge University Press.

Blinder, A. 2006. "Offshoring: The Next Industrial Revolution?" *Foreign Affairs* 85 (2): 113.

Block, F. 2008. "Swimming Against the Current: The Rise of a Hidden Developmental State in the United States." *Politics and Society* 36 (2): 169–206.

———. **2013.** "Can the Path of the World's Richer Nations be Sustained? The Future of the U.S. Model." Human Development Research Paper. United Nations Development Programme, Human Development Report Office, New York.

Bloom, D.E., D. Canning, G. Fink, and J.E. Finlay. 2009. "Fertility, Female Labor Force Participation, and the Demographic Dividend." *Journal of Economic Growth* 14 (2): 79–101.

———. **2012.** "Microeconomic Foundations of the Demographic Dividend." Working Paper 93. Harvard University, Program on the Global Demography of Aging, Cambridge, MA. www.hsph.harvard.edu/pgda/WorkingPapers/2012/PGDA_WP_93.pdf. Accessed 27 December 2012.

Bloom, D.E., D. Canning, and J. Sevilla. 2003. *The Demographic Dividend: A New Perspective on the*

Economic Consequences of Population Change. Santa Monica, CA: Rand Corporation.

———. **2007.** "The Effect of Health on Economic Growth: A Production Function Approach." Working Paper 28. Harvard University, Program on the Global Demography of Aging, Cambridge, MA. www.hsph.harvard.edu/pgda/WorkingPapers/2007/PGDA_WP_28.pdf. Accessed 10 August 2012.

Bolton, P, F. Samama, and J. Stiglitz. 2011. *Sovereign Wealth Funds and Long-Term Investing*. New York: Columbia University Press.

Bourguignon, F., F.H.G. Ferreira, and M. Menéndez. 2007. "Inequality of Opportunity in Brazil." *Review of Income and Wealth* 53 (4): 585–618.

Bourguignon, F., and C. Morrison. 2002. "Inequality among World Citizens: 1820–1992." *American Economic Review* 92 (4): 727–744.

BRAC. n.d. "About BRAC Bangladesh." www.brac.net/content/about-brac-bangladesh. Accessed 15 May 2012.

Bradsher, K. 2010. "China Leading Global Race to Make Clean Energy." *The New York Times*, 30 January. www.nytimes.com/2010/01/31/business/energy-environment/31renew.html. Accessed 15 May 2012.

Branczik, A. 2004. "Humanitarian Aid and Development Assistance." Beyond Intractability. www.beyondintractability.org/bi-essay/humanitarian-aid. Accessed 15 May 2012.

Bräutigam, D. 2009. *The Dragon's Gift: The Real Story of China in Africa*. Oxford, UK: Oxford University Press.

Bremmer, I. 2012. "Africa and the Power of the Pivot." *The New York Times*, 14 May. www.nytimes.com/2012/05/15/opinion/africa-and-the-power-of-the-pivot.html. Accessed 15 May 2012.

Broder, J.M. 2012. "Climate Talks Yield Commitment to Ambitious, but Unclear, Actions." *The New York Times*, 8 December. www.nytimes.com/2012/12/09/science/earth/talks-on-climate-produce-promises-and-complaints.html. Accessed 8 December 2012.

Brookings Institution. 2012. "Middle Class Measures." Development, Aid and Governance Indicators. Washington, DC. www.brookings.edu/research/interactives/development-aid-governance-indicators. Accessed 4 October 2012.

Burawoy, M. 2003. "For A Sociological Marxism: The Complementary Convergence of Antonio Gramsci and Karl Polanyi." *Politics and Society* 31 (2): 193–261.

Burd-Sharp, S., and K. Lewis. 2010. *The Measure of America 2010–2011: Mapping Risks and Resilience*. New York: NYU Press.

Cammett, M. 2007. "Business-Government Relations and Industrial Change: The Politics of Upgrading in Morocco and Tunisia." *World Development* 35 (11): 1889–1903.

Campante, F., and D. Chor. 2012. "Why Was the Arab Spring Poised for Revolution? Schooling, Economic Opportunities, and the Arab Spring." *Journal of Economic Perspectives* 26 (2): 167–188.

Castells, M. 2003. *The Power of Identity*. Malden, MA: Blackwell.

Castle, S., and M. Landler. 2008. "After 7 Years, Talks Collapse on World Trade." *The New York Times*, 30 July.

Celasun, M. 1994. "Trade and Industrialization in Turkey: Initial Conditions, Policy and Performance in the 1990s."

In G. Helleiner, ed., *Trade and Industrialization in Turbulent Times*. London: Routledge.

Center for Systemic Peace. 2012. "Global Conflict Trends: Measuring Systemic Peace." Vienna, VA. www.systemicpeace.org/conflict.htm. Accessed 15 May 2012.

Chandhoke, N. 2009. "What Is the Relationship Between Participation and Representation?" In O. Törnquist, N. Webster, and K. Stokke, eds. *Rethinking Popular Representation*. New York: Palgrave Macmillan.

Chang, H.J. 2010. "How to 'Do' a Developmental State: Political, Organizational and Human Resource Requirements for the Developmental State." In O. Edigheji, ed., *Constructing a Democratic Developmental State in South Africa, Potentials and Challenges*. Cape Town: HSRC Press.

Chen, S., and M. Ravallion. 2012. "More Relatively-Poor People in a Less Absolutely-Poor World." Policy Research Working Paper 6114. Washington, DC, World Bank.

Cheng, H., Y. Hu, and J. Zhao. 2009. "Meeting China's Water Shortage Crisis: Current Practices and Challenges." *Environmental Science & Technology* 43 (2): 240–244.

Chibber, V. 1999. "Building a Developmental State: The Korean Case Reconsidered." *Politics & Society* 27 (3): 309–346.

Chin, G. 2010. "Remaking the Architecture: The Emerging Powers, Self-Insuring and Regional Insulation." *International Affairs* 86 (3): 693–715.

———. **2012.** "Responding to the Global Financial Crisis: The Evolution of Asian Regionalism and Economic Globalization." Working Paper 343. Asian Development Bank Institute, Tokyo. www.adbi.org/working-paper/2012/01/31/4846.gfc.evolution.asian.regionalism.economic.globalization/. Accessed 15 May 2012.

China Daily. **2012.** "Overseas M&A Deals Hit $43b in 2011." 27 February. www.chinadaily.com.cn/bizchina/2012-02-27/content_14703801.htm. Accessed 15 May 2012.

Chorev, N. 2012. *The World Health Organization between North and South*. Ithaca, NY: Cornell University Press.

Chowla, P. 2012. "Spotlight G20: Does BRICS Money for the IMF Mean They Are Bailing Out Europe?" 21 June. Triple Crisis: Global Perspectives on Finance, Development, and Environment. http://triplecrisis.com/spotlight-g-20-does-brics-money-for-the-imf-mean-they-are-bailing-out-europe/. Accessed 8 December 2012.

Chuhan-Pole, P., and M. Angwafo, eds. 2011. *Yes Africa Can: Success Stories From A Dynamic Continent*. Washington, DC: World Bank. http://siteresources.worldbank.org/AFRICAEXT/Resources/258643-1271798012256/YAC_Consolidated_Web.pdf. Accessed 10 August 2012.

Ciorciari, J. 2011. "Chiang Mai Initiative, Multilateralization International Politics and Institution-Building in Asia." *Asian Survey* 51 (5): 926–952.

Clapp, R.A. 1995. "Creating Comparative Advantage: Forest Policy as Industrial Policy in Chile." *Economic Geography* 71 (3): 273–296.

Cleland, J. 2002. "Education and Future Fertility Trends with Special Reference to Mid-Transitional Countries." United Nations Department of Economic and Social Affairs, Population Division, New York. www.un.org/esa/population/publications/completingfertility/RevisedCLELANDpaper.PDF. Accessed 15 May 2012.

Cochrane, S.H. 1979. *Fertility and Education: What Do We Really Know?* Baltimore, MD: Johns Hopkins University Press.

Commission on Growth and Development. 2008. *The Growth Report: Strategies for Sustained Growth and Inclusive Development*. Washington, DC: World Bank.

Cornia, G.A. 2004. *Inequality, Growth and Poverty in an Era of Liberalization and Globalization*. Oxford, UK: Oxford University Press.

Dahal, S.H., H. Gazdar, S.I. Keethaponcalan, and P. Murthy. 2003. "Internal Conflict and Regional Security in South Asia." United Nations Institute for Disarmament Research, Geneva. www.unidir.org/pdf/ouvrages/pdf-1-92-9045-148-3-en.pdf. Accessed 15 May 2012.

Dalton, R., A. Van Sickle, and S. Weldon. 2010. "The Individual–Institutional Nexus of Protest Behaviour." *British Journal of Political Science* 40 (1): 51–73.

Daniell, J., and A. Vervaeck. 2012. "Damaging Earthquakes Database 2011—the Year in Review." Center for Disaster Management and Risk Reduction Technology, Potsdam, Germany. http://reliefweb.int/sites/reliefweb.int/files/resources/Full_Report_3285.pdf.

Das, G. 2000. *India Unbound: The Social and Economic Revolution from Independence to the Global Information Age*. New York: Anchor Books.

Davies, J.E. 2011. "Washington's Growth and Opportunity Act or Beijing's Overarching Brilliance: Will African Governments Choose Neither?" *Third World Quarterly* 32 (6): 1147–1163.

De Hoyos, R., J.M. Martínez de la Calle, and M. Székely. 2009. "Education and Social Mobility in Mexico." Mexico Education Ministry, Mexico City. www.pegnet.ifw-kiel.de/activities/de_hoyos_de_la_calle_szekely2009.pdf. Accessed 15 May 2012.

Deloitte. 2011. "The Connected Archipelago: The Role of the Internet in Indonesia's Economic Development." Deloitte Access Economics, Sydney. www.deloitte.com/view/en_gx/global/bde64a5db2134310VgnVCM1000001a56f00aRCRD.htm. Accessed 15 May 2012.

———. **2012a.** "Lateral Trades, Breathing Fire into the BRICS: China Outbound M&A Activity into Brazil, Russia, India and South Africa." China Services Group, Beijing. www.deloitte.com.mx/documents/BoletinFactorChina/LateralTrades-BreathingFireintotheBRICS-English.pdf. Accessed 21 June 2012.

———. **2012b.** "Turkish Outbound M&A." Corporate Finance, Istanbul. www.deloitte.com/assets/Dcom-Turkey/Local%20Assets/Documents/turkey_tr_mnaoutbound_27012012.pdf. Accessed 10 May 2012.

DeLong, J.B. 2004. "India since Independence: An Analytic Growth Narrative." In D. Rodrik, ed., *Modern Economic Growth: Analytical Country Studies*. Princeton, NJ: Princeton University Press.

Diamond, I., M. Newby, and S. Varle. 1999. "Female Education and Fertility: Examining the Links." In C. Bledsoe, J. Casterline, J. Johnson-Kuhn, and J. Haaga, eds., *Critical Perspectives on Schooling and Fertility in the Developing World*. Washington, DC: National Academy of Science Press.

Dobbs, R., J. Remes, J. Manyika, C. Roxburgh, S. Smit, F. Schaer. 2012. *Urban World: Cities and the Rise of the Consuming Class*. New York: McKinsey Global Institute. www.mckinsey.com/insights/mgi/research/urbanization/

urban_world_cities_and_the_rise_of_the_consuming_class. Accessed 28 August 2012.

Dolan, P., R. Layard, and R. Metcalfe. 2011. *Measuring Subjective Well-Being for Public Policy.* London: UK Office for National Statistics.

Dollar. D. 1992. "Outward-Oriented Developing Countries Really Do Grow More Rapidly: Evidence from 95 LDCs, 1976–85." *Economic Development and Cultural Change* 40 (30): 523–544.

Done, K. 2011. "Embraer Faces Headwinds." *Financial Times*, 10 October.

Drèze, J., and M. Murthi. 1999. "Fertility, Education and Development: Further Evidence from India." Research Paper DEDPS20. London School of Economics, Suntory and Toyota Centres for Economics and Related Disciplines, London, UK.

Duhigg, C., and K. Bradsher. 2012. "How the U.S. Lost Out on iPhone Work." *The New York* Times, 21 January. www.nytimes.com/2012/01/22/business/apple-america-and-a-squeezed-middle-class.html. Accessed 22 January 2012.

Duhigg, C., and S. Greenhouse. 2012. "Electronic Giant Vowing Reforms in China Plants." *The New York Times*, 30 March. www.nytimes.com/2012/03/30/business/apple-supplier-in-china-pledges-changes-in-working-conditions.html. Accessed 15 May 2012.

The Economist. **2011a.** "The Magic of Diasporas." 19 November. www.economist.com/node/21538742. Accessed 15 May 2012.

———. **2011b.** "South-North FDI: Role Reversal." 24 September. www.economist.com/node/21528982. Accessed 15 May 2012.

———. **2012a.** "Indian Takeovers Abroad: Running with the Bulls." 3 March. www.economist.com/node/21548965. Accessed 15 May 2012.

———. **2012b.** "Points of Light." 14 July. www.economist.com/node/21558591. Accessed 4 November 2012.

Edigheji, O. 2010. *Constructing a Democratic Developmental State in South Africa: Potentials and Challenges.* Cape Town: HSRC Press.

Edwards, S. 1998. "Openness, Productivity, and Growth: What Do We Really Know?" *Economic Journal* 108 (447): 383–398.

Elson, D. 2002. "Gender Justice, Human Rights and Neo-liberal Economic Policies." In M. Molyneux and S. Razavi, eds., *Gender Justice, Development and Rights.* Oxford, UK: Oxford University Press.

Engerman, S.L., and K.L. Sokoloff. 2002. *Factor Endowments, Inequality, and Paths of Development among New World Economics.* Working Paper 9259. Cambridge, MA: National Bureau of Economic Research. www.nber.org/papers/w9259. Accessed 15 May 2012.

Essama-Nssah, B. 2011. "Achieving Universal Primary Education through School Fee Abolition: Some Policy Lessons from Uganda." In P. Chuhan-Pole and M. Angwafo, eds., *Yes Africa Can: Success Stories From A Dynamic Continent.* Washington, DC: World Bank. http://siteresources.worldbank.org/AFRICAEXT/Resources/258643-1271798012256/YAC_Consolidated_Web.pdf. Accessed 10 August 2012.

Estevadeordal, A., B. Frantz, and A.M. Taylor. 2003. "The Rise and Fall of World Trade, 1870–1939." *Quarterly Journal of Economics* 2 (118): 359–407.

Evans, P.B. 2010. "Constructing the 21st Century Developmental State: Potentialities and Pitfalls." In O. Edigheji, ed., *Constructing a Democratic Developmental State in South Africa: Potentials and Challenges.* Cape Town: HSRC Press.

Fan, S., B. Nestorova, and T. Olofinbiyi. 2010. "China's Agricultural and Rural Development: Implications for Africa." China—Development Assistance Committee Study Group on Agriculture, Food Security and Rural Development, 27–28 April, Bamako. www.ifpri.org/sites/default/files/publications/chinaafricadac.pdf. Accessed 23 October 2012.

Fan, S., and A. Saurkar. 2006. "Public Spending in Developing Countries: Trends, Determination, and Impact." World Bank, Washington, DC. http://siteresources.worldbank.org/EXTRESPUBEXPANAAGR/Resources/ifpri2.pdf. Accessed 23 October 2012.

Felbermayr, G.J., and B. Jung. 2009. "The Pro-Trade Effect of the Brain Drain: Sorting Out Confounding Factors." *Economics Letters* 104 (2): 72–75.

Fine, D., A. van Wamelen, S. Lund, A. Cabral, M. Taoufiki, N. Dörr, A. Leke, C. Roxburgh, J. Schubert, and P. Cook. 2012. *Africa at Work: Job Creation and Inclusive Growth.* New York: McKinsey Global Institute. www.mckinsey.com/insights/mgi/research/africa_europe_middle_east/africa_at_work. Accessed 23 September 2012.

FitzGerald, V., F. Stewart, and R. Venugopal. 2006. *Globalization, Violent Conflict and Self-Determination.* Basingstoke: UK: Palgrave Macmillan.

Foley, C.F., and W. R. Kerr. 2011. "Ethnic Innovation and U.S. Multinational Firm Activity." Working Paper 12-006. Harvard Business School, Cambridge, MA. www.people.hbs.edu/ffoley/foleykerr.pdf. Accessed 15 May 2012.

Foster, M., and P. Mijumbi. 2002. "How, When and Why Does Poverty Get Budget Priority: Poverty Reduction Strategy and Public Expenditure in Uganda." Case Study 1. Working Paper 163. Overseas Development Institute, London. www.odi.org.uk/resources/docs/2061.pdf. Accessed 15 May 2012.

Frankel, J.A., and D. Romer. 1999. "Does Trade Cause Growth?" *American Economic Review* 89 (3) 379–399.

Frenk, J., O. Gómez-Dantés, and F.M. Knaul. 2009. "The Democratization of Health in Mexico: Financial Innovations for Universal Coverage." *Bulletin of the World Health Organization* 87 (7): 542–548.

Fu, X. 2008. "Foreign Direct Investment, Absorptive Capacity and Regional Innovation Capabilities in China." *Oxford Development Studies* 36 (1): 89–110.

Fukuda-Parr, S. 2003. "The Human Development Paradigm: Operationalizing Sen's Ideas on Capabilities." *Feminist Economics* 19 (2–3): 301–317.

Fukuda Parr, S., C. Lopes, and K. Malik. 2002. "Overview. Institutional Innovations for Capacity Development." In *Capacity for Development: New Solutions to Old Problems.* London: Earthscan.

G8 (Group of Eight). 2005. "The Gleneagles Communiqué: Climate Change, Energy and Sustainable Development." 8 July. www.unglobalcompact.org/docs/about_the_gc/government_support/PostG8_Gleneagles_Communique.pdf. Accessed 15 May 2012.

Gallup. 2012. Gallup World Poll Database. http://worldview.gallup.com. Accessed 15 May 2012.

Galor, O. 2006. "Economic Growth in the Very Long-Run." Working Paper 2006-16. Brown University, Department of Economics, Providence, RI.

Giroux, S.C. 2008. "Child Stunting Across Schooling and Fertility Transitions: Evidence from Sub-Saharan Africa." DHS Working Paper 57. United States Agency for International Development, Washington, DC. http://pdf.usaid.gov/pdf_docs/PNADM570.pdf. Accessed 21 December 2012.

Glennie, J. 2011. "Busan Has Been an Expression of Shifting Geopolitical Realities." *The Guardian*, 2 December. www.guardian.co.uk/global-development/poverty-matters/2011/dec/02/busan-shifting-geopolitical-realities. Accessed 15 May 2012.

Glewwe, P., and A.L. Kassouf. 2008. "The Impact of the Bolsa Escola/Família: Conditional Cash Transfer Program on Enrollment, Grade Promotion and Drop-Out Rates in Brazil." Annals of the 36th Brazilian Economics Meeting of the Brazilian Association of Graduate Programs in Economics. www.anpec.org.br/encontro2008/artigos/200807211140170-.pdf. Accessed 15 May 2012.

Global Footprint Network. 2011. "The National Footprint Accounts, 2011 Edition." Oakland, CA. www.footprintnetwork.org/en/index.php/GFN/page/footprint_data_and_results/. Accessed 15 May 2012.

Gooch, L. 2012. "Seeking the Right to Be Female in Malaysia." *The New York Times,* 5 October. www.nytimes.com/2012/10/06/world/asia/seeking-the-right-to-be-female-in-malaysia.html. Accessed 21 December 2012.

Government of India. 2009. "The Right of Children to Free and Compulsory Education Act, 2009." *The Gazette of India,* 2009: 35.

Grabel, I. 2013. "Financial Architectures and Development: Resilience, Policy Space, and Human Development." Human Development Research Paper. United Nations Development Programme, Human Development Report Office, New York.

Grameen Bank. n.d. "A Short History of Grameen Bank". www.grameen-info.org/index.php?option=com_content&task=view&id=19&Itemid=114. Accessed 15 May 2012.

Green, G. 2010. "Imagine There's No Army." *Diplomat Magazine*, 1 September. www.diplomatmagazine.com/index.php?option=com_content&view=article&id=321&Itemid=. Accessed 15 May 2012.

Guajardo, J., D. Leigh, and A. Pescatori. 2011. "Expansionary Austerity: New International Evidence." Working Paper WP/11/158. International Monetary Fund, Washington, DC. www.imf.org/external/pubs/ft/wp/2011/wp11158.pdf. Accessed 15 May 2012.

Gupta, A., and H. Wang. 2012. "India's Misguided China Anxiety." *Businessweek*, 21 March. www.businessweek.com/printer/articles/14394-indias-misguided-china-anxiety. Accessed 15 May 2012.

Hailu, D., and V. Veras Soares. 2008. "Cash Transfers in Africa and Latin America: An Overview." Poverty in Focus 15. International Poverty Centre for Inclusive Growth, Brasilia.

Hamdani, K. 2013. "The Challenge of the South." Human Development Research Paper. United Nations Development Programme, Human Development Report Office, New York.

Han, S. 2012. "South Korean Parliament Approves Carbon Trading System." *Bloomberg*, 2 May. www.bloomberg

.com/news/2012-05-02/south-korean-parliament-approves-carbon-trading-system.html. Accessed 15 May 2012.

Hansen. R. 2010. "An Assessment of Principal Regional Consultative Processes." Migration Research Series 38. International Organization for Migration, Geneva.

Hanushek, E.A., D. Jamison, E. Jamison, and L. Woessmann. 2008. "Education and Economic Growth." *Education Next*, Spring. http://media.hoover.org/sites/default/files/documents/ednext_20082_62.pdf. Accessed 8 August 2012.

Harding, R. 2012. "Interview: Justin Yifu Lin: Funding Developing World Infrastructure Could Buy Time for Europe to Reform, Hears Robin Harding." *Financial Times*, 6 June.

Harrison, A., and A. Rodriguez-Clare. 2010. "Trade, Foreign Investment and Industrial Policy for Developing Countries." In D. Rodrik and M. Rosenzweig, eds., *Handbook of Development Economics*, Vol. 5. New York: North-Holland.

Harvey, F. 2012. "Doha Climate Change Deal Clears Way for 'Damage Aid' to Poor Nations." *The Observer*, 8 December. www.guardian.co.uk/environment/2012/dec/08/doha-climate-change-deal-nations?intcmp=122. Accessed 8 December 2012.

Hausmann, R., J. Hwang, and D. Rodrik. 2007. "What You Export Matters." *Journal of Economic Growth* 12 (1): 1–25.

Hausmann, R., L. Pritchett, D. Rodrik. 2005. "Growth Accelerations." *Journal of Economic Growth* 10 (4): 303–329.

Hausmann, R., D. Rodrik, and A. Velasco. 2005. "Growth Diagnostics." Harvard University, John F. Kennedy School of Government, Cambridge, MA.

Hausmann, R., and M. Székely. 2001. "Inequality and the Family in Latin America." In N. Birdsall, A.C. Kelley, and S. Sinding, eds., *Population Matters: Demographic Change, Economic Growth, and Poverty in the Developing World*. New York: Oxford University Press.

Hazard, E., L. De Vries, M.A. Barry, A.A. Anouan, and N. Pinaud. 2009. "The Developmental Impact of the Asian Drivers in Senegal." *World Economy* 32 (11): 1563–1585.

Heilmann, S. 2008. "Policy Experiments in China's Economic Rise." *Studies in Comparative International Development* 43 (1): 1–26.

Heller, P. 2013. "Civil Society and Social Movements in a Globalizing World." Human Development Research Paper. United Nations Development Programme, Human Development Report Office, New York.

Hiemstra-van der Horst, G. 2011. "We Are Scared to Say No: Facing Foreign Timber Companies in Sierra Leone's Community Woodlands." *Journal of Development Studies* 47 (4): 574–594.

HM Treasury. 2010. *Spending Review*. London. http://cdn.hm-treasury.gov.uk/sr2010_completereport.pdf. Accessed 15 May 2012.

Hoff, K. 2003. "Paths of Institutional Development: A View from Economic History." *World Bank Research Observer* 18 (2): 205–226.

Holland, D., and K. Portes. 2012. "Self-Defeating Austerity?" *National Institute Economic Review* 222 (1): F4–F10.

Hook, L. 2012. "China's Post-90 Generation Make their Mark." *The Financial Times*, 9 July. www.ft.com/intl/

cms/s/0/4fcbab6c-c67d-11e1-963a-00144feabdc0.html. Accessed 15 July 2012.

Hook, L., and P. Clark. 2012. "China's Wind Groups Pick up Speed." *The Financial Times*, 15 July. www.ft.com/intl/cms/s/0/fb4bc872-c674-11e1-963a-00144feabdc0.html. Accessed 15 July 2012.

Hori, T. 2011. "Educational Gender Inequality and Inverted U-Shaped Fertility Dynamics." *Japanese Economic Review* 62 (1): 126–150.

Howell, J. 2004. *Governance in China*. Lanham, MA: Rowman & Littlefield.

Huntington, S. 1968. *Political Order in Changing Societies*. Fredericksburg, VA: BookCrafters, Inc.

Hussain, A., and N. Stern. 2006. "Public Finance: The Role of the State and Economic Transformation in China: 1978–2020." *Comparative Studies* 26: 25–55.

Hvistendahl, M. 2011. "Unnatural Selection." *Psychology Today*, 5 July. www.psychologytoday.com/articles/201107/unnatural-selection. Accessed 24 July 2012.

ICTSD (International Centre for Trade and Sustainable Development). 2011. "Brazil Pushes Forward with Currency Discussion at WTO." *Bridges Weekly Trade News Digest* 15 (32): 5–7. http://ictsd.org/i/news/bridgesweekly/114573/.

IIASA (International Institute for Applied Systems Analysis). 2008. "Economic Growth in Developing Countries: Education Proves Key." Policy Brief 03. Laxenburg, Austria. www.iiasa.ac.at/Admin/PUB/policy-briefs/pb03-web.pdf. Accessed 4 June 2012.

Iley, R.A., and M.K. Lewis. 2011. "Has the Global Financial Crisis Produced a New World Order?" *Accounting Forum* 35 (2): 90–103.

ILO (International Labour Organization). 2012. *World of Work Report 2012: Better Jobs for a Better Economy*. Geneva. www.ilo.org/wcmsp5/groups/public/---dgreports/---dcomm/---publ/documents/publication/wcms_179453.pdf. Accessed 4 June 2012.

IMF (International Monetary Fund). 2010. "IMF Executive Board Approves Major Overhaul of Quotas and Governance." Press release 10/418. Washington, DC. www.imf.org/external/np/sec/pr/2010/pr10418.htm. Accessed 15 May 2012.

———. 2011a. "New Growth Drivers for Low-Income Countries: The Role of BRICs." Strategy, Policy, and Review Department, Washington, DC. www.imf.org/external/np/pp/eng/2011/011211.pdf. Accessed 15 May 2012.

———. 2011b. *World Economic Outlook*. Washington, DC. www.imf.org/external/pubs/ft/weo/2011/02/. Accessed 15 May 2012.

India Ministry of External Affairs. 2012. "Fourth BRICS Summit – Delhi Declaration." 29 March. New Delhi. www.mea.gov.in/mystart.php?id=190019162. Accessed 15 May 2012.

India Ministry of Finance. 2012. "Human Development." In *Economic Survey 2011–2012*. New Delhi. www.indiabudget.nic.in/es2011-12/echap-13.pdf. Accessed 15 May 2012.

Institute for Economics and Peace. 2012. "Global Peace Index Fact Sheet." Sydney. www.visionofhumanity.org/wp-content/uploads/2012/06/2012GPI-Fact-Sheet2.pdf. Accessed 28 August 2012

IPCC (Intergovernmental Panel on Climate Change). 2012. *Managing the Risks of Extreme Events and*

Disasters to Advance Climate Change Adaptation. Special Report of the Intergovernmental Panel on Climate Change. Cambridge, UK: Cambridge University Press. http://ipcc-wg2.gov/SREX/images/uploads/SREX-All_FINAL.pdf. Accessed 15 May 2012.

Islam, I. 2002. "Poverty, Employment and Wages: An Indonesian Perspective." International Labour Organization, Recovery and Reconstruction Department, Geneva.

ITU (International Telecommunications Union). 2012. World Telecommunication/ICT Indicators Database. www.itu.int/ITU-D/ict/statistics/. Accessed 15 May 2012.

Ivanov, A., M. Collins, C. Grosu. J. Kling, S. Milcher, N. O'Higgins, B. Slay, and A. Zhelyazkova. 2006. *At Risk: Roma and the Displaced in Southeast Europe*. Bratislava: United Nations Development Programme Regional Bureau for Europe and the Commonwealth of Independent States.

Ivanov, A., K. Mizsei, B. Slay, D. Mihailov, and N. O'Higgins. 2003. *Avoiding the Dependency Trap: The Roma Human Development Report*. Bratislava: United Nations Development Programme Regional Bureau for Europe and the Commonwealth of Independent States.

Iyer, L. 2009. "The Bloody Millennium: Internal Conflict in South Asia." Working Paper 09-086. Harvard Business School, Cambridge, MA. www.hbs.edu/research/pdf/09-086.pdf. Accessed 15 May 2012.

Jacob, R. 2012. "Flagging Western Demand Drives China's Exporters to New Markets." *Financial Times*, 13 June. www.ftchinese.com/story/001045040/en/. Accessed 15 May 2012.

Jenkins, J.C., and M. Wallace. 1996. "The Generalized Action Potential of Protest Movements: The New Class, Social Trends and Political Exclusion Explanations." *Sociological Forum* 11 (2): 183–207.

Jenkins, R., and A. Barbosa. 2012. "Fear for Manufacturing? China and the Future of Industry in Brazil and Latin America." *The China Quarterly* 209: 59–81.

Jones, R., and H. Kierzkowski. 2001. "Horizontal Aspects of Vertical Fragmentation." In L. Cheng and H. Kierzkowski, eds., *Global Production and Trade in East Asia*. Norwell, MA: Kluwer Academic Publishers.

Justino, P. 2008. "Tackling Civil Unrest: Policing or Redistribution?" MICROCON Policy Briefing Paper 2. Institute of Development Studies, Brighton, UK. http://papers.ssrn.com/sol3/papers.cfm?abstract_id=1141142&http://papers.ssrn.com/sol3/papers.cfm?abstract_id=1141142. Accessed 15 May 2012.

Kabananukye, K. I. B., A. E.K. Kanbananukye, J. Krishnamurty, and D. Owomugasho. 2004. "Economic Growth, Employment, Poverty and Pro-Poor Policies in Uganda." Issues in Employment and Poverty Discussion Paper 16. International Labour Organization, Geneva. www.ilo.org/employment/Whatwedo/Publications/WCMS_120732/lang--en/index.htm. Accessed 24 September 2012.

Kabeer, N., and S. Mahmud. 2004. "Rags, Riches and Women Workers: Export Oriented Garment Manufacturing in Bangladesh." In M. Carr, ed., *Chains of Fortune: Linking Women Producers and Workers with Global Markets*. London: Commonwealth Secretariat.

Kahneman, D., and A. Krueger. 2006. "Developments in the Measurement of Subjective Well-Being." *Journal of Economic Perspectives* 20 (21): 3–24.

Kamau, P., D. McCormick, and N. Pinaud. 2009. "The Developmental Impact of Asian Drivers on Kenya with Emphasis on Textiles and Clothing Manufacturing." *World Economy* 32 (11): 1586–1612.

Kaminski, B., and F. Ng. 2006. "Turkey's Evolving Trade Integration into Pan-European Markets." Working Paper 3908. World Bank, Development Research Group, Washington, DC. http://papers.ssrn.com/sol3/papers.cfm?abstract_id=1294804. Accessed 15 May 2012.

Kanbur, R. 2004. "Growth, Inequality and Poverty: Some Hard Questions." Commentary prepared for the State of the World Conference at the Princeton Institute for International and Regional Studies, 13–14 February, Princeton, NJ. www.arts.cornell.edu/poverty/kanbur/GroIneqPov.pdf. Accessed 15 May 2012.

Kaplinsky, R. 2008. "What Does the Rise of China do for Industrialisation in Sub-Saharan Africa?" *Review of African Political Economy* 35 (1): 7–22.

Kaplinsky, R., and M. Morris. 2009. "The Asian Drivers and SSA: Is There a Future for Export-Oriented African Industrialization?" *The World Economy* 32 (11): 1638–1655.

Kaplinsky, R., A. Terheggen, and J. Tijaja. 2011. "China as a Final Market: The Gabon Timber and Thai Cassava Value Chains." *World Development* 39 (7): 1177–1190.

Karimuddin, A. 2011. "MarkPlus Insight Survey: Indonesia Has 55 Million Internet Users." *DailySocial.net*, 1 November. http://dailysocial.net/en/2011/11/01/markplus-insight-survey-indonesia-has-55-million-internet-users/. Accessed 15 May 2012.

Kaul, I. 2013. "The Rise of the Global South: Implications for the Provisioning of Global Public Goods." Human Development Research Paper. United Nations Development Programme, Human Development Report Office, New York.

Keohane, R., and D. Victor. 2010. "The Regime Complex for Climate Change." Discussion Paper 10-33. Harvard University, John F. Kennedy School of Government, Harvard Project on International Climate Agreements. http://belfercenter.ksg.harvard.edu/files/Keohane_Victor_Final_2.pdf. Accessed 15 May 2012.

Keynes, J.M. 1937. "How to Avoid a Slump." *The Times*, 12–14 January. Reprinted in *The Collected Writings of John Maynard Keynes* Vol. 21. London: Macmillan.

Khan, A.R. 2005. "Growth, Employment and Poverty: An Analysis of the Vital Nexus Based on Some Recent UNDP and ILO/SIDA Studies." Issues in Employment and Poverty Discussion Paper 19. International Labour Office, Geneva. www.ilo.org/wcmsp5/groups/public/---ed_emp/documents/publication/wcms_120683.pdf. Accessed 24 September 2012.

Kharas, H., K. Makino, and W. Jung, eds. 2011. *Catalyzing Development: A New Vision of Aid.* Washington, DC: Brookings Institution Press.

King, D., K. Richards, and S. Tyldesley. 2011. "International Climate Change Negotiations: Key Lessons and Next Steps." University of Oxford, Smith School of Enterprise and the Environment, UK. www.smithschool.ox.ac.uk/wp-content/uploads/2011/03/Climate-Negotiations-report_Final.pdf. Accessed 15 May 2012.

Kraemer, K., G. Linden, and J. Dedrick. 2011. "Capturing Value in Global Networks: Apple's iPad and iPhone." University of California, Irvine, University of California, Berkeley, and Syracuse University, NY. http://pcic.merage.uci.edu/papers/2011/Value_iPad_iPhone.pdf. Accessed 15 May 2012.

Kragelund, P. 2013. "New Development Partnerships." Human Development Research Paper. United Nations Development Programme, Human Development Report Office, New York.

Krueger, A.B., and D.A. Schkade. 2008. "The Reliability of Subjective Well-Being Measures." *Journal of Public Economics* 92 (8–9): 1833–1845.

Krugman, P. 1991. "The Move Towards Free Trade Zones." Symposium of the Federal Reserve Bank of Kansas City, 22–24 August, Jackson Hole, WY. www.kansascityfed.org/publicat/sympos/1991/S91krugm.pdf. Accessed 23 October 2012.

Kugler, M., and H. Rapoport. 2011. "Migration, FDI, and the Margins of Trade." Working Paper 222. Harvard University, Center for International Development, Cambridge, MA.

LaFraniere, S. 2011. "Five Days Later, Chinese Concede Design Flaw Had Role in Wreck." *The New York Times*, 28 July. www.nytimes.com/2011/07/29/world/asia/29trains.html. Accessed 15 May 2012.

Lamberte, M., and P.J. Morgan. 2012. "Regional and Global Monetary Cooperation." Working Paper 346. Asian Development Bank Institute, Tokyo. www.adbi.org/working-paper/2012/02/21/5006.regional.global.monetary.cooperation/. Accessed 15 May 2012.

Lautier, M. 2008. "Export of Health Services from Developing Countries: The Case of Tunisia." *Social Science and Medicine* 67: 101–110.

Leape, J. 2012. "It's Happening, But Not in Rio." *The New York Times*, 24 June. www.nytimes.com/2012/06/25/opinion/action-is-happening-but-not-in-rio.html. Accessed 24 June 2012

Li, J. 2010. "Decarbonising Power Generation in China—Is the Answer Blowing in the Wind?" *Renewable and Sustainable Energy Reviews* 14 (4): 1154–1171.

López-Calva, L., and N. Lustig, eds. 2010. *Declining Inequality in Latin America: A Decade of Progress?* Harrisonburg, VA: RR Donnelley.

Luedi, T. 2008. "China's Track Record in M&A." *McKinsey Quarterly*, June. www.mckinseyquarterly.com/Chinas_track_record_in_MA_2151. Accessed 15 May 2012.

Lutz, W., and S. KC. 2013. "Demography and Human Development: Education and Population Projections." Human Development Research Paper. United Nations Development Programme, Human Development Report Office, New York.

Maddison, A. 2010. Statistics on World Population, GDP and Per Capita GDP, 1–2008 AD. Groningen Growth and Development Centre, The Netherlands. www.ggdc.net/MADDISON/oriindex.htm. Accessed 15 May 2012.

Malik, M. 2006. "Bilateral Investment Treaties of South Asian States: Implications for Development." United Nations Development Programme, Asia-Pacific Trade and Investment Initiative, Colombo.

———. **2012.** *Why Has China Grown So Fast For So Long?* New Delhi: Oxford University Press India.

Martin, T.C., and F. Juarez. 1995. "The Impact of Women's Education on Fertility in Latin America: Searching for Explanations." *International Family Planning Perspectives* 12 (2): 52–57, 80.

Milanović, B. 2009. "Global Inequality and the Global Inequality Extraction Ratio." Policy Research Working Paper 5044. World Bank, Development Research Group, Poverty and Inequality Team, Washington, DC. http://www-wds.worldbank.org/servlet/WDSContentServer/WDSP/IB/2009/09/09/000158349_20090909092401/Rendered/PDF/WPS5044.pdf. Accessed 15 May 2012.

———. **2010.** *The Haves and the Have-Nots: A Brief and Idiosyncratic History of Global Inequality.* New York: Basic Books.

Milanović, B., and S. Yitzhaki. 2002. "Decomposing World Income Distribution: Does the World Have a Middle Class?" *Review of Income and Wealth* 48(2): 155–178.

Moyo, D. 2012. "Beijing, a Boon for Africa." *The New York Times*, 27 June. www.nytimes.com/2012/06/28/opinion/beijing-a-boon-for-africa.html. Accessed 28 August 2012.

Mwase, N., and Y. Yang. 2012. "BRICs' Philosophies for Development Financing and Their Implications for LICs." Working Paper WP/12/74. International Monetary Fund, Washington, DC.

Nagel, T. 1974. "What Is It Like To Be a Bat?" *The Philosophical Review* 83 (4): 435–450.

Naqvi, H., and V.V. Acharya. 2012. "Bank Liquidity and Bubbles: Why Central Banks Should Lean Against Liquidity. In D. Evanoff, G. Kaufman, and A.G. Malliaris, eds., *New Perspectives on Asset Price Bubbles: Theory, Evidence and Policy.* Oxford, UK: Oxford University Press.

Nayyar, D. 2012. "Macroeconomics and Human Development." *Journal of Human Development and Capabilities* 13 (1): 7–30.

NEAC (Malaysia National Economic Advisory Council). 2010. "New Economic Model for Malaysia, Parts 1 and 2." Kuala Lumpur.

Nielsen H., and A. Spenceley. 2011. "The Success of Tourism in Rwanda: Gorillas and More." In P. Chuhan-Pole and M. Angwafo, eds., *Yes Africa Can: Success Stories from a Dynamic Continent.* Washington, DC: World Bank. http://siteresources.worldbank.org/AFRICAEXT/Resources/258643-1271798012256/YAC_Consolidated_Web.pdf. Accessed 10 August 2012.

Ocampo, J.A. 2010. "Rethinking Global Economic and Social Governance." *Journal of Globalization and Development* 1 (1).

Ocampo J.A., S. Griffith-Jones, A. Noman, A. Ortiz, J. Vallejo, and J. Tyson. 2010. "The Great Recession and the Developing World." Paper presented at the conference on Development Cooperation in Times of Crisis and on Achieving the MDGs, 9–10 June, Madrid.

Ocampo, J.A., and D. Titelman. 2009. "Subregional Financial Cooperation: the South American Experience." *Journal of Post-Keynesian Economics* 32 (2): 249–68.

———. **2012.** "Regional Monetary Cooperation in Latin America." Columbia University, Initiative for Policy Dialogue, New York, and United Nations Economic Commission for Latin America and the Caribbean, Financing for Development Division, Santiago.

OECD (Organisation for Economic Co-operation and Development). 2006. *Promoting Pro-Poor Growth: Agriculture.* Paris. www.oecd.org/dac/povertyreduction/37922155.pdf. Accessed 23 October 2012.

———. **2007.** "Economic Survey of India, 2007." *OECD Observer*, October. Policy Brief. www.oecd.org/economy/

economicsurveysandcountrysurveillance/39452196.pdf. Accessed 6 August 2012.

———. 2010a. *Perspectives on Global Development 2010: Shifting Wealth*. Paris.

———. 2010b. *PISA 2009 Results: What Students Know and Can Do*. Vol. I. Paris. www.oecd.org/dataoecd/10/61/48852548.pdf. Accessed 24 July 2012.

———. 2011a. "Brazil." In *Agricultural Policy Monitoring and Evaluation 2011*. Paris. www.oecd-ilibrary.org/agriculture-and-food/agricultural-policy-monitoring-and-evaluation-2011/brazil_agr_pol-2011-22-en. Accessed 23 October 2012.

———. 2011b. *Divided We Stand: Why Inequality Keeps Rising*. Paris.

———. 2011c. "Busan Partnership for Effective Development Cooperation." Paris. www.oecd.org/dac/aideffectiveness/busanpartnership.htm. Accessed 24 July 2011.

Ofosu-Asare, K. 2011. "Mobile Phone Revolution in Ghana's Cocoa Industry." *International Journal of Business and Social Science* 2 (13): 91–99.

Osmani, S.R. 2005. "The Employment Nexus between Growth and Poverty: An Asian Perspective." Swedish International Development Cooperation Agency, Stockholm.

Osmani, S.R., W. Mahmud, B. Sen, H. Dagdeviren, and A. Seth. 2006. "The Macroeconomics of Poverty Reduction: The Case Study of Bangladesh." United Nations Development Programme, Asia-Pacific Regional Programme on the Macroeconomics of Poverty Reduction, New York.

Pardee Center for International Futures. 2013. "Development-Oriented Policies and Alternative Human Development Paths." Background paper for the 2013 *Human Development Report*. United Nations Development Programme, Human Development Report Office, New York.

Park, K. 2011. "New Development Partners and a Global Development Partnership." In H. Kharas, K. Makino, and W. Jung, eds., *Catalyzing Development: A New Vision for Aid*. Washington, DC: Brookings Institution Press.

Pasha, H.A., and T. Palanivel. 2004. "Pro-Poor Growth and Policies: The Asian Experience." United Nations Development Programme, Asia-Pacific Regional Programme on the Macroeconomics of Poverty Reduction, New York.

Pinker, S. 2011. "Violence Vanquished." *The Wall Street Journal*, 24 September. http://online.wsj.com/article/SB10001424053111904106704576583203589408180.html. Accessed 15 May 2012.

Polanyi, K. 1944. *The Great Transformation*. New York: Rinehart.

Population Reference Bureau. 2000. "Is Education the Best Contraceptive?" Policy Brief. Population Reference Bureau, Washington, DC. www.prb.org/Publications/PolicyBriefs/IsEducationtheBestContraceptive.aspx. Accessed 15 May 2012.

Psacharopoulos G., and Z. Tzannatos. 1992. "Latin American Women's Earnings and Participation in the Labor Force." Working Paper 856. World Bank, Washington, DC. http://econ.worldbank.org/external/default/main?pagePK=64165259&theSitePK=469372&piPK=64165421&menuPK=64166322&entityID=000009265_3961002093302. Accessed 15 May 2012.

Radelet, S., J. Sachs, and J.-W., Lee. 1997. "Economic Growth in Asia." Development Discussion Paper 609. Harvard Institute for International Development, Cambridge, MA.

Ranis, G., and F. Stewart. 2005. "Dynamic Links Between the Economy and Human Development." Working Paper 8. United Nations Department of Economic and Social Affairs, New York. www.un.org/esa/desa/papers/2005/wp8_2005.pdf. Accessed 15 May 2012.

Ratha, D., and W. Shaw. 2007. "South-South Migration and Remittances." Working Paper 102. World Bank, Washington, DC. http://siteresources.worldbank.org/INTPROSPECTS/Resources/334934-1110315015165/SouthSouthMigrationandRemittances.pdf. Accessed 15 May 2012.

Ravallion, M. 2009. "A Comparative Perspective on Poverty Reduction in Brazil, China and India." Policy Research Working Paper 5080. World Bank, Washington, DC. http://econ.worldbank.org/external/default/main?pagePK=64165259&theSitePK=469382&piPK=64165421&menuPK=64166093&entityID=000158349_20091130085835. Accessed 15 May 2012.

REN21 (Renewable Energy Policy Network for the 21st Century). 2012. *Renewables Global Status Report*. Paris. www.map.ren21.net/GSR/GSR2012.pdf. Accessed 15 May 2012.

Reserve Bank of India. 2012. "Reserve Bank of India Announces SAARC Swap Arrangement." Press Release, 16 May. Mumbai. www.rbi.org.in/scripts/BS_PressRelease Display.aspx?prid=26475. Accessed 15 May 2012.

Revkin, A. 2012. "Beyond Rio: Pursuing 'Ecological Citizenship.'" *The New York Times*, 25 June. http://dotearth.blogs.nytimes.com/2012/06/25/beyond-rio-pursuing-ecological-citizenship/. Accessed 25 June 2012.

Ribas, R., V. Veras Soares, and G. Hirata. 2008. "The Impact of CCTs: What We Know and What We Are Not Sure About." Poverty in Focus 15. International Poverty Centre for Inclusive Growth, Brasilia.

Rockström, J., W. Steffen, K. Noone, Å. Persson, F.S. Chapin, III, E. Lambin, T.M. Lenton, M. Scheffer, C. Folke, H. Schellnhuber, B. Nykvist, C.A. De Wit, T. Hughes, S. van der Leeuw, H. Rodhe, S. Sörlin, P.K. Snyder, R. Costanza, U. Svedin, M. Falkenmark, L. Karlberg, R.W. Corell, V.J. Fabry, J. Hansen, B. Walker, D. Liverman, K. Richardson, P. Crutzen, and J. Foley. 2009. "Planetary Boundaries: Exploring the Safe Operating Space for Humanity." *Ecology and Society* 14 (2). www.ecologyandsociety.org/vol14/iss2/art32/. Accessed 15 May 2012.

Rodriguez, F., and D. Rodrik. 2001. "Trade Policy and Economic Growth: A Skeptic's Guide to the Cross-National Evidence." *NBER Macroeconomics Annual 2000* 15: 261–338.

Rodrik, D. 1998. *Democracies Pay Higher Wages*. Working Paper 6364. Cambridge, MA: National Bureau of Economic Research.

———. 2001. "The Global Governance of Trade as if Development Really Mattered." Background Paper prepared for the United Nations Development Programme. www.wcfia.harvard.edu/sites/default/files/529__Rodrik5.pdf. Accessed 6 August 2012.

———. 2004. "Industrial Policy for the Twenty-first Century." Draft prepared for the United Nations Industrial

Development Organization. Harvard University, John F. Kennedy School of Government, Cambridge, MA. www.hks.harvard.edu/fs/drodrik/Research%20papers/UNIDOSep.pdf. Accessed 6 August 2012.

———. 2005. "Notes on Trade and Industrialization Policy, in Turkey and Elsewhere." *METU Studies in Development* 32 (1): 259–274.

———. 2006. *The Social Cost of Foreign Exchange Reserves*. Working Paper 11952. Cambridge, MA: National Bureau of Economic Research. www.nber.org/papers/w11952. Accessed 15 May 2012.

———. 2011. *The Globalization Paradox: Democracy and the Future of the World Economy*. New York: W.W. Norton.

———. 2012. "Global Poverty amid Global Plenty: Getting Globalization Right." *Americas Quarterly*, Spring: 40–45.

Romero, S. 2012. "Brazil Gains Business and Influence as It Offers Aid and Loans in Africa." *The New York Times*, 7 August. www.nytimes.com/2012/08/08/world/americas/brazil-gains-in-reaching-out-to-africa.html. Accessed 8 August 2012.

Romero, S., and J.M. Broder. 2012. "Progress on the Sidelines as Rio Conference Ends." *The New York Times*, 23 June. www.nytimes.com/2012/06/24/world/americas/rio20-conference-ends-with-some-progress-on-the-sidelines.html. Accessed 4 November 2012.

Rose, P. 1995. "Female Education and Adjustment Programs: A Cross-Country Statistical Analysis." *World Development* 23 (11): 1931–1949.

Rosenfeld, R., S. Messner, and E. Baumer. 2001. "Social Capital and Homicide." *Social Forces* 80 (1): 283–310.

Sachs, J.D., and A. Warner. 1995. "Economic Reform and the Process of Global Integration." *Brookings Papers on Economic Activity* 1: 1–118.

Sala-i-Martin, X. 2006. "The World Distribution of Income: Falling Poverty and . . . Convergence, Period." *Quarterly Journal of Economics* 121 (2): 351–397.

Samake, I., and Y. Yang. 2011. "Low-Income Countries' BRIC Linkage: Are There Growth Spillovers?" Working Paper 11/267. International Monetary Fund, Washington, DC. www.imf.org/external/pubs/ft/wp/2011/wp11267.pdf. Accessed 15 May 2012.

Sen, A. 2007. "Unity and Discord in Social Development." Keynote lecture delivered at the 15th Symposium of the International Consortium for Social Development at the Polytechnic University of Hong Kong, 16–20 July, Hong Kong, China (SAR).

———. 2012. "A Crisis of European Democracy." *The New York Times*, 22 May. www.nytimes.com/2012/05/23/opinion/the-crisis-of-european-democracy.html. Accessed 15 July 2012.

Serbessa, D.D. 2002. "Differential Impact of Women's Educational Level on Fertility in Africa: The Case of Ethiopia." Hiroshima University, Japan. http://home.hiroshima-u.ac.jp/cice/e-forum/69Differential%20Impact%20Ed%20on%20Pop%20_Final_.pdf. Accessed 15 May 2012.

Serra, N., and J. E. Stiglitz. 2008. *The Washington Consensus Reconsidered: Towards a New Global Governance*. Oxford, UK: Oxford University Press.

Sharma, R. 2012. *Breakout Nations: In Pursuit of the Next Economic Miracles*. New York: W.W. Norton.

Sivananthiran, A., and C.S. Venkata Ratnam, eds. 2005. *Informal Economy: The Growing Challenge for*

Labor Administration. Geneva: International Labour Office.

Smith, A. 1776. *An Inquiry into the Nature and Causes of the Wealth of Nations*. New York: Modern Library.

Sobhan, R. 2010. *Challenging the Injustice of Poverty*. Washington, DC: Sage.

———. 2013. "Commentary on Financial Architectures and Development: Resilience, Policy Space, and Human Development in the Global South by Prof. Ilene Grabel." Human Development Research Paper. United Nations Development Programme, Human Development Report Office, New York.

Socialbakers.com. 2012. Facebook Statistics by Country. www.socialbakers.com/facebook-statistics/. Accessed 15 May 2012.

Sonobe, T., J.E. Akoten, and K. Otsuka. 2009. "An Exploration into the Successful Development of the Leather-Shoe Industry in Ethiopia." *Review of Development Economics* 13 (4): 719–736.

South Commission. 1990. *The Challenge to the South: The Report of the South Commission*. Oxford, UK: Oxford University Press. www.southcentre.org/files/Old%20 Books/The%20Challenge%20to%20the%20Southresized. pdf. Accessed 23 October 2012.

Ssewanyana, S., J.M. Matovu, and E. Twimukye. 2011. "Building on Growth in Uganda." In P. Chuhan-Pole and M. Angwafo, eds., *Yes Africa Can: Success Stories From A Dynamic Continent*. Washington, DC: World Bank. http://siteresources.worldbank.org/AFRICAEXT/ Resources/258643-1271798012256/YAC_Consolidated_ Web.pdf. Accessed 10 August 2012.

Stads, G.-J., and N.M. Beintema. 2009. *Public Agricultural Research in Latin America and the Caribbean: Investment and Capacity Trends*. ASTI Synthesis Report. Washington: International Food Policy Research Institute. www.asti. cgiar.org/pdf/LAC_Syn_Report.pdf. Accessed 23 October 2012.

Stern, N. 2003. "Public Policy for Growth and Poverty Reduction." *CESifo Economic Studies* 49 (1): 5–25.

———. 2006. *The Stern Review Report on the Economics of Climate Change*. Cambridge, UK: Cambridge University Press.

Stewart, F. 2013. "Capabilities and Human Development: Beyond the Individual: The Critical Role of Social Institutions and Social Competencies." Human Development Research Paper. United Nations Development Programme, Human Development Report Office, New York.

Stiglitz, J.E. 2012. "Macroeconomic Fluctuations, Inequality, and Human Development." *Journal of Human Development and Capabilities* 13 (1): 31–58.

Stiglitz, J.E., A. Sen, and J.-P. Fitoussi. 2009. *Report by the Commission on the Measurement of Economic Performance and Social Progress*. Paris: Commission on the Measurement of Economic Performance and Social Progress.

Subramanian, A., and D. Roy. 2001. "Who Can Explain the Mauritian Miracle: Meade, Romer, Sachs, or Rodrik?" Working Paper 01/116. International Monetary Fund, Washington, DC. www.imf.org/external/pubs/cat/longres. cfm?sk=15215.0. Accessed 15 May 2012.

Supreme Court of India. 2012. "Society for Un-aided Private Schools of Rajasthan Petitioner(s) versus U.O.I. &

Anr." Supreme Court judgement of 12 April 2012 on Writ Petition (C) No. 95 of 2010.

Suri, T., M.A. Boozer, G. Ranis, and F. Stewart. 2011. "Paths to Success: The Relationship between Human Development and Economic Growth." *World Development* 39 (4): 506–522.

Tangcharoensathien, V., W. Patcharanarumol, P. Ir, S.M. Aljunid, A.G. Mukti, K. Akkhavong, E. Banzon, D.B. Huong, H. Thabrany, and A. Mills. 2011. "Health-Financing Reforms in Southeast Asia: Challenges in Achieving Universal Coverage." *The Lancet* 377 (9768): 863–873.

Taylor, C.E., J.S. Newman, and N.U. Kelly. 1976. "The Child Survival Hypothesis." *Population Studies* 30 (2): 263–278.

Tejada, C. 2012. "China Cancels Waste Project after Protests Turn Violent." *Wall Street Journal*, 28 July. http://business .newsplurk.com/2012/07/china-cancels-waste-project -after.html. Accessed 21 December 2012.

Thorp, R., and M. Paredes. 2011. *Ethnicity and the Persistence of Inequality: The Case of Peru*. Basingstoke, UK: Palgrave Macmillan.

Tomlinson, B.R. 2003. "What Was the Third World?" *Journal of Contemporary History* 38 (2): 307–321.

Tsounta, E. 2009. "Universal Health Care 101: Lessons from the Eastern Caribbean and Beyond." Working Paper WP/09/61. International Monetary Fund, Washington, DC. www.imf.org/external/pubs/ft/wp/2009/wp0961.pdf. Accessed 15 May 2012.

UNCTAD (United Nations Conference on Trade and Development). 2003. *World Investment Report 2003: FDI Policies for Development: National and International Perspectives*. New York and Geneva.

———. 2006. *A Case Study of the Salmon Industry in Chile*. New York and Geneva. http://unctad.org/en/docs/ iteiit200512_en.pdf. Accessed 15 May 2012.

———. 2011a. World Investment Report 2011 Annex Tables. http://archive.unctad.org/Templates/Page. asp?intItemID=5823&lang=1. Accessed 15 May 2012.

———. 2011b. "South-South Integration Is Key to Rebalancing the Global Economy." Policy Brief 22. United Nations Conference on Trade and Development, Geneva. http://unctad.org/en/Docs/presspb20114_en.pdf. Accessed 2 November 2012.

UNDESA (United Nations Department of Economic and Social Affairs). 2007. *World Economic and Social Survey 2007: Development in an Ageing World*. New York: United Nations Publications.

———. 2010. *Development Cooperation for the MDGs: Maximizing Results*. New York: United Nations.

UNDP (United Nations Development Programme). 1991. *Human Development Report 1991*. New York: Oxford University Press.

———. 1993. *Human Development Report 1993*. New York: Oxford University Press.

———. 1994. *Human Development Report 1994*. New York: Oxford University Press.

———. 1995. *Human Development Report 1995*. New York: Oxford University Press.

———. 1996. *Human Development Report 1996*. New York: Oxford University Press.

———. 2008. *China Human Development Report 2007/08: Access for All: Basic Public Services for 1.3 Billion People*. Beijing: China Translation and Publishing Corporation.

———. 2009. *Human Development Report 2009: Overcoming Barriers: Human Mobility and Development*. New York: Palgrave Macmillan.

———. 2010a. *Human Development Report 2010: The Real Wealth of Nations: Pathways to Human Development*. New York: Oxford University Press.

———. 2010b. *Regional Human Development Report for Latin America and the Caribbean 2010: Acting on the Future: Breaking the Intergenerational Transmission of Inequality*. New York.

———. 2010c. *China Human Development Report 2009/10: China and A Sustainable Future: Towards a Low Carbon Economy and Society*. Beijing: China Translation and Publishing Corporation.

———. 2011a. *Human Development Report 2011: Sustainability and Equality: A Better Future for All*. New York: Palgrave Macmillian

———. 2011b. *Regional Human Development Report: Beyond Transition: Towards Inclusive Societies*. Bratislava.

———. 2012. *Caribbean Human Development Report 2012: Human Development and the Shift to Better Citizen Security*. New York.

UNESCAP (United Nations Economic and Social Commission for Asia and the Pacific). 2011. *The Promise of Protection: Social Protection and Development in Asia and the Pacific*. Bangkok.

UNESCO (United Nations Educational, Scientific, and Cultural Organization) Institute for Statistics. Various years. Data Centre. http://stats.uis.unesco.org. Accessed 15 May 2012.

UNIDO (United Nations Industrial Development Organization). 2009. *Industrial Development Report 2009: Breaking In and Moving Up: New Industrial Challenges for the Bottom Billion and the Middle-Income Countries*. Vienna.

United Kingdom, Office of the Deputy Prime Minister, Social Exclusion Unit. 2002. "Reducing Re-Offending by Ex-Prisoners." London. www.thelearningjourney.co.uk/ file.2007-10-01.1714894439/file_view. Accessed 15 May 2012.

United Nations. 2012a. "The State of South-South Cooperation: Report of the Secretary-General." Sixty-Seventh Session of the General Assembly. New York.

———. 2012b. *The Millennium Development Goals Report 2012*. New York. www.un.org/millenniumgoals/pdf/ MDG%20Report%202012.pdf. Accessed 15 May 2012.

United Nations Enable. 2012. "Factsheet on Persons with Disabilities." www.un.org/disabilities/default.asp?id=18. Accessed 24 July 2012.

United Nations Office for Disaster Risk Reduction. 2009. "Terminology." Geneva. www.unisdr.org/we/inform/ terminology. Accessed 8 December 2012.

United Nations Secretary-General's High Level Panel on Global Sustainability. 2012. *Resilient People, Resilient Planet: A Future Worth Choosing*. New York: United Nations.

United Nations Security Council. 2011. "Letter Dated 9 November 2011 from the Permanent Representative of Brazil to the United Nations Addressed to the

Secretary-General." Sixty-Sixth Session, Agenda Items 14 and 117. UN-Doc A/66/551-S/2011/701. www.un.int/brazil/speech/Concept-Paper-%20RwP.pdf. Accessed 15 May 2012.

UNODC (United Nations Office on Drug and Crime). 2012. *2011 Global Study on Homicide: Trends, Contexts, Data.* www.unodc.org/documents/data-and-analysis/statistics/Homicide/Globa_study_on_homicide_2011_web.pdf. Accessed 30 May 2012.

UNSD (United Nations Statistics Division). 2012. United Nations Commodity Trade Statistics Database. http://comtrade.un.org. Accessed 15 May 2012.

UNWTO (World Tourism Organization). 2011. *Tourism Highlights: 2011 Edition.* Geneva.

Vos, R. 2010. "The Crisis of Globalization as an Opportunity to Create a Fairer World." *Journal of Human Development and Capabilities* 11 (1): 143–160.

Wacziarg, R., and K.H. Welch. 2008. "Trade Liberalization and Growth: New Evidence." *World Bank Economic Review* 22 (2): 187–231.

Westaway, J. 2012. "Globalization, Sovereignty and Social Unrest." *Journal of Politics and Law* 5 (2): 132–139.

Whalley, J., and A. Weisbrod. 2011. "The Contribution of Chinese FDI to Africa's Pre-Crisis Growth Surge." VoxEU, 21 December. www.voxeu.org/article/contribution-chinese-fdi-africa-s-growth. Accessed 15 May 2012.

Wilkinson, R., and K. Pickett. 2009. *The Spiritual Level.* New York: Bloomsbury Press.

———. **2012.** "Sorry Nick Clegg – Social Mobility and Austerity Just Don't Mix." *The Guardian,* 15 May. www.guardian.co.uk/commentisfree/2012/may/15/nick-clegg-social-mobility-austerity. Accessed 15 May 2012.

Wines, M., and S. LaFraniere. 2011. "In Baring Facts of Train Crash, Blogs Erode China Censorship." *The New York Times,* 28 July. www.nytimes.com/2011/07/29/world/asia/29china.html. Accessed 15 May 2012.

Winters, L.A. 2004. "Trade Liberalisation and Economic Performance: An Overview." *Economic Journal* 114 (493): F4–F21.

Wiseman, P. 2002. "China Thrown Off Balance as Boys Outnumber Girls." *USA Today,* 19 June. www.usatoday.com/news/world/2002/06/19/china-usat.htm. Accessed 24 July 2012.

Woods, N. 2010. "Global Governance after the Financial Crisis: A New Multilateralism or the Last Gasp of the Great Powers?" *Global Policy* 1 (1): 51–63.

World Bank. 2003. *Private Participation in Infrastructure: Trends in Developing Countries in 1990–2001.* Washington, DC. http://documents.worldbank.org/curated/en/2003/01/2522708/private-participation-infrastructure-trends-developing-countries-1990-2001. Accessed 15 May 2012.

———. **2006.** *Global Economic Prospects: Economic Implications of Remittances and Migration.* Washington, DC. http://go.worldbank.org/0G6XW1UPP0. Accessed 15 May 2012.

———. **2008.** *World Development Report 2009: Reshaping Economic Geography.* Washington, DC. http://web.worldbank.org/WBSITE/EXTERNAL/EXTDEC/EXTRESEARCH/EXTWDRS/0,,contentMDK:23062295~pagePK:478093~piPK:477627~theSitePK:477624,00.html. Accessed 15 May 2012.

———. **2010a.** Bilateral Migration and Remittances. http://go.worldbank.org/JITC7NYTT0 . Accessed 15 May 2012.

———. **2010b.** *Thailand Economic Monitor.* Bangkok. http://siteresources.worldbank.org/THAILANDEXTN/Resources/333295-1280288892663/THM_June2010_fullreport.pdf. Accessed 15 May 2012.

———. **2010c.** *Arab Development Assistance: Four Decades of Cooperation.* Washington, DC. http://siteresources.worldbank.org/INTMENA/Resources/ADAPub82410web.pdf. Accessed 15 May 2012.

———. **2010d.** "World Bank Reforms Voting Power, Gets $86 Billion Boost." Press Release, 25 April. Washington, DC. http://web.worldbank.org/WBSITE/EXTERNAL/NEWS/0,,contentMDK:22556045~pagePK:64257043~piPK:437376~theSitePK:4607,00.html. Accessed 15 May 2012.

———. **2011a.** *Malaysia Economic Monitor: Brain Drain.* Washington, DC. http://documents.worldbank.org/curated/en/2011/04/14134061/malaysia-economic-monitor-brain-drain. Accessed 15 May 2012.

———. **2011b.** *Growing Old in Older Brazil.* Washington, DC.

———. **2012a.** World Development Indicators Database. http://data.worldbank.org/. Accessed 15 May 2012.

———. **2012b.** "An Update to World Bank's Estimates of Consumption Poverty in the Developing World." Briefing Note. Washington, DC. http://siteresources.worldbank.org/INTPOVCALNET/Resources/Global_Poverty_Update_2012_02-29-12.pdf. Accessed 15 May 2012.

———. **n.d.** "India Transport: Public Private Partnership." http://web.worldbank.org/WBSITE/EXTERNAL/COUNTRIES/SOUTHASIAEXT/0,,contentMDK:22020973~pagePK:146736~piPK:146830~theSitePK:223547,00.html. Accessed 15 May 2012.

WTO (World Trade Organization). n.d. "The Doha Round." www.wto.org/english/tratop_e/dda_e/dda_e.htm. Accessed 28 December 2012.

Xing, Y., and N. Detert. 2010. "How the iPhone Widens the United States Trade Deficit with the People's Republic of China." Working Paper 257. Asian Development Bank Institute, Tokyo. www.adbi.org/working-paper/2010/12/14/4236.iphone.widens.us.trade.deficit.prc/. Accessed 15 May 2012.

Zafar. A. 2011. "Mauritius: An Economic Success Story." In P. Chuhan-Pole and M. Angwafo, eds., *Yes Africa Can: Success Stories From A Dynamic Continent.* Washington, DC: World Bank. http://siteresources.worldbank.org/AFRICAEXT/Resources/258643-1271798012256/YAC_Consolidated_Web.pdf. Accessed 10 August 2012.

Zuckerberg, M. 2012. "One Billion People on Facebook." http://newsroom.fb.com/News/457/One-Billion-People-on-Facebook. Accessed 4 October 2012.

Zuzana, B., and L. Ndikumana. Forthcoming. "The Global Financial Crisis and Africa: The Effects and Policy Responses." In G. Epstein and M. H. Wolfson, eds., *The Oxford Handbook of the Political Economy of Financial Crisis.* Oxford, UK: Oxford University Press.

Statistical annex

Readers guide

The 14 statistical tables provide an overview of key aspects of human development. The tables include composite indices estimated by the Human Development Report Office (HDRO) using data available to the HDRO on 15 October 2012. All indicators, along with the technical notes on the calculation of composite indicators and additional sources of information, are available online at http://hdr.undp.org/en/statistics.

Countries and territories are ranked by their 2012 HDI value. Robustness and reliability analysis has shown that for most countries the HDI is not statistically significant at the third decimal place (see Aguna and Kovacevic 2011 and Høyland, Moene and Willumsen 2011). For this reason countries with the same HDI value at the third decimal place are listed with tied ranks.

Sources and definitions

The HDRO uses data from international data agencies with the mandate, resources and expertise to collect national data on specific indicators, unless otherwise noted.

Definitions of indicators and sources for original data components are given at the end of each table, with full source details in *Statistical references*.

Comparisons over time and across editions of the Report

Because national and international data agencies continually improve their data series, the data—including the HDI values and ranks—presented in this Report are not comparable to those published in earlier editions. For the HDI, trends using consistent data calculated at five-year intervals for 1980–2012 are presented in table 2.

Discrepancies between national and international estimates

National and international data estimates can vary because international agencies harmonize national data for comparability across countries, produce an estimate of missing data or do not incorporate the most recent national data. When HDRO becomes aware of discrepancies, these are brought to the attention of national and international data authorities.

Country groupings and aggregates

Several weighted aggregates are presented in the tables. In general, an aggregate is shown only when data are available for at least half the countries and represent at least two-thirds of the available population in that classification. Aggregates for each classification represent only the countries for which data are available.

Human development classification

HDI classifications are relative—based on quartiles of HDI distribution across the 187 countries denoted as very high, high, medium (each with 47 countries) and low (with 46 countries).

Regional groupings

Regional groupings are based on United Nations Development Programme regional classification. Least Developed Countries and Small Island Developing States are defined according to UN classifications. The composition of each region is presented in *Regions*.

Country notes

Data for China do not include Hong Kong Special Administrative Region of China, Macao Special Administrative Region of China or Taiwan Province of China, unless otherwise noted. Data for Sudan include South Sudan unless otherwise noted.

Symbols

A dash between two years, as in 2005–2012, indicates that the data are the most recent year available in the period specified. A slash between years, as in 2005/2012, indicates average for the period defined. Growth rates are usually average annual rates of growth between the first and last years of the period shown.

The following symbols are used in the tables:

..	Not available
0 or 0.0	Nil or negligible
—	Not applicable

Statistical acknowledgements

The Report's composite indices and other statistical resources draw on a wide variety of the most respected international data providers in their specialized fields. We are particularly grateful to the Carbon Dioxide Information Analysis Center of the US Department of Energy; Centre for Research on the Epidemiology of Disasters; Eurostat; Food and Agricultural Organization; Gallup; ICF Macro; International Energy Agency; International Labour Organization; International Monetary Fund; International Telecommunication Union; International Union for Conservation of Nature; Inter-Parliamentary Union; Luxembourg Income Study; Organisation for Economic Co-operation and Development; Stockholm International Peace Research Institute; United Nations Children's Fund; United Nations Conference on Trade and Development; United Nations Department of Economic and Social Affairs; United Nations Economic Commission for Latin America and the Caribbean; United Nations Educational, Scientific and Cultural Organization Institute for Statistics; United Nations Office on Drug and Crime; United Nations World Tourism Organization; World Bank; World Health Organization; and World Intellectual Property Organization. The international educational database maintained by Robert Barro (Harvard University) and Jong-Wha Lee (Korea University) is another invaluable source for the calculation of the Report's indices.

Statistical tables

The first five tables contain the composite human development indices and their components; the remaining nine tables present a broader set of indicators related to human development. Four composite human development indices—the Human Development Index (HDI), the Inequality-adjusted Human Development Index (IHDI), the Gender Inequality Index (GII) and the Multidimensional Poverty Index (MPI)—have been presented since the 2010 *Human Development Report*. The GII and the MPI remain experimental indices.

HDI values along with values of the four component indicators on life expectancy, educational attainment and income are presented in **table 1**. Countries are ranked according to HDI value. The difference between rank by gross national income and HDI indicates whether a country is efficiently using its income for advancement in the two nonincome HDI dimensions. The nonincome HDI is calculated to provide an additional means of cross-country comparison and to order countries by achievements in the nonincome dimensions. A time series of HDI values based on data available in 2012, thus using the most recent revision of historical data and methodology, is presented in **table 2**. It is the only means for comparing HDI values for 2012 with those for past years. The change in HDI rank over the last five years and between 2011 and 2012 as well as the average annual HDI growth rate across four time periods allow for easy assessment of the direction and speed of HDI changes.

Table 3 presents the IHDI, which goes beyond a country's average achievements in health, education and income to show how the achievements are distributed among residents by discounting the value of each dimension according to its level of inequality. The IHDI can be interpreted as the actual level of human development (accounting for inequality), while the HDI is the potential human development that could be obtained if achievements were distributed equally among residents. The difference between the HDI and IHDI, expressed as a percentage, defines the loss in potential human development due to inequality. The difference in ranking by the HDI and the IHDI indicates that taking inequality into account would either lower a country's rank (negative value) or improve it (positive).

Table 4 presents the Gender Inequality Index, an experimental composite measure of inequality in achievement between women and men in three dimensions: reproductive health, empowerment and the labour market. The GII is designed to provide empirical foundations for policy analysis and advocacy efforts. A high value indicates high inequality between women and men.

The Multidimensional Poverty Index, an experimental measure designed to capture the overlapping deprivations that people face in education, health and living standards, is presented in **table 5**. The MPI gives both the incidence of nonincome multidimensional poverty (a headcount of those in multidimensional poverty) and its intensity (the relative number of deprivations people experience at the same time). The contributions of deprivations in each dimension to overall poverty are included to provide a comprehensive picture of people living in poverty. Countries are presented alphabetically in two groups according to the year of the survey used to estimate the MPI.

Table 6 combines macroeconomic indicators such as gross domestic product (GDP), gross fixed capital formation and the consumer price index with public spending indicators. During economic uncertainty or recession, gross fixed capital formation typically declines. The consumer price index is presented as a measure of inflation. Indicators of public spending are given for two points in time to allow for analysis of change in spending. These indicators can be used to examine priorities in public spending and the pattern of expenditure and how it relates to human development outcomes.

Several indicators on the health of children, youth and adults as well as two indicators of health care quality are presented in **table 7**. **Table 8** comprises standard education indicators along with indicators on education quality, including average test scores (and deviations from the average scores) in reading, mathematics and science. The education quality indicators are based on standardized tests assigned to 15-year-old students by the Organisation for Economic Co-operation and Development–managed Programme on International Student Assessment using the 2009 dataset for 63 UN Member States. Two additional indicators of education quality, primary education teachers trained to teach and a perception-based indicator of satisfaction with the quality of education, complement the test-based quality indicators.

Table 9's data on social integration indicate whether a society is inclusive and integrated. In particular, indicators show the extent of equal rights and opportunities for employment, overall inequality, human safety, and trust and community satisfaction. Complementary objective indicators and perception-based indicators allow for a more nuanced picture of social integration. Life, freedom and job satisfaction focus on individuals' views of their personal conditions, while trust in people and government, along with community satisfaction, give insight into people's satisfaction with broader society.

The extent to which a country is integrated into the global economy is reflected in **table 10**. A distinction between trade in final goods and trade in parts and components is made to capture the phenomenon of global value added and production sharing, which have important policy implications for the growth of world trade and for economic development in countries of the South.

Indicators on two aspects of globalization: capital flows and human mobility are shown in **table 11**. Increasing foreign investment is one measure of growing economic globalization. Migration is an opportunity for work and to send funds back home while expanding the labour force in recipient countries. Human mobility in all forms is also a potential factor in cross-cultural understanding.

Table 12 captures the importance of investment in research and development to advancing human development and building country capacities to effectively adopt and use technologies. **Table 13** sheds light on environmental sustainability. It shows the proportion of fossil fuels and renewable energy sources in the energy supply, presents three ways of looking at carbon dioxide and greenhouse gas emissions data and shows important measures for ecosystems and natural resources. The table also presents indicators on the direct human impacts of changes to the physical environment.

Major population indicators needed to understand current population conditions and the direction of changes are presented in **table 14**. Statistics on median age of the population, dependency ratios and total fertility rates can be compared to assess the burden on the labour force and the ability of societies to sustain themselves. Deviations from the natural sex ratio at birth have implications for population replacement levels and indicate gender bias and potential future social and economic problems.

Key to HDI countries and ranks, 2012

Country	Rank	Country	Rank	Country	Rank
Afghanistan	175	Georgia	72	Norway	1
Albania	70	Germany	5	Oman	84
Algeria	93	Ghana	135	Pakistan	146
Andorra	33	Greece	29	Palau	52
Angola	148	Grenada	63	Palestine, State of	110
Antigua and Barbuda	67	Guatemala	133	Panama	59
Argentina	45	Guinea	178	Papua New Guinea	156
Armenia	87	Guinea-Bissau	176	Paraguay	111
Australia	2	Guyana	118	Peru	77
Austria	18	Haiti	161	Philippines	114
Azerbaijan	82	Honduras	120	Poland	39
Bahamas	49	Hong Kong, China (SAR)	13	Portugal	43
Bahrain	48	Hungary	37	Qatar	36
Bangladesh	146	Iceland	13	Romania	56
Barbados	38	India	136	Russian Federation	55
Belarus	50	Indonesia	121	Rwanda	167
Belgium	17	Iran, Islamic Republic of	76	Saint Kitts and Nevis	72
Belize	96	Iraq	131	Saint Lucia	88
Benin	166	Ireland	7	Saint Vincent and the Grenadines	83
Bhutan	140	Israel	16	Samoa	96
Bolivia, Plurinational State of	108	Italy	25	Sao Tome and Principe	144
Bosnia and Herzegovina	81	Jamaica	85	Saudi Arabia	57
Botswana	119	Japan	10	Senegal	154
Brazil	85	Jordan	100	Serbia	64
Brunei Darussalam	30	Kazakhstan	69	Seychelles	46
Bulgaria	57	Kenya	145	Sierra Leone	177
Burkina Faso	183	Kiribati	121	Singapore	18
Burundi	178	Korea, Republic of	12	Slovakia	35
Cambodia	138	Kuwait	54	Slovenia	21
Cameroon	150	Kyrgyzstan	125	Solomon Islands	143
Canada	11	Lao People's Democratic Republic	138	South Africa	121
Cape Verde	132	Latvia	44	Spain	23
Central African Republic	180	Lebanon	72	Sri Lanka	92
Chad	184	Lesotho	158	Sudan	171
Chile	40	Liberia	174	Suriname	105
China	101	Libya	64	Swaziland	141
Colombia	91	Liechtenstein	24	Sweden	7
Comoros	169	Lithuania	41	Switzerland	9
Congo	142	Luxembourg	26	Syrian Arab Republic	116
Congo, Democratic Republic of the	186	Madagascar	151	Tajikistan	125
Costa Rica	62	Malawi	170	Tanzania, United Republic of	152
Côte d'Ivoire	168	Malaysia	64	Thailand	103
Croatia	47	Maldives	104	The former Yugoslav Republic of Macedonia	78
Cuba	59	Mali	182	Timor-Leste	134
Cyprus	31	Malta	32	Togo	159
Czech Republic	28	Mauritania	155	Tonga	95
Denmark	15	Mauritius	80	Trinidad and Tobago	67
Djibouti	164	Mexico	61	Tunisia	94
Dominica	72	Micronesia, Federated States of	117	Turkey	90
Dominican Republic	96	Moldova, Republic of	113	Turkmenistan	102
Ecuador	89	Mongolia	108	Uganda	161
Egypt	112	Montenegro	52	Ukraine	78
El Salvador	107	Morocco	130	United Arab Emirates	41
Equatorial Guinea	136	Mozambique	185	United Kingdom	26
Eritrea	181	Myanmar	149	United States	3
Estonia	33	Namibia	128	Uruguay	51
Ethiopia	173	Nepal	157	Uzbekistan	114
Fiji	96	Netherlands	4	Vanuatu	124
Finland	21	New Zealand	6	Venezuela, Bolivarian Republic of	71
France	20	Nicaragua	129	Viet Nam	127
Gabon	106	Niger	186	Yemen	160
Gambia	165	Nigeria	153	Zambia	163
				Zimbabwe	172

TABLE 1

Human Development Index and its components

HDI rank	Human Development Index (HDI) Value 2012	Life expectancy at birth (years) 2012	Mean years of schooling (years) 2010[a]	Expected years of schooling (years) 2011[b]	Gross national income (GNI) per capita (2005 PPP $) 2012	GNI per capita rank minus HDI rank 2012	Nonincome HDI Value 2012
VERY HIGH HUMAN DEVELOPMENT							
1 Norway	0.955	81.3	12.6	17.5	48,688	4	0.977
2 Australia	0.938	82.0	12.0[c]	19.6[d]	34,340	15	0.978
3 United States	0.937	78.7	13.3	16.8	43,480	6	0.958
4 Netherlands	0.921	80.8	11.6[c]	16.9	37,282	8	0.945
5 Germany	0.920	80.6	12.2	16.4[e]	35,431	10	0.948
6 New Zealand	0.919	80.8	12.5	19.7[d]	24,358	26	0.978
7 Ireland	0.916	80.7	11.6	18.3[d]	28,671	19	0.960
7 Sweden	0.916	81.6	11.7[c]	16.0	36,143	6	0.940
9 Switzerland	0.913	82.5	11.0[c]	15.7	40,527	2	0.926
10 Japan	0.912	83.6	11.6[c]	15.3	32,545	11	0.942
11 Canada	0.911	81.1	12.3	15.1	35,369	5	0.934
12 Korea, Republic of	0.909	80.7	11.6	17.2	28,231	15	0.949
13 Hong Kong, China (SAR)	0.906	83.0	10.0	15.5	45,598	−6	0.907
13 Iceland	0.906	81.9	10.4	18.3[d]	29,176	12	0.943
15 Denmark	0.901	79.0	11.4[c]	16.8	33,518	4	0.924
16 Israel	0.900	81.9	11.9	15.7	26,224	13	0.942
17 Belgium	0.897	80.0	10.9[c]	16.4	33,429	3	0.917
18 Austria	0.895	81.0	10.8	15.3	36,438	−5	0.908
18 Singapore	0.895	81.2	10.1[c]	14.4[f]	52,613	−15	0.880
20 France	0.893	81.7	10.6[c]	16.1	30,277	4	0.919
21 Finland	0.892	80.1	10.3	16.9	32,510	2	0.912
21 Slovenia	0.892	79.5	11.7	16.9	23,999	12	0.936
23 Spain	0.885	81.6	10.4[c]	16.4	25,947	8	0.919
24 Liechtenstein	0.883	79.8	10.3[g]	11.9	84,880[h]	−22	0.832
25 Italy	0.881	82.0	10.1[c]	16.2	26,158	5	0.911
26 Luxembourg	0.875	80.1	10.1	13.5	48,285	−20	0.858
26 United Kingdom	0.875	80.3	9.4	16.4	32,538	−5	0.886
28 Czech Republic	0.873	77.8	12.3	15.3	22,067	10	0.913
29 Greece	0.860	80.0	10.1[c]	16.3	20,511	13	0.899
30 Brunei Darussalam	0.855	78.1	8.6	15.0	45,690	−23	0.832
31 Cyprus	0.848	79.8	9.8	14.9	23,825	4	0.869
32 Malta	0.847	79.8	9.9	15.1	21,184	9	0.876
33 Andorra	0.846	81.1	10.4[i]	11.7	33,918[i]	−15	0.839
33 Estonia	0.846	75.0	12.0	15.8	17,402	13	0.892
35 Slovakia	0.840	75.6	11.6	14.7	19,696	9	0.872
36 Qatar	0.834	78.5	7.3	12.2	87,478[k]	−35	0.761
37 Hungary	0.831	74.6	11.7	15.3	16,088	13	0.874
38 Barbados	0.825	77.0	9.3	16.3	17,308	10	0.859
39 Poland	0.821	76.3	10.0	15.2	17,776	7	0.851
40 Chile	0.819	79.3	9.7	14.7	14,987	13	0.863
41 Lithuania	0.818	72.5	10.9	15.7	16,858	7	0.850
41 United Arab Emirates	0.818	76.7	8.9	12.0	42,716	−31	0.783
43 Portugal	0.816	79.7	7.7	16.0	19,907	0	0.835
44 Latvia	0.814	73.6	11.5[c]	14.8	14,724	10	0.856
45 Argentina	0.811	76.1	9.3	16.1	15,347	7	0.848
46 Seychelles	0.806	73.8	9.4[i]	14.3	22,615	−9	0.808
47 Croatia	0.805	76.8	9.8[c]	14.1	15,419	4	0.837
HIGH HUMAN DEVELOPMENT							
48 Bahrain	0.796	75.2	9.4	13.4[e]	19,154	−3	0.806
49 Bahamas	0.794	75.9	8.5	12.6	27,401	−21	0.777
50 Belarus	0.793	70.6	11.5[i]	14.7	13,385	11	0.830
51 Uruguay	0.792	77.2	8.5[c]	15.5	13,333	11	0.829
52 Montenegro	0.791	74.8	10.5[i]	15.0	10,471	24	0.850
52 Palau	0.791	72.1	12.2	13.7[e]	11,463[m]	18	0.840
54 Kuwait	0.790	74.7	6.1	14.2	52,793	−51	0.730
55 Russian Federation	0.788	69.1	11.7	14.3	14,461	0	0.816
56 Romania	0.786	74.2	10.4	14.5	11,011	16	0.836
57 Bulgaria	0.782	73.6	10.6[c]	14.0	11,474	12	0.826
57 Saudi Arabia	0.782	74.1	7.8	14.3	22,616	−21	0.774
59 Cuba	0.780	79.3	10.2	16.2	5,539[n]	44	0.894
59 Panama	0.780	76.3	9.4	13.2	13,519	1	0.810
61 Mexico	0.775	77.1	8.5	13.7	12,947	4	0.805

HDI rank	Human Development Index (HDI) Value 2012	Life expectancy at birth (years) 2012	Mean years of schooling (years) 2010[a]	Expected years of schooling (years) 2011[b]	Gross national income (GNI) per capita (2005 PPP $) 2012	GNI per capita rank minus HDI rank 2012	Nonincome HDI Value 2012
62 Costa Rica	0.773	79.4	8.4	13.7	10,863	12	0.816
63 Grenada	0.770	76.1	8.6[e]	15.8	9,257	21	0.827
64 Libya	0.769	75.0	7.3	16.2	13,765	−8	0.791
64 Malaysia	0.769	74.5	9.5	12.6	13,676	−7	0.791
64 Serbia	0.769	74.7	10.2[c]	13.6	9,533	16	0.823
67 Antigua and Barbuda	0.760	72.8	8.9	13.3	13,883	−12	0.776
67 Trinidad and Tobago	0.760	70.3	9.2	11.9	21,941	−28	0.743
69 Kazakhstan	0.754	67.4	10.4	15.3	10,451	8	0.791
70 Albania	0.749	77.1	10.4	11.4	7,822	21	0.807
71 Venezuela, Bolivarian Republic of	0.748	74.6	7.6[c]	14.4	11,475	−2	0.774
72 Dominica	0.745	77.6	7.7[l]	12.7	10,977	−1	0.771
72 Georgia	0.745	73.9	12.1[o]	13.2	5,005	37	0.845
72 Lebanon	0.745	72.8	7.9[l]	13.9	12,364	−5	0.762
72 Saint Kitts and Nevis	0.745	73.3	8.4[e]	12.9	12,460	−5	0.763
76 Iran, Islamic Republic of	0.742	73.2	7.8	14.4	10,695	−1	0.769
77 Peru	0.741	74.2	8.7	13.2	9,306	6	0.780
78 The former Yugoslav Republic of Macedonia	0.740	75.0	8.2[o]	13.4	9,377	2	0.777
78 Ukraine	0.740	68.8	11.3	14.8	6,428	22	0.813
80 Mauritius	0.737	73.5	7.2	13.6	13,300	−17	0.745
81 Bosnia and Herzegovina	0.735	75.8	8.3[l]	13.4	7,713	13	0.787
82 Azerbaijan	0.734	70.9	11.2[l]	11.7	8,153	5	0.780
83 Saint Vincent and the Grenadines	0.733	72.5	8.6[e]	13.3	9,367	−1	0.767
84 Oman	0.731	73.2	5.5[l]	13.5	24,092	−51	0.694
85 Brazil	0.730	73.8	7.2	14.2	10,152	−8	0.755
85 Jamaica	0.730	73.3	9.6	13.1	6,701	14	0.792
87 Armenia	0.729	74.4	10.8	12.2	5,540	16	0.808
88 Saint Lucia	0.725	74.8	8.3[e]	12.7	7,971	1	0.768
89 Ecuador	0.724	75.8	7.6	13.7	7,471	7	0.772
90 Turkey	0.722	74.2	6.5	12.9	13,710	−32	0.720
91 Colombia	0.719	73.9	7.3	13.6	8,711	−6	0.751
92 Sri Lanka	0.715	75.1	9.3[c]	12.7	5,170	18	0.792
93 Algeria	0.713	73.4	7.6	13.6	7,418	4	0.755
94 Tunisia	0.712	74.7	6.5	14.5	8,103	−6	0.746
MEDIUM HUMAN DEVELOPMENT							
95 Tonga	0.710	72.5	10.3[c]	13.7	4,153	26	0.807
96 Belize	0.702	76.3	8.0[c]	12.5	5,327	8	0.767
96 Dominican Republic	0.702	73.6	7.2[c]	12.3	8,506	−11	0.726
96 Fiji	0.702	69.4	10.7[c]	13.9	4,087	24	0.794
96 Samoa	0.702	72.7	10.3[l]	13.0	3,928	28	0.800
100 Jordan	0.700	73.5	8.6	12.7	5,272	8	0.766
101 China	0.699	73.7	7.5	11.7	7,945	−11	0.728
102 Turkmenistan	0.698	65.2	9.9[p]	12.6[e]	7,782	−10	0.727
103 Thailand	0.690	74.3	6.6	12.3	7,722	−10	0.715
104 Maldives	0.688	77.1	5.8[c]	12.5	7,478	−9	0.715
105 Suriname	0.684	70.8	7.2[o]	12.4	7,327	−7	0.710
106 Gabon	0.683	63.1	7.5	13.0	12,521	−40	0.668
107 El Salvador	0.680	72.4	7.5	12.0	5,915	−5	0.723
108 Bolivia, Plurinational State of	0.675	66.9	9.2	13.5	4,444	7	0.740
108 Mongolia	0.675	68.8	8.3	14.3	4,245	10	0.746
110 Palestine, State of	0.670	73.0	8.0[l]	13.5	3,359[q]	20	0.761
111 Paraguay	0.669	72.7	7.7	12.1	4,497	4	0.730
112 Egypt	0.662	73.5	6.4	12.1	5,401	−6	0.702
113 Moldova, Republic of	0.660	69.6	9.7	11.8	3,319	19	0.747
114 Philippines	0.654	69.0	8.9[c]	11.7	3,752	11	0.724
114 Uzbekistan	0.654	68.6	10.0[o]	11.6	3,201	19	0.740
116 Syrian Arab Republic	0.648	76.0	5.7[c]	11.7[e]	4,674[r]	−2	0.692
117 Micronesia, Federated States of	0.645	69.2	8.8[p]	11.4[e]	3,352[m]	14	0.719
118 Guyana	0.636	70.2	8.5	10.3	3,387	11	0.703
119 Botswana	0.634	53.0	8.9	11.8	13,102	−55	0.596
120 Honduras	0.632	73.4	6.5	11.4	3,426	8	0.695
121 Indonesia	0.629	69.8	5.8	12.9	4,154	−3	0.672
121 Kiribati	0.629	68.4	7.8[e]	12.0	3,079	13	0.701
121 South Africa	0.629	53.4	8.5[c]	13.1[e]	9,594	−42	0.608

TABLE 1 Human Development Index and its components | 145

TABLE 1 HUMAN DEVELOPMENT INDEX AND ITS COMPONENTS

	Human Development Index (HDI)	Life expectancy at birth	Mean years of schooling	Expected years of schooling	Gross national income (GNI) per capita	GNI per capita rank minus HDI rank	Nonincome HDI
	Value	(years)	(years)	(years)	(2005 PPP $)		Value
HDI rank	2012	2012	2010[a]	2011[b]	2012	2012	2012
124 Vanuatu	0.626	71.3	6.7[e]	10.6	3,960	−1	0.672
125 Kyrgyzstan	0.622	68.0	9.3	12.6	2,009	24	0.738
125 Tajikistan	0.622	67.8	9.8	11.5	2,119	19	0.731
127 Viet Nam	0.617	75.4	5.5	11.9	2,970	9	0.686
128 Namibia	0.608	62.6	6.2	11.3	5,973	−27	0.611
129 Nicaragua	0.599	74.3	5.8	10.8	2,551	10	0.671
130 Morocco	0.591	72.4	4.4	10.4	4,384	−13	0.608
131 Iraq	0.590	69.6	5.6	10.0	3,557	−4	0.623
132 Cape Verde	0.586	74.3	3.5[e]	12.7	3,609	−6	0.617
133 Guatemala	0.581	71.4	4.1	10.7	4,235	−14	0.596
134 Timor-Leste	0.576	62.9	4.4[s]	11.7	5,446	−29	0.569
135 Ghana	0.558	64.6	7.0	11.4	1,684	22	0.646
136 Equatorial Guinea	0.554	51.4	5.4[o]	7.9	21,715	−97	0.463
136 India	0.554	65.8	4.4	10.7	3,285	−3	0.575
138 Cambodia	0.543	63.6	5.8	10.5	2,095	9	0.597
138 Lao People's Democratic Republic	0.543	67.8	4.6	10.1	2,435	2	0.584
140 Bhutan	0.538	67.6	2.3[s]	12.4	5,246	−31	0.516
141 Swaziland	0.536	48.9	7.1	10.7	5,104	−30	0.515
LOW HUMAN DEVELOPMENT							
142 Congo	0.534	57.8	5.9	10.1	2,934	−5	0.553
143 Solomon Islands	0.530	68.2	4.5[p]	9.3	2,172	1	0.572
144 Sao Tome and Principe	0.525	64.9	4.7[s]	10.8	1,864	7	0.579
145 Kenya	0.519	57.7	7.0	11.1	1,541	15	0.588
146 Bangladesh	0.515	69.2	4.8	8.1	1,785	9	0.567
146 Pakistan	0.515	65.7	4.9	7.3	2,566	−9	0.534
148 Angola	0.508	51.5	4.7[s]	10.2	4,812	−35	0.479
149 Myanmar	0.498	65.7	3.9	9.4	1,817	5	0.537
150 Cameroon	0.495	52.1	5.9	10.9	2,114	−4	0.520
151 Madagascar	0.483	66.9	5.2[p]	10.4	828	28	0.601
152 Tanzania, United Republic of	0.476	58.9	5.1	9.1	1,383	10	0.527
153 Nigeria	0.471	52.3	5.2[s]	9.0	2,102	−6	0.482
154 Senegal	0.470	59.6	4.5	8.2	1,653	4	0.501
155 Mauritania	0.467	58.9	3.7	8.1	2,174	−12	0.473
156 Papua New Guinea	0.466	63.1	3.9	5.8[e]	2,386	−15	0.464
157 Nepal	0.463	69.1	3.2	8.9	1,137	11	0.526
158 Lesotho	0.461	48.7	5.9[c]	9.6	1,879	−8	0.476
159 Togo	0.459	57.5	5.3	10.6	928	16	0.542
160 Yemen	0.458	65.9	2.5	8.7	1,820	−7	0.474
161 Haiti	0.456	62.4	4.9	7.6[e]	1,070	7	0.521
161 Uganda	0.456	54.5	4.7	11.1	1,168	5	0.511
163 Zambia	0.448	49.4	6.7	8.5	1,358	0	0.483
164 Djibouti	0.445	58.3	3.8[o]	5.7	2,350	−22	0.435
165 Gambia	0.439	58.8	2.8	8.7	1,731	−9	0.448
166 Benin	0.436	56.5	3.2	9.4	1,439	−5	0.459
167 Rwanda	0.434	55.7	3.3	10.9	1,147	0	0.476
168 Côte d'Ivoire	0.432	56.0	4.2	6.5	1,593	−9	0.444
169 Comoros	0.429	61.5	2.8[p]	10.2	986	4	0.484
170 Malawi	0.418	54.8	4.2	10.4	774	10	0.492
171 Sudan	0.414	61.8	3.1	4.5	1,848	−19	0.405
172 Zimbabwe	0.397	52.7	7.2	10.1	424[t]	14	0.542
173 Ethiopia	0.396	59.7	2.2[s]	8.7	1,017	−2	0.425
174 Liberia	0.388	57.3	3.9	10.5[e]	480	11	0.502
175 Afghanistan	0.374	49.1	3.1	8.1	1,000	−3	0.393
176 Guinea-Bissau	0.364	48.6	2.3[o]	9.5	1,042	−6	0.373
177 Sierra Leone	0.359	48.1	3.3	7.3[e]	881	0	0.380
178 Burundi	0.355	50.9	2.7	11.3	544	4	0.423
178 Guinea	0.355	54.5	1.6[s]	8.8	941	−4	0.368
180 Central African Republic	0.352	49.1	3.5	6.8	722	1	0.386
181 Eritrea	0.351	62.0	3.4[e]	4.6	531	3	0.418
182 Mali	0.344	51.9	2.0[c]	7.5	853	−4	0.359
183 Burkina Faso	0.343	55.9	1.3[o]	6.9	1,202	−18	0.332
184 Chad	0.340	49.9	1.5[p]	7.4	1,258	−20	0.324
185 Mozambique	0.327	50.7	1.2	9.2	906	−9	0.327

HDI rank	Human Development Index (HDI) Value 2012	Life expectancy at birth (years) 2012	Mean years of schooling (years) 2010[a]	Expected years of schooling (years) 2011[b]	Gross national income (GNI) per capita (2005 PPP $) 2012	GNI per capita rank minus HDI rank 2012	Nonincome HDI Value 2012
186 Congo, Democratic Republic of the	0.304	48.7	3.5	8.5	319	0	0.404
186 Niger	0.304	55.1	1.4	4.9	701	−4	0.313
OTHER COUNTRIES OR TERRITORIES							
Korea, Democratic People's Rep. of	..	69.0	..	..	..	..	..
Marshall Islands	..	72.3	..	11.7	..	..	..
Monaco	..	82.3	..	..	..	..	..
Nauru	..	80.0	..	9.3	..	..	..
San Marino	..	81.9	..	12.5	..	..	..
Somalia	..	51.5	..	2.4	..	..	..
South Sudan	..	..	..	..	..	..	..
Tuvalu	..	67.5	..	10.8	..	..	..
Human Development Index groups							
Very high human development	0.905	80.1	11.5	16.3	33,391	—	0.927
High human development	0.758	73.4	8.8	13.9	11,501	—	0.781
Medium human development	0.640	69.9	6.3	11.4	5,428	—	0.661
Low human development	0.466	59.1	4.2	8.5	1,633	—	0.487
Regions							
Arab States	0.652	71.0	6.0	10.6	8,317	—	0.658
East Asia and the Pacific	0.683	72.7	7.2	11.8	6,874	—	0.712
Europe and Central Asia	0.771	71.5	10.4	13.7	12,243	—	0.801
Latin America and the Caribbean	0.741	74.7	7.8	13.7	10,300	—	0.770
South Asia	0.558	66.2	4.7	10.2	3,343	—	0.577
Sub-Saharan Africa	0.475	54.9	4.7	9.3	2,010	—	0.479
Least developed countries	0.449	59.5	3.7	8.5	1,385	—	0.475
Small island developing states	0.648	69.8	7.3	10.7	5,397	—	0.673
World	**0.694**	**70.1**	**7.5**	**11.6**	**10,184**	—	**0.690**

NOTES

a Data refer to 2010 or the most recent year available.

b Data refer to 2011 or the most recent year available.

c Updated by HDRO based on UNESCO Institute for Statistics (2012) data.

d For the HDI calculation this value is capped at 18 years.

e Based on cross-country regression.

f Calculated by the Singapore Ministry of Education.

g Assumes the same adult mean years of schooling as Switzerland before the most recent update.

h Estimated using the purchasing power parity (PPP) rate and the projected growth rate of Switzerland.

i Assumes the same adult mean years of schooling as Spain before the most recent update.

j Estimated using the PPP rate and the projected growth rate of Spain.

k Based on implied PPP conversion factors from IMF (2012).

l Based on the UNESCO Institute for Statistics (2012) estimate of educational attainment distribution.

m Based on projected growth rates by ADB (2012).

n PPP estimate based on cross-country regression; projected growth rate based on ECLAC (2012) and UNDESA (2012c) projected growth rates.

o Based on data from UNICEF Multiple Indicator Cluster Surveys for 2002–2012.

p Based on data on years of schooling of adults from household surveys in the World Bank's International Income Distribution Database.

q Based on an unpublished estimate of the PPP conversion rate from the World Bank and projected growth rates from UNESCWA (2012) and UNDESA (2012c).

r Based on projected growth rates from UNDESA (2012c).

s Based on data from ICF Macro (2012).

t Based on PPP data from IMF (2012).

DEFINITIONS

Human Development Index (HDI): A composite index measuring average achievement in three basic dimensions of human development—a long and healthy life, knowledge and a decent standard of living. See *Technical note 1* at http://hdr.undp.org/en/media/HDR_2013_EN_TechNotes.pdf for details on how the HDI is calculated.

Life expectancy at birth: Number of years a newborn infant could expect to live if prevailing patterns of age-specific mortality rates at the time of birth stay the same throughout the infant's life.

Mean years of schooling: Average number of years of education received by people ages 25 and older, converted from educational attainment levels using official durations of each level.

Expected years of schooling: Number of years of schooling that a child of school entrance age can expect to receive if prevailing patterns of age-specific enrolment rates persist throughout the child's life.

Gross national income (GNI) per capita: Aggregate income of an economy generated by its production and its ownership of factors of production, less the incomes paid for the use of factors of production owned by the rest of the world, converted to international dollars using PPP rates, divided by midyear population.

GNI per capita rank minus HDI rank: Difference in rankings by GNI per capita and by the HDI. A negative value means that the country is better ranked by GNI than by the HDI.

Nonincome HDI: Value of the HDI computed from the life expectancy and education indicators only.

MAIN DATA SOURCES

Column 1: HDRO calculations based on data from UNDESA (2011), Barro and Lee (2011), UNESCO Institute for Statistics (2012), World Bank (2012a) and IMF (2012).

Column 2: UNDESA (2011).

Column 3: Barro and Lee (2011) and HDRO updates based on data on educational attainment from UNESCO Institute for Statistics (2012) and on methodology from Barro and Lee (2010).

Column 4: UNESCO Institute for Statistics (2012).

Column 5: HDRO calculations based on data from World Bank (2012a), IMF (2012) and UNSD (2012a).

Column 6: Calculated based on data in columns 1 and 5.

Column 7: Calculated based on data in columns 2, 3 and 4.

TABLE 1   Human Development Index and its components | 147

TABLE 2

Human Development Index trends, 1980–2012

		Human Development Index (HDI)								HDI rank		Average annual HDI growth			
		Value								Change		(%)			
HDI rank		1980	1990	2000	2005	2007	2010	2011	2012	2007–2012a	2011–2012a	1980/1990	1990/2000	2000/2010	2000/2012
VERY HIGH HUMAN DEVELOPMENT															
1	Norway	0.804	0.852	0.922	0.948	0.952	0.952	0.953	0.955	0	0	0.59	0.79	0.32	0.29
2	Australia	0.857	0.880	0.914	0.927	0.931	0.935	0.936	0.938	0	0	0.27	0.37	0.23	0.22
3	United States	0.843	0.878	0.907	0.923	0.929	0.934	0.936	0.937	0	−1	0.40	0.33	0.29	0.27
4	Netherlands	0.799	0.842	0.891	0.899	0.911	0.919	0.921	0.921	2	0	0.52	0.56	0.31	0.28
5	Germany	0.738	0.803	0.870	0.901	0.907	0.916	0.919	0.920	5	0	0.85	0.81	0.53	0.47
6	New Zealand	0.807	0.835	0.887	0.908	0.912	0.917	0.918	0.919	−1	0	0.34	0.60	0.33	0.29
7	Ireland	0.745	0.793	0.879	0.907	0.918	0.916	0.915	0.916	−3	0	0.62	1.04	0.42	0.35
7	Sweden	0.792	0.823	0.903	0.905	0.909	0.913	0.915	0.916	0	0	0.38	0.93	0.11	0.12
9	Switzerland	0.818	0.840	0.882	0.898	0.901	0.912	0.912	0.913	3	0	0.27	0.49	0.33	0.29
10	Japan	0.788	0.837	0.878	0.896	0.903	0.909	0.910	0.912	1	0	0.61	0.48	0.35	0.32
11	Canada	0.825	0.865	0.887	0.906	0.909	0.909	0.910	0.911	−4	−1	0.48	0.25	0.24	0.22
12	Korea, Republic of	0.640	0.749	0.839	0.875	0.890	0.905	0.907	0.909	4	0	1.58	1.14	0.76	0.67
13	Hong Kong, China (SAR)	0.712	0.788	0.815	0.857	0.877	0.900	0.904	0.906	10	1	1.02	0.34	1.00	0.89
13	Iceland	0.769	0.815	0.871	0.901	0.908	0.901	0.905	0.906	−4	0	0.58	0.67	0.34	0.33
15	Denmark	0.790	0.816	0.869	0.893	0.898	0.899	0.901	0.901	−2	0	0.33	0.63	0.34	0.30
16	Israel	0.773	0.809	0.865	0.885	0.892	0.896	0.899	0.900	−2	0	0.45	0.68	0.34	0.33
17	Belgium	0.764	0.817	0.884	0.884	0.891	0.896	0.897	0.897	−2	0	0.67	0.79	0.14	0.12
18	Austria	0.747	0.797	0.848	0.867	0.879	0.892	0.894	0.895	2	0	0.66	0.62	0.51	0.46
18	Singapore	..	0.756	0.826	0.852	..	0.892	0.894	0.895	7	0	..	0.89	0.77	0.67
20	France	0.728	0.784	0.853	0.877	0.885	0.891	0.893	0.893	−1	0	0.75	0.85	0.44	0.38
21	Finland	0.766	0.801	0.845	0.882	0.890	0.890	0.892	0.892	−5	0	0.45	0.54	0.52	0.45
21	Slovenia	..	..	0.842	0.876	0.888	0.892	0.892	0.892	−3	0	..	..	0.58	0.48
23	Spain	0.698	0.756	0.847	0.865	0.874	0.884	0.885	0.885	1	0	0.80	1.15	0.43	0.37
24	Liechtenstein	..	..	..	..	..	0.882	0.883	0.883	..	0	..	..	..	..
25	Italy	0.723	0.771	0.833	0.869	0.878	0.881	0.881	0.881	−2	0	0.64	0.78	0.56	0.46
26	Luxembourg	0.735	0.796	0.861	0.875	0.879	0.875	0.875	0.875	−5	0	0.81	0.78	0.16	0.14
26	United Kingdom	0.748	0.784	0.841	0.865	0.867	0.874	0.875	0.875	2	0	0.47	0.70	0.39	0.33
28	Czech Republic	..	..	0.824	0.862	0.869	0.871	0.872	0.873	−1	0	..	..	0.56	0.48
29	Greece	0.726	0.772	0.810	0.862	0.865	0.866	0.862	0.860	0	0	0.62	0.48	0.67	0.50
30	Brunei Darussalam	0.765	0.782	0.830	0.848	0.853	0.854	0.854	0.855	0	0	0.22	0.59	0.28	0.25
31	Cyprus	0.715	0.779	0.808	0.817	0.827	0.849	0.849	0.848	4	0	0.86	0.36	0.50	0.41
32	Malta	0.713	0.757	0.801	0.827	0.829	0.844	0.846	0.847	2	1	0.59	0.57	0.52	0.46
33	Andorra	..	..	..	..	..	0.846	0.847	0.846	..	−1	..	..	..	..
33	Estonia	..	0.728	0.786	0.830	0.841	0.839	0.844	0.846	−2	1	..	0.76	0.65	0.62
35	Slovakia	..	0.754	0.785	0.814	0.830	0.836	0.838	0.840	−1	0	..	0.40	0.64	0.57
36	Qatar	0.729	0.743	0.801	0.828	0.833	0.827	0.832	0.834	−3	0	0.18	0.76	0.32	0.33
37	Hungary	0.709	0.714	0.790	0.820	0.826	0.829	0.830	0.831	1	0	0.07	1.02	0.48	0.42
38	Barbados	0.706	0.760	0.790	0.798	0.808	0.823	0.824	0.825	2	0	0.73	0.38	0.41	0.37
39	Poland	..	..	0.778	0.798	0.806	0.817	0.819	0.821	3	0	..	..	0.49	0.46
40	Chile	0.638	0.702	0.759	0.789	0.800	0.813	0.817	0.819	5	0	0.96	0.78	0.68	0.64
41	Lithuania	..	0.732	0.756	0.802	0.810	0.810	0.814	0.818	−2	2	..	0.32	0.68	0.65
41	United Arab Emirates	..	..	..	0.831	0.827	0.816	0.817	0.818	−5	−1	..	..	..	..
43	Portugal	0.644	0.714	0.783	0.796	0.806	0.817	0.817	0.816	−1	−3	1.04	0.93	0.43	0.35
44	Latvia	0.675	0.699	0.738	0.792	0.808	0.805	0.809	0.814	−4	1	0.35	0.55	0.87	0.82
45	Argentina	0.675	0.701	0.755	0.771	0.787	0.805	0.810	0.811	4	−1	0.38	0.74	0.64	0.60
46	Seychelles	..	..	0.774	0.781	0.792	0.799	0.804	0.806	1	0	..	..	0.31	0.33
47	Croatia	..	0.716	0.755	0.787	0.798	0.804	0.804	0.805	−1	−1	..	0.52	0.63	0.54
HIGH HUMAN DEVELOPMENT															
48	Bahrain	0.644	0.713	0.781	0.802	0.802	0.794	0.795	0.796	−4	0	1.02	0.92	0.16	0.15
49	Bahamas	..	..	..	..	..	0.791	0.792	0.794	..	0	..	..	..	..
50	Belarus	..	..	..	0.730	0.756	0.785	0.789	0.793	12	1	..	..	..	..
51	Uruguay	0.664	0.693	0.741	0.744	0.771	0.785	0.789	0.792	3	0	0.42	0.68	0.58	0.55
52	Montenegro	..	..	..	0.756	0.775	0.787	0.791	0.791	0	−2	..	..	..	..
52	Palau	..	..	0.765	0.786	0.792	0.779	0.786	0.791	−4	2	..	..	0.18	0.27
54	Kuwait	0.695	0.712	0.781	0.784	0.787	0.786	0.788	0.790	−4	−1	0.25	0.92	0.06	0.10
55	Russian Federation	..	0.730	0.713	0.753	0.770	0.782	0.784	0.788	0	0	..	−0.23	0.93	0.84
56	Romania	..	0.706	0.709	0.756	0.772	0.783	0.784	0.786	−3	−1	..	0.05	0.99	0.86
57	Bulgaria	0.673	0.704	0.721	0.756	0.766	0.778	0.780	0.782	0	0	0.45	0.24	0.77	0.67
57	Saudi Arabia	0.575	0.653	0.717	0.748	0.756	0.777	0.780	0.782	5	0	1.29	0.93	0.81	0.74
59	Cuba	0.626	0.681	0.690	0.735	0.770	0.775	0.777	0.780	−4	0	0.83	0.14	1.17	1.02
59	Panama	0.634	0.666	0.724	0.746	0.758	0.770	0.776	0.780	1	1	0.49	0.85	0.62	0.62
61	Mexico	0.598	0.654	0.723	0.745	0.758	0.770	0.773	0.775	−1	0	0.89	1.00	0.64	0.59
62	Costa Rica	0.621	0.663	0.705	0.732	0.744	0.768	0.770	0.773	4	0	0.65	0.62	0.85	0.76

	Human Development Index (HDI)								HDI rank		Average annual HDI growth			
	Value								Change		(%)			
HDI rank	1980	1990	2000	2005	2007	2010	2011	2012	2007–2012[a]	2011–2012[a]	1980/1990	1990/2000	2000/2010	2000/2012
63 Grenada	..	..	..	..	..	0.768	0.770	0.770	..	−1	..	..	..	..
64 Libya	..	..	..	0.746	0.760	0.773	0.725	0.769	−5	23[b]	..	..	..	..
64 Malaysia	0.563	0.635	0.712	0.742	0.753	0.763	0.766	0.769	1	1	1.21	1.15	0.69	0.64
64 Serbia	..	..	0.726	0.751	0.760	0.767	0.769	0.769	−5	0	..	..	0.56	0.49
67 Antigua and Barbuda	..	..	..	..	..	0.761	0.759	0.760	..	−1	..	..	..	..
67 Trinidad and Tobago	0.680	0.685	0.707	0.741	0.752	0.758	0.759	0.760	−1	−1	0.08	0.32	0.70	0.60
69 Kazakhstan	..	..	0.663	0.721	0.734	0.744	0.750	0.754	2	−1	..	..	1.15	1.08
70 Albania	..	0.661	0.698	0.729	0.737	0.746	0.748	0.749	0	−1	..	0.54	0.66	0.59
71 Venezuela, Bolivarian Republic of	0.629	0.635	0.662	0.694	0.712	0.744	0.746	0.748	9	−1	0.11	0.41	1.17	1.03
72 Dominica	..	..	0.722	0.732	0.739	0.743	0.744	0.745	−3	0	..	..	0.28	0.26
72 Georgia	..	..	..	0.713	0.732	0.735	0.740	0.745	0	3	..	..	..	..
72 Lebanon	..	..	..	0.714	0.728	0.743	0.744	0.745	3	0	..	..	..	..
72 Saint Kitts and Nevis	..	..	..	..	..	0.745	0.745	0.745	..	−1	..	..	..	..
76 Iran, Islamic Republic of	0.443	0.540	0.654	0.685	0.706	0.740	0.742	0.742	7	−2	1.99	1.94	1.25	1.05
77 Peru	0.580	0.619	0.679	0.699	0.716	0.733	0.738	0.741	3	−1	0.65	0.93	0.78	0.73
78 The former Yugoslav Republic of Macedonia	..	..	..	0.711	0.719	0.736	0.738	0.740	1	−2	..	..	..	..
78 Ukraine	..	0.714	0.673	0.718	0.732	0.733	0.737	0.740	−5	0	..	−0.58	0.85	0.80
80 Mauritius	0.551	0.626	0.676	0.708	0.720	0.732	0.735	0.737	−2	−1	1.28	0.77	0.81	0.73
81 Bosnia and Herzegovina	..	..	..	0.724	0.729	0.733	0.734	0.735	−6	−1	..	..	..	..
82 Azerbaijan	..	..	..	..	..	0.734	0.732	0.734	..	−1	..	..	..	..
83 Saint Vincent and the Grenadines	..	..	..	..	..	0.731	0.732	0.733	..	−2	..	..	..	..
84 Oman	..	..	..	..	..	0.728	0.729	0.731	..	−1	..	..	..	..
85 Brazil	0.522	0.590	0.669	0.699	0.710	0.726	0.728	0.730	0	0	1.23	1.26	0.82	0.73
85 Jamaica	0.612	0.642	0.679	0.695	0.701	0.727	0.729	0.730	4	−2	0.47	0.57	0.69	0.61
87 Armenia	..	0.628	0.648	0.695	0.723	0.722	0.726	0.729	−7	−1	..	0.33	1.08	0.98
88 Saint Lucia	..	..	..	..	..	0.723	0.724	0.725	..	0	..	..	..	..
89 Ecuador	0.596	0.635	0.659	0.682	0.688	0.719	0.722	0.724	10	0	0.63	0.37	0.89	0.79
90 Turkey	0.474	0.569	0.645	0.684	0.702	0.715	0.720	0.722	−1	0	1.85	1.26	1.04	0.95
91 Colombia	0.556	0.600	0.658	0.681	0.698	0.714	0.717	0.719	0	0	0.76	0.93	0.82	0.75
92 Sri Lanka	0.557	0.608	0.653	0.683	0.693	0.705	0.711	0.715	5	0	0.88	0.72	0.78	0.76
93 Algeria	0.461	0.562	0.625	0.680	0.691	0.710	0.711	0.713	5	−1	2.01	1.07	1.28	1.10
94 Tunisia	0.459	0.553	0.642	0.679	0.694	0.710	0.710	0.712	2	0	1.87	1.51	1.01	0.86
MEDIUM HUMAN DEVELOPMENT														
95 Tonga	..	0.656	0.689	0.704	0.705	0.709	0.709	0.710	−7	0	..	0.49	0.28	0.25
96 Belize	0.621	0.653	0.672	0.694	0.696	0.700	0.701	0.702	−4	0	0.51	0.29	0.40	0.35
96 Dominican Republic	0.525	0.584	0.641	0.669	0.683	0.697	0.700	0.702	4	2	1.07	0.93	0.85	0.76
96 Fiji	0.572	0.614	0.670	0.693	0.695	0.699	0.700	0.702	−3	2	0.71	0.87	0.43	0.39
96 Samoa	..	..	0.663	0.689	0.695	0.699	0.701	0.702	−3	0	..	..	0.52	0.48
100 Jordan	0.545	0.592	0.650	0.684	0.695	0.699	0.699	0.700	−7	0	0.83	0.95	0.72	0.62
101 China	0.407	0.495	0.590	0.637	0.662	0.689	0.695	0.699	4	0	1.96	1.78	1.55	1.42
102 Turkmenistan	..	..	..	..	..	0.688	0.693	0.698	..	0	..	..	..	..
103 Thailand	0.490	0.569	0.625	0.662	0.676	0.686	0.686	0.690	−1	1	1.50	0.94	0.93	0.82
104 Maldives	..	..	0.592	0.639	0.663	0.683	0.687	0.688	1	−1	..	..	1.43	1.26
105 Suriname	..	..	..	0.666	0.672	0.679	0.681	0.684	−2	0	..	..	..	..
106 Gabon	0.526	0.610	0.627	0.653	0.662	0.676	0.679	0.683	0	0	1.49	0.27	0.75	0.72
107 El Salvador	0.471	0.528	0.620	0.655	0.671	0.678	0.679	0.680	−3	−1	1.14	1.62	0.90	0.78
108 Bolivia, Plurinational State of	0.489	0.557	0.620	0.647	0.652	0.668	0.671	0.675	0	0	1.31	1.08	0.75	0.71
108 Mongolia	..	0.559	0.564	0.622	0.638	0.657	0.668	0.675	4	2	..	0.08	1.54	1.51
110 Palestine, State of	..	..	..	..	..	0.662	0.666	0.670	..	1	..	..	..	..
111 Paraguay	0.549	0.578	0.617	0.641	0.650	0.668	0.670	0.669	−1	−2	0.52	0.66	0.79	0.67
112 Egypt	0.407	0.502	0.593	0.625	0.640	0.661	0.661	0.662	0	0	2.12	1.68	1.08	0.92
113 Moldova, Republic of	..	0.650	0.592	0.636	0.644	0.652	0.657	0.660	−2	0	..	−0.93	0.96	0.91
114 Philippines	0.561	0.581	0.610	0.630	0.636	0.649	0.651	0.654	0	0	0.35	0.49	0.61	0.58
114 Uzbekistan	..	..	..	0.617	0.630	0.644	0.649	0.654	1	1	..	..	..	..
116 Syrian Arab Republic	0.501	0.557	0.596	0.618	0.623	0.646	0.646	0.648	0	0	1.07	0.67	0.80	0.70
117 Micronesia, Federated States of	..	..	..	..	..	0.639	0.640	0.645	..	0	..	..	..	..
118 Guyana	0.513	0.502	0.578	0.610	0.617	0.628	0.632	0.636	1	1	−0.21	1.41	0.83	0.79
119 Botswana	0.449	0.586	0.587	0.604	0.619	0.633	0.634	0.634	−1	−1	2.71	0.00	0.77	0.66
120 Honduras	0.456	0.520	0.563	0.582	0.594	0.629	0.630	0.632	3	0	1.33	0.79	1.12	0.97
121 Indonesia	0.422	0.479	0.540	0.575	0.595	0.620	0.624	0.629	1	3	1.26	1.21	1.39	1.28
121 Kiribati	..	..	..	..	..	0.628	0.627	0.629	..	0	..	..	..	..
121 South Africa	0.570	0.621	0.622	0.604	0.609	0.621	0.625	0.629	0	1	0.87	0.01	−0.01	0.11
124 Vanuatu	..	..	..	..	..	0.623	0.625	0.626	..	−2	..	..	..	..
125 Kyrgyzstan	..	0.609	0.582	0.601	0.612	0.615	0.621	0.622	−3	0	..	−0.45	0.54	0.56

TABLE 2   Human Development Index trends, 1980–2012 | 149

TABLE 2 HUMAN DEVELOPMENT INDEX TRENDS, 1980–2012

		Human Development Index (HDI)								HDI rank		Average annual HDI growth			
		Value								Change		(%)			
HDI rank		1980	1990	2000	2005	2007	2010	2011	2012	2007–2012[a]	2011–2012[a]	1980/1990	1990/2000	2000/2010	2000/2012
125	Tajikistan	..	0.615	0.529	0.582	0.587	0.612	0.618	0.622	3	1	..	−1.50	1.47	1.36
127	Viet Nam	..	0.439	0.534	0.573	0.590	0.611	0.614	0.617	0	0	..	1.98	1.37	1.22
128	Namibia	..	0.569	0.564	0.579	0.592	0.604	0.606	0.608	−2	0	..	−0.10	0.69	0.64
129	Nicaragua	0.461	0.479	0.529	0.572	0.583	0.593	0.597	0.599	0	0	0.37	1.01	1.15	1.04
130	Morocco	0.371	0.440	0.512	0.558	0.571	0.586	0.589	0.591	0	0	1.71	1.54	1.35	1.20
131	Iraq	..	..	..	0.564	0.567	0.578	0.583	0.590	1	1	..	..	..	..
132	Cape Verde	..	..	0.532	..	..	0.581	0.584	0.586	..	−1	..	..	0.88	0.81
133	Guatemala	0.432	0.464	0.523	0.551	0.570	0.579	0.580	0.581	−1	0	0.72	1.20	1.02	0.89
134	Timor-Leste	..	..	0.418	0.461	0.519	0.565	0.571	0.576	5	0	..	..	3.06	2.71
135	Ghana	0.391	0.427	0.461	0.491	0.506	0.540	0.553	0.558	7	0	0.90	0.77	1.58	1.60
136	Equatorial Guinea	..	..	0.498	0.523	0.533	0.547	0.551	0.554	−2	0	..	..	0.96	0.90
136	India	0.345	0.410	0.463	0.507	0.525	0.547	0.551	0.554	−1	0	1.75	1.23	1.67	1.50
138	Cambodia	..	..	0.444	0.501	0.520	0.532	0.538	0.543	−1	0	..	..	1.82	1.68
138	Lao People's Democratic Republic	..	0.379	0.453	0.494	0.510	0.534	0.538	0.543	3	0	..	1.80	1.66	1.53
140	Bhutan	..	..	..	..	..	0.525	0.532	0.538	..	1	..	..	..	..
141	Swaziland	..	0.533	0.502	0.504	0.520	0.532	0.536	0.536	−3	−1	..	−0.59	0.58	0.55
LOW HUMAN DEVELOPMENT															
142	Congo	0.470	0.510	0.482	0.506	0.511	0.529	0.531	0.534	−1	0	0.82	−0.56	0.94	0.86
143	Solomon Islands	..	..	0.486	0.510	0.522	0.522	0.526	0.530	−6	0	..	..	0.70	0.71
144	Sao Tome and Principe	..	..	..	0.488	0.503	0.520	0.522	0.525	0	0	..	..	..	..
145	Kenya	0.424	0.463	0.447	0.472	0.491	0.511	0.515	0.519	1	0	0.88	−0.33	1.34	1.24
146	Bangladesh	0.312	0.361	0.433	0.472	0.488	0.508	0.511	0.515	1	1	1.49	1.83	1.61	1.46
146	Pakistan	0.337	0.383	0.419	0.485	0.498	0.512	0.513	0.515	−1	0	1.29	0.89	2.03	1.74
148	Angola	..	..	0.375	0.406	0.472	0.502	0.504	0.508	1	0	..	..	2.97	2.56
149	Myanmar	0.281	0.305	0.382	0.435	0.464	0.490	0.494	0.498	1	0	0.83	2.27	2.52	2.23
150	Cameroon	0.373	0.431	0.429	0.453	0.459	0.488	0.492	0.495	1	0	1.46	−0.05	1.29	1.20
151	Madagascar	..	..	0.428	0.467	0.478	0.484	0.483	0.483	−3	0	..	..	1.24	1.02
152	Tanzania, United Republic of	..	0.353	0.369	0.395	0.408	0.466	0.470	0.476	15	1	..	0.43	2.36	2.15
153	Nigeria	..	..	..	0.434	0.448	0.462	0.467	0.471	1	1	..	..	..	..
154	Senegal	0.322	0.368	0.405	0.441	0.454	0.470	0.471	0.470	−2	−2	1.32	0.97	1.50	1.25
155	Mauritania	0.340	0.357	0.418	0.441	0.454	0.464	0.464	0.467	−3	0	0.48	1.61	1.04	0.92
156	Papua New Guinea	0.324	0.368	0.415	0.429	..	0.458	0.462	0.466	1	0	1.29	1.22	0.99	0.96
157	Nepal	0.234	0.341	0.401	0.429	0.440	0.458	0.460	0.463	2	0	3.85	1.62	1.35	1.21
158	Lesotho	0.422	0.474	0.429	0.425	0.431	0.452	0.456	0.461	2	1	1.18	−0.99	0.53	0.61
159	Togo	0.357	0.382	0.426	0.436	0.442	0.452	0.455	0.459	−2	1	0.67	1.11	0.60	0.62
160	Yemen	..	0.286	0.376	0.428	0.444	0.466	0.459	0.458	−4	−2	..	2.78	2.16	1.66
161	Haiti	0.335	0.399	0.422	0.437	..	0.450	0.453	0.456	−6	1	1.77	0.56	0.64	0.65
161	Uganda	..	0.306	0.375	0.408	0.427	0.450	0.454	0.456	0	0	..	2.06	1.84	1.65
163	Zambia	0.405	0.398	0.376	0.399	0.411	0.438	0.443	0.448	3	0	−0.18	−0.56	1.52	1.46
164	Djibouti	..	..	..	0.405	0.419	0.431	0.442	0.445	0	0	..	..	..	..
165	Gambia	0.279	0.323	0.360	0.375	0.383	0.437	0.440	0.439	5	0	1.47	1.09	1.95	1.65
166	Benin	0.253	0.314	0.380	0.414	0.420	0.432	0.434	0.436	−3	0	2.16	1.95	1.28	1.14
167	Rwanda	0.277	0.233	0.314	0.377	0.400	0.425	0.429	0.434	2	0	−1.74	3.05	3.07	2.73
168	Côte d'Ivoire	0.348	0.360	0.392	0.405	0.412	0.427	0.426	0.432	−3	1	0.34	0.85	0.86	0.81
169	Comoros	..	..	..	0.425	0.425	0.426	0.428	0.429	−7	−1	..	..	..	..
170	Malawi	0.272	0.295	0.352	0.363	0.381	0.413	0.415	0.418	1	1	0.83	1.78	1.61	1.44
171	Sudan	0.269	0.301	0.364	0.390	0.401	0.411	0.419	0.414	−3	−1	1.15	1.89	1.22	1.08
172	Zimbabwe	0.367	0.427	0.376	0.352	0.355	0.374	0.387	0.397	0	1	1.53	−1.26	−0.04	0.46
173	Ethiopia	..	..	0.275	0.316	0.350	0.387	0.392	0.396	1	−1	..	..	3.49	3.09
174	Liberia	0.298	..	0.304	0.301	0.334	0.367	0.381	0.388	3	0	..	..	1.88	2.04
175	Afghanistan	0.209	0.246	0.236	0.322	0.346	0.368	0.371	0.374	0	0	1.63	−0.41	4.54	3.91
176	Guinea-Bissau	..	..	..	0.348	0.355	0.361	0.364	0.364	−4	0	..	..	..	..
177	Sierra Leone	0.255	0.247	0.244	0.315	0.331	0.346	0.348	0.359	1	2	−0.28	−0.15	3.58	3.29
178	Burundi	0.217	0.272	0.270	0.298	0.323	0.348	0.352	0.355	2	−1	2.26	−0.07	2.59	2.31
178	Guinea	..	..	..	0.331	0.342	0.349	0.352	0.355	−2	−1	..	..	..	..
180	Central African Republic	0.285	0.312	0.294	0.308	0.316	0.344	0.348	0.352	2	−1	0.94	−0.59	1.59	1.50
181	Eritrea	..	..	..	..	..	0.342	0.346	0.351	..	1	..	..	..	..
182	Mali	0.176	0.204	0.270	0.312	0.328	0.344	0.347	0.344	−2	−1	1.50	2.86	2.45	2.04
183	Burkina Faso	..	..	..	0.301	0.314	0.334	0.340	0.343	1	0	..	..	..	..
184	Chad	..	..	0.290	0.317	0.319	0.336	0.336	0.340	−2	0	..	..	1.47	1.32
185	Mozambique	0.217	0.202	0.247	0.287	0.301	0.318	0.322	0.327	0	0	−0.70	2.00	2.57	2.37
186	Congo, Democratic Republic of the	0.286	0.297	0.234	0.258	0.280	0.295	0.299	0.304	0	0	0.37	−2.34	2.35	2.19
186	Niger	0.179	0.198	0.234	0.269	0.278	0.298	0.297	0.304	1	1	0.98	1.72	2.42	2.20

	Human Development Index (HDI)								HDI rank		Average annual HDI growth			
	Value								Change		(%)			
HDI rank	1980	1990	2000	2005	2007	2010	2011	2012	2007–2012[a]	2011–2012[a]	1980/1990	1990/2000	2000/2010	2000/2012
OTHER COUNTRIES OR TERRITORIES														
Korea, Democratic People's Rep. of	..	..	..	..	..	..	..	..	..	..	..	..	..	..
Marshall Islands	..	..	..	..	..	..	..	..	..	..	..	..	..	..
Monaco	..	..	..	..	..	..	..	..	..	..	..	..	..	..
Nauru	..	..	..	..	..	..	..	..	..	..	..	..	..	..
San Marino	..	..	..	..	..	..	..	..	..	..	..	..	..	..
Somalia	..	..	..	..	..	..	..	..	..	..	..	..	..	..
South Sudan	..	..	..	..	..	..	..	..	..	..	..	..	..	..
Tuvalu	..	..	..	..	..	..	..	..	..	..	..	..	..	..
Human Development Index groups														
Very high human development	0.773	0.817	0.867	0.889	0.896	0.902	0.904	0.905	—	—	0.56	0.59	0.40	0.36
High human development	0.605[c]	0.656[c]	0.695	0.725	0.738	0.753	0.755	0.758	—	—	0.81	0.58	0.80	0.72
Medium human development	0.419[c]	0.481	0.549	0.589	0.609	0.631	0.636	0.640	—	—	1.38	1.32	1.41	1.29
Low human development	0.315	0.350	0.385	0.424	0.442	0.461	0.464	0.466	—	—	1.05	0.95	1.82	1.62
Regions														
Arab States	0.443	0.517	0.583	0.622	0.633	0.648	0.650	0.652	—	—	1.56	1.21	1.07	0.94
East Asia and the Pacific	0.432[c]	0.502[c]	0.584	0.626	0.649	0.673	0.678	0.683	—	—	1.51	1.51	1.43	1.31
Europe and Central Asia	0.651[c]	0.701[c]	0.709	0.743	0.757	0.766	0.769	0.771	—	—	0.74	0.12	0.77	0.70
Latin America and the Caribbean	0.574	0.623	0.683	0.708	0.722	0.736	0.739	0.741	—	—	0.83	0.93	0.74	0.67
South Asia	0.357	0.418	0.470	0.514	0.531	0.552	0.555	0.558	—	—	1.58	1.19	1.60	1.43
Sub-Saharan Africa	0.366	0.387	0.405	0.432	0.449	0.468	0.472	0.475	—	—	0.58	0.44	1.47	1.34
Least developed countries	0.290[c]	0.327[c]	0.367	0.401	0.421	0.443	0.446	0.449	—	—	1.22	1.15	1.91	1.70
Small island developing states	0.530[c]	0.571[c]	0.600[c]	0.623	0.658	0.645	0.647	0.648	—	—	0.75	0.50	0.73	0.65
World	**0.561[c]**	**0.600**	**0.639**	**0.666**	**0.678**	**0.690**	**0.692**	**0.694**	**—**	**—**	**0.68**	**0.64**	**0.77**	**0.68**

NOTES

a A positive value indicates an improvement in rank.

b The substantial change in rank is due to an updated International Monetary Fund estimate of Libya's GDP growth in 2011.

c Based on fewer than half the countries in the group or region.

DEFINITIONS

Human Development Index (HDI): A composite index measuring average achievement in three basic dimensions of human development—a long and healthy life, knowledge and a decent standard of living. See *Technical note 1* at http://hdr.undp.org/en/media/HDR_2013_EN_TechNotes.pdf for details on how the HDI is calculated.

Average annual HDI growth: A smoothed annualized growth of the HDI in a given period calculated as the annual compound growth rate.

MAIN DATA SOURCES

Columns 1–8: HDRO calculations based on data from UNDESA (2011), Barro and Lee (2011), UNESCO Institute for Statistics (2012), World Bank (2012a) and IMF (2012).

Columns 9–14: Calculated based on HDI values in the relevant year.

TABLE 2   Human Development Index trends, 1980–2012 | 151

TABLE 3

Inequality-adjusted Human Development Index

HDI rank	Human Development Index (HDI) Value	Inequality-adjusted HDI (IHDI) Value	Overall loss (%)	Difference from HDI rank[a]	Inequality-adjusted life expectancy index Value	Loss (%)	Inequality-adjusted education index Value	Loss (%)	Inequality-adjusted income index Value	Loss (%)	Quintile income ratio	Income Gini coefficient
	2012	2012	2012	2012	2012	2012	2012[b]	2012	2012[b]	2012	2000–2010[c]	2000–2010[c]
VERY HIGH HUMAN DEVELOPMENT												
1 Norway	0.955	0.894	6.4	0	0.928	3.7	0.968	2.2	0.797	12.8	3.9	25.8
2 Australia	0.938	0.864	7.9	0	0.930	4.7	0.965	1.7	0.719	16.6	..	..
3 United States	0.937	0.821	12.4	−13	0.863	6.6	0.941	5.3	0.681	24.1 [d]	8.4	40.8
4 Netherlands	0.921	0.857	6.9	0	0.916	4.3	0.897	3.9	0.766	12.3	..	..
5 Germany	0.920	0.856	6.9	0	0.915	4.0	0.927	1.8	0.741	14.5	4.3	28.3
6 New Zealand	0.919	..	..	..	0.907	5.2	..	..	..	..	..	..
7 Ireland	0.916	0.850	7.2	0	0.915	4.3	0.933	3.2	0.720	13.8	5.7	34.3
7 Sweden	0.916	0.859	6.2	3	0.937	3.3	0.878	3.8	0.772	11.2	4.0	25.0
9 Switzerland	0.913	0.849	7.0	1	0.942	4.1	0.856	2.0	0.760	14.3	5.5	33.7
10 Japan	0.912	..	..	..	0.965	3.5	..	..	..	..	..	..
11 Canada	0.911	0.832	8.7	−4	0.913	5.0	0.879	3.2	0.718	17.1	5.5	32.6
12 Korea, Republic of	0.909	0.758	16.5	−18	0.915	4.3	0.702	25.5	0.679	18.4	..	..
13 Hong Kong, China (SAR)	0.906	..	..	..	0.962	2.9	..	..	..	..	..	..
13 Iceland	0.906	0.848	6.4	3	0.945	3.0	0.889	2.5	0.727	13.2	..	..
15 Denmark	0.901	0.845	6.2	3	0.887	4.4	0.891	3.1	0.764	11.0	..	..
16 Israel	0.900	0.790	12.3	−8	0.935	3.9	0.840	7.9	0.627	23.7	7.9	39.2
17 Belgium	0.897	0.825	8.0	−1	0.903	4.4	0.822	7.6	0.756	11.9	4.9	33.0
18 Austria	0.895	0.837	6.6	3	0.919	4.2	0.838	2.5	0.760	12.7	4.4	29.2
18 Singapore	0.895	..	..	..	0.935	2.9	..	..	..	..	..	..
20 France	0.893	0.812	9.0	−2	0.930	4.2	0.788	9.4	0.732	13.3	..	..
21 Finland	0.892	0.839	6.0	6	0.909	3.9	0.859	2.4	0.757	11.3	3.8	26.9
21 Slovenia	0.892	0.840	5.8	7	0.898	4.1	0.905	3.3	0.729	9.9	4.8	31.2
23 Spain	0.885	0.796	10.1	−1	0.930	4.1	0.823	5.5	0.659	19.7	6.0	34.7
24 Liechtenstein	0.883	..	..	..	..	..	..	..	..	..	..	..
25 Italy	0.881	0.776	11.9	−4	0.937	3.9	0.740	13.1	0.673	18.1	6.5	36.0
26 Luxembourg	0.875	0.813	7.2	4	0.913	3.5	0.729	6.3	0.807	11.6	4.6	30.8
26 United Kingdom	0.875	0.802	8.3	2	0.903	4.8	0.806	2.6	0.709	16.9	..	..
28 Czech Republic	0.873	0.826	5.4	9	0.874	3.9	0.904	1.3	0.712	10.7	..	..
29 Greece	0.860	0.760	11.5	−3	0.899	4.8	0.759	11.3	0.644	18.1	6.2	34.3
30 Brunei Darussalam	0.855	..	..	..	0.862	5.8	..	..	..	..	..	..
31 Cyprus	0.848	0.751	11.5	−4	0.901	4.1	0.672	16.3	0.698	13.6	..	..
32 Malta	0.847	0.778	8.2	3	0.893	5.1	0.771	5.5	0.683	13.6	..	..
33 Andorra	0.846	..	..	..	..	..	..	..	..	..	..	..
33 Estonia	0.846	0.770	9.0	2	0.813	6.0	0.894	2.6	0.627	17.7	6.4	36.0
35 Slovakia	0.840	0.788	6.3	6	0.825	5.7	0.856	1.5	0.692	11.3	3.6	26.0
36 Qatar	0.834	..	..	..	0.854	7.2	..	..	..	..	13.3	41.1
37 Hungary	0.831	0.769	7.4	3	0.810	5.7	0.854	4.1	0.658	12.2	4.8	31.2
38 Barbados	0.825	..	..	..	0.814	9.2	..	..	..	..	..	..
39 Poland	0.821	0.740	9.9	0	0.834	5.8	0.767	6.3	0.634	17.1	5.5	34.1
40 Chile	0.819	0.664	19.0	−10	0.871	6.6	0.689	13.7	0.488	34.1	13.5	52.1
41 Lithuania	0.818	0.727	11.0	−1	0.767	7.2	0.830	5.0	0.605	20.1	6.7	37.6
41 United Arab Emirates	0.818	..	..	..	0.836	6.3	..	..	..	..	..	..
43 Portugal	0.816	0.729	10.8	1	0.893	4.9	0.700	5.6	0.619	20.8	..	..
44 Latvia	0.814	0.726	10.9	−1	0.784	7.1	0.837	3.6	0.583	20.9	6.6	36.6
45 Argentina	0.811	0.653	19.5	−8	0.796	9.7	0.716	12.1	0.487	34.4	11.3	44.5
46 Seychelles	0.806	..	..	..	..	..	..	..	..	..	18.8	65.8
47 Croatia	0.805	0.683	15.1	−3	0.845	5.5	0.703	10.4	0.537	27.8	5.2	33.7
HIGH HUMAN DEVELOPMENT												
48 Bahrain	0.796	..	..	..	0.815	6.2	..	..	..	..	..	..
49 Bahamas	0.794	..	..	..	0.783	10.9	..	..	..	..	..	..
50 Belarus	0.793	0.727	8.3	3	0.737	7.4	0.819	5.4	0.636	12.1	4.0	27.2
51 Uruguay	0.792	0.662	16.4	−4	0.815	9.3	0.682	10.8	0.521	27.9	10.3	45.3
52 Montenegro	0.791	0.733	7.4	8	0.803	6.8	0.817	2.5	0.600	12.6	4.6	30.0
52 Palau	0.791	..	..	..	..	..	..	..	..	..	..	..
54 Kuwait	0.790	..	..	..	0.803	6.7	..	..	..	..	..	..
55 Russian Federation	0.788	..	..	..	0.689	10.8	..	..	0.647	11.9	7.3	40.1
56 Romania	0.786	0.687	12.6	2	0.770	9.6	0.779	5.0	0.540	22.2	4.6	30.0
57 Bulgaria	0.782	0.704	9.9	5	0.776	7.8	0.760	6.1	0.592	15.4	4.3	28.2
57 Saudi Arabia	0.782	..	..	..	0.754	11.5	..	..	..	..	..	..
59 Cuba	0.780	..	..	..	0.882	5.4	..	..	..	..	..	..
59 Panama	0.780	0.588	24.6	−15	0.776	12.4	0.609	17.8	0.431	40.5	17.1	51.9

	Human Development Index (HDI)	Inequality-adjusted HDI (IHDI)			Inequality-adjusted life expectancy index		Inequality-adjusted education index		Inequality-adjusted income index		Quintile income ratio	Income Gini coefficient
	Value	Value	Overall loss (%)	Difference from HDI rank[a]	Value	Loss (%)	Value	Loss (%)	Value	Loss (%)		
HDI rank	2012	2012	2012	2012	2012	2012	2012[b]	2012	2012[b]	2012	2000–2010[c]	2000–2010[c]
61 Mexico	0.775	0.593	23.4	−12	0.801	10.9	0.564	21.9	0.463	35.6	11.3	48.3
62 Costa Rica	0.773	0.606	21.5	−10	0.862	7.8	0.601	15.7	0.430	37.9	14.5	50.7
63 Grenada	0.770	..	..	..	0.798	9.6	..	..	..	..	..	..
64 Libya	0.769	..	..	..	0.782	9.7	..	..	..	..	..	..
64 Malaysia	0.769	..	..	..	0.799	6.7	..	..	..	..	11.3	46.2
64 Serbia	0.769	0.696	9.5	8	0.788	8.3	0.709	9.9	0.603	10.3	4.2	27.8
67 Antigua and Barbuda	0.760	..	..	..	..	..	..	..	..	..	..	..
67 Trinidad and Tobago	0.760	0.644	15.3	−3	0.660	16.6	0.652	6.6	0.621	21.9	..	..
69 Kazakhstan	0.754	0.652	13.6	3	0.624	16.2	0.781	6.9	0.567	17.3	4.2	29.0
70 Albania	0.749	0.645	13.9	0	0.797	11.2	0.640	11.9	0.526	18.3	5.3	34.5
71 Venezuela, Bolivarian Republic of	0.748	0.549	26.6	−17	0.754	12.2	0.571	18.1	0.385	44.9	11.5	44.8
72 Dominica	0.745	..	..	..	..	..	..	..	..	..	..	..
72 Georgia	0.745	0.631	15.3	−2	0.720	15.1	0.814	3.3	0.428	25.9	8.9	41.3
72 Lebanon	0.745	0.575	22.8	−9	0.718	13.5	0.531	24.1	0.498	30.0	..	..
72 Saint Kitts and Nevis	0.745	..	..	..	..	..	..	..	..	..	..	..
76 Iran, Islamic Republic of	0.742	..	..	..	0.703	16.1	..	..	..	..	7.0	38.3
77 Peru	0.741	0.561	24.3	−10	0.727	14.8	0.538	24.6	0.452	32.5	13.5	48.1
78 The former Yugoslav Republic of Macedonia	0.740	0.631	14.7	2	0.784	9.4	0.612	12.3	0.524	21.8	9.5	43.2
78 Ukraine	0.740	0.672	9.2	13	0.687	10.5	0.808	6.1	0.548	10.9	3.8	26.4
80 Mauritius	0.737	0.639	13.3	5	0.760	9.8	0.570	13.5	0.602	16.6	..	..
81 Bosnia and Herzegovina	0.735	0.650	11.5	11	0.794	9.6	0.668	5.2	0.518	19.2	6.5	36.2
82 Azerbaijan	0.734	0.650	11.4	11	0.636	20.6	0.697	8.3	0.620	4.5	5.3	33.7
83 Saint Vincent and the Grenadines	0.733	..	..	..	0.710	14.0	..	..	..	..	..	..
84 Oman	0.731	..	..	..	0.777	7.2	..	..	..	..	..	..
85 Brazil	0.730	0.531	27.2	−12	0.725	14.4	0.503	25.3	0.411	39.7	20.6	54.7
85 Jamaica	0.730	0.591	19.1	2	0.710	15.3	0.669	10.6	0.434	30.1	9.6	45.5
87 Armenia	0.729	0.649	10.9	13	0.728	14.9	0.735	3.7	0.510	13.9	4.5	30.9
88 Saint Lucia	0.725	..	..	..	0.773	10.4	..	..	..	..	..	..
89 Ecuador	0.724	0.537	25.8	−8	0.754	14.1	0.529	22.1	0.390	38.8	12.5	49.3
90 Turkey	0.722	0.560	22.5	−1	0.743	12.8	0.442	27.4	0.534	26.5	7.9	39.0
91 Colombia	0.719	0.519	27.8	−11	0.732	13.7	0.523	21.5	0.366	44.5	20.1	55.9
92 Sri Lanka	0.715	0.607	15.1	11	0.786	9.4	0.618	14.6	0.461	20.8	6.9	40.3
93 Algeria	0.713	..	..	..	0.717	14.5	..	..	..	..	..	..
94 Tunisia	0.712	..	..	..	0.752	12.6	..	..	..	..	8.1	41.4
MEDIUM HUMAN DEVELOPMENT												
95 Tonga	0.710	..	..	..	0.712	13.8	..	..	..	..	..	..
96 Belize	0.702	..	..	..	0.777	12.2	..	..	..	..	..	..
96 Dominican Republic	0.702	0.510	27.3	−15	0.708	16.0	0.458	26.8	0.410	37.6	11.3	47.2
96 Fiji	0.702	..	..	..	0.676	13.0	..	..	..	..	8.0	42.8
96 Samoa	0.702	..	..	..	0.718	13.4	..	..	..	..	..	..
100 Jordan	0.700	0.568	19.0	5	0.732	13.1	0.541	22.4	0.462	21.1	5.7	35.4
101 China	0.699	0.543	22.4	0	0.731	13.5	0.481	23.2	0.455	29.5	9.6	42.5
102 Turkmenistan	0.698	..	..	..	0.521	26.7	..	..	..	..	..	..
103 Thailand	0.690	0.543	21.3	0	0.768	10.1	0.491	18.0	0.424	34.0	7.1	40.0
104 Maldives	0.688	0.515	25.2	−8	0.834	7.3	0.335	41.2	0.489	23.2	6.8	37.4
105 Suriname	0.684	0.526	23.0	−2	0.680	15.0	0.504	20.1	0.426	32.8	..	..
106 Gabon	0.683	0.550	19.5	6	0.489	27.8	0.611	7.3	0.556	22.1	7.8	41.5
107 El Salvador	0.680	0.499	26.6	−11	0.699	15.2	0.429	32.4	0.415	31.1	14.3	48.3
108 Bolivia, Plurinational State of	0.675	0.444	34.2	−12	0.553	25.1	0.537	27.6	0.294	47.4	27.8	56.3
108 Mongolia	0.675	0.568	15.9	13	0.623	18.8	0.661	8.9	0.444	19.7	6.2	36.5
110 Palestine, State of	0.670	..	..	..	0.725	13.1	..	..	..	..	5.8	35.5
111 Paraguay	0.669	..	..	..	0.681	17.8	..	..	0.374	33.4	17.3	52.4
112 Egypt	0.662	0.503	24.1	−7	0.724	13.9	0.347	40.9	0.505	14.2	4.4	30.8
113 Moldova, Republic of	0.660	0.584	11.6	18	0.693	11.2	0.670	6.1	0.429	17.0	5.3	33.0
114 Philippines	0.654	0.524	19.9	4	0.654	15.2	0.587	13.5	0.375	30.0	8.3	43.0
114 Uzbekistan	0.654	0.551	15.8	13	0.578	24.3	0.706	1.4	0.409	20.1	6.2	36.7
116 Syrian Arab Republic	0.648	0.515	20.4	3	0.793	10.0	0.372	31.5	0.464	18.3	5.7	35.8
117 Micronesia, Federated States of	0.645	..	..	..	0.625	19.2	..	..	..	..	40.2	61.1
118 Guyana	0.636	0.514	19.1	2	0.618	21.7	0.559	10.5	0.393	24.4	..	..
119 Botswana	0.634	..	..	..	0.394	24.3	..	..	..	..	..	..
120 Honduras	0.632	0.458	27.5	−3	0.694	17.4	0.413	28.2	0.335	35.8	29.7	57.0
121 Indonesia	0.629	0.514	18.3	3	0.652	16.8	0.459	20.4	0.453	17.7	5.1	34.0

TABLE 3   Inequality-adjusted Human Development Index | 153

TABLE 3 INEQUALITY-ADJUSTED HUMAN DEVELOPMENT INDEX

	Human Development Index (HDI)	Inequality-adjusted HDI (IHDI)			Inequality-adjusted life expectancy index		Inequality-adjusted education index		Inequality-adjusted income index		Quintile income ratio	Income Gini coefficient
	Value	Value	Overall loss (%)	Difference from HDI rank[a]	Value	Loss (%)	Value	Loss (%)	Value	Loss (%)		
HDI rank	2012	2012	2012	2012	2012	2012	2012[b]	2012	2012[b]	2012	2000–2010[c]	2000–2010[c]
121 Kiribati	0.629	..	..	..	..	..	..	..	..	..	..	..
121 South Africa	0.629	..	..	..	0.376	28.4	0.558	20.8	..	..	25.3	63.1
124 Vanuatu	0.626	..	..	..	0.681	15.6	..	..	..	..	..	..
125 Kyrgyzstan	0.622	0.516	17.1	8	0.606	19.8	0.674	6.5	0.336	24.1	6.4	36.2
125 Tajikistan	0.622	0.507	18.4	2	0.548	27.2	0.623	12.2	0.383	15.0	4.7	30.8
127 Viet Nam	0.617	0.531	14.0	14	0.755	13.4	0.447	17.1	0.444	11.4	5.9	35.6
128 Namibia	0.608	0.344	43.5	−16	0.528	21.1	0.402	27.8	0.191	68.3	21.8	63.9
129 Nicaragua	0.599	0.434	27.5	1	0.735	13.9	0.351	33.3	0.317	33.6	7.6	40.5
130 Morocco	0.591	0.415	29.7	0	0.686	16.7	0.243	45.8	0.430	23.0	7.3	40.9
131 Iraq	0.590	..	..	..	0.622	20.3	0.334	33.0	..	..	4.6	30.9
132 Cape Verde	0.586	..	..	..	0.746	12.7	..	..	..	..	12.3	50.5
133 Guatemala	0.581	0.389	33.1	−3	0.659	18.6	0.280	36.1	0.318	42.5	19.6	55.9
134 Timor-Leste	0.576	0.386	33.0	−3	0.471	30.2	0.251	47.6	0.485	17.8	4.6	31.9
135 Ghana	0.558	0.379	32.2	−3	0.508	27.5	0.352	40.9	0.303	27.2	9.3	42.8
136 Equatorial Guinea	0.554	..	..	..	0.270	45.4	..	..	..	..	..	..
136 India	0.554	0.392	29.3	1	0.525	27.1	0.264	42.4	0.434	15.8	4.9	33.4
138 Cambodia	0.543	0.402	25.9	3	0.488	28.8	0.372	28.3	0.358	20.3	6.1	37.9
138 Lao People's Democratic Republic	0.543	0.409	24.7	4	0.589	21.7	0.311	31.2	0.374	20.6	5.9	36.7
140 Bhutan	0.538	0.430	20.0	8	0.568	24.1	0.312	12.2	0.450	23.1	6.8	38.1
141 Swaziland	0.536	0.346	35.4	−3	0.296	35.0	0.409	29.8	0.343	40.9	14.0	51.5
LOW HUMAN DEVELOPMENT												
142 Congo	0.534	0.368	31.1	1	0.374	37.0	0.384	25.4	0.348	30.3	10.7	47.3
143 Solomon Islands	0.530	..	..	..	0.602	20.7	..	..	..	..	..	..
144 Sao Tome and Principe	0.525	0.358	31.7	1	0.503	28.8	0.379	20.0	0.241	44.2	10.8	50.8
145 Kenya	0.519	0.344	33.6	−2	0.390	34.1	0.405	30.7	0.259	36.0	11.0	47.7
146 Bangladesh	0.515	0.374	27.4	5	0.595	23.2	0.252	39.4	0.350	17.7	4.7	32.1
146 Pakistan	0.515	0.356	30.9	2	0.487	32.3	0.217	45.2	0.426	11.0	4.2	30.0
148 Angola	0.508	0.285	43.9	−12	0.267	46.1	0.303	34.6	0.286	50.0	30.9	58.6
149 Myanmar	0.498	..	..	..	0.537	25.3	..	..	..	..	..	..
150 Cameroon	0.495	0.330	33.4	−1	0.288	43.0	0.346	35.3	0.361	19.9	6.9	38.9
151 Madagascar	0.483	0.335	30.7	1	0.549	25.6	0.342	30.1	0.199	36.1	9.3	44.1
152 Tanzania, United Republic of	0.476	0.346	27.3	5	0.414	32.4	0.326	28.3	0.307	20.9	6.6	37.6
153 Nigeria	0.471	0.276	41.4	−13	0.286	43.8	0.250	45.2	0.295	34.5	12.2	48.8
154 Senegal	0.470	0.315	33.0	2	0.432	30.7	0.223	44.6	0.325	21.6	7.4	39.2
155 Mauritania	0.467	0.306	34.4	1	0.391	36.2	0.212	42.1	0.346	23.8	7.8	40.5
156 Papua New Guinea	0.466	..	..	..	0.508	25.2	..	..	..	..	..	..
157 Nepal	0.463	0.304	34.2	0	0.622	19.5	0.202	43.6	0.225	37.4	5.0	32.8
158 Lesotho	0.461	0.296	35.9	−1	0.297	34.3	0.379	24.3	0.229	47.0	19.0	52.5
159 Togo	0.459	0.305	33.5	3	0.371	37.2	0.291	41.5	0.263	20.0	5.6	34.4
160 Yemen	0.458	0.310	32.3	6	0.541	25.1	0.156	49.8	0.353	17.6	6.3	37.7
161 Haiti	0.456	0.273	40.2	−7	0.461	30.9	0.241	40.7	0.182	47.9	26.6	59.2
161 Uganda	0.456	0.303	33.6	3	0.331	39.1	0.327	32.2	0.257	29.1	8.7	44.3
163 Zambia	0.448	0.283	36.7	−2	0.269	41.9	0.383	23.8	0.221	42.6[e]	16.6	54.6
164 Djibouti	0.445	0.285	36.0	1	0.380	36.9	0.166	47.0	0.365	21.7	7.7	40.0
165 Gambia	0.439	..	..	..	0.404	33.9	..	..	..	..	11.0	47.3
166 Benin	0.436	0.280	35.8	−1	0.343	40.3	0.213	42.0	0.301	23.6	6.6	38.6
167 Rwanda	0.434	0.287	33.9	6	0.330	41.3	0.285	29.4	0.251	30.2	12.7	53.1
168 Côte d'Ivoire	0.432	0.265	38.6	−3	0.352	37.8	0.197	43.2	0.268	34.4	8.5	41.5
169 Comoros	0.429	..	..	..	0.440	32.6	0.189	47.4	..	..	26.7	64.3
170 Malawi	0.418	0.287	31.4	7	0.329	39.9	0.309	30.2	0.232	23.1	6.6	39.0
171 Sudan	0.414	..	..	..	0.440	33.0	..	..	..	..	6.2	35.3
172 Zimbabwe	0.397	0.284	28.5	5	0.357	30.6	0.469	17.8	0.137	35.8	..	..
173 Ethiopia	0.396	0.269	31.9	1	0.404	35.4	0.179	38.3	0.271	20.8	4.3	29.8
174 Liberia	0.388	0.251	35.3	0	0.367	37.6	0.230	46.4	0.188	19.0	7.0	38.2
175 Afghanistan	0.374	..	..	..	0.225	50.9	0.205	39.3	..	..	4.0	27.8
176 Guinea-Bissau	0.364	0.213	41.4	−3	0.224	50.1	0.185	40.3	0.234	32.5	5.9	35.5
177 Sierra Leone	0.359	0.210	41.6	−3	0.242	45.3	0.171	47.4	0.222	31.0	8.1	42.5
178 Burundi	0.355	..	..	..	0.264	45.6	..	..	..	..	4.8	33.3
178 Guinea	0.355	0.217	38.8	0	0.311	42.7	0.145	42.0	0.228	31.1	7.3	39.4
180 Central African Republic	0.352	0.209	40.5	−2	0.247	46.0	0.176	45.9	0.210	28.1	18.0	56.3
181 Eritrea	0.351	..	..	..	0.485	26.6	..	..	..	..	..	..
182 Mali	0.344	..	..	..	0.269	46.3	0.162	36.9	..	..	5.2	33.0

HDI rank	Human Development Index (HDI) Value 2012	Inequality-adjusted HDI (IHDI) Value 2012	Overall loss (%) 2012	Difference from HDI rank[a] 2012	Inequality-adjusted life expectancy index Value 2012	Loss (%) 2012	Inequality-adjusted education index Value 2012[b]	Loss (%) 2012	Inequality-adjusted income index Value 2012[b]	Loss (%) 2012	Quintile income ratio 2000–2010[c]	Income Gini coefficient 2000–2010[c]
183 Burkina Faso	0.343	0.226	34.2	4	0.329	41.7	0.125	36.2	0.281	23.4	7.0	39.8
184 Chad	0.340	0.203	40.1	−1	0.226	52.0	0.126	43.4	0.295	21.0	7.4	39.8
185 Mozambique	0.327	0.220	32.7	5	0.286	40.8	0.182	18.2	0.205	37.0[f]	9.8	45.7
186 Congo, Democratic Republic of the	0.304	0.183	39.9	−1	0.226	50.0	0.249	31.2	0.108	36.8	9.3	44.4
186 Niger	0.304	0.200	34.2	0	0.317	42.6	0.107	39.5	0.236	17.9	5.3	34.6
OTHER COUNTRIES OR TERRITORIES												
Korea, Democratic People's Rep. of	..	..	..	..	..	..	..	..	..	..	..	..
Marshall Islands	..	..	..	..	..	..	..	..	..	..	..	..
Monaco	..	..	..	..	..	..	..	..	..	..	..	..
Nauru	..	..	..	..	..	..	..	..	..	..	..	..
San Marino	..	..	..	..	..	..	..	..	..	..	..	..
Somalia	..	..	..	..	..	..	..	..	..	..	..	..
South Sudan	..	..	..	..	..	..	..	..	..	..	..	45.5
Tuvalu	..	..	..	..	..	..	..	..	..	..	..	..
Human Development Index groups												
Very high human development	0.905	0.807	10.8	—	0.897	5.2	0.851	6.8	0.688	19.8	—	—
High human development	0.758	0.602	20.6	—	0.736	12.4	0.592	19.9	0.500	28.6	—	—
Medium human development	0.640	0.485	24.2	—	0.633	19.3	0.395	30.2	0.456	22.7	—	—
Low human development	0.466	0.310	33.5	—	0.395	35.7	0.246	38.7	0.307	25.6	—	—
Regions												
Arab States	0.652	0.486	25.4	—	0.669	16.7	0.320	39.6	0.538	17.5	—	—
East Asia and the Pacific	0.683	0.537	21.3	—	0.711	14.2	0.480	21.9	0.455	27.2	—	—
Europe and Central Asia	0.771	0.672	12.9	—	0.716	11.7	0.713	10.5	0.594	16.3	—	—
Latin America and the Caribbean	0.741	0.550	25.7	—	0.744	13.4	0.532	23.0	0.421	38.5	—	—
South Asia	0.558	0.395	29.1	—	0.531	27.0	0.267	42.0	0.436	15.9	—	—
Sub-Saharan Africa	0.475	0.309	35.0	—	0.335	39.0	0.285	35.3	0.308	30.4	—	—
Least developed countries	0.449	0.303	32.5	—	0.406	34.6	0.240	36.2	0.287	26.1	—	—
Small island developing states	0.648	0.459	29.2	—	0.633	19.2	0.412	30.1	0.370	37.2	—	—
World	**0.694**	**0.532**	**23.3**	**—**	**0.638**	**19.0**	**0.453**	**27.0**	**0.522**	**23.5**	**—**	**—**

NOTES

a Based on countries for which the Inequality-adjusted Human Development Index is calculated.

b The list of surveys used to estimate inequalities is available at http://hdr.undp.org.

c Data refer to the most recent year available during the period specified.

d Based on the 2010 Current Population Survey (from the Luxembourg Income Study database). In the 2011 *Human Development Report* income inequality was based on the 2005 American Community Survey (from the World Bank's International Income Distribution Database). The two sources seem to be inconsistent.

e Based on simulated income distribution from the 2007 Demographic and Health Survey. In the 2011 *Human Development Report* inequality in consumption was based on the 2002–2003 Living Conditions Monitoring Survey.

f Based on simulated income distribution from the 2009 Demographic and Health Survey. In the 2011 *Human Development Report* inequality in consumption was based on the 2003 National Household Survey of Living Conditions.

DEFINITIONS

Human Development Index (HDI): A composite index measuring average achievement in three basic dimensions of human development—a long and healthy life, knowledge and a decent standard of living. See *Technical note 1* at http://hdr.undp.org/en/media/HDR_2013_EN_TechNotes.pdf for details on how the HDI is calculated.

Inequality-adjusted HDI (IHDI): HDI value adjusted for inequalities in the three basic dimensions of human development. See *Technical note 2* at http://hdr.undp.org/en/media/HDR_2013_EN_TechNotes.pdf for details on how the IHDI is calculated.

Overall loss: The loss in potential human development due to inequality, calculated as the percentage difference between the HDI and the IHDI.

Inequality-adjusted life expectancy index: The HDI life expectancy index adjusted for inequality in distribution of expected length of life based on data from life tables listed in *Main data sources*.

Inequality-adjusted education index: The HDI education index adjusted for inequality in distribution of years of schooling based on data from household surveys listed in *Main data sources*.

Inequality-adjusted income index: The HDI income index adjusted for inequality in income distribution based on data from household surveys listed in *Main data sources*.

Quintile income ratio: Ratio of the average income of the richest 20% of the population to the average income of the poorest 20% of the population.

Income Gini coefficient: Measure of the deviation of the distribution of income (or consumption) among individuals or households within a country from a perfectly equal distribution. A value of 0 represents absolute equality, a value of 100 absolute inequality.

MAIN DATA SOURCES

Column 1: HDRO calculations based on data from UNDESA (2011), Barro and Lee (2011), UNESCO Institute for Statistics (2012), World Bank (2012a) and IMF (2012).

Column 2: Calculated as the geometric mean of the values in columns 5, 7 and 9 using the methodology in *Technical note 2*.

Column 3: Calculated based on data in columns 1 and 2.

Column 4: Calculated based on data in column 2 and recalculated HDI ranks for countries with the IHDI.

Column 5: Calculated based on abridged life tables from UNDESA (2011).

Column 6: Calculated based on data in column 5 and the unadjusted life expectancy index.

Columns 7 and 9: Calculated based on data from LIS (2012), Eurostat (2012), World Bank (2012b), UNICEF Multiple Indicator Cluster Surveys for 2002–2012 and ICF Macro (2012) using the methodology in *Technical note 2*.

Column 8: Calculated based on data in column 7 and the unadjusted education index.

Column 10: Calculated based on data in column 9 and the unadjusted income index.

Columns 11 and 12: World Bank (2012a).

TABLE 3 Inequality-adjusted Human Development Index | 155

TABLE 4

Gender Inequality Index

HDI rank		Gender Inequality Index Rank 2012	Gender Inequality Index Value 2012	Maternal mortality ratio[a] (deaths per 100,000 live births) 2010	Adolescent fertility rate[b] (births per 1,000 women ages 15–19) 2012[d]	Seats in national parliament[c] (% female) 2012	Population with at least secondary education (% ages 25 and older) Female 2006–2010[e]	Population with at least secondary education (% ages 25 and older) Male 2006–2010[e]	Labour force participation rate (% ages 15 and older) Female 2011	Labour force participation rate (% ages 15 and older) Male 2011
VERY HIGH HUMAN DEVELOPMENT										
1	Norway	5	0.065	7	7.4	39.6	95.6	94.7	61.7	70.1
2	Australia	17	0.115	7	12.5	29.2	92.2	92.2	58.8	72.3
3	United States	42	0.256	21	27.4	17.0[f]	94.7	94.3	57.5	70.1
4	Netherlands	1	0.045	6	4.3	37.8	87.5	90.4	58.3	71.3
5	Germany	6	0.075	7	6.8	32.4	96.2	96.9	53.0	66.5
6	New Zealand	31	0.164	15	18.6	32.2	82.8	84.7	61.6	74.1
7	Ireland	19	0.121	6	8.8	19.0	74.8	73.0	52.6	68.5
7	Sweden	2	0.055	4	6.5	44.7	84.4	85.5	59.4	68.1
9	Switzerland	3	0.057	8	3.9	26.8	95.1	96.6	60.6	75.0
10	Japan	21	0.131	5	6.0	13.4	80.0[g]	82.3[g]	49.4	71.7
11	Canada	18	0.119	12	11.3	28.0	100.0	100.0	61.9	71.4
12	Korea, Republic of	27	0.153	16	5.8	15.7	79.4[g]	91.7[g]	49.2	71.4
13	Hong Kong, China (SAR)	..	..	..	4.2	..	68.7	76.4	51.0	68.1
13	Iceland	10	0.089	5	11.6	39.7	91.0	91.6	70.8	78.4
15	Denmark	3	0.057	12	5.1	39.1	99.3	99.4	59.8	69.1
16	Israel	25	0.144	7	14.0	20.0	82.7	85.5	52.5	62.4
17	Belgium	12	0.098	8	11.2	38.9	76.4	82.7	47.7	60.6
18	Austria	14	0.102	4	9.7	28.7	100.0	100.0	53.9	67.6
18	Singapore	13	0.101	3	6.7	23.5	71.3	78.9	56.5	76.6
20	France	9	0.083	8	6.0	25.1	75.9	81.3	51.1	61.9
21	Finland	6	0.075	5	9.3	42.5	100.0	100.0	55.9	64.2
21	Slovenia	8	0.080	12	4.5	23.1	94.2	97.1	53.1	65.1
23	Spain	15	0.103	6	10.7	34.9	63.3	69.7	51.6	67.4
24	Liechtenstein	..	..	..	6.0	24.0	..	..	..	..
25	Italy	11	0.094	4	4.0	20.7	68.0	78.1	37.9	59.6
26	Luxembourg	26	0.149	20	8.4	25.0	77.1	78.7	49.2	65.2
26	United Kingdom	34	0.205	12	29.7	22.1	99.6	99.8	55.6	68.5
28	Czech Republic	20	0.122	5	9.2	21.0	99.8	99.8	49.6	68.2
29	Greece	23	0.136	3	9.6	21.0	57.7	66.6	44.8	65.0
30	Brunei Darussalam	..	..	24	22.7	..	66.6[g]	61.2[g]	55.5	76.5
31	Cyprus	22	0.134	10	5.5	10.7	71.0	78.1	57.2	71.5
32	Malta	39	0.236	8	11.8	8.7	58.0	67.3	35.2	67.4
33	Andorra	..	..	..	7.3	50.0	49.5	49.3	..	..
33	Estonia	29	0.158	2	17.2	19.8	94.4[g]	94.6[g]	56.7	68.2
35	Slovakia	32	0.171	6	16.7	17.3	98.6	99.1	51.2	68.1
36	Qatar	117	0.546	7	15.5	0.1[h]	70.1	62.1	51.8	95.2
37	Hungary	42	0.256	21	13.6	8.8	93.2[g]	96.7[g]	43.8	58.4
38	Barbados	61	0.343	51	40.8	19.6	89.5[g]	87.6[g]	64.8	76.2
39	Poland	24	0.140	5	12.2	21.8	76.9	83.5	48.2	64.3
40	Chile	66	0.360	25	56.0	13.9	72.1	75.9	47.1	74.2
41	Lithuania	28	0.157	8	16.1	19.1	87.9	93.1	54.1	63.9
41	United Arab Emirates	40	0.241	12	23.4	17.5	73.1[g]	61.3[g]	43.5	92.3
43	Portugal	16	0.114	8	12.5	28.7	40.9	40.2	56.5	68.0
44	Latvia	36	0.216	34	12.8	23.0	98.6	98.2	55.2	67.2
45	Argentina	71	0.380	77	54.2	37.7	57.0[g]	54.9[g]	47.3	74.9
46	Seychelles	..	..	..	47.6	43.8	66.9	66.6	..	..
47	Croatia	33	0.179	17	12.8	23.8	57.4[g]	72.3[g]	46.0	59.7
HIGH HUMAN DEVELOPMENT										
48	Bahrain	45	0.258	20	14.8	18.8	74.4[g]	80.4[g]	39.4	87.3
49	Bahamas	53	0.316	47	28.3	16.7	91.2	87.6	69.3	79.3
50	Belarus	..	..	4	20.5	29.7	..	..	50.2	62.6
51	Uruguay	69	0.367	29	59.0	12.3	50.6	48.8	55.6	76.5
52	Montenegro	..	..	8	14.8	12.3	97.5	98.8	..	..
52	Palau	..	..	..	12.7	6.9	..	..	..	..
54	Kuwait	47	0.274	14	14.4	6.3	53.7	46.6	43.4	82.3
55	Russian Federation	51	0.312	34	23.2	11.1	93.5[g]	96.2[g]	56.3	71.0
56	Romania	55	0.327	27	28.8	9.7	83.4	90.5	48.6	64.9
57	Bulgaria	38	0.219	11	36.2	20.8	90.9	94.4	48.6	60.3
57	Saudi Arabia	145	0.682	24	22.1	0.1[h]	50.3[g]	57.9[g]	17.7	74.1
59	Cuba	63	0.356	73	43.9	45.2	73.9[g]	80.4[g]	43.3	69.9
59	Panama	108	0.503	92	75.9	8.5	63.5[g]	60.7[g]	49.6	82.5

HDI rank	Gender Inequality Index Rank	Gender Inequality Index Value	Maternal mortality ratio[a] (deaths per 100,000 live births)	Adolescent fertility rate[b] (births per 1,000 women ages 15–19)	Seats in national parliament[c] (% female)	Population with at least secondary education (% ages 25 and older) Female	Population with at least secondary education (% ages 25 and older) Male	Labour force participation rate (% ages 15 and older) Female	Labour force participation rate (% ages 15 and older) Male
	2012	2012	2010	2012[d]	2012	2006–2010[e]	2006–2010[e]	2011	2011
61 Mexico	72	0.382	50	65.5	36.0	51.2	57.0	44.3	80.5
62 Costa Rica	62	0.346	40	61.9	38.6	54.4[g]	52.8[g]	46.4	78.9
63 Grenada	..	..	24	35.4	17.9	..	..	..	..
64 Libya	36	0.216	58	2.6	16.5	55.6[g]	44.0[g]	30.1	76.8
64 Malaysia	42	0.256	29	9.8	13.2	66.0[g]	72.8[g]	43.8	76.9
64 Serbia	..	..	12	19.2	32.4	80.1	90.7	..	..
67 Antigua and Barbuda	..	..	..	49.1	19.4	..	..	..	..
67 Trinidad and Tobago	50	0.311	46	31.6	27.4	59.4	59.2	54.9	78.3
69 Kazakhstan	51	0.312	51	25.5	18.2	99.3	99.4	66.6	77.2
70 Albania	41	0.251	27	14.9	15.7	78.8	85.0	49.6	71.3
71 Venezuela, Bolivarian Republic of	93	0.466	92	87.3	17.0	55.1	49.8	52.1	80.2
72 Dominica	..	..	..	18.9	12.5	29.7	23.2	..	..
72 Georgia	81	0.438	67	39.5	6.6	89.7	92.7	55.8	74.2
72 Lebanon	78	0.433	25	15.4	3.1	53.0	55.4	22.6	70.8
72 Saint Kitts and Nevis	..	..	..	33.2	6.7	..	..	..	..
76 Iran, Islamic Republic of	107	0.496	21	25.0	3.1	62.1	69.1	16.4	72.5
77 Peru	73	0.387	67	48.7	21.5	47.3	59.1	67.8	84.7
78 The former Yugoslav Republic of Macedonia	30	0.162	10	17.8	30.9	72.0	85.3	42.9	68.9
78 Ukraine	57	0.338	32	26.1	8.0	91.5[g]	96.1[g]	53.3	66.6
80 Mauritius	70	0.377	60	31.8	18.8	45.2[g]	52.9[g]	44.1	75.5
81 Bosnia and Herzegovina	..	..	8	13.4	19.3	..	..	35.2	58.6
82 Azerbaijan	54	0.323	43	31.4	16.0	90.0	95.7	61.6	68.5
83 Saint Vincent and the Grenadines	..	..	48	54.1	17.4	..	..	55.7	78.4
84 Oman	59	0.340	32	9.3	9.6	47.2	57.1	28.3	81.6
85 Brazil	85	0.447	56	76.0	9.6	50.5	48.5	59.6	80.9
85 Jamaica	87	0.458	110	69.7	15.5	74.0[g]	71.1[g]	56.0	71.8
87 Armenia	59	0.340	30	33.2	10.7	94.1[g]	94.8[g]	49.4	70.2
88 Saint Lucia	..	..	35	55.9	17.2	..	..	64.2	77.3
89 Ecuador	83	0.442	110	80.6	32.3	36.6	36.6	54.3	82.7
90 Turkey	68	0.366	20	30.5	14.2	26.7	42.4	28.1	71.4
91 Colombia	88	0.459	92	68.1	13.6	43.8	42.4	55.8	79.7
92 Sri Lanka	75	0.402	35	22.1	5.8	72.6	75.5	34.7	76.3
93 Algeria	74	0.391	97	6.1	25.6	20.9	27.3	15.0	71.9
94 Tunisia	46	0.261	56	4.4	26.7	29.9	44.4	25.5	70.0
MEDIUM HUMAN DEVELOPMENT									
95 Tonga	90	0.462	110	18.0	3.6[i]	71.6[g]	76.7[g]	53.6	75.0
96 Belize	79	0.435	53	70.8	13.3	35.2[g]	32.8[g]	48.3	81.8
96 Dominican Republic	109	0.508	150	103.6	19.1	43.3	41.7	51.0	78.6
96 Fiji	..	..	26	42.8	..	57.5	58.1	39.3	79.5
96 Samoa	..	..	..	25.5	4.1	64.3	60.0	42.8	77.8
100 Jordan	99	0.482	63	23.7	11.1	68.9	77.7	15.6	65.9
101 China	35	0.213	37	9.1	21.3	54.8[g]	70.4[g]	67.7	80.1
102 Turkmenistan	..	..	67	16.9	16.8	..	..	46.4	76.0
103 Thailand	66	0.360	48	37.0	15.7	29.0	35.6	63.8	80.0
104 Maldives	64	0.357	60	10.2	6.5	20.7	30.1	55.7	76.8
105 Suriname	94	0.467	130	34.9	11.8	40.5	47.1	40.5	68.7
106 Gabon	105	0.492	230	81.0	16.7	53.8[g]	34.7[g]	56.3	65.0
107 El Salvador	82	0.441	81	76.2	26.2	34.8	40.8	47.4	78.6
108 Bolivia, Plurinational State of	97	0.474	190	74.7	30.1	39.8	49.7	64.1	80.9
108 Mongolia	56	0.328	63	18.7	12.7	83.0[g]	81.8[g]	54.3	65.5
110 Palestine, State of	..	..	64	48.3	..	48.0	56.2	15.1	66.3
111 Paraguay	95	0.472	99	66.7	13.6	35.0	39.0	57.9	86.3
112 Egypt	126	0.590	66	40.6	2.2	43.4[g]	59.3[g]	23.7	74.3
113 Moldova, Republic of	49	0.303	41	29.1	19.8	91.6	95.3	38.4	45.1
114 Philippines	77	0.418	99	46.5	22.1	65.9[g]	63.7[g]	49.7	79.4
114 Uzbekistan	..	..	28	12.8	19.2	..	..	47.7	74.7
116 Syrian Arab Republic	118	0.551	70	36.5	12.0	27.4	38.2	13.1	71.6
117 Micronesia, Federated States of	..	..	100	18.5	0.1	..	..	..	..
118 Guyana	104	0.490	280	53.9	31.3	61.5[g]	48.8[g]	41.8	79.1
119 Botswana	102	0.485	160	43.8	7.9	73.6[g]	77.5[g]	71.7	81.6
120 Honduras	100	0.483	100	85.9	19.5	20.7	18.8	42.3	82.8
121 Indonesia	106	0.494	220	42.3	18.2	36.2	46.8	51.2	84.2

TABLE 4 Gender Inequality Index | 157

TABLE 4 GENDER INEQUALITY INDEX

		Gender Inequality Index		Maternal mortality ratio[a]	Adolescent fertility rate[b]	Seats in national parliament[c]	Population with at least secondary education		Labour force participation rate	
							(% ages 25 and older)		(% ages 15 and older)	
		Rank	Value	(deaths per 100,000 live births)	(births per 1,000 women ages 15–19)	(% female)	Female	Male	Female	Male
HDI rank		2012	2012	2010	2012[d]	2012	2006–2010[e]	2006–2010[e]	2011	2011
121	Kiribati	..	..	..	16.4	8.7	..	..	..	..
121	South Africa	90	0.462	300	50.4	41.1[i]	68.9	72.2	44.0	60.8
124	Vanuatu	..	..	110	50.6	1.9	..	..	61.3	79.7
125	Kyrgyzstan	64	0.357	71	33.0	23.3	81.0[g]	81.2[g]	55.5	78.6
125	Tajikistan	57	0.338	65	25.7	17.5	93.2[g]	85.8[g]	57.4	75.1
127	Viet Nam	48	0.299	59	22.7	24.4	24.7[g]	28.0[g]	73.2	81.2
128	Namibia	86	0.455	200	54.4	25.0	33.0[g]	34.0[g]	58.6	69.9
129	Nicaragua	89	0.461	95	104.9	40.2	30.8[g]	44.7[g]	46.7	80.0
130	Morocco	84	0.444	100	10.8	11.0	20.1[g]	36.3[g]	26.2	74.7
131	Iraq	120	0.557	63	85.9	25.2	22.0[g]	42.7[g]	14.5	69.3
132	Cape Verde	..	..	79	69.2	20.8	..	..	50.8	83.3
133	Guatemala	114	0.539	120	102.4	13.3	12.6	17.4	49.0	88.3
134	Timor-Leste	..	..	300	52.3	38.5	..	..	38.4	74.1
135	Ghana	121	0.565	350	62.4	8.3	45.7[g]	61.8[g]	66.9	71.8
136	Equatorial Guinea	..	..	240	114.6	10.0	..	..	80.6	92.3
136	India	132	0.610	200	74.7	10.9	26.6[g]	50.4[g]	29.0	80.7
138	Cambodia	96	0.473	250	32.9	18.1	11.6	20.6	79.2	86.7
138	Lao People's Democratic Republic	100	0.483	470	30.1	25.0	22.9[g]	36.8[g]	76.5	79.5
140	Bhutan	92	0.464	180	44.9	13.9	34.0	34.5	65.8	76.5
141	Swaziland	112	0.525	320	67.9	21.9	49.9[g]	46.1[g]	43.6	70.8
LOW HUMAN DEVELOPMENT										
142	Congo	132	0.610	560	112.6	9.6	43.8[g]	48.7[g]	68.4	72.9
143	Solomon Islands	..	..	93	64.6	..	..	..	53.2	79.9
144	Sao Tome and Principe	..	..	70	55.4	18.2	..	..	43.7	76.6
145	Kenya	130	0.608	360	98.1	9.8	25.3	52.3	61.5	71.8
146	Bangladesh	111	0.518	240	68.2	19.7	30.8[g]	39.3[g]	57.2	84.3
146	Pakistan	123	0.567	260	28.1	21.1	18.3	43.1	22.7	83.3
148	Angola	..	..	450	148.1	38.2[k]	..	..	62.9	77.1
149	Myanmar	80	0.437	200	12.0	4.6	18.0[g]	17.6[g]	75.0	82.1
150	Cameroon	137	0.628	690	115.1	13.9	21.1[g]	34.9[g]	64.2	77.4
151	Madagascar	..	..	240	122.7	15.9	..	..	83.4	88.7
152	Tanzania, United Republic of	119	0.556	460	128.7	36.0	5.6[g]	9.2[g]	88.2	90.3
153	Nigeria	..	..	630	111.3	6.7	..	..	47.9	63.3
154	Senegal	115	0.540	370	89.7	41.6	4.6	11.0	66.1	88.4
155	Mauritania	139	0.643	510	71.3	19.2	8.0[g]	20.8[g]	28.7	79.2
156	Papua New Guinea	134	0.617	230	62.0	2.7	6.8[g]	14.1[g]	70.6	74.1
157	Nepal	102	0.485	170	86.2	33.2	17.9[g]	39.9[g]	80.4	87.6
158	Lesotho	113	0.534	620	60.8	26.1	21.9	19.8	58.9	73.4
159	Togo	122	0.566	300	54.3	11.1	15.3[g]	45.1[g]	80.4	81.4
160	Yemen	148	0.747	200	66.1	0.7	7.6[g]	24.4[g]	25.2	72.0
161	Haiti	127	0.592	350	41.3	4.0	22.5[g]	36.3[g]	60.1	70.6
161	Uganda	110	0.517	310	126.4	35.0	23.0	23.9	76.0	79.5
163	Zambia	136	0.623	440	138.5	11.5	25.7	44.2	73.2	85.6
164	Djibouti	..	..	200	19.5	13.8	..	..	36.0	67.2
165	Gambia	128	0.594	360	66.9	7.5	16.9[g]	31.4[g]	72.4	83.1
166	Benin	135	0.618	350	97.0	8.4	11.2[g]	25.6[g]	67.4	78.2
167	Rwanda	76	0.414	340	35.5	51.9	7.4[g]	8.0[g]	86.4	85.4
168	Côte d'Ivoire	138	0.632	400	105.7	11.0	13.7[g]	29.9[g]	51.8	81.2
169	Comoros	..	..	280	51.1	3.0	..	..	35.1	80.4
170	Malawi	124	0.573	460	105.6	22.3	10.4[g]	20.4[g]	84.8	81.3
171	Sudan	129	0.604	730	53.0	24.1	12.8[g]	18.2[g]	30.9	76.5
172	Zimbabwe	116	0.544	570	53.4	17.9	48.8[g]	62.0[g]	83.0	89.5
173	Ethiopia	..	..	350	48.3	25.5	..	..	78.4	89.8
174	Liberia	143	0.658	770	123.0	11.7	15.7[g]	39.2[g]	57.9	64.4
175	Afghanistan	147	0.712	460	99.6	27.6	5.8[g]	34.0[g]	15.7	80.3
176	Guinea-Bissau	..	..	790	96.2	10.0	..	..	68.0	78.2
177	Sierra Leone	139	0.643	890	104.2	12.9	9.5[g]	20.4[g]	66.3	69.1
178	Burundi	98	0.476	800	20.9	34.9	5.2[g]	9.2[g]	83.7	82.1
178	Guinea	..	..	610	133.7	..[l]	..	..	65.4	78.3
180	Central African Republic	142	0.654	890	98.6	12.5	10.3[g]	26.2[g]	72.5	85.1
181	Eritrea	..	..	240	53.7	22.0	..	..	79.8	90.0
182	Mali	141	0.649	540	168.9	10.2	11.3	9.2	36.8	70.0

HDI rank	Gender Inequality Index Rank	Gender Inequality Index Value	Maternal mortality ratio[a] (deaths per 100,000 live births)	Adolescent fertility rate[b] (births per 1,000 women ages 15–19)	Seats in national parliament[c] (% female)	Population with at least secondary education (% ages 25 and older) Female	Population with at least secondary education (% ages 25 and older) Male	Labour force participation rate (% ages 15 and older) Female	Labour force participation rate (% ages 15 and older) Male
	2012	2012	2010	2012[d]	2012	2006–2010[e]	2006–2010[e]	2011	2011
183 Burkina Faso	131	0.609	300	117.4	15.3	0.9	3.2	77.5	90.4
184 Chad	..	..	1,100	138.1	12.8	..	..	64.4	80.2
185 Mozambique	125	0.582	490	124.4	39.2	1.5[g]	6.0[g]	86.0	82.9
186 Congo, Democratic Republic of the	144	0.681	540	170.6	8.2	10.7[g]	36.2[g]	70.2	72.5
186 Niger	146	0.707	590	193.6	13.3	2.5[g]	7.6[g]	39.9	89.9
OTHER COUNTRIES OR TERRITORIES									
Korea, Democratic People's Rep. of	..	..	81	0.6	15.6	..	..	71.6	83.7
Marshall Islands	..	..	..	37.7	3.0	..	..	..	..
Monaco	..	..	..	1.5	19.0	..	..	..	..
Nauru	..	..	..	23.0	0.1	..	..	..	..
San Marino	..	..	..	2.5	18.3	..	..	..	..
Somalia	..	..	1,000	68.0	13.8	..	..	37.7	76.8
South Sudan	..	..	..	..	24.3	..	..	..	..
Tuvalu	..	..	..	21.5	6.7	..	..	..	..
Human Development Index groups									
Very high human development	..	0.193	15	18.7	25.0	84.7	87.1	52.7	68.7
High human development	..	0.376	47	45.9	18.5	62.9	65.2	46.8	75.3
Medium human development	..	0.457	121	44.7	18.2	42.1	58.8	50.5	79.9
Low human development	..	0.578	405	86.0	19.2	18.0	32.0	56.4	79.9
Regions									
Arab States	..	0.555	176	39.2	13.0	31.8	44.7	22.8	74.1
East Asia and the Pacific	..	0.333	73	18.5	17.7	49.6	63.0	65.2	80.6
Europe and Central Asia	..	0.280	28	23.1	16.7	81.4	85.8	49.6	69.0
Latin America and the Caribbean	..	0.419	74	70.6	24.4	49.8	51.1	53.7	79.9
South Asia	..	0.568	203	66.9	18.5	28.3	49.7	31.3	81.0
Sub-Saharan Africa	..	0.577	475	105.2	20.9	23.7	35.1	64.7	76.2
Least developed countries	..	0.566	394	90.9	20.3	16.9	27.1	64.8	82.4
Small island developing states	..	0.481	193	61.1	22.0	48.0	53.0	53.0	73.9
World	..	0.463	145	51.2	20.3	52.3	62.9	51.3	77.2

NOTES

a Data were computed to ensure comparability across countries and are thus not necessarily the same as official country statistics, which may be based on alternative rigorous methods. Data are rounded according to the following scheme: less than 100, no rounding; 100–999, rounded to the nearest 10; and greater than 1,000, rounded to the nearest 100.

b Based on medium-fertility variant.

c For countries with bicameral legislative systems the share of seats in national parliament is calculated based on both houses.

d Data are annual average of projected values for 2010–2015.

e Data refer to the most recent year available during the period specified.

f The denominator of the calculation refers to voting members of the House of Representatives only.

g Barro and Lee (2011) estimate for 2010.

h For calculating the Gender Inequality Index, a value of 0.1% was used.

i No women were elected in 2010; however, one woman was appointed to the cabinet.

j Does not include the 36 rotating delegates appointed on an ad hoc basis.

k Estimate is for prior to the 31 August 2012 elections.

l The parliament was dissolved following the December 2008 coup.

DEFINITIONS

Gender Inequality Index: A composite measure reflecting inequality in achievements between women and men in three dimensions: reproductive health, empowerment and the labour market. See *Technical note 3* at http://hdr.undp.org/en/media/HDR_2013_EN_TechNotes.pdf for details on how the Gender Inequality Index is calculated.

Maternal mortality ratio: Ratio of the number of maternal deaths to the number of live births in a given year, expressed per 100,000 live births.

Adolescent fertility rate: Number of births to women ages 15–19 per 1,000 women ages 15–19.

Seats in national parliament: Proportion of seats held by women in a lower or single house or an upper house or senate, expressed as percentage of total seats.

Population with at least secondary education: Percentage of the population ages 25 and older that have reached secondary education.

Labour force participation rate: Proportion of a country's working-age population that engages in the labour market, either by working or actively looking for work, expressed as a percentage of the working-age population.

MAIN DATA SOURCES

Columns 1 and 2: HDRO calculations based on WHO and others (2012), UNDESA (2011), IPU (2012), Barro and Lee (2010), UNESCO Institute for Statistics (2012) and ILO (2012).

Column 3: WHO and others (2012).

Column 4: UNDESA (2011).

Column 5: IPU (2012).

Columns 6 and 7: UNESCO Institute for Statistics (2012).

Columns 8 and 9: ILO (2012).

TABLE 4   Gender Inequality Index | 159

TABLE 5

Multidimensional Poverty Index

	Multidimensional Poverty Index		Population in multidimensional poverty[a]			Population vulnerable to poverty	Population in severe poverty	Contribution of deprivation to overall poverty (%)			Population below income poverty line (%)	
			Headcount		Intensity of deprivation						PPP $1.25 a day	National poverty line
	Year[b]	Value[a]	(%)	(thousands)	(%)	(%)	(%)	Education	Health	Living standards	2002–2011[c]	2002–2012[c]
ESTIMATES BASED ON SURVEYS FOR 2007–2011												
Albania	2008/2009 (D)	0.005	1.4	45	37.7	7.4	0.1	32.0	44.9	23.0	0.6	12.4
Armenia	2010 (D)	0.001	0.3	6	35.2	3.0	0.0	25.8	64.8	9.4	1.3	35.8
Bangladesh	2007 (D)	0.292	57.8	83,207	50.4	21.2	26.2	18.7	34.5	46.8	43.3	31.5
Bhutan	2010 (M)	0.119	27.2	198	43.9	17.2	8.5	40.4	21.2	38.4	10.2	23.2
Bolivia, Plurinational State of	2008 (D)	0.089	20.5	1,972	43.7	18.7	5.8	19.8	27.5	52.6	15.6	60.1
Burkina Faso	2010 (D)	0.535	84.0	13,834	63.7	7.1	65.7	36.2	27.9	35.9	44.6	
Cambodia	2010 (D)	0.212	45.9	6,415	46.1	21.4	17.0	22.1	32.7	45.1	22.8	30.1
Colombia	2010 (D)	0.022	5.4	2,500	40.9	6.4	1.1	31.8	33.5	34.7	8.2	37.2
Congo	2009 (D)	0.208	40.6	1,600	51.2	17.7	22.9	10.4	45.6	44.0	54.1	50.1
Congo, Democratic Republic of the	2010 (M)	0.392	74.0	48,815	53.0	15.1	45.9	18.0	25.1	56.9	87.7	71.3
Dominican Republic	2007 (D)	0.018	4.6	439	39.4	8.6	0.7	39.1	22.6	38.2	2.2	34.4
Egypt	2008 (D)	0.024	6.0	4,699	40.7	7.2	1.0	48.1	37.3	14.5	1.7	22.0
Ethiopia	2011 (D)	0.564	87.3	72,415	64.6	6.8	71.1	25.9	27.6	46.5	39.0	38.9
Ghana	2008 (D)	0.144	31.2	7,258	46.2	21.6	11.4	32.1	19.5	48.4	28.6	28.5
Guyana	2009 (D)	0.030	7.7	58	39.2	12.3	1.0	17.4	50.4	32.2	..	..
Indonesia	2007 (D)	0.095	20.8	48,352	45.9	12.2	7.6	15.7	50.6	33.8	18.1	12.5
Jordan	2009 (D)	0.008	2.4	145	34.4	1.3	0.1	49.6	47.4	3.1	0.1	13.3
Kenya	2008/2009 (D)	0.229	47.8	18,863	48.0	27.4	19.8	12.7	30.1	57.2	43.4	45.9
Lesotho	2009 (D)	0.156	35.3	759	44.1	26.7	11.1	21.9	18.9	59.2	43.4	56.6
Liberia	2007 (D)	0.485	83.9	3,218	57.7	9.7	57.5	29.7	25.0	45.3	83.8	63.8
Madagascar	2008/2009 (D)	0.357	66.9	13,463	53.3	17.9	35.4	34.3	16.7	49.1	81.3	68.7
Malawi	2010 (D)	0.334	66.7	9,633	50.1	23.4	31.4	19.5	27.1	53.3	73.9	52.4
Maldives	2009 (D)	0.018	5.2	16	35.6	4.8	0.3	13.6	81.1	5.3	..	..
Mauritania	2007 (M)	0.352[d]	61.7[d]	1,982[d]	57.1[d]	15.1[d]	40.7[d]	32.0	21.6	46.5	23.4	42.0
Morocco	2007 (N)	0.048[d]	10.6[d]	3,287[d]	45.3[d]	12.3[d]	3.3[d]	35.5	27.5	37.0	2.5	9.0
Mozambique	2009 (D)	0.512	79.3	18,127	64.6	9.5	60.7	23.9	36.2	39.9	59.6	54.7
Namibia	2006/2007 (D)	0.187	39.6	855	47.2	23.6	14.7	15.1	31.0	53.9	31.9	38.0
Nepal	2011 (D)	0.217	44.2	13,242	49.0	17.4	20.8	21.8	33.7	44.4	24.8	25.2
Nigeria	2008 (D)	0.310	54.1	83,578	57.3	17.8	33.9	27.0	32.2	40.8	68.0	54.7
Pakistan	2006/2007 (D)	0.264[d]	49.4[d]	81,236[d]	53.4[d]	11.0[d]	27.4[d]	30.8	37.9	31.2	21.0	22.3
Palestine, State of	2006/2007 (N)	0.005	1.4	52	37.3	8.8	0.1	33.9	55.3	10.8	0.0	21.9
Peru	2008 (D)	0.066	15.7	4,422	42.2	14.9	3.9	18.6	20.8	60.6	4.9	31.3
Philippines	2008 (D)	0.064	13.4	12,083	47.4	9.1	5.7	15.8	56.5	27.7	18.4	26.5
Rwanda	2010 (D)	0.350	69.0	6,900	50.8	19.4	34.7	19.5	30.9	49.6	63.2	44.9
Sao Tome and Principe	2008/2009 (D)	0.154	34.5	56	44.7	24.3	10.7	28.8	27.5	43.6	..	66.2
Senegal	2010/2011 (D)	0.439	74.4	7,642	58.9	11.7	50.6	31.8	40.6	27.6	33.5	50.8
Sierra Leone	2008 (D)	0.439	77.0	4,321	57.0	13.1	53.2	31.5	19.3	49.2	53.4	66.4
South Africa	2008 (N)	0.057	13.4	6,609	42.3	22.2	2.4	7.5	50.5	42.0	13.8	23.0
Swaziland	2010 (M)	0.086	20.4	242	41.9	23.1	3.3	16.7	29.9	53.4	40.6	69.2
Tanzania, United Republic of	2010 (D)	0.332	65.6	28,552	50.7	21.0	33.4	18.3	26.4	55.3	67.9	33.4
Timor-Leste	2009/2010 (D)	0.360	68.1	749	52.9	18.2	38.7	21.3	31.0	47.7	37.4	49.9
Ukraine	2007 (D)	0.008	2.2	1,018	35.5	1.0	0.2	4.7	91.1	4.2	0.1	2.9
Uganda	2011 (D)	0.367	69.9	24,122	52.5	19.0	31.2	15.6	34.1	50.4	51.5	31.1
Vanuatu	2007 (M)	0.129	30.1	67	42.7	33.5	6.5	29.7	17.3	53.0	..	..
Viet Nam	2010/2011 (M)	0.017	4.2	3,690	39.5	7.9	0.7	32.8	25.1	42.1	40.1	28.9
Zambia	2007 (D)	0.328	64.2	7,740	51.2	17.2	34.8	17.5	27.9	54.7	68.5	59.3
Zimbabwe	2010/2011 (D)	0.172	39.1	4,877	44.0	25.1	11.5	10.2	33.6	56.3	..	72.0
ESTIMATES BASED ON SURVEYS FOR 2002–2006												
Argentina	2005 (N)	0.011[f]	2.9[f]	1,160[f]	37.6[f]	5.8[f]	0.2[f]	41.9	12.9	45.2	0.9	..
Azerbaijan	2006 (D)	0.021	5.3	461	39.4	12.5	0.6	24.4	49.4	26.2	0.4	15.8
Belarus	2005 (M)	0.000	0.0	0	35.1	0.8	0.0	16.6	61.8	21.7	0.1	5.4
Belize	2006 (M)	0.024	5.6	16	42.6	7.6	1.1	22.8	35.8	41.4	..	33.5
Benin	2006 (D)	0.412	71.8	5,652	57.4	13.2	47.2	33.6	25.1	41.3	47.3	39.0
Bosnia and Herzegovina	2006 (M)	0.003	0.8	30	37.2	7.0	0.1	29.2	51.8	19.0	0.0	14.0
Brazil	2006 (N)	0.011	2.7	5,075	39.3	7.0	0.2	39.0	40.2	20.7	6.1	21.4
Burundi	2005 (M)	0.530	84.5	6,128	62.7	12.2	61.9	31.5	22.4	46.1	81.3	66.9
Cameroon	2004 (D)	0.287	53.3	9,149	53.9	19.3	30.4	25.7	24.5	49.8	9.6	39.9
Chad	2003 (W)	0.344	62.9	5,758	54.7	28.2	44.1	40.9	4.6	54.5	61.9	55.0
China	2002 (W)	0.056	12.5	161,675	44.9	6.3	4.5	64.8	9.9	25.2	13.1	2.8
Croatia	2003 (W)	0.016	4.4	196	36.3	0.1	0.3	45.0	46.7	8.3	0.1	11.1
Czech Republic	2002/2003 (W)	0.010	3.1	316	33.4	0.0	0.0	0.0	99.9	0.1	..	..

	Multidimensional Poverty Index		Population in multidimensional poverty[a]			Population vulnerable to poverty	Population in severe poverty	Contribution of deprivation to overall poverty (%)			Population below income poverty line (%)	
			Headcount		Intensity of deprivation						PPP $1.25 a day	National poverty line
	Year[b]	Value[a]	(%)	(thousands)	(%)	(%)	(%)	Education	Health	Living standards	2002–2011[c]	2002–2012[c]
Côte d'Ivoire	2005 (D)	0.353	61.5	11,083	57.4	15.3	39.3	32.0	38.7	29.3	23.8	42.7
Djibouti	2006 (M)	0.139	29.3	241	47.3	16.1	12.5	38.3	24.6	37.1	18.8	..
Ecuador	2003 (W)	0.009	2.2	286	41.6	2.1	0.6	78.6	3.3	18.1	4.6	32.8
Estonia	2003 (W)	0.026	7.2	97	36.5	1.3	0.2	91.2	1.2	7.6	0.5	..
Gambia	2005/2006 (M)	0.324	60.4	935	53.6	17.6	35.5	33.5	30.7	35.8	33.6	48.4
Georgia	2005 (M)	0.003	0.8	36	35.2	5.3	0.0	23.2	33.8	43.0	15.3	24.7
Guatemala	2003 (W)	0.127 d	25.9 d	3,134 d	49.1 d	9.8 d	14.5 d	57.2	10.0	32.8	13.5	51.0
Guinea	2005 (D)	0.506	82.5	7,459	61.3	9.3	62.3	35.5	23.0	41.5	43.3	53.0
Haiti	2005/2006 (D)	0.299	56.4	5,346	53.0	18.8	32.3	27.0	21.5	51.5	..	..
Honduras	2005/2006 (D)	0.159	32.5	2,281	48.9	22.0	11.3	38.0	18.5	43.6	17.9	60.0
Hungary	2003 (W)	0.016	4.6	466	34.3	0.0	0.0	1.8	95.6	2.7	0.2	..
India	2005/2006 (D)	0.283	53.7	612,203	52.7	16.4	28.6	21.8	35.7	42.5	32.7	29.8
Iraq	2006 (M)	0.059	14.2	3,996	41.3	14.3	3.1	47.5	32.1	20.4	2.8	22.9
Kazakhstan	2006 (M)	0.002	0.6	92	36.9	5.0	0.0	14.6	56.8	28.7	0.1	8.2
Kyrgyzstan	2005/2006 (M)	0.019	4.9	249	38.8	9.2	0.9	36.6	36.9	26.4	6.2	33.7
Lao People's Democratic Republic	2006 (M)	0.267	47.2	2,757	56.5	14.1	28.1	33.1	27.9	39.0	33.9	27.6
Latvia	2003 (W)	0.006 d	1.6 d	37 d	37.9 d	0.0 d	0.0 d	0.0	88.0	12.0	0.1	5.9
Mali	2006 (D)	0.558	86.6	11,771	64.4	7.6	68.4	34.5	26.2	39.3	50.4	47.4
Mexico	2006 (N)	0.015	4.0	4,313	38.9	5.8	0.5	38.6	23.9	37.5	1.2	51.3
Moldova, Republic of	2005 (D)	0.007	1.9	72	36.7	6.4	0.1	24.7	34.3	41.1	0.4	21.9
Mongolia	2005 (M)	0.065	15.8	403	41.0	20.6	3.2	15.4	27.9	56.6	..	35.2
Montenegro	2005/2006 (M)	0.006	1.5	9	41.6	1.9	0.3	37.5	47.6	14.9	0.1	6.6
Nicaragua	2006/2007 (D)	0.128	28.0	1,538	45.7	17.4	11.2	27.9	13.6	58.5	11.9	46.2
Niger	2006 (D)	0.642	92.4	12,437	69.4	4.0	81.8	35.4	21.5	43.2	43.6	59.5
Paraguay	2002/2003 (W)	0.064	13.3	755	48.5	15.0	6.1	35.1	19.0	45.9	7.2	34.7
Russian Federation	2003 (W)	0.005 d	1.3 d	1,883 d	38.9 d	0.8 d	0.2 d	84.2	2.5	13.3	0.0	11.1
Serbia	2005/2006 (M)	0.003	0.8	79	40.0	3.6	0.1	30.5	40.1	29.4	0.3	9.2
Slovakia	2003 (W)	0.000 e	0.0 e	0 e	0.0 e	0.0 e	0.0 e	0.0	0.0	0.0	0.1	..
Slovenia	2003 (W)	0.000 e	0.0 e	0 e	0.0 e	0.4 e	0.0 e	0.0	0.0	0.0	0.1	..
Somalia	2006 (M)	0.514	81.2	6,941	63.3	9.5	65.6	34.2	18.6	47.2	..	..
Sri Lanka	2003 (W)	0.021 d	5.3 d	1,027 d	38.7 d	14.4 d	0.6 d	6.3	35.4	58.3	7.0	8.9
Suriname	2006 (M)	0.039	8.2	41	47.2	6.7	3.3	36.1	18.8	45.1	..	..
Syrian Arab Republic	2006 (M)	0.021 e	5.5 e	1,041 e	37.5 e	7.1 e	0.5 e	45.4	42.7	11.8	1.7	..
Tajikistan	2005 (M)	0.068	17.1	1,104	40.0	23.0	3.1	18.7	45.0	36.3	6.6	46.7
Thailand	2005/2006 (M)	0.006	1.6	1,067	38.5	9.9	0.2	40.7	31.2	28.1	0.4	8.1
The former Yugoslav Republic of Macedonia	2005 (M)	0.008	1.9	39	40.9	6.7	0.3	59.9	12.8	27.3	0.0	19.0
Togo	2006 (M)	0.284	54.3	3,003	52.4	21.6	28.7	28.3	25.4	46.3	38.7	61.7
Trinidad and Tobago	2006 (M)	0.020	5.6	74	35.1	0.4	0.3	1.3	94.3	4.4	..	..
Tunisia	2003 (W)	0.010 d	2.8 d	272 d	37.1 d	4.9 d	0.2 d	25.0	47.3	27.6	1.4	3.8
Turkey	2003 (D)	0.028	6.6	4,378	42.0	7.3	1.3	42.3	38.4	19.2	0.0	18.1
United Arab Emirates	2003 (W)	0.002	0.6	20	35.3	2.0	0.0	94.4	0.4	5.2	..	..
Uruguay	2002/2003 (W)	0.006	1.7	57	34.7	0.1	0.0	96.0	0.6	3.4	0.2	18.6
Uzbekistan	2006 (M)	0.008	2.3	603	36.2	8.1	0.1	23.2	55.7	21.1	..	..
Yemen	2006 (M)	0.283	52.5	11,176	53.9	13.0	31.9	27.0	40.5	32.4	17.5	34.8

NOTES

a Not all indicators were available for all countries; caution should thus be used in cross-country comparisons. Where data are missing, indicator weights are adjusted to total 100%. For details on countries missing data, see Alkire and others (2011) and Alkire, Conconi and Roche (2012).

b *D* indicates data are from Demographic and Health Surveys, *M* indicates data are from Multiple Indicator Cluster Surveys, *W* indicates data are from World Health Surveys and *N* indicates data are from national surveys.

c Data refer to the most recent year available during the period specified.

d Lower bound estimate.

e Upper bound estimate.

f Refers to only part of the country.

DEFINITIONS

Multidimensional Poverty Index: Percentage of the population that is multidimensionally poor adjusted by the intensity of the deprivations. See *Technical note 4* at http://hdr.undp.org/en/media/HDR_2013_EN_TechNotes.pdf for details on how the Multidimensional Poverty Index is calculated.

Multidimensional poverty headcount: Percentage of the population with a weighted deprivation score of at least 33%.

Intensity of deprivation of multidimensional poverty: Average percentage of deprivation experienced by people in multidimensional poverty.

Population vulnerable to poverty: Percentage of the population at risk of suffering multiple deprivations— that is, those with a deprivation score of 20%–33%.

Population in severe poverty: Percentage of the population in severe multidimensional poverty—that is, those with a deprivation score of 50% or more.

Contribution of deprivation to overall poverty: Percentage of the Multidimensional Poverty Index attributed to deprivations in each dimension.

Population below PPP $1.25 a day: Percentage of the population living below the international poverty line $1.25 (in purchasing power parity terms) a day.

Population below national poverty line: Percentage of the population living below the national poverty line, which is the poverty line deemed appropriate for a country by its authorities. National estimates are based on population-weighted subgroup estimates from household surveys.

MAIN DATA SOURCES

Columns 1 and 2: Calculated from various household surveys, including ICF Macro Demographic and Health Surveys, United Nations Children's Fund Multiple Indicator Cluster Surveys and World Health Organization World Health Surveys conducted between 2000 and 2010.

Columns 3–10: Calculated based on data on household deprivations in education, health and living standards from various household surveys as listed in column 1.

Columns 11 and 12: World Bank (2012a).

TABLE 5 Multidimensional Poverty Index | 161

TABLE 6

Command over resources

HDI rank	GDP (2005 PPP $ billions) 2011	GDP per capita (2005 PPP $) 2011	Gross fixed capital formation (% of GDP) 2011	Consumer Price Index (2005 = 100) 2010	General government final consumption expenditure (% of GDP) 2000	2011	Health (% of GDP) 2010	2010	Education (% of GDP) 2000	2005–2010[b]	Military[a] (% of GDP) 2000	2010	Total debt service (% of GDP) 2000	2009
VERY HIGH HUMAN DEVELOPMENT														
1 Norway	232.7	46,982	20.2	112	19.3	21.5	6.4	8.0	6.6	7.3	1.7	1.5	..	..
2 Australia	781.5	34,548	27.1	116	17.6	18.0	5.4	5.9	4.7	5.1	1.8	1.9	..	..
3 United States	13,238.3	42,486	14.7 c	112	14.3	17.5 c	5.8	9.5	..	5.4	3.0	4.8	..	..
4 Netherlands	621.9	37,251	18.6	108	22.0	28.1	5.0	9.4	5.0	5.9	1.5	1.4	..	..
5 Germany	2,814.4	34,437	18.2	108	19.0	19.5	8.2	9.0	..	4.6	1.5	1.4	..	..
6 New Zealand	108.4 c	24,818 c	18.9 c	115	17.3	20.3 c	6.0	8.4	..	7.2	1.2	1.2	..	..
7 Ireland	159.9	35,640	11.5 c	107	14.2	18.9 c	4.6	6.4	4.2	5.7	0.7	0.6 .	..	..
7 Sweden	331.3	35,048	18.4	108	25.8	26.6	7.0	7.8	7.2	7.3	2.0	1.3	..	..
9 Switzerland	300.3	37,979	20.9 c	104	11.1	11.5 c	5.6	6.8	5.2	5.4	1.1	0.8	..	..
10 Japan	3,918.9	30,660	20.1 c	100	16.9	19.8	6.2	7.8	3.7	3.8	1.0	1.0	..	..
11 Canada	1,231.6	35,716	22.1 c	109	18.6	21.8 c	6.2	8.0	5.6	4.8	1.1	1.5	..	..
12 Korea, Republic of	1,371.0	27,541	28.6 c	116	12.0	15.3 c	2.2	4.1	..	5.0	2.6	2.7	..	..
13 Hong Kong, China (SAR)	310.0	43,844	21.5 c	112	9.1	8.4 c	..	..	..	3.6	..	..	..	..
13 Iceland	10.7	33,618	14.1	149	23.4	25.2	7.7	7.6	6.7	7.8	0.0	0.1 d	..	..
15 Denmark	180.6	32,399	17.2	111	25.1	28.6	6.8	9.7	8.3	8.7	1.5	1.5	..	..
16 Israel	207.5	26,720	18.7	114	25.8	23.9	4.7	4.6	6.5	5.8	8.0	6.5	..	..
17 Belgium	364.7	33,127	20.9	111	21.3	24.1	6.1	8.0	..	6.4	1.4	1.1	..	..
18 Austria	306.1	36,353	21.1	109	19.0	19.3	7.6	8.5	5.7	5.5	1.0	0.9	..	..
18 Singapore	277.8	53,591	23.4	114	10.9	10.3	1.3	1.4	3.4	3.3	4.6	3.7	..	..
20 France	1,951.2	29,819	20.1	108	22.9	24.5	8.0	9.3	5.7	5.9	2.5	2.3	..	..
21 Finland	173.8	32,254	19.2	110	20.6	23.9	5.1	6.7	5.9	6.8	1.3	1.4	..	..
21 Slovenia	51.2	24,967	19.5	115	18.7	20.6	6.1	6.9	..	5.7	1.1	1.6	..	..
23 Spain	1,251.3	27,063	21.7	112	17.1	20.3	5.2	6.9	4.3	5.0	1.2	1.0	..	..
24 Liechtenstein	..	..	..	..	..	..	..	..	..	2.1	..	..	..	..
25 Italy	1,645.0	27,069	19.5	110	18.3	20.5	5.8	7.4	4.4	4.7	2.0	1.7	..	..
26 Luxembourg	35.4	68,459	19.0	111	15.1	16.5	5.2	6.6	..	..	0.6	0.6	..	..
26 United Kingdom	2,034.2	32,474	14.3	114	18.6	22.5	5.6	8.1	4.5	5.6	2.4	2.6	..	..
28 Czech Republic	252.8	23,967	23.9	115	20.3	20.9	5.9	6.6	4.0	4.5	2.0	1.3	..	..
29 Greece	255.0	22,558	14.0	117	18.9	17.5	4.7	6.1	3.4	4.1	3.6	2.3	..	..
30 Brunei Darussalam	18.2 c	45,507 c	15.9 c	105	25.8	22.4 c	2.6	2.4	3.7	2.0	5.7	3.2	..	..
31 Cyprus	21.0	26,045	18.4 c	113	16.0	19.7 c	2.4	2.5	5.3	7.9	3.0	2.1	..	..
32 Malta	9.6	23,007	15.0	112	18.2	21.1	4.9	5.7	..	5.8	0.7	0.7	..	..
33 Andorra	..	..	..	..	..	..	4.9	5.3	..	2.9	..	..	..	..
33 Estonia	24.0	17,885	21.5	126	19.8	19.5	4.1	4.7	5.4	5.7	1.4	1.7	..	..
35 Slovakia	112.9	20,757	22.4	115	20.1	18.1	5.6	5.8	3.9	4.1	1.7	1.3	..	..
36 Qatar	145.8	77,987	39.6 d	136	19.7	24.8 d	1.6	1.4	..	2.4	..	2.3 e	..	..
37 Hungary	172.5	17,295	16.7	130	21.5	10.0	5.0	5.1	5.0	5.1	1.7	1.0	..	..
38 Barbados	4.8 d	17,564 d	14.6 c	132	21.2	20.3 c	4.1	5.2	5.6	6.7	..	..	..	..
39 Poland	691.2	18,087	19.9 c	115	17.4	18.9 c	3.9	5.4	5.0	5.1	1.8	1.9	..	..
40 Chile	263.7	15,272	23.2	101	12.5	11.8	3.4	3.8	3.9	4.5	3.8	3.2	8.2	6.2
41 Lithuania	54.1	16,877	17.6	129	22.8	18.9	4.5	5.2	..	5.7	1.7	1.1	9.7	24.3
41 United Arab Emirates	333.7	42,293	23.8 c	115	..	8.2 c	2.5	2.7	1.3	1.0	9.4	6.9	..	..
43 Portugal	226.8	21,317	18.1	109	19.0	20.1	6.4	7.5	5.2	5.8	1.9	2.1	..	..
44 Latvia	30.6	13,773	22.4	139	20.8	15.6	3.2	4.1	5.4	5.6	0.9	1.1	7.7	43.9
45 Argentina	631.9	15,501	22.6	154	13.8	15.1	5.0	4.4	4.6	6.0	1.1	0.9	9.4	3.8
46 Seychelles	2.0	23,172	22.0 d	185	24.2	11.1 d	4.0	3.1	..	5.0	1.7	1.3	3.4	5.0
47 Croatia	71.2	16,162	21.9	117	23.8	21.2	6.7	6.6	..	4.3	3.1	1.7	..	..
HIGH HUMAN DEVELOPMENT														
48 Bahrain	26.9 c	21,345 c	26.6 d	114	17.6	15.5 d	2.7	3.6	..	2.9	4.0	3.4	..	..
49 Bahamas	9.8	28,239	26.0	113	10.8	15.0	2.8	3.6	2.8	..	..	..	..	..
50 Belarus	125.0	13,191	37.6	162	19.5	13.5	4.9	4.4	6.2	4.5	1.3	1.4	2.9	2.6
51 Uruguay	44.9	13,315	19.0	142	12.4	13.0	6.1	5.6	2.4	2.9	2.8	2.0	5.3	3.5
52 Montenegro	6.6	10,402	22.1	122	21.9	18.2	5.4	6.1	..	..	..	1.9	..	2.4
52 Palau	0.3	13,176	..	..	..	..	8.5	7.9	9.8	..	..	..	..	..
54 Kuwait	135.1	47,935	17.8 d	130	21.5	13.5	1.9	2.1	..	3.8	7.2	3.6	..	..
55 Russian Federation	2,101.8	14,808	23.1	163	15.1	16.9	3.2	3.2	2.9	4.1	3.7	3.9	4.6	4.2
56 Romania	233.3	10,905	32.2	135	7.2	15.8	3.5	4.4	2.9	4.3	2.5	1.3	6.7	11.5
57 Bulgaria	88.2	11,799	23.3	138	19.0	15.4	3.6	3.7	..	4.4	2.7	1.9	10.0	8.4
57 Saudi Arabia	601.8	21,430	19.0	129	26.0	19.8	3.1	2.7	5.9	5.6	10.6	10.1	..	..
59 Cuba	..	..	9.9 c	..	29.6	37.9 c	6.1	9.7	7.7	12.9	..	..	..	..

		ECONOMY				PUBLIC SPENDING									
		GDP	GDP per capita	Gross fixed capital formation	Consumer Price Index	General government final consumption expenditure		Health		Education		Military[a]		Total debt service	
		(2005 PPP $ billions)	(2005 PPP $)	(% of GDP)	(2005 = 100)	(% of GDP)		(% of GDP)		(% of GDP)		(% of GDP)		(% of GDP)	
HDI rank		2011	2011	2011	2010	2000	2011	2010	2010	2000	2005–2010[b]	2000	2010	2000	2009
59	Panama	49.2	13,766	27.5c	123	13.2	11.2c	5.3	6.1	5.0	3.8	0.0	0.0	7.6	4.0
61	Mexico	1,466.6	12,776	20.4	124	11.1	12.0	2.4	3.1	4.9	5.3	0.6	0.5	10.1	3.0
62	Costa Rica	50.7	10,732	19.8	158	13.3	17.6c	5.0	7.4	4.4	6.3	0.0	0.0	4.1	3.0
63	Grenada	1.0	9,806	23.1d	121	11.7	15.6d	4.2	2.6	..	..	..	..	2.8	3.3
64	Libya	96.2d	15,361d	..	125	20.8	..	1.9	2.7	..	..	3.1	1.2e	..	..
64	Malaysia	394.6	13,672	20.3c	114	10.2	12.7c	1.7	2.4	6.0	5.8	1.6	1.6	6.9	5.6
64	Serbia	71.2	9,809	25.3	153	19.6	18.2	5.2	6.4	..	5.0	5.5	2.2	2.0	11.2
67	Antigua and Barbuda	1.3	14,139	18.3d	112	19.0	17.6d	3.3	4.3	..	2.5	..	..	..	..
67	Trinidad and Tobago	30.6	22,761	..	155	9.3	..	1.7	3.4	3.8	..	..	..	..	..
69	Kazakhstan	191.5	11,568	23.9	162	12.1	9.8	2.1	2.5	3.3	3.1	0.8	1.1	18.4	32.3
70	Albania	25.3	7,861	24.9	115	8.9	9.3	2.3	2.6	..	..	1.2	1.6	0.8	3.9
71	Venezuela, Bolivarian Republic of	329.6	11,258	17.0	163	12.4	10.4	2.4	1.7	..	3.7	1.5	0.9	5.4	1.5
72	Dominica	0.8	11,120	22.3c	116	18.5	17.2c	4.1	5.2	..	3.6	..	..	3.3	3.3
72	Georgia	21.6	4,826	17.2	143	8.5	9.4	1.2	2.4	2.2	3.2	0.6	3.9	3.9	7.0
72	Lebanon	54.9	12,900	30.0	105	17.3	12.3	3.2	2.8	1.9	1.8	5.4	4.2	8.6	10.9
72	Saint Kitts and Nevis	0.7	13,291	30.3d	122	17.6	16.0d	3.3	4.0	5.2	4.5	..	..	5.1	6.7
76	Iran, Islamic Republic of	765.2d	10,462d	..	206	13.9	..	1.9	2.2	4.4	4.7	3.7	1.8e	2.9	..
77	Peru	266.0	9,049	23.8	115	10.6	9.8	2.8	2.7	..	2.7	1.8	1.3	4.8	4.4
78	The former Yugoslav Republic of Macedonia	19.5	9,451	21.5	115	18.2	18.0	4.9	4.5	..		1.9	1.4	3.9	7.3
78	Ukraine	290.6	6,359	19.3	195	20.9	18.8	2.9	4.4	4.2	5.3	3.6	2.7	11.7	22.1
80	Mauritius	16.4	12,737	24.4	137	14.1	14.0	2.0	2.5	3.8	3.1	0.2	0.1	9.9	1.3
81	Bosnia and Herzegovina	28.5	7,607	20.7	118	..	22.1	4.1	6.8	..	..	..	1.2	5.8	8.2
82	Azerbaijan	81.5	8,890	17.2	164	9.5	11.8	0.9	1.2	3.9	3.2	2.3	2.9	2.5	0.8
83	Saint Vincent and the Grenadines	1.0	9,482	23.5d	124	16.4	19.5d	3.6	3.9	7.9	4.9	..	..	3.3	4.7
84	Oman	72.1c	25,330d	..	131	20.7	19.9d	2.5	2.2	3.1	4.3	10.8	8.5	..	..
85	Brazil	2,021.3	10,278	19.3	126	19.2	20.7	2.9	4.2	4.0	5.7	1.8	1.6	10.1	2.1
85	Jamaica	19.2	7,074	22.9	179	14.3	17.7	2.9	2.6	5.0	6.1	0.5	0.8	7.8	8.5
87	Armenia	15.8	5,112	30.9	131	11.8	11.8	1.1	1.8	2.8	3.2	3.6	4.2	2.4	10.3
88	Saint Lucia	1.4	8,231	33.5c	115	18.2	16.0c	3.2	5.3	7.1	4.4	..	..	4.2	3.6
89	Ecuador	109.2	7,443	24.2	124	9.8	15.8	1.3	3.0	1.3	..	1.6	3.6	11.8	3.2
90	Turkey	991.7	13,466	20.0	153	11.7	8.1	3.1	5.1	2.6	2.9	3.7	2.4	7.8	8.0
91	Colombia	415.8	8,861	21.9	126	16.7	10.6	5.5	5.5	3.5	4.8	3.0	3.6	5.1	3.4
92	Sri Lanka	102.9	4,929	34.6	172	10.5	7.5	1.8	1.3	..	2.1	5.0	3.0	4.8	2.9
93	Algeria	275.0	7,643	38.3d	122	13.6	14.2d	2.6	3.2	..	4.3	3.4	3.6	8.2	0.4
94	Tunisia	88.1	8,258	24.0	123	16.7	13.4	3.3	3.4	6.2	6.3	1.8	1.4	8.9	5.3
MEDIUM HUMAN DEVELOPMENT															
95	Tonga	0.4	4,092	24.3c	131	18.2	18.9c	4.0	4.1	4.9	..	..	..	2.4	1.4
96	Belize	2.1	5,896	..	113	12.9	..	2.2	3.3	5.0	6.1	0.9	1.1	9.2	7.2
96	Dominican Republic	87.0	8,651	16.7	136	7.8	5.2	2.2	2.7	1.9	2.2	1.0	0.7	2.2	2.6
96	Fiji	3.6	4,199	..	127	17.2	..	3.2	3.4	5.9	4.5	1.9	1.6	1.5	0.7
96	Samoa	0.7	4,008	..	131	..	..	4.0	5.7	4.0	5.3	..	..	2.2	1.8
100	Jordan	32.6	5,269	21.3	134	23.7	18.9	4.7	5.4	..	..	6.3	5.0	8.7	2.5
101	China	9,970.6	7,418	45.5	115	15.8	13.1	1.8	2.7	..	..	1.9	2.1	2.2	1.0
102	Turkmenistan	41.1	8,055	60.0	..	14.2	11.1	3.2	1.5	..	..	..	..	16.1	0.8
103	Thailand	530.6	7,633	25.8	116	11.3	13.3	1.9	2.9	5.4	3.8	1.5	1.5	11.4	3.5
104	Maldives	2.5	7,834	..	138	22.9	..	4.1	3.8	..	8.7	..	..	3.2	9.8
105	Suriname	3.7c	7,110c	..	145	37.5	..	3.9	3.4	..	..	..	..	..	..
106	Gabon	21.5	13,998	25.1	113	9.6	8.8	1.0	1.8	3.8	..	1.8	0.9	6.9	3.4
107	El Salvador	37.6	6,032	14.2	119	10.2	11.1	3.6	4.3	2.5	3.2	1.3	1.1	2.8	5.0
108	Bolivia, Plurinational State of	45.4	4,499	16.6c	137	14.5	13.2	3.7	3.0	5.5	6.3	2.1	1.7	7.6	3.3
108	Mongolia	11.7	4,178	48.6	168	15.3	14.0	3.9	3.0	5.6	5.4	2.1	1.1	3.4	2.8
110	Palestine, State of	..	..	..	..	27.0	..	..	..	..	..	..	..	..	..
111	Paraguay	31.2	4,752	21.3	140	12.7	10.4	3.7	2.1	5.3	4.0	1.1	0.9	5.0	2.5
112	Egypt	457.8	5,547	19.4	173	11.2	11.3	2.2	1.7	..	3.8	3.2	2.0	1.8	1.4
113	Moldova, Republic of	10.6	2,975	23.9	153	10.3	22.7	3.2	5.4	4.5	9.1	0.4	0.3	11.6	6.7
114	Philippines	344.4	3,631	15.8	127	11.4	10.2	1.6	1.3	3.3	2.7	1.6	1.2	8.7	6.5
114	Uzbekistan	85.2	2,903	23.5	..	18.7	16.6	2.5	2.8	..	..	1.2	..	6.4	1.5
116	Syrian Arab Republic	96.9c	4,741c	18.8c	142	12.4	10.1c	2.0	1.6	..	4.9	5.5	4.1	2.5	1.1
117	Micronesia, Federated States of	0.3	3,017	..	..	..	..	7.7	12.9	6.7	..	..	..	..	..
118	Guyana	2.3c	3,104c	26.3c	136	24.7	15.1c	4.6	5.1	8.5	3.7	1.5	2.1	9.7	1.4
119	Botswana	26.3	12,939	27.9	156	25.4	19.9	2.9	6.0	..	7.8	3.3	2.4	1.2	0.5

TABLE 6 Command over resources | 163

TABLE 6 COMMAND OVER RESOURCES

		ECONOMY				PUBLIC SPENDING									
		GDP	GDP per capita	Gross fixed capital formation	Consumer Price Index	General government final consumption expenditure		Health		Education		Military[a]		Total debt service	
		(2005 PPP $ billions)	(2005 PPP $)	(% of GDP)	(2005 = 100)	(% of GDP)		(% of GDP)		(% of GDP)		(% of GDP)		(% of GDP)	
HDI rank		2011	2011	2011	2010	2000	2011	2010	2010	2000	2005–2010[b]	2000	2010	2000	2009
120	Honduras	27.7	3,566	22.2	139	13.4	17.1	3.0	4.4	..	..	0.7	1.1	5.5	3.4
121	Indonesia	992.1	4,094	32.4	146	6.5	4.5	0.7	1.3	..	3.0	..	0.7	10.1	4.1
121	Kiribati	0.2	2,220	..	..	..	..	7.5	9.3	11.0	..	..	..	..	..
121	South Africa	489.6	9,678	18.9	140	18.1	21.5	3.4	3.9	5.6	6.0	1.5	1.3	2.9	1.4
124	Vanuatu	1.0	4,062	..	119	20.8	..	2.7	4.8	7.0	5.2	..	..	0.7	0.9
125	Kyrgyzstan	11.7	2,126	24.8	167	20.0	19.1	2.1	3.5	3.5	6.2	2.9	4.4	12.6	11.6
125	Tajikistan	14.3	2,052	18.7	170	8.3	28.9	0.9	1.6	2.3	4.0	1.2	..	7.3	12.1
127	Viet Nam	264.6	3,013	31.9	167	6.4	5.7	1.6	2.6	..	5.3	..	2.5	4.2	1.3
128	Namibia	13.9	5,986	26.5	141	23.5	21.6	4.2	4.0	7.9	8.1	2.7	3.9	..	..
129	Nicaragua	15.1	2,579	29.7	159	12.2	10.1	3.7	4.9	3.9	..	0.8	0.7	7.3	7.9
130	Morocco	143.5	4,373	30.6	111	18.4	15.4	1.2	2.0	5.8	5.4	2.3	3.5	7.3	3.6
131	Iraq	112.5	3,412	..	171	..	..	0.4	6.8	..	..	..	2.4	..	..
132	Cape Verde	1.8	3,616	36.5	121	30.7	20.7	3.4	3.1	..	5.6	1.3	0.5	3.0	2.2
133	Guatemala	64.2	4,351	14.6	134	7.0	10.5	2.2	2.5	..	3.2	0.8	0.4	2.0	3.8
134	Timor-Leste	1.6	1,393	..	134	35.2	..	6.3	5.1	..	14.0	..	4.9	..	..
135	Ghana	41.3	1,652	21.8	189	10.2	8.5	3.0	3.1	..	5.5	0.7	0.4	7.8	1.0
136	Equatorial Guinea	23.1	32,026	60.1 [d]	129	4.6	3.9 [d]	1.0	3.4	0.7	..	..	..	..	..
136	India	3,976.5	3,203	29.5	152	12.6	11.7 [c]	1.3	1.2	4.4	3.1	3.1	2.7	2.3	1.2
138	Cambodia	29.8	2,080	16.2 [c]	148	5.2	6.3 [c]	1.3	2.1	1.7	2.6	2.2	1.6	0.9	0.6
138	Lao People's Democratic Republic	15.5	2,464	27.4	127	6.7	9.8	1.0	1.5	1.5	3.3	0.8	0.3	2.3	4.3
140	Bhutan	3.8	5,096	41.3 [d]	134	20.4	21.4 [d]	5.3	4.5	5.8	4.0	..	..	1.6	5.6
141	Swaziland	5.7	5,349	10.4	144	18.2	19.4	3.3	4.2	5.5	7.4	1.5	3.0	2.0	1.1
LOW HUMAN DEVELOPMENT															
142	Congo	16.1	3,885	23.4	130	11.6	9.7	1.2	1.1	..	6.2	..	1.1	1.4	1.6
143	Solomon Islands	1.4	2,581	..	152	25.2	..	4.8	8.0	..	6.1	..	..	2.1	3.0
144	Sao Tome and Principe	0.3	1,805	..	260	..	..	3.6	2.7	..	..	..	..	..	0.8
145	Kenya	62.7	1,507	24.3	180	15.1	13.3	1.9	2.1	5.2	6.7	1.3	1.9	4.7	1.2
146	Bangladesh	236.0	1,568	24.7	145	4.6	5.5	1.1	1.2	2.4	2.2	1.3	1.1	1.6	1.0
146	Pakistan	428.4	2,424	11.8	181	8.6	8.2	0.6	0.8	1.8	2.4	3.7	2.8	3.9	2.5
148	Angola	102.0	5,201	10.7	186	..	17.7	1.9	2.4	2.6	3.4	6.4	4.2	18.7	2.8
149	Myanmar	..	..	..	225	..	..	0.3	0.2	0.6	..	2.3	..	..	..
150	Cameroon	41.9	2,090	..	117	9.5	..	1.0	1.5	1.9	3.5	1.3	1.6	5.5	0.9
151	Madagascar	18.2	853	33.0 [d]	159	9.0	11.6 [d]	2.5	2.3	2.9	3.2	1.2	0.7	3.0	0.6
152	Tanzania, United Republic of	59.8	1,334	28.1	151	11.7	18.2	1.6	4.0	..	6.2	1.5	1.2	1.6	0.9
153	Nigeria	360.8	2,221	..	161	..	..	1.5	1.9	..	..	0.8	1.0	4.0	0.2
154	Senegal	22.2	1,737	30.7	115	12.8	8.8	1.6	3.1	3.2	5.6	1.3	1.6	4.8	2.3
155	Mauritania	8.0	2,255	25.9	133	20.2	12.3	3.1	2.3	..	4.3	3.5	3.8	6.4	3.0
156	Papua New Guinea	16.6	2,363	14.8	130	16.6	8.4	3.3	2.6	..	..	0.9	0.4	8.6	8.6
157	Nepal	33.6	1,102	21.2	155	8.9	9.6	1.3	1.8	3.0	4.7	0.8	1.4	1.9	1.2
158	Lesotho	3.3	1,504	34.9	141	41.7	32.6	3.4	8.5	11.8	13.0	4.0	3.1	8.2	1.6
159	Togo	5.6	914	19.4	116	10.5	..	1.4	3.4	4.4	4.5	..	1.7	2.3	1.1
160	Yemen	51.1	2,060	11.7 [c]	167	13.6	11.8 [c]	2.4	1.3	9.7	5.2	4.4	3.9 [e]	2.5	0.8
161	Haiti	10.5	1,034	..	150	7.8	..	1.7	1.5	..	..	0.0	0.0	..	2.0
161	Uganda	41.0	1,188	24.4	150	14.5	11.3	1.8	2.0	2.5	3.2	2.5	1.6	1.2	0.4
163	Zambia	19.2	1,423	21.3	167	9.5	11.6	2.9	3.6	2.0	1.3	..	1.7	5.7	0.9
164	Djibouti	..	2,087 [d]	..	129	29.7	..	3.9	4.7	9.7	8.4	5.1	3.7 [e]	2.4	..
165	Gambia	3.3	1,873	17.5	123	11.2	9.9	1.9	2.9	2.7	5.0	1.0	0.6	2.7	1.9
166	Benin	13.0	1,428	27.4	119	11.6	..	1.9	2.0	3.3	4.5	0.6	1.0 [e]	3.3	0.6
167	Rwanda	12.0	1,097	21.0 [c]	155	11.0	15.5 [c]	1.7	5.2	4.1	4.7	3.5	1.3	2.1	0.3
168	Côte d'Ivoire	31.9	1,581	16.4	114	7.2	9.1	1.3	1.1	3.8	4.6	..	1.6	9.8	1.7
169	Comoros	0.7	980	12.4 [d]	118	11.7	15.3 [d]	1.5	3.0	..	7.6	..	..	1.6	0.8
170	Malawi	12.4	805	20.8	156	14.6	15.7	2.8	4.0	5.2	5.7	0.7	1.1	3.6	0.4
171	Sudan	83.8	1,878	24.7	166	7.6	17.7	0.9	1.9	..	..	4.5	3.4	2.0	0.7
172	Zimbabwe	..	..	6.5	..	24.3	18.3	0.0	..	..	2.5	4.7	1.3	6.3	1.5
173	Ethiopia	83.0	979	19.0	223	17.9	9.0	2.3	2.6	3.9	4.7	7.5	0.9	1.7	0.6
174	Liberia	2.1	506	33.3	162	7.5	20.2	1.3	3.9	..	2.8	..	0.9	0.1	0.6
175	Afghanistan	37.2 [c]	1,083 [c]	16.3 [c]	141	..	10.7 [c]	2.3	0.9	..	..	..	3.8	..	0.1
176	Guinea-Bissau	1.7	1,097	..	119	14.0	..	1.0	0.9	..	..	4.4	..	2.4	2.1
177	Sierra Leone	4.6	769	14.9	163	14.3	11.1	1.1	1.5	4.9	4.3	3.7	1.2	7.3	0.6
178	Burundi	4.6	533	18.4	163	15.5	26.3	2.1	4.4	3.2	9.2	6.0	3.8 [e]	2.6	0.2
178	Guinea	10.1	990	20.0 [c]	237	6.8	7.5 [c]	0.7	0.6	2.5	2.4	1.5	..	5.0	1.8

	ECONOMY				PUBLIC SPENDING									
	GDP	GDP per capita	Gross fixed capital formation	Consumer Price Index	General government final consumption expenditure		Health		Education		Military[a]		Total debt service	
	(2005 PPP $ billions)	(2005 PPP $)	(% of GDP)	(2005 = 100)	(% of GDP)		(% of GDP)		(% of GDP)		(% of GDP)		(% of GDP)	
HDI rank	2011	2011	2011	2010	2000	2011	2010	2010	2000	2005–2010[b]	2000	2010	2000	2009
180 Central African Republic	3.2	716	10.8[d]	124	14.0	4.5[d]	1.6	1.4	1.5	1.2	..	2.6	1.5	0.1
181 Eritrea	2.8	516	..	..	63.8	..	2.5	1.3	3.2	2.1	32.7	..	0.5	1.1
182 Mali	15.3	964	..	116	8.6	..	2.1	2.3	3.6	4.5	2.2	1.9	3.8	0.6
183 Burkina Faso	19.5	1,149	..	115	20.8	..	2.0	3.4	..	4.0	1.2	1.3	1.8	0.6
184 Chad	15.5	1,343	31.8[c]	117	7.7	13.2[c]	2.7	1.1	2.6	2.8	1.9	2.7	1.8	0.9
185 Mozambique	20.6	861	24.3	157	9.0	12.3	4.2	3.7	..	5.0	1.3	0.9[d]	2.3	1.0
186 Congo, Democratic Republic of the	22.3	329	28.7[d]	..	7.5	7.6[d]	0.1	3.4	..	2.5	1.0	1.3	0.6	2.0
186 Niger	10.3	642	..	117	13.0	..	1.8	2.6	3.2	3.8	1.2	0.9	1.4	0.5
OTHER COUNTRIES OR TERRITORIES														
Korea, Democratic People's Rep. of	..	..	..	..	..	..	..	..	..	..	..	..	..	..
Marshall Islands	..	..	..	..	..	..	19.8	15.0	14.6	..	..	..	..	..
Monaco	..	..	..	..	..	..	2.8	3.8	1.3	1.2	..	..	..	..
Nauru	..	..	..	..	..	..	..	..	..	..	..	..	..	..
San Marino	..	..	..	114	..	..	6.5	6.1	..	..	..	..	..	..
Somalia	..	..	..	..	..	..	..	..	..	..	..	..	..	..
South Sudan	..	..	..	..	..	..	..	..	..	..	..	..	..	..
Tuvalu	..	..	..	..	..	..	12.3	14.2	..	..	..	..	..	..
Human Development Index groups														
Very high human development	37,231.3	32,931	18.4	—	16.7	19.4	6.0	8.2	4.5	5.1	2.2	2.7	..	..
High human development	11,740.8	11,572	21.4	—	15.5	15.8	2.9	3.6	..	4.7	2.8	2.7	8.1	4.7
Medium human development	18,095.7	5,203	38.4	—	13.9	12.4	1.8	2.4	..	3.6	2.2	2.0	3.7	1.6
Low human development	1,948.5	1,623	18.4	—	10.1	11.1	1.4	1.8	..	3.5	2.5	2.0	3.9	1.3
Regions														
Arab States	2,808.0	8,104	24.3	—	19.2	15.4	2.4	2.6	..	3.9	6.8	5.5	..	..
East Asia and the Pacific	12,580.2	6,616	..	—	..	..	1.7	2.5	..	..	..	..	..	..
Europe and Central Asia	5,946.1	12,458	22.5	—	15.7	15.4	3.7	4.3	..	4.1	2.8	2.7	6.8	8.3
Latin America and the Caribbean	6,046.4	10,429	20.1	—	14.7	16.1	3.2	3.8	4.3	5.3	1.4	1.4	8.9	2.8
South Asia	5,586.1	3,241	27.6	—	11.8	10.9	1.3	1.2	4.0	3.2	3.2	2.5	2.6	1.3
Sub-Saharan Africa	1,691.4	2,094	20.8	—	15.9	16.9	2.5	3.0	..	5.2	1.9	1.5	4.1	1.2
Least developed countries	1,065.9	1,346	..	—	9.7	..	1.7	2.2	..	3.7	..	2.2	3.1	1.3
Small island developing states	223.2	5,340	..	—	17.3	..	3.6	3.0	..	..	..	..	..	..
World	**69,016.4**	**10,103**	**22.3**	**—**	**16.3**	**17.5**	**5.3**	**6.5**	**..**	**4.9**	**2.3**	**2.6**	**..**	**..**

NOTES

a For country-specific footnotes, see the Stockholm International Peace Research Institute's Military Expenditure database at www.sipri.org/research/armaments/milex/milex_database.

b Data refer to the most recent year available during the period specified.

c Refers to 2010.

d Refers to 2009.

e Refers to 2008.

DEFINITIONS

Gross domestic product (GDP): Sum of gross value added by all resident producers in the economy plus any product taxes and minus any subsidies not included in the value of the products, expressed in 2005 international dollars using purchasing power parity rates.

GDP per capita: Sum of gross value added by all resident producers in the economy plus any product taxes and minus any subsidies not included in the value of the products, expressed in international dollars using purchasing power parity rates and divided by total population during the same period.

Gross fixed capital formation: Value of acquisitions of new or existing fixed assets by the business sector, governments and households (excluding their unincorporated enterprises) less disposals of fixed assets, expressed as a percentage of GDP. No adjustment is made for depreciation of fixed assets.

Consumer Price Index: An index that reflects changes in the cost to the average consumer of acquiring a basket of goods and services that may be fixed or changed at specified intervals, such as yearly.

General government final consumption expenditure: All government current expenditures for purchases of goods and services (including compensation of employees and most expenditures on national defense and security but excluding government military expenditures that are part of government capital formation), expressed as a percentage of GDP.

Public spending on health: Current and capital spending from government (central and local) budgets, external borrowings and grants (including donations from international agencies and nongovernmental organizations), and social (or compulsory) health insurance funds, expressed as a percentage of GDP.

Public spending on education: Total public expenditure (current and capital) on education, expressed as a percentage of GDP.

Public spending on the military: All expenditures of the defense ministry and other ministries on recruiting and training military personnel and on the construction and purchase of military supplies and equipment, expressed as a percentage of GDP.

Total debt service: Sum of principal repayments and interest actually paid in foreign currency, goods, or services on long-term debt, interest paid on short-term debt, and repayments (repurchases and charges) to the International Monetary Fund, expressed as a percentage of GDP.

MAIN DATA SOURCES

Columns 1–10: World Bank (2012a).

Columns 11 and 12: SIPRI (2012).

Columns 13 and 14: HDRO calculations based on data on total debt service as a percentage of GNI from World Bank (2012a).

TABLE 6 Command over resources | 165

TABLE 7

Health

		IMMUNIZATION COVERAGE			HIV PREVALENCE, YOUTH		MORTALITY RATES							HEALTH CARE QUALITY	
				Underweight children (moderate and severe)					Adult		Cause-specific				Satisfaction with health care quality
		DTP	Measles		Female	Male	Infant	Under-five	Female	Male	Due to malaria	Due to cholera	Due to cardiovascular diseases and diabetes[a]	Physicians	
		(% of one-year-olds)		(% of children under age 5)	(% ages 15–24)		(deaths per 1,000 live births)		(per 1,000 adults)		(per 100,000 people per year)	(number)	(per 1,000 people)	(per 1,000 people)	(% satisfied)
HDI rank		2010	2010	2006–2010[b]	2009	2009	2010	2010	2009	2009	2008	2005–2010[b]	2008	2005–2010[b]	2007–2009[b]
VERY HIGH HUMAN DEVELOPMENT															
1	Norway	99	93	..	0.1	0.1	3	3	50	83	0.0	0	124	4.1	68
2	Australia	97	94	..	0.1	0.1	4	5	45	79	0.0	0	112	3.0	60
3	United States	99	92	..	0.2	0.3	7	8	78	134	0.0	0	156	2.7	56
4	Netherlands	99	96	..	0.1	0.1	4	4	56	75	0.0	0	122	3.9	77
5	Germany	97	96	..	0.1	0.1	3	4	53	99	0.0	0	170	3.5	47
6	New Zealand	95	91	..	0.1	0.1	5	6	57	86	0.0	0	138	2.4	64
7	Ireland	98	90	..	0.1	0.1	3	4	57	97	0.0	..	141	3.2	47
7	Sweden	99	96	..	0.1	0.1	2	3	47	74	0.0	0	141	3.6	81
9	Switzerland	98	90	..	0.1	0.2	4	5	43	74	0.0	0	114	4.1	81
10	Japan	99	94	..	0.1	0.1	2	3	42	86	0.0	0	91	2.1	54
11	Canada	92	93	..	0.1	0.1	5	6	53	87	0.0	0	121	1.9	73
12	Korea, Republic of	96	98	..	0.1	0.1	4	5	46	109	0.0	0	141	2.0	60
13	Hong Kong, China (SAR)	..	..	..	..	..	..	..	..	..	..	..	..	..	67
13	Iceland	98	93	..	0.1	0.1	2	2	43	65	0.0	..	121	3.9	87
15	Denmark	93	85	..	0.1	0.1	3	4	65	107	0.0	0	143	3.4	82
16	Israel	96	98	..	0.1	0.1	4	5	45	78	0.0	..	116	3.6	70
17	Belgium	99	94	..	0.1	0.1	4	4	59	105	0.0	0	131	3.0	88
18	Austria	93	76	..	0.2	0.3	4	4	50	102	0.0	0	155	4.7	89
18	Singapore	98	95	..	0.1	0.1	2	3	42	76	0.0	..	140	1.8	86
20	France	99	90	..	0.1	0.2	3	4	54	117	0.0	0	98	3.5	84
21	Finland	99	98	..	0.1	0.1	2	3	56	124	0.0	0	157	2.7	85
21	Slovenia	98	95	..	0.1	0.1	2	3	54	131	0.0	0	168	2.5	68
23	Spain	99	95	..	0.1	0.2	4	5	43	94	0.0	0	113	3.7	84
24	Liechtenstein	..	..	..	..	..	2	2	..	..	..	..	..	..	..
25	Italy	98	90	..	0.1	0.1	3	4	41	77	0.0	0	128	4.2	59
26	Luxembourg	99	96	..	0.1	0.1	2	3	57	95	0.0	..	150	2.9	90
26	United Kingdom	98	93	..	0.1	0.2	5	5	58	95	0.0	0	133	2.7	81
28	Czech Republic	99	98	..	0.1	0.1	3	4	63	138	0.0	..	258	3.6	63
29	Greece	99	99	..	0.1	0.1	3	4	44	106	0.0	..	186	6.0	45
30	Brunei Darussalam	98	94	..	..	..	6	7	82	105	0.0	..	284	1.4	..
31	Cyprus	99	87	..	..	..	3	4	41	81	0.0	..	188	2.3	60
32	Malta	97	73	..	0.1	0.1	5	6	44	76	0.0	..	175	3.1	81
33	Andorra	99	99	..	..	..	3	4	44	94	0.0	..	..	3.7	..
33	Estonia	96	95	..	0.2	0.3	4	5	77	234	0.0	..	342	3.4	47
35	Slovakia	99	98	..	0.1	0.1	7	8	74	184	0.0	..	343	3.0	..
36	Qatar	98	99	..	0.1	0.1	7	8	48	69	0.0	0	195	2.8	..
37	Hungary	99	99	..	0.1	0.1	5	6	99	229	0.0	..	324	3.1	50
38	Barbados	95	85	..	1.1	0.9	17	20	80	136	0.1	..	233	1.8	..
39	Poland	99	98	..	0.1	0.1	5	6	76	197	0.0	0	283	2.1	45
40	Chile	93	93	..	0.1	0.2	8	9	59	116	0.0	..	156	1.1	45
41	Lithuania	98	96	..	0.1	0.1	5	7	95	274	0.0	..	375	3.7	29
41	United Arab Emirates	94	94	..	..	..	6	7	66	84	0.0	..	277	1.9	..
43	Portugal	99	96	..	0.2	0.3	3	4	54	123	0.0	..	154	3.8	69
44	Latvia	97	93	..	0.1	0.2	8	10	105	284	0.0	..	420	3.0	42
45	Argentina	98	99	2.3[c]	0.2	0.3	12	14	88	160	0.0	..	207	3.2	66
46	Seychelles	99	99	..	..	..	12	14	108	227	0.0	0	..	1.5	..
47	Croatia	98	95	..	0.1	0.1	5	6	60	153	0.0	..	294	2.6	..
HIGH HUMAN DEVELOPMENT															
48	Bahrain	99	99	..	..	..	9	10	87	127	0.1	..	339	1.4	..
49	Bahamas	99	94	..	3.1	1.4	14	16	126	202	0.0	..	239	..	..
50	Belarus	99	99	1.3	0.1	0.1	4	6	117	324	0.0	..	525	4.9	45
51	Uruguay	98	95	5.4	0.2	0.3	9	11	84	156	0.0	..	211	3.7	77
52	Montenegro	97	90	1.7	..	..	7	8	85	161	0.0	..	419	..	..
52	Palau	99	75	..	..	..	15	19	110	229	0.0	..	..	1.3	..
54	Kuwait	98	98	..	..	..	10	11	50	66	0.0	..	274	1.8	..
55	Russian Federation	99	98	..	0.3	0.2	9	12	144	391	0.0	0	580	4.3	35
56	Romania	99	95	3.5	0.1	0.1	11	14	90	219	0.0	..	398	1.9	44

HDI rank		IMMUNIZATION COVERAGE			HIV PREVALENCE, YOUTH		MORTALITY RATES							HEALTH CARE QUALITY	
		DTP	Measles	Underweight children (moderate and severe)	Female	Male	Infant	Under-five	Adult Female	Adult Male	Due to malaria	Due to cholera	Due to cardiovascular diseases and diabetes[a]	Physicians	Satisfaction with health care quality
		(% of one-year-olds)		(% of children under age 5)	(% ages 15–24)		(deaths per 1,000 live births)		(per 1,000 adults)		(per 100,000 people per year)	(number)	(per 1,000 people)	(per 1,000 people)	(% satisfied)
		2010	2010	2006–2010[b]	2009	2009	2010	2010	2009	2009	2008	2005–2010[b]	2008	2005–2010[b]	2007–2009[b]
57	Bulgaria	96	97	..	0.1	0.1	11	13	86	205	0.0	..	464	3.6	..
57	Saudi Arabia	98	98		..	..	15	18	102	186	0.0	..	456	0.9	69
59	Cuba	98	99	..	0.1	0.1	5	6	78	120	0.0	..	215	6.4	..
59	Panama	98	95	3.9	0.3	0.4	17	20	82	145	0.0	..	174	..	54
61	Mexico	96	95	3.4	0.1	0.2	14	17	88	157	0.0	0	237	2.9	69
62	Costa Rica	96	83	1.1	0.1	0.2	9	10	69	115	0.0	..	159	..	75
63	Grenada	99	95	..	..	..	9	11	143	248	0.0	..	299	..	..
64	Libya	98	98		..	..	13	17	101	175	0.0	..	396	1.9	..
64	Malaysia	98	96	12.9	0.1	0.1	5	6	95	175	0.1	2	278	0.9	89
64	Serbia	97	95	1.4	0.1	0.1	6	7	90	184	0.0	..	422	2.0	..
67	Antigua and Barbuda	99	98	..	..	..	7	8	158	197	0.0	..	..	..	..
67	Trinidad and Tobago	96	92	..	0.7	1.0	24	27	120	225	0.0	..	427	1.2	32
69	Kazakhstan	99	99	3.9	0.2	0.1	29	33	185	432	0.0	0	696	3.9	49
70	Albania	99	99	5.2	..	..	16	18	88	126	0.0	..	443	1.1	..
71	Venezuela, Bolivarian Republic of	90	79	3.7	..	..	16	18	92	196	0.1	..	237	..	75
72	Dominica	99	99	..	..	..	11	12	103	192	0.0	..	..	..	..
72	Georgia	99	94	1.1	0.1	0.1	20	22	97	235	0.0	..	505	4.5	61
72	Lebanon	83	53	..	0.1	0.1	19	22	85	166	0.0	0	332	3.5	50
72	Saint Kitts and Nevis	98	99	..	..	..	7	8	90	185	0.0	..	..	..	..
76	Iran, Islamic Republic of	99	99	..	0.1	0.1	22	26	90	144	0.0	11	385	0.9	73
77	Peru	97	94	4.2	0.1	0.2	15	19	96	123	0.1	..	135	0.9	48
78	The former Yugoslav Republic of Macedonia	98	98	1.5	..	..	10	12	79	144	0.0	..	465	2.5	..
78	Ukraine	96	94	..	0.3	0.2	11	13	148	395	0.0	0	593	3.1	23
80	Mauritius	99	99	..	0.2	0.3	13	15	99	219	0.0	0	444	1.1	..
81	Bosnia and Herzegovina	95	93	1.4	..	..	8	8	67	145	0.0	..	398	1.4	..
82	Azerbaijan	80	67	7.7	0.1	0.1	39	46	134	221	0.0	..	619	3.8	53
83	Saint Vincent and the Grenadines	99	99	..	..	..	19	21	110	204	0.0	..	340	..	..
84	Oman	99	97	8.6	0.1	0.1	8	9	85	157	0.0	..	455	1.9	..
85	Brazil	99	99	1.7	..	..	17	19	102	205	0.1	0	264	1.7	44
85	Jamaica	99	88	2.0	0.7	1.0	20	24	131	224	0.0	..	248	0.9	..
87	Armenia	98	97	4.7	0.1	0.1	18	20	103	246	0.0	..	537	3.7	61
88	Saint Lucia	98	95	..	..	..	14	16	90	188	0.0	..	278	0.5	..
89	Ecuador	99	98	6.2	0.2	0.2	18	20	96	173	0.0	..	167	..	64
90	Turkey	97	97	1.7	0.1	0.1	14	18	73	134	0.0	..	362	1.5	67
91	Colombia	96	88	3.4	0.1	0.2	17	19	80	166	0.3	..	186	1.4	63
92	Sri Lanka	99	99	21.1	0.1	0.1	14	17	82	275	0.0	..	312	0.5	83
93	Algeria	99	95	3.2	0.1	0.1	31	36	105	135	0.0	0	277	1.2	52
94	Tunisia	98	97	3.3	0.1	0.1	14	16	70	129	0.1	..	257	1.2	80
MEDIUM HUMAN DEVELOPMENT															
95	Tonga	99	99	..	..	..	13	16	233	135	0.8	..	396	0.3	..
96	Belize	99	98	4.3	1.8	0.7	14	17	129	202	0.0	..	256	0.8	50
96	Dominican Republic	96	79	7.1	0.7	0.3	22	27	149	172	0.1	0	320	..	58
96	Fiji	99	94	..	0.1	0.1	15	17	157	263	0.0	..	457	0.5	..
96	Samoa	97	61	..	..	..	17	20	167	198	0.9	..	427	0.3	..
100	Jordan	98	98	1.9	..	..	18	22	111	195	0.0	..	468	2.5	66
101	China	99	99	3.8[c]	..	..	16	18	87	142	0.0	4	287	1.4	..
102	Turkmenistan	99	99	8.2	..	..	47	56	212	380	0.0	..	773	2.4	..
103	Thailand	99	98	7.0	..	..	11	13	139	270	0.4	0	311	0.3	85
104	Maldives	97	97	17.3	0.1	0.1	14	15	70	97	0.9	..	351	1.6	..
105	Suriname	99	89	7.2	0.4	0.6	27	31	124	217	2.5	..	351	..	..
106	Gabon	69	55	..	3.5	1.4	54	74	262	321	31.0	0	370	0.3	..
107	El Salvador	97	92	5.5	0.3	0.4	14	16	128	281	0.0	..	203	1.6	59
108	Bolivia, Plurinational State of	87	79	4.3	0.1	0.1	42	54	132	203	0.0	..	290	..	59
108	Mongolia	98	97	5.0	0.1	0.1	26	32	141	305	0.0	0	379	2.8	52
110	Palestine, State of	..	..	..	..	..	20	22	..	..	..	..	..	..	50
111	Paraguay	96	94	3.4	0.1	0.2	21	25	98	168	0.0	0	249	1.1	66
112	Egypt	97	96	6.0	0.1	0.1	19	22	130	215	0.2	..	406	2.8	53
113	Moldova, Republic of	93	97	3.2	0.1	0.1	16	19	134	309	0.0	..	525	2.7	41

TABLE 7 Health | 167

TABLE 7 HEALTH

HDI rank	DTP	Measles	Underweight children (moderate and severe)	Female	Male	Infant	Under-five	Female	Male	Due to malaria	Due to cholera	Due to cardiovascular diseases and diabetes[a]	Physicians	Satisfaction with health care quality
	(% of one-year-olds)		(% of children under age 5)	(% ages 15–24)		(deaths per 1,000 live births)		(per 1,000 adults)		(per 100,000 people per year)	(number)	(per 1,000 people)	(per 1,000 people)	(% satisfied)
	2010	2010	2006–2010[b]	2009	2009	2010	2010	2009	2009	2008	2005–2010[b]	2008	2005–2010[b]	2007–2009[b]
114 Philippines	89	88	21.6[c]	0.1	0.1	23	29	130	240	0.2	2	345	1.2	81
114 Uzbekistan	99	98	4.0	0.1	0.1	44	52	139	220	0.0	..	641	2.6	..
116 Syrian Arab Republic	89	82	10.1	..	..	14	16	95	159	0.0	..	400	1.5	56
117 Micronesia, Federated States of	90	80	..	..	..	34	42	161	183	0.3	0	412	0.6	..
118 Guyana	99	95	10.5	0.8	0.6	25	30	224	286	5.0	..	452	..	63
119 Botswana	98	94	11.2	11.8	5.2	36	48	324	372	1.0	0	346	0.3	72
120 Honduras	99	99	8.1	0.2	0.3	20	24	134	237	0.1	..	376	..	68
121 Indonesia	94	89	18.4	0.1	0.1	27	35	143	234	3.2	19	350	0.3	79
121 Kiribati	97	89	..	..	..	39	49	173	325	2.6	..	..	0.3	..
121 South Africa	73	65	8.7[c]	13.6	4.5	41	57	479	521	0.2	28	321	0.8	63
124 Vanuatu	78	52	..	..	..	12	14	159	200	8.5	..	399	0.1	..
125 Kyrgyzstan	99	99	2.2	0.1	0.1	33	38	162	327	0.0	..	605	2.3	57
125 Tajikistan	95	94	15.0	0.1	0.1	52	63	160	183	0.0	..	523	2.0	64
127 Viet Nam	93	98	20.2	0.1	0.1	19	23	107	173	0.1	0	339	1.2	74
128 Namibia	87	75	16.6	5.8	2.3	29	40	357	540	29.0	0	495	0.4	68
129 Nicaragua	99	99	5.5	0.1	0.1	23	27	122	210	0.0	..	234	0.4	66
130 Morocco	99	98	8.6	0.1	0.1	30	36	87	126	0.0	..	355	0.6	..
131 Iraq	81	73	6.4	..	..	31	39	145	292	0.0	24	424	0.7	44
132 Cape Verde	99	96	..	..	..	29	36	111	272	0.2	0	300	0.6	..
133 Guatemala	96	93	13.0[c]	0.3	0.5	25	32	151	280	0.1	..	190	..	60
134 Timor-Leste	75	66	44.7	..	..	46	55	154	233	83.0	..	318	0.1	..
135 Ghana	96	93	13.9	1.3	0.5	50	74	253	402	48.0	51	386	0.1	74
136 Equatorial Guinea	65	51	..	5.0	1.9	81	121	355	373	98.0	33	484	0.3	..
136 India	83	74	42.5	0.1	0.1	48	63	169	250	1.9	6	336	0.6	67
138 Cambodia	93	93	28.3	0.1	0.1	43	51	190	350	3.7	0	408	0.2	75
138 Lao People's Democratic Republic	81	64	31.1	0.2	0.1	42	54	251	289	2.9	3	430	0.3	69
140 Bhutan	94	95	12.7	0.1	0.1	44	56	194	256	0.2	..	425	0.0	..
141 Swaziland	95	94	5.8	15.6	6.5	55	78	560	674	0.3	0	499	0.2	..
LOW HUMAN DEVELOPMENT														
142 Congo	90	76	11.4	2.6	1.2	61	93	320	409	121.0	0	463	0.1	34
143 Solomon Islands	85	68	11.8	..	..	23	27	119	170	30.0	..	367	0.2	..
144 Sao Tome and Principe	98	92	13.1	..	..	53	80	104	161	9.2	33	308	0.5	..
145 Kenya	93	86	16.1	4.1	1.8	55	85	282	358	12.0	21	363	0.1	62
146 Bangladesh	98	94	41.0	0.1	0.1	38	48	222	246	1.8	..	418	0.3	69
146 Pakistan	90	86	31.3	0.1	0.1	70	87	189	225	0.6	0	422	0.8	41
148 Angola	97	93	15.6[c]	1.6	0.6	98	161	353	377	89.0	0	483	0.1	62
149 Myanmar	93	88	22.6	0.3	0.3	50	66	188	275	34.0	1	369	0.5	..
150 Cameroon	92	79	16.0	3.9	1.6	84	136	409	420	121.0	110	498	0.2	54
151 Madagascar	78	67	..	0.1	0.1	43	62	198	273	8.5	0	376	0.2	82
152 Tanzania, United Republic of	98	92	15.8	3.9	1.7	50	76	311	456	87.0	94	427	0.0	30
153 Nigeria	77	71	23.1	2.9	1.2	88	143	365	377	146.0	174	456	0.4	55
154 Senegal	80	60	13.7	0.7	0.3	50	75	218	266	76.0	458	373	0.1	57
155 Mauritania	82	67	14.7[c]	0.3	0.4	75	111	262	315	36.0	70	422	0.1	31
156 Papua New Guinea	80	55	18.4	0.8	0.3	47	61	221	274	45.0	0	428	0.1	..
157 Nepal	85	86	38.6	0.1	0.2	41	50	159	234	0.0	0	350	0.2	80
158 Lesotho	93	85	13.2	14.2	5.4	65	85	573	676	0.1	0	452	0.1	..
159 Togo	97	84	16.6	2.2	0.9	66	103	278	338	65.0	15	403	0.1	22
160 Yemen	94	73	43.1	..	..	57	77	180	237	4.9	3	494	0.3	..
161 Haiti	83	59	17.7	1.3	0.6	70	165	227	278	5.7	3,990	411	..	35
161 Uganda	83	55	15.9	4.8	2.3	63	99	348	539	103.0	98	473	0.1	48
163 Zambia	99	91	14.6	8.9	4.2	69	111	477	580	104.0	7	518	0.1	53
164 Djibouti	90	85	22.9	1.9	0.8	73	91	271	326	1.2	27	490	0.2	56
165 Gambia	99	97	18.1	2.4	0.9	57	98	246	296	93.0	13	417	0.0	..
166 Benin	94	69	18.4	0.7	0.3	73	115	246	385	105.0	11	454	0.1	52
167 Rwanda	92	82	11.4	1.9	1.3	59	91	258	304	15.0	0	408	0.0	78
168 Côte d'Ivoire	95	70	15.9	1.5	0.7	86	123	456	528	116.0	6	536	0.1	..
169 Comoros	81	72	..	0.1	0.1	63	86	229	284	58.0	0	450	0.2	..
170 Malawi	97	93	12.8	6.8	3.1	58	92	496	691	87.0	11	587	0.0	66

HDI rank	DTP	Measles	Underweight children (moderate and severe)	Female	Male	Infant	Under-five	Female	Male	Due to malaria	Due to cholera	Due to cardiovascular diseases and diabetes[a]	Physicians	Satisfaction with health care quality
	(% of one-year-olds)		(% of children under age 5)	(% ages 15–24)		(deaths per 1,000 live births)		(per 1,000 adults)		(per 100,000 people per year)	(number)	(per 1,000 people)	(per 1,000 people)	(% satisfied)
	2010	2010	2006–2010[b]	2009	2009	2010	2010	2009	2009	2008	2005–2010[b]	2008	2005–2010[b]	2007–2009[b]
171 Sudan	99	90	27.0	1.3	0.5	66	103	275	291	23.0	1,011	548	0.3	48
172 Zimbabwe	94	84	9.7	6.9	3.3	51	80	574	672	40.0	26	324	0.2	27
173 Ethiopia	90	81	33.2	..	..	68	106	379	445	10.0	0	508	0.0	19
174 Liberia	75	64	14.9 c	0.7	0.3	74	103	337	389	98.0	18	437	0.0	38
175 Afghanistan	86	62	32.9	..	..	103	149	352	440	0.3	0	675	0.2	46
176 Guinea-Bissau	92	61	18.1	2.0	0.8	92	150	369	431	203.0	399	513	0.0	..
177 Sierra Leone	96	82	21.1	1.5	0.6	114	174	363	414	239.0	0	440	0.0	46
178 Burundi	99	92	28.8	2.1	1.0	88	142	407	424	39.0	18	464	0.1	47
178 Guinea	75	51	20.8	0.9	0.4	81	130	337	474	165.0	107	520	0.1	31
180 Central African Republic	64	62	24.4	2.2	1.0	106	159	470	461	192.0	0	498	0.1	..
181 Eritrea	99	99	34.5	0.4	0.2	42	61	179	249	0.7	0	383	0.1	..
182 Mali	90	63	26.7	0.5	0.2	99	178	218	357	131.0	76	406	0.0	44
183 Burkina Faso	98	94	25.7	0.8	0.5	93	176	262	443	221.0	16	463	0.1	50
184 Chad	71	46	30.3	2.5	1.0	99	173	384	412	235.0	14	500	0.0	42
185 Mozambique	77	70	18.3	8.6	3.1	92	135	434	557	171.0	24	512	0.0	69
186 Congo, Democratic Republic of the	67	68	24.2	..	..	112	170	331	442	193.0	244	477	0.1	..
186 Niger	80	71	40.2 c	0.5	0.2	73	143	224	229	184.0	55	381	0.0	46
OTHER COUNTRIES OR TERRITORIES														
Korea, Democratic People's Rep. of	94	99	18.8	..	..	26	33	126	207	0.0	..	303	3.3	..
Marshall Islands	99	97	..	..	..	22	26	386	429	1.1	..	..	0.6	..
Monaco	99	99	..	..	..	3	4	51	112	0.0	..	..	..	..
Nauru	99	99	4.8	..	..	32	40	303	448	0.0	..	..	0.7	..
San Marino	95	93	..	..	..	2	2	48	57	0.0	..	..	..	..
Somalia	55	46	31.6	0.6	0.4	108	180	350	382	28.0	1,182	572	0.0	..
South Sudan	..	..	..	..	..	..	..	..	..	..	..	..	..	..
Tuvalu	99	85	1.6	..	..	27	33	280	255	0.0	..	..	0.6	..
Human Development Index groups														
Very high human development	98	94	..	..	..	5	6	60	114	0.0	..	150	2.9	62
High human development	97	95	..	..	..	16	18	105	221	0.0	..	357	2.3	..
Medium human development	90	85	22.7	..	..	33	42	132	204	1.3	..	324	1.0	..
Low human development	87	78	26.1	..	..	73	110	287	346	65.4	138	450	0.3	50
Regions														
Arab States	93	87	..	..	..	36	48	139	198	3.5	..	409	1.4	..
East Asia and the Pacific	97	95	9.7	..	..	20	24	103	168	1.5	..	305	1.2	..
Europe and Central Asia	98	96	..	..	..	17	21	118	281	0.0	..	492	3.1	45
Latin America and the Caribbean	96	93	4.0	..	..	18	23	99	181	0.2	..	236	..	57
South Asia	86	78	40.2	..	..	50	65	173	245	1.6	..	360	0.6	65
Sub-Saharan Africa	84	75	21.2	..	..	76	120	355	430	98.1	86	447	0.2	..
Least developed countries	88	78	27.3	..	..	71	108	282	357	62.1	190	459	0.2	..
Small island developing states	89	72	..	..	..	41	70	155	207	15.6	..	342	2.6	..
World	**91**	**85**	..	..	..	**40**	**55**	**137**	**211**	**12.2**	..	**323**	**1.4**	..

NOTES

a Estimates are age-standardized and based on a combination of country life tables, cause of death models, regional cause of death patterns, and World Health Organization and Joint United Nations Programme on HIV/AIDS estimates for some major causes (not including chronic diseases).

b Data are for the most recent year available during the period specified.

c Data differ from standard definition or refer to only part of the country.

DEFINITIONS

Immunization coverage for DTP: Percentage of one-year-olds who have received three doses of the combined diphtheria, tetanus toxoid and pertussis (DTP) vaccine.

Immunization coverage for measles: Percentage of one-year-olds who have received at least one dose of a measles vaccine.

Underweight children: Percentage of children under age 5 falling two standard deviations or more below the median weight-for-age of the reference population.

HIV prevalence: Percentage of the population ages 15–24 who are infected with HIV.

Infant mortality rate: Probability of dying between birth and exactly age 1, expressed per 1,000 live births.

Under-five mortality rate: Probability of dying between birth and exactly age 5, expressed per 1,000 live births.

Adult mortality rate: Probability that a 15-year-old person will die before reaching age 60, expressed per 1,000 adults.

Cause-specific deaths: Deaths attributable to a certain disease or cause.

Physicians: Number of physicians (both generalists and specialists), expressed per 1,000 people.

Satisfaction with heath care quality: Percentage of respondents who answered "yes" to the Gallup World Poll question, "In this country, do you have confidence in the healthcare or medical systems?"

MAIN DATA SOURCES

Columns 1, 2, 8 and 9: WHO (2012a).

Columns 3–5: UNICEF (2012).

Columns 6, 10, 11 and 13: WHO (2012b).

Column 7: Inter-agency Group for Child Mortality Estimation (2012).

Column 12: HDRO calculations based on data on female deaths and male deaths due to cardiovascular diseases and diabetes from WHO (2012b) and population data from UNDESA (2011).

Column 14: Gallup (2012).

TABLE 7 Health | 169

TABLE 8

Education

		EDUCATIONAL ATTAINMENT		GROSS ENROLMENT RATIO				EDUCATION QUALITY								
		Adult literacy rate	Population with at least secondary education	Primary	Secondary	Tertiary	Primary school teachers trained to teach	Performance of 15-year-old students						Satisfaction with education quality	Primary school dropout rate
								Mean score			Deviation from mean				
		(% ages 15 and older)	(% ages 25 and older)	(%)			(%)	Readinga	Mathematicsb	Sciencec	Reading	Mathematics	Science	(% satisfied)	(% of primary school cohort)
HDI rank		2005–2010d	2010	2002–2011d	2002–2011d	2002–2011d	2005–2011d	2009	2009	2009	2009	2009	2009	2011	2002–2011d
VERY HIGH HUMAN DEVELOPMENT															
1	Norway	..	95.2	99.0	110.0	73.8	..	503	498	500	91	85	90	..	0.5
2	Australia	..	92.2	104.0	129.0	75.9	..	515	514	527	99	94	101	67.3	..
3	United States	..	94.5	102.0	96.0	94.8	..	500	487	502	97	91	98	62.8	6.9
4	Netherlands	..	88.9	108.0	120.0	62.7	..	508	526	522	89	89	96	60.3	..
5	Germany	..	96.5	102.0	103.0	..	..	497	513	520	95	98	101	65.6e	4.4
6	New Zealand	..	83.7	101.0	119.0	82.6	..	521	519	532	103	96	107	69.9	..
7	Ireland	..	73.9	108.0	117.0	61.0	..	496	487	508	95	86	97	83.6	..
7	Sweden	..	85.0	100.0	100.0	70.8	..	497	494	495	99	94	100	61.6	1.0
9	Switzerland	..	95.8	102.0	95.0	51.5	..	501	534	517	93	99	96	..	..
10	Japan	..	81.1f	103.0	102.0	59.0	..	520	529	539	100	94	100	54.6	0.0
11	Canada	..	100.0	99.0	101.0	60.0	..	524	527	529	90	88	90	75.4	..
12	Korea, Republic of	..	85.4f	104.0	97.0	103.9	..	542	546	538	79	89	82	50.5	1.2
13	Hong Kong, China (SAR)	..	72.3	102.0	83.0	59.7	95.6	533	555	549	84	95	87	49.6	0.5
13	Iceland	..	91.3	99.0	107.0	74.1	..	500	507	496	96	91	95	..	2.5
15	Denmark	..	99.4	99.0	117.0	74.4	..	495	503	499	84	87	92	64.5	0.5
16	Israel	..	84.1	113.0	91.0	62.5	..	474	447	455	112	104	107	64.0	1.1
17	Belgium	..	79.4	105.0	111.0	67.5	..	506	515	507	102	104	105	62.1	6.6
18	Austria	..	100.0	100.0	100.0	60.2	..	470	496	494	100	96	102	63.7	2.3
18	Singapore	96.1g	75.0	101.8	106.9	71.0	94.3	526	562	542	97	104	104	91.8	0.9
20	France	..	78.4	111.0	113.0	54.5	..	496	497	498	106	101	103	58.5	..
21	Finland	..	100.0	99.0	108.0	91.6	..	536	541	554	86	82	89	81.9	0.5
21	Slovenia	99.7h	95.6	98.0	97.0	86.9	..	483	501	512	91	95	94	72.6	0.5
23	Spain	97.7	66.4	107.0	119.0	73.2	..	481	483	488	88	91	87	59.0	0.5
24	Liechtenstein	..	..	106.0	70.0	34.4	..	499	536	520	83	88	87	..	18.2
25	Italy	98.9h	72.8	103.0	99.0	66.0	..	486	483	489	96	93	97	46.7	0.3
26	Luxembourg	..	77.9	100.0	98.0	10.5	..	472	489	484	104	98	104	64.8	..
26	United Kingdom	..	99.7	106.0	102.0	58.5	..	494	492	514	95	87	99	76.9e	..
28	Czech Republic	..	99.8	106.0	90.0	60.7	..	478	493	500	92	93	97	71.4	0.4
29	Greece	97.2h	62.0	100.0	101.0	89.4	..	483	466	470	95	89	92	47.9	2.6
30	Brunei Darussalam	95.2h	63.8f	108.0	110.0	17.2	87.1	..	..	..	..	..	..	..	3.9
31	Cyprus	98.3h	74.5	105.0	98.0	52.0	..	..	..	..	..	..	..	65.6	4.7
32	Malta	92.4	62.5	95.0	105.0	33.4	..	..	..	..	..	..	..	58.5	20.3
33	Andorra	..	49.4	84.0	87.0	11.2	100.0	..	..	..	..	..	..	..	..
33	Estonia	99.8h	94.5f	99.0	104.0	62.7	..	501	512	528	83	81	84	49.5	1.6
35	Slovakia	..	98.8	102.0	89.0	54.2	..	477	497	490	90	96	95	58.4	2.3
36	Qatar	96.3	63.4	103.0	94.0	10.0	42.9	372	368	379	115	98	104	69.9	6.4
37	Hungary	99.0i	94.8f	102.0	98.0	61.7	..	494	490	503	90	92	86	56.4	2.3
38	Barbados	..	88.6f	120.0	101.0	65.9	58.5	..	..	..	..	..	..	..	4.2
39	Poland	99.5i	80.0	97.0	97.0	70.5	..	500	495	508	89	88	87	60.8	2.4
40	Chile	98.6	74.0	106.0	88.0	59.2	..	449	421	447	83	80	81	44.0	2.6
41	Lithuania	99.7h	90.2	97.0	98.0	77.4	..	468	477	491	86	88	85	51.1	1.6
41	United Arab Emirates	90.0	64.3f	104.0	92.0	22.5	100.0	459j	453j	466j	107j	99j	106j	80.6e	3.3
43	Portugal	95.2i	40.4	114.0	107.0	62.2	..	489	487	493	87	91	83	64.9	..
44	Latvia	99.8h	98.4	101.0	95.0	60.1	..	484	482	494	80	79	78	51.0	5.4
45	Argentina	97.8h	56.0f	118.0	89.0	71.2	..	398	388	401	108	93	102	62.6	6.2
46	Seychelles	91.8	66.8	117.0	119.0	..	99.4	..	..	..	..	..	..	..	15.1
47	Croatia	98.8h	64.4f	93.0	95.0	49.2	..	476	460	486	88	88	85	63.7	1.0
HIGH HUMAN DEVELOPMENT															
48	Bahrain	91.9h	78.0f	107.0	103.0	..	..	..	..	..	..	..	..	80.5e	1.8
49	Bahamas	..	89.6	114.0	96.0	..	91.5	..	..	..	..	..	..	..	10.5
50	Belarus	99.6	..	100.0	96.0	83.0	99.8	..	..	..	..	..	..	55.4	0.3
51	Uruguay	98.1	49.8	113.0	90.0	63.3	..	426	427	427	99	91	97	55.8	4.8
52	Montenegro	98.4h	98.2	107.0	104.0	47.6	..	408	403	401	93	85	87	62.1	..
52	Palau	..	..	101.0	96.0	37.9	..	..	..	..	..	..	..	..	..
54	Kuwait	93.9	48.9	106.0	101.0	21.9	100.0	..	..	..	..	..	..	61.2e	4.0
55	Russian Federation	99.6h	94.7f	99.0	89.0	75.9	..	459	468	478	90	85	90	38.0	3.9
56	Romania	97.7h	86.8	96.0	95.0	63.8	..	424	427	428	90	79	79	45.3	4.9

		EDUCATIONAL ATTAINMENT		GROSS ENROLMENT RATIO				EDUCATION QUALITY							
								Performance of 15-year-old students							
		Adult literacy rate	Population with at least secondary education	Primary	Secondary	Tertiary	Primary school teachers trained to teach	Mean score			Deviation from mean			Satisfaction with education quality	Primary school dropout rate
		(% ages 15 and older)	(% ages 25 and older)		(%)		(%)	Reading[a]	Mathematics[b]	Science[c]	Reading	Mathematics	Science	(% satisfied)	(% of primary school cohort)
HDI rank		2005–2010[d]	2010	2002–2011[d]	2002–2011[d]	2002–2011[d]	2005–2011[d]	2009	2009	2009	2009	2009	2009	2011	2002–2011[d]
57	Bulgaria	98.4	92.6	103.0	88.0	53.0	..	429	428	439	113	99	106	35.4	6.2
57	Saudi Arabia	86.6[h]	54.6[f]	106.0	101.0	36.8	91.5	..	..	..	..	..	..	61.8[e]	6.7
59	Cuba	99.8[h]	77.1[f]	103.0	89.0	95.2	100.0	..	..	..	..	..	..	..	3.8
59	Panama	94.1	62.1[f]	108.0	74.0	44.6	91.6	371	360	376	99	81	90	73.2	6.2
61	Mexico	93.1	53.9	115.0	87.0	27.0	95.6	425	419	416	85	79	77	64.5	6.0
62	Costa Rica	96.2[h]	53.6[f]	110.0	100.0	25.6	89.5	..	..	..	..	..	..	80.0	11.2
63	Grenada	..	..	103.0	108.0	52.8	65.3	..	..	..	..	..	..	..	..
64	Libya	89.2[i]	49.6[f]	114.0	110.0	54.4	..	..	..	..	..	..	..	..	..
64	Malaysia	93.1	69.4[f]	96.0	68.0	40.2	..	..	..	..	..	..	..	91.4	2.3
64	Serbia	99.3[h]	85.1	96.0	91.0	49.1	94.2	442	442	443	84	91	84	58.0	1.4
67	Antigua and Barbuda	99.0	..	102.0	105.0	16.4	54.8	..	..	..	..	..	..	..	..
67	Trinidad and Tobago	98.8[h]	59.3	105.0	90.0	11.5	88.0	416	414	410	113	99	108	83.3	10.6
69	Kazakhstan	99.7[h]	99.3	111.0	100.0	40.8	..	390	405	400	91	83	87	49.9	0.2
70	Albania	95.9	81.7	87.0	89.0	18.4	..	385	377	391	100	91	89	54.7	4.8
71	Venezuela, Bolivarian Republic of	95.5	52.4	103.0	83.0	78.1	88.4	..	..	..	..	..	..	81.2	7.9
72	Dominica	..	26.5	112.0	98.0	3.6	60.8	..	..	..	..	..	..	..	11.9
72	Georgia	99.7[h]	91.0	109.0	86.0	28.2	94.6	..	..	..	..	..	..	65.7	3.8
72	Lebanon	89.6	54.2	105.0	81.0	54.0	..	..	..	..	..	..	..	67.6[e]	8.2
72	Saint Kitts and Nevis	..	..	93.0	97.0	18.2	61.6	..	..	..	..	..	..	..	26.5
76	Iran, Islamic Republic of	85.0	66.0	108.0	84.0	42.8	98.4	..	..	..	..	..	..	67.9	5.7
77	Peru	89.6	52.9	109.0	92.0	35.0	..	370	365	369	98	90	89	49.1	..
78	The former Yugoslav Republic of Macedonia	97.3[h]	78.6	89.0	83.0	40.4	..	..	..	..	..	..	..	61.6	2.5
78	Ukraine	99.7[h]	93.5[f]	99.0	96.0	79.5	99.9	..	..	..	..	..	..	50.1	2.3
80	Mauritius	88.5[h]	49.0[f]	99.0	89.0	24.9	100.0	..	..	..	..	..	..	83.5	2.2
81	Bosnia and Herzegovina	97.9[h]	..	88.0	90.0	35.9	..	..	..	..	..	..	..	67.9	26.8
82	Azerbaijan	99.8	92.7	94.0	85.0	19.3	100.0	362	431	373	76	64	74	53.0	3.6
83	Saint Vincent and the Grenadines	..	..	105.0	107.0	..	84.1	..	..	..	..	..	..	..	..
84	Oman	86.6	53.9	105.0	100.0	24.5	100.0	..	..	..	..	..	..	70.0[e]	2.7
85	Brazil	90.3	49.5	127.0	101.0	36.1	..	412	386	405	94	81	84	53.7	24.3
85	Jamaica	86.6[i]	72.6[f]	89.0	93.0	29.0	..	..	..	..	..	..	..	73.7	4.8
87	Armenia	99.6[h]	94.4[f]	103.0	92.0	51.5	77.5	..	..	..	..	..	..	45.7	2.3
88	Saint Lucia	..	..	94.0	96.0	11.3	86.8	..	..	..	..	..	..	..	7.9
89	Ecuador	91.9	36.6	114.0	80.0	39.8	82.6	..	..	..	..	..	..	74.5	19.4
90	Turkey	90.8	34.5	102.0	78.0	45.8	..	464	445	454	82	93	81	54.3	8.2
91	Colombia	93.4	43.1	115.0	96.0	39.1	100.0	413	381	402	87	75	81	71.7	15.5
92	Sri Lanka	91.2	73.9	99.0	87.0	15.5	..	..	..	..	..	..	..	77.9	1.4
93	Algeria	72.6	24.1	110.0	95.0	30.8	99.3	..	..	..	..	..	..	67.1[e]	5.0
94	Tunisia	77.6	37.0	109.0	90.0	34.4	..	404	371	401	85	78	81	54.8[e]	5.3
MEDIUM HUMAN DEVELOPMENT															
95	Tonga	99.0	74.0[f]	110.0	101.0	6.5	..	..	..	..	..	..	..	..	9.6
96	Belize	..	34.0[f]	121.0	75.0	21.5	45.2	..	..	..	..	..	..	..	9.7
96	Dominican Republic	89.5	42.5	108.0	76.0	34.0	84.9	..	..	..	..	..	..	68.9	..
96	Fiji	..	57.8	105.0	86.0	16.1	97.8	..	..	..	..	..	..	..	9.1
96	Samoa	98.8[h]	62.1	108.0	85.0	7.5	..	..	..	..	..	..	..	..	..
100	Jordan	92.6	73.3	97.0	91.0	41.8	..	405	387	415	91	83	89	63.3[e]	6.6
101	China	94.3[h]	62.7[f]	111.0	81.0	25.9	..	556[k]	600[k]	575[k]	80[k]	103[k]	82[k]	62.6	..
102	Turkmenistan	99.6[h]	..	..	..	..	..	..	..	..	..	..	..	74.3	..
103	Thailand	93.5	32.2	91.0	79.0	47.7	..	421	419	425	72	79	80	88.7	..
104	Maldives	98.4	25.4	109.0	71.0	..	77.0	..	..	..	..	..	..	..	..
105	Suriname	94.7	43.7	113.0	75.0	12.1	100.0	..	..	..	..	..	..	..	9.7
106	Gabon	88.4[i]	44.4[f]	182.0	53.0	..	..	..	..	..	..	..	..	46.5	..
107	El Salvador	84.5	37.5	114.0	65.0	23.4	92.7	..	..	..	..	..	..	72.7	13.5
108	Bolivia, Plurinational State of	91.2	44.5	105.0	80.0	38.6	..	..	..	..	..	..	..	68.2	16.3
108	Mongolia	97.4[h]	82.4[f]	100.0	93.0	53.3	97.6	..	..	..	..	..	..	57.9	5.9
110	Palestine, State of	94.9	52.1	91.0	86.0	50.2	100.0	..	..	..	..	..	..	63.5[e]	1.5
111	Paraguay	93.9	36.9	100.0	67.0	36.6	..	..	..	..	..	..	..	66.9	21.9
112	Egypt	72.0	51.2[f]	106.0	85.0	30.4	..	..	..	..	..	..	..	42.6[e]	..
113	Moldova, Republic of	98.5[h]	93.3	94.0	88.0	38.1	..	..	..	..	..	..	..	53.7	4.8

TABLE 8 Education | 171

TABLE 8 EDUCATION

HDI rank		Adult literacy rate	Population with at least secondary education	Primary	Secondary	Tertiary	Primary school teachers trained to teach	Reading[a]	Mathematics[b]	Science[c]	Reading	Mathematics	Science	Satisfaction with education quality	Primary school dropout rate
		(% ages 15 and older)	(% ages 25 and older)	(%)			(%)							(% satisfied)	(% of primary school cohort)
		2005–2010d	2010	2002–2011d	2002–2011d	2002–2011d	2005–2011d	2009	2009	2009	2009	2009	2009	2011	2002–2011d
114	Philippines	95.4	64.8 f	106.0	85.0	28.9	..	..	..	..	..	..	..	79.2	24.2
114	Uzbekistan	99.4 h	..	95.0	106.0	8.9	100.0	..	..	..	..	..	..	85.0	1.9
116	Syrian Arab Republic	83.4 h	32.8	118.0	72.0	..	..	..	..	..	..	..	..	59.1 e	5.4
117	Micronesia, Federated States of	..	..	110.0	83.0	14.2	..	..	..	..	..	..	..	..	..
118	Guyana	..	55.6 f	85.0	91.0	11.9	66.1	..	..	..	..	..	..	..	16.5
119	Botswana	84.5	75.5 f	108.0	80.0	7.4	97.4	..	..	..	..	..	..	66.4	13.2
120	Honduras	84.8	19.8	116.0	73.0	18.8	36.4	..	..	..	..	..	..	63.6	23.8
121	Indonesia	92.6	41.4	118.0	77.0	23.1	..	402	371	383	66	70	69	80.1	20.0
121	Kiribati	..	..	113.0	86.0	..	85.4	..	..	..	..	..	..	..	21.1
121	South Africa	88.7	70.4	102.0	94.0	..	87.4	..	..	..	..	..	..	69.3	23.0
124	Vanuatu	82.6	..	117.0	55.0	4.7	100.0	..	..	..	..	..	..	..	28.5
125	Kyrgyzstan	99.2	81.1 f	100.0	84.0	48.8	68.4	314	331	330	99	81	91	47.7	2.4
125	Tajikistan	99.7 h	89.7 f	102.0	87.0	19.7	92.9	..	..	..	..	..	..	76.4	1.1
127	Viet Nam	93.2	26.3 f	106.0	77.0	22.3	98.3	..	..	..	..	..	..	80.4	7.9
128	Namibia	88.8 h	33.5 f	107.0	64.0	9.0	95.6	..	..	..	..	..	..	..	17.4
129	Nicaragua	78.0	37.6 f	118.0	69.0	18.0	74.9	..	..	..	..	..	..	81.0	51.6
130	Morocco	56.1	28.0 f	114.0	56.0	13.2	100.0	..	..	..	..	..	..	41.6 e	9.5
131	Iraq	78.2 h	32.4 f	105.0	53.0	16.4	..	..	..	..	..	..	..	38.0	33.3
132	Cape Verde	84.3 h	..	110.0	88.0	17.8	90.0	..	..	..	..	..	..	..	14.3
133	Guatemala	75.2 h	14.8	116.0	59.0	17.8	..	..	..	..	..	..	..	71.8	35.2
134	Timor-Leste	58.3	..	117.0	56.0	16.7	..	..	..	..	..	..	..	..	33.4
135	Ghana	67.3 h	53.8 f	107.0	58.0	8.8	50.6	..	..	..	..	..	..	57.2	27.8
136	Equatorial Guinea	93.9 h	..	87.0	27.0	3.3	45.3	..	..	..	..	..	..	..	38.1
136	India	62.8	38.7 f	118.0	60.0	16.2	..	..	..	..	..	..	..	74.8	34.2
138	Cambodia	77.6	15.7 f	127.0	46.0	7.8	99.1	..	..	..	..	..	..	94.1	45.5
138	Lao People's Democratic Republic	72.7	29.7 f	121.0	45.0	13.4	96.9	..	..	..	..	..	..	78.9	33.0
140	Bhutan	52.8	34.4	111.0	70.0	8.8	91.5	..	..	..	..	..	..	..	9.0
141	Swaziland	87.4 h	48.1 f	116.0	58.0	4.4	73.1	..	..	..	..	..	..	77.8	16.1
LOW HUMAN DEVELOPMENT															
142	Congo	..	46.2 f	115.0	45.0	5.5	86.8	..	..	..	..	..	..	46.6	29.7
143	Solomon Islands	..	..	109.0	36.0	..	..	..	..	..	..	..	..	..	..
144	Sao Tome and Principe	89.2 h	..	134.0	59.0	4.5	40.5	..	..	..	..	..	..	..	32.0
145	Kenya	87.4 h	41.9	113.0	60.0	4.0	96.8	..	..	..	..	..	..	59.6	27.2
146	Bangladesh	56.8 h	35.1 f	..	..	10.6	58.4	..	..	..	..	..	..	81.6	33.8
146	Pakistan	54.9	31.2	95.0	34.0	5.4	84.2	..	..	..	..	..	..	60.5	38.5
148	Angola	70.1 h	..	124.0	31.0	3.7	..	..	..	..	..	..	..	42.0	68.1
149	Myanmar	92.3 h	17.8 f	126.0	54.0	11.0	99.9	..	..	..	..	..	..	..	25.2
150	Cameroon	70.7	27.9 f	120.0	42.0	11.5	57.1	..	..	..	..	..	..	62.1	33.8
151	Madagascar	64.5	..	149.0	31.0	3.7	90.4	..	..	..	..	..	..	45.8	65.4
152	Tanzania, United Republic of	73.2 h	7.4 f	102.0	..	2.1	94.5	..	..	..	..	..	..	44.8	18.6
153	Nigeria	61.3 h	..	83.0	44.0	10.3	66.1	..	..	..	..	..	..	47.4	20.1
154	Senegal	49.7	7.5 f	87.0	37.0	7.9	47.9	..	..	..	..	..	..	38.0	40.4
155	Mauritania	58.0 h	14.2 f	102.0	24.0	4.4	100.0	..	..	..	..	..	..	39.2 e	29.3
156	Papua New Guinea	60.6 h	10.5 f	60.0	..	..	..	..	..	..	..	..	..	..	..
157	Nepal	60.3 h	28.3 f	115.0	44.0	5.6	80.7	..	..	..	..	..	..	73.0	38.3
158	Lesotho	89.6 h	20.9	103.0	46.0	3.5	63.4	..	..	..	..	..	..	43.2	30.7
159	Togo	57.1	29.8 f	140.0	46.0	5.9	76.7	..	..	..	..	..	..	45.4	40.6
160	Yemen	63.9	16.0 f	87.0	44.0	10.2	..	..	..	..	..	..	..	37.2 e	40.5
161	Haiti	48.7	29.1 f	..	..	..	..	..	..	..	..	..	..	39.9	..
161	Uganda	73.2	23.4	121.0	28.0	4.2	89.4	..	..	..	..	..	..	48.8	68.2
163	Zambia	71.2	35.0 f	115.0	..	2.4	..	..	..	..	..	..	..	68.0	46.9
164	Djibouti	..	..	59.0	36.0	4.9	100.0	..	..	..	..	..	..	66.6	35.7
165	Gambia	50.0 h	24.0 f	83.0	54.0	4.1	..	..	..	..	..	..	..	..	38.9
166	Benin	42.4 h	18.4 f	126.0	37.0	6.0	42.6	..	..	..	..	..	..	60.7	35.7
167	Rwanda	71.1 h	7.7 f	143.0	32.0	5.5	91.5	..	..	..	..	..	..	83.9	63.0
168	Côte d'Ivoire	56.2 h	22.1 f	88.0	27.0	8.9	100.0	..	..	..	..	..	..	..	39.2
169	Comoros	74.9 h	..	104.0	46.0	7.9	57.4	..	..	..	..	..	..	46.0 e	25.9
170	Malawi	74.8 h	15.3 f	135.0	32.0	0.7	95.9	..	..	..	..	..	..	65.2	47.2

	EDUCATIONAL ATTAINMENT		GROSS ENROLMENT RATIO				EDUCATION QUALITY							
	Adult literacy rate	Population with at least secondary education	Primary	Secondary	Tertiary	Primary school teachers trained to teach	Performance of 15-year-old students						Satisfaction with education quality	Primary school dropout rate
							Mean score			Deviation from mean				
	(% ages 15 and older)	(% ages 25 and older)		(%)		(%)	Reading[a]	Mathematics[b]	Science[c]	Reading	Mathematics	Science	(% satisfied)	(% of primary school cohort)
HDI rank	2005–2010[d]	2010	2002–2011[d]	2002–2011[d]	2002–2011[d]	2005–2011[d]	2009	2009	2009	2009	2009	2009	2011	2002–2011[d]
171 Sudan	71.1[h]	15.5[f]	73.0	39.0	6.1	59.7	..	..	..	..	..	..	43.0	9.1
172 Zimbabwe	92.2[h]	55.4[f]	..	..	6.2	..	..	..	..	..	..	..	66.4	..
173 Ethiopia	39.0	..	102.0	36.0	5.5	39.4	..	..	..	..	..	..	..	52.5
174 Liberia	60.8[i]	27.3[f]	96.0	..	19.1	40.2	..	..	..	..	..	..	49.6	54.4
175 Afghanistan	..	20.3[f]	97.0	46.0	3.3	..	..	..	..	..	..	..	58.5	..
176 Guinea-Bissau	54.2[h]	..	123.0	36.0	2.7	38.9	..	..	..	..	..	..	..	..
177 Sierra Leone	42.1	14.8	125.0	..	2.1	48.0	..	..	..	..	..	..	35.3	..
178 Burundi	67.2[h]	7.1[f]	156.0	25.0	3.2	91.2	..	..	..	..	..	..	70.9	43.8
178 Guinea	41.0[h]	..	94.0	38.0	9.5	65.2	..	..	..	..	..	..	39.0	34.3
180 Central African Republic	56.0[h]	17.9[f]	93.0	13.0	2.6	..	..	..	..	..	..	..	40.7	53.1
181 Eritrea	67.8[h]	..	45.0	32.0	2.0	93.8	..	..	..	..	..	..	..	31.0
182 Mali	31.1	10.3	82.0	39.0	5.8	50.0	..	..	..	..	..	..	34.6	24.5
183 Burkina Faso	28.7	2.0	79.0	23.0	3.3	85.7	..	..	..	..	..	..	53.0	36.4
184 Chad	34.5[h]	..	90.0	26.0	2.2	45.3	..	..	..	..	..	..	60.1	76.7
185 Mozambique	56.1[h]	3.6[f]	115.0	25.0	1.5	75.9	..	..	..	..	..	..	63.2	64.6
186 Congo, Democratic Republic of the	66.8[h]	23.2[f]	94.0	38.0	6.2	91.7	..	..	..	..	..	..	39.3	45.2
186 Niger	28.7	5.1[f]	71.0	13.0	1.5	96.4	..	..	..	..	..	..	55.3	30.7
OTHER COUNTRIES OR TERRITORIES														
Korea, Democratic People's Rep. of	100.0	..	..	..	..	..	539	..	..	..	..	..	..	..
Marshall Islands	..	..	102.0	99.0	16.2	..	..	..	..	..	..	..	..	16.5
Monaco	..	..	..	..	..	..	..	..	..	..	..	..	..	..
Nauru	..	..	93.0	63.0	..	74.2	..	..	..	..	..	..	..	..
San Marino	..	..	94.0	97.0	..	..	..	..	..	..	..	..	..	..
Somalia	..	..	32.0	8.0	..	..	..	..	..	..	..	..	..	..
South Sudan	..	..	..	..	..	..	..	..	..	..	..	..	..	..
Tuvalu	..	..	100.0	..	..	..	..	..	..	..	..	..	..	..
Human Development Index groups														
Very high human development	..	85.9	104.2	100.4	75.8	..	—	—	—	—	—	—	61.3	3.8
High human development	92.7	64.2	110.5	91.0	48.7	..	—	—	—	—	—	—	58.0	7.3
Medium human development	82.3	50.5	113.4	70.7	22.1	..	—	—	—	—	—	—	69.2	18.8
Low human development	60.8	25.2	98.2	37.4	6.8	73.8	—	—	—	—	—	—	56.5	41.7
Regions														
Arab States	74.5	38.4	97.7	71.1	24.1	..	—	—	—	—	—	—	50.0	9.9
East Asia and the Pacific	93.8	..	111.0	78.8	26.1	..	—	—	—	—	—	—	..	..
Europe and Central Asia	98.1	83.5	99.9	91.2	57.5	..	—	—	—	—	—	—	51.8	4.2
Latin America and the Caribbean	91.3	50.4	115.9	90.9	42.5	92.3	—	—	—	—	—	—	..	14.3
South Asia	62.8	39.2	113.6	57.6	15.7	77.2	—	—	—	—	—	—	73.3	21.4
Sub-Saharan Africa	63.0	29.7	100.3	40.3	6.2	73.9	—	—	—	—	—	—	52.0	37.8
Least developed countries	60.7	..	101.8	36.0	6.6	71.9	—	—	—	—	—	—	58.2	40.9
Small island developing states	..	..	97.0	77.0	45.2	89.4	—	—	—	—	—	—	..	..
World	81.3	57.7	107.9	71.2	28.7	..	—	—	—	—	—	—	64.2	18.0

NOTES

a Average score in reading for Organisation for Economic Co-operation and Development (OECD) countries is 493.

b Average score in mathematics for OECD countries is 495.

c Average score in science for OECD countries is 501.

d Data refer to the most recent year available during the period specified.

e Average of two or more surveys during the period.

f Barro and Lee (2011) estimates for 2010.

g Refers to 2011.

h United Nations Educational, Scientific and Cultural Organization Institute for Statistics (UIS) estimate derived from its Global Age-specific Literacy Projections Model, which is based on national data since 2000.

i UIS estimate derived from its Global Age-specific Literacy Projections Model, which is based on national data from before 2000.

j Refers to Dubai only.

k Refers to Shanghai only.

DEFINITIONS

Adult literacy rate: Percentage of the population ages 15 and older who can, with understanding, both read and write a short simple statement on their everyday life.

Population with at least secondary education: Percentage of the population ages 25 and older that reached at least secondary education.

Gross enrolment ratio: Total enrolment in a given level of education (primary, secondary or tertiary), regardless of age, expressed as a percentage of the official school-age population for the same level of education.

School teachers trained to teach: Percentage of primary school teachers that have received the minimum organized teacher training (pre-service or in-service) required for teaching at the primary level.

Performance in reading, mathematics and science: Score obtained in testing of skills and knowledge of 15-year-old students in these subjects essential for participation in society.

Deviation from mean: Spread of scores in reading, mathematics and science relative to the average scores.

Satisfaction with education quality: Percentage of respondents who answered "satisfied" to the Gallup World Poll question, "Are you satisfied or dissatisfied with the education system?"

Primary school dropout rate: Percentage of students from a given cohort that have enrolled in primary school but that drop out before reaching the last grade of primary education. It is calculated as 100 minus the survival rate to the last grade of primary education and assumes that observed flow rates remain unchanged throughout the cohort life and that dropouts do not re-enter school.

MAIN DATA SOURCES

Columns 1, 2–6 and 14: UNESCO Institute for Statistics (2012).

Columns 7–12: OECD (2010).

Column 13: Gallup (2012).

TABLE 8 Education | 173

TABLE 9

Social integration

		EMPLOYMENT, VULNERABILITY AND EQUITY				PERCEPTIONS OF INDIVIDUAL WELL-BEING			PERCEPTIONS OF SOCIETY			HUMAN SAFETY			
		Employment to population ratio	Youth unemployment	Child labour	Overall loss in Human Development Index due to inequality	Overall life satisfaction	Satisfaction with freedom of choice	Satisfaction with job	Trust in people	Satisfaction with community[a]	Trust in national government	Perception of safety	Homicide rate	Suicide rate (per 100,000 people)	
		(% ages 25 and older)	(% ages 15–24)	(% ages 5–14)	(%)	(0, least satisfied, 10, most satisfied)	(% satisfied)			(% answering "yes")		(% answering "yes")	(per 100,000 people)	Female	Male
HDI rank		2011	2005–2011[b]	2001–2010[b]	2012	2007–2011[b]	2007–2011[b]	2007–2011[b]	2011	2007–2011[b]	2007–2011[b]	2007–2011[b]	2004–2011[b]	2001–2010[b]	2001–2010[b]
VERY HIGH HUMAN DEVELOPMENT															
1	Norway	65.9	9.3	..	6.4	7.6	93.0	..	..	92.8	54.0	81.0	0.6	6.5	17.3
2	Australia	62.4	11.9	..	7.9	7.4	94.0	87.4	..	91.9	53.0	64.0	1.0	3.6	12.8
3	United States	61.2	18.7	..	12.4	7.1	85.0	87.4	37.0	83.8	38.0	75.0	4.2	4.5	17.7
4	Netherlands	61.5	7.8	..	6.9	7.6	91.0	94.5	46.0	94.5	60.0	79.0	1.1	5.5	13.1
5	Germany	57.2	9.1	..	6.9	6.7	89.0	89.0	31.0	93.9	43.0	78.0	0.8	6.0	17.9
6	New Zealand	66.2	18.2	..	..	7.2	93.0	89.0	..	88.1	64.0	67.0	0.9	5.5	18.1
7	Ireland	55.8	35.3	..	7.2	7.0	95.0	89.1	30.0	93.6	53.0	70.0	1.2	4.7	19.0
7	Sweden	62.5	23.8	..	6.2	7.5	93.0	91.8	55.0	92.5	64.0	78.0	1.0	6.8	18.7
9	Switzerland	65.5	7.9	..	7.0	7.5	88.0	..	44.0	93.5	58.0	76.0	0.7	11.4	24.8
10	Japan	59.7	8.9	..	..	6.1	78.0	76.2	33.0	84.6	23.0	69.0	0.4	13.2	36.2
11	Canada	62.7	15.9	..	8.7	7.4	94.0	91.5	42.0	91.7	55.0	79.0	1.6	5.4	17.3
12	Korea, Republic of	64.8	12.1	..	16.5	6.9	66.0	71.1	26.0	78.5	28.0	54.0	2.6	22.1	39.9
13	Hong Kong, China (SAR)	61.2	11.0	..	..	5.5	89.0	84.4	29.0	84.1	58.0	88.0	0.2	10.7	19.0
13	Iceland	71.9	18.4	..	6.4	6.9	86.0	..	..	81.8	24.0	77.0	0.3	7.0	16.5
15	Denmark	59.8	15.7	..	6.2	7.8	93.0	94.0	60.0	93.4	47.0	79.0	0.9	6.4	17.5
16	Israel	60.9	11.8	..	12.3	7.4	52.0	84.0	26.0	82.3	45.0	59.0	2.1	1.5	7.0
17	Belgium	54.0	18.7	..	8.0	6.9	86.0	90.3	30.0	91.2	29.0	64.0	1.7	10.3	28.8
18	Austria	58.6	8.8	..	6.6	7.5	92.0	94.1	29.0	94.4	41.0	82.0	0.6	7.1	23.8
18	Singapore	69.2	6.7	..	..	6.5	82.0	86.5	33.0	92.9	83.0	89.0	0.3	7.7	12.9
20	France	54.4	23.2	..	9.0	7.0	90.0	87.4	20.0	89.4	38.0	63.0	1.1	8.5	24.7
21	Finland	57.8	19.3	..	6.0	7.4	93.0	87.7	58.0	91.2	57.0	78.0	2.2	10.0	29.0
21	Slovenia	57.2	16.8	..	5.8	6.0	90.0	85.0	15.0	90.6	18.0	84.0	0.7	9.4	34.6
23	Spain	49.5	48.2	..	10.1	6.5	80.0	85.7	22.0	87.8	31.0	68.0	0.8	3.4	11.9
24	Liechtenstein	..	..	..	..	..	..	..	..	..	..	..	2.8	..	..
25	Italy	47.5	32.0	..	11.9	6.1	55.0	81.0	20.0	75.7	26.0	52.0	0.9	2.8	10.0
26	Luxembourg	59.9	20.8	..	7.2	7.1	95.0	93.5	26.0	94.7	77.0	77.0	2.5	3.2	16.1
26	United Kingdom	58.8	22.0	..	8.3	6.9	90.0	88.3	35.0	86.6	49.0	70.0	1.2	3.0	10.9
28	Czech Republic	59.7	18.1	..	5.4	6.3	73.0	79.9	24.0	88.1	21.0	59.0	1.7	4.4	23.9
29	Greece	49.1	51.5	..	11.5	5.4	52.0	70.3	16.0	74.2	18.0	53.0	1.5	1.0	6.0
30	Brunei Darussalam	69.3	..	..	..	..	..	..	..	..	..	..	0.5	..	..
31	Cyprus	66.2	23.1	..	11.5	6.7	73.0	87.1	11.0	88.7	40.0	70.0	1.7	1.7	7.4
32	Malta	48.3	14.0	..	8.2	6.2	86.0	86.0	16.0	84.1	49.0	64.0	1.0	1.0	5.9
33	Andorra	..	..	..	..	..	..	..	..	..	..	..	1.3	..	..
33	Estonia	58.4	23.8	..	9.0	5.5	69.0	81.1	33.0	86.3	42.0	56.0	5.2	7.3	30.6
35	Slovakia	57.5	33.6	..	6.3	5.9	68.0	78.6	21.0	86.6	28.0	59.0	1.5	3.4	22.3
36	Qatar	89.9	8.9	..	..	6.6	90.0	86.0	23.0	90.4	89.0	87.0	0.9	..	..
37	Hungary	49.6	27.2	..	7.4	4.9	61.0	80.5	13.0	74.2	36.0	57.0	1.3	10.6	40.0
38	Barbados	66.9	..	..	..	..	..	..	..	..	..	..	11.3	0.0	7.3
39	Poland	55.1	28.9	..	9.9	5.6	80.0	77.0	25.0	88.2	27.0	59.0	1.1	4.1	26.4
40	Chile	62.9	21.1	3.0	19.0	6.6	77.0	78.2	15.0	78.4	48.0	46.0	3.2	4.2	18.2
41	Lithuania	55.6	34.6	..	11.0	5.4	52.0	78.2	25.0	84.2	18.0	39.0	6.6	10.4	61.3
41	United Arab Emirates	83.4	21.8	..	..	7.2	87.0	88.7	18.0	93.8	..	90.0	0.8	..	..
43	Portugal	58.0	31.7	3.0	10.8	5.2	79.0	88.7	27.0	90.1	21.0	63.0	1.2	4.0	15.6
44	Latvia	55.1	29.6	..	10.9	5.0	54.0	80.6	13.0	84.8	11.0	48.0	3.1	8.2	40.0
45	Argentina	62.6	22.2	7.0	19.5	6.4	79.0	80.7	23.0	89.0	61.0	50.0	3.4	3.0	12.6
46	Seychelles	..	..	..	..	..	..	..	..	..	..	..	8.3	0.0	8.9
47	Croatia	49.1	36.8	..	15.1	5.6	46.0	..	16.0	66.0	..	64.0	1.4	7.5	28.9
HIGH HUMAN DEVELOPMENT															
48	Bahrain	72.2	..	5.0	..	4.5	73.0	79.3	11.0	88.2	..	60.0	0.6	3.5	4.0
49	Bahamas	71.9	21.7	..	..	..	..	..	..	..	..	..	27.4	0.6	1.9
50	Belarus	54.4	..	5.0	8.3	5.2	57.0	65.7	34.0	76.6	59.0	60.0	4.9	8.8	48.7
51	Uruguay	65.9	21.7	8.0	16.4	6.1	78.0	78.0	27.0	83.8	73.0	48.0	5.9	6.3	26.0
52	Montenegro	..	40.0	10.0	7.4	5.5	50.0	..	21.0	68.3	..	78.0	3.5	..	..
52	Palau	..	..	..	..	..	..	..	..	..	..	..	0.0	..	..
54	Kuwait	75.5	11.8	..	..	6.6	75.0	84.9	11.0	81.5	..	..	2.2	1.7	1.9
55	Russian Federation	62.8	15.7	..	..	5.4	54.0	67.9	24.0	69.4	48.0	40.0	10.2	9.5	53.9

	EMPLOYMENT, VULNERABILITY AND EQUITY				PERCEPTIONS OF INDIVIDUAL WELL-BEING			PERCEPTIONS OF SOCIETY			HUMAN SAFETY			
	Employment to population ratio	Youth unemployment	Child labour	Overall loss in Human Development Index due to inequality	Overall life satisfaction	Satisfaction with freedom of choice	Satisfaction with job	Trust in people	Satisfaction with community[a]	Trust in national government	Perception of safety	Homicide rate	Suicide rate (per 100,000 people)	
	(% ages 25 and older)	(% ages 15–24)	(% ages 5–14)	(%)	(0, least satisfied, 10, most satisfied)	(% satisfied)			(% answering "yes")		(% answering "yes")	(per 100,000 people)	Female	Male
HDI rank	2011	2005–2011[b]	2001–2010[b]	2012	2007–2011[b]	2007–2011[b]	2007–2011[b]	2011	2007–2011[b]	2007–2011[b]	2007–2011[b]	2004–2011[b]	2001–2010[b]	2001–2010[b]
56 Romania	57.3	23.8	1.0	12.6	5.0	60.0	69.5	15.0	78.1	12.0	55.0	2.0	3.5	21.0
57 Bulgaria	52.0	27.6	..	9.9	3.9	60.0	73.3	20.0	74.0	27.0	52.0	2.0	6.2	18.8
57 Saudi Arabia	59.7	45.8	..	..	6.7	57.0	81.8	36.0	85.9	..	77.0	1.0	..	..
59 Cuba	58.7	3.5	..	..	..	..	..	..	..	..	..	5.0	5.5	19.0
59 Panama	68.3	14.6	7.0	24.6	7.3	80.0	88.5	21.0	86.6	46.0	47.0	21.6	1.9	9.0
61 Mexico	63.9	10.4	5.0	23.4	6.8	80.0	74.4	29.0	73.7	38.0	42.0	22.7	1.5	7.0
62 Costa Rica	65.6	21.6	5.0	21.5	7.3	92.0	87.4	14.0	82.5	32.0	41.0	11.3	1.9	10.2
63 Grenada	..	..	..	..	..	..	..	..	..	..	..	11.5	0.0	0.0
64 Libya	53.6	..	..	..	4.9	41.0	64.3	..	68.7	..	91.0	2.9	..	..
64 Malaysia	66.6	11.3	..	..	5.8	79.0	85.6	14.0	87.3	79.0	46.0	2.3	..	..
64 Serbia	..	46.1	4.0	9.5	4.5	41.0	..	17.0	60.0	..	68.0	1.2	10.0	28.1
67 Antigua and Barbuda	..	..	..	..	..	..	..	..	..	..	..	6.8	..	..
67 Trinidad and Tobago	66.6	12.9	1.0	15.3	6.7	81.0	89.9	..	87.3	29.0	42.0	35.2	3.8	17.9
69 Kazakhstan	75.0	5.0	2.0	13.6	5.5	76.0	77.9	33.0	79.7	72.0	56.0	8.8	9.4	43.0
70 Albania	56.5	28.3	12.0	13.9	5.3	46.0	..	7.0	67.7	..	67.0	4.0	3.3	4.7
71 Venezuela, Bolivarian Republic of	68.1	22.0	8.0	26.6	7.5	75.0	85.1	13.0	79.0	59.0	31.0	45.1	1.2	5.3
72 Dominica	..	..	..	..	..	..	..	..	..	..	..	22.1	..	..
72 Georgia	62.8	35.6	18.0	15.3	4.2	58.0	55.0	16.0	78.3	66.0	91.0	4.3	1.7	7.1
72 Lebanon	47.6	22.3	7.0	22.8	5.2	65.0	70.8	7.0	74.1	37.0	69.0	2.2	..	..
72 Saint Kitts and Nevis	..	..	..	..	..	..	..	..	..	..	..	38.2	..	..
76 Iran, Islamic Republic of	46.1	33.9	..	..	4.8	57.0	65.0	..	76.3	56.0	55.0	3.0	..	..
77 Peru	77.4	16.2	34.0	24.3	5.6	72.0	74.1	12.0	75.3	19.0	46.0	10.3	1.0	1.9
78 The former Yugoslav Republic of Macedonia	43.4	55.7	6.0	14.7	4.2	56.0	..	11.0	66.7	..	63.0	1.9	4.0	9.5
78 Ukraine	58.3	18.7	7.0	9.2	5.1	53.0	61.4	29.0	71.4	24.0	48.0	5.2	7.0	37.8
80 Mauritius	60.8	28.0	..	13.3	5.5	83.0	84.6	..	90.5	67.0	55.0	2.5	1.9	11.8
81 Bosnia and Herzegovina	37.2	60.0	5.0	11.5	4.7	33.0	..	18.0	61.7	..	67.0	1.5	..	..
82 Azerbaijan	70.8	15.2	7.0	11.4	4.7	49.0	57.8	27.0	73.4	74.0	74.0	2.2	0.3	1.0
83 Saint Vincent and the Grenadines	..	..	..	..	..	..	..	..	..	..	..	22.9	1.9	5.4
84 Oman	65.7	..	..	..	6.9	91.0	85.3	..	89.9	..	..	0.7	..	..
85 Brazil	68.2	23.1	3.0	27.2	6.8	80.0	81.3	15.0	78.5	51.0	40.0	21.0	2.0	7.7
85 Jamaica	65.9	37.9	6.0	19.1	..	..	68.3	..	72.2	..	..	52.2	..	..
87 Armenia	47.3	54.7	4.0	10.9	4.4	41.0	45.4	15.0	52.7	34.0	75.0	1.4	1.1	2.8
88 Saint Lucia	..	..	..	..	..	..	..	..	..	..	..	25.2	0.0	4.9
89 Ecuador	71.5	18.1	8.0	25.8	5.8	78.0	79.8	9.0	86.0	59.0	49.0	18.2	3.6	10.5
90 Turkey	48.8	20.7	3.0	22.5	5.3	44.0	71.2	8.0	78.9	60.0	51.0	3.3	..	..
91 Colombia	68.3	29.9	9.0	27.8	6.4	81.0	81.5	14.0	82.9	55.0	43.0	33.4	2.0	7.9
92 Sri Lanka	58.2	24.7	..	15.1	4.2	81.0	84.7	17.0	89.7	86.0	77.0	3.6	..	..
93 Algeria	43.9	37.5	5.0	..	5.2	53.0	58.7	16.0	73.9	53.0	49.0	1.5	..	..
94 Tunisia	46.3	31.4	..	..	4.7	58.0	59.4	15.0	66.0	47.0	47.0	1.1	..	..
MEDIUM HUMAN DEVELOPMENT														
95 Tonga	..	..	..	..	..	..	..	..	..	..	..	1.0	..	..
96 Belize	66.3	28.8	40.0	..	6.5	62.0	..	..	67.1	26.0	43.0	41.4	0.7	6.6
96 Dominican Republic	62.4	44.5	10.0	27.3	4.7	82.0	76.3	15.0	79.2	45.0	38.0	25.0	0.7	3.9
96 Fiji	62.7	..	..	..	..	..	..	..	..	..	..	2.8	..	..
96 Samoa	..	..	..	..	..	..	..	..	..	..	..	1.1	..	..
100 Jordan	44.9	46.8	..	19.0	5.7	72.0	74.9	9.0	75.6	77.0	81.0	1.8	0.0	0.2
101 China	74.6	..	..	22.4	5.0	77.0	69.9	57.0	77.1	..	80.0	1.1	..	..
102 Turkmenistan	62.6	..	..	..	5.8	..	93.6	27.0	97.5	..	83.0	4.2	..	..
103 Thailand	76.9	3.0	8.0	21.3	6.7	92.0	96.3	27.0	95.2	54.0	74.0	4.8	3.8	12.0
104 Maldives	64.7	30.5	..	25.2	..	..	..	..	..	..	..	1.6	0.0	0.7
105 Suriname	56.4	..	6.0	23.0	..	..	..	..	..	..	..	4.6	4.8	23.9
106 Gabon	68.2	..	..	19.5	..	77.0	53.7	..	54.8	53.0	39.0	13.8	..	..
107 El Salvador	64.5	13.0	5.0	26.6	6.7	74.0	77.3	18.0	81.9	49.0	42.0	69.2	3.6	12.9
108 Bolivia, Plurinational State of	77.4	..	26.0	34.2	5.8	67.0	83.9	10.0	84.8	38.0	44.0	8.9	..	..
108 Mongolia	67.9	..	18.0	15.9	5.0	64.0	82.1	14.0	80.6	29.0	47.0	8.7	..	..
110 Palestine, State of	41.2	49.6	..	..	4.8	51.0	70.8	9.0	71.5	49.0	59.0	4.1	..	..
111 Paraguay	73.4	17.8	15.0	..	5.8	71.0	85.6	12.0	85.5	48.0	38.0	11.5	2.0	5.1

TABLE 9   Social integration | 175

TABLE 9 SOCIAL INTEGRATION

	EMPLOYMENT, VULNERABILITY AND EQUITY				PERCEPTIONS OF INDIVIDUAL WELL-BEING			PERCEPTIONS OF SOCIETY			HUMAN SAFETY			
	Employment to population ratio	Youth unemployment	Child labour	Overall loss in Human Development Index due to inequality	Overall life satisfaction	Satisfaction with freedom of choice	Satisfaction with job	Trust in people	Satisfaction with community[a]	Trust in national government	Perception of safety	Homicide rate	Suicide rate (per 100,000 people)	
	(% ages 25 and older)	(% ages 15–24)	(% ages 5–14)	(%)	(0, least satisfied, 10, most satisfied)	(% satisfied)			(% answering "yes")		(% answering "yes")	(per 100,000 people)	Female	Male
HDI rank	2011	2005–2011[b]	2001–2010[b]	2012	2007–2011[b]	2007–2011[b]	2007–2011[b]	2011	2007–2011[b]	2007–2011[b]	2007–2011[b]	2004–2011[b]	2001–2010[b]	2001–2010[b]
112 Egypt	51.3	54.1	7.0	24.1	4.1	57.0	64.7	22.0	61.0	63.0	58.0	1.2	0.0	0.1
113 Moldova, Republic of	43.9	15.8	16.0	11.6	5.8	58.0	66.1	12.0	70.6	24.0	50.0	7.5	5.6	30.1
114 Philippines	68.8	19.3	..	19.9	5.0	88.0	81.1	14.0	85.6	72.0	62.0	5.4	..	..
114 Uzbekistan	62.8	..	..	15.8	5.1	90.0	87.3	26.0	93.8	..	80.0	3.1	2.3	7.0
116 Syrian Arab Republic	45.8	40.2	4.0	20.4	4.1	47.0	55.5	9.0	44.8	..	65.0	2.3		
117 Micronesia, Federated States of	..	..	..	..	..	..	..	..	..	..	..	0.9		
118 Guyana	61.0	50.0	16.0	19.1	6.0	66.0	..	..	74.8	46.0	47.0	18.6	13.4	39.0
119 Botswana	73.8	..	9.0	..	3.6	82.0	45.9	9.0	56.5	74.0	31.0	14.5	..	..
120 Honduras	67.3	11.2	16.0	27.5	5.9	77.0	79.4	13.0	82.8	29.0	45.0	91.6	..	..
121 Indonesia	70.1	23.0	7.0	18.3	5.2	86.0	74.1	21.0	92.3	74.0	88.0	8.1	..	..
121 Kiribati	..	..	..	..	..	..	..	..	..	..	..	7.3		
121 South Africa	49.6	55.0	..	..	4.7	84.0	56.5	17.0	62.0	63.0	38.0	31.8	0.4	1.4
124 Vanuatu	..	..	..	..	..	..	..	..	..	..	..	0.9		
125 Kyrgyzstan	70.4	16.2	4.0	17.1	4.9	71.0	75.2	34.0	84.8	44.0	62.0	20.1	3.6	14.1
125 Tajikistan	70.3	..	10.0	18.4	4.3	70.0	82.7	31.0	89.9	89.0	85.0	2.1	2.3	2.9
127 Viet Nam	81.3	..	16.0	14.0	5.8	61.0	71.8	26.0	70.1	77.0	67.0	1.6	..	..
128 Namibia	57.4	63.8	..	43.5	4.9	76.0	..	..	76.5	82.0	33.0	17.2	..	..
129 Nicaragua	66.3	9.7	15.0	27.5	5.7	75.0	79.8	11.0	86.0	54.0	51.0	13.6	2.6	9.0
130 Morocco	50.9	18.1	8.0	29.7	5.1	54.0	65.4	58.0	69.4	60.0	67.0	1.4	..	..
131 Iraq	41.9	..	11.0	..	5.0	30.0	64.2	15.0	66.7	37.0	41.0	2.0	..	..
132 Cape Verde	66.7	..	3.0	..	..	..	..	..	..	..	..	11.6	..	..
133 Guatemala	69.7	7.1	21.0	33.1	6.3	74.0	79.8	15.0	85.7	36.0	41.0	38.5	1.7	5.6
134 Timor-Leste	62.8	..	4.0	33.0	..	..	..	..	..	..	..	6.9	..	..
135 Ghana	81.3	..	34.0	32.2	5.6	85.0	63.8	19.0	68.9	68.0	78.0	15.7	..	..
136 Equatorial Guinea	86.5	..	28.0	..	..	..	..	..	..	..	..	20.7		
136 India	61.0	11.5	12.0	29.3	4.6	80.0	71.2	20.0	82.6	58.0	70.0	3.4	7.8	13.0
138 Cambodia	86.7	3.5	39.0	25.9	4.2	92.0	77.6	9.0	90.2	90.0	68.0	3.4	..	..
138 Lao People's Democratic Republic	85.1	..	11.0	24.7	5.0	87.0	87.9	..	94.3	98.0	84.0	4.6	..	..
140 Bhutan	80.3	10.9	18.0	20.0	..	..	..	..	..	..	..	1.0	..	..
141 Swaziland	55.9	..	9.0	35.4	..	..	55.1	..	62.3	..	..	12.9	..	..
LOW HUMAN DEVELOPMENT														
142 Congo	78.8	..	25.0	31.1	4.5	76.0	56.4	..	67.1	48.0	58.0	30.8	..	..
143 Solomon Islands	73.8	..	..	..	..	..	..	..	..	..	..	3.7	..	..
144 Sao Tome and Principe	..	..	8.0	31.7	..	..	..	..	..	..	..	1.9		
145 Kenya	75.9	..	26.0	33.6	4.4	71.0	50.0	10.0	69.3	46.0	50.0	20.1	..	..
146 Bangladesh	74.0	13.6	13.0	27.4	5.0	78.0	76.4	15.0	91.3	79.0	80.0	2.7	..	..
146 Pakistan	55.4	10.5	..	30.9	5.3	34.0	73.2	20.0	83.6	28.0	46.0	7.8	..	..
148 Angola	75.8	..	24.0	43.9	4.2	69.0	65.2	..	49.8	61.0	53.0	19.0	..	..
149 Myanmar	83.4	..	..	..	..	..	..	..	80.4	..	..	10.2	..	..
150 Cameroon	80.3	..	31.0	33.4	4.4	82.0	62.2	13.0	69.4	65.0	56.0	19.7	..	..
151 Madagascar	90.5	2.8	28.0	30.7	4.4	54.0	38.0	..	72.0	65.0	53.0	8.1	..	..
152 Tanzania, United Republic of	84.2	10.1	21.0	27.3	4.1	74.0	63.0	26.0	67.4	56.0	61.0	24.5	..	..
153 Nigeria	61.7	..	29.0	41.4	4.8	77.0	58.6	13.0	67.4	55.0	69.0	12.2	..	..
154 Senegal	76.3	20.1	22.0	33.0	3.8	64.0	42.2	28.0	52.1	30.0	55.0	8.7	..	..
155 Mauritania	44.7	..	16.0	34.4	5.0	56.0	55.3	30.0	62.2	43.0	62.0	14.7	..	..
156 Papua New Guinea	78.0	..	..	..	..	..	..	..	..	..	..	13.0	..	..
157 Nepal	86.4	..	34.0	34.2	3.8	43.0	87.3	17.0	86.7	33.0	61.0	2.8	..	..
158 Lesotho	59.7	41.9	23.0	35.9	..	..	46.9	..	52.4	..	..	35.2	..	..
159 Togo	84.1	..	47.0	33.5	2.8	56.0	42.4	..	57.7	51.0	52.0	10.9	..	..
160 Yemen	50.9	..	23.0	32.3	3.7	59.0	54.3	27.0	51.9	39.0	67.0	4.2	..	..
161 Haiti	74.6	..	21.0	40.2	3.8	37.0	43.4	30.0	57.9	46.0	42.0	6.9	0.0	0.0
161 Uganda	86.9	5.4	25.0	33.6	4.2	73.0	50.1	17.0	69.7	52.0	42.0	36.3	..	..
163 Zambia	76.6	23.4	41.0	36.7	5.0	65.0	47.3	31.0	62.6	40.0	54.0	38.0	..	..
164 Djibouti	..	..	8.0	36.0	4.4	74.0	70.0	55.0	75.3	68.0	72.0	3.4	..	..
165 Gambia	81.1	..	25.0	..	..	..	..	..	..	..	..	10.8	..	..
166 Benin	80.6	..	46.0	35.8	3.7	76.0	46.7	..	66.8	78.0	58.0	15.1	..	..
167 Rwanda	92.3	..	35.0	33.9	4.0	82.0	58.6	30.0	74.3	95.0	92.0	17.1	..	..
168 Côte d'Ivoire	72.8	..	35.0	38.6	4.2	76.0	..	13.0	40.6	42.0	47.0	56.9	..	..

	EMPLOYMENT, VULNERABILITY AND EQUITY				PERCEPTIONS OF INDIVIDUAL WELL-BEING			PERCEPTIONS OF SOCIETY			HUMAN SAFETY			
	Employment to population ratio	Youth unemployment	Child labour	Overall loss in Human Development Index due to inequality	Overall life satisfaction	Satisfaction with freedom of choice	Satisfaction with job	Trust in people	Satisfaction with community[a]	Trust in national government	Perception of safety	Homicide rate	Suicide rate (per 100,000 people)	
	(% ages 25 and older)	(% ages 15–24)	(% ages 5–14)	(%)	(0, least satisfied, 10, most satisfied)	(% satisfied)		(% answering "yes")			(% answering "yes")	(per 100,000 people)	Female	Male
HDI rank	2011	2005–2011[b]	2001–2010[b]	2012	2007–2011[b]	2007–2011[b]	2007–2011[b]	2011	2007–2011[b]	2007–2011[b]	2007–2011[b]	2004–2011[b]	2001–2010[b]	2001–2010[b]
169 Comoros	62.7	..	27.0	..	3.9	50.0	49.8	35.0	77.2	44.0	78.0	12.2	..	..
170 Malawi	92.0	..	26.0	31.4	5.1	88.0	50.9	33.0	80.8	83.0	55.0	36.0	..	..
171 Sudan	59.4	..	..	..	4.4	56.0	48.8	31.0	72.7	54.0	75.0	24.2	..	..
172 Zimbabwe	89.0	..	..	28.5	4.8	63.0	58.6	15.0	68.4	43.0	39.0	14.3	..	..
173 Ethiopia	84.0	29.4	53.0	31.9	4.4	39.0	..	..	52.1	32.0	49.0	25.5	..	..
174 Liberia	72.1	6.6	21.0	35.3	4.2	82.0	63.0	12.0	63.4	54.0	38.0	10.1	..	..
175 Afghanistan	53.8	..	13.0	..	3.8	47.0	82.0	25.0	71.7	31.0	29.0	2.4	..	..
176 Guinea-Bissau	78.1	..	57.0	41.4	..	..	..	..	..	..	..	20.2	..	..
177 Sierra Leone	77.4	..	48.0	41.6	4.1	77.0	61.3	16.0	52.3	58.0	50.0	14.9	..	..
178 Burundi	88.5	..	19.0	..	3.8	49.0	64.7	38.0	76.0	85.0	65.0	21.7	..	..
178 Guinea	79.1	..	25.0	38.8	4.0	79.0	58.9	..	75.3	77.0	62.0	22.5	..	..
180 Central African Republic	82.8	..	47.0	40.5	3.6	68.0	66.5	37.0	75.8	75.0	62.0	29.3	..	..
181 Eritrea	84.1	..	..	..	..	..	..	..	..	..	..	17.8	..	..
182 Mali	56.0	..	36.0	..	3.8	75.0	54.9	45.0	63.9	71.0	80.0	8.0	..	..
183 Burkina Faso	86.0	4.6	38.0	34.2	4.0	58.0	60.1	26.0	78.2	55.0	62.0	18.0	..	..
184 Chad	77.0	..	48.0	40.1	3.7	54.0	72.0	21.0	70.1	39.0	30.0	15.8	..	..
185 Mozambique	90.1	..	22.0	32.7	5.0	64.0	63.1	..	83.1	63.0	42.0	8.8	..	..
186 Congo, Democratic Republic of the	82.8	..	42.0	39.9	4.0	62.0	45.6	39.0	60.2	35.0	38.0	21.7	..	..
186 Niger	66.2	..	43.0	34.2	4.1	82.0	69.7	40.0	85.2	78.0	81.0	3.8	..	..
OTHER COUNTRIES OR TERRITORIES														
Korea, Democratic People's Rep. of	78.7	..	..	..	..	..	..	..	..	..	..	15.2	..	..
Marshall Islands	..	..	..	..	..	..	..	..	..	..	..	..	..	..
Monaco	..	..	..	..	..	..	..	..	..	..	..	0.0	..	..
Nauru	..	..	..	..	..	..	..	..	..	..	..	9.8	..	..
San Marino	..	..	..	..	..	..	..	..	..	..	..	..	..	..
Somalia	59.9	..	49.0	..	..	..	..	..	..	..	..	1.5	..	..
South Sudan	..	..	..	..	..	..	..	..	..	..	..	..	..	..
Tuvalu	..	..	..	..	..	..	..	..	..	..	..	..	..	..
Human Development Index groups														
Very high human development	58.8	19.5	..	10.8	6.7	81.5	84.3	30.9	85.9	38.1	68.4	2.1	6.6	20.6
High human development	61.2	22.4	..	20.6	5.9	66.3	73.4	19.3	76.4	..	47.6	13.0	..	..
Medium human development	68.4	..	..	24.2	4.9	77.8	71.4	..	79.9	..	73.4	3.9	..	..
Low human development	72.2	..	29.7	33.5	4.5	61.8	63.4	..	72.2	50.8	57.7	14.6	..	..
Regions														
Arab States	52.6	..	..	25.4	4.8	54.6	63.9	24.9	67.6	..	62.9	4.5	..	..
East Asia and the Pacific	74.5	..	..	21.3	..	..	..	..	..	..	..	2.8	..	..
Europe and Central Asia	58.4	20.9	..	12.9	5.3	58.5	71.0	21.5	76.5	43.9	53.5	5.5	6.9	35.4
Latin America and the Caribbean	67.2	19.6	8.5	25.7	6.5	77.9	..	..	79.0	47.1	42.0	22.2	2.1	8.1
South Asia	61.2	12.9	..	29.1	4.7	72.9	72.1	19.5	83.2	56.1	66.9	3.7	..	..
Sub-Saharan Africa	74.5	..	33.5	35.0	4.4	69.1	56.2	..	65.2	53.6	55.3	20.4	..	..
Least developed countries	77.4	..	30.2	32.5	4.3	64.2	63.2	..	72.3	56.4	59.5	14.6	..	..
Small island developing states	65.9	..	..	29.2	..	..	..	..	..	..	..	14.6	..	..
World	65.8	..	..	23.3	5.3	73.9	73.1	29.8	79.0	52.0	66.0	6.9	..	..

NOTES

a Based on the Gallup survey question on overall satisfaction with city.

b Data refer to the most recent year available during the period specified.

DEFINITIONS

Employment to population ratio: Percentage of the population ages 25 years or older that is employed.

Youth unemployment: Percentage of the labour force population ages 15–24 that is not in paid employment or self-employed but is available for work and has taken steps to seek paid employment or self-employment.

Child labour: Percentage of children ages 5–11 who, during the reference week, did at least one hour of economic activity or at least 28 hours of household chores, or children ages 12–14 who, during the reference week, did at least 14 hours of economic activity or at least 28 hours of household chores.

Overall loss in Human Development Index (HDI) due to inequality: Loss in potential human development due to inequality, calculated as the percentage difference between the HDI and Inequality-adjusted HDI. See *Technical note 2* for details on how the Inequality-adjusted HDI is calculated.

Overall life satisfaction: Average response to the Gallup World Poll Question: Please imagine a ladder, with steps numbered from zero at the bottom to ten at the top. Suppose we say that the top of the ladder represents the best possible life for you, and the bottom of the ladder represents the worst possible life for you. On which step of the ladder would you say you personally feel you stand at this time, assuming that the higher the step the better you feel about your life, and the lower the step the worse you feel about it? Which step comes closest to the way you feel?

Satisfaction with freedom of choice: Percentage of respondents answering "yes" to the Gallup World Poll question, "In this country, are you satisfied or dissatisfied with your freedom to choose what you do with your life?"

Satisfaction with job: Percentage of respondents answering "satisfied" to the Gallup World Poll question, "Are you satisfied or dissatisfied with your job?"

Trust in people: Percentage of respondents answering "yes" to the Gallup World Poll question, "Generally speaking, would you say that most people can be trusted or that you have to be careful in dealing with people?"

Satisfaction with community: Percentage of respondents answering "yes" to the Gallup World Poll question, "Right now, do you think that economic conditions in the city or area where you live, as a whole, are getting better or getting worse?"

Trust in national government: Percentage of respondents answering "yes" to the Gallup World Poll question, "In this country, do you have confidence in the national government?"

Perception of safety: Percentage of respondents answering "yes" to the Gallup World Poll question, "Do you feel safe walking alone at night in the city or area where you live?"

Homicide rate: Number of intentional homicides—that is, unlawful deaths purposefully inflicted on a person by another person—expressed per 100,000 people.

Suicide rate: Estimated total number of deaths from purposely self-inflicted injuries, in the total population or of a given sex or age, divided by the total number of the reference population, expressed per 100,000 people.

MAIN DATA SOURCES

Columns 1 and 2: ILO (2012).

Column 3: UNICEF (2012).

Column 4: Calculated based on HDI and Inequality-adjusted HDI values from tables 1 and 3.

Columns 5–11: Gallup (2012).

Column 12: UNODC (2012).

Columns 13 and 14: WHO (2012c).

TABLE 9   Social integration | 177

TABLE 10

International trade flows of goods and services

	TRADE OF GOODS[a]				TRADE OF SERVICES				COMPOSITION OF MERCHANDISE GOODS					
	Exports of merchandise goods		Imports of merchandise goods		Exports of services		Imports of services		Share of merchandise exports (%)		Share of merchandise imports (%)		Parts and components[b]	
	($ billions)	(% of GDP)[c]	($ billions)	(% of GDP)[c]	($ billions)	(% of GDP)[c]	($ billions)	(% of GDP)[c]	Agricultural exports	Manufactured exports	Agricultural imports	Manufactured imports	(% of manufactured exports)	(% of manufactured imports)
HDI rank	2010	2010	2010	2010	2010	2010	2010	2010	2010	2010	2010	2010	2010	2010
VERY HIGH HUMAN DEVELOPMENT														
1 Norway	130.7	33.0	77.3	19.5	39.7	10.0	42.8	10.8	7.8	18.6	9.4	75.1	37.0	21.5
2 Australia	206.7	20.1	187.9	18.3	48.5	4.7	51.5	5.0	13.1	12.8	5.9	72.4	24.2	21.6
3 United States	1,121.8	7.9	1,966.5	13.9	544.4	3.9	402.0	2.8	12.3	65.2	5.9	68.8	30.3	28.8
4 Netherlands	492.6	62.9	440.0	56.2	95.4	12.2	85.2	10.9	16.2	56.5	11.4	56.5	26.0	28.9
5 Germany	1,271.1	38.8	1,066.8	32.5	237.6	7.2	263.2	8.0	6.0	81.8	8.6	67.4	28.1	32.0
6 New Zealand	29.7	22.9	30.2	23.3	8.7	6.7	9.1	7.1	65.6	20.3	11.2	70.0	16.0	18.6
7 Ireland	118.3	55.3	60.5	28.3	97.1	45.4	108.4	50.7	9.7	84.2	13.0	66.4	13.5	22.6
7 Sweden	158.4	36.5	148.8	34.3	64.4	14.8	48.5	11.2	8.8	74.5	10.2	69.2	28.6	31.1
9 Switzerland	195.6	38.3	176.3	34.5	83.6	16.4	39.6	7.8	4.1	87.6	6.8	79.6	15.9	16.9
10 Japan	769.8	14.6	692.6	13.2	141.5	2.7	157.6	3.0	1.3	88.3	11.2	50.0	36.0	31.8
11 Canada	362.1	24.8	388.3	26.6	69.2	4.7	91.3	6.3	14.2	46.7	8.2	74.7	22.7	29.5
12 Korea, Republic of	466.4	50.6	425.2	46.1	..	..	..	..	2.0	88.3	6.3	56.4	36.8	35.3
13 Hong Kong, China (SAR)	14.8	6.8	441.4	203.9	..	..	..	..	5.7	46.3	4.7	84.7	18.1	56.9
13 Iceland	4.6	37.3	3.9	31.9	2.5	20.0	2.2	17.7	41.9	14.6	12.2	58.8	8.9	29.0
15 Denmark	96.5	31.0	84.5	27.1	59.9	19.2	50.7	16.3	21.3	60.4	16.0	72.7	22.1	22.8
16 Israel	58.4	28.4	59.2	28.7	24.7	12.0	18.1	8.8	4.0	65.4	8.5	57.4	28.7	24.1
17 Belgium	411.1	87.5	389.5	82.9	83.3	17.7	78.5	16.7	10.3	70.7	9.8	66.9	13.5	17.6
18 Austria	144.9	38.2	150.6	39.7	54.5	14.4	36.9	9.7	8.7	79.5	9.5	72.5	30.2	27.0
18 Singapore	351.9	180.9	310.8	159.8	112.3	57.7	96.5	49.6	2.2	72.1	3.5	64.7	64.5	61.4
20 France	511.7	19.8	592.1	22.9	143.7	5.6	129.8	5.0	12.9	78.2	9.9	73.1	26.5	25.8
21 Finland	70.1	29.5	68.8	28.9	24.6	10.3	21.7	9.1	8.5	76.5	9.6	60.5	23.1	26.2
21 Slovenia	24.4	50.9	26.5	55.2	5.8	12.0	4.4	9.1	6.0	84.8	11.2	69.1	25.6	26.4
23 Spain	246.3	17.3	315.5	22.2	124.1	8.7	87.1	6.1	16.2	71.9	11.8	65.3	21.3	26.7
24 Liechtenstein	..	..	..	..	..	..	..	..	..	..	..	..	..	..
25 Italy	446.8	21.5	487.0	23.5	98.3	4.7	110.1	5.3	8.6	81.7	11.3	63.0	24.2	23.0
26 Luxembourg	13.8	26.4	20.3	38.8	67.5	128.6	37.3	71.2	11.3	79.3	12.3	63.3	19.0	17.7
26 United Kingdom	405.9	18.4	559.3	25.3	237.9	10.8	168.8	7.6	7.0	68.2	10.9	67.1	26.0	26.1
28 Czech Republic	132.1	67.1	125.7	63.8	21.7	11.0	18.2	9.2	5.3	86.4	6.7	76.9	40.6	43.2
29 Greece	21.7	7.0	63.9	20.6	37.5	12.1	20.2	6.5	27.5	49.1	13.4	59.2	14.7	12.5
30 Brunei Darussalam	..	..	..	..	1.1[d]	7.9	1.4[d]	12.4	..	..	..	..	..	..
31 Cyprus	0.8	3.2	8.6	37.0	11.5	49.5	4.2	17.9	36.1	50.2	15.6	61.6	34.2	14.6
32 Malta	3.7	45.7	5.7	70.5	4.0	49.0	2.6	31.6	5.3	67.6	11.3	62.6	60.4	37.1
33 Andorra	..	..	..	..	..	..	..	..	..	..	..	..	..	..
33 Estonia	12.8	67.3	13.2	69.4	4.5	23.7	2.8	14.6	15.2	62.2	13.6	63.8	24.9	27.1
35 Slovakia	64.0	73.4	64.0	73.5	..	..	..	..	5.6	86.3	7.7	75.5	26.6	43.9
36 Qatar	48.3	43.0	..	..	2.3	2.0	6.2	5.5	0.1	6.8	..	..	0.9	..
37 Hungary	94.7	74.0	87.4	68.3	19.1	14.9	15.9	12.4	8.1	81.7	5.8	71.8	50.1	51.6
38 Barbados	0.2	6.1	1.2	31.1	1.5	38.1	0.8	19.6	33.5	63.9	26.7	70.0	15.7	16.7
39 Poland	157.1	34.9	174.1	38.7	32.5	7.2	29.0	6.4	12.0	79.1	9.4	74.2	30.6	29.2
40 Chile	70.9	36.5	59.4	30.5	10.8	5.6	11.8	6.1	22.2	12.0	7.7	68.7	9.7	19.3
41 Lithuania	20.8	56.9	23.4	63.9	4.1	11.3	2.8	7.7	19.7	54.0	14.2	49.9	13.4	16.4
41 United Arab Emirates	..	..	..	..	11.7	4.1	41.7	14.7	..	..	..	..	..	..
43 Portugal	48.7	21.2	75.6	32.8	23.3	10.1	14.4	6.2	13.9	73.1	15.1	66.7	24.8	22.1
44 Latvia	8.9	35.5	11.1	44.7	3.7	14.7	2.2	8.8	30.0	57.6	16.3	59.1	13.7	16.0
45 Argentina	68.2	20.2	56.8	16.8	13.2	3.9	14.1	4.2	50.8	32.2	3.7	84.4	13.1	29.1
46 Seychelles	..	..	..	..	0.4	47.7	0.3	36.8	..	..	..	..	..	..
47 Croatia	11.8	19.0	20.1	32.3	11.0	17.7	3.5	5.6	15.0	68.0	11.5	67.2	24.6	17.2
HIGH HUMAN DEVELOPMENT														
48 Bahrain	15.5	73.3	16.0	75.7	4.0	19.2	1.9	9.0	1.9	5.6	8.1	38.8	1.4	25.1
49 Bahamas	0.3	3.9	2.9	37.0	..	..	..	..	25.6	63.4	19.3	52.9	0.0	14.1
50 Belarus	25.2	48.3	34.9	66.7	4.5	8.6	2.9	5.5	14.7	52.9	9.4	47.5	10.7	20.2
51 Uruguay	5.4[d]	15.4	6.9[d]	19.8	2.5	7.1	1.4	4.1	73.5	23.7	12.2	62.5	10.5	15.6
52 Montenegro	..	..	..	..	1.0	24.0	0.4	9.7	..	..	..	..	..	..
52 Palau	..	..	..	..	..	..	..	..	..	..	..	..	..	..
54 Kuwait	50.3	43.8	..	..	7.7	6.7	13.6	11.8	0.4	6.2	..	..	3.4	..
55 Russian Federation	400.1	29.5	248.7	18.4	44.3	3.3	73.5	5.4	4.1	14.1	14.0	68.6	9.7	21.7
56 Romania	49.4	30.6	62.0	38.4	8.6	5.3	9.4	5.8	10.1	78.5	9.1	75.3	37.0	32.6
57 Bulgaria	20.6	42.8	25.4	52.7	7.0	14.5	4.5	9.3	17.5	49.3	10.6	54.9	22.1	20.4
57 Saudi Arabia	245.9	59.4	106.9	25.8	10.7	2.6	76.8	18.5	1.2	11.0	16.5	76.1	2.7	23.0

	TRADE OF GOODS[a]				TRADE OF SERVICES				COMPOSITION OF MERCHANDISE GOODS					
	Exports of merchandise goods		Imports of merchandise goods		Exports of services		Imports of services		Share of merchandise exports (%)		Share of merchandise imports (%)		Parts and components[b]	
	($ billions)	(% of GDP)[c]	($ billions)	(% of GDP)[c]	($ billions)	(% of GDP)[c]	($ billions)	(% of GDP)[c]	Agricultural exports	Manufactured exports	Agricultural imports	Manufactured imports	(% of manufactured exports)	(% of manufactured imports)
HDI rank	2010	2010	2010	2010	2010	2010	2010	2010	2010	2010	2010	2010	2010	2010
59 Cuba	..	..	..	..	8.0[d]	..	1.4[d]	..	..	..	..	..	..	..
59 Panama	0.7	2.8	16.7	65.8	6.1	24.0	2.8	10.9	67.6	11.9	8.2	89.7	0.1	11.8
61 Mexico	298.3	31.0	301.5	31.4	15.4	1.6	25.6	2.7	6.3	74.5	7.8	79.5	40.3	46.2
62 Costa Rica	9.0	27.6	13.9	42.4	4.2	12.7	1.8	5.4	37.3	60.7	10.1	73.0	43.9	31.8
63 Grenada	..	..	0.3[d]	36.2	0.1	17.7	0.1	13.0	..	..	25.8	58.8	..	14.1
64 Libya	..	..	..	..	..	..	..	..	..	..	..	..	..	..
64 Malaysia	198.8	92.3	164.5	76.3	34.0	15.8	33.7	15.6	14.5	67.0	9.8	73.2	54.5	54.5
64 Serbia	..	..	..	..	3.5	9.0	3.5	9.0	..	..	..	..	..	..
67 Antigua and Barbuda	0.0	0.2	0.5	42.3	0.5	43.2	0.2	18.8	50.7	47.6	22.5	48.3	0.0	23.1
67 Trinidad and Tobago	10.0	49.1	6.5	31.9	0.9	4.2	0.4	2.1	2.6	31.0	11.9	49.9	1.0	20.0
69 Kazakhstan	..	..	..	..	4.2	3.2	11.3	8.6	..	..	..	..	..	..
70 Albania	1.5	12.9	4.6	38.4	2.2	18.7	2.0	16.8	6.9	62.0	19.0	63.6	5.7	12.5
71 Venezuela, Bolivarian Republic of	67.0	18.5	32.3	9.0	..	..	..	..	0.2	4.0	16.7	80.8	7.2	25.0
72 Dominica	0.0	5.9	0.2	47.1	0.1	24.7	0.1	13.2	27.1	66.0	25.1	57.1	0.9	16.2
72 Georgia	1.3	11.5	5.1	45.5	1.6	14.3	1.1	9.7	21.5	46.3	18.9	60.2	6.0	13.3
72 Lebanon	4.3	11.5	18.0	48.6	15.3	41.3	13.0	35.2	12.6	54.6	16.7	54.8	18.4	11.7
72 Saint Kitts and Nevis	0.0	3.9	0.3	39.6	..	..	..	..	12.7	87.2	21.6	73.7	87.8	17.5
76 Iran, Islamic Republic of	83.8	25.3	54.7	16.5	..	..	..	..	6.5	15.6	17.6	70.0	4.3	21.3
77 Peru	35.2	25.1	30.0	21.4	4.0	2.8	6.0	4.3	16.9	10.9	12.0	72.5	4.5	17.9
78 The former Yugoslav Republic of Macedonia	2.7[d]	29.2	5.0[d]	54.7	..	..	..	..	25.4	69.0	17.4	74.8	7.0	11.8
78 Ukraine	51.4	40.7	60.7	48.0	17.1	13.5	12.2	9.7	20.4	63.7	10.3	52.9	13.9	16.9
80 Mauritius	1.5	16.1	4.4	47.5	2.7	29.1	2.0	21.4	39.5	56.3	23.1	54.6	1.6	15.6
81 Bosnia and Herzegovina	4.8	28.5	9.2	54.7	1.3	7.6	0.6	3.5	13.2	54.7	19.7	57.8	27.6	15.6
82 Azerbaijan	21.3	43.8	6.6	13.6	2.1	4.3	3.8	7.8	2.8	2.5	20.2	76.3	6.0	23.1
83 Saint Vincent and the Grenadines	0.0	5.2	0.4	56.3	..	..	..	..	82.4	15.7	24.0	53.3	0.2	15.1
84 Oman	31.6	60.4	19.8	37.8	1.8	3.4	6.5	12.5	2.6	10.5	12.7	73.3	8.6	21.9
85 Brazil	197.4	10.5	179.7	9.6	31.8	1.7	62.6	3.3	34.8	35.8	6.0	73.9	22.8	30.7
85 Jamaica	1.2	9.5	5.2	39.7	2.6	20.0	1.8	13.9	24.8	7.9	18.7	48.7	1.5	14.5
87 Armenia	0.9	9.6	3.7	41.5	0.8	8.5	1.0	11.1	17.3	21.2	18.6	52.5	10.4	17.1
88 Saint Lucia	..	..	..	..	..	..	..	..	..	..	..	..	..	..
89 Ecuador	17.5	31.8	20.6	37.4	1.4	2.5	3.0	5.4	34.1	9.6	9.4	67.8	12.9	17.4
90 Turkey	114.0	16.9	185.5	27.6	34.4	5.1	19.7	2.9	10.9	77.7	6.9	62.5	14.8	21.3
91 Colombia	39.5	15.0	40.5	15.4	4.4	1.7	8.0	3.0	14.6	21.0	11.1	80.9	8.4	17.3
92 Sri Lanka	8.3	18.1	12.4	27.0	2.5	5.4	3.1	6.8	30.8	61.2	16.7	61.8	5.5	13.7
93 Algeria	57.1	38.0	41.0	27.3	3.6	2.4	11.9	7.9	0.6	0.8	17.9	78.4	2.9	20.5
94 Tunisia	16.4	37.4	22.2	50.6	5.8	13.2	3.3	7.6	8.2	76.0	11.5	72.3	28.9	26.8
MEDIUM HUMAN DEVELOPMENT														
95 Tonga	0.0	2.4	0.2	47.0	0.0	12.2	0.0	13.5	90.6	7.6	31.3	44.8	0.2	16.3
96 Belize	0.3	20.5	0.7	50.9	0.4	25.7	0.2	11.8	62.3	1.3	17.4	60.9	0.3	12.3
96 Dominican Republic	4.8	9.7	15.1	30.8	5.1	10.3	2.1	4.4	28.5	67.6	14.6	59.4	10.4	18.7
96 Fiji	0.6	18.6	1.8	60.2	0.7[d]	23.3	0.5[d]	14.9	62.2	22.1	18.7	48.1	5.7	19.1
96 Samoa	0.1	10.6	0.3	55.3	0.2	28.3	0.1	15.5	21.5	78.2	26.9	54.0	97.8	17.4
100 Jordan	5.9	23.6	15.3	60.8	5.2	20.5	4.3	17.0	16.5	72.0	17.6	56.3	5.4	18.4
101 China	1,577.8	28.9	1,289.1	23.6	171.2	3.1	193.3	3.5	3.3	93.4	8.4	60.9	28.7	44.8
102 Turkmenistan	..	..	..	..	..	..	..	..	..	..	..	..	..	..
103 Thailand	195.3	67.0	180.1	61.8	34.0	11.7	45.9	15.7	18.0	71.6	6.6	66.2	38.1	40.9
104 Maldives	0.1	3.7	1.1	54.5	0.8	38.3	0.3	15.3	96.2	0.1	24.6	50.2	0.0	21.1
105 Suriname	2.0	49.2	1.4	33.9	0.2	5.9	0.3	6.3	2.9	1.9	15.3	63.7	27.8	18.3
106 Gabon	5.4[d]	44.4	2.5[d]	20.7	0.4	3.3	1.9	15.9	9.6	4.2	17.6	74.1	30.3	26.1
107 El Salvador	4.5	21.4	8.5	40.3	1.0	4.6	1.1	5.1	21.9	71.5	18.5	63.8	7.8	14.1
108 Bolivia, Plurinational State of	7.0	37.7	5.6	30.3	..	..	..	..	16.1	6.3	8.4	78.1	2.6	12.3
108 Mongolia	..	..	..	..	0.5	9.0	0.8	14.5	..	..	..	..	..	..
110 Palestine, State of	0.4[d]	..	4.0[d]	..	..	..	..	..	17.2	66.9	22.9	43.8	1.5	10.1
111 Paraguay	4.5	27.8	10.0	61.6	1.5	9.2	0.7	4.4	88.5	10.7	8.1	79.4	7.4	20.1
112 Egypt	26.3	12.9	53.0	26.0	..	..	..	..	19.5	41.7	22.4	59.9	8.4	18.1
113 Moldova, Republic of	0.9	16.6	3.9	68.5	..	..	..	..	73.0	22.6	16.2	62.4	8.2	15.6
114 Philippines	51.5	28.0	58.5	31.8	13.2	7.2	11.3	6.1	8.0	85.1	11.7	66.8	72.8	58.4
114 Uzbekistan	..	..	..	..	1.1	3.1	0.6	1.7	..	..	..	..	..	..
116 Syrian Arab Republic	11.4	20.1	17.6	31.1	5.2	8.5	..	..	22.7	24.7	23.4	54.1	6.6	16.0
117 Micronesia, Federated States of	..	..	..	..	..	..	..	..	..	..	..	..	..	..

TABLE 10   International trade flows of goods and services | 179

TABLE 10 INTERNATIONAL TRADE FLOWS OF GOODS AND SERVICES

		TRADE OF GOODS[a]				TRADE OF SERVICES				COMPOSITION OF MERCHANDISE GOODS					
		Exports of merchandise goods		Imports of merchandise goods		Exports of services		Imports of services		Share of merchandise exports (%)		Share of merchandise imports (%)		Parts and components[b]	
		($ billions)	(% of GDP)[c]	($ billions)	(% of GDP)[c]	($ billions)	(% of GDP)[c]	($ billions)	(% of GDP)[c]	Agricultural exports	Manufactured exports	Agricultural imports	Manufactured imports	(% of manufactured exports)	(% of manufactured imports)
HDI rank		2010	2010	2010	2010	2010	2010	2010	2010	2010	2010	2010	2010	2010	2010
118	Guyana	0.9	43.2	1.4	67.6	0.3	12.7	0.3	16.3	49.0	3.8	15.3	54.8	2.1	15.5
119	Botswana	4.7	35.5	5.7	42.8	0.8	6.1	1.2	9.3	5.2	10.5	13.2	57.2	16.3	21.8
120	Honduras	2.6 d	17.8	6.0 d	40.4	1.0	6.9	1.3	9.0	53.1	33.8	20.1	59.9	18.3	15.0
121	Indonesia	157.8	25.3	135.5	21.7	16.8	2.7	26.1	4.2	22.8	37.0	11.5	63.4	18.8	32.9
121	Kiribati	0.0	2.8	0.1	52.4	..	..	..	..	68.3	27.6	41.7	32.0	0.1	18.3
121	South Africa	71.5	22.1	79.9	24.7	14.0	4.3	18.5	5.7	11.0	43.2	6.8	64.1	15.0	27.3
124	Vanuatu	..	..	..	..	0.2 d	38.2	0.1 d	16.8	..	..	..	..	..	..
125	Kyrgyzstan	1.3	27.4	3.2	68.0	..	..	..	..	17.1	18.6	18.1	53.9	14.6	12.8
125	Tajikistan	..	..	..	..	0.2	3.9	0.4	7.4	..	..	..	..	..	..
127	Viet Nam	72.2 d	71.1	84.8 d	83.5	..	..	..	..	23.3	64.0	12.1	71.9	19.0	23.6
128	Namibia	5.8	58.3	6.0	59.6	0.9	8.5	0.7	7.0	25.5	23.3	15.5	69.6	6.7	16.4
129	Nicaragua	1.8	28.9	4.2	65.5	0.5	7.4	0.7	10.8	78.7	6.3	17.1	60.8	5.7	14.5
130	Morocco	17.8	19.6	35.4	38.9	12.5	13.8	7.4	8.2	20.6	63.4	13.6	59.9	28.2	21.5
131	Iraq	..	..	..	..	..	..	..	..	..	..	..	..	..	..
132	Cape Verde	0.0	2.9	0.7	44.8	0.5	31.3	0.4	23.2	81.6	17.5	29.1	57.8	0.0	18.2
133	Guatemala	8.5	21.4	13.8	35.0	2.2	5.6	2.4	6.0	46.3	42.6	14.6	66.0	3.0	15.7
134	Timor-Leste	..	..	..	..	..	..	..	..	..	..	..	..	..	..
135	Ghana	5.2	18.0	8.1	27.7	1.5	5.1	3.0	10.3	24.2	7.3	16.4	81.3	8.9	19.0
136	Equatorial Guinea	..	..	..	..	0.1	0.5	2.2	16.7	..	..	..	..	..	..
136	India	220.4	14.5	350.0	23.0	123.8	8.1	116.8	7.7	10.5	52.4	5.1	36.9	14.5	29.8
138	Cambodia	5.6	51.7	4.9	45.3	1.8	17.0	1.2	10.8	3.7	96.1	8.6	79.4	0.2	7.3
138	Lao People's Democratic Republic	..	..	..	..	..	..	..	..	..	..	..	..	..	..
140	Bhutan	0.4	29.7	0.9	61.4	0.1 d	4.2	0.1 d	5.3	7.4	69.5	13.7	60.8	0.0	19.1
141	Swaziland	..	..	..	..	0.2	7.2	0.6	17.6	..	..	..	..	..	..
LOW HUMAN DEVELOPMENT															
142	Congo	6.9	64.1	4.4	40.5	..	..	..	..	2.1	30.2	7.4	86.7	2.5	9.1
143	Solomon Islands	0.2	32.9	0.4	65.6	0.1	14.7	0.2	28.8	29.2	0.1	18.7	20.1	14.5	21.6
144	Sao Tome and Principe	0.0	3.2	0.1	56.4	0.0 d	5.3 d	0.0 d	9.6 d	95.3	4.7	30.6	52.0	20.1	13.5
145	Kenya	5.2	16.5	12.1	38.5	3.7	11.7	2.0	6.4	57.6	33.9	13.6	62.8	6.3	16.1
146	Bangladesh	..	..	..	..	2.4	2.6	4.4	4.6	..	..	..	..	..	..
146	Pakistan	21.0	12.4	37.5	22.1	6.4	3.8	7.1	4.2	18.8	74.0	18.0	48.4	0.6	17.1
148	Angola	..	..	..	..	0.6	0.8	17.3	22.0	..	..	..	..	..	..
149	Myanmar	7.6	..	4.2	..	0.3	..	0.7	..	30.2	5.5	8.7	67.9	2.3	14.3
150	Cameroon	3.9	17.4	5.1	22.9	1.2	5.2	1.7	7.8	39.2	6.9	19.3	51.3	18.6	17.5
151	Madagascar	0.9	11.0	2.5	29.6	1.0 d	9.9	1.2 d	14.2	29.9	46.7	14.6	69.6	1.5	22.5
152	Tanzania, United Republic of	3.9	17.7	8.0	36.2	..	..	..	..	29.6	17.2	10.8	60.5	8.0	15.0
153	Nigeria	86.6	47.3	44.2	24.2	3.1	1.7	22.3	12.2	5.0	6.7	11.0	86.5	8.0	24.0
154	Senegal	2.2	16.9	4.8	37.3	1.1	8.9	1.1	8.9	27.2	36.4	23.9	44.4	3.2	15.9
155	Mauritania	0.7	21.9	1.7	52.0	0.2	4.8	0.8	23.2	38.4	0.0	19.9	52.8	0.0	30.7
156	Papua New Guinea	..	..	..	..	0.2	2.4	2.8	32.7	..	..	..	..	..	..
157	Nepal	0.8	5.8	5.1	35.5	0.7	4.7	0.9	6.0	23.0	72.3	13.4	56.5	3.0	15.5
158	Lesotho	0.6	32.3	1.4	69.7	0.0	2.5	0.5	26.5	12.9	84.7	30.4	57.8	8.4	16.2
159	Togo	0.4	13.9	1.0	31.3	0.3	8.6	0.3	11.0	18.8	70.2	17.0	67.2	0.3	12.1
160	Yemen	6.2 d	22.1	9.3 d	33.0	..	..	..	..	6.8	1.1	31.6	46.7	5.3	13.7
161	Haiti	..	..	..	..	0.4	5.8	0.9	13.6	..	..	..	..	..	..
161	Uganda	1.2	7.0	4.7	28.3	1.3	7.9	1.8	11.1	74.0	22.8	13.5	65.3	2.7	18.0
163	Zambia	7.2	49.7	5.3	36.7	0.3	2.2	0.9	6.5	6.8	8.7	5.3	61.7	14.0	18.5
164	Djibouti	0.2 d	15.0	0.6 d	61.7	0.3 d	30.7	0.1 d	12.2	0.5	92.7	30.1	62.7	47.0	19.0
165	Gambia	0.0	3.4	0.3	28.0	..	..	..	..	79.0	10.5	35.9	42.9	5.7	22.2
166	Benin	0.4	6.6	1.5	22.7	0.3	5.3	0.4	6.6	84.4	14.7	35.5	43.1	4.8	8.0
167	Rwanda	0.2 d	4.4	1.1 d	20.5	0.4	6.9	0.6	11.0	52.9	20.8	14.9	75.8	3.0	17.5
168	Côte d'Ivoire	10.3	44.8	7.8	34.2	..	..	..	..	58.1	16.1	20.1	54.9	5.8	11.7
169	Comoros	..	..	..	..	0.1	11.3	0.1	17.9	..	..	..	..	..	..
170	Malawi	1.1	21.8	2.2	44.4	0.1	1.7	0.4	7.7	79.8	9.0	14.8	74.1	11.6	10.1
171	Sudan	9.0 d	14.9	8.6 d	14.1	0.3	0.4	2.9	4.8	6.2	0.4	16.1	78.9	4.4	16.8
172	Zimbabwe	3.2	48.1	9.1	136.0	0.2	3.6	0.4	6.6	24.7	29.5	20.7	49.2	1.9	11.3
173	Ethiopia	2.3	7.4	8.6	27.9	2.4	7.6	2.5	8.2	82.7	8.2	11.5	68.8	17.7	18.8
174	Liberia	..	..	..	..	0.2	16.9	1.1	115.7	..	..	..	..	..	..
175	Afghanistan	0.4	2.5	5.2	32.8	..	..	..	..	50.8	19.6	13.7	19.1	0.0	27.1
176	Guinea-Bissau	..	..	..	..	..	..	..	..	..	..	..	..	..	..

	TRADE OF GOODS[a]				TRADE OF SERVICES				COMPOSITION OF MERCHANDISE GOODS					
	Exports of merchandise goods		Imports of merchandise goods		Exports of services		Imports of services		Share of merchandise exports (%)		Share of merchandise imports (%)		Parts and components[b]	
	($ billions)	(% of GDP)[c]	($ billions)	(% of GDP)[c]	($ billions)	(% of GDP)[c]	($ billions)	(% of GDP)[c]	Agricultural exports	Manufactured exports	Agricultural imports	Manufactured imports	(% of manufactured exports)	(% of manufactured imports)
HDI rank	2010	2010	2010	2010	2010	2010	2010	2010	2010	2010	2010	2010	2010	2010
177 Sierra Leone	..	..	..	..	0.1	3.2	0.1	7.6	..	..	..	..	..	..
178 Burundi	0.1	6.2	0.4	21.0	0.1	4.1	0.2	8.8	76.8	5.3	15.1	81.7	16.1	13.9
178 Guinea	..	..	..	..	0.1	1.4	0.4	8.9	..	..	..	..	..	..
180 Central African Republic	0.1[d]	4.5	0.2[d]	10.6	0.1	3.3	0.2	8.7	37.4	3.1	30.2	67.2	13.2	18.4
181 Eritrea	..	..	..	..	..	..	..	..	..	..	..	..	..	..
182 Mali	1.9	21.0	4.7	51.2	0.4	3.8	0.9	9.8	14.2	3.7	12.1	61.3	11.0	21.3
183 Burkina Faso	1.3	15.0	2.0	23.9	0.1	1.4	0.6	7.1	28.0	2.9	15.9	61.3	13.3	15.7
184 Chad	..	..	..	..	0.2	2.0	2.4	30.4	..	..	..	..	..	..
185 Mozambique	2.2	23.3	3.6	37.7	0.6	6.9	1.1	12.1	20.1	2.0	12.6	49.6	20.9	17.4
186 Congo, Democratic Republic of the	..	..	..	..	..	..	..	..	..	..	..	..	..	..
186 Niger	0.5	9.1	2.3	43.0	0.1	2.5	1.1	19.8	20.7	11.9	17.3	69.3	2.6	18.3
OTHER COUNTRIES OR TERRITORIES														
Korea, Democratic People's Rep. of	..	..	..	..	..	..	..	..	..	..	..	..	..	..
Marshall Islands	..	..	..	..	..	..	..	..	..	..	..	..	..	..
Monaco	..	..	..	..	..	..	..	..	..	..	..	..	..	..
Nauru	..	..	..	..	..	..	..	..	..	..	..	..	..	..
San Marino	..	..	..	..	..	..	..	..	..	..	..	..	..	..
Somalia	..	..	..	..	..	..	..	..	..	..	..	..	..	..
South Sudan	..	..	..	..	..	..	..	..	..	..	..	..	..	..
Tuvalu	..	..	..	..	..	..	..	..	..	..	..	..	..	..
Human Development Index groups														
Very high human development	8,889.2	21.6	9,960.0	24.2	2,682.8	6.6	2,333.0	5.8	9.4	70.1	8.5	67.4	29.5	30.6
High human development	2,088.2	26.8	1,769.7	23.2	302.6	4.0	426.9	5.9	10.5	37.4	11.3	71.6	30.0	30.4
Medium human development	2,475.3	27.0	2,409.2	26.2	418.1	4.7	446.8	5.1	7.9	79.9	8.7	59.0	28.5	38.8
Low human development	188.8	24.9	210.0	27.9	29.1	3.3	82.6	9.8	18.0	19.4	14.1	66.9	3.8	18.9
Regions														
Arab States	546.6	38.9	367.5	..	86.4	5.8	..	..	4.4	17.8	16.7	70.5	12.5	21.0
East Asia and the Pacific	..	..	..	..	..	..	..	..	..	..	..	..	..	..
Europe and Central Asia	1,226.6	33.5	1,218.4	33.1	251.7	6.6	232.3	6.2	8.5	54.9	10.3	68.3	28.7	29.1
Latin America and the Caribbean	857.8	18.9	842.6	18.5	120.0	2.7	151.8	3.6	21.0	42.0	8.5	76.3	31.5	32.3
South Asia	335.2	14.2	466.8	23.3	136.6	7.4	132.7	7.2	10.6	44.8	8.7	44.2	11.8	26.1
Sub-Saharan Africa	237.5	28.3	246.3	29.1	39.6	4.3	93.5	10.3	15.7	21.5	11.4	69.1	12.4	22.2
Least developed countries	..	..	..	..	16.8	3.5	49.9	11.0	..	..	..	..	..	..
Small island developing states	..	..	..	..	..	..	..	..	..	..	..	..	..	..
World	**13,641.6**	**23.2**	**14,348.9**	**24.5**	**3,432.6**	**5.9**	**3,289.3**	**5.7**	**9.4**	**66.5**	**9.0**	**66.6**	**29.2**	**31.6**

NOTES

a All data on merchandise trade are extracted at the six-digit level of the 1996 Harmonized System nomenclature; for definitional purposes, they are concorded with the Standard International Trade Classification using concordance tables.

b For methodology of classification of parts and components, see Athukorala (2012) and its discussion paper version cited therein.

c GDP in current dollars is averaged for 2009 and 2010.

d Refers to 2009.

DEFINITIONS

Exports of merchandise goods: Goods that subtract from the stock of material resources of a country by leaving its economic territory.

Imports of merchandise goods: Goods that add to the stock of material resources of a country by entering its economic territory.

Exports of services: Exports of a heterogeneous range of intangible products and activities that changes the conditions of the consuming units or facilitates the exchange of products or financial assets.

Imports of services: Imports of a heterogeneous range of intangible products and activities that changes the conditions of the consuming units or facilitates the exchange of products or financial assets.

Agricultural or manufacured goods as share of merchandise exports: Exports of agricultural or manufactured goods, expressed as a percentage of total merchandise exports.

Agricultural or manufactured goods as share of merchandise imports: Imports of agricultural or manufactured goods, expressed as a percentage of total merchandise imports.

Parts and components: Intermediate goods used as an input in the production of manufactures for final consumption, expressed as a percentage of manufactured exports or imports.

MAIN DATA SOURCES

Columns 1, 3, and 9–14: UNSD (2012b).

Columns 2 and 4: HDRO calculations based on UNSD (2012b) and World Bank (2012a).

Columns 5 and 7: UNCTAD (2012).

Columns 6 and 8: HDRO calculations based on UNCTAD (2012) and World Bank (2012a).

TABLE 10 International trade flows of goods and services | 181

TABLE 11

International capital flows and migration

		FINANCIAL FLOWS						HUMAN MOBILITY					
								Migration			International inbound tourism	International telephone traffic (minutes per person)	
		Foreign direct investment, net inflows	Net official development assistance received[a]	Private capital flows	Remittances (% of GDP)		Total reserves minus gold	Stock of emigrants[b]	Stock of immigrants	Net migration rate			
		(% of GDP)	(% of GNI)	(% of GDP)	Inflows	Outflows	(% of GDP)	(% of population)		(per 1,000 people)	(thousands)	Incoming	Outgoing
HDI rank		2007–2011c	2010	2007–2011c	2010	2010	2007–2011c	2010	2010	2005/2010d	2010	2005–2010c	2005–2010c
VERY HIGH HUMAN DEVELOPMENT													
1	Norway	2.8	−1.1	−4.9	0.16	0.97	10.2	3.8	10.0	7.2	4,767	..	241.9
2	Australia	2.7	−0.3	6.5	0.43	0.33	3.1	2.1	25.7	10.5	5,885	..	..
3	United States	1.5	−0.2	−0.2	0.04	0.36	0.9	0.8	13.5	3.3	59,791	82.5	237.1
4	Netherlands	1.9	−0.8	1.1	0.50	1.67	2.4	6.0	10.5	0.6	10,883	..	96.5
5	Germany	1.1	−0.4	1.2	0.35	0.49	1.9	4.3	13.1	1.3	26,875	..	182.5
6	New Zealand	0.5	−0.3	1.7	0.59e	0.82e	11.7	14.5	22.4	3.1	2,492	..	173.3
7	Ireland	6.4	−0.5	25.3	0.29	0.85	0.6	16.1	19.6	4.6	7,189	..	441.8
7	Sweden	2.3	−1.0	2.2	0.15	0.15	8.2	3.4	14.1	5.8	4,951	..	160.5
9	Switzerland	0.4	−0.4	−9.0	0.49	4.09	44.0	5.4	23.2	4.8	8,628	..	409.3
10	Japan	0.0	−0.2	0.7	0.03	0.08	21.4	0.6	1.7	0.4	8,611	13.8	..
11	Canada	2.4	−0.3	4.1	..	..	3.8	3.5	21.3	6.6	16,097	..	..
12	Korea, Republic of	0.4	−0.1	−0.5	0.86	1.12	27.3	4.3	1.1	−0.1	8,798	22.2	47.7
13	Hong Kong, China (SAR)	34.1	..	−0.8	0.15	0.19	117.1	10.2	38.8	5.1	20,085	524.3	1,446.9
13	Iceland	7.2	−0.3	−55.2	0.20	0.10	60.1	13.0	11.3	6.8	1,213	233.1	148.0
15	Denmark	4.6	−0.9	−1.6	0.20	1.02	24.6	4.7	8.8	3.3	8,744	183.9	190.6
16	Israel	4.7	..	−0.2	0.65	1.72	30.8	14.0	40.4	7.8	2,803	..	..
17	Belgium	18.0	−0.6	−0.2	2.18	0.87	3.5	4.2	13.7	3.8	7,186	..	255.0
18	Austria	3.3	−0.3	0.6	0.86	0.92	2.6	7.1	15.6	3.8	22,004	..	171.6
18	Singapore	18.1	..	−1.4	..	..	99.1	6.1	40.7	30.9	9,161	447.5	1,525.2
20	France	1.5	−0.5	10.8	0.61	0.21	1.8	2.8	10.7	1.6	77,148	182.1	192.1
21	Finland	0.0	−0.6	2.9	0.35	0.18	3.0	6.2	4.2	2.7	3,670	..	..
21	Slovenia	2.2	..	6.8	0.66	0.34	1.7	6.5	8.1	2.2	1,869f	88.2	112.0
23	Spain	1.7	..	−3.2	0.76	0.88	2.2	3.0	15.2	10.1	52,677	..	118.9
24	Liechtenstein	..	..	..	..	..	..	17.1	34.6	..	52	..	..
25	Italy	1.5	−0.2	−3.4	0.33	0.60	2.2	5.8	7.4	6.7	43,626	..	152.0
26	Luxembourg	542.9	−1.1	214.8	2.99	19.69	1.5	11.8	35.2	17.6	849	810.6	822.5
26	United Kingdom	2.2	−0.6	−4.9	0.33	0.16	3.3	7.5	11.2	3.3	28,295	..	147.5
28	Czech Republic	2.5	..	2.1	0.57	0.92	18.4	3.6	4.4	4.6	8,185	120.1	50.5
29	Greece	0.6	..	−7.8	0.50	0.65	0.4	10.8	10.1	2.7	15,007g	96.1	201.3
30	Brunei Darussalam	4.0	..	4.3	..	3.60	12.6	6.0	36.4	1.8	157f	..	..
31	Cyprus	1.0	..	35.1	0.63	1.75	2.0	17.0	17.5	8.3	2,173	314.7	555.4
32	Malta	12.2	..	−42.2	0.58	0.56	5.6	26.2	3.8	2.4	1,332	..	144.0
33	Andorra	..	..	..	..	..	..	10.7	64.4	..	1,830	638.6	708.3
33	Estonia	0.8	..	15.0	1.71	0.50	0.9	12.6	13.6	0.0	2,120	102.9	80.8
35	Slovakia	0.6	..	1.4	1.83	0.08	0.9	9.6	2.4	1.3	1,298h	137.2	140.6
36	Qatar	4.3	..	..	..	..	9.4	0.7	86.5	132.9	1,866	422.7	484.8
37	Hungary	17.1	..	6.5	1.76	0.98	34.8	4.6	3.7	1.5	9,510	116.2	48.2
38	Barbados	16.3	0.3e	10.4	2.99	0.97	22.1	41.0	10.9	0.0	532	..	..
39	Poland	2.8	..	4.9	1.62	0.34	18.0	8.3	2.2	0.3	12,470	..	24.9
40	Chile	7.0	0.1	−0.3	0.00	0.00	16.9	3.7	1.9	0.4	2,766	26.2	12.2
41	Lithuania	2.9	..	6.1	4.34	1.48	18.5	13.2	4.0	−2.1	1,507	75.1	34.4
41	United Arab Emirates	1.3	..	..	..	..	10.3	1.2	70.0	106.3	7,126	..	643.1
43	Portugal	4.3	−0.3	−3.8	1.56	0.62	0.8	20.8	8.6	2.8	6,756f	173.9	111.2
44	Latvia	5.5	..	2.9	2.56	0.18	21.2	12.3	15.0	−0.9	1,373	..	94.1
45	Argentina	1.6	0.0	0.9	0.17	0.27	9.7	2.4	3.6	−1.0	5,325	..	18.4
46	Seychelles	17.4	6.3	19.3	1.13	2.72	25.1	14.6	12.8	..	175	64.7	111.3
47	Croatia	2.3	0.3	3.8	2.16	0.27	22.7	17.1	15.9	0.5	9,111	224.1	90.9
HIGH HUMAN DEVELOPMENT													
48	Bahrain	0.7	..	19.9	..	7.16e	22.2	3.7	39.1	90.2	4,935	..	..
49	Bahamas	7.6	..	7.1	..	1.18	13.7	12.8	9.7	3.9	1,370	..	..
50	Belarus	7.2	0.3	8.7	0.68	0.19	10.9	18.4	11.4	−1.0	119	69.6	52.2
51	Uruguay	4.1	0.1	9.0	0.26	0.02	22.0	10.5	2.4	−3.0	2,353	76.2	46.3
52	Montenegro	18.5	2.0	..	7.32	0.67	8.6	0.0	6.8	−0.8	1,088	..	..
52	Palau	1.4	19.5	..	..	..	..	38.8	28.1	..	84	179.9	205.1
54	Kuwait	0.1	..	−7.8	..	9.47e	14.6	8.5	68.8	22.2	207	..	..
55	Russian Federation	2.8	..	−1.7	0.35	1.26	24.4	7.9	8.7	1.6	22,281	..	..
56	Romania	1.5	..	3.0	2.40	0.22	23.9	13.1	0.6	−0.9	7,575	105.4	..
57	Bulgaria	3.4	..	2.2	2.91	0.05	28.5	16.0	1.4	−1.3	6,047	107.1	47.4
57	Saudi Arabia	2.8	..	−0.5	0.05	6.00	93.7	0.7	27.8	8.2	10,850	..	..

		FINANCIAL FLOWS					HUMAN MOBILITY					
	Foreign direct investment, net inflows	Net official development assistance received[a]	Private capital flows	Remittances (% of GDP)		Total reserves minus gold	Migration			International inbound tourism	International telephone traffic (minutes per person)	
							Stock of emigrants[b]	Stock of immigrants	Net migration rate			
	(% of GDP)	(% of GNI)	(% of GDP)	Inflows	Outflows	(% of GDP)	(% of population)		(per 1,000 people)	(thousands)	Incoming	Outgoing
HDI rank	2007–2011[c]	2010	2007–2011[c]	2010	2010	2007–2011[c]	2010	2010	2005/2010[d]	2010	2005–2010[c]	2005–2010[c]
59 Cuba	0.0	0.2	..	..	..	8.1	10.9	0.1	−3.4	2,507	32.7	2.5
59 Panama	8.8	0.5	7.5	0.86	0.93	7.5	4.0	3.4	0.7	1,324	54.4	75.5
61 Mexico	1.7	0.0	4.5	2.13	..	12.5	10.7	0.7	−3.3	22,260	..	..
62 Costa Rica	5.1	0.3	5.8	1.52	0.75	11.6	2.7	10.5	3.4	2,100	85.7	43.1
63 Grenada	7.7	4.6	6.0	6.96	0.47	14.8	65.5	12.1	−9.7	114	488.1	315.8
64 Libya	2.2	0.1[e]	−5.0	0.03[e]	..	..	1.7	10.4	−0.7	34[h]	..	..
64 Malaysia	3.9	0.0	−1.4	0.55	2.75	47.3	5.3	8.4	0.6	24,577[e]	..	..
64 Serbia	6.0	1.8	10.6	8.72	0.18	33.0	2.0	5.3	0.0	683	104.4	32.1
67 Antigua and Barbuda	8.4	1.7	5.2	2.15	0.19	13.1	47.6	23.6	..	230	487.3	247.8
67 Trinidad and Tobago	2.6	0.0	2.6	0.57	..	46.3	26.7	2.6	−3.0	413	243.7	200.6
69 Kazakhstan	6.9	0.2	−2.7	0.20	2.04	13.5	23.6	19.5	0.1	3,393	40.1	38.9
70 Albania	9.4	2.9	6.7	9.75	0.20	18.5	45.4	2.8	−3.0	2,417	224.3	23.6
71 Venezuela, Bolivarian Republic of	1.7	0.0	2.4	0.04	0.20	3.1	1.8	3.5	0.3	615	..	20.1
72 Dominica	5.2	7.0	6.6	5.56	0.04	16.8	104.8	8.3	..	77	140.8	172.6
72 Georgia	6.8	5.5	6.7	6.93	0.43	19.6	25.1	4.0	−6.8	2,033	125.6	36.4
72 Lebanon	11.0	1.2	2.1	19.38	9.58	80.0	15.6	17.8	−0.6	2,168	318.4	87.3
72 Saint Kitts and Nevis	17.9	1.8	14.4	6.52	0.85	34.5	61.1	9.6	..	92	820.6	629.7
76 Iran, Islamic Republic of	0.9	0.0	..	0.32[e]	..	16.3	1.7	2.8	−0.5	2,034	3.5	10.9
77 Peru	4.8	−0.2	7.8	1.65	0.08	26.7	3.7	0.1	−5.1	2,299	92.7	19.6
78 The former Yugoslav Republic of Macedonia	4.0	2.1	3.4	4.25	0.25	22.9	21.9	6.3	0.2	262	..	23.3
78 Ukraine	4.4	0.5	5.2	4.11	0.02	18.4	14.4	11.6	−0.2	21,203	..	..
80 Mauritius	4.4	1.3	19.9	2.33	0.14	22.8	10.9	3.3	0.0	935	140.8	108.5
81 Bosnia and Herzegovina	2.4	3.0	2.4	11.44	0.33	22.9	38.9	0.7	−0.5	365	213.8	49.6
82 Azerbaijan	2.3	0.3	1.0	2.71	1.82	16.2	16.0	3.0	1.2	1,280	74.8	17.5
83 Saint Vincent and the Grenadines	15.3	2.6	15.5	4.54	1.05	13.0	37.7	7.9	−9.2	72	..	..
84 Oman	1.1	−0.1	−0.8	0.07[e]	9.86[e]	20.0	0.5	28.4	11.7	1,048[e]	223.1	206.9
85 Brazil	2.7	0.0	4.1	0.19	0.06	14.1	0.7	0.4	−0.5	5,161	..	2.3
85 Jamaica	1.6	1.1	−1.5	14.50	2.26	15.1	36.1	1.1	−7.4	1,922	252.4	828.6
87 Armenia	6.5	3.5	4.3	10.63	1.67	18.9	28.2	10.5	−4.9	575	174.9	243.8
88 Saint Lucia	9.2	3.6	9.7	2.62	0.37	17.3	23.3	5.9	−1.2	306	292.7	203.6
89 Ecuador	0.3	0.3	0.9	4.43	0.14	2.5	8.3	2.9	−1.7	1,047	62.7	11.7
90 Turkey	2.1	0.1	4.6	0.12	0.02	10.1	5.6	1.9	−0.1	27,000	57.8	43.4
91 Colombia	4.0	0.3	3.7	1.41	0.04	9.5	4.6	0.2	−0.5	2,147	..	..
92 Sri Lanka	1.0	1.2	3.3	8.38	1.10	10.6	9.1	1.7	−2.5	654	28.6	..
93 Algeria	1.4	0.1	1.1	1.26	0.03	96.9	3.4	0.7	−0.8	1,912	36.5	17.1
94 Tunisia	3.2	1.3	3.0	4.45	0.03	21.4	6.3	0.3	−0.4	6,903	58.0	16.1
MEDIUM HUMAN DEVELOPMENT												
95 Tonga	4.5	19.5	0.0	23.65	2.60	32.9	45.4	0.8	−16.0	45	..	..
96 Belize	6.2	2.0	5.2	5.68	1.65	16.1	16.1	15.0	−0.7	239	135.8	178.5
96 Dominican Republic	3.2	0.4	5.6	6.53	0.06	7.4	10.1	4.2	−2.9	4,125	309.4	52.2
96 Fiji	6.2	2.5	6.0	5.78	0.69	21.8	21.3	2.2	−6.8	632	..	..
96 Samoa	0.1	25.5	1.8	24.11	1.21	25.7	67.3	5.0	−17.3	130	..	..
100 Jordan	6.4	3.6	6.0	13.78	1.87	39.8	11.3	45.9	7.0	4,557	95.8	6.8
101 China	3.1	0.0	2.6	0.89	0.03	43.8	0.6	0.1	−0.3	55,664	9.2	2.9
102 Turkmenistan	10.4	0.2	..	..	..	..	5.0	4.0	−2.2	8	..	..
103 Thailand	3.0	0.0	4.2	0.55	..	48.4	1.2	1.7	1.5	15,936	20.5	..
104 Maldives	7.9	5.6	7.9	0.20	5.31	17.0	0.6	1.0	0.0	792	..	428.6
105 Suriname	−5.9	2.4	−6.2	0.10[e]	0.03[e]	13.8	39.0	7.5	−2.0	205	..	..
106 Gabon	1.3	0.9	..	..	..	12.7	1.7	18.9	0.7	358	..	..
107 El Salvador	1.5	1.4	2.1	16.10	0.11	9.3	20.5	0.7	−9.5	1,150	223.3	175.7
108 Bolivia, Plurinational State of	3.2	3.6	4.2	5.54	0.53	40.6	6.8	1.5	−3.5	807	85.6	11.4
108 Mongolia	23.5	5.4	54.9	4.46	2.73	26.6	1.2	0.4	−1.1	457	35.2	17.2
110 Palestine, State of	..	..	..	..	..	..	68.4	43.6	−4.7	522	..	..
111 Paraguay	2.1	0.6	2.0	3.67	..	20.7	7.9	2.5	−1.3	465	37.6	19.4
112 Egypt	2.9	0.3	7.2	3.53	0.12	6.5	4.4	0.3	−0.9	14,051	55.4	7.8
113 Moldova, Republic of	3.9	7.5	3.7	23.57	2.01	28.1	21.5	11.4	−9.4	8	198.1	59.8
114 Philippines	0.6	0.3	3.0	10.73	0.03	29.9	4.6	0.5	−2.8	3,520	..	..
114 Uzbekistan	2.1	0.6	..	..	..	..	7.0	4.2	−3.9	975	..	..
116 Syrian Arab Republic	2.5	0.2	2.2	2.78	0.36	32.9	4.2	9.8	−0.6	8,546	..	23.4
117 Micronesia, Federated States of	3.4	40.2	..	..	..	23.6	19.7	2.4	−16.3	26	..	..

TABLE 11 International capital flows and migration | 183

TABLE 11 INTERNATIONAL CAPITAL FLOWS AND MIGRATION

		FINANCIAL FLOWS					HUMAN MOBILITY					
	Foreign direct investment, net inflows	Net official development assistance received[a]	Private capital flows	Remittances (% of GDP)		Total reserves minus gold	Migration			International inbound tourism	International telephone traffic (minutes per person)	
							Stock of emigrants[b]	Stock of immigrants	Net migration rate			
	(% of GDP)	(% of GNI)	(% of GDP)	Inflows	Outflows	(% of GDP)	(% of population)		(per 1,000 people)	(thousands)	Incoming	Outgoing
HDI rank	2007–2011[c]	2010	2007–2011[c]	2010	2010	2007–2011[c]	2010	2010	2005/2010[d]	2010	2005–2010[c]	2005–2010[c]
118 Guyana	11.9	6.7	11.8	13.65	3.41	34.6	56.9	1.5	−10.7	150	103.4	26.8
119 Botswana	1.8	1.1	4.6	0.67	0.68	45.8	3.2	5.8	1.9	2,145	..	26.3
120 Honduras	5.9	3.9	5.8	17.27	0.08	15.9	7.5	0.3	−2.8	896	96.0	139.9
121 Indonesia	2.1	0.2	1.7	0.98	0.40	12.6	1.1	0.1	−1.1	7,003	..	..
121 Kiribati	2.4	10.5	..	..	..	..	6.5	2.0	..	5 [f]	..	..
121 South Africa	1.4	0.3	1.6	0.31	0.38	10.4	1.7	3.7	2.9	8,074	..	..
124 Vanuatu	5.6	16.2	7.1	0.93	0.38	21.2	1.6	0.3	0.0	97	..	..
125 Kyrgyzstan	6.6	8.5	3.9	26.60	6.19	28.8	11.2	4.0	−5.1	1,316	23.6	50.0
125 Tajikistan	0.3	7.8	0.4	39.96	15.17	4.4	11.2	4.0	−8.9	325	..	..
127 Viet Nam	7.5	2.9	6.4	7.76	..	10.9	2.5	0.1	−1.0	3,747	..	..
128 Namibia	7.1	2.4	4.5	0.13	0.14	14.5	0.7	6.3	−0.1	984	..	..
129 Nicaragua	13.3	9.8	13.3	12.48	..	25.9	12.5	0.7	−7.1	1,011	..	..
130 Morocco	2.5	1.1	2.0	7.07	0.07	19.5	9.3	0.2	−4.3	9,288	114.1	14.5
131 Iraq	1.8	2.8	−1.1	0.09	0.04	52.6	4.9	0.3	−1.0	1,518	..	..
132 Cape Verde	6.7	20.7	4.8	8.36	0.71	17.8	37.6	2.4	−7.1	382	110.4	28.5
133 Guatemala	2.2	1.0	1.5	10.23	0.05	12.4	6.1	0.4	−3.0	1,876	119.6	50.0
134 Timor-Leste	32.0	9.2	..	..	..	43.8	1.4	1.2	−9.4	40	6.9	11.4
135 Ghana	7.9	5.3	9.8	0.42	..	14.0	3.4	7.6	−0.4	803	45.3	24.5
136 Equatorial Guinea	4.8	0.9	..	..	..	15.4	14.9	1.1	6.1	..	..	..
136 India	1.4	0.2	3.0	3.21	0.23	14.7	0.9	0.4	−0.5	5,776	20.1	7.5
138 Cambodia	7.0	6.9	6.5	3.29	1.91	26.8	2.3	2.2	−3.7	2,399	..	..
138 Lao People's Democratic Republic	3.9	6.2	4.6	0.57	0.11	9.8	5.7	0.3	−2.5	1,670	..	..
140 Bhutan	1.3	9.2	..	0.32	5.41	46.8	6.3	5.7	4.9	27	..	..
141 Swaziland	3.7	2.6	5.0	2.95	0.30	15.1	13.4	3.4	−1.0	868	38.2	3.7
LOW HUMAN DEVELOPMENT												
142 Congo	23.5	14.5	..	0.12	0.85	38.3	5.6	3.8	2.6	85	..	..
143 Solomon Islands	35.1	61.4	34.3	0.43	0.65	49.2	1.0	1.3	0.0	21	..	..
144 Sao Tome and Principe	12.3	24.2	12.2	0.99	0.27	20.7	21.9	3.2	−8.2	8	40.7	14.6
145 Kenya	0.6	5.1	0.8	5.52	0.19	12.7	1.1	2.0	−1.0	1,469	16.5	7.6
146 Bangladesh	0.7	1.3	0.8	10.81	0.01	7.7	3.3	0.7	−4.0	267	..	..
146 Pakistan	1.1	1.6	0.6	5.48	0.01	6.9	2.5	2.3	−2.4	855	24.8	13.1
148 Angola	−3.9	0.3	−5.9	0.10 [h]	0.87	28.5	2.8	0.3	0.9	425	..	..
149 Myanmar	..	..	..	..	..	..	1.0	0.2	−2.1	311	2.9	0.2
150 Cameroon	0.0	2.4	0.5	0.87	0.24	12.6	1.4	1.0	−0.2	298	23.2	5.4
151 Madagascar	9.9	5.4	..	..	..	12.9	0.4	0.2	−0.1	196	5.5	2.1
152 Tanzania, United Republic of	1.9	13.0	4.6	0.11	0.55	15.7	0.7	1.5	−1.4	783	3.8	3.2
153 Nigeria	3.1	1.2	4.9	5.10	0.02	14.9	0.6	0.7	−0.4	1,414	18.7	11.8
154 Senegal	1.8	7.3	3.1	10.47	1.12	13.6	5.0	1.6	−2.3	875	86.5	26.9
155 Mauritania	0.4	10.6	..	..	..	11.9	3.5	2.9	−0.6	..	39.9	15.8
156 Papua New Guinea	0.3	5.5	−0.8	0.16	3.41	32.9	0.9	0.4	0.0	114 [h]	..	..
157 Nepal	0.5	5.1	0.5	21.66	0.20	19.2	3.3	3.2	−0.7	603	12.9	..
158 Lesotho	5.4	9.5	5.5	34.23	0.88	..	20.5	0.3	−1.9	414	..	..
159 Togo	1.3	13.3	−0.6	10.49	2.27	21.5	5.4	2.7	−0.2	150	34.9	10.2
160 Yemen	0.2	2.3	−1.8	3.99	1.09	13.2	4.7	2.1	−1.2	536	76.6	4.6
161 Haiti	2.3	45.5	2.3	22.59	2.03	16.3	9.9	0.3	−5.0	423	..	..
161 Uganda	4.7	10.2	6.3	5.32	3.50	15.6	2.2	1.9	−0.9	946	..	4.9
163 Zambia	10.3	6.4	4.6	0.27	0.42	12.1	1.4	1.8	−1.4	815	..	..
164 Djibouti	9.2	14.9 [e]	9.2	3.09 [e]	..	..	1.5	13.0	0.0	53	41.1	209.2
165 Gambia	3.2	11.9	3.2	11.02	5.53	20.1	3.7	16.6	−1.7	91 [h]	..	..
166 Benin	1.7	10.5	1.1	3.78	1.34	12.2	5.8	2.5	1.2	199 [h]	40.8	23.9
167 Rwanda	0.8	18.5	1.1	1.63	1.27	16.5	2.6	4.5	0.3	666	9.2	3.0
168 Côte d'Ivoire	1.8	3.9	1.4	0.78	3.29	17.9	5.4	11.2	−3.8	..	..	..
169 Comoros	1.7	12.5	..	..	..	25.4	5.6	2.0	−2.9	15	..	..
170 Malawi	2.8	20.8	1.4	..	..	3.5	1.4	1.8	−0.3	746	..	0.9
171 Sudan	3.1	3.4	3.1	2.95	0.00	0.3	2.2	1.7	0.7	420	10.4	16.0
172 Zimbabwe	1.4	10.1	..	..	..	..	9.9	2.9	−14.3	2,239	16.0	21.8
173 Ethiopia	1.0	11.9	2.0	0.76	0.09	..	0.7	0.6	−0.8	330	5.7	0.4
174 Liberia	45.8	175.5	45.8	2.71	0.10	..	10.5	2.3	16.7	..	24.5	28.0
175 Afghanistan	0.4	42.4	..	..	..	25.9	8.1	0.3	−2.6	..	4.9	2.5
176 Guinea-Bissau	1.1	16.7	1.4	5.76	2.03	22.6	6.8	1.2	−1.4	30	..	..

		FINANCIAL FLOWS					HUMAN MOBILITY					
	Foreign direct investment, net inflows	Net official development assistance received[a]	Private capital flows	Remittances (% of GDP)		Total reserves minus gold	Migration			International inbound tourism	International telephone traffic (minutes per person)	
							Stock of emigrants[b]	Stock of immigrants	Net migration rate			
	(% of GDP)	(% of GNI)	(% of GDP)	Inflows	Outflows	(% of GDP)	(% of population)		(per 1,000 people)	(thousands)	Incoming	Outgoing
HDI rank	2007–2011[c]	2010	2007–2011[c]	2010	2010	2007–2011[c]	2010	2010	2005/2010[d]	2010	2005–2010[e]	2005–2010[e]
177 Sierra Leone	4.5	24.4	36.9	3.01	0.31	19.6	4.6	1.8	2.2	39	..	..
178 Burundi	0.0	31.0	0.1	1.39	0.06	12.6	4.2	0.7	9.5	201	..	..
178 Guinea	2.1	5.1	22.7	1.28	0.92	..	5.2	3.8	–6.3	30[i]	..	..
180 Central African Republic	3.6	13.2	..	..	..	7.1	2.9	1.8	0.2	52	5.5	6.6
181 Eritrea	2.6	7.7	..	..	..	4.4	18.0	0.3	2.3	84	22.9	1.7
182 Mali	1.6	12.1	–0.6	4.63	1.77	13.0	7.6	1.2	–1.4	169	8.8	14.1
183 Burkina Faso	0.4	12.0	0.4	1.08	1.13	9.4	9.7	6.4	–1.6	274	..	..
184 Chad	9.1	6.2	..	..	..	10.0	2.1	3.4	–1.4	31	..	..
185 Mozambique	8.6	21.4	16.1	1.43	0.87	19.3	5.0	1.9	–0.2	2,224	5.9	2.6
186 Congo, Democratic Republic of the	22.4	29.0	..	..	..	8.1	1.3	0.7	–0.1	53	3.9	3.1
186 Niger	17.5	13.8	13.4	1.63	0.41	11.2	2.4	1.3	–0.4	66	..	..
OTHER COUNTRIES OR TERRITORIES												
Korea, Democratic People's Rep. of	..	..	..	..	..	..	1.3	0.2	0.0	..	..	..
Marshall Islands	5.3	45.9	..	..	..	..	16.6	2.7	..	5	..	..
Monaco	..	..	..	..	..	..	56.3	71.6	..	279	..	..
Nauru	..	..	..	..	..	..	..	..	..	..	..	..
San Marino	..	..	..	..	..	1.2	9.9	37.0	..	120	..	..
Somalia	..	..	..	..	..	20.7	8.7	0.2	–6.8	..	..	..
South Sudan	..	..	..	..	..	..	..	..	..	..	..	..
Tuvalu	4.8	26.2	..	..	..	..	..	..	..	2	..	..
Human Development Index groups												
Very high human development	2.7	..	0.9	0.31	0.50	7.8	3.6	11.3	4.0	534,968	..	189.8
High human development	2.7	0.2	2.2	0.99	1.25	23.2	6.7	4.5	–0.3	199,071	62.5	24.9
Medium human development	2.8	0.2	2.8	1.81	0.13	33.8	1.6	0.7	–0.6	163,618	..	..
Low human development	2.3	5.5	1.9	4.91	0.46	13.6	2.8	1.6	–1.5	19,020	..	..
Regions												
Arab States	2.4	..	0.5	2.29	3.76	43.7	5.4	8.0	3.3	76,540	..	..
East Asia and the Pacific	3.1	0.1	..	..	..	40.3	1.1	0.3	–0.5	116,484	..	..
Europe and Central Asia	3.4	..	1.8	1.22	0.81	19.4	10.3	6.5	–0.1	149,901	90.3	49.2
Latin America and the Caribbean	2.7	0.2	3.7	1.15	0.12	13.1	5.3	1.1	–1.8	66,379	101.7	23.9
South Asia	1.3	0.7	2.6	3.60	0.23	14.0	1.6	0.8	–1.1	11,008	19.5	..
Sub-Saharan Africa	2.7	3.8	2.8	1.99	0.52	15.0	2.5	2.1	–0.5	30,141	..	..
Least developed countries	2.4	8.3	1.5	5.09	..	14.8	3.3	1.4	–1.4	16,915	..	..
Small island developing states	2.7	3.4	5.0	6.13	1.05	16.7	12.5	1.8	–3.5	15,782	..	..
World	**2.7**	**0.0**	**1.4**	**0.76**	**0.53**	**14.7**	**2.9**	**3.1**	**0.0**	**917,082**	**..**	**..**

NOTES

a A negative value refers to net official development assistance disbursed by donor countries.

b Some values may exceed 100% (see *Definitions*).

c Data refer to the most recent year available during the period specified.

d Data are average annual estimates for 2005–2010.

e Refers to 2009.

f Refers to 2007.

g Refers to 2006.

h Refers to 2008.

DEFINITIONS

Foreign direct investment, net inflows: Sum of equity capital, reinvestment of earnings, other long-term capital and short-term capital, expressed as a percentage of GDP.

Net official development assistance received: Disbursements of loans made on concessional terms (net of repayments of principal) and grants by official agencies to promote economic development and welfare in countries and territories in part I of the Development Assistance Committee list of aid recipients, expressed as a percentage of the recipient country's GNI.

Private capital flows: Net foreign direct investment and portfolio investment, expressed as a percentage of GDP.

Remittances, inflows: Earnings and material resources transferred by international migrants or refugees to recipients in their country of origin or countries where they formerly resided.

Remittances, outflows: Current transfers by migrant workers and wages and salaries earned by nonresident workers. Remittances are classified as current private transfers from migrant workers resident in the host country for more than a year, irrespective of their immigration status, to recipients in their country of origin. Migrants' transfers are defined as the net worth of migrants who are expected to remain in the host country for more than one year that is transferred from one country to another at the time of migration. Compensation of employees is the income of migrants who have lived in the host country for less than a year. Data are expressed as a share of GDP.

Total reserves minus gold: Sum of special drawing rights, reserves of International Monetary Fund (IMF) members held by the IMF and holdings of foreign exchange under the control of monetary authorities, excluding gold holdings, expressed as a percentage of GDP.

Stock of emigrants: Ratio of the stock of emigrants from a country to the population (not to the sum of population and emigrants), expressed as a percentage of the country's population. The definition of emigrant varies across countries but generally refers to residents that left the country with the intention to remain abroad for more than a year.

Stock of immigrants: Ratio of the stock of immigrants into a country, expressed as a percentage of the country's population. The definition of immigrant varies across countries but generally includes the stock of foreign-born people or the stock of foreign people (according to citizenship) or the combination of the two.

Net migration rate: Ratio of the difference between the number of in-migrants and out-migrants from a country during a specified period to the average population during the period, expressed per 1,000 people.

International inbound tourism: Arrivals of nonresident visitors (overnight visitors, tourists, same-day visitors, excursionists) at national borders.

International telephone traffic, incoming: Effective (completed) telephone calls (fixed and mobile) originating outside a given country with a destination inside the country, expressed in minutes of traffic per person.

International telephone traffic, outgoing: Effective (completed) telephone calls (fixed and mobile) originating in a given country with a destination outside the country, expressed in minutes of traffic per person.

MAIN DATA SOURCES

Columns 1 and 3–6: World Bank (2012a).

Column 2: World Bank (2012a) and OECD–DAC (2012).

Column 7: HDRO calculations based on data from World Bank (2011) and UNDESA (2011).

Column 8: HDRO calculations based on data from World Bank (2011) and population data from World Bank (2012a).

Column 9: UNDESA (2011).

Column 10: UN WTO (2012).

Columns 11 and 12: HDRO calculations based on incoming and outgoing total telephone traffic data from ITU (2012).

TABLE 11 International capital flows and migration | 185

TABLE 12

Innovation and technology

HDI rank		RESEARCH AND DEVELOPMENT			INNOVATION		TECHNOLOGY ADOPTION				
		Expenditure	Researchers	Graduates in science and engineering[a]	Patents granted to residents and nonresidents	Royalty and licence fees receipts	Electrification rate	Personal computers	Internet users	Fixed broadband Internet subscriptions	Fixed and mobile telephone subscribers
		(% of GDP)	(per million people)	(% of total)	(per million people)	($ per capita)	(% of population)			(per 100 people)	
		2005–2010[b]	2002–2010[b]	2002–2011[b]	2005–2010[b]	2005–2011[b]	2009	2002–2009[b]	2010	2010	2010
VERY HIGH HUMAN DEVELOPMENT											
1	Norway	1.8	5,503.7	15.3	334.0	101.9	99.7[c]	62.9	93.3	35.3	149.3
2	Australia	2.3	4,258.5	18.1	653.7	32.7	99.7[c]	60.3	75.9	24.2	139.7
3	United States	2.8	4,673.2	15.5	707.6	387.1	99.7[c]	80.6	74.2	27.6	139.0
4	Netherlands	1.8	2,817.6	14.0	117.6	320.8	99.7[c]	91.2	90.7	38.1	158.9
5	Germany	2.8	3,780.1	28.6	166.2	174.9	99.7[c]	65.6	82.5	31.7	183.7
6	New Zealand	1.2	4,323.7	20.5	995.2	53.5	99.7[c]	52.6	83.0	24.9	157.7
7	Ireland	1.8	3,372.5	21.6	54.4	574.2	99.7[c]	58.2	69.8	21.1	151.5
7	Sweden	3.6	5,017.6	25.0	147.1	619.4	99.7[c]	88.1	90.0	31.8	168.6
9	Switzerland	3.0	3,319.8	21.6	96.7	..	99.7[c]	96.2	82.2	37.9	177.7
10	Japan	3.4	5,189.3	20.6	1,759.9	226.8	99.7[c]	40.7	77.6	26.9	126.4
11	Canada	2.0	4,334.7	21.1	562.1	114.4	99.7[c]	94.5	81.3	29.8	120.3
12	Korea, Republic of	3.4	4,946.9	31.5	1,428.8	86.8	99.7[c]	57.6	82.5	35.7	162.3
13	Hong Kong, China (SAR)	0.8	2,759.5	34.7	758.9	56.6	99.7[c]	69.3	71.8	29.9	256.9
13	Iceland	2.6	7,428.1	14.5	434.2	0.1	99.7[c]	52.7	95.6	34.1	168.1
15	Denmark	3.0	6,390.3	19.6	27.9	..	99.7[c]	54.9	88.8	37.7	172.2
16	Israel	4.3	..	..	502.0	137.3	99.7	24.2	65.4	25.1	172.5
17	Belgium	2.0	3,490.7	16.3	49.7	232.1	99.7[c]	37.7	73.7	31.5	154.1
18	Austria	2.7	4,122.1	28.8	134.6	92.6	99.7[c]	60.7	72.7	23.9	184.6
18	Singapore	2.7	5,834.0	..	873.3	367.7	100.0	74.3	71.1	24.9	184.8
20	France	2.2	3,689.8	26.2	157.7	240.0	99.7[c]	63.1	77.5	34.0	151.8
21	Finland	3.8	7,647.4	29.4	172.1	556.5	99.7[c]	50.0	86.9	28.6	179.7
21	Slovenia	1.9	3,678.8	18.2	123.2	42.7	99.7[c]	42.5	69.3	24.2	148.0
23	Spain	1.4	2,931.8	25.3	60.2	23.0	99.7[c]	39.3	65.8	22.9	155.9
24	Liechtenstein	..	..	19.8	..	..	99.7[c]	..	80.0	63.8	152.9
25	Italy	1.3	1,690.0	20.5	303.4	59.8	99.7[c]	36.7	53.7	21.9	185.3
26	Luxembourg	1.7	4,824.8	32.5	171.4	890.0	99.7[c]	67.3	90.1	33.2	197.1
26	United Kingdom	1.8	3,794.2	21.7	90.2	226.3	99.7[c]	80.2	84.7	31.6	184.0
28	Czech Republic	1.5	2,754.8	23.8	86.8	10.2	99.7[c]	27.4	68.6	14.5	159.7
29	Greece	0.6	1,849.5	24.9	42.2	6.1	99.7[c]	9.4	44.6	19.9	154.6
30	Brunei Darussalam	..	286.3	21.9	107.2	..	99.7[c]	9.1	50.0	5.4	129.1
31	Cyprus	0.5	752.0	13.7	17.2	2.1	99.7[c]	30.9	53.0	17.6	131.2
32	Malta	0.6	1,168.1	15.0	9.6	81.0	..	..	63.1	28.0	169.2
33	Andorra	..	..	..	..	..	99.7[c]	..	81.0	28.9	122.2
33	Estonia	1.4	3,210.3	19.4	89.5	16.9	99.7[c]	25.5	74.2	25.1	159.3
35	Slovakia	0.5	2,437.7	20.6	68.8	0.7	99.7[c]	58.1	79.9	12.7	129.4
36	Qatar	..	..	24.0	..	..	98.7	16.0	81.6	8.2	149.4
37	Hungary	1.1	2,005.9	15.1	6.5	102.8	99.7[c]	25.6	65.2	19.6	149.9
38	Barbados	..	..	8.7	..	12.6	99.7[c]	14.8	70.0	20.6	177.9
39	Poland	0.7	1,597.5	15.7	78.5	7.1	99.7[c]	16.9	62.5	13.0	143.0
40	Chile	0.4	354.8	20.4	59.6	3.7	98.5	14.1	45.0	10.5	136.2
41	Lithuania	0.8	2,541.1	21.0	25.3	0.2	99.7[c]	24.2	62.8	20.6	171.1
41	United Arab Emirates	..	..	27.3	..	..	100.0	30.0	78.0	10.5	165.1
43	Portugal	1.7	4,307.8	33.8	13.1	5.7	99.7[c]	18.2	51.3	19.2	185.0
44	Latvia	0.5	1,601.2	14.3	81.7	4.5	99.7[c]	32.7	71.5	19.3	126.8
45	Argentina	0.5	1,045.5	14.3	30.6	4.7	97.2	9.0	36.0	9.6	166.5
46	Seychelles	0.3	155.7	..	..	21.6	99.7[c]	21.2	40.8	7.3	160.5
47	Croatia	0.8	1,571.3	24.4	18.6	5.3	99.7[c]	18.0	60.1	18.3	186.2
HIGH HUMAN DEVELOPMENT											
48	Bahrain	..	..	..	..	..	99.4	55.0	55.0	5.4	142.2
49	Bahamas	..	..	..	..	..	..	12.5	43.0	7.2	162.6
50	Belarus	0.6	..	26.6	127.4	2.1	..	..	32.1	17.4	152.5
51	Uruguay	0.7	346.1	13.6	8.6	0.1	98.3	13.6	47.9	10.9	160.8
52	Montenegro	1.1	..	..	418.1	..	..	..	52.0	8.3	211.9
52	Palau	..	..	..	..	..	..	..	..	1.2	105.0
54	Kuwait	0.1	151.9	..	..	..	100.0	26.5	38.3	1.7	181.5
55	Russian Federation	1.3	3,091.4	28.1	212.1	6.1	..	13.3	43.4	11.0	199.4
56	Romania	0.5	894.8	21.7	20.8	13.7	..	19.2	40.0	13.9	135.9
57	Bulgaria	0.5	1,586.7	18.8	33.5	2.5	..	11.0	46.0	14.5	164.9
57	Saudi Arabia	0.1	..	35.8	7.1	..	99.0	65.7	41.0	5.5	203.0

		RESEARCH AND DEVELOPMENT			INNOVATION		TECHNOLOGY ADOPTION				
		Expenditure	Researchers	Graduates in science and engineering[a]	Patents granted to residents and nonresidents	Royalty and licence fees receipts	Electrification rate	Personal computers	Internet users	Fixed broadband Internet subscriptions	Fixed and mobile telephone subscribers
		(% of GDP)	(per million people)	(% of total)	(per million people)	($ per capita)	(% of population)			(per 100 people)	
HDI rank		2005–2010[b]	2002–2010[b]	2002–2011[b]	2005–2010[b]	2005–2011[b]	2009	2002–2009[b]	2010	2010	2010
59	Cuba	0.5	..	3.3	12.4	..	97.0	5.6	15.9	0.0	19.2
59	Panama	0.2	111.3	19.2	107.5	..	88.1	6.3	42.7	7.8	200.4
61	Mexico	0.4	347.3	25.6	82.9	..	..	13.9	31.1	10.0	98.1
62	Costa Rica	0.4	257.4	11.9	9.7	0.9	99.3	23.2	36.5	6.2	96.9
63	Grenada	..	..	..	..	0.7	..	15.6	33.6	13.8	144.5
64	Libya	..	..	..	..	..	99.8	2.3	14.0	1.1	190.8
64	Malaysia	0.6	364.6	37.7	76.7	9.5	99.4	22.7	56.3	7.3	135.3
64	Serbia	0.9	1,060.1	23.7	43.3	7.8	..	17.6	43.1	11.2	178.7
67	Antigua and Barbuda	..	..	..	104.7	..	..	20.6	80.6	8.0	232.2
67	Trinidad and Tobago	0.0	..	30.4	67.6	..	99.0	13.2	48.5	10.8	163.1
69	Kazakhstan	0.2	..	..	10.9	0.0	..	..	33.4	8.9	143.7
70	Albania	0.2	146.8	6.1	108.9	4.1	..	4.6	45.0	3.3	152.3
71	Venezuela, Bolivarian Republic of	..	182.6	..	..	..	99.0	9.3	35.9	5.4	121.3
72	Dominica	..	..	..	..	0.2	..	18.8	47.3	13.9	178.0
72	Georgia	0.2	..	8.2	59.3	1.0	..	5.4	26.3	5.8	114.2
72	Lebanon	..	..	25.0	..	1.7	99.9	10.3	31.0	4.7	89.0
72	Saint Kitts and Nevis	..	..	..	..	..	..	22.7	76.6	27.9	191.9
76	Iran, Islamic Republic of	0.8	750.7	44.4	63.9	..	98.4	10.5	13.0	0.7	127.5
77	Peru	..	..	..	12.6	0.1	85.7	10.2	34.3	3.1	111.0
78	The former Yugoslav Republic of Macedonia	0.2	471.6	21.4	163.7	4.7	..	36.6	51.9	12.5	124.6
78	Ukraine	0.9	1,353.1	26.3	85.2	2.3	..	4.5	44.6	6.5	145.8
80	Mauritius	0.4	..	..	6.2	1.7	99.4	17.6	28.7	6.1	123.2
81	Bosnia and Herzegovina	0.0	197.2	..	46.0	3.4	..	6.4	52.0	8.2	109.3
82	Azerbaijan	0.3	..	16.6	22.9	0.0	..	8.0	46.7	5.0	117.1
83	Saint Vincent and the Grenadines	..	..	..	..	..	..	15.2	..	11.4	140.8
84	Oman	..	..	38.9	..	..	98.0	18.0	62.0	1.6	175.6
85	Brazil	1.1	695.7	12.2	16.7	3.0	98.3	16.1	40.7	6.8	125.7
85	Jamaica	..	..	..	15.9	1.8	92.0	6.8	26.5	4.3	127.5
87	Armenia	0.3	..	15.9	40.1	..	..	9.7	44.0	2.8	144.2
88	Saint Lucia	..	..	..	203.6	..	..	16.0	40.1	11.6	135.9
89	Ecuador	0.3	106.1	12.8	1.9	..	92.2	12.5	29.0	1.4	116.6
90	Turkey	0.8	803.9	20.9	9.0	..	..	6.4	39.8	9.7	107.2
91	Colombia	0.2	157.2	23.2	13.8	1.3	93.6	11.2	36.5	5.6	111.6
92	Sri Lanka	0.1	96.3	..	24.2	..	76.6	3.7	12.0	1.1	100.4
93	Algeria	0.1	170.1	28.0	6.3	0.1	99.3	1.1	12.5	2.5	100.7
94	Tunisia	1.1	1,862.5	..	..	2.4	99.5	9.7	36.6	4.6	117.6
MEDIUM HUMAN DEVELOPMENT											
95	Tonga	..	..	..	..	..	..	5.9	12.0	1.0	82.0
96	Belize	..	..	..	24.4	7.0	..	14.4	12.6	2.9	65.1
96	Dominican Republic	..	..	..	..	..	95.9	2.2	39.5	3.6	99.8
96	Fiji	..	..	..	..	0.6	..	6.1	14.8	2.7	96.3
96	Samoa	..	..	..	60.7	..	..	2.3	7.0	0.1	110.2
100	Jordan	0.4	..	25.1	10.3	..	99.9	7.6	38.9	3.2	117.5
101	China	1.5	1,198.9	..	100.7	0.6	99.4	5.7	34.4	9.4	86.2
102	Turkmenistan	..	..	..	..	..	..	7.3	2.2	0.0	73.7
103	Thailand	0.2	315.5	..	11.2	2.2	99.3	6.6	21.2	4.6	113.6
104	Maldives	..	..	..	..	26.5	..	20.0	28.3	4.8	171.6
105	Suriname	..	..	..	..	1.3	..	4.0	31.6	3.0	185.7
106	Gabon	0.6	..	..	..	..	36.7	3.4	7.2	0.3	109.0
107	El Salvador	0.1	..	26.4	..	0.0	86.4	5.8	15.9	2.8	140.5
108	Bolivia, Plurinational State of	..	120.3	..	..	0.7	77.5	2.4	20.0	1.0	80.8
108	Mongolia	0.2	..	17.1	34.8	0.8	67.0	25.8	12.9	2.6	98.1
110	Palestine, State of	..	144.3	16.5	..	1.4	..	5.5	36.4	..	..
111	Paraguay	0.1	74.8	..	..	45.2	96.7	7.8	19.8	0.4	97.3
112	Egypt	0.2	420.4	..	4.0	1.6	99.6	4.1	26.7	1.8	99.0
113	Moldova, Republic of	0.5	794.1	..	36.9	1.5	..	11.8	40.1	7.5	121.5
114	Philippines	0.1	78.5	23.8	3.8	0.1	89.7	7.2	25.0	1.8	92.9
114	Uzbekistan	..	..	21.1	7.0	..	..	3.1	19.4	0.3	80.8
116	Syrian Arab Republic	..	..	..	2.4	0.1	92.7	9.4	20.7	0.3	77.6
117	Micronesia, Federated States of	..	..	..	..	..	..	5.5	20.0	0.9	32.4

TABLE 12 Innovation and technology | 187

TABLE 12 INNOVATION AND TECHNOLOGY

	RESEARCH AND DEVELOPMENT			INNOVATION			TECHNOLOGY ADOPTION			
	Expenditure	Researchers	Graduates in science and engineering[a]	Patents granted to residents and nonresidents	Royalty and licence fees receipts	Electrification rate	Personal computers	Internet users	Fixed broadband Internet subscriptions	Fixed and mobile telephone subscribers
	(% of GDP)	(per million people)	(% of total)	(per million people)	($ per capita)	(% of population)		(per 100 people)		
HDI rank	2005–2010[b]	2002–2010[b]	2002–2011[b]	2005–2010[b]	2005–2011[b]	2009	2002–2009[b]	2010	2010	2010
118 Guyana	..	..	14.4	..	62.2	..	3.6	29.9	1.5	93.4
119 Botswana	0.5	..	13.0	..	0.1	45.4	6.1	6.0	0.6	124.6
120 Honduras	..	..	6.8	..	..	70.3	2.5	11.1	1.0	133.9
121 Indonesia	0.1	89.6	22.8	..	0.3	64.5	2.0	9.9	0.8	107.5
121 Kiribati	..	..	..	..	..	..	1.1	9.0	0.9	14.1
121 South Africa	0.9	395.6	..	106.3	1.3	75.0	8.4	12.3	1.5	109.2
124 Vanuatu	..	..	..	..	0.7	..	1.4	8.0	0.2	121.0
125 Kyrgyzstan	0.2	..	15.2	20.4	0.3	..	1.9	19.6	0.3	105.8
125 Tajikistan	0.1	..	26.0	0.4	0.1	..	1.3	11.5	0.1	91.7
127 Viet Nam	..	115.9	..	9.4	..	97.6	9.7	27.9	4.1	196.0
128 Namibia	..	..	2.6	..	0.0	34.0	23.2	6.5	0.4	73.9
129 Nicaragua	..	..	..	..	..	72.1	4.1	10.0	0.8	69.6
130 Morocco	0.6	661.0	34.9	25.3	0.2	97.0	5.7	49.0	1.6	111.8
131 Iraq	..	49.5	29.4	..	43.5	86.0	0.8	2.5	0.0	79.9
132 Cape Verde	..	132.5	..	..	0.0	..	14.3	30.0	3.2	89.5
133 Guatemala	0.1	39.4	16.8	7.2	1.0	80.5	2.1	10.5	1.8	136.0
134 Timor-Leste	..	..	..	..	..	22.0	..	0.2	0.0	53.7
135 Ghana	0.2	17.3	16.7	..	..	60.5	1.1	9.5	0.2	72.6
136 Equatorial Guinea	..	..	..	..	..	..	1.5	6.0	0.2	59.0
136 India	0.8	135.8	..	5.1	0.1	75.0	3.2	7.5	0.9	64.3
138 Cambodia	..	17.4	12.5	..	0.0	24.0	0.4	1.3	0.3	60.2
138 Lao People's Democratic Republic	..	15.8	12.8	..	..	55.0	1.7	7.0	0.2	66.2
140 Bhutan	..	..	..	..	..	..	1.9	13.6	1.2	57.9
141 Swaziland	..	..	2.7	..	0.2	..	4.1	9.0	0.1	73.6
LOW HUMAN DEVELOPMENT										
142 Congo	..	..	..	..	..	37.1	0.5	5.0	0.0	94.2
143 Solomon Islands	..	..	..	..	0.0	..	4.7	5.0	0.4	7.1
144 Sao Tome and Principe	..	..	..	..	..	..	3.9	18.8	0.4	66.8
145 Kenya	0.4	56.2	..	0.5	1.3	16.1	1.4	25.9	0.0	62.6
146 Bangladesh	..	..	10.6	0.6	0.0	41.0	2.5	3.7	0.0	46.8
146 Pakistan	0.5	161.9	..	1.0	0.0	62.4	0.5	16.8	0.3	59.1
148 Angola	..	..	11.9	..	0.7	26.2	0.7	10.0	0.1	48.3
149 Myanmar	..	18.4	..	..	..	13.0	1.0	..	0.0	2.5
150 Cameroon	..	..	21.0	..	0.0	48.7	1.1	4.0	0.0	46.8
151 Madagascar	0.1	46.2	18.2	2.7	0.1	19.0	0.6	1.7	0.0	37.9
152 Tanzania, United Republic of	0.4	..	21.1	..	0.0	13.9	0.9	11.0	0.0	47.2
153 Nigeria	0.2	38.6	..	..	..	50.6	0.9	28.4	0.1	55.8
154 Senegal	0.4	384.1	..	..	0.1	42.0	2.3	16.0	0.6	69.9
155 Mauritania	..	..	..	..	..	..	4.4	3.0	0.2	81.4
156 Papua New Guinea	..	..	..	0.2	..	..	6.4	1.3	0.1	29.6
157 Nepal	..	58.7	23.2	0.0	..	43.6	0.5	7.9	0.2	33.5
158 Lesotho	0.0	21.3	..	..	..	16.0	0.2	3.9	0.0	47.3
159 Togo	..	38.2	..	..	0.0	20.0	3.4	5.4	0.1	44.2
160 Yemen	..	..	..	..	1.4	39.6	2.8	12.3	0.3	50.4
161 Haiti	..	..	..	..	..	38.5	5.2	8.4	..	40.5
161 Uganda	0.4	..	9.5	..	0.8	9.0	1.7	12.5	0.2	39.4
163 Zambia	0.3	43.3	..	..	..	18.8	1.1	10.1	0.1	42.8
164 Djibouti	..	..	46.5	..	..	..	4.2	6.5	0.9	20.7
165 Gambia	0.0	..	..	4.4	..	..	3.6	9.2	0.0	88.3
166 Benin	..	..	..	..	0.0	24.8	0.7	3.1	0.0	81.5
167 Rwanda	..	11.9	..	2.1	0.0	..	0.3	13.0	0.0	33.8
168 Côte d'Ivoire	..	70.4	..	..	0.0	47.3	1.8	2.6	0.0	77.6
169 Comoros	..	..	12.0	..	..	..	0.8	5.1	0.0	25.3
170 Malawi	..	29.9	..	..	..	9.0	0.2	2.3	0.0	21.5
171 Sudan	0.3	..	..	4.4	0.1	35.9	10.8	..	0.4	41.4
172 Zimbabwe	..	..	24.8	..	..	41.5	7.6	11.5	0.3	64.3
173 Ethiopia	0.2	20.8	20.9	0.2	0.0	17.0	0.7	0.7	0.0	9.4
174 Liberia	..	..	..	..	..	..	..	7.0	0.0	39.5
175 Afghanistan	..	..	..	..	..	15.5	0.3	3.7	0.0	38.2
176 Guinea-Bissau	..	..	..	..	..	..	0.2	2.5	..	39.5
177 Sierra Leone	..	..	..	..	0.2	..	..	..	..	34.3

	RESEARCH AND DEVELOPMENT			INNOVATION		TECHNOLOGY ADOPTION				
	Expenditure	Researchers	Graduates in science and engineering[a]	Patents granted to residents and nonresidents	Royalty and licence fees receipts	Electrification rate	Personal computers	Internet users	Fixed broadband Internet subscriptions	Fixed and mobile telephone subscribers
	(% of GDP)	(per million people)	(% of total)	(per million people)	($ per capita)	(% of population)			(per 100 people)	
HDI rank	2005–2010[b]	2002–2010[b]	2002–2011[b]	2005–2010[b]	2005–2011[b]	2009	2002–2009[b]	2010	2010	2010
178 Burundi	..	..	9.6	..	0.0	..	0.9	2.1	0.0	14.1
178 Guinea	..	..	..	..	0.0	..	0.5	1.0	0.0	40.3
180 Central African Republic	..	..	..	..	..	..	0.3	2.3	..	22.4
181 Eritrea	..	..	7.9	..	..	32.0	1.0	5.4	0.0	4.6
182 Mali	0.2	37.7	..	..	0.0	..	0.7	2.7	0.0	49.2
183 Burkina Faso	0.2	45.1	23.3	..	0.0	14.6	0.6	1.4	0.1	35.5
184 Chad	..	..	..	..	..	..	0.2	1.7	0.0	24.3
185 Mozambique	0.2	15.8	12.1	1.8	0.0	11.7	1.4	4.2	0.1	31.3
186 Congo, Democratic Republic of the	0.5	..	..	..	..	11.1	0.0	0.7	0.0	18.0
186 Niger	..	7.8	..	..	0.0	..	0.1	0.8	0.0	25.1
OTHER COUNTRIES OR TERRITORIES										
Korea, Democratic People's Rep. of	..	..	..	258.4	..	26.0	..	..	..	6.6
Marshall Islands	..	..	..	..	..	..	9.6	..	..	15.2
Monaco	0.0	308.1	..	141.2	..	..	..	..	..	..
Nauru	..	..	..	..	..	..	..	..	3.9	..
San Marino	..	..	..	..	..	..	78.9	..	32.0	144.9
Somalia	..	..	..	..	..	..	0.9	..	..	8.0
South Sudan	..	..	..	..	..	..	..	..	..	..
Tuvalu	..	..	..	..	..	..	8.7	25.0	3.3	41.9
Human Development Index groups										
Very high human development	2.5	3,854.0	20.3	566.2	210.9	99.6	58.3	72.8	26.5	153.2
High human development	0.8	..	..	63.4	..	..	13.6	35.8	7.1	133.5
Medium human development	..	..	..	..	..	..	4.6	20.8	4.4	84.5
Low human development	..	..	..	..	..	..	1.5	10.7	0.1	42.7
Regions										
Arab States	..	..	..	..	..	86.7	10.8	27.2	2.0	99.6
East Asia and the Pacific	..	..	..	..	..	..	5.6	29.8	7.2	92.2
Europe and Central Asia	1.0	1,948.2	23.9	93.8	8.2	..	12.3	43.4	10.0	150.0
Latin America and the Caribbean	..	..	..	..	..	93.4	12.2	34.1	6.6	116.7
South Asia	..	..	..	7.0	..	70.1	3.0	8.4	0.7	64.4
Sub-Saharan Africa	..	..	..	..	..	..	1.6	11.3	0.2	47.1
Least developed countries	..	..	..	..	..	..	1.7	4.8	0.1	34.5
Small island developing states	..	..	..	..	..	..	5.6	18.7	2.2	62.7
World	..	..	..	..	..	..	14.1	30.0	7.7	95.2

NOTES

a Includes graduates in manufacturing and construction.

b Data refer to the most recent year available during the period specified.

c In the absence of data on electrification rate, 99.7% is assumed.

DEFINITIONS

Research and development expenditure: Current and capital expenditures (both public and private) on creative work undertaken systematically to increase knowledge and the use of knowledge for new applications. It covers basic research, applied research and experimental development.

Researchers in research and development: Professionals engaged in the conception or creation of new knowledge, products, processes, methods or systems and in the management of the projects concerned. Postgraduate doctoral students (ISCED97 level 6) engaged in research and development are included.

Graduates in science and engineering: People who have successfully completed the final year of a level or sublevel of education in science and engineering.

Patents granted to residents and nonresidents: Number of exclusive rights granted for an invention, which is a product or a process that provides a new way of doing something or offers a new technical solution to a problem, expressed per 1 million people.

Royalty and licence fee receipts: Payments and receipts between residents and nonresidents for the authorized use of intangible, nonproduced, nonfinancial assets and proprietary rights (such as patents, copyrights, trademarks, industrial processes and franchises) and for the use, through licensing agreements, of produced originals of prototypes (such as films and manuscripts).

Electrification rate: Number of people with access to electricity, expressed as a percentage of total population. It includes electricity sold commercially (both on-grid and off-grid) and self-generated electricity but not unauthorized connections.

Personal computers: Number of self-contained computers designed for use by a single individual, expressed per 100 people.

Internet users: People with access to the worldwide network, expressed per 100 people.

Fixed broadband Internet subscriptions: Broadband high-speed access to the public Internet (a TCP/IP connection), at speeds equal to or greater than 256 kilobits per second, in one or both directions, expressed per 100 people

Fixed and mobile telephone subscribers: Sum of telephone lines and mobile subscribers, expressed per 100 people.

MAIN DATA SOURCES

Columns 1 and 2: World Bank (2012a).

Column 3: UNESCO Institute for Statistics (2012).

Column 4: HDRO calculation based on data from WIPO (2012) and population data from UNDESA (2011).

Column 5: HDRO calculations based on data on royalty and licence fee receipts from World Bank (2012b).

Column 6: IEA (2012).

Column 7: World Bank (2012c).

Columns 8 and 9: ITU (2012).

Column 10: HDRO calculations based on data on cellular subscribers and telephone lines from ITU (2012) and population data from UNDESA (2011).

TABLE 12 Innovation and technology | 189

TABLE 13

Environment

		PRIMARY ENERGY SUPPLY		EMISSIONS			Greenhouse gas	Natural resource depletion	NATURAL RESOURCES					IMPACTS	
				Carbon dioxide					Forest area		Fresh water withdrawals	Endangered species	Agricultural land	Number of deaths due to natural disasters	Population living on degraded land
		Fossil fuels	Renewables	Total	Per capita		Per capita								
						(average annual % growth)	(tonnes of carbon dioxide equivalent)	(% of GNI)	(% of land area)	(% change)	(% of total renewable water resources)	(% of all species)	(% of land area)	(annual average per million people)	(%)
		(% of total)		(megatonnes)	(tonnes)										
HDI rank		2009	2009	2008	2008	1970/2008	2005	2010	2010	1990/2010	2003–2012ᵃ	2011	2009	2005/2011	2010
VERY HIGH HUMAN DEVELOPMENT															
1	Norway	58.8	43.3	50	10.5	1.0	5.8	10.2	33.1	10.2	0.8	6.9	3.3	0	..
2	Australia	94.4	5.6	399	18.6	1.2	9.6	6.5	19.4	−3.4	4.6	18.5	53.2	3	9.0
3	United States	84.1	5.4	5,461	18.0	−0.4	3.7	0.9	33.2	2.6	15.6	19.9	44.1	1	1.0
4	Netherlands	93.1	4.0	174	10.6	−0.1	2.4	0.8	10.8	5.8	11.7	5.4	56.8	12	5.0
5	Germany	79.5	8.7	787	9.6	..	1.9	0.1	31.8	3.1	21.0	10.5	48.4	12	8.0
6	New Zealand	63.7	36.1	33	7.8	1.1	10.0	..	30.9	7.1	1.5	20.4	43.6	0	5.0
7	Ireland	95.0	4.5	44	9.9	1.1	5.8	0.2	10.7	58.9	1.5	7.3	60.8	0	..
7	Sweden	32.7	34.8	49	5.3	−2.0	2.1	0.4	68.7	3.4	1.5	4.9	7.5	0	..
9	Switzerland	53.3	17.7	40	5.3	−0.6	1.2	0.0	31.0	7.7	4.9	6.6	38.1	14	..
10	Japan	81.0	3.3	1,208	9.5	0.7	1.0	0.0	68.5	0.1	20.9	13.7	12.6	1	..
11	Canada	74.9	16.9	544	16.3	0.1	4.7	2.3	34.1	0.0	1.6	7.2	7.4	0	3.0
12	Korea, Republic of	..	..	509	10.5	4.9	1.2	0.0	63.0	−2.3	36.5	9.5	19.1	1	3.0
13	Hong Kong, China (SAR)	95.1	0.4	39	5.5	2.6	0.5	0.0	..	..	..	8.3	..	0	..
13	Iceland	15.7	84.2	2	7.0	0.1	3.3	0.0	0.3	243.7	0.1	8.4	22.8	..	..
15	Denmark	80.4	17.4	46	8.4	−1.1	2.9	1.7	12.8	22.3	10.8	6.3	62.1	0	9.0
16	Israel	96.5	5.0	38	5.2	−0.2	1.1	0.2	7.1	16.7	101.9	11.2	24.1	1	13.0
17	Belgium	73.6	3.9	105	9.8	−0.7	1.8	0.0	22.4	0.1	34.0	5.5	45.0	20	10.0
18	Austria	70.2	27.8	68	8.1	0.5	1.9	0.2	47.1	2.9	4.7	11.6	38.4	4	3.0
18	Singapore	99.8	0.1	32	6.7	−0.7	1.4	0.0	3.3	0.0	31.7	13.7	1.0	..	..
20	France	51.0	7.7	377	5.9	−1.0	2.3	0.0	29.0	9.8	15.0	12.8	53.4	33	4.0
21	Finland	54.0	23.8	57	10.6	0.5	3.4	0.1	72.9	1.2	1.5	4.4	7.6	0	..
21	Slovenia	69.3	12.7	17	8.5	..	2.6	0.3	62.2	5.5	3.0	11.8	23.2	15	8.0
23	Spain	79.9	9.6	329	7.2	2.0	1.7	0.0	36.4	31.5	29.0	17.7	55.5	33	1.0
24	Liechtenstein	..	..	..	..	..	..	..	43.1	6.2	..	1.1	40.6	..	..
25	Italy	87.5	9.7	445	7.4	0.8	1.4	0.1	31.1	20.5	23.7	13.5	47.3	33	2.0
26	Luxembourg	88.8	3.1	11	21.5	−1.7	3.5	0.0	33.5	1.1	1.9	2.8	50.6	33	..
26	United Kingdom	87.3	3.2	523	8.5	−0.8	1.8	1.3	11.9	10.3	8.8	10.1	71.6	1	3.0
28	Czech Republic	79.6	5.8	117	11.2	..	2.1	0.5	34.4	1.1	14.8	5.0	54.9	5	4.0
29	Greece	92.4	6.4	98	8.7	3.1	1.4	0.3	30.3	18.3	12.7	16.3	63.6	1	1.0
30	Brunei Darussalam	100.0	0.0	11	27.5	−2.3	17.9	..	72.1	−8.0	1.1	8.4	2.2	..	..
31	Cyprus	95.7	3.9	9	7.9	2.8	1.3	0.0	18.7	7.5	19.3	7.7	13.5	0	11.0
32	Malta	99.9	0.1	3	6.2	2.8	0.9	..	1.1	0.0	71.3	6.8	29.1	..	..
33	Andorra	..	..	1	6.5	..	..	..	35.6	0.0	..	3.7	38.3	..	..
33	Estonia	84.8	15.1	18	13.6	..	2.3	1.6	52.3	6.1	14.0	3.5	22.0	0	5.0
35	Slovakia	69.5	7.3	38	6.9	..	1.4	0.4	40.2	0.6	1.4	5.2	40.1	2	9.0
36	Qatar	100.0	0.0	68	49.1	−0.9	18.0	..	0.0	0.0	455.2	7.3	5.6	..	..
37	Hungary	74.2	7.4	55	5.4	−0.6	1.6	0.5	22.6	12.7	5.4	8.0	63.9	7	17.0
38	Barbados	..	..	1	5.0	2.7	..	..	19.4	0.0	76.1	8.7	44.2	0	..
39	Poland	92.8	6.7	316	8.3	−0.3	2.7	1.4	30.5	5.1	19.4	5.7	53.0	3	13.0
40	Chile	74.5	25.1	73	4.4	1.4	1.6	12.4	21.7	6.3	1.2	9.9	21.2	1	1.0
41	Lithuania	55.8	10.4	15	4.5	..	2.5	0.6	34.5	11.1	9.6	4.1	42.9	1	5.0
41	United Arab Emirates	100.0	0.0	155	25.0	−2.5	6.2	..	3.8	29.5	2,032.0	7.7	6.8	..	2.0
43	Portugal	78.0	19.7	56	5.3	2.9	1.8	0.1	38.1	3.9	12.3	17.0	40.3	26	2.0
44	Latvia	59.5	37.1	8	3.3	..	2.3	0.5	53.8	5.7	1.2	4.6	29.5	4	2.0
45	Argentina	89.4	7.0	192	4.8	0.9	3.9	4.9	10.7	−15.5	4.0	9.0	51.3	0	2.0
46	Seychelles	..	..	1	7.8	7.3	..	0.0	88.5	0.0	..	16.1	6.5	0	..
47	Croatia	83.4	10.9	23	5.3	..	1.5	0.9	34.3	3.8	0.6	14.3	23.2	18	18.0
HIGH HUMAN DEVELOPMENT															
48	Bahrain	99.9	0.0	22	21.4	1.5	4.3	..	0.7	143.5	219.8	7.2	10.3	..	..
49	Bahamas	..	..	2	6.5	−2.2	..	..	51.5	0.0	..	10.0	1.4	3	..
50	Belarus	92.5	5.0	63	6.5	..	2.4	1.0	41.6	10.9	7.5	4.2	44.0	0	5.0
51	Uruguay	60.3	37.1	8	2.5	0.5	8.1	0.6	10.0	89.6	2.6	10.8	84.6	1	6.0
52	Montenegro	..	..	2	3.1	..	..	..	40.4	0.0	..	10.5	38.2	0	8.0
52	Palau	..	..	0	10.5	−0.3	..	..	87.6	5.6	..	11.4	10.9	..	..
54	Kuwait	100.0	0.0	77	30.1	−0.3	6.3	..	0.4	81.2	2,465.0	7.4	8.5	..	1.0
55	Russian Federation	90.2	2.8	1,709	12.0	..	4.9	14.3	49.4	0.0	1.5	10.2	13.2	40	3.0
56	Romania	76.3	15.3	95	4.4	−0.8	1.7	1.6	28.6	3.2	3.2	9.4	58.8	3	13.0
57	Bulgaria	73.1	6.2	51	6.6	−0.2	2.0	2.0	36.1	18.0	28.7	9.3	46.3	1	8.0

		PRIMARY ENERGY SUPPLY		EMISSIONS				NATURAL RESOURCES						IMPACTS	
		Fossil fuels	Renewables	Carbon dioxide			Greenhouse gas	Natural resource depletion	Forest area		Fresh water withdrawals	Endangered species	Agricultural land	Number of deaths due to natural disasters	Population living on degraded land
				Total	Per capita		Per capita								
						(average annual % growth)	(tonnes of carbon dioxide equivalent)	(% of GNI)	(% of land area)	(% change)	(% of total renewable water resources)	(% of all species)	(% of land area)	(annual average per million people)	(%)
		(% of total)		(megatonnes)	(tonnes)										
HDI rank		2009	2009	2008	2008	1970/2008	2005	2010	2010	1990/2010	2003–2012[a]	2011	2009	2005/2011	2010
57	Saudi Arabia	100.0	0.0	434	16.6	2.0	2.5	..	0.5	0.0	943.3	8.8	80.7	1	4.0
59	Cuba	84.1	15.9	31	2.8	0.7	1.4	..	26.1	39.5	19.8	18.1	62.5	0	17.0
59	Panama	78.6	21.5	7	2.0	0.9	1.4	0.0	43.7	−14.3	0.3	7.2	30.0	2	4.0
61	Mexico	88.9	9.6	476	4.3	1.8	1.7	5.7	33.3	−7.8	17.5	17.3	52.9	1	4.0
62	Costa Rica	44.7	55.3	8	1.8	2.5	0.9	0.1	51.0	1.6	2.4	8.0	35.3	2	1.0
63	Grenada	..	..	0	2.4	4.4	..	..	50.0	0.0	..	10.5	36.8	38	..
64	Libya	99.2	0.8	58	9.5	−1.4	2.7	..	0.1	0.0	718.0	8.7	8.8	..	8.0
64	Malaysia	94.7	5.3	208	7.6	4.7	2.4	6.9	62.3	−8.6	2.3	15.4	24.0	0	1.0
64	Serbia	92.4	8.1	50	6.8	..	2.3	..	31.0	17.3	..	7.2	57.8	0	19.0
67	Antigua and Barbuda	..	..	0	5.1	−0.8	..	..	22.3	−4.9	3.3	8.3	29.5	0	..
67	Trinidad and Tobago	99.9	0.1	50	37.4	3.7	7.8	32.0	44.1	−5.9	6.0	6.8	10.5	0	..
69	Kazakhstan	99.0	1.1	237	15.1	..	4.3	23.4	1.2	−3.3	28.9	8.4	77.2	1	24.0
70	Albania	54.0	38.8	4	1.3	−0.8	1.1	2.5	28.3	−1.6	4.4	12.7	44.0	1	6.0
71	Venezuela, Bolivarian Republic of	87.7	12.4	170	6.1	−0.4	3.0	12.4	52.5	−11.1	0.7	8.3	24.3	1	2.0
72	Dominica	..	..	0	1.9	4.4	..	0.0	59.5	−10.7	..	8.6	32.7	15	..
72	Georgia	68.0	33.3	5	1.2	..	1.4	0.6	39.5	−1.3	2.6	9.3	36.1	0	2.0
72	Lebanon	95.9	2.6	17	4.1	2.5	0.4	..	13.4	4.5	28.1	10.0	67.3	0	1.0
72	Saint Kitts and Nevis	..	..	0	4.9	..	..	..	42.3	0.0	..	8.6	21.2	..	..
76	Iran, Islamic Republic of	99.5	0.5	538	7.4	2.2	2.1	..	6.8	0.0	67.7	8.8	29.8	1	25.0
77	Peru	73.5	26.5	41	1.4	0.1	0.9	8.1	53.1	−3.1	1.0	8.4	16.8	6	1.0
78	The former Yugoslav Republic of Macedonia	84.3	11.3	12	5.8	..	1.0	5.9	39.2	9.4	16.1	13.3	40.2	1	7.0
78	Ukraine	80.0	1.6	324	7.0	..	2.1	3.7	16.8	4.7	27.6	8.2	71.2	2	6.0
80	Mauritius	..	..	4	3.1	4.4	..	0.0	17.3	−9.8	26.4	15.2	48.3	1	..
81	Bosnia and Herzegovina	92.2	12.1	31	8.3	..	1.2	..	42.7	−1.1	0.9	9.8	41.7	0	6.0
82	Azerbaijan	98.2	1.7	47	5.4	..	4.7	34.5	11.3	0.0	35.2	8.2	57.6	0	4.0
83	Saint Vincent and the Grenadines	..	..	0	1.8	4.7	..	0.0	68.5	5.5	..	9.0	25.6	0	..
84	Oman	100.0	0.0	46	17.3	11.1	7.1	..	0.0	0.0	86.6	8.5	5.9	5	6.0
85	Brazil	51.3	45.8	393	2.1	2.0	4.0	3.4	62.4	−9.6	0.7	10.0	31.3	1	8.0
85	Jamaica	83.7	16.3	12	4.5	1.4	0.7	0.6	31.1	−2.2	6.2	15.2	41.5	3	3.0
87	Armenia	68.4	6.7	6	1.8	..	1.3	1.0	9.3	−24.5	36.4	7.9	61.6	0	10.0
88	Saint Lucia	..	..	0	2.3	3.4	..	..	77.0	7.3	..	9.4	18.0	6	..
89	Ecuador	86.7	12.4	27	1.9	2.6	1.7	12.9	35.6	−28.6	3.6	12.7	30.3	1	2.0
90	Turkey	89.9	10.2	284	4.0	3.2	1.4	0.4	14.7	17.1	18.8	15.3	50.6	0	5.0
91	Colombia	75.2	25.1	68	1.5	0.3	1.8	7.8	54.5	−3.2	0.6	11.5	38.3	4	2.0
92	Sri Lanka	45.3	54.7	12	0.6	1.8	0.6	0.3	28.8	−20.9	24.5	17.8	41.6	2	21.0
93	Algeria	99.8	0.2	111	3.2	2.9	1.8	18.1	0.6	−10.5	52.7	12.2	17.4	4	29.0
94	Tunisia	85.7	14.2	25	2.4	3.2	1.0	5.1	6.5	56.5	61.7	11.2	63.0	0	37.0
MEDIUM HUMAN DEVELOPMENT															
95	Tonga	..	..	0	1.7	4.6	..	0.0	12.5	0.0	..	8.5	43.1	0	..
96	Belize	..	..	0	1.3	0.7	..	0.0	61.1	−12.2	0.8	6.4	6.7	13	1.0
96	Dominican Republic	76.6	23.4	22	2.2	3.1	0.9	0.2	40.8	0.0	16.6	16.1	51.1	9	7.0
96	Fiji	..	..	1	1.5	1.0	..	0.0	55.5	6.4	0.3	13.1	22.9	8	..
96	Samoa	..	..	0	0.9	3.9	..	0.3	60.4	31.5	..	10.8	23.7	5	..
100	Jordan	98.0	1.8	21	3.7	3.4	0.5	1.0	1.1	0.0	99.4	9.1	11.5	0	22.0
101	China	87.4	11.9	7,032	5.3	4.7	1.5	5.1	21.9	31.6	19.5	12.1	56.2	1	9.0
102	Turkmenistan	100.7	0.0	48	9.7	..	6.7	..	8.8	0.0	100.8	8.4	69.4	..	11.0
103	Thailand	79.4	20.5	286	4.2	6.3	1.6	2.4	37.1	−3.0	13.1	12.5	38.7	2	17.0
104	Maldives	..	..	1	3.0	..	..	0.0	3.0	0.0	15.7	9.1	26.7	0	..
105	Suriname	..	..	2	4.7	0.2	..	..	94.6	−0.1	0.5	3.5	0.5	2	..
106	Gabon	33.9	66.1	2	1.7	−2.2	6.4	33.1	85.4	0.0	0.1	5.9	19.9	0	..
107	El Salvador	37.8	62.0	6	1.0	2.6	0.8	0.4	13.9	−23.9	5.5	3.8	74.5	7	6.0
108	Bolivia, Plurinational State of	79.1	20.9	13	1.3	2.2	4.9	12.3	52.7	−8.9	0.3	4.7	34.1	5	2.0
108	Mongolia	96.4	3.2	11	4.1	1.6	3.7	32.3	7.0	−13.1	1.4	6.4	74.5	4	31.0
110	Palestine, State of	..	..	2	0.5	..	..	..	1.5	1.0	49.9	6.2	61.0	0	..
111	Paraguay	28.5	153.2	4	0.7	2.1	4.1	0.0	44.3	−16.9	0.1	3.9	52.6	0	1.0
112	Egypt	96.3	3.8	210	2.7	4.0	0.9	7.1	0.1	59.1	119.0	8.9	3.7	0	25.0
113	Moldova, Republic of	91.3	3.1	5	1.3	..	1.1	0.2	11.7	21.0	16.4	6.7	75.2	1	22.0
114	Philippines	57.0	43.0	83	0.9	0.7	0.8	2.1	25.7	16.7	17.0	16.8	40.1	9	2.0
114	Uzbekistan	98.4	1.6	125	4.6	..	1.9	19.2	7.7	7.6	118.3	7.9	62.6	0	27.0

TABLE 13 Environment | 191

TABLE 13 ENVIRONMENT

		PRIMARY ENERGY SUPPLY		EMISSIONS				NATURAL RESOURCES						IMPACTS	
				Carbon dioxide			Greenhouse gas	Natural resource depletion	Forest area		Fresh water withdrawals	Endangered species	Agricultural land	Number of deaths due to natural disasters	Population living on degraded land
		Fossil fuels	Renewables	Total	Per capita	Per capita	Per capita								
						(average annual % growth)	(tonnes of carbon dioxide equivalent)	(% of GNI)	(% of land area)	(% change)	(% of total renewable water resources)	(% of all species)	(% of land area)	(annual average per million people)	(%)
		(% of total)		(megatonnes)	(tonnes)										
HDI rank		2009	2009	2008	2008	1970/2008	2005	2010	2010	1990/2010	2003–2012[a]	2011	2009	2005/2011	2010
116	Syrian Arab Republic	99.3	0.7	72	3.6	3.3	0.9	11.9	2.7	32.0	99.8	10.9	75.7	1	33.0
117	Micronesia, Federated States of	..	..	0	0.6	..	..	..	91.7	0.9	..	13.7	31.4	45	..
118	Guyana	..	..	2	2.0	−0.2	..	6.0	77.2	0.0	0.7	3.8	8.5	4	..
119	Botswana	64.3	23.6	5	2.5	..	4.1	3.4	20.0	−17.3	1.6	2.0	45.6	0	22.0
120	Honduras	50.3	49.8	9	1.2	2.2	1.2	0.5	46.4	−36.2	1.2	8.3	28.5	4	15.0
121	Indonesia	65.6	34.4	406	1.7	4.7	1.5	6.6	52.1	−20.3	5.6	14.3	29.6	2	3.0
121	Kiribati	..	..	0	0.3	−1.0	..	..	15.0	0.0	..	12.4	42.0	0	..
121	South Africa	87.8	10.0	436	8.9	0.7	1.9	6.1	7.6	0.0	25.0	14.1	81.7	1	17.0
124	Vanuatu	..	..	0	0.4	−0.4	..	0.0	36.1	0.0	..	12.0	15.3	0	..
125	Kyrgyzstan	72.5	28.4	6	1.2	..	1.0	6.9	5.0	14.0	43.7	5.9	55.4	2	10.0
125	Tajikistan	41.2	58.6	3	0.5	..	0.9	0.8	2.9	0.5	74.8	6.4	33.9	3	10.0
127	Viet Nam	56.2	43.3	127	1.5	2.2	1.3	9.4	44.5	47.4	9.3	12.1	33.1	3	8.0
128	Namibia	70.5	19.2	4	1.8	..	4.4	0.7	8.9	−16.8	1.7	5.6	47.1	7	28.0
129	Nicaragua	44.7	55.3	4	0.8	0.7	1.7	1.6	25.7	−31.0	0.7	4.8	42.8	7	14.0
130	Morocco	92.5	4.9	48	1.5	3.1	0.5	1.6	11.5	1.6	43.4	15.2	67.3	1	39.0
131	Iraq	97.6	0.9	103	3.4	0.9	0.7	45.7	1.9	2.6	87.3	8.2	20.1	0	5.0
132	Cape Verde	..	..	0	0.6	4.2	..	0.1	21.1	47.3	6.8	12.5	21.8	0	..
133	Guatemala	46.1	53.9	12	0.9	1.9	1.1	1.7	33.7	−23.0	2.6	9.3	41.0	14	9.0
134	Timor-Leste	..	..	0	0.2	..	..	..	49.9	−23.2	..	5.2	25.2	1	..
135	Ghana	24.3	76.2	9	0.4	0.5	0.6	8.0	21.7	−33.7	1.8	5.7	68.1	1	1.0
136	Equatorial Guinea	..	..	5	7.3	11.3	..	49.4	58.0	−12.6	0.1	6.4	10.9	..	..
136	India	73.0	26.1	1,743	1.5	3.8	0.7	4.4	23.0	7.0	39.8	14.0	60.5	2	10.0
138	Cambodia	27.8	70.8	5	0.3	1.8	1.9	0.1	57.2	−22.0	0.5	12.1	31.5	1	39.0
138	Lao People's Democratic Republic	..	..	2	0.3	0.5	..	8.3	68.2	−9.0	1.3	10.5	10.2	0	4.0
140	Bhutan	..	..	1	1.0	12.4	..	3.6	69.1	7.1	0.4	6.8	13.2	1	..
141	Swaziland	..	..	1	1.1	0.7	..	0.1	32.7	19.3	23.1	2.7	71.0	0	..
LOW HUMAN DEVELOPMENT															
142	Congo	44.2	53.1	2	0.5	0.4	2.7	59.6	65.6	−1.4	0.0	4.4	30.9	0	..
143	Solomon Islands	..	..	0	0.4	1.1	..	15.6	79.1	−4.8	..	14.8	3.0	4	..
144	Sao Tome and Principe	..	..	0	0.8	3.7	..	0.8	28.1	0.0	0.3	14.9	58.3	..	..
145	Kenya	16.8	83.2	10	0.3	0.0	0.9	1.1	6.1	−6.5	8.9	8.4	48.1	2	31.0
146	Bangladesh	69.8	30.2	47	0.3	..	0.7	2.3	11.1	−3.5	2.9	8.6	70.3	6	11.0
146	Pakistan	61.8	37.4	163	1.0	2.3	1.1	2.8	2.2	−33.2	79.5	8.6	34.1	3	4.0
148	Angola	37.6	62.4	24	1.4	2.1	5.1	35.1	46.9	−4.1	0.4	4.6	46.8	2	3.0
149	Myanmar	27.7	72.3	13	0.3	1.1	2.2	..	48.3	−19.0	2.8	7.9	19.0	287	19.0
150	Cameroon	30.9	69.1	5	0.3	3.0	1.6	4.8	42.1	−18.1	0.3	10.9	19.8	0	15.0
151	Madagascar	..	..	2	0.1	−1.1	..	1.0	21.6	−8.3	4.4	21.0	70.2	5	..
152	Tanzania, United Republic of	11.1	88.9	6	0.2	0.4	1.4	3.2	37.7	−19.4	5.4	12.3	40.1	0	25.0
153	Nigeria	14.7	85.3	96	0.6	1.4	1.1	22.0	9.9	−47.5	3.6	6.6	81.8	0	12.0
154	Senegal	57.8	41.8	5	0.4	0.7	1.0	0.8	44.0	−9.4	5.7	6.9	49.4	0	16.0
155	Mauritania	..	..	2	0.6	1.2	..	34.3	0.2	−41.7	14.0	8.1	38.5	1	24.0
156	Papua New Guinea	..	..	2	0.3	0.3	..	22.2	63.4	−8.9	0.0	11.4	2.5	4	..
157	Nepal	11.1	88.5	4	0.1	5.0	1.0	2.5	25.4	−24.5	4.7	6.1	29.6	6	2.0
158	Lesotho	..	..	..	..	..	..	1.0	1.4	10.0	1.7	3.0	77.0	0	64.0
159	Togo	14.4	83.4	1	0.2	1.7	0.8	3.4	5.3	−58.1	1.2	4.2	62.1	1	5.0
160	Yemen	98.7	1.3	23	1.0	2.5	0.5	14.5	1.0	0.0	168.6	9.3	44.4	2	32.0
161	Haiti	28.1	71.9	2	0.3	3.0	0.6	..	3.7	−12.9	8.6	19.4	66.8	65	15.0
161	Uganda	..	..	4	0.1	−0.6	..	4.5	15.2	−37.1	0.5	7.6	69.9	2	23.0
163	Zambia	7.6	92.2	2	0.2	−4.6	3.8	18.9	66.5	−6.3	1.7	3.3	31.5	1	5.0
164	Djibouti	..	..	1	0.6	−0.9	..	..	0.2	0.0	6.3	8.2	73.4	6	8.0
165	Gambia	..	..	0	0.3	2.3	..	0.8	48.0	8.6	0.9	4.9	66.5	1	18.0
166	Benin	40.4	57.4	4	0.5	4.3	0.9	0.3	41.2	−20.8	0.5	4.5	29.8	1	2.0
167	Rwanda	..	..	1	0.1	4.0	..	3.1	17.6	36.8	1.6	5.7	81.1	1	10.0
168	Côte d'Ivoire	23.5	76.9	7	0.4	−0.5	1.0	3.9	32.7	1.8	1.7	6.7	63.8	0	1.0
169	Comoros	..	• ..	0	0.2	1.0	..	1.1	1.6	−75.0	0.8	11.7	83.3	0	..
170	Malawi	..	..	1	0.1	−0.4	..	1.8	34.4	−16.9	5.6	8.6	59.1	4	19.0
171	Sudan	30.2	69.8	14	0.3	0.1	3.0	12.9	29.4	−8.4	57.6	4.8	57.5	1	40.0
172	Zimbabwe	25.7	69.4	9	0.7	−2.0	1.3	2.7	40.4	−29.5	21.0	3.3	42.4	0	29.0
173	Ethiopia	7.1	92.9	7	0.1	1.2	1.1	4.2	11.2	−18.6	4.6	6.7	35.0	2	72.0
174	Liberia	..	..	1	0.2	−4.6	..	6.4	44.9	−12.2	0.1	8.4	27.1	0	..

		PRIMARY ENERGY SUPPLY		EMISSIONS					NATURAL RESOURCES						IMPACTS	
		Fossil fuels	Renewables	Carbon dioxide			Greenhouse gas	Natural resource depletion	Forest area		Fresh water withdrawals	Endangered species	Agricultural land	Number of deaths due to natural disasters	Population living on degraded land
				Total	Per capita	Per capita	Per capita								
						(average annual % growth)	(tonnes of carbon dioxide equivalent)	(% of GNI)	(% of land area)	(% change)	(% of total renewable water resources)	(% of all species)	(% of land area)	(annual average per million people)	(%)
		(% of total)		(megatonnes)	(tonnes)										
HDI rank		2009	2009	2008	2008	1970/2008	2005	2010	2010	1990/2010	2003–2012a	2011	2009	2005/2011	2010
175	Afghanistan	..	..	1	0.0	−4.4	..	2.6	2.1	0.0	35.6	5.8	58.1	11	11.0
176	Guinea-Bissau	..	..	0	0.2	1.4	..	0.5	71.9	−8.8	0.6	5.7	58.0	1	1.0
177	Sierra Leone	..	..	1	0.2	−0.9	..	2.1	38.1	−12.6	0.3	6.5	47.7	3	..
178	Burundi	..	..	0	0.0	0.6	..	12.7	6.7	−40.5	2.3	4.5	83.7	2	19.0
178	Guinea	..	..	1	0.1	−0.7	..	14.3	26.6	−9.9	0.7	7.3	58.0	0	1.0
180	Central African Republic	..	..	0	0.1	−1.6	..	0.0	36.3	−2.6	0.0	1.6	8.4	0	..
181	Eritrea	22.6	77.4	0	0.1	..	0.8	0.0	15.2	−5.5	9.2	7.4	75.2	0	59.0
182	Mali	..	..	1	0.0	0.5	..	9.8	10.2	−11.2	6.5	2.8	33.7	0	60.0
183	Burkina Faso	..	..	2	0.1	4.2	..	4.3	20.6	−17.5	7.9	2.7	43.7	0	73.0
184	Chad	..	..	0	0.0	0.8	..	29.0	9.2	−12.1	0.9	3.7	39.2	2	45.0
185	Mozambique	7.7	96.7	2	0.1	−2.9	1.1	3.3	49.6	−10.0	0.3	7.0	62.7	1	2.0
186	Congo, Democratic Republic of the	3.7	96.6	3	0.0	−2.8	1.9	13.7	68.0	−3.9	0.0	6.4	9.9	0	..
186	Niger	..	..	1	0.1	0.5	..	2.4	1.0	−38.1	7.0	3.6	34.6	0	25.0
OTHER COUNTRIES OR TERRITORIES															
	Korea, Democratic People's Rep. of	81.7	0.7	78	3.2	..	1.0	..	47.1	−30.9	11.2	8.6	24.1	5	3.0
	Marshall Islands	..	..	0	1.9	..	..	..	70.2	0.0	..	11.0	72.2	0	..
	Monaco	..	..	..	..	..	..	..	0.0	0.0	..	6.8	..	..	..
	Nauru	..	..	..	3.9	..	..	..	0.0	0.0	..	12.1	20.0	..	..
	San Marino	..	..	..	..	..	..	..	0.0	0.0	..	0.0	16.7	..	..
	Somalia	..	..	1	0.1	0.5	..	..	10.8	−18.5	22.4	6.8	70.2	2	26.0
	South Sudan	..	..	..	..	..	..	..	..	..	..	..	..	..	..
	Tuvalu	..	..	..	..	..	..	..	33.3	0.0	..	13.0	60.0	..	..
Human Development Index groups															
	Very high human development	81.0	7.5	12,643	11.4	−0.2	2.7	0.9	29.1	1.1	8.2	13.6	42.6	8	..
	High human development	86.7	9.5	5,765	5.8	1.0	2.8	..	38.0	−4.1	2.8	11.4	26.5	7	8.4
	Medium human development	..	..	10,877	3.2	3.8	..	5.3	24.6	1.3	16.4	12.8	60.9	2	..
	Low human development	..	..	473	0.4	0.5	..	9.5	28.8	−10.6	4.4	7.6	45.8	14	20.2
Regions															
	Arab States	96.7	3.1	1,509	4.6	1.1	1.5	..	7.1	−7.8	87.4	9.4	63.1	1	24.9
	East Asia and the Pacific	..	..	8,255	4.3	4.5	..	..	29.4	2.1	..	12.5	44.9	9	..
	Europe and Central Asia	88.3	4.7	3,723	7.9	..	3.0	7.3	38.5	0.7	5.8	9.6	20.5	13	8.5
	Latin America and the Caribbean	72.6	26.3	1,637	2.9	1.2	2.7	5.7	47.2	−8.9	1.5	11.5	37.5	3	5.4
	South Asia	76.7	22.6	2,509	1.5	3.2	0.8	4.0	14.5	2.4	28.6	12.5	33.9	2	10.1
	Sub-Saharan Africa	..	..	670	0.9	0.4	..	11.6	28.4	−10.2	1.6	7.5	54.7	1	25.0
Least developed countries		..	..	191	0.2	−0.5	..	9.0	29.6	−9.4	2.8	7.6	47.1	20	26.0
Small island developing states		..	..	137	2.7	1.4	..	..	63.1	−3.5	..	14.9	3.3	16	..
World		80.7	13.1	29,837	4.5	0.4	1.7	3.3	31.1	−3.3	7.3	11.7	38.6	6	10.6

NOTE

a Data refer to the most recent year available during the period specified.

DEFINITIONS

Fossil fuels: Percentage of total energy supply that comes from natural resources formed from biomass in the geological past (such as coal, oil and natural gas).

Renewables: Percentage of total energy supply that comes from constantly replenished natural processes, including solar, wind, biomass, geothermal, hydropower and ocean resources and some waste. Nuclear energy is not included.

Carbon dioxide emissions: Human-originated carbon dioxide emissions stemming from the burning of fossil fuels, gas flaring and the production of cement, including carbon dioxide emitted by forest biomass through depletion of forest areas.

Carbon dioxide emissions per capita: Carbon dioxide emissions divided by midyear population.

Greenhouse gas emissions per capita: Emissions from methane, nitrous oxide and other greenhouse gases, including hydrofluorocarbons, per fluorocarbons and sulfur hexafluoride, divided by midyear population. Carbon dioxide emissions are not included.

Natural resource depletion: Monetary expression of energy, mineral and forest depletion, expressed as a percentage of total gross national income (GNI).

Forest area: Land spanning more than 0.5 hectare with trees taller than 5 metres and a canopy cover of more than 10%, or trees able to reach these thresholds in situ. It excludes land predominantly under agricultural or urban land use, tree stands in agricultural production systems (for example, in fruit plantations and agroforestry systems) and trees in urban parks and gardens. Areas under reforestation that have not yet reached but are expected to reach a canopy cover of 10% and a tree height of 5 meters are included, as are temporarily unstocked areas, resulting from human intervention or natural causes, which are expected to regenerate.

Fresh water withdrawals: Total fresh water withdrawn in a given year, expressed as a percentage of total renewable water resources.

Endangered species: Percentage of animal species (including mammals, birds, reptiles, amphibians, fish and invertebrates) classified as critically endangered, endangered or vulnerable by the International Union for the Conservation of Nature.

Agricultural land: The sum of areas under arable land (land under temporary agricultural crops; multiple-cropped areas are counted only once), temporary meadows for mowing or pasture, land under market and kitchen gardens and land temporarily fallow (less than five years), expressed as a percentage of total land. Abandoned land resulting from shifting cultivation is excluded.

Number of deaths due to natural disasters: Number of people confirmed as dead and missing and presumed dead as a result of a natural disaster. Natural disasters are classified as climatological, hydrological and meteorological disasters, which include drought, extreme temperature, flood, mass movement, wet storm and wildfire.

Population living on degraded land: Percentage of the population living on severely or very severely degraded land. Land degradation estimates consider biomass, soil health, water quantity and biodiversity and range in severity.

MAIN DATA SOURCES

Columns 1 and 2: HDRO calculations based on data on total primary energy supply from IEA (2012).

Columns 3 and 4: World Bank (2012a).

Columns 5 and 7: HDRO calculations based on data from World Bank (2012a).

Column 6: HDRO calculations based on data from World Bank (2012a) and UNDESA (2011).

Columns 8 and 9: HDRO calculations based on data on forest and total land area from FAO (2012).

Column 10: FAO (2011).

Column 11: IUCN (2012).

Column 12: HDRO calculations based on data from FAO (2012).

Column 13: CRED EM-DAT (2012) and UNDESA (2011).

Column 14: FAO (2012).

TABLE 13 Environment | 193

TABLE 14

Population trends

		Population													
		Total[a]		Annual growth		Urban		Median age		Total dependency ratio		Total fertility rate		Sex ratio at birth[b]	
		(millions)		(%)		(% of total)		(years)		(per 100 people ages 15–64)		(births per woman)		(male to female births)	
HDI rank		2012	2030	2000/2005	2010/2015[a,c]	2000	2012	2000	2010	2000	2012	2000	2012[a,c]	2000[d]	2012[c]
VERY HIGH HUMAN DEVELOPMENT															
1	Norway	5.0[e]	5.6[e]	0.6[e]	0.7[e]	76.1	79.7	36.9	38.7	54.2	51.5	1.8	2.0	1.05	1.06
2	Australia	22.9[f]	27.8[f]	1.3[f]	1.3[f]	87.2	89.4	35.4	36.9	49.6	49.3	1.7	2.0	1.06	1.06
3	United States	315.8	361.7	1.0	0.9	79.1	82.6	35.3	36.9	51.0	50.7	2.0	2.1	1.05	1.05
4	Netherlands	16.7	17.3	0.6	0.3	76.8	83.6	37.3	40.7	47.3	50.6	1.7	1.8	1.06	1.06
5	Germany	82.0	79.5	0.0	−0.2	73.1	74.1	39.9	44.3	47.0	51.7	1.3	1.4	1.06	1.06
6	New Zealand	4.5	5.2	1.4	1.0	85.7	86.3	34.3	36.6	52.7	51.4	1.9	2.1	1.05	1.06
7	Ireland	4.6	5.4	1.8	1.1	59.1	62.5	32.5	34.7	49.2	50.8	1.9	2.1	1.07	1.07
7	Sweden	9.5	10.4	0.4	0.6	84.0	85.4	39.4	40.7	55.3	55.5	1.6	1.9	1.06	1.06
9	Switzerland	7.7	8.1	0.7	0.4	73.3	73.8	38.6	41.4	48.7	47.9	1.4	1.5	1.05	1.05
10	Japan	126.4	120.2	0.1	−0.1	78.6	91.9	41.3	44.7	46.6	59.6	1.3	1.4	1.06	1.06
11	Canada	34.7	39.8	1.0	0.9	79.5	80.8	36.8	39.9	46.3	45.1	1.5	1.7	1.05	1.06
12	Korea, Republic of	48.6	50.3	0.5	0.4	79.6	83.5	32.1	37.9	39.5	38.0	1.3	1.4	1.10	1.10
13	Hong Kong, China (SAR)	7.2	8.5	0.1	1.0	100.0	100.0	36.5	41.8	39.3	32.3	0.8	1.1	1.07	1.07
13	Iceland	0.3	0.4	1.1	1.2	92.4	93.8	32.8	34.8	53.5	49.6	2.0	2.1	1.04	1.05
15	Denmark	5.6	5.9	0.3	0.3	85.1	87.1	38.4	40.6	50.0	54.1	1.8	1.9	1.06	1.06
16	Israel	7.7	9.8	1.9	1.7	91.2	91.9	28.0	30.1	61.6	61.6	2.9	2.9	1.05	1.05
17	Belgium	10.8	11.2	0.5	0.3	97.1	97.5	39.1	41.2	51.6	53.3	1.6	1.8	1.05	1.05
18	Austria	8.4	8.6	0.6	0.2	65.8	67.9	38.2	41.8	48.0	48.1	1.4	1.3	1.06	1.06
18	Singapore	5.3	6.0	1.7	1.1	100.0	100.0	34.1	37.6	40.5	35.4	1.4	1.3	1.07	1.07
20	France	63.5	68.5	0.6	0.5	76.9	86.4	37.7	39.9	53.6	55.7	1.8	2.0	1.05	1.05
21	Finland	5.4	5.6	0.3	0.3	82.2	83.8	39.3	42.0	49.3	53.5	1.7	1.9	1.05	1.05
21	Slovenia	2.0	2.1	0.2	0.2	50.8	49.8	38.0	41.7	42.7	45.0	1.2	1.5	1.05	1.05
23	Spain	46.8[g]	50.0[g]	1.5[g]	0.6[g]	76.3	77.6	37.6	40.1	46.3	48.4	1.2	1.5	1.06	1.06
24	Liechtenstein	0.0	0.0	1.1	0.8	15.1	14.3	..	..	..	..	..	..	..	..
25	Italy	61.0	60.9	0.6	0.2	67.2	68.5	40.2	43.2	48.3	53.8	1.2	1.5	1.06	1.06
26	Luxembourg	0.5	0.6	1.0	1.4	83.8	85.7	37.3	38.9	49.1	46.1	1.7	1.7	1.06	1.06
26	United Kingdom	62.8	69.3	0.4	0.6	78.7	79.7	37.7	39.8	53.4	52.7	1.7	1.9	1.05	1.05
28	Czech Republic	10.6	10.8	0.0	0.3	74.0	73.4	37.4	39.4	43.7	42.9	1.1	1.5	1.06	1.06
29	Greece	11.4	11.6	0.4	0.2	59.7	61.7	38.3	41.4	47.1	50.6	1.3	1.5	1.07	1.07
30	Brunei Darussalam	0.4	0.5	2.1	1.7	71.2	76.4	25.8	28.9	49.8	41.6	2.4	2.0	1.06	1.06
31	Cyprus	1.1	1.3	1.8	1.1	68.6	70.7	31.8	34.2	48.4	41.4	1.7	1.5	1.07	1.07
32	Malta	0.4	0.4	0.6	0.3	92.4	95.0	36.1	39.5	46.6	42.1	1.6	1.3	1.06	1.06
33	Andorra	0.1	0.1	3.7	1.5	92.4	86.7	..	..	..	..	..	..	..	..
33	Estonia	1.3	1.3	−0.4	−0.1	69.4	69.5	37.9	39.7	49.8	50.0	1.3	1.7	1.06	1.06
35	Slovakia	5.5	5.5	0.0	0.2	56.2	54.7	33.6	36.9	45.4	37.9	1.3	1.4	1.05	1.05
36	Qatar	1.9	2.4	6.6	2.9	96.3	98.9	30.3	31.6	38.4	18.3	3.1	2.2	1.05	1.04
37	Hungary	9.9	9.6	−0.2	−0.2	64.6	69.9	38.5	39.8	46.8	46.2	1.3	1.4	1.06	1.06
38	Barbados	0.3	0.3	0.2	0.2	38.3	44.9	33.6	37.5	50.3	40.0	1.6	1.6	1.04	1.04
39	Poland	38.3	37.8	−0.1	0.0	61.7	60.8	35.3	38.0	46.3	40.5	1.3	1.4	1.06	1.06
40	Chile	17.4	19.5	1.1	0.9	85.9	89.4	28.8	32.1	54.0	45.2	2.1	1.8	1.04	1.04
41	Lithuania	3.3	3.1	−0.5	−0.4	67.0	67.2	35.9	39.3	51.2	44.9	1.3	1.5	1.06	1.05
41	United Arab Emirates	8.1	10.5	5.9	2.2	80.2	84.7	28.1	30.1	36.3	20.9	2.6	1.7	1.05	1.05
43	Portugal	10.7	10.3	0.4	0.0	54.4	61.6	37.7	41.0	47.8	50.0	1.5	1.3	1.06	1.06
44	Latvia	2.2	2.1	−0.7	−0.4	68.1	67.7	38.1	40.2	49.9	47.3	1.2	1.5	1.05	1.06
45	Argentina	41.1	46.8	0.9	0.9	90.1	92.7	27.9	30.4	60.7	54.4	2.5	2.2	1.04	1.04
46	Seychelles	0.1	0.1	1.2	0.3	50.4	54.0	..	..	..	..	..	..	..	..
47	Croatia	4.4	4.2	−0.3	−0.2	55.6	58.1	39.1	41.5	48.4	47.9	1.4	1.5	1.06	1.06
HIGH HUMAN DEVELOPMENT															
48	Bahrain	1.4	1.7	2.5	2.1	88.4	88.7	27.4	30.1	44.1	29.2	2.7	2.5	1.05	1.05
49	Bahamas	0.4	0.4	1.4	1.1	82.0	84.5	27.0	30.9	52.9	40.9	2.1	1.9	1.06	1.06
50	Belarus	9.5	8.9	−0.5	−0.3	70.0	75.5	36.3	38.3	47.5	40.5	1.2	1.5	1.06	1.06
51	Uruguay	3.4	3.6	0.0	0.3	91.3	92.6	31.6	33.7	60.2	56.2	2.2	2.0	1.05	1.05
52	Montenegro	0.6	0.6	−0.2	0.1	58.5	63.5	33.5	35.9	47.1	46.5	1.8	1.6	1.08	1.08
52	Palau	0.0	0.0	0.8	0.8	70.0	85.1	..	..	..	..	..	..	..	..
54	Kuwait	2.9	4.0	3.1	2.4	98.1	98.3	28.3	28.2	42.3	41.1	2.6	2.3	1.03	1.03
55	Russian Federation	142.7	136.4	−0.4	−0.1	73.4	74.0	36.5	37.9	44.1	39.8	1.2	1.5	1.06	1.06
56	Romania	21.4	20.3	−0.4	−0.2	53.0	52.8	34.7	38.5	46.7	43.6	1.3	1.4	1.06	1.06
57	Bulgaria	7.4	6.5	−0.7	−0.7	68.9	73.7	39.7	41.6	47.7	47.3	1.2	1.5	1.06	1.06
57	Saudi Arabia	28.7	38.5	3.6	2.1	79.8	82.5	20.9	25.9	72.5	49.0	4.0	2.7	1.03	1.03
59	Cuba	11.2	11.0	0.3	0.0	75.6	75.1	32.8	38.4	45.8	41.8	1.6	1.4	1.06	1.06
59	Panama	3.6	4.5	1.8	1.5	65.8	75.9	24.8	27.3	59.6	54.3	2.7	2.4	1.05	1.05

		Population						Median age		Total dependency ratio		Total fertility rate		Sex ratio at birth[b]	
		Total[a]		Annual growth		Urban				(per 100 people ages 15–64)		(births per woman)		(male to female births)	
		(millions)		(%)		(% of total)		(years)							
HDI rank		2012	2030	2000/2005	2010/2015[a,c]	2000	2012	2000	2010	2000	2012	2000	2012[a,c]	2000[d]	2012[c]
61	Mexico	116.1	135.4	1.3	1.1	74.7	78.4	23.4	26.6	62.5	53.5	2.6	2.2	1.05	1.05
62	Costa Rica	4.8	5.7	1.9	1.4	59.0	65.1	24.8	28.4	58.5	44.5	2.4	1.8	1.05	1.05
63	Grenada	0.1	0.1	0.2	0.4	35.9	39.5	21.8	25.0	74.9	51.9	2.6	2.2	1.05	1.05
64	Libya	6.5	7.8	2.0	0.8	76.3	77.9	21.9	25.9	55.6	55.0	3.1	2.4	1.06	1.06
64	Malaysia	29.3	37.3	2.2	1.6	62.0	73.5	23.8	26.0	59.1	52.8	3.1	2.6	1.06	1.06
64	Serbia	9.8[h]	9.5[h]	−0.6[h]	−0.1[h]	53.0	56.7	35.7	37.6	50.5	46.7	1.7	1.6	1.08	1.08
67	Antigua and Barbuda	0.1	0.1	1.6	1.0	32.1	29.8	..	..	..	..	..	..	..	..
67	Trinidad and Tobago	1.4	1.4	0.4	0.3	10.8	14.0	26.9	30.8	47.3	38.6	1.6	1.6	1.04	1.04
69	Kazakhstan	16.4	18.9	0.3	1.0	55.7	53.5	27.7	29.0	52.6	47.2	1.9	2.5	1.07	1.07
70	Albania	3.2	3.3	0.5	0.3	41.7	54.5	27.4	30.0	59.6	46.1	2.2	1.5	1.07	1.07
71	Venezuela, Bolivarian Republic of	29.9	37.0	1.8	1.5	89.9	93.7	23.3	26.1	62.0	53.3	2.8	2.4	1.05	1.05
72	Dominica	0.1	0.1	−0.2	0.0	67.2	67.2	..	..	..	..	..	..	..	..
72	Georgia	4.3	3.8	−1.2	−0.6	52.6	52.9	34.4	37.3	52.5	44.8	1.6	1.5	1.11	1.11
72	Lebanon	4.3	4.7	1.6	0.7	86.0	87.4	25.6	29.1	59.4	45.1	2.4	1.8	1.05	1.05
72	Saint Kitts and Nevis	0.1	0.1	1.3	1.2	32.8	32.0	..	..	..	..	..	..	..	..
76	Iran, Islamic Republic of	75.6	84.4	1.3	1.0	64.0	69.2	20.8	27.1	65.2	38.7	2.2	1.6	1.05	1.05
77	Peru	29.7	35.5	1.3	1.1	73.0	77.6	23.0	25.6	63.8	54.9	2.9	2.4	1.05	1.05
78	The former Yugoslav Republic of Macedonia	2.1	2.0	0.3	0.1	59.4	59.4	32.5	35.9	47.7	41.2	1.7	1.4	1.08	1.08
78	Ukraine	44.9	40.5	−0.8	−0.5	67.1	69.1	37.7	39.3	46.0	42.8	1.1	1.5	1.06	1.06
80	Mauritius	1.3	1.4	1.0	0.5	42.7	41.8	28.6	32.4	48.0	39.6	2.0	1.6	1.04	1.04
81	Bosnia and Herzegovina	3.7	3.5	0.5	−0.2	43.0	48.8	35.1	39.4	44.5	40.5	1.4	1.1	1.07	1.07
82	Azerbaijan	9.4	10.8	1.1	1.2	51.4	53.9	25.6	29.5	58.1	38.3	2.0	2.2	1.17	1.15
83	Saint Vincent and the Grenadines	0.1	0.1	0.2	0.0	45.2	49.7	24.2	27.9	62.3	48.3	2.4	2.0	1.03	1.03
84	Oman	2.9	3.6	1.4	1.9	71.6	73.7	21.0	25.3	64.5	42.8	3.6	2.2	1.05	1.05
85	Brazil	198.4	220.5	1.3	0.8	81.2	84.9	25.4	29.1	54.0	46.8	2.4	1.8	1.05	1.05
85	Jamaica	2.8	2.8	0.8	0.4	51.8	52.1	24.5	27.0	67.0	55.9	2.6	2.3	1.05	1.05
87	Armenia	3.1	3.1	−0.1	0.3	64.7	64.1	30.3	32.1	55.9	45.3	1.7	1.7	1.18	1.14
88	Saint Lucia	0.2	0.2	1.0	1.0	28.0	16.8	24.0	27.4	66.5	46.9	2.3	1.9	1.03	1.03
89	Ecuador	14.9	17.9	1.7	1.3	60.3	68.0	22.6	25.5	65.1	56.3	3.0	2.4	1.05	1.05
90	Turkey	74.5	86.7	1.4	1.1	64.7	72.5	24.5	28.3	56.0	46.8	2.4	2.0	1.05	1.05
91	Colombia	47.6	56.9	1.6	1.3	72.1	75.6	23.8	26.8	60.1	51.5	2.6	2.3	1.05	1.05
92	Sri Lanka	21.2	23.1	1.1	0.8	15.7	15.2	27.8	30.7	48.9	50.6	2.2	2.3	1.04	1.04
93	Algeria	36.5	43.5	1.5	1.4	60.8	73.8	21.7	26.2	62.2	45.6	2.6	2.2	1.05	1.05
94	Tunisia	10.7	12.2	0.9	1.0	63.4	66.5	24.7	28.9	57.2	43.2	2.1	1.9	1.05	1.05
MEDIUM HUMAN DEVELOPMENT															
95	Tonga	0.1	0.1	0.6	0.4	23.0	23.5	19.9	21.3	78.9	76.1	4.3	3.8	1.05	1.05
96	Belize	0.3	0.4	2.3	2.0	47.7	44.5	18.8	21.8	83.4	60.8	3.6	2.7	1.03	1.03
96	Dominican Republic	10.2	12.1	1.5	1.2	61.7	70.3	22.7	25.1	67.1	58.3	2.9	2.5	1.05	1.05
96	Fiji	0.9	1.0	0.3	0.8	47.9	52.6	22.1	26.4	62.6	51.7	3.1	2.6	1.06	1.06
96	Samoa	0.2	0.2	0.4	0.5	22.0	19.6	19.7	20.9	81.6	72.7	4.6	3.8	1.08	1.08
100	Jordan	6.5	8.4	2.0	1.9	79.8	83.0	19.4	20.7	75.8	66.9	3.9	2.9	1.05	1.05
101	China	1,353.6[i,j]	1,393.1[i,j]	0.6[i,j]	0.4[i,j]	35.9[j]	51.9	29.7	34.5	48.1	37.6	1.7	1.6	1.21	1.18
102	Turkmenistan	5.2	6.2	1.1	1.2	45.9	49.0	21.6	24.5	68.4	48.4	2.8	2.3	1.05	1.05
103	Thailand	69.9	73.3	1.1	0.5	31.1	34.4	30.2	34.2	44.7	41.1	1.7	1.5	1.06	1.06
104	Maldives	0.3	0.4	1.5	1.3	27.7	42.3	18.8	24.6	79.2	43.6	2.9	1.7	1.06	1.06
105	Suriname	0.5	0.6	1.3	0.9	64.9	70.1	25.7	27.6	57.1	52.3	2.7	2.3	1.08	1.08
106	Gabon	1.6	2.1	2.1	1.9	80.1	86.5	19.3	21.6	84.2	64.0	4.1	3.2	1.03	1.03
107	El Salvador	6.3	7.1	0.4	0.6	58.9	65.3	20.7	23.2	78.2	60.6	2.9	2.2	1.05	1.05
108	Bolivia, Plurinational State of	10.2	13.4	1.9	1.6	61.8	67.2	20.0	21.7	78.1	66.9	4.1	3.2	1.05	1.05
108	Mongolia	2.8	3.5	1.1	1.5	57.1	69.5	21.8	25.4	63.9	46.8	2.2	2.5	1.03	1.03
110	Palestine, State of	4.3	6.8	2.1	2.8	72.0	74.6	16.2	18.1	98.7	79.5	5.4	4.3	1.05	1.05
111	Paraguay	6.7	8.7	2.0	1.7	55.3	62.5	20.4	24.4	74.0	61.4	3.7	2.9	1.05	1.05
112	Egypt	84.0	106.5	1.9	1.7	42.8	43.6	21.4	24.4	67.9	57.2	3.3	2.7	1.05	1.05
113	Moldova, Republic of	3.5	3.1	−1.7	−0.7	44.6	48.4	32.3	35.2	50.8	38.8	1.6	1.5	1.06	1.06
114	Philippines	96.5	126.3	2.0	1.7	48.0	49.1	20.4	22.2	71.5	62.4	3.8	3.1	1.06	1.06
114	Uzbekistan	28.1	33.4	0.9	1.1	37.4	36.2	20.9	24.2	71.4	48.7	2.7	2.3	1.05	1.05
116	Syrian Arab Republic	21.1	27.9	2.9	1.7	51.9	56.5	19.1	21.1	77.7	65.2	3.6	2.8	1.05	1.05
117	Micronesia, Federated States of	0.1	0.1	0.4	0.5	22.3	22.7	18.9	20.8	78.2	65.1	4.3	3.3	1.07	1.07
118	Guyana	0.8	0.8	0.4	0.2	28.7	28.4	23.0	23.8	66.7	55.8	2.5	2.2	1.05	1.05
119	Botswana	2.1	2.3	1.3	1.1	53.2	62.3	20.0	22.9	69.5	56.7	3.4	2.6	1.03	1.03
120	Honduras	7.9	10.7	2.0	2.0	45.5	52.7	18.4	21.0	86.0	66.9	4.0	3.0	1.05	1.05
121	Indonesia	244.8	279.7	1.3	1.0	42.0	51.5	24.4	27.8	54.7	47.3	2.5	2.1	1.05	1.05

TABLE 14   Population trends | 195

TABLE 14   POPULATION TRENDS

HDI rank	Population Total (millions)		Annual growth (%)		Urban (% of total)		Median age (years)		Total dependency ratio (per 100 people ages 15–64)		Total fertility rate (births per woman)		Sex ratio at birth (male to female births)	
	2012	2030	2000/2005	2010/2015[a,c]	2000	2012	2000	2010	2000	2012	2000	2012[a,c]	2000[d]	2012[c]
121 Kiribati	0.1	0.1	1.8	1.5	43.0	44.0	..	..	..	..	..	..	..	..
121 South Africa	50.7	54.7	1.3	0.5	56.9	62.4	22.9	24.9	59.6	52.9	2.9	2.4	1.03	1.03
124 Vanuatu	0.3	0.4	2.6	2.4	21.7	25.2	18.9	20.6	81.3	70.0	4.4	3.8	1.07	1.07
125 Kyrgyzstan	5.4	6.7	0.4	1.1	35.3	35.4	22.5	23.8	67.9	51.9	2.7	2.6	1.05	1.06
125 Tajikistan	7.1	9.0	0.9	1.5	26.5	26.5	18.5	20.4	84.9	65.3	4.0	3.2	1.05	1.05
127 Viet Nam	89.7	101.5	1.1	1.0	24.4	31.7	23.8	28.2	60.5	40.9	2.0	1.8	1.05	1.05
128 Namibia	2.4	3.0	1.9	1.7	32.4	39.0	19.5	21.2	77.6	64.8	4.0	3.1	1.03	1.03
129 Nicaragua	6.0	7.2	1.3	1.4	54.7	57.8	18.9	22.1	80.4	61.2	3.3	2.5	1.05	1.05
130 Morocco	32.6	37.5	1.1	1.0	53.3	57.4	22.6	26.3	62.0	49.2	2.7	2.2	1.06	1.06
131 Iraq	33.7	55.3	2.7	3.1	67.8	66.4	18.0	18.3	89.5	84.3	5.3	4.6	1.07	1.07
132 Cape Verde	0.5	0.6	1.6	0.9	53.4	63.4	18.5	22.8	88.9	55.8	3.7	2.3	1.03	1.03
133 Guatemala	15.1	22.7	2.5	2.5	45.1	50.2	17.7	18.9	92.4	82.4	4.8	3.9	1.05	1.05
134 Timor-Leste	1.2	2.0	3.9	2.9	24.3	28.7	15.3	16.6	106.8	93.0	7.1	6.0	1.05	1.05
135 Ghana	25.5	36.5	2.4	2.3	44.0	52.6	19.1	20.5	79.9	73.0	4.7	4.0	1.06	1.06
136 Equatorial Guinea	0.7	1.1	3.1	2.7	38.8	39.6	19.5	20.3	85.9	72.0	5.8	5.0	1.03	1.03
136 India	1,258.4	1,523.5	1.6	1.3	27.7	31.6	22.7	25.1	63.8	53.8	3.1	2.6	1.08	1.08
138 Cambodia	14.5	17.4	1.4	1.2	18.6	20.1	18.1	22.9	80.5	53.2	3.8	2.4	1.05	1.05
138 Lao People's Democratic Republic	6.4	7.8	1.6	1.3	22.0	35.4	18.6	21.5	85.0	58.4	4.2	2.6	1.05	1.05
140 Bhutan	0.8	0.9	2.9	1.5	25.4	36.4	19.4	24.6	79.2	49.7	3.7	2.3	1.04	1.04
141 Swaziland	1.2	1.5	0.8	1.4	22.6	21.2	17.2	19.5	90.8	69.4	4.2	3.2	1.03	1.03
LOW HUMAN DEVELOPMENT														
142 Congo	4.2	6.2	2.4	2.2	58.7	64.1	18.9	19.6	82.7	79.3	4.9	4.5	1.03	1.03
143 Solomon Islands	0.6	0.8	2.8	2.5	15.8	20.0	18.8	19.9	80.6	74.1	4.7	4.1	1.09	1.09
144 Sao Tome and Principe	0.2	0.2	1.6	2.0	53.4	63.4	17.8	19.3	88.3	75.8	4.6	3.5	1.03	1.03
145 Kenya	42.7	65.9	2.6	2.7	19.9	24.4	17.4	18.5	89.0	82.1	5.0	4.6	1.03	1.03
146 Bangladesh	152.4	181.9	1.6	1.3	23.6	28.9	20.8	24.2	70.4	53.0	3.1	2.2	1.05	1.05
146 Pakistan	180.0	234.4	1.9	1.8	33.1	36.5	19.0	21.7	82.8	63.4	4.5	3.2	1.05	1.05
148 Angola	20.2	30.8	3.4	2.7	49.0	60.0	16.1	16.6	100.5	93.9	6.8	5.2	1.03	1.03
149 Myanmar	48.7	54.3	0.6	0.8	27.2	33.2	24.7	28.2	55.2	43.0	2.4	2.0	1.03	1.03
150 Cameroon	20.5	28.8	2.3	2.1	45.5	52.7	18.2	19.3	86.3	78.3	5.0	4.3	1.03	1.03
151 Madagascar	21.9	35.3	3.0	2.8	27.1	33.2	17.4	18.2	93.8	83.7	5.5	4.5	1.02	1.03
152 Tanzania, United Republic of	47.7	81.9	2.6	3.1	22.3	27.2	17.4	17.5	91.0	92.6	5.7	5.5	1.03	1.03
153 Nigeria	166.6	257.8	2.5	2.5	42.4	50.3	18.1	18.5	86.4	86.1	5.9	5.5	1.06	1.06
154 Senegal	13.1	20.0	2.7	2.6	40.3	42.8	17.0	17.8	92.1	84.3	5.5	4.7	1.03	1.03
155 Mauritania	3.6	5.2	2.8	2.2	40.0	41.7	18.4	19.8	83.0	73.1	5.2	4.4	1.05	1.05
156 Papua New Guinea	7.2	10.2	2.5	2.2	13.2	12.5	19.6	20.4	74.7	70.3	4.5	3.8	1.08	1.08
157 Nepal	31.0	39.9	2.2	1.7	13.4	17.3	19.2	21.4	80.5	64.1	4.1	2.6	1.05	1.05
158 Lesotho	2.2	2.6	1.0	1.0	20.0	28.3	18.6	20.3	84.1	69.1	4.1	3.1	1.03	1.03
159 Togo	6.3	8.7	2.4	2.0	32.9	38.5	18.0	19.7	86.4	73.6	5.1	3.9	1.02	1.02
160 Yemen	25.6	41.3	3.1	3.0	26.3	32.9	15.5	17.4	105.6	86.4	6.5	5.0	1.05	1.05
161 Haiti	10.3	12.5	1.6	1.3	35.6	54.8	19.1	21.5	79.2	65.5	4.3	3.2	1.05	1.05
161 Uganda	35.6	59.8	3.2	3.1	12.1	16.0	15.6	15.7	106.0	103.1	6.9	6.0	1.03	1.03
163 Zambia	13.9	24.5	2.3	3.0	34.8	39.6	17.1	16.7	93.2	99.0	6.1	6.3	1.03	1.03
164 Djibouti	0.9	1.3	2.0	1.9	76.5	77.1	18.9	21.4	78.8	62.8	4.8	3.6	1.04	1.04
165 Gambia	1.8	2.8	3.0	2.7	48.8	57.9	16.9	17.8	92.1	83.8	5.6	4.7	1.03	1.03
166 Benin	9.4	14.6	3.2	2.7	38.3	45.6	17.1	17.9	94.5	86.9	6.0	5.1	1.04	1.04
167 Rwanda	11.3	17.6	2.6	2.9	13.8	19.4	16.9	18.7	92.4	84.2	5.8	5.3	1.01	1.01
168 Côte d'Ivoire	20.6	29.8	1.7	2.2	43.5	52.0	18.7	19.2	81.6	79.3	5.2	4.3	1.02	1.02
169 Comoros	0.8	1.2	2.7	2.5	28.1	28.1	18.5	18.9	79.2	82.8	5.3	4.8	1.05	1.05
170 Malawi	15.9	28.2	2.7	3.2	14.6	15.8	17.0	16.9	95.6	96.3	6.1	6.0	1.03	1.03
171 Sudan	35.0	50.8	2.3	2.4	32.5	33.3	18.6[k]	19.7[k]	83.7[k]	76.0[k]	5.5[k]	..	1.05[k]	1.05[k]
172 Zimbabwe	13.0	17.6	0.1	2.2	33.8	39.1	18.2	19.3	82.3	71.6	3.9	3.1	1.02	1.02
173 Ethiopia	86.5	118.5	2.5	2.1	14.7	17.2	17.0	18.7	95.7	77.3	6.1	3.9	1.03	1.03
174 Liberia	4.2	6.5	2.2	2.6	44.3	48.5	17.9	18.2	85.9	86.0	5.8	5.1	1.06	1.06
175 Afghanistan	33.4	53.3	3.8	3.1	20.6	23.8	15.9	16.6	101.3	92.6	7.7	6.0	1.06	1.06
176 Guinea-Bissau	1.6	2.3	2.0	2.1	35.9	44.6	18.2	19.0	86.7	79.7	5.8	4.9	1.03	1.03
177 Sierra Leone	6.1	8.5	4.4	2.1	35.8	39.6	18.5	18.4	80.2	80.8	5.7	4.8	1.02	1.02
178 Burundi	8.7	11.4	2.6	1.9	8.2	11.2	16.7	20.2	96.5	67.7	5.8	4.1	1.03	1.03
178 Guinea	10.5	15.9	1.6	2.5	31.0	35.9	17.7	18.3	90.7	85.0	6.0	5.1	1.06	1.06
180 Central African Republic	4.6	6.4	1.6	2.0	37.6	39.3	18.7	19.4	85.1	78.0	5.4	4.5	1.03	1.03
181 Eritrea	5.6	8.4	4.0	2.9	17.6	21.8	17.1	19.0	89.7	78.9	5.4	4.3	1.03	1.03
182 Mali	16.3	26.8	3.1	3.0	28.1	35.6	16.3	16.3	98.8	97.3	6.8	6.2	1.05	1.05

HDI rank	Population Total[a] (millions) 2012	2030	Annual growth (%) 2000/2005	2010/2015[a,c]	Urban (% of total) 2000	2012	Median age (years) 2000	2010	Total dependency ratio (per 100 people ages 15–64) 2000	2012	Total fertility rate (births per woman) 2000	2012[a,c]	Sex ratio at birth[b] (male to female births) 2000[d]	2012[c]
183 Burkina Faso	17.5	29.1	2.9	3.0	17.8	27.4	16.5	17.1	95.3	90.5	6.3	5.8	1.05	1.05
184 Chad	11.8	18.4	3.5	2.6	21.5	21.9	16.9	17.1	96.2	92.6	6.6	5.8	1.03	1.03
185 Mozambique	24.5	35.9	2.6	2.2	29.1	31.4	17.9	17.8	88.8	89.1	5.7	4.8	1.03	1.03
186 Congo, Democratic Republic of the	69.6	106.0	2.9	2.6	29.3	34.8	16.0	16.7	102.6	94.0	6.9	5.5	1.03	1.03
186 Niger	16.6	30.8	3.5	3.5	16.2	18.1	15.8	15.5	102.3	104.8	7.5	7.0	1.05	1.05
OTHER COUNTRIES OR TERRITORIES														
Korea, Democratic People's Rep. of	24.6	26.2	0.7	0.4	59.4	60.4	29.9	32.9	49.5	47.0	2.1	2.0	1.05	1.05
Marshall Islands	0.1	0.1	0.0	1.6	68.4	72.2	..	..	..	..	..	..	..	..
Monaco	0.0	0.0	0.1	0.0	100.0	100.0	..	..	..	..	..	..	..	..
Nauru	0.0	0.0	0.1	0.6	100.0	100.0	..	..	..	..	..	..	..	..
San Marino	0.0	0.0	2.3	0.6	93.4	94.1	..	..	..	..	..	..	..	..
Somalia	9.8	16.4	2.4	2.6	33.2	38.2	18.0	17.5	88.3	91.0	6.5	6.3	1.03	1.03
South Sudan	10.7	16.1	2.8[i]	3.2[i]	16.5	18.2	..	..	..	..	..	..	..	..
Tuvalu	0.0	0.0	0.6	0.2	46.0	51.0	..	..	..	..	..	..	..	..
Human Development Index groups														
Very high human development	1,134.3	1,216.9	0.7	0.5	77.0	81.2	36.8	39.3	49.1	50.3	1.6	1.8	1.05	1.06
High human development	1,039.2	1,150.1	0.9	0.8	70.1	74.1	27.6	30.4	54.7	46.4	2.2	1.9	1.05	1.05
Medium human development	3,520.5	4,017.4	1.2	1.0	34.8	43.7	25.6	28.9	56.8	47.0	2.5	2.1	1.10	1.10
Low human development	1,280.7	1,845.3	2.3	2.2	28.6	33.6	18.4	19.8	85.2	75.5	5.1	4.2	1.04	1.04
Regions														
Arab States	357.3	480.8	2.2	2.0	53.2	57.2	20.6	23.3	72.3	59.7	3.9	3.0	1.05	1.05
East Asia and the Pacific	1,991.4	2,135.3	0.8	0.6	36.7	49.7	28.1	32.3	50.8	40.9	2.0	1.8	1.14	1.12
Europe and Central Asia	481.6	491.3	0.0	0.2	63.2	64.8	32.9	34.9	49.5	43.4	1.6	1.7	1.06	1.06
Latin America and the Caribbean	597.7	696.0	1.3	1.1	75.3	79.3	24.4	27.5	60.3	52.1	2.6	2.2	1.05	1.05
South Asia	1,753.0	2,141.8	1.6	1.4	29.0	32.9	22.0	24.6	66.7	54.6	3.3	2.6	1.07	1.07
Sub-Saharan Africa	852.5	1,284.0	2.5	2.5	32.0	37.0	17.8	18.5	88.6	83.4	5.6	4.8	1.04	1.04
Least developed countries	870.4[T]	1,256.8[T]	2.2[T]	2.2[T]	24.3[T]	28.9[T]	18.3[T]	19.7[T]	85.5[T]	75.5[T]	5.1[T]	4.1[T]	1.04[T]	1.04[T]
Small island developing states	53.8	63.8	1.3	1.1	48.2	52.6	24.0	26.6	64.6	57.3	3.1	2.7	1.06	1.06
World	7,052.1[T]	8,321.3[T]	1.2[T]	1.2[T]	46.7[T]	52.6[T]	26.7[T]	29.2[T]	59.0[T]	52.0[T]	2.7[T]	2.5[T]	1.07[T]	1.07[T]

NOTES

a Projections based on medium-fertility variant.

b The natural sex ratio at birth is commonly assumed and empirically confirmed to be 105 male births to 100 female births.

c Data are annual average of projected values for 2010–2015.

d Data are average annual estimates for 2000–2005.

e Includes Svalbard and Jan Mayen Islands.

f Includes Christmas Island, Cocos (Keeling) Islands and Norfolk Island.

g Includes Canary Islands, Ceuta and Melilla.

h Includes Kosovo.

i Includes Taiwan, China, and excludes Hong Kong Special Administrative Region and Macao Special Administrative Region.

j Excludes Hong Kong Special Administrative Region and Macao Special Administrative Region.

k Estimates are for Sudan only and do not include South Sudan.

l HDRO calculations based on population data from UNDESA (2012b).

T Aggregate from original data source.

DEFINITIONS

Population: De facto population in a country, area or region as of 1 July.

Annual population growth rate: Average annual exponential growth rate for the period specified.

Urban population: De facto population living in areas classified as urban according to the criteria used by each area or country as of 1 July.

Median age: Age that divides the population distribution into two equal parts—that is, 50% of the population is above that age and 50% is below it.

Total dependency ratio: Ratio of the sum of the population ages 0–14 and ages 65 and older to the population ages 15–64.

Total fertility rate: Number of children that would be born to each woman if she were to live to the end of her child-bearing years and bear children at each age in accordance with prevailing age-specific fertility rates.

Sex ratio at birth: Number of male births per female birth.

MAIN DATA SOURCES

Columns 1, 2, 13 and 14: UNDESA (2012b).

Columns 3, 4 and 7–12: UNDESA (2011).

Columns 5 and 6: UNDESA (2012a).

TABLE 14   Population trends | 197

Regions

Arab States (20 countries or territories)
Algeria, Bahrain, Djibouti, Egypt, Iraq, Jordan, Kuwait, Lebanon, Libya, Morocco, Oman, State of Palestine, Qatar, Saudi Arabia, Somalia, Sudan, Syrian Arab Republic, Tunisia, United Arab Emirates, Yemen

East Asia and the Pacific (24 countries)
Cambodia, China, Fiji, Indonesia, Kiribati, Democratic People's Republic of Korea, Lao People's Democratic Republic, Malaysia, Marshall Islands, Federated States of Micronesia, Mongolia, Myanmar, Nauru, Palau, Papua New Guinea, Philippines, Samoa, Solomon Islands, Thailand, Timor-Leste, Tonga, Tuvalu, Vanuatu, Viet Nam

Europe and Central Asia[1] (31 countries)
Albania, Armenia, Azerbaijan, Belarus, Bosnia and Herzegovina, Bulgaria, Croatia, Cyprus, Czech Republic, Estonia, Georgia, Hungary, Kazakhstan, Kyrgyzstan, Latvia, Lithuania, Malta, Republic of Moldova, Montenegro, Poland, Romania, Russian Federation, Serbia, Slovakia, Slovenia, Tajikistan, The former Yugoslav Republic of Macedonia, Turkey, Turkmenistan, Ukraine, Uzbekistan

Latin America and the Caribbean (33 countries)
Antigua and Barbuda, Argentina, Bahamas, Barbados, Belize, Plurinational State of Bolivia, Brazil, Chile, Colombia, Costa Rica, Cuba, Dominica, Dominican Republic, Ecuador, El Salvador, Grenada, Guatemala, Guyana, Haiti, Honduras, Jamaica, Mexico, Nicaragua, Panama, Paraguay, Peru, Saint Kitts and Nevis, Saint Lucia, Saint Vincent and the Grenadines, Suriname, Trinidad and Tobago, Uruguay, Bolivarian Republic of Venezuela

South Asia (9 countries)
Afghanistan, Bangladesh, Bhutan, India, Islamic Republic of Iran, Maldives, Nepal, Pakistan, Sri Lanka

Sub-Saharan Africa (46 countries)
Angola, Benin, Botswana, Burkina Faso, Burundi, Cameroon, Cape Verde, Central African Republic, Chad, Comoros, Congo, Democratic Republic of the Congo, Côte d'Ivoire, Equatorial Guinea, Eritrea, Ethiopia, Gabon, Gambia, Ghana, Guinea, Guinea-Bissau, Kenya, Lesotho, Liberia, Madagascar, Malawi, Mali, Mauritania, Mauritius, Mozambique, Namibia, Niger, Nigeria, Rwanda, Sao Tome and Principe, Senegal, Seychelles, Sierra Leone, South Africa, South Sudan, Swaziland, United Republic of Tanzania, Togo, Uganda, Zambia, Zimbabwe

Note: Countries included in aggregates for Least Developed Countries and Small Island Developing States follow UN classifications, which are available at www.unohrlls.org.
1. The former socialist countries of Europe and Central Asia that have undergone a political and economic transformation since 1989–1991 as well as Cyprus, Malta and Turkey.

Statistical references

ADB (Asian Development Bank). 2012. *Asian Development Outlook 2012: Confronting Rising Inequality in Asia.* www.adb.org/sites/default/files/pub/2012/ado2012.pdf. Accessed 30 April 2012.

Aguna, C., and M. Kovacevic 2011. "Uncertainty and Sensitivity Analysis of the Human Development Index." Human Development Research Paper 2010/11. UNDP–HDRO, New York. http://hdr.undp.org/en/reports/global/hdr2010/papers/HDRP_2010_47.pdf.

Alkire, S., A. Conconi, and J.M. Roche. 2012. "Multidimensional Poverty Index 2012: Brief Methodological Note and Results." University of Oxford, Department of International Development, Oxford Poverty and Human Development Initiative, Oxford, UK.

Alkire, S., J.M. Roche, M.E. Santos, and S. Seth. 2011. "Multidimensional Poverty Index 2011: Brief Methodological Note." University of Oxford, Department of International Development, Oxford Poverty and Human Development Initiative, Oxford, UK. www.ophi.org.uk/multidimensional -poverty-index-2011-brief-methodological-note/. Accessed 15 February 2012.

Alkire, S., and J. Foster. 2010. "Designing the Inequality-Adjusted Human Development Index (HDI)." Human Development Research Paper 2010/28. UNDP–HDRO, New York. http://hdr.undp.org/en/reports/global/hdr2010/papers/HDRP_2010_28.pdf.

Anand, S., and A. Sen. 2000. "The Income Component of the Human Development Index." *Journal of Human Development and Capabilities* 1(1): 83–106.

Athukorala, Prema-chandra. 2012. "Asian Trade Flows: Trends, Patterns and Prospects." *Japan and the World Economy* 24: 150–62.

Barro, R. J., and J. W. Lee. 2010. *A New Data Set of Educational Attainment in the World, 1950–2010.* Working Paper 15902. Cambridge, MA: National Bureau of Economic Research. www.nber.org/papers/w15902. Accessed 15 April 2012.

———. **2011.** Dataset of educational attainment. www.barrolee.com. Accessed 15 April 2012.

CRED EM-DAT (Centre for Research on the Epidemiology of Disasters). 2012. The International Disaster Database. www.emdat.be. Accessed 30 March 2012.

ECLAC (Economic Commission for Latin America and the Caribbean). 2012. *Preliminary Overview of the Economies of Latin America and the Caribbean.* Santiago. www.eclac.org/cgi-bin/getProd.asp?xml=/publicaciones/xml/4/41974/P41974.xml&xsl=/. Accessed 30 April 2012.

Eurostat. 2012. "European Union Statistics on Income and Living Conditions (EUSILC)." Brussels. http://epp.eurostat.ec.europa.eu/portal/page/portal/microdata/eu_silc. Accessed 15 April 2012.

FAO (Food and Agriculture Organization). 2011. AQUASTAT database. www.fao.org/nr/water/aquastat/data. Accessed 15 April 2012.

———. **2012.** Statistics Division Database. www.fao.org/corp/statistics/en/. Accessed 15 April 2012.

Gallup. 2012. Gallup World Poll database. https://worldview.gallup.com. Accessed 30 April 2012.

Høyland, B., K. Moene, and F. Willumsen. 2011. "The Tyranny of International Rankings." *Journal of Development Economics* 97(1): 1–14.

ICF Macro. 2012. Measure DHS (Demographic and Health Survey). www.measuredhs.com.

IEA (International Energy Agency). 2012. *World Energy Outlook 2011.* Paris. www.iea.org/weo/electricity.asp. Accessed 30 March 2012.

ILO (International Labour Organization). 2012. *Key Indicators of the Labour Market.* 7th edition. Geneva. www.ilo.org/empelm/what/WCMS_114240/lang--en/index.htm. Accessed 15 October 2012.

IMF (International Monetary Fund). 2012. World Economic Outlook database, October 2012. www.imf.org/external/pubs/ft/weo/2012/01/weodata/index.aspx. Accessed 15 October 2012.

Inter-agency Group for Child Mortality Estimation. 2012. Database on child mortality. www.childinfo.org/mortality_igme.html. Accessed 15 October 2012.

IPU (Inter-Parliamentary Union). 2012. PARLINE database. www.ipu.org/wmn-e/classif.htm. Accessed 15 May 2012.

ITU (International Telecommunication Union). 2012. World Telecommunication/ICT Indicators database. www.itu.int/ITU-D/ict/statistics/. Accessed 15 October 2012.

IUCN (International Union for Conservation of Nature and Natural Resources). 2012. IUCN Red List of Threatened Species. Version 2011.2. www.iucnredlist.org. Accessed 15 April 2012.

LIS (Luxembourg Income Study). 2012. "Luxembourg Income Study Project." www.lisproject.org/techdoc.htm. Accessed 15 May 2012.

OECD (Organisation for Economic Co-operation and Development). 2010. Programme for International Student Assessment. www.oecd.org/edu/pisa/2009. Accessed 30 March 2012.

OECD-DAC (Organisation for Economic Co-operation and Development–Development Assistance Committee). 2012. Aid statistics database. www.oecd.org/dac/aidstatistics/. Accessed 15 October 2012.

SIPRI (Stockholm International Peace Research Institute). 2012. SIPRI Military Expenditure Database. www.sipri.org. Accessed 30 March 2012.

UNCTAD (United Nations Conference on Trade and Development). 2012. Statistics. http://unctadstat.unctad.org/ReportFolders/reportFolders.aspx?sCS_referer=&sCS_ChosenLang=en. Accessed 1 May 2012.

UNDESA (United Nations Department of Economic and Social Affairs). 2011. *World Population Prospects: The 2010 Revision.* New York. http://esa.un.org/unpd/wpp/index.htm. Accessed 15 April 2012.

———. **2012a.** *World Urbanization Prospects: The 2011 Revision.* New York. http://esa.un.org/unpd/wup/index.htm. Accessed 30 April 2012.

———. **2012b.** Population Division Database. Detailed Indicators. http://esa.un.org/undp/wpp/unpp/. Accessed 1 May 2012.

———. **2012c.** *World Economic Situation and Prospects: Mid-2012 Update.* New York. www.un.org/en/development/desa/policy/wesp/. Accessed 30 April 2012.

UNESCO (United Nations Educational, Scientific and Cultural Organization) Institute for Statistics. 2012. Data Centre. http://stats.uis.unesco.org. Accessed 15 October 2012.

UNESCWA (United Nations Economic and Social Commission for Western Asia). 2012. "Summary of the Survey of Economic and Social Developments in Western Asia, 2011–2012." Beirut. www.escwa.un.org/information/publications/edit/upload/E_ESCWA_EDGD_12_1_e.pdf. Accessed 30 April 2012.

UNICEF (United Nations Children's Fund). 2012. *The State of the World's Children 2012.* New York. www.unicef.org/sowc2012/. Accessed 30 March 2012.

———. **Various years.** Multiple Indicator Cluster Surveys. New York. www.unicef.org/statistics/index_24302.html. Accessed 15 October 2012.

UNODC (United Nations Office on Drug and Crime). 2012. *2011 Global Study on Homicide: Trends, Contexts, Data.* www.unodc.org/documents/data-and-analysis/statistics/Homicide/Globa_study_on_homicide_2011_web.pdf. Accessed 30 May 2012.

UNSD (United Nations Statistics Division). 2012a. National Accounts Main Aggregate Database. http://unstats.un.org/unsd/snaama. Accessed 1 May 2012.

———. **2012b.** International Merchandise Trade Statistics. Comtrade Database. http://comtrade.un.org/. Accessed 15 October 2012.

UN WTO (World Tourism Organization). 2012. Compendium of Tourism Statistics database. http://statistics.unwto.org/en/content/compendium-tourism-statistics. Accessed 30 April 2012.

WHO (World Health Organization). 2012a. *World Health Statistics 2011.* Geneva. www.who.int/gho/publications/world_health_statistics/EN_WHS2011_Full.pdf. Accessed 30 March 2012.

———. **2012b.** Global Health Observatory. www.apps.who.int/ghodata. Accessed 30 March 2012.

———. **2012c.** Mental Health. www.who.int/mental_health/en. Accessed 30 April 2012.

WHO (World Health Organization), UNICEF (United Nations Children's Fund), UNFPA (United Nations Population Fund) and World Bank. 2012. "Trends in Estimates of Maternal Mortality Ratio." www.childinfo.org/maternal_mortality_ratio.php. Accessed 15 May 2012.

WIPO (World Intellectual Property Organization). 2012. Intellectual Property Statistics. www.wipo.int/ipstats/en/. Accessed 22 March 2012.

World Bank. 2011. *Migration and Remittances Factbook.* 2nd Edition. Washington, DC. http://siteresources.worldbank.org/INTLAC/Resources/Factbook2011-Ebook.pdf. Accessed 15 April 2012.

———. **2012a.** *World Development Indicators 2012.* Washington, DC. http://data.worldbank.org. Accessed 15 October 2012.

———. **2012b.** International Income Distribution Database. [Not publicly available]. 15 April 2012.

———. **2012c.** Correspondence on personal computers data. 15 April 2012.

Technical appendix: explanatory note for projections exercise

This technical appendix summarizes the two projection models discussed in chapter 4.

Lutz and KC (2013) Model for demography, education and human development

The Lutz and KC (2013) Model is used to project demographic trends through to 2050. It is based on the premise that trends in population growth are affected by improvements in education quality and quantity. This Report employs a dataset covering 120 countries, with their populations disaggregated by age, sex and education level.

Lutz and KC's multistate population modelling approach was developed in the 1970s at the International Institute for Applied Systems Analysis in Austria and is well accepted among technical demographers. The idea behind the projection is straightforward: with a baseline year of 2000 (the latest year for which internationally comparable data are available for most countries) and assuming that education level remains invariant after a certain age, the proportion of women ages 50–54 without any formal education in 2005 can be derived directly from the proportion of women ages 45–49 without any formal education in 2000.

Given that the size of a birth cohort as it ages over time can change only through mortality and migration, these proportions would be constant only if no individual moved up to the primary education category after age 15 and if mortality and migration did not differ by education level. However, strong links exist between education level and mortality, fertility and migration behaviour, so the approach must be adjusted to correct for these effects. The size of a birth cohort depends on the education level of women of childbearing age, where a negative relationship is traditionally observed. In projecting these cohorts forward, differential survival rates, based on a comprehensive literature review and modelling exercises using past data, are applied to the education groups.

In reality, the likelihood of an individual transitioning from one education level to the next highest strongly depends on the education level of his or her parents. But this educational inheritance mechanism is not explicitly modelled here. Instead, assumptions regarding transition rates and their future development are statistically derived from the aggregate behaviour of education systems in the past. Since this expansion is partly the result of the inheritance mechanism—the fact that many parents desire that their children reach an education level at least as high as their own—inheritance is implicitly reflected in the projection, even though it is not formally part of the model. Such an approach appears preferable because data on the aggregate growth patterns of education systems, on which assumptions for the future can be based, are much more readily available than robust data on the microprocess of educational inheritance.

The procedure for each country can be summarized as follows:

- A baseline population distribution by five-year age group cohorts, sex and education level is derived for 2000.
- For each five-year time step, cohorts move to the next five-year age group.
- Mortality rates specific to each age cohort, sex and education group and to each period are applied.
- Age- and sex-specific education transition rates are applied.
- Age-, sex- and education-specific net migrants are added to or removed from the population. In the projections presented here the migration assumptions correspond to those used in the UN population projections.
- Fertility rates, specific to each age, sex and education group and to each period, are applied to determine the size of the new 0–5 age group.
- The new population distribution by age, sex and education level is noted, and the above steps are repeated for the next five-year time step.

The projection aims to yield a dataset with the population distributed by five-year age groups (from ages 15–20 to ages 100 and older), by sex, and by four education levels over 50 years from 2000 (the base year) to 2050 in five-year intervals.

Pardee Center for International Futures (2013) Model for prospects of human development and policy scenarios

This Report uses the International Futures Model for long-term human development projections based on closely interacting policy-related issues, including income, health, education, poverty, gender, social change (instability and risk) and environmental sustainability. For more detailed information on how the model was developed, see Pardee Center for International Futures (2013) and the University of Denver Korbel School website (www.ifs.du.edu/introduction).

The International Futures Model is a large-scale, long-term, integrated global modelling system that incorporates demographic, economic, education, health, energy, agricultural, sociopolitical, infrastructural, technological and environmental submodels for 183 countries interacting in the global system.

The model was used in the 2011 *Human Development Report* to project long-term environmental trend scenarios and evaluate their impact on human development.